Convergence of Blockchain, Internet of Everything, and Federated Learning for Security

Fasee Ullah
Universiti Teknologi Petronas, Malaysia

Arfat Ahmad Khan
Khon Kaen University, Thailand

Asad Ullah
Department of Computer Science, Bahria University, Pakistan

IGI Global
Scientific Publishing
Publishing Tomorrow's Research Today

Vice President of Editorial	Melissa Wagner
Managing Editor of Acquisitions	Mikaela Felty
Managing Editor of Book Development	Jocelynn Hessler
Production Manager	Mike Brehm
Cover Design	Phillip Shickler

Published in the United States of America by
IGI Global Scientific Publishing
701 East Chocolate Avenue
Hershey, PA, 17033, USA
Tel: 717-533-8845
Fax: 717-533-7115
Website: https://www.igi-global.com E-mail: cust@igi-global.com

Library of Congress Cataloging-in-Publication Data

Names: Ullah, Fasee, 1983- editor | Khan, Arfat Ahmad, 1991- editor | Ullah, Asad, 1988- editor
Title: Convergence of blockchain, internet of everything, and federated learning for security / edited by Fasee Ullah, Arfat Ahmad Khan, Asad Ullah.
Description: Hershey, PA : IGI Global Scientific Publishing, [2025] | Includes bibliographical references and index. | Summary: "This book aims to bridge the gap between theory and practice in integrating Blockchain, IoE, and Federated Learning, specifically addressing existing security challenges. By systematically exploring the convergence of these transformative technologies, the book seeks to provide a broad understanding of the technology's foundational principles and highlight the technical, operational, and ethical challenges in integrating these technologies and their proposed practical solutions"-- Provided by publisher.
Identifiers: LCCN 2025001364 (print) | LCCN 2025001365 (ebook) | ISBN 9798337314242 h/c | ISBN 9798337314259 s/c | ISBN 9798337314266 ebook
Subjects: LCSH: Computer security | Computer networks--Security measures | Blockchains (Databases)--Security measures | Internet of things--Security measures | Federated learning (Machine learning) | Data privacy
Classification: LCC QA76.9.A25 C66783 2025 (print) | LCC QA76.9.A25 (ebook) | DDC 005.75/88--dc23/eng/20250606
LC record available at https://lccn.loc.gov/2025001364
LC ebook record available at https://lccn.loc.gov/2025001365

British Cataloguing in Publication Data
A Cataloguing in Publication record for this book is available from the British Library.

Table of Contents

Detailed Table of Contents

The convergence of Blockchain and the Internet of Everything (IoE) is a paradigm shift in the evolution of interconnected systems. IoE is a unification of all aspects of people, processes, data, and devices into a single large network. In addition to these tremendous opportunities, it also poses challenges, especially where security, transparency, trust are concerned. These specific challenges are dealt with promisingly by Blockchain, which essentially is a decentralized and immutable ledger. This chapter elaborates on the interaction of Blockchain and IoE and how Blockchain technologies would influence the security, transparency, and trustworthiness of IoE ecosystems. Through their realistic applications such as supply chain management, smart cities, and healthcare, practical insights into these implementations within IoE systems are offered. The chapter also considers the technical and operational synergies and challenges of the integration as well as future prospects, which provide valuable insights into the transformative possibilities of merging these two technology paradigms.

Data protection relies on cryptography to secure data across Blockchain, IoE, and Federated Learning systems. Strong cryptographic methods ensure confidentiality, authenticity, and integrity, safeguarding evolving digital security needs. Key techniques include symmetric and asymmetric encryption, hash functions, digital signatures, and zero-knowledge proofs. Cryptography enables secure protocols like

the system's effectiveness, offering a comprehensive security solution for protecting IoT networks and connected devices.

Security and trust are two critical challenges of IoE, which refers to the interconnection of electronic devices providing intelligent services. The IoE ecosystem works using smart contracts based on pre-specified rules and dynamic automated transactions that self-eject contracts, permitting the removal of intermediaries from the process. This dynamism reduces human error and fraud while enhancing assurance and transparency. The chapter offers insights into the data integrity, better authenticity, and efficiency of identified communications provided by smart contracts in IoE architectures. Smart contracts are essentially platforms through which security and public confidence in IoE are reinforced by alleviating risks. Because they depend on tamper-free immutable blockchain ledgers, event information is recorded safely, creating immense efficiency, command over fraud, and been further improved with standards. They scale, interoperate, and comply with regulation—three key points—when constructing a secure and trusted IoE ecosystem.

Recent technological developments make users vulnerable to several cyber-attacks, where phishing attacks compromise users' sensitive information. To identify these attacks, there are different social techniques, which bring user awareness. However, they are incapable of significantly identifying phishing attacks that demands technology-assisted techniques. The existing literature provides several blacklist-whitelist, fuzzy rule, and Machine Learning (ML) based techniques, where ML techniques are the most efficient. However, there is a lack of comprehensive

Preface

The rapid evolution of digital technologies has significantly transformed the landscape of security, connectivity, and data management. The convergence of Blockchain, the Internet of Everything (IoE), and Federated Learning represents a groundbreaking shift in approaching security in an increasingly interconnected world. As digital ecosystems expand, so do the risks associated with cyber threats, making traditional security frameworks inadequate. Blockchain provides a decentralized mechanism to ensure data integrity and trust, IoE fosters a hyper-connected environment, and Federated Learning enables secure, privacy-preserving analytics. The integration of these technologies presents a promising yet complex avenue for building robust, scalable, and adaptive security systems. However, challenges such as scalability, interoperability, and ethical concerns surrounding data privacy and ownership must be addressed to fully realize their potential.

This book, *Convergence of Blockchain, Internet of Everything, and Federated Learning for Security*, seeks to provide a comprehensive exploration of the synergies among these technologies. It offers theoretical foundations, practical applications, and real-world case studies to demonstrate their integration's impact on security frameworks. We aim to bridge the gap between theoretical research and practical implementation, equipping researchers, practitioners, and policymakers with the knowledge necessary to navigate this evolving domain.

In pursuit of this goal, this book is structured to achieve the following objectives:

1. Fundamental Understanding – Establishing the core principles of Blockchain, IoT, and Federated Learning while highlighting the technical, operational, and ethical challenges in their integration.
2. Practical Insights – Showcasing real-world case studies that demonstrate successful implementations, lessons learned, and best practices.
3. Future Research and Policy Development – Identifying emerging trends, research gaps, and policy factors to guide future advancements in these fields.

This book is designed for a wide range of readers, including researchers, technology practitioners, policymakers, academics, and students. Researchers will discover valuable insights into interdisciplinary approaches that integrate transformative technologies. Technology developers and practitioners focused on creating scalable and secure system designs will benefit from the book's practical applications and case studies. Policymakers and regulators responsible for overseeing digital transformation and cybersecurity will gain perspectives on ethical, legal, and operational challenges, which will assist them in developing strong regulatory frameworks. Lastly, academics and students will acquire foundational knowledge and a roadmap for further exploration.

This book addresses both theoretical and practical aspects, making it an essential resource for anyone looking to leverage the combined potential of Blockchain, the Internet of Everything (IoE), and Federated Learning. Our aim is to shape the future of secure and sustainable digital ecosystems. We hope this work encourages further research, collaboration, and innovation in enhancing digital security and transformation.

ORGANIZATION OF THE BOOK

Chapter 1: Blockchain Synergies with the Internet of Everything (IoE) The convergence of blockchain technology and the Internet of Everything (IoE) represents a significant advancement in interconnected systems, bringing together people, processes, data, and devices into a cohesive network. However, this interconnectedness also introduces challenges related to security, transparency, and trust. Blockchain, with its decentralized and immutable ledger, provides effective solutions to these issues. This chapter explores how blockchain enhances the security and reliability of IoE systems, offering practical insights through applications in supply chain management, smart cities, and healthcare. Additionally, the chapter examines the technical synergies, operational challenges, and future prospects of this integration, highlighting its transformative potential.

Chapter 2: Cryptography Securing Data in Motion within Blockchain, Internet of Everything, and Federated Learning Ensuring secure data transmission is crucial in the interconnected digital landscape of Blockchain, the Internet of Everything (IoE), and Federated Learning. Cryptography plays a key role in protecting data confidentiality, authenticity, and integrity. This chapter examines important cryptographic techniques, such as symmetric and asymmetric encryption, hash functions, digital signatures, and zero-knowledge proofs. Additionally, it explores advanced security protocols like TLS, homomorphic encryption, and differential privacy, while addressing the challenges posed by quantum computing.

The discussion provides a thorough understanding of cryptographic advancements that enhance digital security and privacy.

Chapter 3: Integration of Blockchain Mechanisms in Cybersecurity: Enhancing Data Integrity and Trustworthiness Blockchain technology has emerged as a vital tool in enhancing cybersecurity by ensuring data integrity and authentication. This chapter explores the role of Blockchain in mitigating cybersecurity threats through its decentralized and tamper-resistant framework. By utilizing cryptographic techniques and distributed ledger technology (DLT), Blockchain improves authentication mechanisms, especially through decentralized identity verification systems. Real-world applications demonstrate how Blockchain strengthens digital security, protects identities, and builds trust in digital environments. The findings highlight Blockchain's potential to transform cybersecurity frameworks.

Chapter 4: A Novel Tri-Layered Security Protocol for Enhancing IoT Networks Security The growth of the Internet of Things (IoT) has increased security risks, making it essential to develop innovative protection strategies. This chapter introduces a novel tri-layer security protocol aimed at enhancing IoT security by combining lightweight cryptography, fog computing, and an Intrusion Detection System (IDS). This multi-layered approach ensures secure communication, minimizes latency, and proactively identifies cyber threats. Extensive simulations and real-world testing have validated the protocol's effectiveness in protecting IoT networks, providing a robust security solution for interconnected devices.

Chapter 5: Leveraging Smart Contracts for Enhanced IoE Security The IoE ecosystem faces challenges in security and trust, which can be addressed through smart contracts. Operating on predefined rules, smart contracts automate transactions, eliminate intermediaries, and enhance transparency. This chapter discusses how smart contracts improve data integrity, authentication, and efficiency in IoE architectures. By leveraging Blockchain's immutable ledger, smart contracts provide secure and scalable solutions, reinforcing public confidence and regulatory compliance in IoE systems.

Chapter 6: Machine Learning-Based Phishing Websites Classification Using Diverse Datasets: An Empirical Analysis Cybercriminals increasingly exploit phishing attacks to compromise sensitive information. While user awareness remains vital, technological solutions such as Machine Learning (ML) have proven more effective in identifying phishing attempts. This chapter presents an empirical analysis of eleven ML techniques, including WiSARD, CHIRP, and Ridor, in detecting phishing attacks. Utilizing diverse datasets and a 10-fold cross-validation approach, the study demonstrates the superior accuracy and efficiency of J48, offering valuable insights into phishing detection mechanisms.

Chapter 7: Blockchain and IoE Transforming Industry Applications Blockchain and IoE have emerged as transformative technologies across various industries, driving operational efficiency, data accuracy, and automation. This chapter explores their combined impact on healthcare, manufacturing, and smart cities, highlighting their role in enhancing security, resource allocation, and regulatory compliance. Case studies and real-world implementations underscore the potential of these technologies in shaping future industry landscapes.

Chapter 8: Industry Applications of Blockchain and IoE in Supply Chains, Healthcare, Manufacturing, and Smart Cities The integration of Blockchain and IoE is revolutionizing multiple sectors by addressing challenges related to security, transparency, and efficiency. This chapter examines sector-specific applications, focusing on supply chains, healthcare, manufacturing, and smart cities. It also explores security benefits, scalability issues, regulatory concerns, and resource constraints. Through real-world case studies, the chapter provides a roadmap for leveraging these technologies to build intelligent and resilient digital ecosystems.

Chapter 9: MediBlock: A Consent-Based EHR Sharing System Electronic Health Records (EHRs) require secure and efficient management, a challenge that Blockchain technology can effectively address. This chapter introduces a decentralized, secure EHR management system utilizing Blockchain. The proposed architecture integrates smart contracts for access control, a consensus mechanism for data integrity, and a distributed network for storage. The discussion highlights the advantages of Blockchain-based EHR management, including enhanced security, privacy, and interoperability, alongside implementation challenges.

Chapter 10: IoT-Powered IPMS and AIPRA Revolutionize Healthcare with AI-Driven Pandemic Detection, Resource Optimization, Remote Monitoring, and Global Health Pandemics pose severe challenges to global healthcare systems, necessitating advanced technological interventions. This chapter explores how IoT-powered Intelligent Pandemic Management Systems (IPMS) and AI-Powered Resource Allocation (AIPRA) leverage AI, Blockchain, and IoT for real-time detection, resource optimization, and data security. The hybrid system achieves high accuracy in pandemic detection, resource utilization, and privacy protection, ensuring effective global health crisis management.

Chapter 11: Smart Water Governance with Blockchain Technology Water management faces challenges related to efficiency, transparency, and accountability. This chapter investigates how Blockchain technology can revolutionize water governance by enabling secure, immutable data recording of water usage, quality, and distribution. By reducing inefficiencies and fostering stakeholder trust, Blockchain presents a viable solution for sustainable water resource management.

Chapter 12: Exploring the Potential of Blockchain-Embedded Smart Grids in the Quantum Era The integration of green and renewable energy into power systems has led to the emergence of smart grids. This chapter explores how Blockchain-embedded smart grids facilitate secure, transparent, and decentralized energy transactions. As the energy sector transitions toward quantum-era technologies, this discussion highlights Blockchain's role in ensuring efficiency, resilience, and security in energy distribution networks.

Chapter 13: Regulation and Innovation in Financial Markets: The Impact of FinTech on Traditional Banking and Financial Systems This chapter provides a thorough examination of how distributed ledger technology (DLT) and blockchain are transforming financial markets, with a specific emphasis on their effects on traditional banking and financial systems. As the FinTech sector develops, the decentralized and anonymous features of these technologies have driven innovation across various areas, including finance, healthcare, and supply chains. The chapter begins by outlining the foundational principles of DLT and blockchain, then explores their significant applications in FinTech. These applications include cryptocurrencies, smart contracts, risk management, corporate finance, governance, crowdfunding, and derivative markets. By discussing both the opportunities and regulatory challenges associated with these innovations, this chapter offers a nuanced perspective on how blockchain is continuously disrupting and redefining the traditional financial landscape.

CONCLUSION

As the financial landscape continues to evolve, the integration of emerging technologies such as blockchain, distributed ledger technology (DLT), and FinTech innovations is reshaping traditional banking, investment strategies, and regulatory frameworks. The chapters in this volume provide a comprehensive examination of how these advancements are enhancing efficiency, security, and accessibility in financial systems, while also presenting new challenges for governance and compliance.

Through critical analyses and empirical studies, this book emphasizes the transformative potential of blockchain across various sectors, including finance, healthcare, supply chains, and sustainability. At the same time, it acknowledges the complexities and trade-offs involved in adopting these technologies, particularly in balancing innovation with regulatory oversight. The discussions presented highlight the need for a nuanced approach to implementation—one that ensures transparency, security, and equitable access, while also mitigating risks associated with decentralization and anonymity.

Looking ahead, the ongoing evolution of FinTech and blockchain will require collaborative efforts among policymakers, industry leaders, and researchers to fully harness their potential while addressing ethical and legal considerations. We hope that this collection of insights serves as a valuable resource for academics, practitioners, and decision-makers navigating the rapidly changing financial and technological landscape. The future of financial innovation will be shaped by those who can effectively bridge the gap between regulation and disruption, ensuring that technological advancements promote not only economic growth but also broader societal progress.

Chapter 1
Blockchain Synergies With the Internet of Everything (IoE)

Md Tahmid Ashraf Chowdhury
https://orcid.org/0009-0003-8886-1138
Universiti Teknologi Petronas, Malaysia

Mohammad Ahsanul Islam
https://orcid.org/0009-0003-7569-8175
Daffodil International University, Bangladesh

ABSTRACT

The convergence of Blockchain and the Internet of Everything (IoE) is a paradigm shift in the evolution of interconnected systems. IoE is a unification of all aspects of people, processes, data, and devices into a single large network. In addition to these tremendous opportunities, it also poses challenges, especially where security, transparency, trust are concerned. These specific challenges are dealt with promisingly by Blockchain, which essentially is a decentralized and immutable ledger. This chapter elaborates on the interaction of Blockchain and IoE and how Blockchain technologies would influence the security, transparency, and trustworthiness of IoE ecosystems. Through their realistic applications such as supply chain management, smart cities, and healthcare, practical insights into these implementations within IoE systems are offered. The chapter also considers the technical and operational synergies and challenges of the integration as well as future prospects, which provide valuable insights into the transformative possibilities of merging these two technology paradigms.

DOI: 10.4018/979-8-3373-1424-2.ch001

INTRODUCTION

The newness of technology brought an entirely new dimension to modern society that offered alternate channels of connection, collaboration, and functionality through very flexible aspects. Internet of Everything (IoE) is primarily a phrase that opens up to new ideas, which are far beyond what is meant by the Internet of Things (IoT) as such(Tyagi & Nair, 2020a). The IoE incorporates not only devices into the web but also a network that integrates both people and processes with data into a full network(Majeed et al., 2016a). This extension of interconnected systems only drives a better efficient functioning and a smarter kind of decision making. Still, it promises far-reaching transformational changes in all sectors of industry, improvements on quality of life, and automation that is the most extreme possible.

IoE is a classroom of interactions, where human interfaces converge with automated systems and data exchanges(Thesis et al., 2022). It harbors enormous opportunities for innovation in several areas, including healthcare, transportation, energy management, and urban planning. Smart cities powered by IoE would develop systems through which optimized resource utilization with decreased environmental footprint would raise living standards. However, the rapid growth of IoE systems has also brought to the table huge challenges regarding security, scalability, and trustworthiness, among many others(Iftikhar & Qureshi, 2024). Making these issues relevant and tackling them will become very necessary for the sustainability and effectiveness of IoE ecosystems.

The primary challenges that Internet of Everything (IoE) encounters are security issues(Akan et al., 2023). By the sheer amount of data resulting from IoE devices, coupled with the decentralized nature of those networks, there exist several door openings from which a malicious actor can penetrate. It could be unauthorized access, data breach, denial-of-service, or cyberattack, which would have to be guarded against, lest it endanger sensitive information or destroy user trust. Besides lacking standard protocols or interoperability among the IoE devices, communication and coordination can also get hampered, leading systems to fragment rather than develop their full capabilities(Rafique & Qadir, 2024a).

This problem is overcome, increasingly, by Blockchain technology facing organizations. In providing apt solutions for the IoE ecosystem regarding transparency and safety and the building of trust, blockchain provides a decentralized immutable ledger(Fowdur et al., 2024). This will thus allow tamper-proof data records and enable safe peer-to-peer transaction without any kind of intermediaries via Blockchain technology. The integration of Blockchain with IoE can redefine how interconnected systems work; it can give a base to the security and efficiency of interactions among devices, processes, and humans(Rafique & Qadir, 2024b).

Figure 1. Integration of blockchain technology with IoE systems for secure and efficient energy management and data exchange

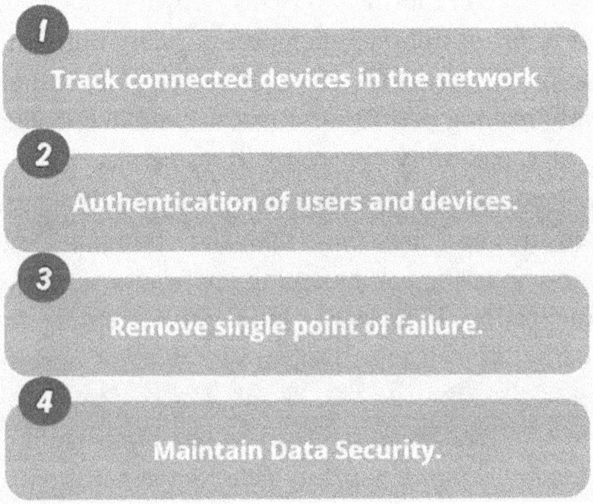

It does address a host of key weaknesses found within IoE ecosystems: for example, the improvement of data integrity, since all the transactions and data exchanged in it find their place in an immutable ledger; hence, this trait can be extremely useful in certain use cases related to tracking authenticity, as in supply chain management. Secondly, the decentralized design of Blockchain reduces dependence on the hub-like central authorities and minimizes a single point of failure, hence adding resilience to IoE networks(Yengkhom & Mukhopadhyay, 2022).

Scalability is another field within which Blockchain complements IoE(Javed & Qureshi, 2024). Most of the systems developed on traditional IoE tend to have difficulties concerning scalability with an increase in the number of gadgets and data upon exponential growth. Blockchain has a distributed nature, which efficiently allows data management and hence its processing to make sure scaling of IoE networks goes seamlessly. In addition, smart contracts-automating agreements encoded on Blockchain-facilitate more efficient processes and streamline interactions among players in IoE ecosystems(Ismail et al., 1 C.E.).

Blockchain and IoE are the twins, which connect quite well with each other in terms of not only technical capacity but also transformational real-world applications(Hakiri et al., 2024). For example, it helps make information about patients secure, manage medical records better, and foster interoperability among various healthcare service providers in the healthcare sector. Likewise, in supply chain management-either transparency, traceability, or authenticity-associated with Blockchain assures reduce chances of fraud and optimizes logistics. Smart cities, which are also among the emerging IoE applications, leverage key Blockchain applications such as energy management, traffic control, and public services to develop sustainable urban areas with citizens in focus(Makani et al., 2022).

Blockchain and IoE can be termed as twins, showing much potential to connect with each other in terms of not only technical capacity but also transformational real-world applications(Hakiri et al., 2024). This helps, for instance, in the healthcare sector: securely making patient information available, better managing medical records, and interoperability between various service providers. Similarly, in supply chain management, either transparency, traceability, or authenticity linked with Blockchain ensures less chance of fraud and optimizing logistics. The smart city, integrated into one of the IoE emerging applications, takes advantage of the key Blockchain applications in areas like energy management, traffic control, and public services and builds a sustained urban area with citizens in focus(Mishra & Singh, 2023).

The integration of Blockchain with IoE shows immense promise toward the future(Rafique & Qadir, 2024c). These might be complemented with emerging technologies like edge computing, artificial intelligence, and 5G to make IoE ecosystems more intelligent, responsive, and secure. For example, edge computing can enhance the processing capability of data at the edge of the network for reduced latency in real-time decision-making. AI can analyze the IoE data to provide actionable insights, whereas 5G connectivity may provide high-speed, low-latency infrastructure to support complex IoE applications(D. Sharma et al., 2024).

In other words, it has marked a paradigm shift in the evolutionary cycle of connected systems. Solving the inherent problems of IoE and opening up new dimensions of innovation, it opens a window of opportunities which Blockchain can promise: to redraw the interaction between devices, processes, and people within one unified network(Imoize et al., 2021). A discussion is, therefore, presented in this chapter, regarding the technical synergies, practical applications, and future prospects of this integration, giving useful insights into the transformed possibilities from these two emerging paradigms.

KEY CHALLENGES IN IOE ECOSYSTEMS

The Internet of Everything is a complete transformation when it comes to how people, processes, data and devices join together to create one grand interconnected ecosystem(*Internet of Things: Converging Technologies for Smart Environments and ... - Google Books*, n.d.). There is so much hidden potential in IoE, but it faces serious challenges that should be addressed fully so that all of such promises can be realized. Some of these challenges are security, scalability, standardization, data integrity, and sustainability. Security and privacy are still some of the most complicated issues regarding IoE environments. Its interconnectedness involves an unending flow of sensitive information among devices, users and systems. Such interconnectedness completely enhances the attack area for a myriad of cybercriminals. IoE devices, especially those with undersized computing power, provide little, if any, security features, causing them to be very vulnerable in front of various malicious activities such as hacking, data breach, or even malware assault. Apart from this, the greatest bane of user privacy, which is in tandem with the continuous collecting and analyzing of data. All other measures in these contexts would involve encryption, secure communication protocols, and the management of identities to protect user IoE systems.

Data integrity and reliability are yet another major hurdle. The ecosystem of the IoE is dependent on data derived from an array of devices, which operate with various formats, sources, and standards(Tyagi & Nair, 2020b). Diversity in the data leads to conflicts, inconsistencies, inaccuracies, and duplications that act as undermining agents to IoE applications. For instance, applications like healthcare and self-navigating vehicles require accuracy to facilitate safe and effective operation. Therefore, the validation, authentication, and integration of data into generic and differentiated platforms are paramount for these applications in mitigation against such hazards.

Definitely, scalability is the next big technical challenge with the ever-growing size of IoE networks(Civas et al., 2021). With connection devices, the explosion in numbers creates huge demands on infrastructure that require advanced computing as well as highly efficient communication protocols, coupled with data storage solutions. The task of streaming high volumes of real-time data through IoE systems is becoming increasingly complex without lagging behind in performance regarding latency, bandwidth, or overall performance quality. Indeed, another challenge in scalability is achieving multibillion devices by innovative network architectures and resource optimization techniques to ensure seamless operation and, most important, user experience.

Standardization and interoperability are major issues in IoE ecosystems(Costa et al., 2021). At present, there is no universal standard or governing principle about how IoE devices should communicate with one another, thus leading to fragmentation and limiting the interoperability of devices that originate from various manufacturers. The absence of standardization also complicates efforts to upgrade existing IoE networks with newer devices and technologies, thus hindering innovation and development. All stakeholders should thus collaborate to develop common protocols and frameworks for IoE systems because that is what will lead them to realize their true potential. Issues related to energy efficiency these days and continued sustainability. Most of the IoE devices operate less due to battery restriction, particularly in far-off or deprived areas(Siddiki Abir et al., 2023). The constant requirement for communities and computing further deteriorates the energy crisis as well as sustainability. It was necessary to think creatively about the hardware and renewable sources of energy and algorithms set up in energy efficient hardware. Minimized environmental impact would be achieved through IoE systems. More advanced technology, security, sustainable development, and international cooperation should be setting the stage for this complete "Introduction of IoE, a fully integrated transformative ecosystem."

HOW BLOCKCHAIN ENHANCES IOE

In turn, the blockchain would prove to be the ultimate remedy to most of the above issues and will enable Internet of Everything networks to be efficient, secure, and trustworthy(Dananjayan et al., 2023). IoE networks are envisioned as networks of millions of devices that generate data and transmit the same. Architectures of most IoE deployments are centralized in nature. This makes architecture vulnerable against cyber threats, data tampering, or scaling. Blockchain, being decentralized, secure, and transparent, addresses these challenges completely and is going to change how IoE operates.

Among the leading issues within IoE systems, data security is considered the most crucial(Majeed et al., 2016b). As sensitive data is obtained from the devices, those are very liable to get compromised due to unauthorized access or tampering, which again compromises the integrity of the entire network, blockchain with a decentralized structure provides that crucial solution, which helps nullify such possibilities. While the concept of traditional centralized systems rests their functionalities on a single point of control, Blockchain disperses the data over a network of nodes, and any malicious actor will practically not be able to tamper with the records without detection. This guarantees the safety and privacy of sensitive data from IoE devices, thereby gaining users' and stakeholders' confidence.

Besides enhancing data security, Blockchain significantly enhances the scope of device authentication in IoE networks. Keeping in mind the billions of devices connected in IoE ecosystems, ensuring the legitimacy and authorization of each device remains an extremely challenging task. Stronger authentication mechanisms in Blockchain therefore do not require any sort of centralized authority and employ cryptographic techniques in validating devices in a decentralized fashion. In this way, it prevents unauthorized access and reduces administrative overhead related to device authentication processes(Hammi et al., 2018).

In particular, IoE networks require data transparency and integrity, which become crucial in many critical verticals, such as supply chain management and healthcare, where trust and accountability are needed(Malathi, n.d.). This ability of blockchain to provide verifiable, tamper-proof records of transactions is invaluable in these areas. Examples include tracking goods in supply chain management from origin to final destination with Blockchain. It ensures that the correct information and a permanent record reach every stakeholder. The result of this transparency: fraud reduction, smooth conduct of operations, and a trustworthy atmosphere. For instance, in health, Blockchain secures medical records and facilitates sharing between providers in a manner that preserves privacy.

Another revolutionary feature of Blockchain that helps IoE networks is the smart contract(Saia et al., 2019a). Smart contracts are sets of rules written on the Blockchain that automatically get executed once a particular condition for execution is met. This ability especially comes in handy within an IoE ecosystem, where most of the transactions happen between devices themselves.

The scalability problem in IoE networks is rooted in the exponential growth in numbers of connected devices and, hence, the data generated. This usually causes a bottleneck and performance problems for traditional centralized architectures, which cannot handle such immense growth. The distributed nature of blockchain allows efficient data management and processing across multiple nodes, solving this problem. It follows that such scalability will enable IoE networks to easily absorb increased demand without any performance or reliability compromise(Babar & Akan, 2024).

Interoperability within heterogeneous IoE devices is another added advantage of Blockchain. Generally, IoE ecosystems consist of multiple devices provided by various manufacturers using different communication protocols. Such fragmentation makes the efficient sharing and coordination of actions within the network difficult. Blockchain acts as a unifying framework that allows all kinds of different devices to securely and compatibly interact with each other, despite their respective underlying protocols(Bhushan et al., 2020). Blockchain acts as the global shield for safe data exchange, building on a resilient and functional IoE network.

This further opens the door to new innovative and efficient frontiers for many industries, ranging from smart homes and cities to health care. For instance, in the case of smart cities, Blockchain can provide improved management of some elements such as energy, water, and transportation. Blockchain-powered IoE systems will optimize energy distribution by reducing waste and generally enhancing urban quality thanks to real-time data and a record of transactions. In turn, this will help develop the automotive industry's most ambitious dream: autonomous vehicles, securely communicating and exchanging data with each other and infrastructure, enabled by Blockchain(Rafique & Qadir, 2024d).

While Blockchain integrated with IoE has many advantages, it also faces certain challenges. Ensuring that IoE systems run seamlessly on Blockchain requires overcoming some of the key technical barriers to high energy consumption, bounded processing power, and latency. Moreover, regulatory and governance challenges around data privacy laws and their compliance requirements that need to be met if wide adaptation is to be achieved. This can be achieved only through collaborative efforts at the government, industry leadership, and academia levels for the complete integration of this technology.

It will be further complemented by the convergence of emerging technologies, including Edge Computing, Artificial Intelligence, and 5G connectivity with Blockchain and IoE(Babbar et al., 2023). It would be said that edge computing enhances data processing capability at the edge of the network, reducing latency for quick decision-making. AI can analyze IoE data and mine out some actionable insight, whereas 5G provides the low-latency and high-speed infrastructure to carry such complex IoE applications. All put together, these constitute a strong ecosystem wherein Blockchain fortifies the functionality of IoE.

Thus, such technologies form the complete remedy against all the inherent IoE network challenges with respect to data security, scalability, and interoperability. Decentralization, transparency, and tamper-proof framework which is created by Blockchain can bring efficiency, reliability, and trustworthiness to the IoE ecosystems. Smart contracts, scalability, and interoperability enable a wide range of very innovative applications across many sectors(Yang et al., 2020). In IoE, while its growth itself is fast-moving, its merger with Blockchain will take very long in writing the future of interconnected systems for progress and opening new horizons for innovation and collaboration.

Technical Synergies Between Blockchain and IoE

It integrates Blockchain with the IoE and involves a new milestone in interconnected systems development due to the deep technical synergies it offers in solving critical problems and opening new opportunities(Allioui et al., 2023). At its core, Blockchain is a distributed ledger system that lets one get secure, tamper-proof infrastructure in place to preserve the integrity and transparency of vast data generated from IoE devices. While traditional centralized servers remain vulnerable to the risks of single failure and cyber-attacks, Blockchain, on the contrary, is developed on a distributed model that will enhance the resilience of any system and significantly improve data security. A combination of technologies that makes such an ecosystem robust, scalable, and supportive of IoE network growth in leaps and bounds.

By its very nature, the Internet of Everything (IoE) consists of billions of connected devices operating at an individual level, ranging from consumer gadgets and industrial sensors(Reddy et al., 2021). The effective operation of such small networks involving such large-scale devices and data flows, which mystically encrypts, preserves security, and safe data at all levels. But the performance of IoT requires secure communication to ensure safety and prevent unauthorized access. Take, for example, with the aid of wearable monitors, IoE systems collect crucial patient data.

With blockchain, such information must be encrypted so that only authorized parties can access it Internet of Things (IoT), thus preserving personal patient confidentiality with the possibility of appropriate data sharing by the health-care ecosystem.

The most transformative use of Blockchain in IoE is smart contracts-self-executing agreements encoded with predefined conditions. These smart contracts will, in turn, enable IoE devices to perform tasks autonomously and independently without the intervention of human beings. In a smart home environment, for instance, devices can themselves monitor energy consumption and trigger automated billing through smart contracts(Kirli et al., 2022). Similarly, the IIoT system can utilize smart contracts for predictive maintenance, serving to have machinery serviced at the right time without the involvement of a person. This makes the process faster, sometimes without human intervention, while decreasing the costs associated with operations and minimizing the scope for human error.

Another significant challenge which IoE is likely to face in this regard is scalability. Blockchain has a distinct advantage here(Miglani et al., 2020). Traditional systems simply cannot keep up with the geometric explosion in numbers of connected devices and volumes of data. Blockchain can help mitigate this problem because each entity participating within the Blockchain network acts as a different node, thereby becoming responsible for storing and processing data. The smart city infrastructure is literally dependent upon thousands of sensors and devices. Blockchain is ideal for processing massive amounts of data produced there so that real-time decision-making is allowed in traffic management, energy distribution, and public safety systems, for example.

Interoperability is another domain where Blockchain is complementary to IoE(Abdalla et al., 2021). Most IoE ecosystems comprise devices of various manufacturers, with varied sets of communication protocols and standards in use. Blockchain enables a common platform for easily exchanging data across heterogeneous systems. Such interoperability will be useful in complex cases like smart cities, wherein diverse devices and networks would have to come together and provide integrated solutions. It could be an intelligent transportation system that makes use of Blockchain for integrating data from traffic sensors, autonomous vehicles, and public transit systems to optimize routes and reduce congestion through real-time analytics.

The transparency and trust surrounding Blockchain ledger are truly unchangeable. In systems whereby tracking ought to be done in real-time and where assets need to be verified at all times, Blockchain ensures that any transaction and data entry once made is registered in the ledger and which cannot thereafter be manipulated by anybody. This factors in the aspect of transparency among the stakeholders, building the trust factor alongside increasing accountability. In the sense of the food industry, Blockchain could track anything like how the produce moves from farms to the consuming table to make sure buyers can have proof about the origin and quality. In the pharma industry, Blockchain is busy decrementing counterfeit trading by guaranteeing that each phase in the entire supply chain is accounted for and is traceable(Rana et al., 2024).

Blockchain and IoE are co-dependent phenomena and way beyond their discrete usage thematic(Knight, 2022). They create such a general ecosystem which enables the whole society to greatly leverage far-reaching advantages. In agriculture, sensors in IoE monitor soil and crop health and weather patterns that directly interact with Blockchain in secure mechanisms of saving important data and sharing it among parties involved. This will ensure farm-specific meticulous understanding and resource optimization, hence strengthening productivity. In finance, again, Blockchain can be used to establish secure peer-to-peer transactions absent intermediaries, this is also advisable with IoE's capacity of powerfully effecting microtransactions, such as one-click toll payments or spare energy purchase within smart grids.

Further, Blockchain is for useful data origin and data integrity within IoE systems, important in business sectors demanding high levels of accountability(Wylde et al., 2022). For instance, in disaster management, with IoE sensing devices, the environment is under watch, but this data being observed by the Blockchain means it is more trustworthy and not tampered with. Therefore, that person posing with this information can be of great reliance and hence aid in arriving at a faster emergency response.

The integration of Blockchain into IoE demands it to continuously trail the path of Innovation and create a secure framework for continuous innovation within technologies like AI and ML(Verma et al., 2022). These technologies are mostly run by large data sets, and Blockchain verifies and keeps the fidelity of data. This brings greater accuracy to AI-driven insights. While crafting out a successful predictive insight into manufacturing, the ML algorithm is supported by operational data from various IoE devices through Blockchain, ensuring its integrity and thus leveraging against malicious disruptions.

On the other hand, an intriguing domain for Blockchain-IoE synergies could be energy efficiency(Malathy et al., 2023). Here, Blockchain could potentially set up a platform that facilitates transactions occurring in peer-to-peer energy trade, primarily conducted by consumers or prosumers who generate and use power as well. As powered enforcement tools, smart contracts will help to make the payment for completion of fair, successful, and legal transactions, thus facilitating interaction with these consumer-producers. This will offer further support for the decentralized scenario that goes against the conventional power utility companies and their quest for renewable energy technologies.

In closing, Blockchain and IoE indeed illustrate that the ultimate utility of networked systems and processes is possible with alliances(Arefkhani et al., n.d.). IoE networks backed up with Blockchain technologies, having challenged certain inherent shortcomings—security, scalability, and interoperability—in current generation networks, are releasing new realms of innovative solutions that have greatly heightened trust in really fast-moving worlds of technology. Given the benefit of acculturation in industries, the next generation will see more transformational progress and will eventually define the character of the future for devices, for systems, and for people.

Table 1. Key synergies and applications of blockchain in IoE

Aspect	Blockchain Contribution to IoE
Data Security	Provides a tamper-proof, distributed ledger to enhance resilience and protect IoE-generated data.
Smart Contracts	Enables autonomous device operations, e.g., energy billing, predictive maintenance.
Scalability	Handles the exponential growth of IoE devices by distributing data storage and processing.
Interoperability	Creates a unified platform for communication across diverse IoE devices and protocols.
Transparency & Trust	Ensures immutable, real-time tracking for industries like food and pharma supply chains.
Use Cases in Sectors	Agriculture (crop monitoring), Finance (peer-to-peer transactions), Disaster management (trustworthy data for emergencies).
Integration with AI/ML	Enhances data integrity for better predictive insights and operational accuracy.
Energy Efficiency	Facilitates decentralized peer-to-peer energy trading via smart contracts.

REAL-WORLD APPLICATIONS OF BLOCKCHAIN IN IOE

Blockchain and IoE will change the way industries operate and make transactions infinitely more effective, transparent, and secure(Inclusive Fintech: Blockchain, Cryptocurrency and Ico - David Kuo Chuen Lee, Linda Low - Google Books, *n.d.).* Using this marriage of 19 billion devices that are networked and connected by IoE and the decentralization and immutability of Blockchain, innovators can find solutions to age-old problems while businesses and governments innovate on their own. Based on the infrastructural implications of synergies that create changes in a manner that is holistic and using examples from across industries, this section reveals various sectors including smart cities, supply chains, healthcare, agriculture, and finance.

Smart Cities

It is a transformation that might happen in smart cities through the introduction of Blockchain in the Internet of Everything, allowing better management of infrastructure and services for a sustainable, connected, and intelligent future of urban centers(Kundu, 2019). With the presence of Blockchain, this could provide greater security and operational efficiencies to all IoE verticals in the following fields: traffic management systems, energy grid supply systems, public services, and security.

Traffic Management

Urbanization and technology issues are responsible for important problems in traffic management, both in the physical and the sky. Congestion severely smothers our cities, hence the necessity of Intelligent Traffic Management Systems (ITMS) to maintain undemanding regulations in traffic. UAVs have presented their share of problems because they introduce airspace management that proposes new challenges in itself. This may be alleviated by the use of blockchain technology.

Automobile sensors connected by the IoE into the vehicle, roads, and traffic lights are showering a lot of traffic data that could fill up the entire 21st century(Rayes & Salam, 2022). The blockchain retrieves data and securely stores it. In this way, accurate and adequately authorized information exchange with the rest of the world takes place.

Figure 2. Architecture of the blockchain-powered Traffic Management System (TMS) for UAVs

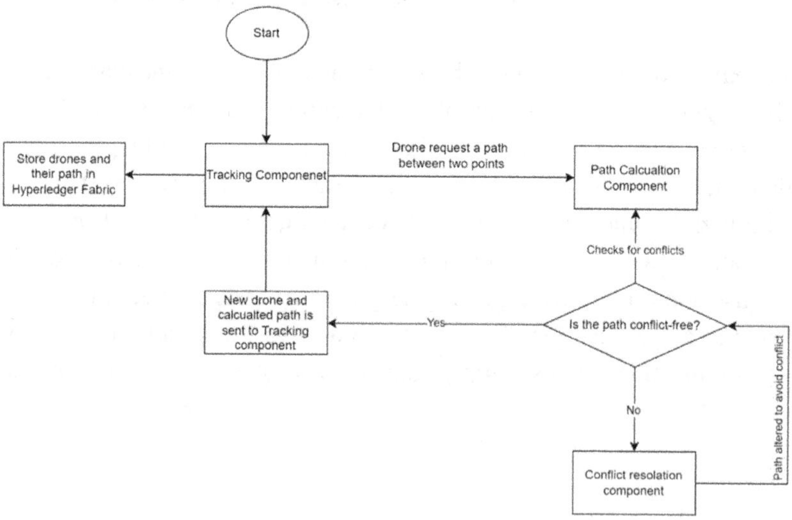

Drone-tracking, geofencing, and interdrone communication enabled by a new TMS architecture-authority show in Figure 1-inverse architectures; Hyperledger Fabric autonomously calculates ways and resolves conflicts for drone expeditions. The system team comprises critical components, namely the Tracking Component, recording drones and flight paths; Path Calculation Component, discovering novel routes; and Conflict Resolution Component, untangling route conflicts. TMS validates and adjusts these paths causing drones to navigate safe courses.

Energy Grids

Renewable energy and smart grids form the basis of any sustainable urban development(Khalil et al., 2021). Smart grids fitted with IoE devices track energy consumption, production, and distribution for proper resource management. Blockchain provides such systems with an immutable and transparent ledger of energy transactions that enable peer-to-peer energy exchange among households that are equipped with renewable sources of energy, such as solar panels. This would reduce waste by better distribution and energy efficiency through real-time tracking and verification of energy use. For example, a peer-to-peer robust energy ecosystem can be built simply by transferring excess energy generated by one home to another.

Table 2. Blockchain enhancing energy management in the Internet of Everything (IoE)

Aspect	Description	Role of IoE	Role of Blockchain	Example/Use Case Data
Energy Consumption	Monitoring and tracking household energy usage.	IoE devices like smart meters track real-time data.	Immutable ledger records consumption data transparently.	A household consumes 250 kWh/month, recorded securely.
Energy Production	Generation of renewable energy through sources like solar panels.	IoE monitors energy production levels.	Blockchain verifies and records energy production securely.	A solar panel generates 500 kWh/month of energy.
Energy Distribution	Efficiently distributing energy among households.	IoE enables real-time communication between grids.	Blockchain facilitates secure and transparent peer-to-peer energy exchanges.	20% excess energy is shared among neighboring homes.
Waste Reduction	Minimizing energy waste by optimizing distribution and usage.	IoE devices ensure real-time adjustments.	Blockchain tracks energy flows to prevent misallocation and ensure efficient use.	Waste reduced by 15% through optimized distribution.
Peer-to-Peer Energy Trade	Households with excess energy transfer it to others in need.	IoEfacilitates connections between homes.	Blockchain provides trustless, secure transactions for energy exchange.	A family sells 50 kWh of excess energy monthly.

Aspect	Description	Role of IoE	Role of Blockchain	Example/Use Case Data
Verification	Ensuring accurate and trusted records of energy generation and usage.	IoE collects and communicates data in real-time.	Blockchain guarantees data integrity and prevents tampering.	Verified 100% accuracy of energy production logs.
Efficiency	Enhancing overall energy utilization for sustainability.	IoE optimizes processes based on real-time data.	Blockchain ensures transparency and automates energy transactions through	Efficiency improved by 25% through automated trading.

Public Services

Public services delivery is critical to smart cities in improving people's living quality(De Guimarães et al., 2020). Blockchain can innovate the approach to identity management in such a way that digital identities are assured with blockchain-secured modes, enabling residents to seek out government services without any threats related to identity theft. In this case, there will be complete assurance of security and hassle-free interaction between citizens and municipal authorities. IoE-enabled sensors-equipped waste management systems track waste levels in real time. The blockchain can store this information and record it, and thereby, account for the exact waste management providers while improving resource utilization. This ensures timely collections, reduces operation inefficiencies, and enables a cleaner urban environment.

Security and Privacy

Security and privacy of sensitive data generated from the IoE systems ensure one of the crucial challenges in a smart city. These systems handle vast volumes of information, starting from personal data to infrastructure metrics, rendering them targets for cyberattacks. Blockchain's cryptographic algorithms and decentralized design provide robust protection against unauthorized access and tampering(P. Sharma et al., 2021). Encryption of the data and sharing on the nodes in the network, Blockchain allows sensitive information to be secured with transparency to the operation. Examples include safeguarding against breaches of residents' data for urban planning or delivery of public service that would create a lot of trust and confidence in the smart city initiative.

Integration and Scalability

Integration of IoE systems and devices is becoming more complex due to smart city evolution("Intelligent Systems for IoE Based Smart Cities," 2023). Blockchain provides a unified framework wherein different platforms and ecosystems can easily interoperate. In such a case, various IoE devices ranging from smart homes to industrial systems will be able to communicate and work with each other effectively. For example, a transport system in a smart city will have to integrate data from connected vehicles, public transit, and pedestrian sensors into one mobility solution. Blockchain, due to its scalability nature, will guarantee efficiency and resiliency when such systems come to handle growing numbers of connected devices.

Sustainability and Future Outlook

Sustainability is at the core of smart city development, for which Blockchain-espoused IoE is effectively meeting their requirements. It would be plausible that the footprints of carbon, energy usage, and other resources could be modified as per the Blockchain method to perform synchronization between the applications. The real-time utilization of data from the sensors could identify marks of inefficiencies in all stages of energy or waste management, leading to taking urgent action on the same. Furthermore, there can be links adaptably moving toward controlled stimuli, such as giving rewards to citizens for taking up eco-friendly stances or using mass transit.

Blockchain synergizes with IoE to provide pure and virtually unlimited potentiality to craft smarter, cleaner, and environment-sensitive metropolitan settings(Taylor et al., 2019). Just by overcoming traffic congestion problems, energy robustness, public services, and data security courses, the collaboration supposedly outlines our upcoming cities. Future advancements and inventions will see the broad spousal of Blockchain-based IoE systems in creating scenarios of smart urban environments naturally based on productive measures and green-earth sensitivity for human well-being.

Supply Chain Management

Blockchain's transparency and immutability are invaluable in supply chain networks(Afrin & Pathak, 2023). When it comes to issues like fraud, counterfeiting, and lack of transparency, supply chains are now even more ready to accept IoT devices to help track their goods. The secure and visible management of supply chains, however, is easily provided by blockchain.

Tracking and Tracing

Embedded with a temperature sensor, location sensor, and humidity sensor, IoT sensors are attached to products. Blockchain records such parameters from IoT sensors into an immutable ledger so that products can be traced from production till point of consumption. It becomes the most critical for those products that have expiration such as those in pharmaceuticals and food.

Reducing Fraud

Counterfeit goods are somehow a source of concern to most sectors-industry inclusive, especially luxury goods and electronics. Blockchain guarantees that products are not fake because it gives proof in the form of a digital history that is ascertainable regarding their manufacturing and proof of ownership.

Optimizing Logistics

IoT devices aboard shipping containers collate delivery schedule performance data and data from ships on how the vehicle actually performed.

The combination of this data with block-induced effectiveness enables efficient route planning and reduces delays. Automated smart contracts would release payments instantaneously as soon as the conditions in the delivery process have been met, freeing reconciling activities from manual processes.

Healthcare

The key concerns that always hover around the sector of healthcare, having sensitive patient information and critical operations, include privacy, accuracy, and safety. Integration of Blockchain with IoE has ensured unprecedented security and reliability in major aspects of the healthcare sector. Blockchain works on ensuring that patient records are tamper-proof and accessible to only those who have concerned access, thus safeguarded privacy while sharing it smoothly between healthcare providers. It also enhances medical research in the verification of data integrity and, therefore, research findings on accurate, unchanged information.

Secure Patient Records

IoT-enabled medical devices are increasingly the customers that collect health data on an ongoing basis. Blockchain now provides storage for said data, however entirely secured and immune from tampering, which guarantees access to any specific data only to those with authority. Permission also enables patients to control their medical records and give authorized health professionals access to it during the particular time needed.

Telemedicine and Remote Monitoring

Telemedicine has provided IoT devices facilitating wearables that have made remote-monitoring systems essential to patients. The blockchain would enable transferring data from telemonitoring devices without being hacked and altered to build a bond of trust between patients and health providers.

Authenticity in Vaccines and Medicines

Most world healthcare systems are at risk due to counterfeit medicines and vaccines. Blockchain ensures the traceability of medical goods in their entire life cycle such that they are delivered intact to the patient(Siyal et al., 2019). IoT sensor humidity and temperature measured during the shipment will be confirmed by blockchain that such conditions were met.

Medical Research

Blockchain is an important manifestation of technology that can introduce IoT sharing of data across diverse institutions for rapid advancements in medicine. Blockchain, through its decentralized ledger, thus provides a tamper-proof mechanism for authenticity of data, therefore tending to do away with the apprehension of data manipulation and hence helping to build up a relationship amongst people based on mutual trust(Nasir et al., 2024). Ultimately, the system cannot just help to uphold the integrity of shared data but also foster understanding and collaboration across institutions in support of the more rapid progress they would necessarily harness in strategies for drug discovery or disease prevention. Through the proof of access and validation, blockchain ensures that research efforts are repetitious only with permissioned entries of already existing data. Thus, institutions will complement each other's findings, leading to a modus operandi of innovation. The sustainable energy of trust and transparency, which is pairing the credibility of blockchain with the pandemic rise of IoT to generate data, will transform the research landscape, ensuring accurate, efficient, and ethically reasonable use of data resulting in translational success in biomedicine(Tkachuk et al., 2023).

Agriculture

Blockchain just complements these advances by extending a secure, transparent infrastructure that increases trust and efficiency(Bodkhe et al., 2020). With Blockchain, data collected through IoT is immutably stored for authenticity and its reliability. It thus can have farmers, suppliers, and stakeholders pool the data collaboratively to drive smarter decision-making down the value chain. For example, Blockchain can ensure supply chain traceability-record each phase of handling produce from farm to market-to assure its quality and compliance. It will integrate the data-driven resilient agricultural ecosystem for less wastage, increasing the productivity for better sustainability that helps in overcoming challenges to modern agriculture for meeting the demand of the increasing global population.

Figure 3. Blockchain applications in smart agriculture

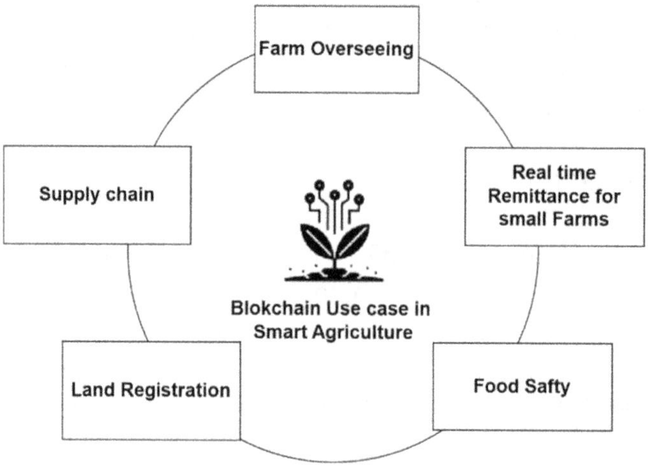

Precision Farming

IoT devices such as soil sensors, weather monitors and drones provide an exhaustive array of data regarding the quality of the soil, weather patterns and crop health. All this data get stored by blockchain, and thus it helps farmers to take data-backed decisions determining their crop yield.

Supply Chains Transparency

It provides traceability in the agricultural products, farms, and ends at the table of consumers. People can track their food and where its source came from, thus creating trust in organic and fair-trade practices. Such consumers can help farmers to bargain for higher prices as they can verify quality and authenticity with them.

Resource Management

Blockchain would work well with IoT to improve any resource like water and fertilizer. For instance, they created a smart contract to irrigate a field using real-time data collected by IoT sensors, therefore reducing wastage and helping with sustainability.

Finance

The finance sector is one such industry that is currently ahead in adopting Blockchain technology, and it is quite necessary to come to the point of integration with IoE in order to provide an extra level of security and automation along with comfort for consumers(Javaid et al., 2022).

Table 3. Blockchain applications in finance within IoE

Application	Description	Benefits
Automated Payments	Secure and transparent processing of routine payments for utilities, subscriptions, etc.	Reduced disputes, increased trust
Fraud Prevention	Real-time detection and prevention of fraudulent transactions through IoT sensors and Blockchain-secured data.	Enhanced security, minimized losses
Micropayments	Enabling efficient and secure micropayment systems for digital services.	Low-cost transactions, improved accessibility
Digital Identity	Secure management of digital identities using Blockchain-secured biometric data.	Reduced identity theft risk, enhanced authentication
Cross-Border Transactions	Facilitating secure and transparent cross-border transactions with reduced fees and increased clarity.	Enhanced global trade, improved financial inclusion

Automated Payments

The ability to deal with routine payments, such as utility bills or services with regular subscription, is inherent in smart home IoT devices. The Blockchain provides security and transparency, reducing disputes and enhancing trust(Rijal & Saranani, 2023). Fraud Prevention: IoE devices that have Blockchain functionality can detect and stop fraudulent transactions in real-time. For instance, IoT sensors on ATMs can monitor physical manipulation, while Blockchain safeguards the transaction data from online tampering. Micropayments: It is IoT that will enable this pop up at the end of micropayment systems given for account usage per digital service such as library or office space and will use Blockchain towards these end-of-life recharge transactions in low cost and secure infrastructures. Digital Identity: These IoT systems that are enabled with Blockchain have a secure space to keep managing a digital identity. For instance, these connected devices authenticate users for financial transactions through Blockchain secured biometrical data, minimizing identity theft risks. Cross Border Transactions: IoT devices brought out in global trade networks have the potential to bring forward a cashless seamless cross-border transfer. Their exchange value and the transaction fee can be kept opaque to other people through Blockchain technology while ensuring a higher degree of clarity towards one another.

CHALLENGES AND LIMITATIONS

The convergence of Blockchain with the Internet of Everything will bring a paradigm shift in the way emergent secure, transparent, and efficient ecosystems manifest themselves. Such a scenario generates a number of challenges. Technical, operational, and economic barriers limit the seamless execution of these technologies. For maximum utilization of Blockchain-IoE synergy among organizations, such issues need to be addressed(Akkaoui et al., 2022).

A comprehensive overview of these challenges is presented in Table 1 below:

Table 4. Challenges in blockchain-IoE integration

Challenge Category	Specific Challenge	Description
Performance	Scalability	Low throughput
	Energy Consumption	High energy use
	Latency & Bandwidth	Slow transactions
Technical	Interoperability	Device incompatibility
	Data Privacy & Security	Privacy risks

Challenge Category	Specific Challenge	Description
Economic	Cost	High implementation costs
Regulatory	Regulations & Standards	Lack of clear rules

Another challenge is scalability, IoE applications will involve billions of interconnected devices, each potentially producing an enormous amount of data(Touati et al., 2018). Taking the estimation by Cisco, the number of IoT-connected devices is expected to increase to 29.3 billion by the end of 2030, producing 79.4 ZB of data annually. Public blockchains, including Bitcoin and Ethereum, are not intrinsically designed to manage transaction throughput that would be demanded in such scenarios. For example, Ethereum can handle a mere 15-30 transactions per second-a figure far from the 24,000 TPS handled by Visa. This large discrepancy brings big obstacles for the real-time IoE applications of autonomous vehicles and smart cities that will rely on high transaction throughput.

Another critical challenge is power consumption by Blockchain, which is boundlessly high. Most of the Blockchain networks depend on consensus mechanisms that require very high levels of power consumption, such as PoW. The Bitcoin network itself consumes around 120 TWh of electricity every year, comparable to the amount used by an entire country like Argentina(Náñez Alonso et al., 2021). In the context of IoE, where many devices are resource-constrained, such energy demands are unsustainable. An example lies in the fact that most smart agriculture systems use soil monitoring sensors, which are powered with meager energy supplies. Therefore, integration with energy-intensive Blockchain processes contradicts the design principle of IoE systems today.

More challenges arise around data privacy and security. While Blockchain is made famous for its immutability and transparency, these very characteristics often run in conflict with data privacy regulations like the GDPR(Ramsay, 2018). IoE devices collect very sensitive data, such as personal health records or location information, which must be handled with care to keep your device compliant with the laws on privacy. Such data, if stored on a public and immutable Blockchain, is vulnerable to unauthorized access and misuse. The development of privacy-preserving mechanisms within Blockchain systems is considered key to overcoming these challenges.

Interoperability remains another big challenge to integrating Blockchain and IoE(Sadawi et al., 2021). The IoE ecosystem is constituted of various devices from various manufacturers, each with different communication protocols and standards. Though Blockchain provides a standard platform for data exchange, facilitating seamless interoperation among heterogeneous systems is quite complicated. For example, applications in smart cities require the collaboration of different types of devices and networks in real time, such as traffic sensors, autonomous vehicles, and public transportation systems. In IoE-Blockchain, compatibility and efficiency in communications between these components are indispensable to any successful solutions.

Another factor that makes the adoption of Blockchain-IoE solutions not widespread is cost. The implementation of Blockchain technology involves huge infrastructure investment, software development, and maintenance costs. Most SMEs that will greatly benefit from IoE innovations usually have very limited resources to invest in Blockchain integration. The operational cost related to running Blockchain nodes and processing transactions may also be expensive for resource-constrained IoE applications such as environmental monitoring or rural healthcare systems(Xu et al., 2020).

In addition to less-than-ideal latency and bandwidth, Blockchain-IoE integration is hindered. IoE applications that require real-time data processing and decision-making simply can't afford any delays that blockchains give them with consensus mechanisms. Like a single millisecond, in a self-driving car, can separate life and death. The current transaction verification system for the Blockchain spans from minutes to hours and is not an ideal fit for immediate applications. Furthermore, the bandwidth required for sending large amounts of IoE data to the Blockchain network strains the infrastructure considerably, mainly for the far-off or undeveloped regions(Saia et al., 2019b).

The adoption and greater acceptance of Blockchain-IoE systems are challenged by regulations and laws. Identity, internet of things, ledger technology (Blockchain), smart contract, and regulations present commercial real-world problems that have no real solution direction(Sam et al., 2023). The legal landscape shaping AI and Blockchain technologies is still a subject of contention, while definitions and possibilities will differ from jurisdiction to jurisdiction. Other issues that plague regulators and innovators alike include data ownership, cross-border data transfer, and liability in case of IoT/Blockchain system breakdowns. It is indeed a profound challenge to determine the responsibility-an obligation—liability relationship in instances of system accidents within IoE systems. To build trust and encourage the broader acceptance of these technologies, it is of utmost importance that there are clear and uniform regulations that guide them.

A critical issue is also the constant lack of standardization in Blockchain and IoT contexts(Upadhyay, 2020). No universally accepted standard of blockchain protocols and IoE communication frameworks is thus presented with a problem of fragmentation hindering a degree of connection and scalability. Efforts are called for so that various stakeholders of industry, policy, and standardization could be involved to develop a consensus on certain guidelines and protocols that will facilitate smooth integration.

There is strong hope that the breakthroughs made are heading to the curb of limitations. Scaling at Layer 2 and sharding prove enormous benefits in diminishing the throughput and high energy consumptions on the blockchain networks. The switch to Ethereum 2.0-PoS, that assures an increase in transaction throughput, calls for reducing the need for as much energy by 99%(Han et al., 2021). Other such advancements in edge computing and fog computing ease IoE systems' rightfulness by some means by computing data near the points, resulting in lessening latencies and disbanding bandwidth requirements altogether.

Privacy-oriented technologies such as zero-knowledge proofs (ZKPs) and homomorphic encryption forms an identity piece in Blockchain to address data privacy(Abid et al., 2025). Being such, these technologies blind any verification of sensitive data without showing what that information is, thus ensuring that those involved in the protection of the assets being carried in the system, which clearly adheres to the principles of privacy with what the blockchain transparently means.

When it comes to interoperability, there are certain proposals being considered for the same, such as International Livelihood Program (ILP) and the IoT Blockchain Standards Alliance which extends towards creating standards for interfacing various platforms. They open the pathway for the effortless trading of data works toward extending collaboration that reaches all corners of the diverse IoE devices and networks(Friess & Vermesan, 2015).

While in the case of Blockchain, the development and cost-related barriers are getting addressed by lightweight Blockchain protocols and decentralized infrastructure models. For example, federated Blockchain systems split the cost of maintaining a Blockchain network among multiple organizations so that SMEs can afford it(Ilbiz & Durst, 2019).

FUTURE TRENDS AND OPPORTUNITIES

A lot has been said about Blockchain and the Internet of Everything, bringing new business models and great opportunities during the transformation in technology in all industries. Security and privacy have become further enhancements ensured by decentralized Blockchain security for IoE networks. Crypto techniques and distributed public ledgers form the two barrier walls separating data exchanges within IoE systems from outside access, thereby ensuring not only security but also a chain that is tamper-proof. In the long run, data exchanges through Blockchain will allow confidential data to be shared between benign actors and considerably enhance the level of user privacy.

Robotic automation and smart contracts are some major buzzes. With the promised smart contracts by Blockchain revolutionizing interactions between IoE gadgets, will be responsible for the inclusion of actors themselves in the system of routines. Facilitated at every step will be the __pre-predetermined controls__- empowering this much-less manual involvement. Subsequently, areas such as supply chain, healthcare, automotive, etc. The supply chain, for example, will automate shipment confirmation and updating records by autonomous IoE devices upon conformance to preset conditions, proving convenience and transparency. Smart contracts will be everywhere and energy-efficient operation of the one with efficient results.

There is a significant upside to the decentralized IoE network. The traditional centralized IoE systems are painfully unable to scale and make good of most similarity-laden cost related issues in superficies: Blockchain deals with these new challenges in the best way possible, ensuring full distribution and explicit communication. Devices understanding each other without authority will fuel a grand leap in the robustness, scalability, and efficiency of the network of the IoE at large, most notably in logistics, energy, and agriculture. For instance, blockchain-powered energy grids, among others, will support free-market power exchange between peers, optimize resource management, and reduce reliance on the central government for payments. Thus, decentralized models of the network ensure that IoE ecosystems remain whip-fast under heavy-traffic or sudden disruptions.

Tokenization ensures Blockchain potential at its best in the IoE ecosystem. By usage of the Blockchain platform, the money-laden value of IoE device tokens could be rentable. This allows for a different avenue of cashing in on businesses and buyers to lead to open, viable marketing. For instance, a company could tokenize its fleet of IoE-enabled delivery drones, leasing them out to others for particular jobs, thus creating additional revenue streams. Tokenized assets, procuring simplified ownership and transfer, further help provide a much more efficient economic model.

The Interoperability among IoE Platforms appears to be a critical trend due to an increasing number of connected devices. The successful integration of IoE technologies and applications in fatal social development requires uninterrupted, secure commutation across various platforms, hence defining Blockchain. The analytics set by the blockchain framework help unite systems and services, providing mutual communication among devices, tabs, and networks of various manufacturers. By hitting this point, interoperability will enable a sequence of multiple IoE platforms from smart homes to industrial IoT systems to act with each other to advance mass acceptance and demand improvement. If supported on multiple ecosystems, interoperability will spark creativity by prompting developers to form a solid set of applications for use through several ecosystems.

The benefits of Blockchain integration with energy have massive potential in some respects, namely, energy efficiency and sustainability. By incorporating renewable energy sources and smart grids, Blockchain could optimize energy management within IoE ecosystems-such activities include monitoring of energy use, carbon outputs and real-time production data. With such capabilities, there will be less waste and much increased transparency exploitable on a global basis for sustainable growth. For instance, Blockchain-smart grid-enabled systems could ensure the efficient distribution of excess energy for real-time optimizing utilization. In addition, Blockchain's ability to create and verify carbon credits could contribute to ongoing mitigation of global warming cause against climate change.

The association of this new technology could bring about a better future in the world of smart technology. Such cities of the future will fight to appeal to IoE-enabled features like smart traffic lights, waste management, and grid dynamics for data-sharing purposes and collaborative decision-making. This would effectively bring about swift decision-making, optimal resource utilization, improved urban planning, motivated citizens, and up-to-date setoffs for sustainable and intelligent urban development. In one instance, a smart city might be able to use Blockchain technology to manage traffic flow with the help of a reciprocal interconnection of all forms of data from connected cars, traffic sensors, and public transport, thus undesirably reducing congestion and ensuring better traffic movements. Moreover, everything would be kept very securely among the citizens as long as the privacy and security of all are a matter of concern.

Similarly transformative sights is endowed in integrating AI with IoE and Blockchain. In that critical chain of technological operations, from generating massive data, AI or IoE is the one who crafts these insights, and Blockchain who is instrumental in ensuring the trust and integrity of the data remain viable. Integration of these technologies in orthogonal ways gives rise to groundbreaking applications. Sectors like autonomous transport, predictive maintenance, and consumer experience get a shot in the arm. For example, in the ever-vital area of autonomous conveyances, and where Blockchain acts as a highly secure means of multifaceted varying authentic information to be linked with an IoE-enabled infrastructure traversed by autonomous-driving AI. The same can go a step further, feeding the diagnostics and prognosis of screwed-up health with clean and assured patient data right down to its core.

The Blockchain and IoE regulation and ethics sectors are massively proliferating and evolving, with ample challenges and opportunities as well. Governments and legislators are developing various regulations (along with the industry players) in foreign/joint partnership to guarantee that they stand overseas from the factor of both innovation and user protection. Ensuring trust and implementation of these new technologies responsibly means shaping-off fears concerning privacy and ethical repercussions. To that end, a clear statutory framework will go a long way to define accountability for IoE systems powered by Blockchain and see that they operate in transparent and fair manners. This will have a future need for further debate between policymakers and industry in order to develop a conducive environment for innovation with minimal risk exposure.

Secondly, the advancements in different blockchain protocols and IoE technologies have been removing constraints to scalability and energy efficiency. Other developments, for instance, perfecting Layer 2 solutions, sharding, and energy-efficient consensus mechanism, such as Proof of Stake, are already capable of solving the existing Blockchain systems' current drawbacks. In this particular case, Ethereum migrating to Ethereum 2.0 will likely bring about massive improvement in both transaction throughput and energy consumption-making it better suited for IoE applications. The growth of edge computing or fog computing is that it processes near sources; hence, consequently, latency and bandwidth consumption can be minimized. Therefore, technological advancement would complement effective integration of IoE and Blockchain.

Convergence of Blockchain and IoE is creating many different trends and opportunities that will revolutionize industries, making lives so much simpler. Convergence, on the other hand, opens several challenges concerning scalability, interoperability, and energy efficiency to achieve real transformative potential. Truly speaking, mainstreaming the solutions based on Blockchain-IoE requires collaborative contributions from researchers, industry leaders, policy planners, and technologists and will yield in a better-connected, more secure, and sustainable future.

CONCLUSION

The affiliation of blockchain with the Internet of Everything (IoE) is a continuous important change in today's digital ecosystem and has enabled new horizons for industries, businesses, and individuals alike. Combined, they indeed are the changes promised: trustworthy, decentralized, and more efficient when it holds the networks of devices forming the backbone of IoE. When the number of IoE devices multiplies, issues concerning security, privacy, interoperability, and scalability have pronounced presence. Therefore, blockchain holds great promise as the solution to address such concerns while creating new avenues for innovation due to the intrinsic characteristics of transparency, immutability, and decentralization.

Traditional centralized systems make devices vulnerable to cyberattacks and data breaches, resulting in many ramifications for users and organizations. Blockchain uses cryptography to ensure that the data is made available and is intact, protecting it from the aforementioned threats. It does so by virtue of a distributed ledger, which eliminates single points of failure since no one entity can steal the entire network.

This security level would matter a lot for areas, including healthcare, finance, and smart cities, where trust and data integrity would matter most.

Smart contracts are enabled in the IoE devices housing the blockchains, letting them function independently. Self-executing smart contracts stored in the Blockchain empower the devices to coordinate and decide based on pre-specified rules without any interference from humans. Smart devices in a home, for instance, may place orders for supplies or carry out maintenance tasks based on their states. The industrial case is that connected IoE machines adjust production schedules or optimize supply chain logistics. This saves significant operational costs, error reductions, efficiency gains, and competitive advantages for these organizations.

Next amazing part of Blockchain is decentralized networks, which it is able to create. Traditional IoE networks rely entirely on core cloud servers, as this set-up would control communication and storage of data. Inevitably, these types of sets will bring bottlenecks, latencies, and make them vulnerable to attacks. Hence with the decentralized nature of the architecture, it created using blockchains into decentralization that enables the devices themselves to interact with one another privately. This peer-to-peer communication can reduce further reliance on the third party, such networks become more future-proof, and scalability improves. Applications in critical areas like energy grids, disaster management, and transportation could exponentially benefit from decentralization.

Innovation of economic opportunities towards the tokenization of IoE assets is enabled by Blockchain. The main purpose of tokenization is to represent physical or digital assets as digital tokens on a Blockchain. As an example, IoE-enabled resources or devices - like renewable energy units - can be monetized and traded for cost efficiency. In addition, an electric vehicle could trade its surplus energy stored in its battery with the grid or among other vehicles in real-time. This not only encourages new business models but serves as the democratization of resources and the development of new and inclusive economic ecosystems.

Interoperability continues to be one of the most significant issues with the IoE. Devices and platforms manufactured by different manufacturers may barely communicate with each other properly. Blockchain makes it possible to provide a global standard to exchange and harmonize the data-integration and communication aspect. Such interoperability leaves no space for breakage, making devices across the spectrum compatible. For industries like health care, where diverse systems need to collaborate to provide seamless patient care-beyond the walls of a hospital-Blockchain can be a real game-changer.

The convergence of Blockchain and IoE arguably has some of the most serious implications on sustainability. IoE devices are the major monitors of optimal resource consumption, whereas Blockchain facilitates transparent visibility in terms of accountability. In smart grids, for example, Blockchain can fairly distribute renewable energy and efficiently reduce waste. In this case, Blockchain and IoE technologies are at the center of important responses for global issues such as climate change and resource depletion.

Although the Blockchain-IoE integration is a competing potential, it is not a seamless flow. Scalability and energy consumption therefore remain prominent to this lesser growing army of IoE devices. Blockchain has a very high energy demand due to its proof-of-work, which can defeat sustainability goals. Therefore, continual advancements in blockchain technology, such as proof-of-stake and other energy-efficient consensus mechanisms, should solve these problems. It is also essential to form regulatory and ethical frameworks that would ensure well-guided use of the technologies. Setting up global standards in collaboration with governments, industry, and researchers would also be a significant step toward confronting these challenges.

Thus, the integration of Blockchain with the Internet of Everything promises to be a watershed moment beyond technology by which lives and ways of working and socializing are transformed. On the one hand, the IoE will have the capacity to build new levels of security, efficiency, and innovative application from the achievements of Blockchain. On the other hand, the entire spectrum of industries-from health-care and energy through transport and urban development-is likely to transform in their very foundations. New endeavors targeted at different technical, ethical, and regulatory challenges will produce appropriate outcomes. But at this point, organizations and stakeholders that catch this wave will find an element of innovation leadership and actively participate in building a sustainable and equitable future. There lies a tremendous potential resource in the amalgamation of Blockchain and IoE, which can forge ahead with great impetus in terms of prosperity, security, and inter-connectivity in this world, generation after generation.

REFERENCES

Abdalla, R. S., Mahbub, S. A., Mokhtar, R. A., Ali, E. S., & Saeed, R. A. (2021). IoE Design Principles and Architecture. *Internet of Energy for Smart Cities*, 145–170. https://doi.org/DOI: 10.1201/9781003047315-6

Abid, A., Cheikhrouhou, S., Kallel, S., & Jmaiel, M. (2025). A privacy-preserving traceability system for self-sovereign identity-based inter-organizational business processes. *Computer Standards & Interfaces*, *92*, 103930. DOI: 10.1016/j.csi.2024.103930

Afrin, N., & Pathak, A. (2023). Blockchain-Powered Security and Transparency in Supply Chain: Exploring Traceability and Authenticity through Smart Contracts. *International Journal of Computer Applications*, *185*(49), 975–8887. DOI: 10.5120/ijca2023923318

Akan, O. B., Dinc, E., Kuscu, M., Cetinkaya, O., & Bilgin, B. A. (2023). Internet of Everything (IoE) - From Molecules to the Universe. *IEEE Communications Magazine*, *61*(10), 122–128. DOI: 10.1109/MCOM.001.2200594

Akkaoui, R., Stefanov, A., Palensky, P., & Epema, D. H. J. (2022). A Taxonomy and Lessons Learned From Blockchain Adoption Within the Internet of Energy Paradigm. *IEEE Access : Practical Innovations, Open Solutions*, *10*, 106708–106739. DOI: 10.1109/ACCESS.2022.3212148

Al Sadawi, A., Hassan, M. S., & Ndiaye, M. (2021). A Survey on the Integration of Blockchain with IoT to Enhance Performance and Eliminate Challenges. *IEEE Access : Practical Innovations, Open Solutions*, *9*, 54478–54497. DOI: 10.1109/ACCESS.2021.3070555

Allioui, H. ;, Mourdi, Y., Allioui, H., & Mourdi, Y. (2023). Exploring the Full Potentials of IoT for Better Financial Growth and Stability: A Comprehensive Survey. *Sensors 2023, Vol. 23, Page 8015*, *23*(19), 8015. https://doi.org/DOI: 10.3390/s23198015

Arefkhani, R., Husain, A. J., Tech, M., & Student, C. (n.d.). *Optimized Resource Allocation in Blockchain Fog-based IOE*. Retrieved February 7, 2025, from www.ijert.org

Babar, A. Z., & Akan, O. B. (2024). *Sustainable and Precision Agriculture with the Internet of Everything (IoE)*. https://arxiv.org/abs/2404.06341v3

Babbar, H., Rani, S., Bouachir, O., & Aloqaily, M. (2023). From Massive IoT Toward IoE: Evolution of Energy Efficient Autonomous Wireless Networks. *IEEE Communications Standards Magazine*, *7*(2), 32–39. DOI: 10.1109/MCOMSTD.0001.2100116

Bhushan, B., Sahoo, C., Sinha, P., & Khamparia, A. (2020). Unification of Blockchain and Internet of Things (BIoT): requirements, working model, challenges and future directions. *Wireless Networks 2020 27:1, 27*(1), 55–90. https://doi.org/DOI: 10.1007/s11276-020-02445-6

Bodkhe, U., Tanwar, S., Parekh, K., Khanpara, P., Tyagi, S., Kumar, N., & Alazab, M. (2020). Blockchain for Industry 4.0: A comprehensive review. *IEEE Access : Practical Innovations, Open Solutions, 8*, 79764–79800. DOI: 10.1109/ACCESS.2020.2988579

Civas, M., Cetinkaya, O., Kuscu, M., & Akan, O. B. (2021). Universal Transceivers: Opportunities and Future Directions for the Internet of Everything (IoE). *Frontiers in Communications and Networks, 2*, 733664. DOI: 10.3389/frcmn.2021.733664

da Costa, V. C. F., Oliveira, L. F., & de Souza, J. (2021). A collaborative approach to support interoperability and awareness of Internet of Everything (IoE) enablers. *Proceedings of the 2021 IEEE International Conference on Human-Machine Systems, ICHMS 2021*. https://doi.org/DOI: 10.1109/ICHMS53169.2021.9582657

De Guimarães, J. C. F., Severo, E. A., Felix Júnior, L. A., Da Costa, W. P. L. B., & Salmoria, F. T. (2020). Governance and quality of life in smart cities: Towards sustainable development goals. *Journal of Cleaner Production, 253*, 119926. DOI: 10.1016/j.jclepro.2019.119926

Fowdur, T. P., Hurbungs, V., & Babooram, L. (2024). Leveraging the Power of Blockchain in Industry 4.0 and Intelligent Real-Time Systems for Achieving the SDGs. *Artificial Intelligence, Engineering Systems and Sustainable Development: Driving the UN SDGs*, 109–121. https://doi.org/DOI: 10.1108/978-1-83753-540-820241009/FULL/XML

Friess, P., & Vermesan, O. (2015). Building the Hyperconnected Society- Internet of Things Research and Innovation Value Chains, Ecosystems and Markets. *Building the Hyperconnected Society- Internet of Things Research and Innovation Value Chains. Ecosystems and Markets, 332*. Advance online publication. DOI: 10.1201/9781003337454

Hakiri, A., Gokhale, A., Ben Yahia, S., & Mellouli, N. (2024). A comprehensive survey on digital twin for future networks and emerging Internet of Things industry. *Computer Networks, 244*, 110350. DOI: 10.1016/j.comnet.2024.110350

Hammi, M. T., Bellot, P., & Serhrouchni, A. (2018). BCTrust: A decentralized authentication blockchain-based mechanism. *IEEE Wireless Communications and Networking Conference, WCNC, 2018-April*, 1–6. https://doi.org/DOI: 10.1109/WCNC.2018.8376948

Han, R., Yu, J., Lin, H., Chen, S., & Esteves-Veríssimo, P. (2021). On the Security and Performance of Blockchain Sharding. *Cryptology EPrint Archive*. https://eprint.iacr.org/2021/1276

Iftikhar, A., & Qureshi, K. N. (2024). Future Privacy and Trust Challenges for IoE Networks. *Internet of Things, Part F1832*, 193–218. https://doi.org/DOI: 10.1007/978-3-031-45162-1_12

Ilbiz, E., & Durst, S. (2019). The Appropriation of Blockchain for Small and Medium-sized Enterprises. *Journal of Innovation Management*, *7*(1), 26–45. DOI: 10.24840/2183-0606_007.001_0004

Imoize, A. L., Adedeji, O., Tandiya, N., & Shetty, S. (2021). 6G Enabled Smart Infrastructure for Sustainable Society: Opportunities, Challenges, and Research Roadmap. *Sensors 2021, Vol. 21, Page 1709, 21*(5), 1709. https://doi.org/DOI: 10.3390/s21051709

Inclusive Fintech: Blockchain, Cryptocurrency And Ico - David Kuo Chuen Lee, Linda Low - Google Books. (n.d.). Retrieved February 7, 2025, from https://books.google.com.my/books?hl=en&lr=&id=HCpjDwAAQBAJ&oi=fnd&pg=PR5&dq=Blockchain+and+IoE+will+change+the+way+industries+operate+and+make+transactions+infinitely+more+effective,+transparent,+and+secure&ots=ip4uuRl7Ru&sig=lXN4Pid0Eoa9Qwt8GnleCueSig0&redir_esc=y#v=onepage&q&f=false

Intelligent Systems for IoE Based Smart Cities. (2023). *Intelligent Systems for IoE Based Smart Cities*. https://doi.org/DOI: 10.2174/97898151249651230101

Internet of Things: Converging Technologies for Smart Environments and ... - Google Books. (n.d.). Retrieved February 5, 2025, from https://books.google.com.my/books?hl=en&lr=&id=rHYGZ0wxLP0C&oi=fnd&pg=PR1&dq=The+Internet+of+Everything+is+a+complete+transformation+when+it+comes+to+how+people,+processes,+data+and+devices+join+together+to+create+one+grand+interconnected+ecosystem&ots=N_FsvVywDj&sig=mD1qXt7RGotNnn07VSFN8kwpPxk&redir_esc=y#v=onepage&q&f=false

Ismail, F. S. M., Mushtaque, S. G. M., & Adane, D. (1 C.E.). Struggles, Potential, and Research Angles in the Amalgamation of Blockchain Technology With 6G Networks. Https://Services.Igi-Global.Com/Resolvedoi/Resolve.Aspx?Doi=10.4018/978-1-6684-5376-6.Ch007, 167–196. https://doi.org/DOI: 10.4018/978-1-6684-5376-6.ch007

Javaid, M., Haleem, A., Singh, R. P., Suman, R., & Khan, S. (2022). A review of Blockchain Technology applications for financial services. *BenchCouncil Transactions on Benchmarks. Standards and Evaluations*, *2*(3), 100073. DOI: 10.1016/j.tbench.2022.100073

Javed, I. T., & Qureshi, K. N. (2024). Role of Blockchain for IoE Infrastructures and Applications. *Internet of Things, Part F1832*, 127–139. https://doi.org/DOI: 10.1007/978-3-031-45162-1_8

Khalil, M. I., Jhanjhi, N. Z., Humayun, M., Sivanesan, S. K., Masud, M., & Hossain, M. S. (2021). Hybrid smart grid with sustainable energy efficient resources for smart cities. *Sustainable Energy Technologies and Assessments*, *46*, 101211. DOI: 10.1016/j.seta.2021.101211

Kirli, D., Couraud, B., Robu, V., Salgado-Bravo, M., Norbu, S., Andoni, M., Antonopoulos, I., Negrete-Pincetic, M., Flynn, D., & Kiprakis, A. (2022). Smart contracts in energy systems: A systematic review of fundamental approaches and implementations. *Renewable & Sustainable Energy Reviews*, *158*, 112013. DOI: 10.1016/j.rser.2021.112013

Knight, B. (2022). The classroom as a complex adaptive system (CAS): Credible framing, useful metaphor or mis-designation? *International Journal of Complexity in Education*, *3*(1). https://uwe-repository.worktribe.com/output/8809354/the-classroom-as-a-complex-adaptive-system-cas-credible-framing-useful-metaphor-or-mis-designation

Kundu, D. (2019). Blockchain and Trust in a Smart City. Https://Doi.Org/10.1177/0975425319832392, *10*(1), 31–43. https://doi.org/DOI: 10.1177/0975425319832392

Majeed, A., Haq, A. U., Jamal, A., Bhana, R., Banigo, F., & Baadel, S. (2016a). Internet of everything (IoE) exploiting organisational inside threats: Global network of smart devices (GNSD). *ISSE 2016 - 2016 International Symposium on Systems Engineering - Proceedings Papers*. https://doi.org/DOI: 10.1109/SysEng.2016.7753152

Majeed, A., Haq, A. U., Jamal, A., Bhana, R., Banigo, F., & Baadel, S. (2016b). Internet of everything (IoE) exploiting organisational inside threats: Global network of smart devices (GNSD). *ISSE 2016 - 2016 International Symposium on Systems Engineering - Proceedings Papers*. https://doi.org/DOI: 10.1109/SysEng.2016.7753152

Makani, S., Pittala, R., Alsayed, E., Aloqaily, M., & Jararweh, Y. (2022). A survey of blockchain applications in sustainable and smart cities. *Cluster Computing*, *25*(6), 3915–3936. DOI: 10.1007/s10586-022-03625-z

Malathi, K. (n.d.). *Improved Dynamic Regression Framework for Effective Data Management in Wireless Networks on Cloud-assisted Internet of Everything Platform*. https://doi.org/DOI: 10.58346/JISIS.2024.I2.011

Malathy, S., Vanitha, C. N., Dhanaraj, R. K., & Kotteswari, C. (2023). Impact of Blockchain-IoE on economy. *Blockchain-Based Systems for the Modern Energy Grid*, 135–156. https://doi.org/DOI: 10.1016/B978-0-323-91850-3.00007-X

Miglani, A., Kumar, N., Chamola, V., & Zeadally, S. (2020). Blockchain for Internet of Energy management: Review, solutions, and challenges. *Computer Communications*, *151*, 395–418. DOI: 10.1016/j.comcom.2020.01.014

Mishra, P., & Singh, G. (2023). Energy Management Systems in Sustainable Smart Cities Based on the Internet of Energy: A Technical Review. *Energies 2023, Vol. 16, Page 6903, 16*(19), 6903. https://doi.org/DOI: 10.3390/en16196903

Náñez Alonso, S. L., Jorge-vázquez, J., Echarte Fernández, M. Á., & Reier Forradellas, R. F. (2021). Cryptocurrency Mining from an Economic and Environmental Perspective. Analysis of the Most and Least Sustainable Countries. *Energies 2021, Vol. 14, Page 4254, 14*(14), 4254. https://doi.org/DOI: 10.3390/en14144254

Nasir, N. M., Hassan, S., & Zaini, K. M. (2024). *Securing Permissioned Blockchain-based Systems: An Analysis on the Significance of Consensus Mechanisms*. IEEE., DOI: 10.1109/ACCESS.2024.3465869

Rafique, W., & Qadir, J. (2024). Internet of everything meets the metaverse: Bridging physical and virtual worlds with blockchain. *Computer Science Review*, *54*, 100678. DOI: 10.1016/j.cosrev.2024.100678

Ramsay, S. (2018). *The General Data ProtectionRegulation vs. The Blockchain : A legal study on the compatibility between blockchain technology and the GDPR*. https://urn.kb.se/resolve?urn=urn:nbn:se:su:diva-157498

Rana, M. T., Numan, M., Yousif, M., Hussain, T., Khan, A. Z., & Zhao, X. (2024). Enhancing sustainability in electric mobility: Exploring blockchain applications for secure EV charging and energy management. *Computers & Electrical Engineering*, *119*, 109503. DOI: 10.1016/j.compeleceng.2024.109503

Rayes, A., & Salam, S. (2022). Internet of Things from Hype to Reality: The Road to Digitization: Third Edition. *Internet of Things from Hype to Reality: The Road to Digitization: Third Edition*, 1–451. https://doi.org/DOI: 10.1007/978-3-030-90158-5/COVER

Reddy, K. S., Agarwal, K., & Tyagi, A. K. (2021). Beyond Things: A Systematic Study of Internet of Everything. *Advances in Intelligent Systems and Computing, 1180 AISC*, 226–242. https://doi.org/DOI: 10.1007/978-3-030-49339-4_23

Rijal, S., & Saranani, F. (2023). The Role of Blockchain Technology in Increasing Economic Transparency and Public Trust. [TACIT]. *Technology and Society Perspectives*, *1*(2), 56–67. DOI: 10.61100/tacit.v1i2.51

Saia, R., Carta, S., Recupero, D. R., & Fenu, G. (2019a). Internet of entities (IoE): A blockchain-based distributed paradigm for data exchange between wireless-based devices. *SENSORNETS 2019 - Proceedings of the 8th International Conference on Sensor Networks*, 77–84. https://doi.org/DOI: 10.5220/0007379600770084

Saia, R., Carta, S., Recupero, D. R., & Fenu, G. (2019b). Internet of entities (IoE): A blockchain-based distributed paradigm for data exchange between wireless-based devices. *SENSORNETS 2019 - Proceedings of the 8th International Conference on Sensor Networks*, 77–84. https://doi.org/DOI: 10.5220/0007379600770084

Sam, D., Jayanthi, K., Tiwari, R., Ebenezer, A. S., Kanmani, S. D., & Sheeba, A. (2023). Blockchain in internet of entities - issues and challenges. *Blockchain-Based Systems for the Modern Energy Grid*, 83–99. https://doi.org/DOI: 10.1016/B978-0-323-91850-3.00012-3

Sharma, D., Tilwari, V., & Pack, S. (2024). An overview for Designing 6G Networks: Technologies, Spectrum Management, Enhanced Air Interface and AI/ML Optimization. *IEEE Internet of Things Journal*. Advance online publication. DOI: 10.1109/JIOT.2024.3505617

Sharma, P., Jindal, R., & Borah, M. D. (2021). Blockchain-based decentralized architecture for cloud storage system. *Journal of Information Security and Applications*, *62*, 102970. DOI: 10.1016/j.jisa.2021.102970

Siddiki Abir, M. A. B., Chowdhury, M. Z., & Jang, Y. M. (2023). Software-Defined UAV Networks for 6G Systems: Requirements, Opportunities, Emerging Techniques, Challenges, and Research Directions. *IEEE Open Journal of the Communications Society*, *4*, 2487–2547. DOI: 10.1109/OJCOMS.2023.3323200

Siyal, A. A., Junejo, A. Z., Zawish, M., Ahmed, K., Khalil, A., & Soursou, G. (2019). Applications of Blockchain Technology in Medicine and Healthcare: Challenges and Future Perspectives. *Cryptography 2019, Vol. 3, Page 3, 3*(1), 3. https://doi.org/DOI: 10.3390/cryptography3010003

Taylor, A., Raleigh, N. A. B., Kurki, S., Ferreira-Aulu, M. B., & Wilenius, M. (2019). *PRECURSORS TO A "GOOD" BIOECONOMY IN 2125: MAKING SENSE OF BIOECONOMY & JUSTICE HORIZONS First Foresight Report of the BioEcoJust Project.*

Thesis, P. D., Luis González Ramírez, P., & Lloret Mauri Jesús Tomás Gironés Valencia, J. (2022). *Interconnection Architecture of Proximity Smart IoE-Networks with Centralised Management.* https://doi.org/DOI: 10.4995/Thesis/10251/181892

Tkachuk, R. V., Ilie, D., Robert, R., Kebande, V., & Tutschku, K. (2023). Towards efficient privacy and trust in decentralized blockchain-based peer-to-peer renewable energy marketplace. *Sustainable Energy. Grids and Networks, 35*, 101146. DOI: 10.1016/j.segan.2023.101146

Touati, F., Tariq, H., Crescini, D., & Ben Mnaouer, A. (2018). Development of Prototype for IoT and IoE Scalable Infrastructures, Architectures and Platforms. *Lecture Notes in Computer Science (Including Subseries Lecture Notes in Artificial Intelligence and Lecture Notes in Bioinformatics), 11277 LNCS*, 202–216. https://doi.org/DOI: 10.1007/978-3-030-02849-7_18

Tyagi, A. K., Dananjayan, S., Agarwal, D., & Thariq Ahmed, H. F. (2023). Blockchain—Internet of Things applications: Opportunities and challenges for industry 4.0 and society 5.0. *Sensors (Basel), 23*(2), 947.

Tyagi, A. K., & Nair, M. (2020a). Internet of Everything (IoE) and Internet of Things (IoTs): Threat Analyses, Possible Opportunities for Future. *Journal of Information Assurance and Security, 15*, 153–177. www.mirlabs.net/jias/index.html

Tyagi, A. K., & Nair, M. (2020b). Internet of Everything (IoE) and Internet of Things (IoTs): Threat Analyses, Possible Opportunities for Future. *Journal of Information Assurance and Security, 15*, 153–177. www.mirlabs.net/jias/index.html

Upadhyay, N. (2020). Demystifying blockchain: A critical analysis of challenges, applications and opportunities. *International Journal of Information Management, 54*, 102120. DOI: 10.1016/j.ijinfomgt.2020.102120

Verma, A., Bhattacharya, P., Madhani, N., Trivedi, C., Bhushan, B., Tanwar, S., Sharma, G., Bokoro, P. N., & Sharma, R. (2022). Blockchain for Industry 5.0: Vision, Opportunities, Key Enablers, and Future Directions. *IEEE Access : Practical Innovations, Open Solutions, 10*, 69160–69199. DOI: 10.1109/ACCESS.2022.3186892

Wylde, V., Rawindaran, N., Lawrence, J., Balasubramanian, R., Prakash, · Edmond, Jayal, A., Khan, I., Hewage, C., & Platts, J. (2022). Cybersecurity, Data Privacy and Blockchain: A Review. *SN Computer Science 2022 3:2, 3*(2), 1–12. https://doi.org/DOI: 10.1007/s42979-022-01020-4

Xu, H., Klaine, P. V., Onireti, O., Cao, B., Imran, M., & Zhang, L. (2020). Blockchain-enabled resource management and sharing for 6G communications. *Digital Communications and Networks*, *6*(3), 261–269. DOI: 10.1016/j.dcan.2020.06.002

Yang, J., Wen, J., Jiang, B., & Wang, H. (2020). Blockchain-based sharing and tamper-proof framework of big data networking. *IEEE Network*, *34*(4), 62–67. DOI: 10.1109/MNET.011.1900374

Yengkhom, A., & Mukhopadhyay, D. (2022). A survey on various applications of internet of things on blockchain platform. *Blockchain for IoT*, 21–48. https://doi.org/DOI: 10.1201/9781003188247-2/SURVEY-VARIOUS-APPLICATIONS-INTERNET-THINGS-BLOCKCHAIN-PLATFORM-ARCHANA-YENGKHOM-DEBARKA-MUKHOPADHYAY

Chapter 2 Cryptography Securing Data in Motion Within Blockchain, Internet of Everything, and Federated Learning

S. Aarthi
https://orcid.org/0009-0006-9064-2091
Marwadi University, India

K. Aravinthan
https://orcid.org/0000-0002-7923-1842
Adaikalamatha College, India

R. N. Ravikumar
https://orcid.org/0009-0009-3705-1681
Marwadi University, India

N. Sivakumar
Marwadi University, India

Soram Wanglen
Marwadi University, India

ABSTRACT

Data protection relies on cryptography to secure data across Blockchain, IoE, and Federated Learning systems. Strong cryptographic methods ensure confidentiality, authenticity, and integrity, safeguarding evolving digital security needs. Key

DOI: 10.4018/979-8-3373-1424-2.ch002

techniques include symmetric and asymmetric encryption, hash functions, digital signatures, and zero-knowledge proofs. Cryptography enables secure protocols like TLS, homomorphic encryption, and differential privacy while addressing quantum-resistant security challenges, ensuring robust digital privacy solutions.

1. INTRODUCTION TO CRYPTOGRAPHY IN MODERN SYSTEMS

1.1. Definition and Evolution of Cryptography

Cryptography is the science of securing communication by converting data into forms that are-reader: more difficult to understand by persons outside of the software development team. not to be seen by other people who for one reason or another cannot read that kind of information. It derives from prehistoric ages where some of the earliest cultures developing on the Earth used them. basic aspects of encryption are still in some extent easy and thus the ancient practices of techniques such as the Caesar cipher were employed in encrypting messages. Over centuries, Cryptography over the years advanced and became a method that is very complicated in using mathematics in the theoretical representation, in form of a mathematical formula to guard against information loss in the computer revolution. Today, it underpins secure, which are confidentiality of the communicated information, its integrity and authentication, (Pooja *et al.,* 2024).

1.2. Importance of Securing Data in Motion in Digital Ecosystems

The real of data often flows over networks in a world that appears to be more connected than ever before. communications to monetary transfers, and various other forms of switching. Protection of data in motion is very important to avoid interception of such data. altered, corruption, or breach by any unauthorized person. If there are no strong safeguards, information that is executed becomes vulnerable to cyber threats such as:

- **Eavesdropping:** Unauthorized interception of communication.
- **Man-in-the-Middle Attacks:** Interception and manipulation of data between two parties.
- **Data Tampering:** Malicious modification of data during transmission.

Cryptography mitigates these threats by encoding data, ensuring only authorized entities can interpret or modify it,. (Nwakeze, 2024).

1.3. Overview of Blockchain, IoE, and Federated Learning

- **Blockchain:** A peer-to-peer electronic currency system that provides secure record of financial transactions. Multiple nodes. It uses cryptography for achieving data efficacy and enabling trust. without central authority.
- **Internet of Everything (IoE):** Expands the IoT concept to cover people, processes, and data. IoE is characterized by large volumes of communication between connected devices. thus making cryptography necessary to secure communication.
- **Federated Learning:** A machine learning model of cooperative training of algorithms on decentralized data while at the same time, keeping such data local. It maintains security in data passed across, several different types of cryptography can be distinguished, namely and improved secure aggregation during updates of the model.

These domains demonstrate various aspects of using cryptography in protecting different advanced ecosystems.

1.4. Cryptography as a Foundation of Data Security

Cryptography can be defined as the pillar on which current methods of data protection are based. It provides secure communication systems, qualified its users and the channels through which information is passed, and guarantees that information being passed cannot be manipulated. By using cryptographic techniques including encryption, digital signatures, and secure protocols cryptography solves these problems in specific confidentiality, integrity, and authenticity as shown in Figure 1.

Figure 1. Key roles in data security

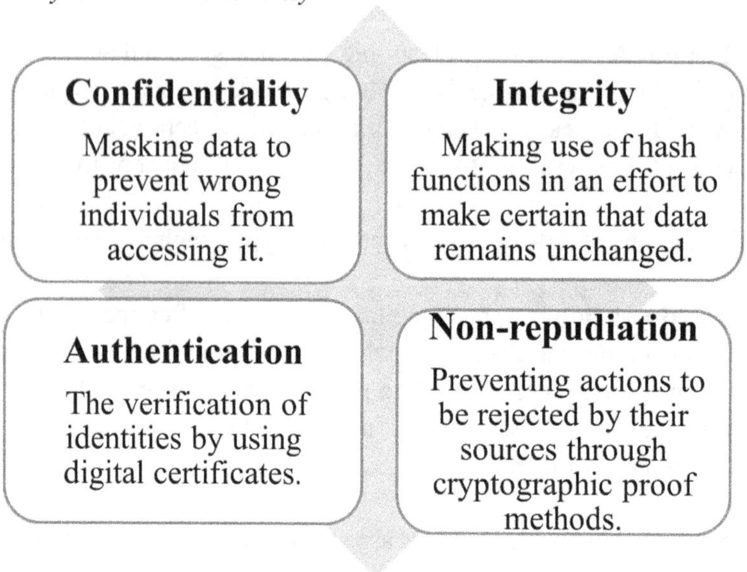

With the development of new connected digital structures, cryptography also grows, safeguarding the newly qualified as well as the blockchain and IoE technologies as well as federated learning, (Rupam *et al.*, 2024).

2. FUNDAMENTALS OF CRYPTOGRAPHY

2.1. Symmetric Encryption vs. Asymmetric Encryption

Symmetric Encryption: Encrypted data can be decrypted with key which means that symmetric encryption involves use of single key. This method is highly effective and known for encryption of large data set as shown in Figure 2.

Figure 2. Symmetric encryption

Algorithms:

- **AES (Advanced Encryption Standard)**: A reliable and known encryption standard, which can be used for protecting data storage media, as well as for data in motion.
- **DES/Triple DES:** Older algorithms which has been rendered useless due to some slight vulnerabilities which they were not able to fix.

  Strengths: High speeds, minimal computer resource utilization and Suitable for safe working environments isolated from other networks.

  Limitations: The system demands a secure key distribution which often could be difficult in large-scale networks.

  Asymmetric Encryption: Asymmetric encryption uses a pair of keys. one public key for the encryption and one private key for decryption. It is widely necessary in secure communication over the open networks as shown in Figure 3.

Figure 3. Asymmetric encryption

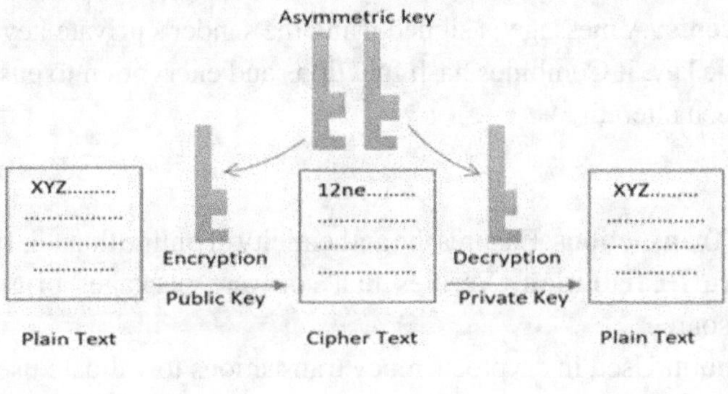

Algorithms:

- **RSA**: A widely used algorithm, though computationally intensive.
- **ECC (Elliptic Curve Cryptography)**: Offers equivalent security to RSA with smaller key sizes, improving efficiency.

  Strengths: Eliminates the need for secure key distribution and Ideal for public-key infrastructure (PKI) and digital certificates.
  Limitations: Slower than symmetrical encryption and Time-consuming for large dataset.

2.2. Hash Functions and Their Role in Data Integrity

Hash functions translate the input data in works of fixed size output (hash) which are unique to the input. Since data should be safeguarded against unauthorized modification, audit trails also need to guarantee it, (Urs & Lugrin, 2023).

Examples:

- **SHA-256:** SHA512 is one of the SHA-2 class, which used predominantly in the blockchain environment for creating block identifiers.
- **SHA-3**: A newer standard offering resilience against cryptographic vulnerabilities.

Role in Data Integrity: Any alteration to input data results in a completely different hash, making tampering detectable and used in verifying file authenticity, digital signatures, and password storage.

2.3. Digital Signatures and Authentication

Digital signatures provide a means of verifying the authenticity and integrity of digital data or messages. They rely on asymmetric encryption principles.

Key Concepts: A message is signed using the sender's private key and verified with the public key. It Combines hash functions and encryption to ensure the message hasn't been altered.

Use Cases:

- **Secure Transactions**: Ensures the authenticity of online financial transactions.
- **Software Distribution**: Verifies that software packages originate from a trusted source.
- **Blockchain**: Used in cryptocurrency transactions to validate user identities.

2.4. Zero-Knowledge Proofs: Ensuring Security Without Revealing Data

Zero-knowledge proofs (ZKPs) are cryptographic methods that enable one party (the prover) to prove to another (the verifier) that a statement is true without revealing any additional information. This proof confirms the possession of a secret such as a password, without revealing the secret itself. It relies on the challenges and responses more than once to make sure that it is credible.

Applications:

- Authentication: Confirm people's identities without their having to reveal other delicate information.
- Blockchain Privacy: Shield transaction details while demonstrating their genuine nature (ZK proof protocols such as zk-SNARKs in anonymous coins).
- Federated Learning: Yields confirmation of the model's accuracy without compromising on the clients' information secrecy, (Tarun *et al.*, 2024).

Advantages: Improves information privacy and security. It cuts down the chances of exposure to important information. In so doing, cryptography offers the prerequisite essentials for securing information in new, complex, connected systems.

3. CRYPTOGRAPHY IN BLOCKCHAIN TECHNOLOGY

Blockchain cryptography technologies are described as the use of highly developed mathematical concepts and algorithms to make Blockchain Technology secure by safeguarding the quality and authenticity of a block chain network data and transactions. It has a fundamental importance in the protection of information, assurance that users are trustworthy and allowing for the construction of self-governing network systems not reliant on central points of trust as shown in Figure 4.

Figure 4. Cryptography in blockchain technology

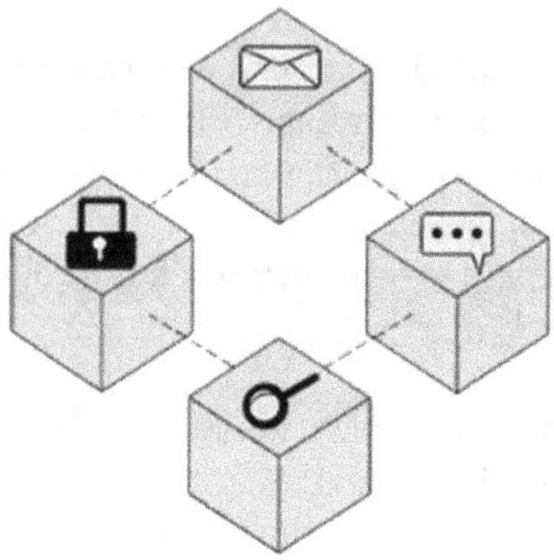

3.1. Cryptographic Mechanisms in Blockchain Architecture

3.1.1. Hashing for Immutability

Hashing is the cornerstone of blockchain structure since it guarantees the absolute identification of the information stored in the blocks. Every block in blockchain comprises an encrypted hash of the previous block. Any change to a block modifies hash and disrupts the integrity of the chain and tampering evident.

> **Key Algorithm:** SHA-256: Typically employed to produce a determined output size and which may have only one corresponding unique identifier and input data.
>
> **Benefits:** This helps to guarantee the honesty of the blockchain ledger and avoids changes that are not sanctioned by the system and as such, it is a measure against tampering.

3.1.2. Digital Signatures for Transaction Authentication

Digital signatures will ensure the validity and genuineness of transactions that transpire on the blockchain. A transaction is signed with the sender's private key and vice versa with the use of the sender's public key. Making certain that, when the money is accepted, it was authorized by the rightful owner and has not gone tampered with.

Role in Security: Ensures that no one does not make transaction of any kind on the bank without governmental consent. It Offers privacy, users cannot deny that they engaged in certain activity.

3.2. Secure Communication Between Nodes in a Decentralized Network

In blockchain networks, the structure of implementations of nodes to achieve secure communication is an important aspect of trust integrity. The Techniques are:

- **Transport Layer Security (TLS)**: Encrypts data transmission between nodes.
- **Message Authentication Codes (MACs)**: Ensures the authenticity and integrity of messages exchanged.

  Benefits: Protects against man-in-the-middle attacks and eavesdropping. It Allows for performing transaction and block formation securely across the EOS network.

3.3. Public and Private Keys: Securing Wallets and Transactions

Wallets, as well as safe transactions in blockchain are secured by public and private key cryptography systems.

- **Public Key**: If it is spending or verifying digital signatures, it is a public key available for public use in accepting payments.
- **Private Key**: A secret paragraph with which a user can sign transactions and release money in the respective wallet, (Weihong & Cutsem, 2024).

Key Features:

- Grants are tightly connected to the private key, so only the owner can give permission for its usage transactions.
- Wallets are used to store and safeguard these keys as they are secured with high secure encryption.
- Physical protection of private key (for example in a hardware wallet).
- Multiple signature wallets to improve security.

3.4. Integration of Cryptography in Distributed Contracts and Applications (DCA)

The foundation of smart contracts and decentralized applications is built with assured cryptographic processes interactions.

- **Smart Contracts:** Smart contracts which contain coded clauses rather than being entered into conventional prose language and then enforced on the blockchain. Cryptography makes it possible to electronically execute contracts in such a way that the process is unique, irreversible and predictable. Hashing and digital signatures ensure that inputs and conditions designated to the smart contract system are original.
- **Decentralized Applications (DApps):** Software applications that are developed using block chain platforms, the use of cryptography for the purpose of secure communication. For user authentication and safe interaction, the program employs public and private keys. Encryption safeguards data from end to end, giving a secure environment for passing sensitive data within the DApp. Smart contracts and DApps rely on cryptographic mechanisms to enable secure and automated interactions, (Gbadebo *et al.,* 2019).

The cryptographic approach ensures that blockchain systems are secure, reliable and immune to a number of vices. attacks, thus making it possible for these threats to be implemented in several fields.

4. CRYPTOGRAPHY IN THE INTERNET OF EVERYTHING (IOE)

Figure 5. Cryptography in the Internet of Everything (IoE)

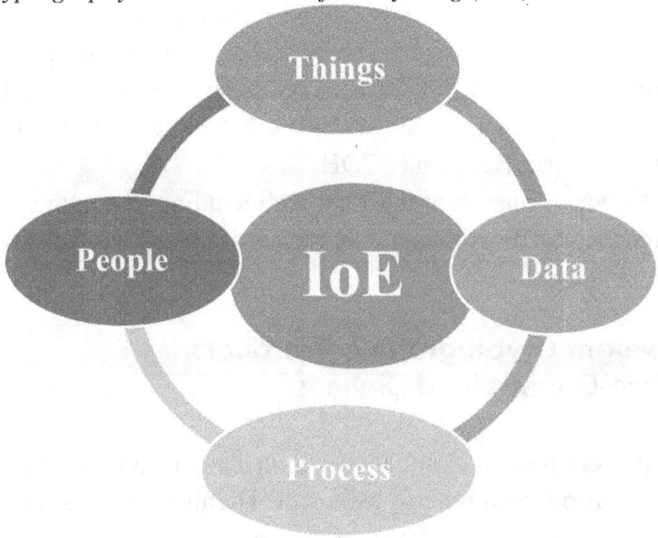

The Internet of everything (IoE), interconnects devices, people, processes and data in one system. environment, and the potential for big prospects and threats to data protection in the presented ecosystem as shown in Figure 5.

4.1. Challenges of Securing Hyper-Connected Ecosystems

- **Resource Constraints:** Few devices, in fact, are equipped with enough computational power for effective cryptographic operations.
- **Scalability:** Strict identities and protocols for navigating interconnecting billions of people devices.
- **Data Privacy:** Protecting the identity information that is required to be kept private in this industry interconnected systems.
- **Vulnerability to Attacks:** IoE systems are vulnerable to attacks such as Distributed Denial of Service (DDoS) attacks and needs CAPTCHA to improve security.

4.2. Device-to-Device Encryption in IoE Networks

In IoE, devices have to send messages to other devices in a secure way in order to exchange information and work jointly actions. Communication that occurs between devices is secure in order to protect privacy and combat eavesdropping.

Key Management: Some cryptographic systems allow devices to develop common secrets for encryption, these are stools through secure key exchange protocols like Elliptic Curve DiffieHellman (ECDH).

Benefits: Conceals important information, including its health status or industry control signals. It affirms which only the certified apparatus is involved in the relevant communication.

4.3. Lightweight Cryptographic Protocols for Resource-Constrained Devices

Most IoE devices present in homes today involve low power devices and lesser memory microcontrollers and energy resources. The above constraints are overcome by lightweight cryptography as shown in Figure 6.

Figure 6. Characteristics of lightweight cryptographic protocols

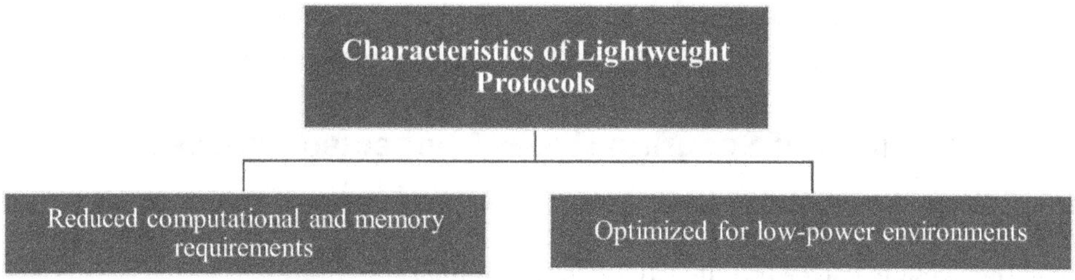

Examples:

- **Advanced Encryption Standard (AES) in CBC-MAC Mode:** Adapted for small devices.
- **Lightweight Ciphers:** SPECK and SIMON are some of the algorithms designed prominently.
- It is very well suited to tiny, constrained devices.

Benefits: Allows for the basic notion of secure communication without the detriment of using up the device resources. It is Not suitable for deployment in large IoE networks.

4.4. TLS, IoT and Making IoT Communication Secure

TLS was identified as the most commonly used protocol to secure communications in the contexts of IoE.

- It helps create a secure communication protocol between two devices together with servers.
- Implement key exchange using asymmetric encryption and the data link level encryption using symmetric encryption.
- It Authenticates Users Identity through Documents and digital certificates. and servers.
- Uses asymmetric encryption for key exchange and symmetric encryption for data transmission.
- Verifies identities through digital certificates, (Ramzi *et al.,* 2019).

Applications in IoE:

- Securing communication between smart home devices and cloud services.
- Protecting medical data in healthcare IoT systems.

Benefits: Eliminates spying and theft of information and it Protects the device from counterfeiting and safeguards the data.

4.5. Use Cases: Smart Homes, Healthcare, and Industrial IoT

Figure 7. Use cases

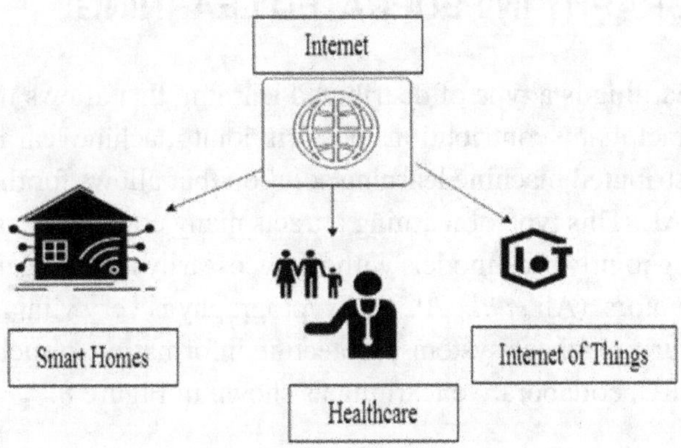

Smart Homes

- **Devices:** Smart homes equipped: thermostats, lights, security cameras.
- **Cryptographic applications:** Ultimately end-to-end encryption ensures and prevents privacy. Sensitive information such as unauthorized video feeds.

Healthcare

- **Devices:** Smart Clothing, Telehealth, Smart Devices Implants.
- **Cryptographic Applications:** This signifies that data entry of a patient is only shielded by lightweight encryption in order to protect the sensitive data.

The voluntary compliances with privacy regulations such as the Health Insurance Portability and Accountability Act –HIPAA, (Haoyong *et al.,* 2024).

Industrial IoT

- **Devices:** Automation devices and systems, products such as sensors and actuators, robotics specifically in manufacturing contexts and processes.
- **Cryptographic Applications:** For key management of data, there are TLS and secure key management systems.

Cryptography in IoE ensures the security and reliability of the operation in the super-connected IoT ecosystem. solving privacy and security issues and at the same time promoting innovation in smart technologies.

5. CRYPTOGRAPHY IN FEDERATED LEARNING

Federated learning is a type of distributed learning that allows multiple parties to TEXT to attract many contributions perform joint machine learning. Federated learning is a distributed machine learning solution that allows for the participation of multiple ICIAL. This type of learning attracts many contributions perform joint machine learning jointly train models without necessarily revealing underlying data to other collaborators, (Ali *et al.,* 2024). Cryptography is very vital in protection of privacy and security in these systems, protecting information in such systems from preying eyesReLU. collaborative learning as shown in Figure 8.

Figure 8. Cryptography in federated learning

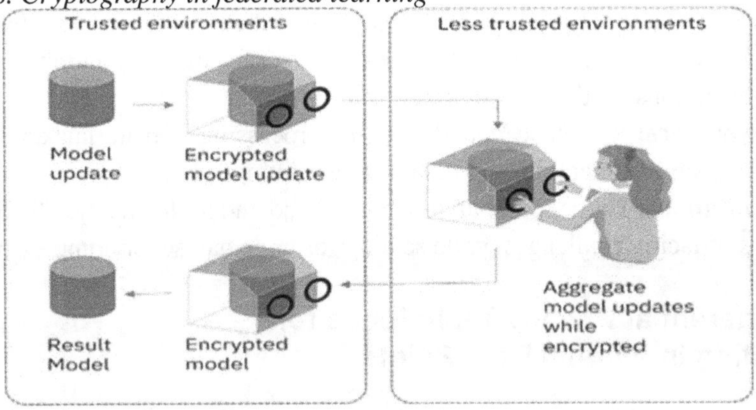

5.1. Privacy-Preserving Data Analytics in Distributed Systems

Concept: In federated learning parameters such as data do not have to be shared but model updates are sent to a central server or insights are shared. The idea of cryptography is important so that the privacy of information is on hold during these exchanges.

Techniques:

- Encrypted communication channels protect data-in-motion.
- Use of cryptographic stuff assures the updates for integrity and authenticity.

Benefits:

- Safeguards information within specific areas such as medical services, money related, and other telecommunications.
- Disallows opponent's from having insight of extra details during exchanges.

5.2. Role of Homomorphic Encryption in Secure Computations

Homomorphic Encryption (HE): Homomorphic Encryption (HE): A technique known as cryptography enables computations to be on. It encrypts with the possibility to read its data without decryption. The results of the computations are kept in encrypted and can only be decoded with the help of the data owner, (Pengkun, Jinshu, & Xiaofeng, 2020).

Applications in Federated Learning: Enables participants to perform encrypted aggregations or model updates without exposing raw data. Facilitates secure calculation in contexts where each party makes a number of input contributions model.
Advantages: It Protects data during the processing of materials and reduces the possible vulnerability of data during training.
Limitations: Higher computational overhead and high latency. The Possibilities of facing challenges while scaling for large dataset or complex models.

5.3. Differential Privacy Techniques for Protecting Individual Data Points

Differential Privacy (DP): Algebraic approach that introduce noise into data in a controlled manner outputs so that individual additions do not compromise results but rather the general value of dataset, (Kairouz *et al.,* 2019).
Benefits: Offers high theoretical privacy protection assurance. It Facilitates consistency with the data protection laws such as the GDPR.
Use Cases: Covering patient data in healthcare with federated learning. Consumer applications like predictive text or recommendation systems.

5.4. Secure Multiparty Computation (SMPC) in Collaborative Learning

SMPC: A cryptographic protocol that enables multiple parties to collaboratively compute a function over their inputs while keeping those inputs private.

- Participants encrypt their inputs, and computations are performed on encrypted values.
- Only the final aggregated output is decrypted, ensuring individual inputs remain confidential, (Kurniawan & Mambo, 2022).

  Applications: Secure aggregation of model updates in federated learning. Collaborative training between entities with competing interests (e.g., competing businesses).
  Advantages: Strong privacy guarantees without relying on a centrally trusted entity and prevents single points of failure or attack.

5.5. Challenges of Scalability and Computational Overhead in Federated Environments

Figure 9. Challenges in federated environments

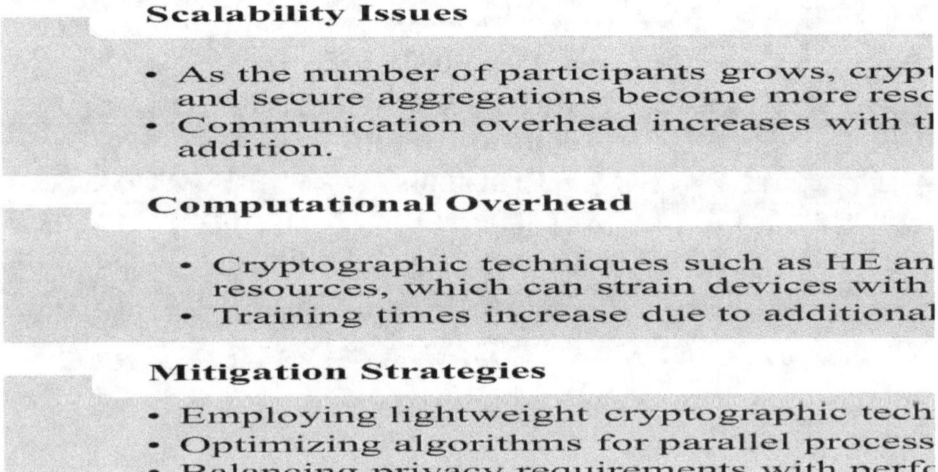

By leveraging advanced cryptographic methods, federated learning ensures data privacy and security, enabling collaboration across diverse organizations and domains while addressing the challenges of scalability and efficiency, (Bhavsingh, 2024)

6. ADVANCED CRYPTOGRAPHIC TECHNIQUES AND PROTOCOLS

Advanced cryptographic techniques provide the foundation for securing modern digital ecosystems. They enable secure communication, data integrity, and future-proof security in the face of evolving threats, including quantum computing as shown in Figure 10.

Figure 10. Advanced cryptographic techniques and protocols

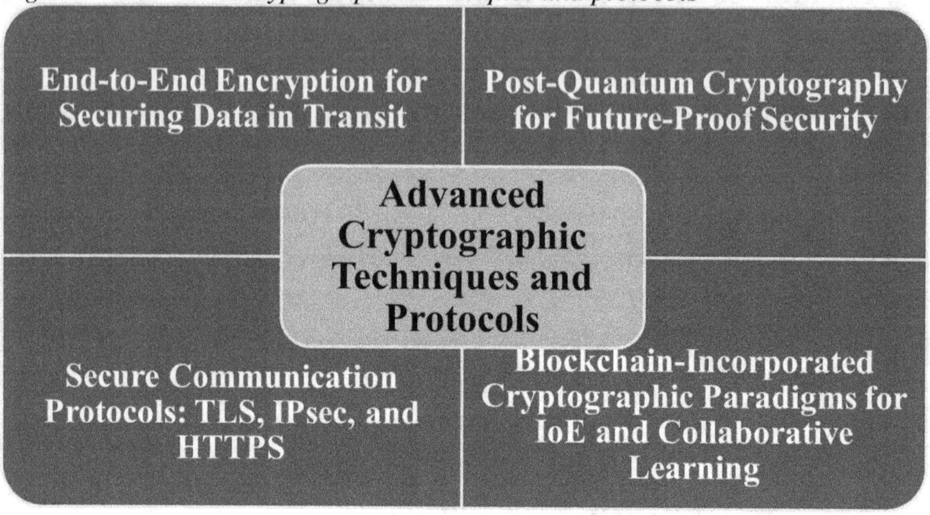

6.1. End-to-End Encryption for Securing Data in Transit

Concept: End-to-end encryption (E2EE) ensures that data is encrypted on the sender's side and decrypted only on the receiver's side, preventing intermediaries from accessing the data. Data is encrypted using the recipient's public key before transmission. Only the recipient's private key can decrypt the data. **Applications**: Instant communication applications that provide end-to-end encryption (Signal, WhatsApp etc.). IoE systems to give an assurance that device-to-device communication should not be compromised, (Kim *et al.*, 2020). **Benefits:** Ensures that third party do not access information intended for other end users and improves the level of security and confidentiality of users in communication processes.

6.2. Post-Quantum Cryptography for Future-Proof Security

- **Threat of Quantum Computing:** The main benefit that quantum computers are believed to be able to develop is decrypting commonly RSA and ECC cryptographic algorithms that were employed leading to a violation of the users' data privacy.
- **Post-Quantum Cryptography:** Cryptosystem – a set of agreed cryptographic algorithms that can effectively withstand a specific attack quantum attack

and, at the same time, remain compatible with the classical ones, (Yunakovsky *et al.,* 2021).

Applications:

- Long-term data protection for sensitive information (e.g., government records, medical data).
- IoE and federated learning systems to be made ready for future Quantum threats by improving them.

Challenges:

- Such additional factors as high computation cost and overhead.
- Transitioning existing systems to quantum-resistant algorithms.

6.3. Secure Communication Protocols: TLS, IPsec, and HTTPS

Secure communication protocols ensure the confidentiality, integrity, and authenticity of data in transit.

Transport Layer Security (TLS) Provides encryption for data transmitted over the internet.

Key Features:

- Uses asymmetric encryption for key exchange and symmetric encryption for data transfer.
- Authenticates the servers and clients by Digital certificates.
- Applications: Protecting web traffic, emails and interactions of IoE devices, (Tzinos, Limniotis, & Kolokotronis, 2022).

IPsec (Internet Protocol Security) It is also referred to as IP-security which is a protocol designed to protect data at the IP layer networks.

Key Features:

- Its smart card related services include, Authentication, encryption, and key management.
- Recognizes the use of VPN to support secure remote access.
- Applications: IoT networks, corporate intranets, and remote work setups.

HTTPS (Hypertext Transfer Protocol Secure) where TLS is used to provide a secure connection MEDIATEK.

Key Features:

- Encipher messages that are transmitted from web browsers to web servers.
- Confirms the identities of servers with the use of certificates.

Applications: E-commerce, online banking, and any web application requiring secure communication.

6.4. Blockchain-Incorporated Cryptographic Paradigms for IoE and Collaborative Learning

IoE and federated learning are enforced by Blockchain because of the improvements to security and, thus, trust it provides decentralized cryptographic structures.

IoE Applications

Blockchain secures IoE ecosystems by providing immutable logs and tamper-resistant data sharing. **Examples:**

- **Smart Contracts**: Enforce automated and secure interactions between IoE devices.
- **Decentralized Identity Management**: Uses blockchain to verify device identities without relying on central authorities, (Lavaur, Lacan, & Chanel, 2022).

Federated Learning Applications

Blockchain enhances federated learning by ensuring trust and transparency between participants. **Examples:**

- **Audit Trails**: Blockchain records all model updates and ensures accountability.
- **Token-Based Incentives**: Cryptographic tokens reward participants for contributing to federated learning tasks.

Benefits:

- Decentralized trust: No single point of failure or authority.
- Enhanced privacy: Cryptographic mechanisms ensure secure data sharing.

The postmodern cryptographic methods and frameworks lay the basis for secure communication which can be established to secure from quantum threats and provide trust in the decentralized systems like IoE and challenging applications of federate learning.

7. PRACTICAL CHALLENGES IN CRYPTOGRAPHY

However, as other research has indicated, the practical use of cryptography is a strong method of establishing a secure environment for protecting data in the developing world currently. The main disadvantage of different complicated lSystem has presented below: These threats stem from an attempt to balance security, cost efficiency that includes both performance and scalability as well as robust usability, (Lavaur, Lacan, & Chanel, 2022).

7.1. Key Management in Distributed Systems Importance

Secure key management is essential for the effectiveness of cryptographic systems. In distributed environments, this task becomes significantly more complex.

Challenges:

- **Key Distribution**: Securely sharing keys among multiple parties without exposing them to interception.
- **Key Storage:** The act of guarding keys from access or theft by other people with the intention of using them.
- **Key Rotation:** They key then can get compromised very easily and updating them frequently.

Scenarios:

- IoE devices, where due to the limited availability of resources, key management becomes an issue.
- Federated learning environments at which secure key exchanges are needed among participants.

Solutions: By employing hardware security modules (HSMs) or trusted platform modules (TPMs). Establishing decentralized key management structures on the blockchain or other distributed ledgers.

7.2. Computational Costs of Advanced Encryption Methods

- **Issue:** Homomorphic encryption or post quantum cryptography for instance; can be quite resource intensive.
- **Impact:** Delayed responsiveness to real time applications.
- Higher power usage in low power constraint devices such as IoT sensors or mobile devices.

Examples:

- Homomorphic encryption enables secure computation but introducing considerable overhead.
- Post-quantum cryptography with additional complicated algorithms and larger keys.

Mitigation Strategies: Adapting of cryptographic algorithms for particular hardware and Lightweight cryptography for constraint contexts, (Kumar *et al.*, 2021).

7.3. Balancing Performance with Security in Real-Time Applications

• **Problem:** Real-time appliances like self-driving cars, IoT in industries etc. need a very quick data processing and decision-making cause a tension with the overhead of strong encryption.

Examples of Conflict:

- Encrypted communication in latency-sensitive applications, such as stock trading or telemedicine.
- Complex authentication protocols delaying critical operations in emergency systems.

Approaches to Balance: It is important to choose cryptographic techniques that are most appropriate to the performance of the various parts of an application requirement. Adopting lightweight encryption methods to be used in real-timescape and models to leverage the best of both types. chores as well as, more robust methods to the less timely data, (Lara-Nino, Diaz-Perez, & Morales-Sandoval, 2018).

7.4. Positioning Risks That Arise from Legacy Interfaces

Legacy Systems: Many organizations rely on older systems that use outdated cryptographic algorithms or protocols, making them vulnerable to modern attacks.

Challenges: Compatibility: Updating cryptographic systems while ensuring compatibility with existing infrastructure.

Obsolete Algorithms: When using insecure algorithms, such as MD5 or DES, its continued utilization is still perhaps worthwhile Previously to system limitations.

Cost: The expenses that companies can encounter when gearing up or altogether changing their outmoded systems.

Examples: New IoT devices that need to retain their firmware and cannot dynamically change it. Environments with Enterprise systems, which use outdated versions of TLS or insecure key lengths.

Solutions: Embracing periodic security and general risk assessment in the premises. The application of patch management and incremental updates of secure connections and applications.

Finally, using gateway devices to provide protection to legacy systems where the systems themselves cannot be overhauled. Implementation issues of cryptography put emphasis on the issue of data security in real environment applications. Solving these challenges is possible only through the usage of new approaches and local management and coordination backed in balanced and prudent provision of resources by design, and consistent efforts during planning and throughout subsequent stages to guarantee strong and reliable cryptographic approaches, (Wenhua *et al.,* 2023).

8. ETHICAL AND REGULATORY CONSIDERATIONS

Blockchain continues to be a part of cryptographic technologies that still have a focus on the protection of data and communication. The need for pragmatic solutions to include addressing ethical and regulatory issues involves getting crucial. CHALLENGE: Where to find a balance between privacy and security and moreover, where to make these new elements fit in with regulations when providing legal services must be followed to create trust with the appropriate legal usage. cryptography in different paradigms of Business.

8.1. Meeting Data Privacy and Global Standard Requirements

Cryptography can be said to play the most important role in the achievement of data privacy. Nevertheless, its implementation must be consistent within regard to privacy of individuals and compliance with international standard and laws for ethical conduct. Of personal data.

8.1.1. GDPR (General Data Protection Regulation)

Overview: A European Union regulation that mandates strict data protection and privacy standards for all organizations handling the personal data of EU citizens.

Relevance to Cryptography:

- Such applications of cryptography as end to end are vital in compliance practices.
- Data minimization: Such methods like differential privacy are adopted in order to avoid having led to an avoidable exposure of personal data, (Qamar, Javed, & Beg, 2021).
- Ensures transparency and accountability in how personal data is stored and processed.

Impact on Cryptographic Practices:

This issue requires organizations to adopt the best form of security measures that can protect data from the public domain. Encryption keys and access control means must be well protected in order freedom to delete as well as freedom to request for his or her data.

CCPA (California Consumer Privacy Act)

Overview: A California state law that provides consumers with the right to know what personal data is being collected and to request its deletion.

Relevance to Cryptography:

- Organizations must implement encryption techniques that protect personal data in storage and during transmission.
- Secure data-sharing protocols are critical to ensure compliance with consumer data requests.

Impact on Cryptographic Practices:

- Cryptography enables secure data transmission and protects privacy during data exchanges.
- Guarantees the consumer's right to data protection in compliance with the GDPR through security systems.

Other Regulatory Frameworks

- **HIPAA (Health Insurance Portability and Accountability Act)**: In the healthcare sector, cryptographic techniques protect patient data and ensure compliance with privacy standards.
- **PCI DSS (Payment Card Industry Data Security Standard)**: Cryptography is vital in securing payment card data during transactions and storage.
- **FATF (Financial Action Task Force) Guidelines**: Ensures financial institutions use encryption to prevent money laundering and fraud, (Ethical considerations in ai-enabled big data research: balancing innovation and privacy, 2020).

8.2. Ethical Implications of Cryptographic Misuse

While cryptography makes it possible to protect the individual's privacy and data security, its abuse can enhance the violation of his/her privacy significant ethical concerns as shown in Figure 11.

Figure 11. Data anonymization and privacy versus surveillance

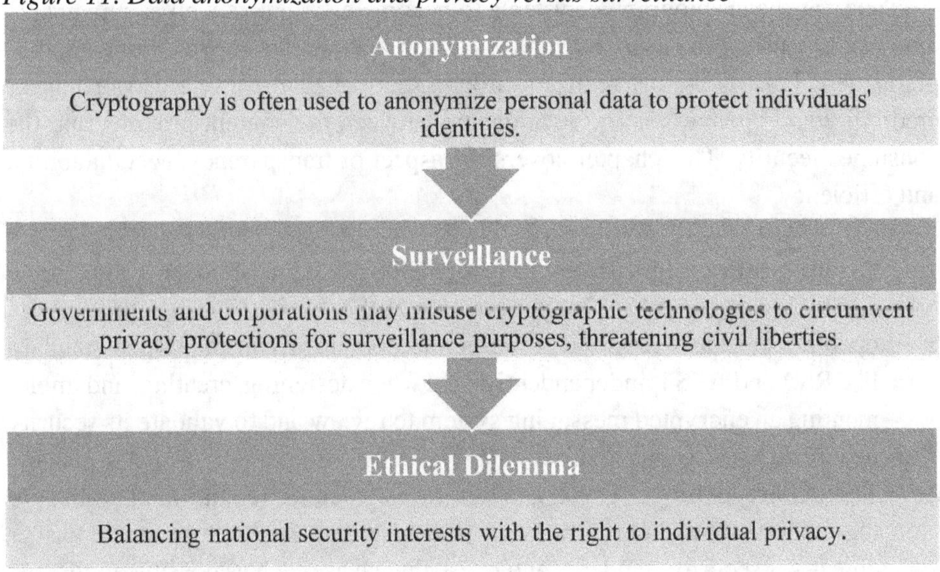

Example: When government tries to put "backdoors" on encryption. Research also reported that algorithms for Law enforcement to decrypt data reduce the overall security and make individuals vulnerable to lose their privacy.

The Use of Cryptography in Malicious Activities

- **Cryptocurrency:** Cryptography drives objects such as Bitcoins; however, its anonymity can be used by criminals for any heinous acts including the use of funding, meager or money laundering terrorism.
- **Ethical Challenge:** Deciding on what degree of control of encryption is appropriate, technologies in such a manner the right to privacy or liberty is not infringed and the development of more technologies is not restricted. Access to Encrypted Data.
- **Ethical Dilemma:** Is it right for governments or any institutions to force corporations to? Decode other's conversation or information for instance in criminal cases?

- **Impact:** This might demoralize users from trusting encrypted systems and introduce security. loopholes that different bad actors would love to capitalize on.

8.3 Trust in Cryptographic Systems of Defending on World Industrialization

Thus, for the cryptographic systems to become efficient as well as universally employed by users, the users must have trust in the systems in which they are implemented. Trust is mainly realized through the management of trustworthiness, credibility and openness in the relationship between the content provider and the consumer security. This chapter covers the aspect of transparency, accountability, and efficiency.

Cryptographic Algorithms: Cryptographic protocols are open-source ones, and their usage is way more popular due to the fact that these entities are an open book; that is they are in the public domain. **Example**: Open standard like RSA and AES is independently used when designing, creating, and implementing an encrypted messaging system to review and to validate its security features, (Nti, Gyamfi, & Osei, 2017).

Third-Party Audits: These goals in mind, keeping regular audits of cryptographic systems help in making assurance that the latter meet the former objectives security standards and resist change as much as possible to threats.

User Education

- **Educating Consumers:** Informing people about the need for encryption and data. Security plays a crucial role in developing confidence in different services offered over the internet such as online shopping, online banking services etc.
- **Training for Developers**: Cryptography, in most cases, is intricate, thus, it is significant to allow developers to have the right tools and the right knowledge to put in secure systems.

Regulatory Assurance

- **Certifications and Compliance**: The industries should go for accreditation from those bodies that have been accorded recognition standards to show compliance with certain norms such as the International Organization for Standardization (ISO 27001) Information Security Management. concerning data protection and privacy commits.
- **Clear Communication**: Organizations must be transparent about their data practices, cryptographic protocols, and how they protect consumer data.

According to the roles of cryptography in present day protection of information, it is of extreme importance to notice this practice 's ethical application. The concepts of privacy, protection of data, safety issues and legal requirements worldwide. By balancing these considerations, industries can design reliable systems that respect people's privacy and liberties and advance the primacy of cryptographic technology, but in its reasonable and proper utilization, (International Research Journal of Modernization in Engineering technology and Science, 2024).

9. CASE STUDIES AND APPLICATIONS

Cryptographic protocols are at the heart of protection of most contemporary systems, ranging from Decentralized Finance to electronic funds transfer, healthcare uses of cryptocurrencies and co-learning intelligent systems. Below are case studies explaining how cryptography is used to solve practical problems and accompanied with the findings and recommendations Shared Among Stakeholders Dissemination of Introduction of measures and plans to avoid future pitfalls and adopt the best strategies in implementing education lessons.

9.1. Blockchain Protecting Financial Operations in Decentralized Finance (DeFi)

DeFi is an emerging domain within the field of cryptocurrency that is defined by decentralized finance. Blockchain ecosystem, which will strive to provide lending and borrowing, trade and exchange services, in addition to many others. Assets without involving other conventional forms of facilities and financial mediators such as banks, brokers, or insurance companies. Blockchain technology is the bedrock of DeFi application to facilitate secure decentralized financial systems. It is intended to provide clear and effective financial transactions in a decentralized and without any kind of trust, (Jafar, 2019).

The major implementation of cryptography is in blockchain systems that have a crucial role in the protection of transactions. compression; anonymity; and decentralization of transactions ensuring privacy and establishing trustless environment. In the platforms of DeFi, the clients transact directly with one another employing smart contracts and digital currency. engagement security in decision making process to maintain the authenticity of the transactions and the security of the user's assets.

Cryptographic Mechanisms Ensuring Security in DeFi

1. **Hashing for Immutability**: Another of the postulates lodged at the core of a blockchain gerektir. Technology is immutability. If a transaction is being made on DeFi platform, it is processed employing a cryptographic hash function (usually SHA-256 or other, based on the blockchain). Transaction details are written in to a block and when the block is filled it goes to the block chain. the moment the transaction is recorded on the blockchain; it is secure information in the blockchain cannot be changed or deleted, (Lo & Medda, 2020).

Every DeFi transaction is assigned a specific numerical representation referred to as a cryptographic hash value for that transaction and therefore creating the fingerprint for that transaction. Once it is validated through network membership and incorporated into the group database, the sender is ready to transmit messages with the hope of having them processed by the addressee. In the case of the blockchain, this hash is important because it will not allow anyone to alter the details of a transaction. without changing the entire blockchain, which would be computationally infeasible.

Example: All trade and transactions that occur in the platform like Uniswap or Compound are all documented. on the block chain with their own hash which makes it more secure and easy to track record of activity.

Uniswap - Decentralized Exchange (DEX): Uniswap is known as a decentralized exchange. where users are afforded an opportunity to trade several cryptocurrencies from their same wallet without having to depend on centralized intermediaries on the contrary, much remains to be desired regarding the current state of centralized intermediaries for facilitating self-organization processes among members of a social network. Funds transfers are protected by the non-changeable nature of the blockchain. The TRADE AUTHENTICATION that has been established through the use of digital signatures as shown in Figure 12, (Brennecke *et al.*, 2022).

Figure 12. How Uniswap works

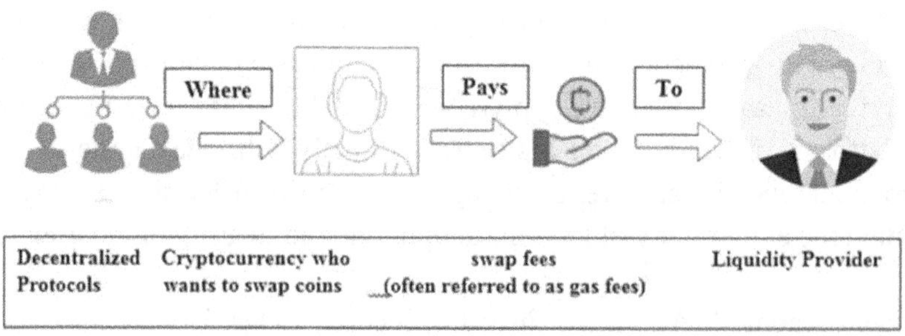

Security Feature: All trades on Uniswap occur through smart contracts written on Ethereum and are documented on the Ethereum blockchain and can confirmed via the transaction hash for instance. Smart contracts are digital self-executing contracts enabling the exchange of tokens through certain pre-specified criteria for tokens; there are no middlemen needed and ensuring transparency.

2. Digital Signatures for Transaction Authentication: Any time something takes place in the DeFi market:

The foreseeable functionality of such approaches as the application of digital signatures, one of the essential cryptographic technologies that guarantee the genuine and real consideration of the transaction. A user signs any transaction with their private key and the network checks for the authenticity of the said transaction using the other party's public key, (Shoetan, 2024). When for instance a user feels that it is time to begin a trade or a withdrawal, among other activities. When any transaction of these funds is to be made, they authorize it in writing using their private key. The digital signature will help to guarantee that only this means that the person possessing the private key can authorize the transaction. The public key enables any member to check this message and attest that it is the signature of the transaction is legitimate.

Example: As in other DeFi protocols such as Aave, users verify their transactions. Private keys to securely engage with the platform without having to fully depend on a central authority.

Aave - Decentralized Lending and Borrowing: Aave is a defi autonomous finance that allows users to make and receive loans in cryptocurrencies with other people's environment. The loans are managed by employing smart contracts, technology that enables the system to make decisions without human intervention. The disadvantageous elements of money, including its reliability as a collateral, and interest rates can be obtained without the support of a central authority as shown in Figure 13.

Figure 13. How Aave works

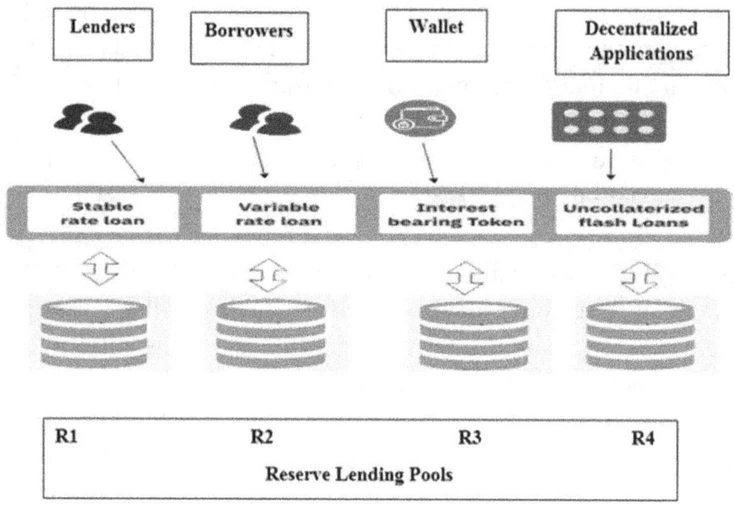

Security Feature: While wallet transactions in Aave operate on public-key cryptography, loans security is employed contracts by smart contracts instead. It also guarantees that the borrower's collateral is frozen and can be sold off to recover the money if the individuals do not meet their debts obligation, (Kuznetsov, 2024).

9.2. IoE in Healthcare: Encrypting Patient Data in Real-Time Monitoring Systems

Internet of Everything (IoE) deals with connecting equipment, sensors and real-time data into healthcare system applications. Data security is important, especially the patient information obtained from the devices, and cryptography plays a critical role in it. It is safe, and your information is not observed by the third party, (V., 2024).

Cryptographic Applications in IoE Healthcare:

- **End-to-End Encryption (E2EE):** Makes certain that the relevant patient information including vital signs is kept encrypted given that it is shared from wearable devices to the health facilities.
- **Public-Key Infrastructure (PKI):** Verifies and additionally manages the connection of healthcare devices and systems enabling safe connection of the devices and medical platforms.
- **Blockchain for Data Integrity:** Blockchain can guarantee the authenticity of the patient's data. which enables them to transfer and accessi-

bility securely across different institutions while at the same time preserving an unalterable audit trail, (Fang & Qian, 2021).

Example:

A healthcare IoE system deals with the usage of wearables such as a wrist band to measure the heart rate, glucose level and other vital signs. The data is encrypted before going through the network to the cloud and for analysis by patients, doctors and other healthcare personnel to enhance their privacy so that there not be any leakage of patient's information.

- **Data Privacy**: Cryptography is essential in safeguarding sensitive patient data from unauthorized access and ensuring compliance with healthcare regulations like HIPAA.
- **Interoperability**: Ensuring that different IoE devices and platforms securely communicate with each other remains a challenge.
- **Latency**: Real-time data processing must balance encryption's computation al cost with the need for quick responses in critical healthcare situations.

9.3. Federated Learning in Personalized Healthcare Analytics and Diagnostics

Overview:

It also allows for multiple healthcare settings to jointly train a model in a manner known as federated learning paradigms where the raw patient data is not disclosed and can still be useful. Secure multi-party computation and homomorphic encryption including ciphering methods which are topical in the field of database security have a great importance in keeping privacy relevant to the training process, (Fang & Qian, 2021).

Cryptographic Applications in Federated Learning:

- **Homomorphic Encryption:** Enables institutions to carry out operations on data in encrypted data or for allowing the machine learning models to learn from the sensitive health care data without exposing patient's identity through disclosing or sharing specific details of that individual patient, (Bagirovs, 2024).
- **Secure Aggregation:** Checking that only model updates sent to a central server are aggregated while keeping non-disclosed most specific details of the input data.

- **Differential Privacy:** Preserves patients' privacy by adding perturbation in the updates of the model that during the training process it is not necessary to transmit information about any certain patient.

Example:

Instead, several health care institutions contribute to training the machine learning algorithm for prognosis of patient outcomes. Conditions incorporated included potential estimates of development of certain diseases such as diabetes. Rather than transmitting patient data, each institution applies a certain encryption of its data and sends models updates to a central server, where they are safely summed up to enhance the overall model.

- **Data Privacy and Compliance**: Federated learning is well-suited for healthcare, as it allows sensitive data to remain private while still enabling valuable insights.
- **Computational Overhead**: Cryptographic techniques like homomorphic encryption can slow down model training, making optimization critical.
- **Collaboration**: Healthcare institutions must establish trust and secure frameworks to participate in federated learning, ensuring that each institution's data remains protected.

9.4. Best Practices from Real-World Implementations

- **Use of Strong, Established Protocols**: Leveraging well-tested cryptographic standards and protocols (e.g., AES, RSA, TLS) helps mitigate vulnerabilities.
- **Transparency and Accountability**: Whether using blockchain or federated learning, ensuring that cryptographic protocols are transparent and auditable builds trust.
- **Continuous Education and Awareness**: Organizations should regularly train staff on cryptographic security best practices and emerging threats to ensure systems remain secure.

The case study below demonstrates how cryptography works in different fields and the lessons executed from practical applications which allow me to gain experience from real-world implementations. As cryptographic systems become more powerful, and integral to the issues of securing the data and the requirement of privacy, constant progress and evolution are crucial to address new opportunities and emerging changes and constraints in regulations.

10. CRYPTOGRAPHY FUTURE EVOLUTION

Given these and other changes in the field of digital security, cryptography has to evolve, too, as the threats that exist within such a system are of high risks that emerging hazards, new technologies and growing rules and regulations present requirements. The developments of the future of cryptography cover aspects such as better algorithms and blending with AI or artificial intelligence, emergence of Moore's law and readiness for quantum computing, (Salih & Abdulrazzaq, 2023).

10.1. New Algorithmic Approaches regarding New Threats

Cryptography has changed its threat environment and the threats it poses to a dangerous level as cyber-attacks become more sophisticated. Hoping to counter these emerging threats, new cryptographic methods are currently being invented threats.

- **Post-Quantum Cryptography (PQC):** Latter, with the development of quantum computers, most of the conventional encryption techniques, such as RSA, ECC, etc. are vulnerable to risk of being broken. PQC is in development to produce encryption mechanisms that are immune to quantum assaults including lattice-based cryptography, hash-based signatures or MV polynomial cryptography, (Sklavos, 2012).
- **Fully Homomorphic Encryption (FHE)**: FHE allows computations to be performed on encrypted data without decrypting it first. This technique has vast potential for secure cloud computing, ensuring data privacy even during processing. Though it is complex and challenging to implement, further research will focus emphasizing the goals that have to do with optimization for practical usage.
- **Quantum Key Distribution (QKD):** This technique employs QM to make communication secure by identifying. I have no idea if anyone is listening to what is being said during the transmission. QKD offers an assurance of a highly secure exchange of keys mechanisms, while it is still in its early stage of development for large-scale applications.
- **Advanced Hash Functions:** However, as attacker's computational capabilities continue to grow, the subtraction dependent trail unpicking is subject to cryptographic hash. While performing the operations of these functions, there is a possibility that the algorithm can suffer from attacks such as pre-image or collision attacks. Research into SAFER use of technologies that provide more security that those of initial hash functions, including cryptographic ones like Will play a role of Sponge functions, will be important.

10.2. Integration of AI in Cryptographic Systems for Dynamic Threat Detection

The utilization of Artificial Intelligence in Cryptographic Systems for prompt threat identification. Modern cryptographic systems are being bolstered with the assistance of AI technology more frequently than before due providing real-time threat identification and controllable security actions

- **AI-Driven Cryptographic Attack Detection**: By means of machine learning algorithms the existence of an abnormal or even a possible security breach can be identified in the message authentication cryptographic systems to enable the system to respond to the caller with a high speed. AI could identify new attacks of marked relationships and cryptographic vulnerabilities in real time thus offering constant surveillance and other defenses of oneself and another person. **Example:** AI enabled traffic analysis of encrypted traffic patterns and raise alarms with regards to peculiar traffic activities that point to a cyber-tip, which in turn means that some type of cyber-attack is underway and can be automatically counteracted, (Kaneko, Saito, & Kikuchi, 2015).
- **AI in Cryptographic Key Management:** This means that through the use AI-powered systems it is possible to predict the management of cryptographic keys. The duration taken by keys, automation of the process of having to change keys frequently and altering the procedures of issuing keys on emerging threats.
- **Automated Cryptanalysis:** In the process of cryptanalysis, AI can help by estimating various attacks approaches for the attack against cryptographic algorithms and to detect vulnerable points at a faster rate than the methods. This can be used to expose cryptographic protocols to conditions which they have not being previously exposed to before they are deployed in sensitive environments.
- **Adaptive Encryption:** In architecture with artificial intelligence, it is possible to introduce the dependence on the fluctuation of the cryptographic key, the level of protection, etc. The type of data being processed, or the threat level. For example, one can encrypt high-risk transactions, and high-risk data could use more powerful algorithms, in contrast, low risk data could use less rigorous cryptographic measures for efficiency.

10.3. Innovations in Hardware for Enhanced Cryptographic Efficiency

Issues such as efficiency of cryptographic systems are influenced totally by the computation costs of encryption and decryption. For that reason, a family of algorithms, increasing the level of complexity of the cryptographic algorithms, hardware introductory changes are crucial to retain performance and effectiveness of an organization.

- **Hardware Security Modules (HSMs)**: HSMs are physical appliances developed to work as a trusted platform for generating, storing and managing cryptographic keys. New developments in HSM technology include quantum-resistant HSMs, are of vital importance to the impending practical schemes of secure cryptography. They are being developed to enable a new generation of cryptographic methods, PQTs, (Vithalkar, 2024).
- **Dedicated Cryptographic Processors (CPUs):** Specific cryptographic accelerators are being directed towards improving the encryption and decryption calculation execution time of highly secured cryptographic algorithms decryption operations. These processors are capable of handling large amounts of data encrypted within them. while providing the required high-end processing speeds and lower levels of security risks, (Sonko, 2024).
- **Quantum-Resistant Cryptographic Hardware:** The current encryption is under the immense threat of the quantum computing as you can consider standards. As a result, researchers are beginning to design hardware that will work efficiently with quantum-resistant algorithms. They will be decisive in maintaining that cryptography held as the innovative safeguard of worldwide net security protocols stay safe even in the environment that utilizes quantum computing.
- **Energy-Efficient Cryptographic Systems:** This is specifically important as more IoT devices enter the market and edge computing environments increase in demand. Newer hardware architectures that in a way cut out so much of the software layer and plumb balance between the amount of computation to be done to enable encryption while at the same time meeting high levels of security that can be used in resource limited environments, (Odour, 2022).

11. CONCLUSION

Cryptography plays an important role in providing the integrity, confidentiality, and authenticity of data in a world that is rapidly becoming more and more connected. With increasing overall complexity of digital ecosystems, such as cryptography steadily remaining at the core of data protection methodologies: encryption, hash functions, digital signatures, secure communication protocols, etc. These technologies allow secure interactions in domains including blockchain, IoT and federated learning systems domains where the need for security keeps increasing. Hence, cryptography continues to serve as the basis of security and networking in formations of technologies for various industries.

In the future, cryptography is going to have a significant part to perform the increasing issues of quantum computing security, AI threats, and privacy-preserving solutions. Advanced quantum-resistant algorithms, artificial-intelligence enhanced cryptographic architectures and progressive hardware solutions define the future of protected digital environment. In order for the development of cryptographic solutions to progress more improvements in research and education are required by governments and academia and in cooperation with private organizations. By taking an innovation and standardization approach, it will be possible to advance on cryptography that will meet future needs of the society by enhancing trust, security, and progress from a rapidly growing technological environment.

REFERENCES

Bagchi, S., Abdelzaher, T. F., Govindan, R., Shenoy, P., Atrey, A., Ghosh, P., & Xu, R. (2020). New frontiers in IoT: Networking, systems, reliability, and security challenges. *IEEE Internet of Things Journal*, *7*(12), 11330–11346.

Bagirovs, E. (2024). Applications of post-quantum cryptography. European Conference on cyber Warfare and Security, 23(1), 49-57. https://doi.org/DOI: 10.34190/eccws.23.1.2247

Bhavsingh, M., Samunnisa, K., & Mallareddy, A. (2024). Enhancing efficiency and security in mtc environments: A novel strategy for dynamic grouping and streamlined management. *Emerg. Technol. Eng. J.*, *1*(1), 43–56. DOI: 10.53898/etej2024114

Brennecke, M., Guggenberger, T., Schellinger, B., & Urbach, N. (2022). the decentral bank in decentralized finance: a case study of makerdao.. https://doi.org/DOI: 10.24251/HICSS.2022.737

Fang, H., & Qian, Q. (2021). Privacy preserving machine learning with homomorphic encryption and federated learning. *Future Internet*, *13*(4), 94. DOI: 10.3390/fi13040094

Gbadebo, Ayoade., Erick, Bauman., Latifur, Khan., Kevin, W., Hamlen. (2019). Smart Contract Defense through Bytecode Rewriting. 384-389. DOI: 10.1109/Blockchain.2019.00059

Haoyang, A., & Debiao, H. (2024). Efficient Certificateless Online/Offline Signcryption Scheme Without Bilinear Pairing for Smart Home Consumer Electronics. *IEEE Transactions on Consumer Electronics*, *70*(1), 4005–4015. DOI: 10.1109/TCE.2023.3307697

Hazra, R., Chatterjee, P., Singh, Y., Podder, G., & Das, T. (2024). Data Encryption and Secure Communication Protocols. In Strategies for E-Commerce Data Security: Cloud, Blockchain, AI, and Machine Learning (pp. 546-570). IGI Global.

Jafar, Q. (2019). digital currency generation using hash function and digital signature (digcur). *Al-Nahrain Journal of Science*, *22*(2), 68–77. DOI: 10.22401/ANJS.22.2.09

Kairouz, P., ... (2019). "Advances and Open Problems in Federated Learning." *arXiv preprint arXiv:1912.04977*.

Kaneko, Y., Saito, T., & Kikuchi, H. (2015). cryptographic operation load-balancing between cryptographic module and cpu., 698-705. https://doi.org/DOI: 10.1109/AINA.2015.256

Kim, S., Yun, S., Lee, E., Bae, S., & Lee, I. (2020). Fast packet inspection for end-to-end encryption. *Electronics (Basel)*, *9*(11), 1937. DOI: 10.3390/electronics9111937

Kumar, A., Ottaviani, C., Gill, S., & Buyya, R. (2021). securing the future internet of things with post-quantum cryptography. *Security and Privacy*, *5*(2), e200. Advance online publication. DOI: 10.1002/spy2.200

Kurniawan, H., & Mambo, M.Kurniawan and Mambo. (2022). Homomorphic Encryption-Based Federated Privacy Preservation for Deep Active Learning. *Entropy (Basel, Switzerland)*, *24*(11), 1545. Advance online publication. DOI: 10.3390/e24111545 PMID: 36359635

Kuznetsov, O., Rusnak, A., Yezhov, A., Kanonik, D., Kuznetsova, K., & Karashchuk, S. (2024). Enhanced security and efficiency in blockchain with aggregated zero-knowledge proof mechanisms. *IEEE Access : Practical Innovations, Open Solutions*, •••, 1–1. DOI: 10.1109/ACCESS.2024.3384705

Lara-Nino, C., Diaz-Perez, A., & Morales-Sandoval, M. (2018). Energy and area costs of lightweight cryptographic algorithms for authenticated encryption in wsn. *Security and Communication Networks*, *2018*, 1–14. DOI: 10.1155/2018/5087065

Lavaur, T., Lacan, J., & Chanel, C. (2022). Enabling blockchain services for ioe with zk-rollups. https://doi.org/DOI: 10.20944/preprints202208.0023.v1

Lo, Y., & Medda, F. (2020). uniswap and the rise of the decentralized exchange. SSRN Electronic Journal. https://doi.org/DOI: 10.2139/ssrn.3715398

Nofal, R. A., Tran, N., Garcia, C., Liu, Y., & Dezfouli, B. (2019, November). A comprehensive empirical analysis of tls handshake and record layer on iot platforms. In *Proceedings of the 22nd International ACM Conference on Modeling, Analysis and Simulation of Wireless and Mobile Systems* (pp. 61-70).

Nti, I., Gyamfi, E., & Osei, M. (2017). Effective cryptographic technique for securing cloud storage systems. *International Journal of Applied Information Systems*, *12*(4), 19–25. DOI: 10.5120/ijais2017451696

Nwakeze, Osita, Miracle. (2024). The Importance of Network Security in Protecting Sensitive Data and Information. International journal of research and innovation in applied science, IX(VI):259-270. DOI: 10.51584/IJRIAS.2024.906024

Oduor, X., & Omariba, Z. B. (2022). Application of cryptography in enhancing privacy of personal data in medical services. *International Journal of Communication and Information Technology*, *3*(1), 16–21. DOI: 10.33545/2707661X.2022.v3.i1a.41

Peivandizadeh, A., & Adarbah, Y., H., Molavi, B., Mohajerzadeh, A., & H. Al-Badi, A. (2024). A Secure Key Exchange and Authentication Scheme for Securing Communications in the Internet of Things Environment. *Future Internet*, *16*(10), 357.

Pengkun, Li., Jinshu, Su., Xiaofeng, Wang. (2020). iTLS: Lightweight Transport-Layer Security Protocol for IoT With Minimal Latency and Perfect Forward Secrecy. IEEE Internet of Things Journal, 7(8):6828-6841. DOI: 10.1109/JIOT.2020.2988126

Pooja, G., Dhawane., P., Navghare., Dr., Sampada, Mashirkar., Nikita, Y., Kapadnis., Dipika, D, Raigar., Kimaya, Urane. (2024). Cryptography in Network Security: a Mini Review. Communications on Applied Nonlinear Analysis, DOI: 10.52783/cana.v32.1960

Qamar, A., Javed, T., & Beg, M. (2021). Detecting compliance of privacy policies with data protection laws. https://doi.org//arxiv.2102.12362DOI: 10.48550

Salih, A., & Abdulrazzaq, M. (2023). cyber security: Performance analysis and challenges for cyber attacks detection. *Indonesian Journal of Electrical Engineering and Computer Science*, *31*(3), 1763. DOI: 10.11591/ijeecs.v31.i3.pp1763-1775

Shoetan, P. O., & Familoni, B. T. (2024). Blockchain's impact on financial security and efficiency beyond cryptocurrency uses. *International Journal of Management & Entrepreneurship Research*, *6*(4), 1211–1235.

Singh, D. S. (2024). Decentralized finance (DeFi): Exploring the role of blockchain and cryptocurrency in financial ecosystems. *International Research Journal of Modernization in Engineering Technology and Science*, •••, 5.

Sklavos, N. (2012). cryptographic hardware & embedded systems for communications.. https://doi.org/DOI: 10.1109/ESTEL.2012.6400096

Sonko, S. (2024). quantum cryptography and u.s. digital security: a comprehensive review: investigating the potential of quantum technologies in creating unbreakable encryption and their future in national security. *Computer Science & It Research Journal*, *5*(2), 390–414. DOI: 10.51594/csitrj.v5i2.790

Tzinos, I., Limniotis, K., & Kolokotronis, N. (2022). Evaluating the performance of post-quantum secure algorithms in the tls protocol. Journal of Surveillance security and Safety, 3(3), 101-127. https://doi.org/DOI: 10.20517/jsss.2022.15

Urs, W. (2023). *Thomas, Lugrin*. Hash Functions., DOI: 10.1007/978-3-031-33386-6_5

Vashishth, T. K., Sharma, V., Kumar, B., Sharma, K. K., Chaudhary, S., & Panwar, R. (2025). Blockchain for Securing Federated Learning Systems: Enhancing Privacy and Trust. Model Optimization Methods for Efficient and Edge AI: Federated Learning Architectures, Frameworks and Applications, 299-320.

Vithalkar, P. (2024). cryptographic protocols resilient to quantum attacks: advancements in post-quantum cryptography. cana, 31(3s), 520-532. https://doi.org/DOI: 10.52783/cana.v31.805

Weihong, W. (2024). Poster: I Know What Crypto You Got Last Summer: A Study on Web3 Wallet. *Security and Privacy*, *1-2*, 1–2. Advance online publication. DOI: 10.1109/BRAINS63024.2024.10732070

Wenhua, Z., Qamar, F., Abdali, T., Hassan, R., Jafri, S., & Nguy n, Q. (2023). Blockchain technology: Security issues, healthcare applications, challenges and future trends. *Electronics (Basel)*, *12*(3), 546. DOI: 10.3390/electronics12030546

Yunakovsky, S., Kot, M., Pozhar, N., Nabokov, D., Kudinov, M., Guglya, A., Kiktenko, E. O., Kolycheva, E., Borisov, A., & Fedorov, A. (2021). Towards security recommendations for public-key infrastructures for production environments in the post-quantum era. *EPJ Quantum Technology*, *8*(1), 14. Advance online publication. DOI: 10.1140/epjqt/s40507-021-00104-z

Chapter 3
Integration of Blockchain Mechanisms in Cybersecurity:
Enhancing Data Integrity and Trustworthiness

Swati Jeevan
Universidad Azteca, Mexico

Srinath Doss
Botho University, Botswana

Kamal Kant Hiran
Sir Padampat Singhania University, India

Ruchi Doshi
https://orcid.org/0000-0002-7259-8481
Universidad Azteca, Mexico

ABSTRACT

Blockchain technology has emerged as a pivotal force in the realm of cybersecurity, particularly in elevating data integrity and authentication. This paper delves into how blockchain's decentralized and tamper-resistant architecture alleviates the mounting challenges of protecting sensitive information and preventing unauthorized access. The technology employs cryptographic techniques and distributed ledger technology (DLT) to ensure that data remains immutable, traceable, and impervious to tampering. The research explores how blockchain enhances authentication mechanisms through decentralized identity verification systems, reducing reliance on traditional

DOI: 10.4018/979-8-3373-1424-2.ch003

centralized entities. Real-world applications are scrutinized to demonstrate how blockchain proficiently fortifies security measures, protects digital identities, and fosters trust within increasingly interconnected digital landscapes. The findings suggest that blockchain holds the potential to revolutionize cybersecurity.

1. INTRODUCTION

In this era of digital transformation, cybersecurity has ascended to a paramount concern for governments, enterprises, and individuals alike. The intricate web of interconnected systems, the astonishing surge in data accumulation, and our escalating reliance on digital ecosystems have all exposed weaknesses that nefarious cybercriminals eagerly exploit. The cyber realm is besieged by intricate threats that challenge the capabilities of traditional cybersecurity measures, including data breaches, ransomware incidents, identity theft, and the pilfering of intellectual property. The flaws inherent in centralized security strategies, which form the cornerstone of cyber defences, are becoming increasingly evident. Due to their dependence on these frameworks, they stand exposed to attacks that could endanger vast troves of sensitive information. In light of the rising tide of frequency and sophistication of cyberattacks, a more resilient, trustworthy, and fortified framework is urgently needed to protect data integrity and facilitate authentication in digital environments (Sharma et al., 2023). A groundbreaking new paradigm for tackling cybersecurity challenges has emerged: blockchain technology. Its architecture is decentralized, transparent, and fortified by cryptographic safeguards. Blockchain technology has transcended its original purpose as the backbone for digital currencies like Bitcoin to unveil applications in realms such as healthcare, supply chain logistics, cybersecurity, and finance. The core concepts of distributed ledger technology (DLT), immutability, cryptographic security, and consensus mechanisms define its essence. These characteristics render it an exceptional instrument for addressing data integrity and authentication, two of the most pressing challenges in the domain of cybersecurity. When we refer to data integrity, we mean the maintenance of accuracy and consistency throughout the lifespan of data. Safeguarding data integrity is a formidable task in antiquated centralized systems, as unauthorized entities can manipulate or distort data with little chance of immediate detection. Breaches of data integrity instigated by malicious hackers, insider threats, or accidental alterations can lead to system breaches, financial repercussions, and damage to reputation. Distributing replicas of data across a network of interconnected nodes that collaboratively authenticate and uphold data fidelity is how blockchain addresses this challenge. The blockchain serves as an unchangeable ledger, where every block encapsulates information about transactions, a timestamp, and a cryptographic hash of its predecessor (Hiran et al.,

2024b; Youssef et al., 2025). The majority of the nodes within the network would resist any attempt to alter a block, as doing so would require the modification of every subsequent block in the chain. With this mechanism in place, blockchain technology ensures data precision, uniformity, and permanence over time.

The reverse holds true for authentication, which involves the verification of user credentials to ensure their permission to access designated resources. Cyber threats like phishing, brute-force attacks, and server exploitation serve as just a few illustrations of how conventional authentication frameworks—such as passwords, security tokens, or centralized identity verification services—can be vulnerable. Catastrophic data breaches and unauthorized infiltration of vital systems are potential consequences of such vulnerabilities. By decentralizing identity management and verification processes, blockchain-based authentication introduces an innovative framework. With the advent of blockchain technology, individuals can now autonomously oversee their digital identities, liberated from reliance on any singular entity, facilitated by cryptographic mechanisms like public and private keys (Khazanchi et al., 2021; Saini et al., 2021). This advancement enhances the security of digital interactions by diminishing the chances of centralized vulnerabilities. The aim of this article is to delve into the groundbreaking opportunities that blockchain offers in the realm of cybersecurity, especially focusing on its potential to enhance data authenticity and integrity. This investigation illustrates how blockchain can fortify digital frameworks, curtail unauthorized access, and generate tamper-proof records by scrutinizing its distinctive attributes, such as its decentralized architecture, cryptographic safeguards, and consensus methodologies. It explores how smart contracts and distributed ledgers within blockchain technology can bolster data integrity by meticulously documenting and validating every transaction and modification across a decentralized network, making it exceedingly challenging for malicious actors to manipulate the data. Additionally, the research highlights the burgeoning trend of blockchain-based identity management systems, which enhance security and empower users with greater control over the authentication process (Umapathi et al., 2024; Unogwu et al., 2022). The distributed trust inherent in blockchain negates the necessity for a central authority to manage user credentials and verify identities, as is customary in traditional approaches.

In order to validate transactions while safeguarding sensitive personal information, blockchain ingeniously encodes every user's digital persona with cryptographic precision. By diminishing the chances of data breaches, this decentralized identity management framework not only elevates security but also grants users enhanced privacy and autonomy. The range and adaptability of blockchain's applications in the realm of cybersecurity are boundless. By establishing an auditable and everlasting ledger of all transactions, blockchain technology is empowering the banking industry to protect its dealings and thwart fraud. Furthermore, blockchain possesses the capability to transform the healthcare sector by securing confidential patient data and thwarting unauthorized access to medical records (Adeniyi et al., 2024; Hiran et al., 2024a). Within supply chain management, blockchain technology boasts numerous applications, including the creation of unalterable transaction records that facilitate the tracking of goods and affirm their authenticity. Each of these applications illustrates the myriad ways blockchain can fortify security across diverse domains. The promise of blockchain technology to enhance cybersecurity extends beyond mere theoretical concepts, as this article will reveal. Enterprises around the world are already harnessing it to bolster their systems, thwart cyber threats, and safeguard their digital resources(Popoola et al., 2024). This research aims to provide a comprehensive insight into how blockchain can address current and future cybersecurity challenges by focusing on both the technical aspects of blockchain, such as its distributed ledger technology and cryptographic foundations, along with its practical applications across various sectors. Ultimately, innovative and unconventional strategies are essential to tackle the continuously evolving complexity of cybersecurity threats. The decentralized, immutable, and transparent nature of blockchain technology has the potential to enhance data security, authentication, and trust within digital ecosystems. As more organizations integrate it into their security infrastructures, blockchain technology offers a more stable, reliable, and secure foundation for future digital interactions, poised to revolutionize the field of cybersecurity.

1.1 Background

While the explosion of digital innovations has enhanced various facets of individual lives and organizational functions, it has simultaneously unveiled a host of new cybersecurity vulnerabilities. Incidents such as ransomware attacks, data breaches, and identity theft are escalating, frequently exploiting flaws in antiquated centralized security infrastructures (Habib et al., 2022). These systems, heavily reliant on singular authorities for data management and authentication, become tantalizing targets for cyber miscreants (Al-Shahwani et al., 2024; Shrivas et al., 2022). A more resilient security framework is imperative, as a breach in centralized servers can jeopardize vast troves of sensitive data. Recently, blockchain technology has emerged as a promising remedy to these challenges. Originally designed to support digital currencies, blockchain offers a decentralized, transparent, and tamper-proof framework that bolsters both authentication and data integrity. Its distributed ledger technology (DLT) disperses data storage across a network of nodes, enhancing resilience against failures stemming from isolated elements. Each data segment, or "block," is bound to its predecessor through cryptographic hashes, rendering it exceedingly difficult for unauthorized entities to manipulate the information. In fields where data accuracy is of utmost importance, blockchain technology truly excels, thanks to the cryptographic safeguards it offers, ensuring data is both enduring and verifiable. By eliminating the necessity for centralized identity verification—a system vulnerable to hacking or phishing—blockchain's decentralized authentication methods significantly elevate security. Industries such as fintech, healthcare, and supply chain management are among the many sectors witnessing a surge in blockchain adoption as organizations explore its potential applications in cybersecurity. In a perpetually evolving digital landscape, blockchain holds the promise of fortifying cybersecurity by enhancing the robustness of data integrity and authentication processes (Uddin et al., 2021).

1.2 Data Integrity and Its Importance

The steadfastness, accuracy, and uniformity of data throughout its lifecycle embody what we refer to as data integrity, a fundamental pillar of cybersecurity. From its inception to its transfer, storage, accessibility, and ultimately its obliteration, it ensures that information remains unblemished and trustworthy. Since impaired or jeopardized data can trigger catastrophic repercussions such as misguided choices, financial setbacks, and damage to reputation, the preservation of data integrity is essential across various sectors (Ahmed et al., 2024; Hiran, K. K., Doshi, R., & Rathi, 2014). For example, in the realm of healthcare, erroneous diagnoses and treatment strategies stemming from flawed medical records pose a grave risk to patient welfare. A parallel domino effect can be witnessed in the financial domain when data breaches lead to erroneous transactions, regulatory violations, or even fraudulent activities, which subsequently destabilize markets and erode trust in financial establishments. Each day, enterprises in our interconnected world handle immense volumes of data, comprising sensitive dialogues, proprietary insights, financial documentation, and personal identifiers. Safeguarding the veracity of this information becomes paramount as an ever-growing number of businesses transition their operations online. Merely one breach or alteration that jeopardizes entire systems can unleash havoc on operations, customer rapport, and legal standing. Cybercriminals frequently target data while it is either in motion or storage, exploiting security vulnerabilities in centralized databases or intercepting data during transit. Organizations face severe peril when tactics like man-in-the-middle attacks, in which hackers manipulate or pilfer data by inserting themselves into a communication stream, jeopardize the sanctity of crucial information. Data integrity is vital as businesses rely on trustworthy data for their decision-making processes. Whether through intentional or unintentional data corruption, operational inefficiencies, flawed projections, and misguided choices can ensue (Jain, R. K., Hiran, K., & Paliwal, 2012). The data utilized for training algorithms and models is essential for automated systems and

AI-powered processes, as flawed data can yield dire consequences. Contemplate the potential fallout of employing tainted data to educate machine learning models: inaccurate predictions, financial losses, and even threats to public safety. As a result, the reliability and effectiveness of data integrity directly influence data-driven technologies and decision-making frameworks. Additionally, adherence to regulations is intricately tied to data integrity. Negligent data management may lead to hefty fines, legal consequences, and a decline in public trust. Businesses face the risk of litigation or penalties if data breaches or integrity issues arise, which can exacerbate the already considerable financial and reputational damage they have endured.

Figure 1. The importance of data integrity

The significance of data integrity is paramount in maintaining the confidence of the public. In this era of digital transformation, the visibility of data breaches and the threats posed by unauthorized access to personal data are increasingly evident to users and consumers alike. A waning trust in an organization's capacity to safeguard personal and financial details can spell disaster for businesses. For sectors like healthcare, e-commerce, and banking, which handle delicate client information, ensuring data integrity is of utmost importance (Mahmood & Al Dabagh, 2023). When it comes to securing the authenticity of information across various domains, blockchain technology has emerged as a brilliant solution. The cryptographic fortification and decentralized architecture of blockchain create an unassailable fortress for data storage and management. Unlike traditional centralized databases that confine data to a single location, making them vulnerable to manipulation during an attack, blockchain distributes data across a network of nodes. By cryptographically hashing each data "block" and interlinking it to its predecessor, an unchangeable "chain" is established, rendering alterations nearly impossible without the consensus of the network. Data integrity remains intact as a result. The cryptographic methods employed by blockchain further bolster data integrity by making modifications to recorded data exceedingly challenging. Each node within the network would swiftly detect any attempts to tamper with the data and promptly reject it. This capability proves invaluable for industries such as healthcare, supply chain management, and finance that depend on trustworthy and unalterable records of transactions or information. In the realm of finance, for example, blockchain technology can be harnessed to create a transparent and verifiable ledger of transactions. This ledger ensures that every transaction is accurately logged and immutable, thus playing a crucial role in preventing fraud and errors. The consensus mechanisms integrated into blockchain serve as yet another layer through which it enhances data integrity.

To authenticate transactions and ensure that every participant is in accord regarding the state of the data, blockchain networks hinge on consensus mechanisms such as Proof of Work (PoW) or Proof of Stake (PoS). This collective validation process makes it exceedingly challenging for a solitary nefarious entity to alter the data or sway the system unnoticed. As such, blockchain presents a greater level of trust and transparency compared to traditional centralized systems, which are more susceptible to attacks and internal vulnerabilities. Beyond safeguarding data, blockchain technology can also enhance authentication methods, bolstering the security of digital frameworks even further. Conventional authentication techniques, like passwords and two-factor authentication, rely on authoritative organizations to verify identities. Such systems are easily vulnerable to human errors, phishing schemes, and the machinations of hackers. Conversely, blockchain technology introduces decentralized identity management solutions, liberating users from reliance on a singular entity for the stewardship of their digital identities. By employing cryptographic keys to restrict data access solely to authorized users, blockchain-based authentication significantly reduces the risk of unauthorized access or data tampering. In conclusion, the integrity of data is essential to cybersecurity and bears tremendous implications for contemporary businesses and organizations. Given the ever-evolving nature of cyber threats and the growing importance of data for operations and decision-making, it is imperative to maintain data accuracy, consistency, and reliability. Blockchain technology offers a formidable solution to mitigate the risks of data manipulation, fraud, and unauthorized access, thanks to its decentralized and cryptographically fortified structure. By harnessing blockchain technology, organizations can create systems that are not only more resilient but also more trustworthy. Such systems will better protect critical information, enhance security, and sustain public confidence in an increasingly digital world.

1.3 How Blockchain Enhances Data Integrity

The unyielding, decentralized, and cryptographic essence of blockchain lays a secure groundwork that ensures the precision, uniformity, and reliability of data throughout its entire journey, thereby fostering data integrity. Traditional systems frequently rely on databases housed in a singular central hub, where all information is stored (Boison et al., 2022). The peril of a solitary breach or unauthorized alteration in these systems could lead to extensive havoc, as cybercriminals might easily manipulate or erase data undetected, owing to the centralization inherent in these architectures. Nevertheless, blockchain revolutionizes the way data is stored, shared, and verified through the implementation of distributed ledger technology (DLT). In a blockchain network, there exists no central server; instead, a myriad of computers, or "nodes," each maintain a precise and identical copy of the entire ledger. Even if one node were to falter, the integrity of data across the remaining nodes remains intact, as this decentralized approach eliminates the risk of a singular point of failure. One of the pivotal methods by which blockchain secures data integrity is through cryptographic hashes. This architecture, known as a blockchain, consists of a series of interconnected blocks, with each block housing a cryptographic hash of its predecessor (Khan & Salah, 2018; Zheng et al., 2017). This hash serves as a singular identifier, crafted through cryptographic techniques that convert the data contained in the block into a fixed-length string of characters. Everyone within the network would instantly recognize if someone attempted to alter any data in a block, as the hash value would shift dramatically. Such a modification would trigger a consensus fracture across the network, rendering it nearly impossible for anyone to tamper with the data undetected. Information added to the blockchain is immune to removal or alteration due to the immutable nature of blockchain technology. Nevertheless, this information remains preserved. To further bolster data integrity, blockchain employs consensus validation of each new block prior to its integration into the chain. Transactions are authenticated and data integrity is upheld through various consensus mechanisms, including Proof of Work (PoW) or Proof of Stake (PoS). In the PoW scenario, new blocks are incorporated into the network by participants, commonly referred to as miners, who must tackle complex mathematical puzzles.

Figure 2. How blockchain works (Technolab Zignuts, 2018)

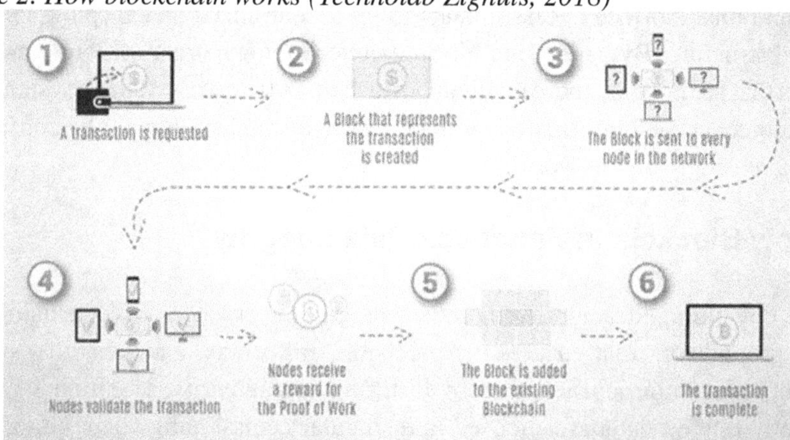

The allure of blockchain's decentralized nature significantly enhances its ability to safeguard data against tampering or unauthorized infiltration. In centralized systems, cybercriminals frequently hone in on the database, exploiting the singular control point that governs access. However, the decentralized architecture of blockchain technology makes this central governing body irrelevant. Each participant employs a public key for transaction validation and a private key for signing; these cryptographic keys govern entry to the blockchain. By shielding data from fraud and unwarranted access, this mechanism guarantees that only users equipped with the appropriate cryptographic credentials can enact changes. Additionally, the distributed ledger characteristic of blockchain ensures that any unauthorized modifications to any segment of the network are swiftly rejected by the collective as soon as they are identified. Moreover, blockchain technology can often serve to enhance existing cybersecurity frameworks by introducing an additional layer of protection for sensitive information. Through the utilization of blockchain, organizations can secure vital files and databases by storing hash values rather than the actual data. This technique allows for real-time integrity checks of sensitive data without exposing it to external threats. If an intruder attempts to manipulate a file, the hash value will no longer align with the one documented on the blockchain, thereby alerting the organization to the integrity violation (Ibrahim et al., 2022). This approach is particularly advantageous for safeguarding highly sensitive materials, such as intellectual property or legal documents. Decentralized identity management systems represent yet another avenue through which blockchain can refine authentication processes and uphold data integrity. Traditional authentication methods, like passwords or multi-factor authentication, are prone to hacking or phishing, as they rely on centralized authorities for identity verification. With blockchain's decentralized identity frameworks, users can demonstrate ownership and authenticity using cryptographic keys, granting them greater command over their digital identities while eliminating the necessity for third-party intermediaries. Individuals can verify their identities on the blockchain without disclosing any personal details, thereby enhancing security and thwarting data breaches. Ultimately, blockchain's decentralized, cryptographic, consensus-driven architecture presents an effective strategy for bolstering data integrity across various applications. This technology ensures that information remains accurate, reliable, and safeguarded against illicit alterations by providing an immutable, tamper-proof ledger of data. By leveraging cryptographic hashes and consensus protocols, blockchain further fortifies data security by distributing it across a network of nodes, thus eliminating the vulnerabilities associated with centralized data storage. As our existence becomes increasingly digital and interconnected, blockchain technology is evolving into an essential ally for cybersecurity, thanks to its decentralized authentication processes, transparency, and auditability that are revolutionizing how enterprises secure data integrity.

2. LITERATURE REVIEW

Table 1. Literature review

Author's	Method	Results
(Baazeem, 2024)	a multilayered Security Model for IoT that integrates advanced cryptographic techniques, blockchain technology for decentralized and immutable data storage, and machine learning algorithms to enhance data confidentiality, integrity, and availability within IoT networks.	proposed multilayered Security Model for IoT, which integrates blockchain technology, advanced cryptographic techniques, and machine learning algorithms, effectively mitigates risks associated with unauthorized access and data tampering, ensuring the secrecy, integrity, and availability of data within IoT networks.
(Adeniyi et al., 2024)	investigates the use of blockchain technology in healthcare cybersecurity, focusing on its capabilities for tamper-proof data storage, effective access control mechanisms, and increased transparency to protect sensitive healthcare data and medical infrastructure.	The study highlights the potential of blockchain technology to enhance cybersecurity in healthcare systems by providing tamper-proof data storage, effective access control mechanisms, and increased transparency, thereby reducing risks associated with data breaches and unauthorized access.
(Dhanalakshmi & Pandeeswari, 2024)	a novel approach that integrates blockchain technology into cloud computing infrastructure to enhance data security and privacy, addressing challenges related to data confidentiality, authentication, and integrity.	addressing critical issues such as data confidentiality, authentication, and integrity. This integration aims to create a more secure environment for cloud service users.
(Leong et al., 2024)	The paper discusses leveraging cryptographic primitives for data encryption and authentication, which are essential for ensuring the confidentiality and integrity of transactions within blockchain networks.	The study emphasizes the importance of a multi-layered approach to enhance blockchain security, which includes leveraging cryptographic techniques for data encryption and authentication, implementing robust consensus mechanisms to prevent tampering, and employing network security measures to mitigate external threats

3. METHODOLOGY

3.1 Research Design

A meticulously designed and interdisciplinary strategy that melds qualitative and quantitative methodologies is employed in the research framework to delve into the realm of blockchain applications within cybersecurity, particularly honing in on the enhancement of data integrity and authentication. During the exploratory segment of the process, pivotal cybersecurity challenges, such as data tampering and unauthorized access, are delineated. To gain deeper insights into the tangible utilizations of blockchain, we will subsequently scrutinize case studies from an array of industries that have adeptly harnessed its power. The premise that blockchain significantly mitigates cybersecurity threats is posited during this phase. To uncover shared challenges and exemplary practices, the qualitative inquiry includes dialogues with blockchain developers, cybersecurity experts, and organizations that have embraced blockchain solutions. Quantitative data encompasses logs of cybersecurity incidents, analytics on blockchain adoption, and performance metrics gathered before and after the integration of blockchain technology. Statistical analyses are employed to corroborate findings, and this information facilitates comparative evaluations of blockchain-driven systems against conventional cybersecurity measures. Moreover, advancements in data integrity and authentication can be examined in real time by crafting and evaluating simulations or prototypes grounded in blockchain within regulated environments.

3.2 Theoretical Analysis

This investigation's conceptual foundation weaves together a tapestry of notions from the realms of blockchain innovation, cryptography, and cybersecurity to unveil the magic of how blockchain elevates digital security. At its essence, this framework is anchored in the tenet of decentralization, asserting that the distributed ledger technology (blockchain) diminishes the perils of centralized authority by dispersing trust across the network and eliminating potential vulnerabilities. Given that central databases have historically been prime targets for cyber assailants, this becomes especially crucial in safeguarding sensitive information. Furthermore, the resilience of blockchain's unalterable ledger is guaranteed by the tenets of immutability and cryptographic integrity, demonstrating that data remains untouchable once inscribed. Additionally, data housed within the blockchain is shielded against alterations and exploitation through cryptographic methods such as digital signatures and hashing. Ultimately, the principles of consensus theory, rooted in game theory, illuminate how blockchain nurtures integrity among network participants, thereby enhancing data security and trustworthiness.

IV. CONCLUSION

In the quest to enhance cybersecurity, blockchain technology unveils an innovative alternative, particularly in fortifying data integrity and authentication. As it operates without a central authority, it becomes significantly less susceptible to cyber threats targeting such frameworks. By distributing information across a vast network of nodes, blockchain technology renders unauthorized access to sensitive data virtually impossible. Furthermore, the immutable nature of blockchain guarantees that information remains undisturbed, making illicit alterations exceedingly improbable. This results in a reliable and permanent ledger of transactions. Embedded within blockchain are cryptographic techniques like digital signatures, encryption, and hashing, which provide robust authentication methods. To bolster identity verification and thwart unauthorized access, these cryptographic instruments ensure that only those with authorization can interact with or modify the data. Moreover, consensus mechanisms such as PoW or PoS enhance network security by thwarting malicious actors from altering the system without widespread consensus. While blockchain offers numerous promising advantages for cybersecurity, it also faces certain limitations, particularly concerning scalability and energy consumption. The rising adoption of blockchain technology underscores the significance of solutions like PoS and other scalable frameworks in addressing these hurdles. Although blockchain technology presents certain challenges, it simultaneously delivers clear advantages, such as a more reliable, transparent, and secure foundation for cybersecurity by enhancing data integrity and authentication. The ongoing evolution of blockchain technology positions it to assume an increasingly pivotal role in the future of secure digital landscapes.

REFERENCES

Adeniyi, A. E., Jimoh, R. G., Awotunde, J. B., Aworinde, H. O., Falola, P. B., & Ninan, D. O. (2024). Blockchain for secured cybersecurity in emerging healthcare systems. *Cybersecurity in Emerging Healthcare Systems*, 335–361. DOI: 10.1049/PBHE064E_ch11

Ahmed, S. F., Alam, M. S., Afrin, S., Rafa, S. J., Taher, S. B., Kabir, M., Muyeen, S. M., & Gandomi, A. H. (2024). Toward a Secure 5G-Enabled Internet of Things: A Survey on Requirements, Privacy, Security, Challenges, and Opportunities. *IEEE Access : Practical Innovations, Open Solutions*, *12*, 13125–13145. DOI: 10.1109/ACCESS.2024.3352508

Al-Shahwani, H. I. W., Mijwil, M. M., Doshi, R., Hiran, K. K., & Bala, I. (2024). Evaluating Antivirus Effectiveness Against Malware in Ascending Order for Increasing Blockchain Endpoint Protection. 150–166. doi:: DOI: 10.4018/979-8-3693-1131-8.ch008

Baazeem, R. (2024). Multilayered Framework for Enhancing Data Confidentiality, Integrity, and Threat Detection through Blockchain, Advanced Cryptography, and Machine Learning. [IJCNA]. *International Journal of Computer Networks and Applications*, *11*(5). Advance online publication. DOI: 10.22247/ijcna/2024/36

Boison, D. K., Malcalm, E., Antwi-Boampong, A., & Hiran, K. K. (2022). Assessing Factors Affecting the Blockchain Adoption in Public Procurement Delivery in Ghana: A Correlational Study Using UTAUT2 Theoretical Framework. *International Journal of Ambient Computing and Intelligence*, *13*(1), 1–13. DOI: 10.4018/ijaci.314568

Dhanalakshmi, J., & Pandeeswari, N. (2024). Blockchain Enabled Security and Integrity in Cloud Computing. *8th International Conference on I-SMAC (IoT in Social, Mobile, Analytics and Cloud), I-SMAC 2024 - Proceedings*, 1076–1082. DOI: 10.1109/I-SMAC61858.2024.10714885

Habib, G., Sharma, S., Ibrahim, S., Ahmad, I., Qureshi, S., & Ishfaq, M. (2022). Blockchain Technology: Benefits, Challenges, Applications, and Integration of Blockchain Technology with Cloud Computing. *Future Internet 2022, Vol. 14, Page 341, 14*(11), 341. DOI: 10.3390/fi14110341

Hiran, K. K., Doshi, R., & Patel, M. (2024a). Applications of Virtual and Augmented Reality for Health and Wellbeing. *Applications of Virtual and Augmented Reality for Health and Wellbeing*, 1–353. DOI: 10.4018/979-8-3693-1123-3

Hiran, K. K., Doshi, R., & Patel, M. (2024b). Modern technology in healthcare and medical education: Blockchain, IoT, AR, and VR. *Modern Technology in Healthcare and Medical Education: Blockchain, IoT, AR, and VR*, 1–310. DOI: 10.4018/979-8-3693-5493-3

Hiran, K. K., Doshi, R., & Rathi, R. (2014). Security & privacy issues of cloud & grid computing networks. *Security & Privacy Issues of Cloud & Grid Computing Networks Article in International Journal on Computational Science & Applications*, *4*(1), 83–91. Advance online publication. DOI: 10.5121/ijcsa.2014.4108

Ibrahim, R. F., Abu Al-Haija, Q., & Ahmad, A. (2022). DDoS Attack Prevention for Internet of Thing Devices Using Ethereum Blockchain Technology. *Sensors 2022, Vol. 22, Page 6806, 22*(18), 6806. DOI: 10.3390/s22186806

Jain, R. K., Hiran, K., & Paliwal, G. (2012). QUANTUM CRYPTOGRAPHY: A NEW GENERATION OF INFORMATION SECURITY SYSTEM. *International Journal of Computers and Distributed Systems*Www.Ijcdsonline.Com*, 2*. https://www.researchgate.net/publication/320404164

Khan, M. A., & Salah, K. (2018). IoT security: Review, blockchain solutions, and open challenges. *Future Generation Computer Systems*, *82*, 395–411. DOI: 10.1016/j.future.2017.11.022

Khazanchi, D., Vyas, A. K., Hiran, K. K., & Padmanaban, S. (2021). Blockchain 3.0 for sustainable development. *Blockchain 3.0 for Sustainable Development*, 1–158. https://doi.org/DOI: 10.1515/9783110702507/EPUB

Leong, W. Y., Leong, Y. Z., & Leong, W. S. (2024). Enhancing Blockchain Security. *IEEE Symposium on Wireless Technology and Applications, ISWTA*, 108–112. DOI: 10.1109/ISWTA62130.2024.10651753

Mahmood, M. S., & Al Dabagh, N. B. (2023). Blockchain technology and internet of things: Review, challenge and security concern. *International Journal of Electrical and Computer Engineering*, *13*(1), 718–735. DOI: 10.11591/ijece.v13i1.pp718-735

Popoola, O., Rodrigues, M., Marchang, J., Shenfield, A., Ikpehai, A., & Popoola, J. (2024). A critical literature review of security and privacy in smart home healthcare schemes adopting IoT & blockchain: Problems, challenges and solutions. *Blockchain: Research and Applications*, *5*(2), 100178. Advance online publication. DOI: 10.1016/j.bcra.2023.100178

Saini, H. K., Jain, K. L., Hiran, K. K., & Bhati, A. (2021). Paradigms to make smart city using blockchain. In *Blockchain 3.0 for Sustainable Development*.

Sharma, P., Sharma, I., Pamecha, S., & Hiran, K. K. (2023). Green Currency Based on Blockchain Technology for Sustainable Development. Https://Services.Igi-Global.Com/Resolvedoi/Resolve.Aspx?Doi=10.4018/978-1-6684-5072-7.Ch005, 102–118. DOI: 10.4018/978-1-6684-5072-7.ch005

Shrivas, M., Bansal, A., Hiran, K. K., & Doshi, R. (2022). *Advancements in quantum blockchain with real-time applications*. IGI Global. DOI: 10.4018/978-1-6684-5072-7

Technolab Zignuts. (2018, May 23). *Understanding of Blockchain Architecture: How It Works & How to Build - Zignuts Technolab*. https://www.zignuts.com/blog/how-blockchain-architecture-works-basic-understanding-of-blockchain-and-its-architecture

Uddin, M. A., Stranieri, A., Gondal, I., & Balasubramanian, V. (2021). A survey on the adoption of blockchain in IoT: Challenges and solutions. *Blockchain: Research and Applications*, *2*(2), 100006. DOI: 10.1016/j.bcra.2021.100006

Umapathi, V., Murugaiah, M., & Doshi, R. (2024). *Bio-Inspired Optimization Techniques in Blockchain Systems*. IGI Global., DOI: 10.4018/979-8-3693-1131-8

Unogwu, O. J., Doshi, R., Hiran, K. K., & Mijwil, M. M. (2022). Introduction to Quantum-Resistant Blockchain. Https://Services.Igi-Global.Com/Resolvedoi/Resolve.Aspx?Doi=10.4018/978-1-6684-5072-7.Ch002, 36–55. DOI: 10.4018/978-1-6684-5072-7.ch002

Youssef, A. B., Dutta, P. K., Doshi, R., & Sajnani, M. (Eds.). (2024). *AI, Blockchain, and Metaverse in Hospitality and Tourism Industry 4.0: Case Studies and Analysis*. CRC Press.

Zheng, Z., Xie, S., Dai, H., Chen, X., & Wang, H. (2017). An Overview of Blockchain Technology: Architecture, Consensus, and Future Trends. *Proceedings - 2017 IEEE 6th International Congress on Big Data, BigData Congress 2017*, 557–564. DOI: 10.1109/BigDataCongress.2017.85

Chapter 4
A Novel Tri-Layered Security Protocol for Enhancing IoT Networks Security

N. Saranya
https://orcid.org/0009-0003-1684-4785
Sri Manakula Vinayagar Engineering College, India

P. Raja
https://orcid.org/0000-0002-9818-6004
Sri Manakula Vinayagar Engineering College, India

M. Muntasir
Sri Manakula Vinayagar Engineering College, India

B. NiranAmalore
Sri Manakula Vinayagar Engineering College, India

B. Balaji
Sri Manakula Vinayagar Engineering College, India

ABSTRACT

The rapid expansion of the Internet of Things (IoT) has revolutionized automation but also introduced significant security challenges. To address these vulnerabilities, this research proposes a novel Tri-layer security protocol that enhances existing security mechanisms while mitigating risks. The proposed system integrates lightweight cryptography at the device level to ensure secure communication without exceeding IoT resource constraints. A fog computing layer functions as an inter-

DOI: 10.4018/979-8-3373-1424-2.ch004

mediary, reducing latency and filtering data before it reaches the central network. Additionally, an Intrusion Detection System (IDS) continuously monitors network traffic, identifying anomalies and triggering proactive security measures against cyber threats. This multi-layered approach significantly strengthens IoT security by reducing exposure to attacks. Extensive simulations and real-world testing validate the system's effectiveness, offering a comprehensive security solution for protecting IoT networks and connected devices.

I. INTRODUCTION

The IoT has redefined electronics communication enabling seamless automation and data sharing. Its integration into various industries, including healthcare, smart infrastructure, agriculture, transportation, and industrial manufacturing, has led to enhanced efficiency and reduced human intervention. IoT applications, such as smart homes, wearable devices, automated industrial systems, intelligent power grids, and advanced transportation networks, optimize resource utilization and minimize operational costs. However, despite its numerous benefits, IoT presents challenges in security, scalability, interoperability, and power sustainability.

IoT systems rely on inter-device communication, cloud-based data processing, and real-time analytics to ensure smooth functionality. Despite these capabilities, security vulnerabilities remain a major concern due to the vast network of interconnected devices handling sensitive data. IoT systems are vulnerable to cyber security risks, including data leaks, unauthorized intrusions, service disruptions, and malware attacks, threatening their confidentiality, reliability, and functionality. The Mirai malware attack, which compromised IoT devices like routers and cameras by exploiting default credentials, demonstrated the potential scale of security threats in IoT ecosystems. This attack led to large-scale distributed denial-of-service (DDoS) disruptions, affecting major online services and highlighting the urgent need for enhanced security frameworks. To address these concerns, there is a critical need for a lightweight encryption model specifically designed for IoT devices. A well-designed model should protect data without hindering operational efficiency, ensuring that security measures do not negatively impact device performance or battery longevity. To secure IoT systems, a range of protective strategies has been employed, including encryption methods, robust authentication protocols, and continuous threat detection mechanisms. However, existing security models often struggle to balance protection with efficiency, especially for resource-constrained IoT devices. To address this issue, researchers and industry experts are exploring advanced security solutions, such as blockchain-based decentralized security models, AI-driven anomaly detection, multi-factor authentication, and hardware-based protections. As IoT continues to evolve, emerging security challenges necessitate the continuous refinement of protection strategies. This paper aims to analyze existing IoT security challenges and propose an efficient, lightweight encryption model that ensures robust protection without compromising device performance or power efficiency.

Numerous researchers have designed and deployed protocols to strengthen security in proposed applications. In Atzori, Iera, and Morabito (2010), a detailed perspective on connected smart technologies was provided, discussing their framework, challenges, and practical applications. This study explores the complexities and potential of IoT, addressing its structural framework and real-world implications. The work remains fundamental in understanding the IoT ecosystem and its evolving technological landscape. Jayavardhana Gubbi *et al.* (2013) carried out a comprehensive review of communication technologies for connected smart systems. Their work explores the diverse landscape of communication technologies crucial for the functioning and connectivity of IoT devices. This survey offers insights into their strengths, weaknesses, and potential applications within the IoT framework. In Blumberg and Rau Chaplin (2016), examined the current state and future directions are examined regarding the security and privacy in IoT. The comprehensive analysis of the existing security measures offers insights into the potential avenues for future developments in safeguarding IoT ecosystems. The Constrained Application Protocol (CoAP), specified for IoT devices that are resource-constrained, was discussed in Schnäbe, Greer, and Zanella (2014), emphasizing its efficiency in IoT environments. The Message Queue Telemetry Transport (MQTT) protocol was investigated in Pfisterer and Römer (2009) for its lightweight message capabilities in IoT networks. In Adel, El-Hoiy, and El-Hennawy (2017) provides an in-depth analysis of LoRaWAN protocols specifically developed for Internet of Things (IoT) applications. A. Kumar et al. developed a detailed survey analysis of lightweight cryptography tailored for resource-constrained Internet of Things (IoT) devices. Furthermore, several studies Kumar, Tripathi, and Sharma (2021) and Arif et al. (2020) have investigated the role of fog computing in IoT security, focusing on intrusion detection and prevention mechanisms in fog-based IoT networks. These collective research efforts contribute significantly to the ongoing development of secure and efficient IoT architectures.

This chapter introduces the development and evaluation of a novel triple-layer security protocol aimed at enhancing the security of IoT systems. The proposed protocol integrates multiple security mechanisms to strengthen resilience against cyber threats while ensuring operational efficiency. The primary goal is to minimize security vulnerabilities by incorporating three protective layers. The first layer involves the implementation of lightweight cryptography directly on IoT devices, enabling secure communication and data exchange without overburdening their limited computational resources. The second layer introduces a fog computing network, which acts as an intermediary to reduce latency while filtering and analyzing data before it reaches the central network. This approach enhances security by preventing unauthorized access at an earlier stage. The final layer incorporates an IDS layer within the proposed system, continuously tracking for anomalies and potential threats. By detecting malicious activities in real-time, the IDS facilitates proactive responses to mitigate cyber-attacks and safeguard the IoT ecosystem. The multi-layered security framework significantly reduces IoT devices' exposure to threats, thereby improving the protection of IoT networks. To assess the effectiveness of the proposed protocol, extensive simulations and real-time implementations are conducted. The research findings provide valuable insights into IoT security, offering a comprehensive strategy for securing connected devices. The chapter is structured into four sessions: the first provides an introduction and a detailed literature review, the second discusses the algorithm and development of the proposed triple-layer security protocol, the third focuses on implementation and result analysis, and the final session presents conclusions along with future research directions for further strengthening IoT security.

II. PROPOSED TRI-LAYERED SECURITY SYSTEM

Figure 1. Block diagram of the proposed tri-layer security protocol

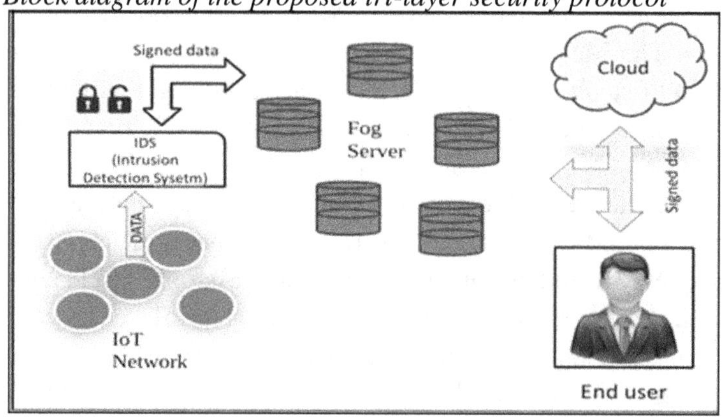

The proposed tri-layer security system is presented in Figure 1. The triple-layered security protocol integrates lightweight cryptography on IoT devices, a network of fog layers for enhanced security, and IDS for real-time vulnerability identification. This comprehensive approach ensures robust protection against threats, minimizing vulnerabilities and fortifying the IoT network with proactive security measures. The proposed triple layers security include,

1. Encryption Layer (AES-CCM & RSA)
2. Fog layer
3. Intrusion Detection system Layer

A) Design of AES-CCM

The AES-CCM is a mode of operation for the AES block cipher, designed to ensure both confidentiality and authenticity. It is widely utilized in low-power IoT devices for secure communication. In the proposed system, this layer integrates the AES cipher, which operates with a block size of 128 bits, enhancing data security and integrity. The proposed AES-CCM algorithm processed various stages such as encryption, decryption, hashing and verification.

Figure 2. Flowchart representation of the proposed AES-CCM layer

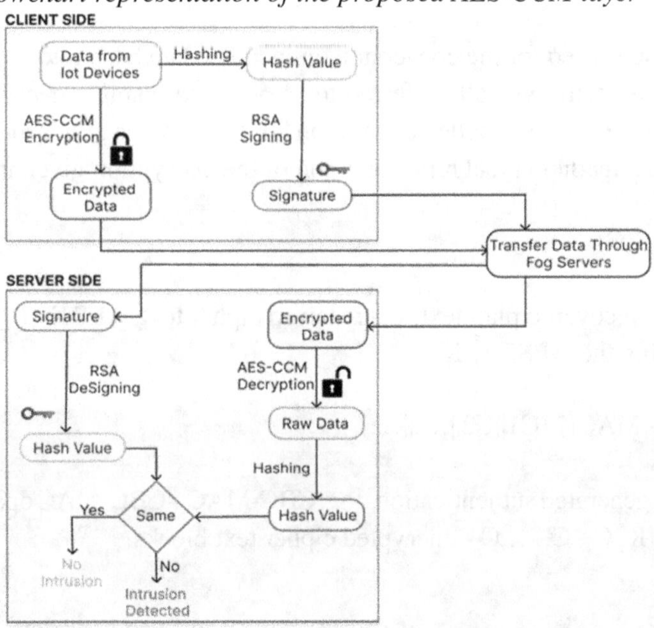

i. AEC Encryption Method

The AEC Encryption is the conversion of data into a code, which is used to secure it from unauthorized access of use. The AES-CCM is a cryptographic algorithm that blends AES encryption and CCM authentication. It ensures data confidentiality using AES encryption and provides message integrity through CCM, making it much suitable choice for secure data transmission. The mathematical model for the encryption represented in Eqs (1-2).

$$C_i = AES_k(N+i) \oplus P_i \tag{1}$$

where, C_i-ith cipher text block. $AES_k(N + i)$result of encrypting the counter block (N + i) with AES key K. P_i- i-th plaintext block.

$$T = CBC - MACK(C_1\|C_2\|.....\|C_n \tag{2}$$

where, T - generated authentication tag. CBC – MAC_K - CBC-MAC operation using the AES key K. C_1, C_2,...C_n- encrypted cipher text blocks

ii. Decryption

Decryption is used for the conversion of encoded data back into its original and understandable form, typically referred to as plaintext, using a decryption key or algorithm. AES-CCM is a mode of operation for the Advanced Encryption Standard algorithm. The mathematical representation of the decryption given in Eqs. (3-4).

$$P = AES\,K^{-1}(C) \tag{3}$$

where, P - recovered plaintext, C - received cipher text. AES $K^{-1}(.)$-decryption operation using the AES key K

$$T = CBC - MACK\,(C1\|C2\|....\|Cn) \tag{4}$$

Where, T-generated authentications tag. CBC-MAC_K-CBC-MAC operating using the AES key K. C_1, C_2,....C_n- encrypted cipher text blocks.

iii. Hashing

Hashing is used for the conversion of input data into a static-size strings, which typically represents the hexadecimal number. The hash value is unique for each data and produces the same output if the hashing data is the same.

iv. Signing Process

Signing is done to the hash value of the message using the private key. The sign 'S' is calculated by the Eq(5)

$$S = H(M)^D modn \quad (5)$$

The digital signature represented by S, H(M) states hash value of the verification process, D represented. This process is done by the public key. In the verification process the hash value is created from the sign and is compared with the actual hash value. If they are equal the signature is valid, if not the signature is invalid. The hash value $H(M)'$ is generated by the Eq.(6).

$$H(M)' = S^e \quad (6)$$

Where, $H(M)'$ - calculated hash value, S - Sign of the message. e - Public exponent. n – modulus.

B) Design of Fog Layer

Cloud computing faces several challenges, including higher response times, increased network usage, high latency, and higher costs. Aazam, Zeadally, and Harras (2018) conducted a comparative analysis of widely used paradigms computing fag layer and found that the fog paradigm exhibits lower latency than the cloud paradigm. Additionally, fog computing consumes significantly fewer network resources than traditional cloud-based systems. In the proposed architecture, fog computing is integrated to minimize frequent data transmissions to the cloud, thereby improving the response rate. The adoption of the fog paradigm within a three-layered architecture enhances scalability. The fog layer protocol consists of geographically distributed fog nodes with substantial computational power, enabling efficient data processing. Its highly adaptable infrastructure and low network bandwidth consumption make fog computing an ideal choice for optimizing performance and resource utilization.

The proposed fog architecture comprises various components, including surveillance cameras, air conditioners, edge devices, a microcontroller chip, a fog node, an Intrusion Detection System (IDS), and a cloud server. The fog node receives the processed data, both the data and the status of edge devices are updated for every five seconds. In this architecture, the controller serves as a mediator for both edge devices and fog nodes, facilitating seamless communication. The fog node interacts with the cloud through the IDS, which also plays a crucial role in managing resources from each fog node. Additionally, fog nodes deployed in different houses within the same street cooperate to share information, enhancing efficiency and data processing capabilities.

Figure 3. Triple layer implementation for fog-enabled single house architecture

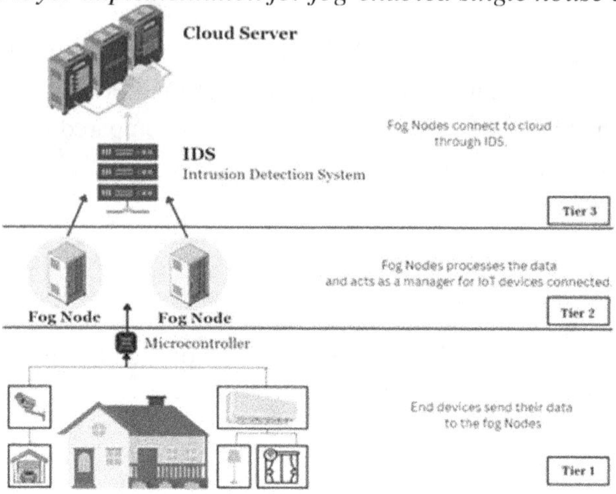

Cloud computing enables long-term data processing and management; however, frequent access to the cloud leads to high network resource consumption, limiting resource availability for other applications and reducing scalability. Integrating a middle layer of fog nodes significantly reduces latency for continuous cloud access. By processing and managing data locally, fog nodes enhance efficiency and optimize resource utilization. The architecture depicted in Figure 3, shows the fog node and cloud have two-way communication, and the tasks of processing and storing the data are taken care of by the fog nodes. The architecture for multiple houses security system is presented in Figure 4, In this case, the resources will share the same for every fog node simultaneously, but the network usage will increase to upload and retrieve the information from the centralized server.

i) Tier-1 Edge Devices and Microcontroller

In the proposed system, edge devices and microcontroller devices are the tier-1 of the fog-enabled smart street architecture. The main work describes to compare the latency rate and utilization of network resources of fog and cloud servers. The miniature edge devices gather data and the devices from a single home are grouped and connected to the microcontroller. At first, all the devices are initialized, and then the data is centralized. The data is collected from the edge devices and fed to the microcontrollers. The steps for processing data and sending it to the fog nodes are listed below:

1) Initialize the system

    a) Set edge devices stationary.
2) Data Acquisition
    a) Data is gathered with the help of edge devices.
3) Data Processing
    a) Data is collected and fed to the Microcontroller.
    b) The microcontroller acts as a manager for these edge devices.
    c) It also acts as a storage to process the data.
4) Data Uploading
    a) Processed data is uploaded to the network of fog nodes.

Figure 4. Smart street security configuration using triple-layer protocol

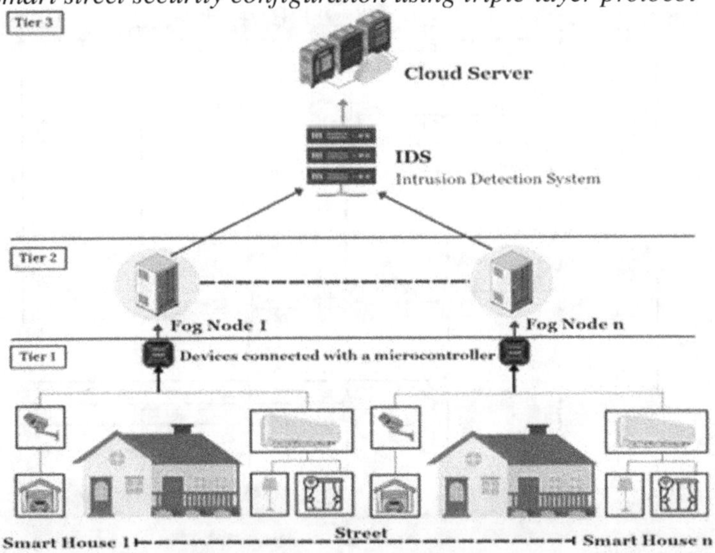

ii) Tier-2 Fog Layer

The Tier-2 Fog layer acts as the middle layer between the edge devices and the IDS to the cloud and it is used to collect the data from edge devices. Each house in the street has specific indexes, for example, Smart House 1 is connected to the Fog Node 1. The fog node updates the data to IDS, which is displayed at the end of the street. The fog nodes store the data for a specific time, which is user-defined, and transfer the data to the cloud. The real-time operating data are collected from the house and processed which is enabled as a supporting middle layer used for collecting, processing, and analyzing the data at the edge.

iii)Tier-3 Cloud Layer

The purpose of this layer, in the proposed architecture, is to acts as storage for the processed data when the data is not needed by the fog node. The communication between the fog network and the cloud is enabled through IDS. The fog node gets through the processed data to the cloud after a specific period, and if the fog needs to process the collected data, it is then provided by the cloud.

Figure 5. Sequence diagram for proposed triple layer security system

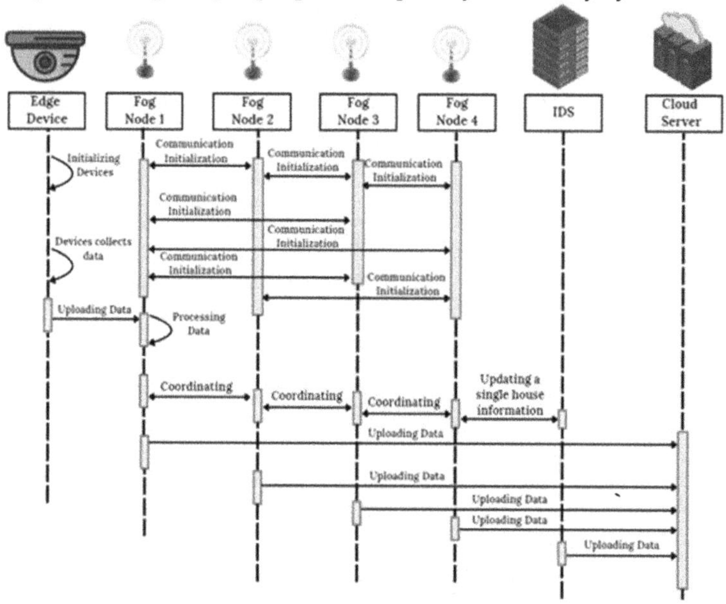

The sequence diagram for the proposed triple layer security system as presented in Figure 5. The Fog nodes allocate network resources, such as bandwidth, to coordinate with each other, fulfilling the storage needs of adjacent nodes. In the proposed architecture, fog nodes are assumed to collaborate through IDS via a proxy server, facilitating communication and sharing essential information among neighboring fog nodes within the network. Since interoperability is a fundamental property of the fog paradigm, the latency associated with communication between fog nodes is not considered.

Consider a house that is not using any IoT devices for a specific period, then the fog node that is connected to the house will coordinate itself to the availability of the requesting node. This is achieved with the help of the IDS which manages the information and sends it to the cloud. The cloud prioritizes and allocates the fog nodes based on the availability of the requesting nodes. The simulated scenario that involves these miniature devices to collect data from the houses as depicted in Figure 6. The data is first sent to the fog node, where it is processed to ensure all information is accurately collected. The processed data is then transmitted to the Intrusion Detection System (IDS) via a Wi-Fi connection. The IDS functions as a proxy server, facilitating the connection between the fog node(s) and the cloud server. To validate the proposed system, iFogSim is utilized for simulation. This tool is employed to monitor and assess network resources, including network usage and latency.

In the simulation environment, variables defined for houses and the number of edge devices. The experimental scenario included four houses, each initially equipped with five edge devices, such as surveillance cameras, automated lamps, air conditioners, garages, windows, or doors. Each house was assigned a dedicated fog node for data processing and communication. A cloud device was established, to which all fog nodes were connected via IDS using Wi-Fi. A notable aspect of this architecture is the assignment of one fog node per area. Since the edge devices are smart (Wi-Fi-enabled) and connected through a microcontroller, they were modelled in the simulators.

Figure 6. Implementation of proposed system using iFogSim topology

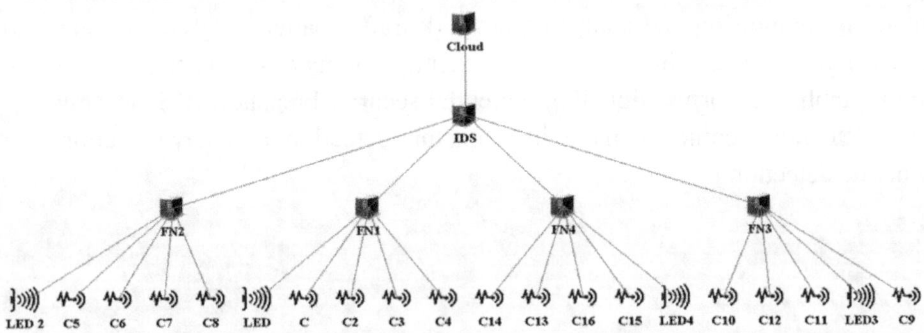

Figure 6 illustrates the topology designed in iFogSim to evaluate the results of the fog computing scenario. The topology consists of four fog nodes, each connected to five end devices. This simulation was conducted to analyze network parameters such as network usage and latency in iFogSim. Additionally, the fog node continuously updates real-time data to the connected IDS.As depicted in Figure 6, increasing the number of houses leads to the creation of additional fog nodes, where resource availability is managed. When more edge devices are connected to a single fog node, latency, and network usage increase accordingly. This alternative topology is illustrated in Figure 7, where edge devices communicate directly with the cloud server through the IDS.

Figure 7. Implementation model for of cloud-enabled scenario with 16 edge devices connected through an IDS

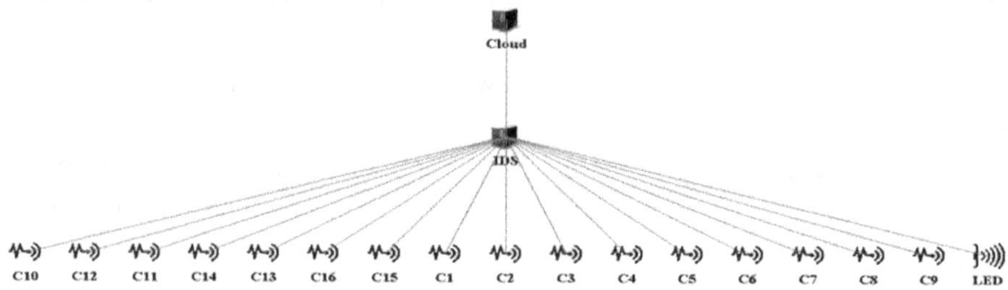

C) Intrusion Detection System (IDS) Layer

An IDS plays a crucial role in cybersecurity, acting as a vigilant safeguard against unauthorized access, malicious attacks, and potential threats within a network or system. At its core, an IDS operates as an intelligent surveillance mechanism, continuously monitoring and analyzing network traffic patterns, system events, and user behaviors. The primary goal is to identify anomalous activities that deviate from established norms, signalling potential security breaches. IDSs leverage diverse detection techniques, including signature detection, anomaly detection, and heuristic detection.

Figure 8. Block diagram of proposed third-layer security system

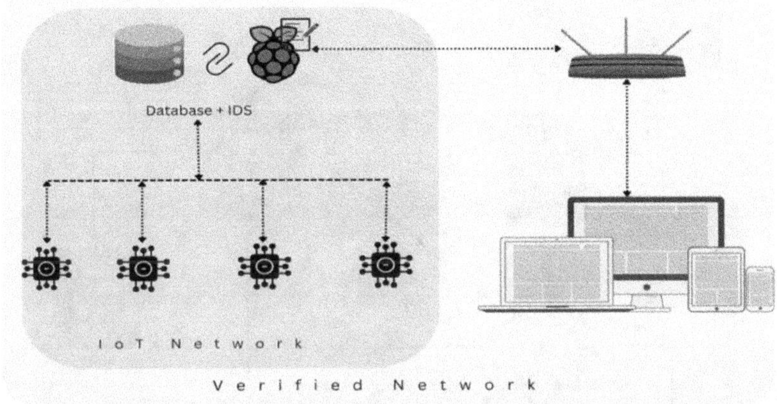

Signature-based detection, similar to antivirus systems, operates by comparing the patterns against a database of known signatures and it generates an alert when the match is identified. In contrast, anomaly-based detection establishes a baseline of normal system behavior by analyzing historical data and system parameters. Any deviations from this established baseline are identified and flagged as possible intrusions. This approach is particularly effective in detecting new, previously unidentified threats, including zero-day attacks.

Figure 9. Working methodology of the IDS system

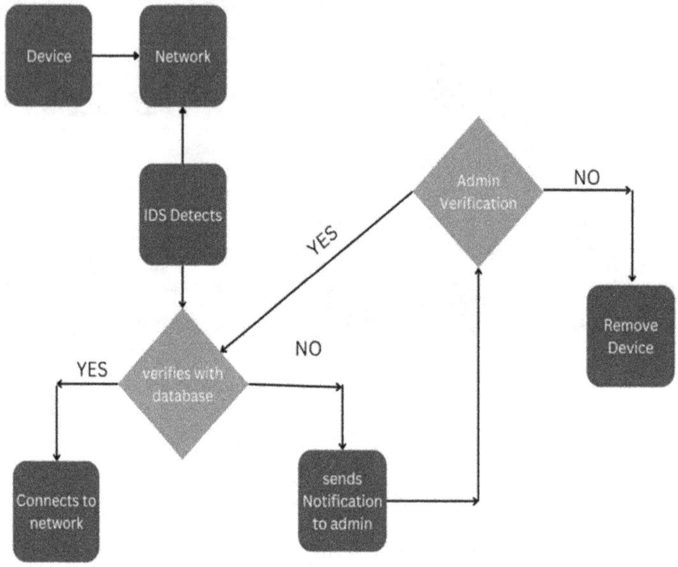

Once an IDS detects an anomaly or potential intrusion, it triggers alerts or responses, depending on its configuration. IDS play a crucial role in bolstering the overall cybersecurity posture, providing real-time threat intelligence, facilitating incident response, and contributing to the prevention and mitigation of cyber threats. As technology evolves, IDSs continue to adapt, incorporating machine learning and artificial intelligence to enhance their capabilities in identifying increasingly sophisticated and dynamic cyber threats. In essence, an IDS serves as an intelligent and proactive guardian, tirelessly monitoring the digital landscape to ensure the integrity, confidentiality, and availability of critical systems and data.

III. RESULTS AND ANALYSIS

a) Encryption Performance Benchmarks

Figure 10. Comparison of payload vs execution time in (a) software (b) hardware

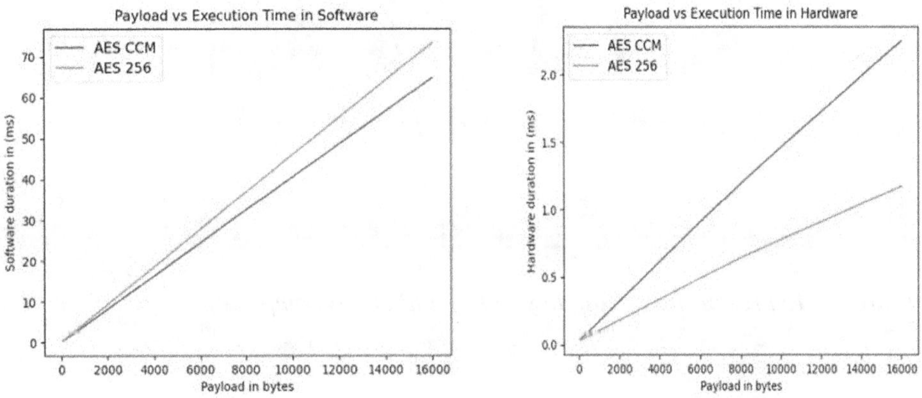

(a) (b)

In real-time applications where performance is critical, minimizing latency is essential. Fog nodes at the network edge, receive and analyze data collected from the home environment. Since each fog node is dedicated to a specific location, the time required to process those images and update device knowledge about the availability of slots which is significantly reduced. Latency can be calculated using Eq. 1,

$$\text{Latency} = \alpha + \mu + \phi \qquad (7)$$

where α represents the Tuple CPU Execution Delay for data gathering and μ represents the upload time of the data. Finally, ϕ represents the amount of time that the data takes to appear on the LED following processing at the fog node. The cloud server's resources are the only ones utilized as traffic volume grows. The increasing load on the network therefore results in a drop in data rates. When servers are spread geographically, each fog node is assigned to a certain region in order to handle requests from that region. Thus, in that scenario, there is a drop in network consumption and an increase in transmission rate. Utilizing, the network use is computed in Eq. 8 which is derived from Gupta *et al.* (2017).

$$NU = t_d * \partial \qquad (8)$$

Figure 11. Representing the network usage in fog and cloud computing

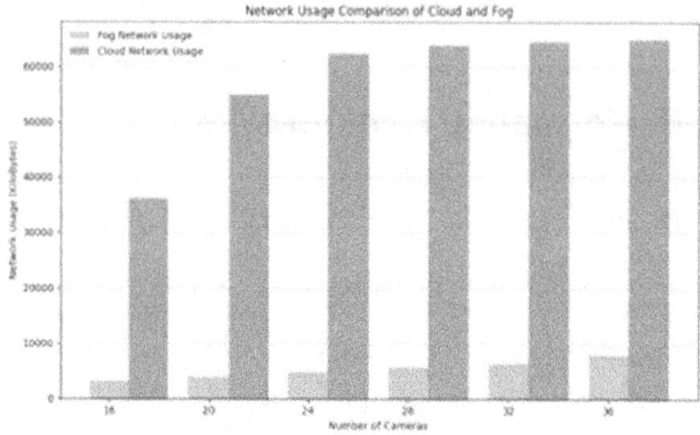

Figure 12. Representing the latency in fog and cloud computing

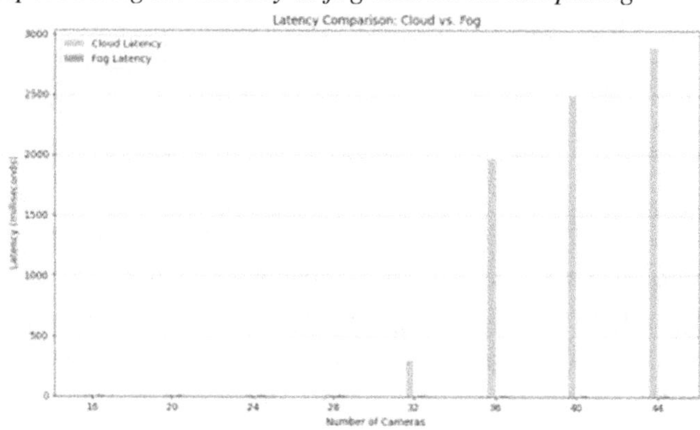

Iv. CONCLUSION

The rapid expansion of IoT has transformed automation by offering seamless connectivity and convenience. However, this advancement has also introduced significant security challenges, necessitating robust protective measures. The proposed Tri-layer security protocol effectively mitigates these risks by integrating lightweight cryptography, fog-layer security, and an Intrusion Detection System (IDS). he proposed fog-based IDS architecture leverages computing algorithms to identify available fog nodes and efficiently distribute resources among them, thereby reducing latency and overall response time. Extensive simulations and practical implementations validate the effectiveness of this security framework, demonstrating its potential to safeguard IoT ecosystems from evolving cyber threats. This method enhances performance as well as security and providing it a robust solution for future smart environments.

REFERENCES

Aazam, M., Zeadally, S., & Harras, K. A. (2018, May). Fog computing architecture, evaluation, and future research directions. *IEEE Communications Magazine*, *56*(5), 46–52. DOI: 10.1109/MCOM.2018.1700707

Alharthi, M. K., Moria, K. M., Alghazzawi, D. M., & Tayeb, H. O. (2022). Epileptic disorder detection of seizures using EEG signals. *Sensors (Basel)*, *22*(17), 6592. DOI: 10.3390/s22176592 PMID: 36081048

Arif, M., Aslam, N., Khan, Z. A., & Aurangzeb, K. (2020). Fog Computing for Secure and Efficient Data Processing in IoT Networks. *IEEE Transactions on Industrial Informatics*, *16*(5), 3120–3130.

Atzori, L., Iera, A., & Morabito, G. (2010). Internet of Things (IoT): A Vision, Architectural Challenges and Applications. *IEEE Transactions on Industrial Informatics*, *7*(4), 469–476.

Blumberg, D. M., & Rau-Chaplin, M. S. (2016). Security and Privacy in the Internet of Things: Current State and Future Directions. *Telecommunications Policy*, *41*(1), 76–96.

El-Hoiy, A. A. A., & El-Hennawy, M. I. (2017). LoRaWAN: A Low-Power Wide-Area Network Protocol for Internet of Things Applications. *IEEE Access : Practical Innovations, Open Solutions*, *5*, 16774–16787.

Gupta, H., Dastjerdi, A. V., Ghosh, S. K., & Buyya, R. (2017). iFogSim: A toolkit for modeling and simulation of resource management techniques in the Internet of Things, edge and fog computing environments. *Software, Practice & Experience*, *47*(9), 1275–1296. DOI: 10.1002/spe.2509

. (2013). Jayavardhana Gubbi, Rajkumar Buyya, Sanjay Marusic, and MarimuthuPalaniswami, "Communication Technologies for the Internet of Things: A Survey,". *IEEE Communications Surveys and Tutorials*, *16*(2), 1060–1074.

Khan, M. A., Ashraf, M. U., & Shafiq, M. (2020). Machine Learning-Based Anomaly Detection for Securing Fog-Based IoT Systems. *IEEE Access : Practical Innovations, Open Solutions*, *8*, 121551–121563.

Khare, S. K., Bajaj, V., & Acharya, U. R. (2021). PDCNNet: An Automatic Framework for the detection of parkinson's disease using EEG signals'. *IEEE Sensors Journal*, *21*(15), 17017–17024. DOI: 10.1109/JSEN.2021.3080135

Kumar, A., Tripathi, A., & Sharma, S. (2021). Lightweight Cryptography for Resource-Constrained IoT Devices: A Survey and Comparative Analysis. *IEEE Internet of Things Journal, 8*(6), 5398–5413.

Li, Y., Li, Z., Li, X., & Lin, X. (2020). Multi-Layered Security Architecture for Industrial IoT Systems. *IEEE Transactions on Industrial Electronics, 67*(11), 8912–8922.

Liu, L., Ren, S., Wang, C., & Zhang, Y. (2021). Secure and Efficient Resource Management in Fog-Based IoT Networks. *IEEE Transactions on Network Science and Engineering, 2*(2), 205–218.

Lu, W., Li, Z., Li, Y., & Xu, X. (2021). Blockchain-Based Trust Management for Fog Computing in IoT Networks. *IEEE Internet of Things Journal, 8*(5), 3401–3412.

Mahato, S., & Paul, S. (2018). *Electroencephalogram (EEG) signal analysis for diagnosis of major depressive disorder (MDD): A Review*. Nanoelectronics, Circuits and Communication Systems., DOI: 10.1007/978-981-13-0776-8_30

Pfisterer, D., & Römer, K. (2009). Message Queue Telemetry Transport (MQTT): A Publish/Subscribe Protocol for the Internet of Things. *IEEE Communications Magazine, 47*(1), 10–19.

Schnäbe, H., Greer, D. C., & Zanella, A. (2014). Constrained Application Protocol (CoAP): A Transport Protocol for the Internet of Things. *IEEE Internet of Things Journal, 1*(1), 112–126.

Sun, J., Cao, R., Zhou, M., Hussain, W., Wang, B., Xue, J., & Xiang, J. (2021). A hybrid deep neural network for classification of schizophrenia using EEG Data. *Scientific Reports, 11*(1), 4706. Advance online publication. DOI: 10.1038/s41598-021-83350-6 PMID: 33633134

Wang, H., Zhang, Y., Zomaya, A., & Li, S. (2022). Lightweight and Efficient Intrusion Detection System for Fog-Based IoT Networks. *IEEE Transactions on Dependable and Secure Computing, 19*(7), 1545–1558.

Wang, J., Zhang, X., Zhang, Y., & Li, Z. (2023). Multi-Agent Reinforcement Learning for Dynamic Security Management in Fog-IoT Networks. *IEEE Transactions on Emerging Topics in Computational Intelligence, 7*(4), 1238–1250.

Wu, Y., Li, Y., Li, X., & Li, Z. (2022). Privacy-Preserving and Secure Data Aggregation in Fog Computing for IoT Applications. *IEEE Transactions on Parallel and Distributed Systems, 33*(8), 1864–1877.

Zhang, D., Li, Z., Zhang, J., & Gu, L. (2019). Anomaly Detection and Intrusion Prevention in Fog-Based IoT Networks: A Survey. *IEEE Access : Practical Innovations, Open Solutions*, *7*, 113067–113082.

Chapter 5
Leveraging Smart Contracts for Enhanced IoE Security

Fasee Ullah
https://orcid.org/0000-0001-6167-5253
Universiti Teknologi Petronas, Malaysia

Md Tahmid Ashraf Chowdhury
https://orcid.org/0009-0003-8886-1138
Universiti Teknologi Petronas, Malaysia

ABSTRACT

Security and trust are two critical challenges of IoE, which refers to the interconnection of electronic devices providing intelligent services. The IoE ecosystem works using smart contracts based on pre-specified rules and dynamic automated transactions that self-eject contracts, permitting the removal of intermediaries from the process. This dynamism reduces human error and fraud while enhancing assurance and transparency. The chapter offers insights into the data integrity, better authenticity, and efficiency of identified communications provided by smart contracts in IoE architectures. Smart contracts are essentially platforms through which security and public confidence in IoE are reinforced by alleviating risks. Because they depend on tamper-free immutable blockchain ledgers, event information is recorded safely, creating immense efficiency, command over fraud, and been further improved with standards. They scale, interoperate, and comply with regulation—three key points—when constructing a secure and trusted IoE ecosystem.

DOI: 10.4018/979-8-3373-1424-2.ch005

1 INTRODUCTION

Understanding that the Internet of Everything (IoE) is the next evolution of the world as an interconnected environment bringing together physical things, people, processes, and data to create a connected whole (Tyagi and Nair 2020a). Go beyond the Internet of Things (IoT) as an evolution of things centered around the human element, including highly sophisticated processes, thus allowing much more dynamic personalized services (Gubbi et al. 2013). Intelligent cities where everything is very smooth as far as traffic management healthcare systems enabling real-time monitoring of patients-they are fundamentally making reverberations in industries and lifestyles across the globe. Real-world opportunities have been made into applications, but it should be acknowledged that it is extremely complex, extensive as well as present new challenges with respect to security, trust, and integrity of data.

Securing the networks, therefore, becomes more imperative because the number of IoE devices increases, thus creating huge amounts of data (Majeed, Haq, et al. 2016a). The decentralized and interlinking nature of IoE would make it a likely candidate for maximum damaging effect of cyber-attacks, data breaches, and unauthorized access. And the distributed and dynamic architecture of IoE makes it necessary to bring in what can be termed as redefined ingenious approaches, most probably not into the traditional centralized models of security (Serôdio et al. 2023). So, the smart contracts, powered by blockchain technology, have been identified as a possible good solution to these issues. This decentralized, immutable, and self-executing nature serves as a very robust environment to increase security as well as trust automation for IoE systems (Miglani et al. 2020a).

Securing the networks, therefore, becomes even more important with an increased understanding of the number of IoE devices that create huge amounts of data (Majeed, Haq, et al. 2016b). Because of its decentralized and interlinking nature, IoE is likely to invite the maximum damage of cyber-attacks, data breaches, and unauthorized access. Reinvented ingenious approaches need to be inducted in IoE architecture which is mostly distributed and highly dynamic hence not fitting into the traditional centralized models of security. It has been identified that smart contracts powered by blockchain technology could be one possible good solution to such issues. Its decentralized, immutable, and self-executing characteristic makes it a truly powerful enabler of security and trust automation in IoE systems (Macrinici, Cartofeanu, and Gao 2018).

Smart contracts are nothing but digital protocols within the blockchains executing predetermined rules and conditions without any human intervention (Nzuva 2019). Such contracts make a mediator unneeded and, therefore, reduce the chances of human error and fraud while also allowing a trustless interaction. It would make smart contracts communicate between different devices in a safe manner; run many complex processes automatically and secure data integrity, to name a few functions. Specifically, this could include a smart contract that authenticates and authorizes any device to access secret data, thus nullifying manual checks in the process (Kushwaha et al. 2022).

One of the main reasons smart contracts will be used in IoE is due to the solution of traditional security models (Saia 2018a). An inability of a single point of failure in a centralized system is its Achilles' heel, whereby such systems are considered fundamentally vulnerable under attack. Smart contracts decentralize control and decision-making, distributing them across a network of nodes to enhance resilience and fault tolerance. The idea also minimizes the risks of centralization and, as such, will fit into the IoE architecture, which is distributed, considering that devices are normally scattered across different locations and domains (Majeed, Haq, et al. 2016b).

Another critical aspect that the smart contracts can contribute towards in IoE is data integrity (Meydani et al. 2024). IoE networks generate information that needs to get collated and processed in real-time to come out with valuable insight about the same. Therefore, integrity validation such data for all this would mean a great deal when it came to service quality and incorrect results. Smart contracts ensure that verification and validation of data are done in a manner that can be automatically guaranteed on its own, data stored and shared over the network is actual and untampered with. It is this capability that makes the technology of more value to sectors, such as in health, where people's lives are threatened by pieces of untruthful data (Lyon 2014).

Besides this, automation enabled through smart contracts goes deeper, going to complex workflows and deeper to transactions, something traditionally done involving multiple intermediaries significantly heightened risks due to such reasons include delayed settlement and frauds (Harder 2017). They have obliterated middlemen altogether-for predefined parameters' fulfillment conditions. Therefore, automating contract executions themselves essentially cut time-cost resources consumed through process execution in different spheres. For instance, on supply chain management, smart contracts trigger the release of payments upon verification of delivery to ensure that the process was transparent and clear-cut right to the end (McKinney, Landy, and Wilka 2017).

However, several challenges hinder the potential of IoE in the development and effective adoption of smart contracts (Miglani et al. 2020b). Among these, scalability issues are paramount. Billions of devices may be associated with IoE networks, and each generates uninterrupted transactions, which no blockchain platform has the potential to handle. For such a challenge, an innovative approach is needed: sharding, layer-2 protocols, or hybrid blockchain architecture will go so far as to ensure scalability concerns about the demands of IoE (Lavaur, Lacan, and Chanel 2022).

Other key challenges that exist in the IoE ecosystem are those related to interoperability issues arising from diversity at devices, platforms, and protocols (Antonios, Konstantinos, and Christos 2023a). Interoperability at all these levels is a prerequisite to ensure seamless communication and compatibility among these heterogeneous constituents for the successful implementation of smart contracts. Besides this, there are also concerns about privacy, since the transparency of blockchain networks is in contrast with the protection of sensitive data. Advanced cryptographic techniques such as zero-knowledge proofs and homomorphic encryption have emerged as promising approaches that balance transparency with privacy (Diro et al. 2024).

The impact of smart contracts on IoE goes beyond society and industry. Such technologies will trigger innovation, efficiency, and new economic opportunities because they will be able to provide secure and automated interactions (Langley et al. 2021). For instance, decentralized marketplaces that use smart contracts will enable peer-to-peer transactions and sharing of resources, hence better utilizing existing assets. In the same way, intelligent energy management systems are optimized in resource allocation and minimize waste, thereby achieving sustainability goals (Mishra and Singh 2023).

Adoption of smart contracts in IoE might completely change governance and regulatory frameworks (Siddiqui et al. 2024a). Traditional models of regulation are struggling to cope with the dynamic and fast-moving pace of technology developments, thus giving way to several lacunas and inconsistencies. Smart contracts offer an open and transparent mechanism of regulating compliance to laws and regulations without burdening regulators, thus guaranteeing equity and uniform enforcement. On the other hand, it does raise some ethical and legal concerns, such as liability for errors in smart contract code and abuse (Sklaroff 2017a).

Continuous development of technologies and collaboration among players are what will create smart contracts in IoE within the near future (Rafique and Qadir 2024a). Innovations in blockchain scalability, cryptography, and artificial intelligence are three ways through which smart contract functionality will be improved, with different-discipline research tending to various technical, legal, and ethical issues in the implementation of smart contracts. Full realization of smart contracts in IoE shall be achieved with proper collaborations between developers, industry leaders, policymakers, and academia (Friess and Vermesan 2015).

It further goes to create a tectonic shift in how IoE conceives of managing and securing the connected systems through smart contracts (Raj, Venkatesh, and Amirtharajan 2013). Automation potential is an assurance and protects data, hence it has become an anchor in the next-generation IoE ecosystem. Further scalability, interoperability, and privacy issues will need to be taken care of, whereas evolution might hold promise with respect to these issues getting tackled. As IoE continues its exponential growth into more and more aspects of life, smart contracts will be major building blocks in securing, simplifying, and making this transformation sustainable (Rafique and Qadir 2024b). This is just a new beginning toward a smart, connected world where the integration of smart contracts and IoE would be at the forefront.

2 UNDERSTANDING SMART CONTRACTS

Smart contracts are a set of agreements implemented on the blockchain that automatically get executed once the predefined rules are satisfied (Governatori et al. 2018). They help in trustless transactions, meaning the interacting parties are assured of not needing any intermediaries to implement the contract terms.The concept of smart contracts was first proposed by Nick Szabo back in the 1990s, envisioning these as computerized transaction protocols that implement the terms of a contract. However, with the advent of blockchain technology, especially through Ethereum, smart contracts have come into practical implementation and are now the cornerstone of decentralized applications ("Learn Ethereum: Build Your Own Decentralized Applications with Ethereum and ... - Xun (Brian) Wu, Zhihong Zou, Dongying Song - Google Books," n.d.).

2.1 Fundamental Principles of Smart Contracts

Smart contracts are based on a few core principles that make them quite reliable and secure in respective applications (Khan et al. 2021). First, the principle of decentralization: it means that contracts are not owned by any one party but managed across a distributed network. This reduces the potential for manipulation and makes the operations more transparent. Another very important principle of smart contracts is automation; smart contracts implement predefined rules, without human intervention. This cuts not only redundant processes but also reduces human errors and delays in operations. The immutability feature related to smart contracts indicates that once the contract has been deployed on the blockchain, it cannot be modified, thus creating trust in the consistency of the contract over its whole life (Salehi, Clark, and Mannan 2023).

2.2 Key Components of Smart Contracts

The key ingredients of a smart contract include the following: First, there is the contract code, which contains the agreement's rules and conditions for execution; this code rests on the blockchain. The execution environment ensures that the logic of the contract plays out according to agreement, usually in a blockchain ecosystem such as the Ethereum Virtual Machine (EVM) (Zou et al. 2021). It finds another critical counterpart in the decentralized ledger, where each interaction in contract performance is recorded to ensure total transparency and audit trails. Also, the integrity of the contract itself, through cryptographic security mechanisms, cannot be compromised-which would ensure it is not allowed to make unauthorized changes (Soltani 2013).

2.3 How Smart Contracts Work

Execution follows a structured course: first, there is creation-where one specifies the terms and then encodes those into the blockchain (Rifat Hossain et al. 2024). Once deployed, it goes into a dormant mode until the conditions originally set are met. In the event of, say, a payment or verification of identity, it triggers the execution of the contract according to pre-set actions. The transaction gets verified in the blockchain network, and once the validation is carried out, the result of the contract gets permanently written on the ledger (Sanwar Hosen et al. 2020). This, therefore, involves the whole process, which grants high reliability and security, meaning that smart contracts will be perfect for automating many tasks within complex ecosystems like IoE.

Figure 1. How smart contracts work

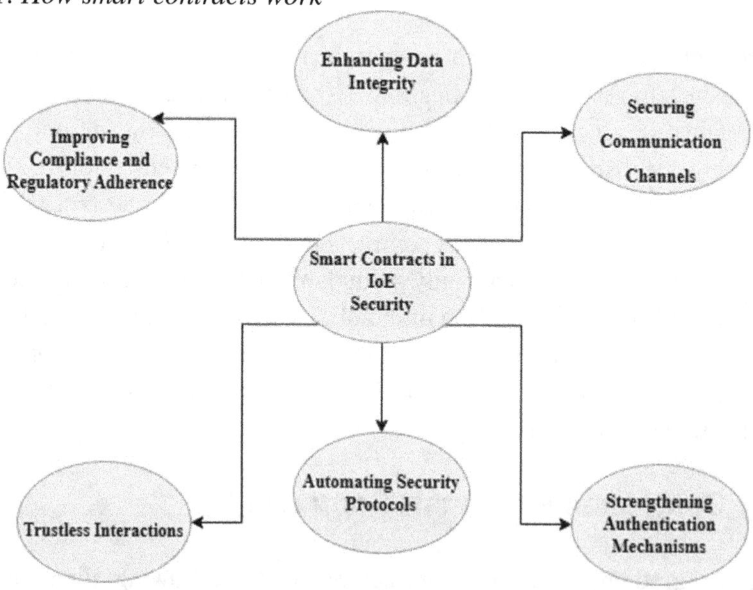

2.4 Benefits of Smart Contracts

There are several advantages that make smart contracts gain wider adoption in a variety of industries. First and most important is the cost-effectiveness since no middlemen are required, hence a reduction in administration and operation costs (Lin et al. 2022). The transparency in all contract details and transactions is also a critical advantage because it is all on the blockchain, where it is very transparent and accountable. Also, the automation feature of smart contracts contributes to faster processing with reduced chances of errors or fraud. Improved security is also among the benefits: cryptographic encryption provides integrity and protection of data from tampering (Othman et al. 2015).

2.5 Challenges in Implementing Smart Contracts

Despite so many advantages, there are a number of challenges which have to be overcome for smart contracts to become widely applicable (Zheng et al. 2020a). First of all, there is a concern about the rigidity of smart contracts. Since it is impossible to change them after being implemented, there arises an inability to fit into the constantly changing requirements. Further, coding bugs and vulnerabilities could lead to disastrous financial losses, as in the case of the DAO hack. Other critical challenges include scalability, whereby blockchain networks are usually congested and slow in processing many transactions. Besides, legal and regulatory uncertainties around smart contracts remain a barrier to their full integration into traditional systems (Mik 2017).

Table 1. Comparison of smart contracts with traditional contracts

Feature	Smart Contracts	Traditional Contracts
Execution	Automated and self-executing	Requires manual enforcement
Intermediaries	No intermediaries required	Typically involves intermediaries such as lawyers or brokers
Transparency	Fully transparent and auditable	Limited transparency, dependent on parties
Security	High security with cryptographic encryption	Susceptible to fraud and human manipulation
Cost	Lower costs due to automation	Higher costs due to intermediary involvement
Flexibility	Limited flexibility once deployed	Can be renegotiated and amended

2.6 Applications of Smart Contracts

Applications have ranged across many sectors, from showing that smart contracts are an exciting area through which innovation will change the usual process to automation in financial services industries for payment settlement, trade, and insurance claims by reducing reliance on intermediaries while increasing the pace of transaction processes. In supply chain management, it allows all logistics operations to be more transparent, traceable, assured of product authenticity, and guaranteed to be in compliance. In healthcare, smart contracts permit secure management and easy access to patient records with maintained privacy. Smart contracts will find a very promising ecosystem in the IoE that enhances security, authentication, and automation of a number of functions across devices (Rafique and Qadir 2024c).

2.7 Security Aspects of Smart Contracts

One of the major concerns while dealing with smart contracts is security, since smart contracts are decentralized in nature and immutable (Singh et al. 2020). Some are doing rigorous audits and formal verifications against vulnerable attacks prior to deployment; hence, trying to make their data safer. These apart, several best practices adopted about security standards by established contract templates, multi-signature mechanisms provide considerable mitigation factors towards a number of potential risks that are there on horizon always. However, such precautions still must be complemented by continuous monitoring and updates owing to the always-emerging risks towards preserving the integrity of the smart-contract-based system.

2.8 The Future of Smart Contracts

In the future, smart contracts look pretty bright, with active development that tries to overcome limitations and extend areas of their possible application (Xie et al. 2019). Among the latest innovations, there are layer-2 scaling solutions for blockchains, which would allow smart contracts to process more transactions without significant slowdowns. Interoperability solutions start to appear that enable smart contracts to work seamlessly on several blockchain platforms. Moreover, the integration of artificial intelligence and machine learning into smart contracts will make contracts more intelligent and adaptive in execution, considering dynamic business environments (Wang et al. 2019).

Smart contracts can change many aspects of different industries: from secure to totally transparent and efficient (Zheng et al. 2020b). Though there are challenges, developments and research are ongoing to further refine their capabilities, and they are considered one of the cornerstones of emerging technologies, including the Internet of Everything.

3 SECURITY CHALLENGES IN IOE

IoE is a paradigm connecting people, processes, and data and things in a way that the digital environment will be intelligent and responsive (da Costa, Oliveira, and de Souza 2021). On the other hand, with all these benefits, the expansion of IoE brings significant security challenges that should be answered in order to make interconnected systems safe, private, and reliable. The complexity and scale of IoE networks make them vulnerable to different classes of cyber threats while ranging from data breaches to sophisticated attacks against device integrity and network communication (Akan et al. 2023).

3.1 Data Security and Privacy Concerns

Data security and privacy are amongst the most rated security challenges in IoE (Mogadem, Li, and Meheretie 2022). With an exponential rise in the number of connected devices, a huge quantity of sensitive information flows continuously across the networks. Severe consequences may be experienced, including identity theft and financial fraud, due to unauthorized access. Performing complete end-to-end encryption, strong authentication mechanisms, and data anonymization techniques are paramount in protecting user data against probable adversaries.

3.2 Scalability and Security Trade-offs

The balance between performance and security is getting tougher with the scaling up of IoE networks (Sharma et al. 2024). The conventional mechanisms for security introduce latency and resource constraints that may impede the IoE applications from operating efficiently. The scalability problem arises when the security framework fails to accommodate a growing number of connected devices, including potential vulnerabilities. A comprehensive approach integrating lightweight encryption algorithms and adaptive security policies has to be followed in order to address this challenge.

3.3 Device Authentication and Trust Management

In this regard, big diversity and heterogeneity of IoE devices is one of the big challenges toward developing secure authentication mechanisms (Iftikhar and Qureshi 2024). Most IoE devices have poor computational resources that limit the implementation of complex cryptographic protocols. Besides this, trust establishment between devices in a hyper-connected environment requires a robust identity management solution with secure device authentication to protect against unauthorized access. A blockchain-based decentralized trust model could be implemented with the integration of smart contracts, reducing the dependency on central entities to a minimum for device authentication.

3.4 Network Security Threats

While several of these concerns and the IoE vulnerability landscapes revolve around network-based threats ranging from DDoS, man-in-the-middle attack, and eavesdropping, the dynamic and distributed nature of IoE networks does introduce varied avenues through which attackers will have chances to exploit vulnerabilities disruptive of network operations (Tyagi and Nair 2020b). Threats can nonetheless be mitigated by the use of intrusion detection systems, firewalls, and secure routing protocols in ascertaining the resiliency of IoE against a variety of malicious activities.

3.5 Regulatory and Compliance Challenges

The other IoE security feature is adherence to regulatory compliance and industrial standards (Tyagi and Nair 2020b). Different regions have different regulations with respect to data protection, privacy, and cybersecurity, among others. It generally tends to get pretty tough for organizations to implement IoE solutions that guarantee all of these regulations without compromising operational efficiency. Organizations must keep pace with the revolution of regulatory demands by introducing corresponding security measures in compliance standards set by GDPR and CCPA.

3.6 Security Risks in IoE Communication Protocols

Variety signal protocols are adopted in IoE, including but not limited to Wi-Fi, Bluetooth, Zigbee, LoRaWAN(Ugwuanyi, Paul, and Irvine 2021). Thus, each comes with different weaknesses an attacker might be well aware of, such as hijacking data, malicious payload injection, and sniffing around critical communication channels. All these factors imply that IoE signal transmission protocols should always be monitored for timely updates while equipped with valid encryption and control mechanisms.

Table 2. Common security threats in IoE

Security Threat	Description	Mitigation Strategies
Data Breaches	Unauthorized access to sensitive information	Encryption, access controls, and monitoring
Device Hijacking	Unauthorized control over IoE devices	Strong authentication and firmware updates
DDoS Attacks	Overloading networks to disrupt services	Traffic filtering and rate limiting
Insider Threats	Security breaches caused by trusted individuals	Role-based access and continuous monitoring
Eavesdropping	Interception of communication between IoE devices	End-to-end encryption and secure protocols

3.7 Physical Security Challenges

While IoE basically deals with digital security, physical security remains of utmost importance (Τσαγδής 2022). Most IoE devices are going to be deployed within industrial facilities, smart homes, and other such places that could be subject to tampering, theft, and unauthorized physical access. In this regard, physical security against unauthorized access and physical attacks will be assured through secure enclosures, tamper-resistant hardware, and mechanisms for location tracking.

3.8 Security Awareness and Training

User and stakeholder ignorance and/or awareness are some of the main causes for IoE security challenges (David et al. 2023). A very few numbers of users were informed about possible security threats for IoE devices, and most of the people failed to apply all best practices in securing the devices and hence the data. Security awareness programs, clear guidelines, and advocating cybersecurity best practices allow the user to take proactive functions in protecting their IoE environment.

3.9 Interoperability and Security Integration

IoE ecosystems are composed of a host of devices provided by different vendors, all having their different set of security capabilities and standards (Majeed, Haq, et al. 2016c). A fine balance of seamless interoperability with a high degree of security can be quite tough to achieve. Incompatible measures may create points of vulnerability which attackers can use to infiltrate. This will ensure that stakeholders in industries, through standardization of security protocols and collaboration, come up with a common security framework where interoperability is guaranteed without compromising security.

4 ROLE OF SMART CONTRACTS IN IOE SECURITY

IoE is a huge transformation in the manner in which devices, people, data, and processes interact and forms an ecosystem where operational efficiency and decision-making get notably improved (Sudharshan 2020). These come with major security risks of their own due to high connectivity. Among the ways the security challenges may be dealt with in IoT is by use of smart contracts-small pieces of self-executing agreements running on a blockchain. Thus, leveraging some unique features of smart contracts, IoE ecosystems can enhance security, bring in better transparency, and automatically enforce security policies (Majeed, Bhana, et al. 2016).

Figure 2. Smart contracts in IoE security

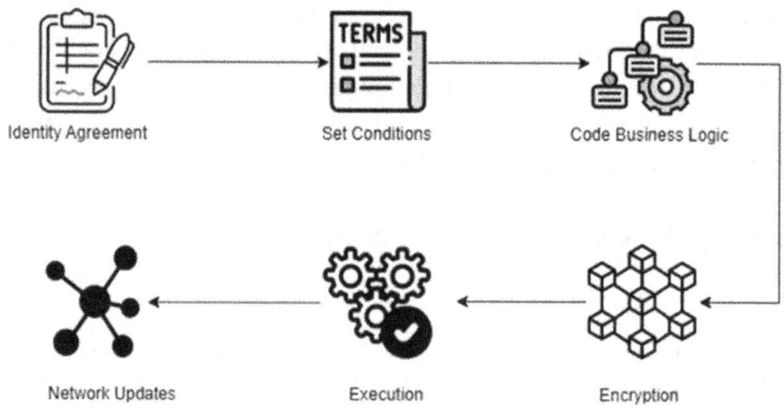

4.1 Enhancing Data Integrity

Data integrity is one of the major roles played by smart contracts in IoE security (Javed and Qureshi 2024). A huge volume of data is transferred across devices and systems within an operating network of IoE; hence, it is very important to ensure authenticity and accuracy of information. Smart contracts provide an immutable ledger to record every transaction of data in a very transparent and secure way. Immutability means, once recorded, nobody at all can alter anything or tamper with the same recording. The recording then is trust-worthy and thus dependable in nature throughout the network.

4.2 Automating Security Protocols

Security protocols can, therefore, be programmed into smart contracts to automatically apply themselves without human intervention (J. Liu and Liu 2019). For instance, smart contracts will carry out the required verifications with regard to the identity of the devices before access is allowed on the network; it ensures communication takes place between the entities only that are authorized within the ecosystem. Automation reduces human error and further reduces unauthorized access, hence making IoE systems secure and efficient.

4.3 Trustless Interactions

Traditional security models in IoE are based on some form of central entity for the validation of a transaction or authorization (Saia 2018b). Smart contracts open newer vistas in conducting trustless interactions between different devices in the IoE environment. Powered by blockchains, smart contracts do away with intermediaries; thus, transactions and information exchanges will happen with assured security and transparency. This level of decentralization further brings added resilience for IoE networks and reduced dependence on trusted third-party entities.

Table 3. Comparison of traditional security vs. smart contract-based security in IoE

Aspect	Traditional Security	Smart Contract-Based Security
Data Integrity	Prone to manipulation	Immutable and tamper-proof
Automation	Limited	High, self-executing rules
Trust Model	Centralized	Decentralized and trustless
Scalability	Challenging	More adaptable with blockchain scaling
Transparency	Limited visibility	Full transparency and auditability

10.4.4 Strengthening Authentication Mechanisms

Amongst the prime IoE security concerns, authentication is considered one of the leading ones, wherein smart contracts have a strong framework to maintain digital identities. (Tyagi et al. 2021) Smart contracts would be able to authenticate devices and users through blockchain-based identity management systems based on predefined criteria that reduce the possibility of identity frauds and unauthorized accesses. The decentralized nature of smart contracts will ensure that all processes related to verification of identity remain tamper-proof and transparent.

4.5 Securing Communication Channels

Another important role of smart contracts relates to the security of communication channels within the IoE network (Gourisetti et al. 2021). Embedding the logic of cryptographic protocols right in the logic of smart contracts will automate data encryption and checking during its transmission. That means that communications among devices are confidential and can't be intercepted by unauthorized parties. In addition, smart contracts will allow network traffic analysis and can perform a security response upon detection of some anomalies, if needed.

4.6 Improving Compliance and Regulatory Adherence

Compliance is now one of the increasingly significant factors for the deployments of IoE, dealing with a host of data protection and privacy legislation that any organization needs to follow strictly (Kambourakis and Neisse 2021). Smart contracts will enable regulatory compliance because all transactions taking place within the network and respective security are auditable; this transparency due to it helps meet the necessary regulatory requirements with reduced human auditing and documentation.

4.7 Challenges and Considerations

However, considering the advantages of using smart contracts in IoE security, there are challenges to be met (Siddiqui et al. 2024b). Specialized expertise is required in creating and deploying smart contracts, and any single bug in coding may disrupt its security. Besides, in making smart contracts compatible with existing IoE infrastructure compatible, huge changes would be made to the prevailing systems, which may include operational disruptions and costs.

5 REDUCING HUMAN ERROR AND FRAUD WITH SMART CONTRACTS

IoE has brought a number of opportunities regarding automation and efficiency (Strielkowski et al. 2019). However, the same developments bring along critical vulnerabilities related to human error and fraudulent activities. Traditional IoE systems rely on centralized control mechanisms and human interventions that increase the probability of operational inefficiencies, data manipulation, and security breaches. Smart contracts utilize blockchain for an automated, tamper-proof, self-executing solution to mitigate these risks and bottom out security by reducing human involvement (Sklaroff 2017b).

5.1 Eliminating Human Error through Automation

Smart contracts help reduce human errors in the IoE ecosystems primarily through automating processes that are often repetitive and complicated (Y. Liu et al. 2024a). Traditional systems are prone to manual intervention in data entry, validation, and processing, which tends to be highly erroneous due to oversight, fatigue, or even lack of proper knowledge. Smart contracts guarantee accurate and consistent application of predefined rules and conditions, allowing no room for human error. This automation enhances accuracy, reliability, and efficiency in operations, hence eradicating discrepancies and reducing inconsistencies that usually arise in manual workflows.

Additionally, automation through smart contracts helps in cutting down delays created by manual intervention. For example, the supply chain network based on IoE requires complete coordination among suppliers, manufacturers, and logistics providers. Smart contracts thus allow for automatic verification and execution of contractual obligations without waiting for approvals manually, hence making the process quicker and reducing human-induced errors.

5.2 Fraud Prevention through Transparency and Immutability

The fraud in the IoE system can be varied from causing a financial loss to bringing disrepute (Bandaranayake 2014). Smart contracts come up with proactive counter fraud due to the inherent properties of blockchain-transparency and immutability. Every transaction that takes place via smart contract gets into a distributed ledger so that no revision or tamper is allowed towards it. It gives an auditable and trustworthy record of every interaction within the IoE ecosystem in such a way that no malicious actor may forge or tamper with it to manipulate the data or commit fraud.

Besides, smart contracts engender trust among stakeholders since activities are transparent. In such areas as health and financial services, the logistic records in regard to smart contract transactions undertaken are verifiable and traceable; such kind of transparency deters fraudulent activities since the parties concerned have to adhere to the set terms and conditions without data manipulation rooms for interests.

5.3 Enhancing Data Security and Integrity

IoE networks generate a lot of sensitive information, which should not be exposed to unauthorized access and tampering (Mathur and Sinha 2023). Traditional security mechanisms are usually inefficient in responding effectively to IoE environments with a large number of interacting devices and systems in real time. Smart contracts have proven viable in this regard, through the provision of cryptographic security mechanisms which ensure data integrity and confidentiality.

These include those in which IoE will introduce a variety of security protocols using smart contracts that guarantee there is an exchange of data between legitimate parties only. In sum, all possible breaches owing to configuration errors, password-related issues, and leaks of sensitive data would be removed automatically. Besides this, smart contracts also introduce strict access control and authentication that check and weed out unauthorized interventions, further bolstering network security on IoE.

5.4 Smart Contracts in Financial Transactions within IoE

Smart contracts reduce human errors and fraud in the IoE ecosystem, and financial transactions are one of the critical areas concerned (Das et al. 2024). Be it billing processes, micropayments, or even financial settlement mechanisms, the manual handling of monetary operations is always prone to certain errors or fraudulent manipulations. While smart contracts automate those transactions under predefined conditions, these make sure that the payments get executed with accuracy and security without any need for manual intervention.

For example, the IoE-enabled smart city project would use IoT devices that remain in place, measure the consumption of electricity and water in real time. Now, smart contracts would read actual usage data and make the payments, reducing possibilities of billing due to erroneous and fraudulent claims at the same time. Automation here lets increased efficiency and consumer trust in the system take place.

5.5 Challenges in Implementing Smart Contracts for Fraud Reduction

Smart contract application to IoE systems faces some challenges in the way of reduction of human-based errors and fraud (Tajjour and Singh Chandel 2023). First of all, challenges are related to the complexity of coding and deployment issues of smart contracts. The error in the code of the smart contract itself may further lead to some vulnerabilities and potential exploits. Thus, testing and auditing of smart contracts have to be performed rigorously in order to make them reliable and secure.

Another challenge is the legal and regulatory framework of smart contracts. Since these are autonomous contracts, there is a possibility of legal disputes arising, as well as issues in compliance, because no human intervenes. The alignment of smart contracts with existing regulatory requirements is very crucial to avoid IoE implementations facing potential conflicts and legal challenges.

Table 4. Comparative analysis of traditional vs. smart contract-based IoE systems

Feature	Traditional IoE Systems	Smart Contract-Based IoE Systems
Error Susceptibility	High (manual processes)	Low (automated execution)
Fraud Vulnerability	High (centralized control)	Low (decentralized ledger)
Transparency	Limited (closed systems)	High (public ledger visibility)
Security	Moderate (human-dependent)	High (cryptographic enforcement)
Operational Efficiency	Low (manual intervention required)	High (automated workflows)

5.6 Future Prospects and Innovations

In the future, smart contracts with AI and ML can do an even better job in fraud detection (L. Liu et al. 2022). AI-powered analytics can also identify suspicious patterns and behaviors for insight, thereby enabling a smart contract to take proactive steps in fraud risk mitigation. Moreover, the development of easier smart contract frameworks will also allow more adopters with less complexity in implementing their IoE ecosystems.

The future of smart contracts in IoE security will also be dictated by the development of regulatory standards and industrial best practices. Ensuring a secure and trustworthy IoE environment using smart contracts calls for collaboration among governments, businesses, and technology providers.

6 SMART CONTRACTS IN ACTION: USE CASES FOR IOE

IoE is the paradigm that reflects the revolution in interaction among devices, systems, and people ("Internet of Energy for Smart Cities: Machine Learning Models and Techniques - Google Books," n.d.). IoE enables seamless integration and intelligent communication of information from diverse domains. In such a networked world, security and trust mechanisms become highly crucial in order to maintain integrity and functionality within the ecosystem. Smart contracts introduce a whole new revolution in dealing with these challenges. They are basically self-executing agreements with pre-set rules encoded in the blockchain technology. Smart contracts have become so relevant in furthering applications of IoE through automation of operations, guaranteeing integrity in data, and ensuring trustless interactions. The section that follows shows some real-world applications where smart contracts are necessary for IoE in security and functionality.

6.1 Supply Chain Transparency and Security

The significant application of smart contracts in the IoE ecosystem pertains to supply chain management (Yang et al. 2023). Sensors integrated with IoT, RFID tags, and GPS trackers track every moment of the life of a product within a supply chain and continuously report their status in real time. This piece of information has to be secure, trustworthy, and tamper-proof for any action to be performed based on it by any stakeholder. Smart contracts define the rules, which are predefined with regard to handling or the way goods are transferred; every step will be automatically checked for validity.

For instance, smart contracts may be designed to automatically generate payments after verification by IoE sensors on transport vehicles that goods have indeed arrived at a certain location. Since blockchain is distributed and immutable in nature, all transactions become fully transparent, and it is virtually impossible for malicious actors to alter the data. Table 1 provides sample applications of smart contracts to supply chain processes in selected industries.

6.2 Secure Smart Homes and Buildings

Smart homes and buildings mean the Internet of Everything (IoE), whereby interconnected devices (smart thermostats, security cameras, lighting systems, etc.) are designed to assist individuals to be more convenient and efficient in their daily routine (Korneeva, Olinder, and Strielkowski 2021). Such systems can, however, compromise end-user privacy and safety as possible risks to security. A good alternative is smart contracts to secure and operate these devices autonomously.

Consider access control in a smart building. Smart contracts allow properly authorized persons (such as leases and employees) to gain access simply by confirming their identity through IoE devices connected to smartphones or the like, such as biometric scanners. Because smart contracts automatically check permissions, they do not require centralized servers. Smart contracts minimize unauthorized access and reduce the chances of data breaches. They also provide improved security and allow for avenues of energy controls at device settings for better optimization of energy-saving results in a fully compliant manner with environmental standards (Márquez-Sánchez et al. 2023).

6.3 Healthcare Data Integrity and Privacy

The health sector boasts numerous IoE devices, including wearable sensors and medical monitoring tools, producing vast quantities of data, aiding personalized care and improving health outcomes (Putra et al. 2024). However, given the fact that healthcare data is quite sensitive, stringent measures must be taken to ensure that, firstly, there is no unauthorized access, and secondly, alteration of data is a far-off possibility. Smart contracts provide a good solution because they automate the processes of data sharing and access control on IoE networks to guarantee data privacy and integrity.

In this case, it is sharing patient information between healthcare providers and insurer companies. Smart contracts will also allow the creation of different conditions under which data can be accessed; for example, whether explicit consent by the patient should be sought or legitimacy needs to be verified. This brings transparency and follows regulations such as HIPAA with regard to privacy, thus making the process of sharing data very secure and reliable ("Beyond the HIPAA Privacy Rule: Enhancing Privacy, Improving Health Through ... - Institute of Medicine, Board on Health Care Services, Board on Health Sciences Policy, Committee on Health Research and the Privacy of Health Information: The HIPAA Privacy Rule - Google Books," n.d.).

6.4 Autonomous Vehicles and Transportation

IoE in autonomous vehicles and smart transportation has redesigned the concept of mobility by making it possible for real-time traffic management, predictive maintenance, and even automation of ride-sharing. Smart contracts would introduce safety and efficiency in those operations (Vermesan et al. 2021).

The smart contract will automatically execute the agreement between the passenger and the service provider in a ride-sharing system. In case of such a ride being completed, the contract confirms the realization of service, hence triggering the payment without any interference from middlemen. Similarly, smart contracts also manage tolls and parking, or even insurance claims with low administrative overhead, hence with minimal disputes. Smart contracts therefore make it possible to coordinate the predictive maintenance times provided through the IoE sensors to help the fleet operator optimize the performance of the fleet by minimizing vehicle downtimes.

6.5 Energy Trading in Smart Grids

IoE in general, and smart grids in particular, enable one to monitor energy production, distribution, and consumption dynamically (Shahinzadeh et al. 2019). Furthermore, driven by the increasing interest in renewable sources, today consumers can sell their surplus energy directly to their neighbors, recently referred to as decentralized energy trading. Security and automation of transactions in P2P energy markets can be ensured through smart contracts.

For example, smart contracts will match energy producers and consumers based on set criteria of price and availability. Once a transaction is agreed upon, the contract automatically executes the trade and updates the blockchain ledger. During this process, no intermediary involvement takes place, reducing transaction costs and increasing transparency. Furthermore, smart contracts assure that energy regulation rules will be followed; hence, all participants must adhere to all environmental and safety standards.

6.6 Industrial IoT and Predictive Maintenance

Integrating smart contracts vastly enhances such IIoT applications using IoE devices in the monitoring and controlling of the manufacturing process (Parhamfar and Zabihi 2024). Predictive maintenance, a key piece of IIoT, is based on data from sensors implanted inside machinery to know in advance when potential failures may happen before actual ones occur, so preventive servicing can be enabled. Smart contracts will automatically trigger the maintenance workflows after real-time sensor data.

An example could be that IoE sensors detect an abnormal level of vibration in a machine, automatically creating a request for maintenance, sending a notice to the relevant technician, and even ordering replacement parts via smart contract. This minimum level of downtime is assured by automation and reduction of human error using smart contracts in such cases. Moreover, the accountability and audits are pretty facile with blockchain records due to their transparent and traceable nature.

6.7 Enhancing Public Safety with Smart Cities

Smart cities represent the integration of IoE into urban living through intelligent infrastructure and services ("Intelligent Systems for IoE Based Smart Cities - Google Books," n.d.). One critical smart city feature that could be developed using smart contracts is public safety. The IoE-enabled surveillance system, emergency response network, and traffic management systems will work much more effectively when run by automated rules.

Emergency response workflows can be improved with smart contracts by automating messaging between IoE devices and emergency services. In this regard, sensors detecting an incident like a fire would automatically trigger a smart contract that sends an alert to the fire department, unlocks escape routes, and notifies the occupants of the building. This increases the degree of automation done, hence reducing response times and making public safety more effective.

7 CHALLENGES AND LIMITATIONS OF SMART CONTRACTS IN IOE

The utilization of smart contracts in the Internet of Everything (IoE) ecosystem is one of the most innovative technologies, which can automate processes, improve security, and form trustless interactions (Rafique and Qadir 2024d). Yet, while these self-executing agreements have a myriad of pros, they also come along with multiple challenges and limitations. The low level of technology development is one of the factors that contribute to the vital errors in the deployment of the smart contracts. That is, they are caused by the inconvenience and cost to simplify the design and functioning of smart contracts. Over the past few years, the use of smart contracts has increasingly grown in terms of volume and their wide use has given birth to various hacking incidents such as The DAO hack. One of the challenges of Blockchain and cryptocurrency security is privacy by design. In other words, some of the tokens and cryptocurrencies, based on the theory, enabled financial transactions running on the blockchain technology are anonymous and irreversible, which makes them perfect for ransoms, blackmails, or for setting up/moving illegal money.

7.1 Scalability and Performance Bottlenecks

One of the aspects in smart contracts embedded in the Internet of Everything (IoE) projects, which present a major problem is the issue of scalability (Rafique and Qadir 2024e). As IoE grows, the number of devices and transactions are increasing exponentially hence requiring more and more advanced infrastructure for handling the massive influx of data. The Blockchain networks, which are underlying almost all of the smart contract uses, usually have performance bottlenecks due to their consensus mechanisms. On the other hand, Public blockchains such as Ethereum and Bitcoin are limited in that they have low transaction throughout and latency is high.

In an IoE (Internet of Everything) scenario, the limitations mentioned above can impede the real-time functioning of the operations. A common example of such a smart contract is a contract monitoring the distribution of electricity in a grid. In the case of peak demand, an efficiency problem will derive if the speed of execution of the contract is not high because it takes too much time to process transactions, which in turn may lead to service disruptions. To fix these problems, scientists are investigating possible solutions such as sharding, layer-2 protocols, and blockchain interoperability, but these technologies are still in their developmental stages.

7.2 Energy Consumption and Resource Constraints

Devices of the Internet of Everything (IoE) are frequently overtaxed because of such factors as battery endurance, computational capacities, and memory (Kelliher 2013). Running smart contracts on IoE apps can only aggravate them, especially when the blockchain network underlying the smart contracts gets choked by energy-wasting consensus algorithms like the Proof of Work (PoW). For example, sensors on IoE that use blockchain may exhaust a battery very quickly, and their potential to work may be compromised.

Additionally, the high computational complexity of smart contracts needed for the execution can cause resource-constrained IoE devices to use up all their processing power. Besides PoW, the PoS and PoA blockchain solutions with better properties can be suggested, but deployment should be optimized properly in order to provide both security and energy efficiency.

7.3 Security Vulnerabilities in Smart Contracts

Although smart contracts are responsible for increased security by cutting out third-parties and automating trust mechanisms, they are still at risk of imperfections (D'Onfro 2020). Unsatisfactorily written code that includes bugs can cause serious economic and working complications. Specifically, the Ethereum blockchain's well-known DAO attack took advantage of a loophole in a smart contract and as a result, millions of dollars were lost.

In the environment of IoE, these attack possibilities could, in extreme cases, lead to devastating situations. A corrupted smart contract that regulates home automation might allow someone unauthorized access to sensitive data or to control devices. Thus, it can bring to the front the problem of user privacy and safety. Making the smart contract safe requires rigorous code audits, formal verification methods, and continuous monitoring. However, the complexity of the maintenance process gets increased because of the dynamic nature of the IoE networks when devices constantly join and leave.

7.4 Legal and Regulatory Challenges

Smart contracts, the act of acting legally without a central organization, is a major legal and regulatory issue due to their decentralized nature (Cuccuru 2017). Conventional legal systems dictate the use of individual enforcement authorities to execute the contracts, but in the case of smart contracts, AI contracts work automatically without people's intervention. This raises the question of liability, jurisdiction, and enforceability, especially when dealing with cross-border IoE applications.

One of the potential scenarios is when a smart contract that represents a supply chain dispute is not executing correctly or simply fails altogether and there is a difficulty in identifying who is accountable. Furthermore, smart contracts' deployments in the global Internet of Everything (IoE) networks are made even harder and more complicated due to the different regulations. In Table 1 are the main legal and regulatory challenges suffered by the smart contracts used in different IoE applications.

Table 5. Legal and regulatory challenges

IoE Application	Legal/Regulatory Challenge	Impact
Smart Healthcare	Data privacy regulations (e.g., GDPR, HIPAA)	Delays in implementation and compliance costs
Autonomous Vehicles	Liability for accidents caused by smart contract failures	Legal disputes and risk of adoption hesitancy
Cross-border Supply Chain	Jurisdictional conflicts over blockchain governance	Complex contract enforcement processes
Energy Trading	Regulatory restrictions on P2P transactions	Limited scalability of decentralized markets

7.5 Interoperability Issues

The Internet of Everything (IoE) space is not homogeneous and its elements can be a mix of devices, platforms, and protocols created by different developers (Chatzigiannakis and Tselios 2021). Through the seamless interoperability of the dissimilar systems, smart contracts are trying to handle a hot issue of divergence. For instance, a smart city capable of Internet of Everything may comprise different players, e.g. government companies, private entrepreneurs, and citizens, each of them utilizing different technologies. Smart contracts' inclusion in such a complex environment will rely on the standardization of protocols and interfaces.

Without the interconnectedness of systems, smart contracts find it impossible to automate the entire process or provide a certain level of data consistency across the IoE ecosystem. The endeavors to deploy common standards, e.g. the IEEE P2418.1 for blockchain use in IoT, are ongoing, but not yet widespread. In the meantime, middleware solutions and communication protocols are being searched for the purpose of solving this problem this way.

7.6 Privacy Concerns

Despite blockchain typically being a transparent system, it may become an issue with privacy needs and the Internet of Everything (IoE) (Rafique and Qadir 2024f). Blocks of data on a blockchain being written cannot be changed and are open to all participants by default, which could put personal information at risk of exposure to bad actors. For example, a smart contract that works directly with health information received by its wearable IoE devices could inadvertently expose private medical information unless adequate privacy measures are implemented.

The use of evidence like zero-knowledge proofs, secure multi-party computation, and private blockchains are the possible ways to address privacy concerns. But still, they have downsides like high complexity, low scalability, and the computational overhead which limits their adaptation to IoE systems.

7.7 Cost Implications

The application of smart contracts and other components of IoE systems can result in noticeable costs (Y. Liu et al. 2024b). The transaction costs pop up on blockchain networks like gas fees which change due to the network load and can conflict with budgets during peak times. In an IoE arena with urgent daily transactions, such as real-time energy trading or micro-payments for data usage, the costs can shake the profitability of smart contracts-based solutions.

Furthermore, the building and resetting of stable smart contracts with the necessary efficiency beyond the budget means the need for additional expertise. To solve these cost problems, they need to be addressed as funds become the savings with the improvement of blockchain scalability due to effective consensus mechanisms.

7.8 Limited Flexibility and Upgradability

The moment smart contracts are on the blockchain, they become unchangeable, the code of these smart contracts cannot be altered (Shermin 2017). The main advantage of such unchangeable smart contracts is the trust and security that they bring. On the other side, these contracts are not capable of their future updates or changes to be made when needed. In such a fast-changing world, where not only the needs of users but also the devices themselves are continuously developing, this software is a major restriction. one device evolves rapidly, and this software can be a significant limitation.

Ideas for the development of smart contracts that will not be put at stake if the security is reached while at the same time cannot be broken down and allow for easier operation and updating of the contracts are necessary. However, the main challenges here are to ensure these new blockchain initiatives are resistant to potential hacks and they can be integrated with the existing IoE system.

8 FUTURE PERSPECTIVES AND INNOVATIONS

The fusion of smart contracts and the Internet of Everything (IoE) inevitable stages along the way to the evolution of whole ecosystems ("Internet of Things: Converging Technologies for Smart Environments and ... - Google Books," n.d.). It has the ability to confront but also to create an entirely new generation of companies at the intersection of safety, automation and mostly scale. Technological advancements have made IoE a prominent aspect in implementing various forms of products that accommodate different human needs and withstand the depletion of natural resources. A significant part of the IoE sector centered on smart farming can be recognized in hi-tech areas because of the planetary connection and thus, the amount of remote access becomes minimum (Brun, Sudheer, and Goud 2023). Thus, the continuous expansion of the concept of the intelligent farm.

8.1 Evolving Blockchain Architectures for IoE

The most promising field of development is related to the emergence of specialized blockchain architectural solutions for IoE (Rafique and Qadir 2024g). Commonsense is that regular blockchain networks are extremely reliable but are not fast and practical enough to efficiently handle the large volume of transcripts resulting from IoE. These new systems are expected to utilize a combination of decentralized public blockchains and the rapid, cheap or cost-efficient private or consortium blockchains.

These hybrid networks are able to provide instant transaction processing, enabling a shared environment of trust and transparency.

Layer-2 solutions such as state channels and side chains are also preparing to play a significant part in scaling up the blockchain functionality (Sguanci, Spatafora, and Vergani 2021). Implementation of off-chain data processing in most cases keeps the pressure off of the main blockchain and hence, ensures smooth operation of the entire network with high frequency where microtransactions prevail as, for instance, in smart cities and transportation systems. Hence, the other side of the application continues to function when the first problem takes place.

8.2 Integration of Artificial Intelligence in Smart Contracts

AI smart contracts that have been combined with artificial intelligence (AI) provide a new way of automating and optimizing the internet of everything IoE processes (Rafique and Qadir 2024h). The AI algorithms are able to sift through all the data that is generated by the various IoE devices and can make up patterns and give predictions, in order to enable the decision-making effectiveness to skyrocket. On the other hand, AI can also be utilized in smart contracts which allow for adaptive contracts to change in accordance with up-to-the-minute data input, therefore to the relevance and efficiency of the contracts.

There are also many applications of AI in the smart healthcare system. For instance, AI-powered contracts could dynamically adjust treatment protocols based on patient vitals collected by wearable devices. Environment includes everything in which an entity lives or operates. AI can study the lifestyle or behavior of a person, and he may adjust through these smart contracts according to that. The application describes more on the synergies that could exist from the compatibility of AI and smart contracts in modifying IoE systems further to be responsive and intelligent.

8.3 Enhanced Privacy Mechanisms

Privacy could be the most significant barrier that has hindered the total adoption of IoE technologies ("Influencable Autonomy and Predictable Freedom in the IoE," n.d.). The new approaches are that private smart contracts could be established on permissioned blockchains, which enable restriction of contract data to contracted entities. Zero-knowledge proofs and homomorphic encryption all appear to provide significant innovations in this space. ZKPs enable the authenticating of data without revealing the actual data.

These techniques may also feature as some of the key benefits in the case of sensitive IoE applications like healthcare, finance, and services under government, the privacy of which is essential; as these technologies develop, they will serve as some of the keystones of the IoE that are likely to be imbibed into the future.

8.4 Interoperability and Cross-Chain Communication

There are many devices and platforms included within the heterogeneous nature of IoE networks, thus requiring seamless interoperability in between all these devices and platforms (Antonios, Konstantinos, and Christos 2023b). The new connections across multiple chains would have to be created for such interoperability, and cross-chain communication protocols should be developed, which will make smart contracts work across different blockchain networks. Technologies such as Polkadot and Cosmos are among the innovators setting trends in the provision of connectivity frameworks for linking blockchains even while individual ones are not compromised.

Future works will be geared towards standardizing interoperability communication protocols in the e-discoverability context and exchanging metadata and sharing metadata over multiple web services for a functional interoperability as well.

8.5 Quantum-Resistant Security for IoE

As quantum computing advances, the traditional cryptographic algorithms that support the security of blockchain and smart contracts might become obsolete. This is why the development of quantum-resistant cryptography is vital for guaranteeing the security of IoE systems in the long run. Post-quantum algorithms like lattice-based, hash-based, and multivariate polynomial cryptography are under development to defend the corresponding ones from quantum attacks.

Quantum-resistant smart contracts will be interrupted in handling the sensitive data and allowing device communication between smart machines under IoE. Not just that, IoE networks will be future-proofed, but also endorsed by various stakeholders to spread the application of smart contract systems more widely.

8.6 Emergence of Decentralized IoE Marketplaces

Smart contracts for decentralized marketplaces will demolish all these walls in IoE through P2P transaction systems without any brokerage. Resource sharing for IoE devices may include things like data trading, services exchanged, and of course, between machines or devices in terms of physical resources like an air conditioner or energy. So, a typical example would be that such smart homes, enabled by IoE, trade energy with each other: surplus energy becomes sold directly to a neighbor, rather than stored or having to pay the mains to store it.

Creating these markets requires the existence of trust mechanisms providing fair trade in the systems: reputation systems and escrow services, to mention a few. Smart contracts would then form something like the blood flowing through the body of these mechanisms, bringing in performance efficiency of decentralized markets.

8.7 Sustainability and Green IoE Initiatives

As the environmental agenda gains momentum, not only the use of smart contracts into the Internet of Everything should be according to the sustainability vision. New applications of green blockchain technologies, e.g., the adoption of energy-efficient consensus mechanisms or the emission trading systems related to carbon in the creation of cryptocurrencies, are the idea to save the environment of IoT devices. Furthermore, smart contracts can be employed in driving sustainability programs for example in keeping track and paying for energy saved in smart cities.

Through smart contracts, for instance, the industrial internet of things (IoE) can use them to control carbon credits among IoT-enabled sectors, and human workers get incentives for behaviors that don't load the environment. They are practical not only in that they help conserve nature to a good extent but also in that they meet global mandates on the environment which in turn improve social and economic dynamics of IoT technologies.

8.8 Future Research Directions

The growth of smart contracts in IoE will rely on the cooperation of various disciplines. Major fields for the future research should be developing lightweight blockchain protocols for the resource-constrained IoE devices, the application of machine learning to identify equipment that requires preventive maintenance and that has an anomaly, and the development of smart contracts that can go with the flow and adjust according to the current instance.

Furthermore, the ethical aspects of smart contracts will begin to have a stronger role in defining the future smart contracts and IoE relations. Mentioning such aspects as algorithmic bias, data sovereignty, and fair access to IoE technologies will be a must for the reason that these technologies should make life easier and fair for their sake.

9 CONCLUSION

The embedding of smart contracts in the Internet of Everything (IoE) is a paradigm shift allowing us to achieve a more secure, effective, and networked digital ecology. As the underlying technology behind IoE matures, the number of devices across industries and domains is growing by the billions, and security protocols are going to have to be strong and reconfigurable, automated operational control must occur more and more rapidly. Due to the decentralized, self-enforcing, and immutable nature of smart contracts, such suffering can be effectively alleviated through them. By means of automation, establish trust, and diminish human interactions they create a pathway for a stronger and more efficient IoE ecosystem.

Among the key results presented in this research, it is that smart contracts play a crucial role in overcoming the cumbersome security challenges that are naturally inherent from IoE. The decentralized nature of smart contracts enables the elimination of central intermediaries, which in turn minimize single points of failure and systemic resilience of IoE systems. As a result of the application of specified rules and limitations, smart contracts ensure data integrity and expedite authentication processes. These capabilities render them irreplaceable in guaranteeing the protection of the information flowing over IoE networks, especially in healthcare, finance, and energy domains, where data security and privacy are the key factors of success.

The potential of smart contracts to reduce human error and fraud is another huge advantage. Traditionally based systems are often hand motions that are error prone and prone to exploitation. In contrast, smart contracts operate in an auto-regulative model that can execute actions in line with a compiler rule regardless of human intervention. With this automation efficiency is improved while simultaneously the chance of fraud is minimized. Furthermore, the openness and immutability of the blockchain technology on which smart contracts are built guarantees the traceability and security of each transaction, which paves the way for trust among participants.

The application potential of smart contracts in IoE is huge and varied. From enabling true seamless M2M communication to decentralized energy trading to supply chain security, smart contracts have made impressive forays into areas where traditional procedures need a complete overhaul. For instance, in a smart city scenario, they can use the systems to create an automatic system of resource distribution and service operations such as traffic routing and waste management. They can also be used for patient record escrow and automated insurance claim processing. Such examples have inspired new applications by illustrating the flexibility and disruptive potential of smart contracts in many applications related to IoE.

Yet, the use of smart contracts integrated with the IoE is nontrivial; their scaling lags since current blockchain networks hold an inefficient level of processing power for a quantity of transactions from IoE devices. To address these issues, ongoing research currently consists of innovations, such as hybrid blockchain designs, layer-2 and sharding technologies, etc. Specifically, the diversity of IoE networks requires interoperability among heterogeneous devices and platforms. Separation of smooth cross-chain communication and protocol standardization will be critical to realize the potential of IoE through smart contracts.

Privacy and data security are also significant concerns. Although smart contracts can help achieve transparency, it is necessary to find a way to ensure protection of private information at the same time. The state-of-the-art cryptographic techniques, such as zero-knowledge proof and homomorphic encryption, offer a viable solution to this issue with the feature that one can check data without disclosing the data in the course of the process. The private smart contract deployment on the permissioned blockchains, their ability to fully mitigate the concerns about privacy, and also, their applicability to suspicious areas, including the health and finance domain, meet these needs.

The emergence of decentralized marketplaces is another promising innovation enabled by smart contracts. These platforms enable one-to-one transactions and joint-use of IoE devices without an intermediary, and they open up new economic prospects. For instance, decentralized energy trading pools enable households to sell excess energy to their neighbors on the spot, thereby maximizing energy efficiency and minimizing cost. Analogously, data marketplaces enable the commercialization of IoE devices through monetization of the data they generate and thus new business models and economic channels emerge. The success of such markets will significantly depend on the development of trust mechanisms, i.e., reputation systems, and escrow mechanisms that can be, if desired, automated as well by implementing smart contracts.

As IoE ecosystems increase in numbers, sustainability becomes a matter that cannot be ignored. Smart contracts have the capability to actually push environmentally responsible actions, such as automating carbon credit trading, and promoting energy efficiency. Green blockchain-based technologies, such as energy-efficient consensus algorithms, have been increasingly studied to decrease IoE system ecological cost. The following steps are in line with global sustainable goals, and also enable the social and economic benefits of IoE technologies.

Interaction of artificial intelligence (AI) and smart contracts is one of the forthcoming steps on the way to automated and improved optimization of the IoE process. Artificial intelligence based smart contracts are able to data analyze real time IoE devices data and dynamically/adaptively take a decision. For instance, in intelligent grids, AI can be exploited to optimize the distribution of things in terms of energy, according to the consumption of energy by people, and in the domain of healthcare, AI can be used to customize the diagnostic protocol of patients based on their medical data.AI integration and smart contracts further enhance the IoE system intelligences and functionalities, and shall remain efficient and intelligent in the foreseeable future.

Quantum computing is one potential threat to various cryptographic schemes securing the smart contract inside. With more sophistication by the quantum computers that are evolving, it is possible to crack conventional crypt-analytic techniques to threaten the very security of the IoE system. Therefore, development of quantum-resistant crypto algorithms is an important research topic. These crown algorithms, that are robust against quantum attacks, will help long term security and sustainability of smart contracts in IoE.

Ethical concerns will play a growing part in shaping the future development of smart contracts and IoE. Issues of algorithmic bias, data ownership and fair access to technology must be dealt with to enable fair benefits sharing of these technologies. Open and participatory decision-making processes will play a key role in the hope of gaining trust, and securing public acceptance of smart-contract-enabled IoE systems.

Predicting the evolution of smart contracts in IoE, will be driven by collaboration and innovation. Interdisciplinary work involving blockchain developers, IoT engineers, AI experts and policymakers will be crucial to developing solutions for technical and regulatory hurdles. Standardization of protocols and the fostering of transnational governance principles for IoE will accelerate the deployment of smart contracts.

In conclusion, smart contracts have the potential to revolutionize the IoE landscape by enhancing security, efficiency, and scalability. Their power to automate, instill trust, and protect data puts them at the heart of future-generation IoE ecosystems. Although challenges associated with scalability, privacy and interoperability persist, progress in blockchain technology, cryptography and AI is opening the door to new solutions. If smart contracts address these challenges and foster interdisciplinary collaboration, IoE's complete potential can bring transformation in industries and the quality of life around the globe. This journey is at its initial stages, and no doubt, one of the vital players in shaping this future will be smart contracts.

REFERENCES

Akan, O. B., Dinc, E., Kuscu, M., Cetinkaya, O., & Bilgin, B. A. (2023). Internet of Everything (IoE) - From Molecules to the Universe. *IEEE Communications Magazine*, *61*(10), 122–128. DOI: 10.1109/MCOM.001.2200594

Antonios, P., Konstantinos, K., & Christos, G. (2023a). A Systematic Review on Semantic Interoperability in the IoE-Enabled Smart Cities. *Internet of Things : Engineering Cyber Physical Human Systems*, *22*(July), 100754. DOI: 10.1016/j.iot.2023.100754

Antonios, P., Konstantinos, K., & Christos, G. (2023b). A Systematic Review on Semantic Interoperability in the IoE-Enabled Smart Cities. *Internet of Things : Engineering Cyber Physical Human Systems*, *22*(July), 100754. DOI: 10.1016/j.iot.2023.100754

Bandaranayake, B. 2014. "Fraud and Corruption Control at Education System Level." Http://Dx.Doi.Org/10.1177/1555458914549669 17 (4): 34–53. https://doi.org/DOI: 10.1177/1555458914549669

Brun, A., Sudheer, B., & Goud, K. 2023. "Implementation of IoT Technologies in Manufacturing Process." https://www.politesi.polimi.it/handle/10589/139316

Chatzigiannakis, I., & Tselios, C. (2021). Internet of Everything. *Intelligent Computing for Interactive System Design*, (February), 21–56. DOI: 10.1145/3447404.3447408

Cuccuru, P. (2017). Beyond Bitcoin: An Early Overview on Smart Contracts. *International Journal of Law and Information Technology*, *25*(3), 179–195. DOI: 10.1093/ijlit/eax003

D'Onfro, D. (2020). Smart Contracts and the Illusion of Automated Enforcement. *Washington University Journal of Law and Policy*, *61*, •••. https://heinonline.org/HOL/Page?handle=hein.journals/wajlp61&id=185&div=&collection=

Das, P., Chitra Jain, A., & Singh, M. (2024). Toward a Trusted Smart City Ecosystem : IoE and Blockchain-Enabled Cognitive Frameworks for Shared Business Services. *Industrial Internet of Things Security*, (October), 208–228. DOI: 10.1201/9781003466284-11

David, Anne, Tan Yigitcanlar, Rita Yi Man Li, Juan M. Corchado, Pauline Hope Cheong, Karen Mossberger, and Rashid Mehmood. 2023. "Understanding Local Government Digital Technology Adoption Strategies: A PRISMA Review." *Sustainability 2023, Vol. 15, Page 9645* 15 (12): 9645. https://doi.org/.DOI: 10.3390/su15129645

Diro, A., Zhou, L., Saini, A., Kaisar, S., & Hiep, P. C. (2024). Leveraging Zero Knowledge Proofs for Blockchain-Based Identity Sharing: A Survey of Advancements, Challenges and Opportunities. *Journal of Information Security and Applications*, *80*(February), 103678. DOI: 10.1016/j.jisa.2023.103678

Farias da Costa, V. C., Oliveira, L., & de Souza, J. (2021). Internet of everything (IoE) taxonomies: A survey and a novel knowledge-based taxonomy. *Sensors (Basel)*, *21*(2), 568.

Gartner, M. (2023). Influencable autonomy and predictable freedom in the IoE.

Gostin, L. O., Levit, L. A., & Nass, S. J. (Eds.). (2009). *Beyond the HIPAA privacy rule: enhancing privacy, improving health through research.*

Gourisetti, S. N. G., Sebastian-Cardenas, D. J., Bhattarai, B., Wang, P., Widergren, S., Borkum, M., & Randall, A. (2021). Blockchain Smart Contract Reference Framework and Program Logic Architecture for Transactive Energy Systems. *Applied Energy*, *304*(December), 117860. DOI: 10.1016/j.apenergy.2021.117860

Governatori, G., Idelberger, F., Milosevic, Z., Riveret, R., Sartor, G., & Xu, X. (2018). On Legal Contracts, Imperative and Declarative Smart Contracts, and Blockchain Systems. *Artificial Intelligence and Law*, *26*(4), 377–409. DOI: 10.1007/s10506-018-9223-3

Gubbi, J., Buyya, R., Marusic, S., & Palaniswami, M. (2013). Internet of Things (IoT): A Vision, Architectural Elements, and Future Directions. *Future Generation Computer Systems*, *29*(7), 1645–1660. DOI: 10.1016/j.future.2013.01.010

Harder, E. F. H. (2017). The future of contracts in a digital economy: The impact of smart contracts on transaction costs in financial markets (Master's thesis, University of Twente).

Hossain, R., Md, F. A. N., Islam, A., Rakin, T. M., & Al-Amin, M. (2024). A Comprehensive Analysis of Blockchain Technology and Consensus Protocols Across Multilayered Framework. *IEEE Access : Practical Innovations, Open Solutions*, *12*, 63087–63129. DOI: 10.1109/ACCESS.2024.3395536

Iftikhar, A., & Qureshi, K. N. (2023). Future privacy and trust challenges for IoE networks. In *Cybersecurity Vigilance and Security Engineering of Internet of Everything* (pp. 193–218). Springer Nature Switzerland.

Javed, I. T., & Qureshi, K. N. (2023). Role of blockchain for IoE infrastructures and applications. In *Cybersecurity Vigilance and Security Engineering of Internet of Everything* (pp. 127–139). Springer Nature Switzerland.

Jindal, A., Kumar, N., & Aujla, G. S. (Eds.). (2021). *Internet of Energy for Smart Cities: Machine Learning Models and Techniques*. CRC Press.

Kambourakis, G., Neisse, R., & Nai-Fovino, I. (2021). *Information security in the age of EU-Institutions digitalisation, a landscape analysis*. European Commission, Joint Research Centre.

Kelliher, D. (2013). An investigation into the effects of iPad/tablet device use in special education and in particular in the case of a student with Williams Syndrome: a case study approach (Doctoral dissertation, University of Limerick).

Khan, S. N., Loukil, F., Ghedira-Guegan, C., Benkhelifa, E., & Bani-Hani, A. (2021). Blockchain Smart Contracts: Applications, Challenges, and Future Trends. *Peer-to-Peer Networking and Applications, 14*(5), 2901–2925. DOI: 10.1007/s12083-021-01127-0 PMID: 33897937

Korneeva, E., Olinder, N., & Strielkowski, W. (2021). Consumer attitudes to the smart home technologies and the internet of things (IOT). *Energies, 14*(23), 7913.

Kushwaha, S. S., Joshi, S., Singh, D., Kaur, M., & Lee, H. N. (2022). Systematic Review of Security Vulnerabilities in Ethereum Blockchain Smart Contract. *IEEE Access : Practical Innovations, Open Solutions, 10*, 6605–6621. DOI: 10.1109/ACCESS.2021.3140091

Langley, D. J., van Doorn, J., Ng, I. C. L., Stieglitz, S., Lazovik, A., & Boonstra, A. (2021). The Internet of Everything: Smart Things and Their Impact on Business Models. *Journal of Business Research, 122*(January), 853–863. DOI: 10.1016/j.jbusres.2019.12.035

Lavaur, T., Lacan, J., & Chanel, C. P. (2022). Enabling blockchain services for ioe with zk-rollups. *Sensors (Basel), 22*(17), 6493.

Lin, S. Y., Zhang, L., Li, J., Ji, L., & Sun, Y. (2022). A Survey of Application Research Based on Blockchain Smart Contract. *Wireless Networks, 28*(2), 635–690. DOI: 10.1007/s11276-021-02874-x

Liu, J., & Liu, Z. (2019). A Survey on Security Verification of Blockchain Smart Contracts. *IEEE Access : Practical Innovations, Open Solutions, 7*, 77894–77904. DOI: 10.1109/ACCESS.2019.2921624

Liu, L., Tsai, W. T., Md, Z. A. B., Peng, H., & Liu, M. (2022). Blockchain-Enabled Fraud Discovery through Abnormal Smart Contract Detection on Ethereum. *Future Generation Computer Systems, 128*(March), 158–166. DOI: 10.1016/j.future.2021.08.023

Liu, Y., He, J., Li, X., Chen, J., Liu, X., Peng, S., Cao, H., & Wang, Y. (2024a). An Overview of Blockchain Smart Contract Execution Mechanism. *Journal of Industrial Information Integration*, *41*(September), 100674. DOI: 10.1016/j.jii.2024.100674

Liu, Y., He, J., Li, X., Chen, J., Liu, X., Peng, S., Cao, H., & Wang, Y. (2024b). An Overview of Blockchain Smart Contract Execution Mechanism. *Journal of Industrial Information Integration*, *41*(September), 100674. DOI: 10.1016/j.jii.2024.100674

Lyon, D. (2014). Surveillance, Snowden, and Big Data: Capacities, Consequences. *Big Data & Society*, *1*(2), 2053951714541861. Advance online publication. Http://Dx.Doi.Org/10.1177/2053951714541861. DOI: 10.1177/2053951714541861

Macrinici, D., Cartofeanu, C., & Gao, S. (2018). Smart Contract Applications within Blockchain Technology: A Systematic Mapping Study. *Telematics and Informatics*, *35*(8), 2337–2354. DOI: 10.1016/j.tele.2018.10.004

Majeed, A., Bhana, R., Haq, A. U., & Williams, M.-L. (2016). "Devising a Secure Architecture of Internet of Everything (IoE) to Avoid the Data Exploitation in Cross Culture Communications." *IJACSA). International Journal of Advanced Computer Science and Applications*, *7*(4). Advance online publication. www.ijacsa.thesai.org. DOI: 10.14569/IJACSA.2016.070443

Majeed, A., Haq, A. U., Jamal, A., Bhana, R., Banigo, F., & Baadel, S. (2016, October). Internet of everything (IoE) exploiting organisational inside threats: Global network of smart devices (GNSD). In *2016 IEEE International Symposium on Systems Engineering (ISSE)* (pp. 1-7). IEEE.

Márquez-Sánchez, S., Calvo-Gallego, J., Erbad, A., Ibrar, M., Fernandez, J. H., Houchati, M., & Corchado, J. M. (2023). Enhancing building energy management: Adaptive edge computing for optimized efficiency and inhabitant comfort. *Electronics (Basel)*, *12*(19), 4179.

Mathur, N., & Sinha, S. (2023). Security Model and Access Control Mechanisms for Attack Mitigation in IoE. *Blockchain Technology for IoE: Security and Privacy Perspectives*, (January), 67–100. DOI: 10.1201/9781003366010-6

McKinney, S. A., Landy, R., & Wilka, R. (2017). "Smart Contracts, Blockchain, and the Next Frontier of Transactional Law." *Washington Journal of Law, Technology & Arts* 13. https://heinonline.org/HOL/Page?handle=hein.journals/washjolta13&id=321&div=&collection=

Meydani, A., Shahinzadeh, H., Ramezani, A., Gharehpetian, G. B., & Tanwar, S. (2024). "Analysis of the Cybersecurity and Privacy Protection of Blockchain-Empowered Internet of Energy (IoE)." *Proceeding of 8th International Conference on Smart Cities, Internet of Things and Applications, SCIoT 2024*, 213–28. https://doi.org/DOI: 10.1109/SCIoT62588.2024.10570124

Miglani, A., Kumar, N., Chamola, V., & Zeadally, S. (2020a). Blockchain for Internet of Energy Management: Review, Solutions, and Challenges. *Computer Communications*, *151*(February), 395–418. DOI: 10.1016/j.comcom.2020.01.014

Miglani, A., Kumar, N., Chamola, V., & Zeadally, S. (2020b). Blockchain for Internet of Energy Management: Review, Solutions, and Challenges. *Computer Communications*, *151*(February), 395–418. DOI: 10.1016/j.comcom.2020.01.014

Mik, E. (2017). Smart Contracts: Terminology, Technical Limitations and Real World Complexity. *Law, Innovation and Technology*, *9*(2), 269–300. DOI: 10.1080/17579961.2017.1378468

Mishra, P., & Singh, G. (2023). Energy management systems in sustainable smart cities based on the internet of energy: A technical review. *Energies*, *16*(19), 6903.

Mogadem, M. M., Li, Y., & Meheretie, D. L. (2022). A Survey on Internet of Energy Security: Related Fields, Challenges, Threats and Emerging Technologies. *Cluster Computing*, *25*(4), 2449–2485. DOI: 10.1007/s10586-021-03423-z

Nzuva, S. M. (2019). Smart Contracts Implementation, Applications, Benefits, and Limitations. *Journal of Information Engineering and Applications*, (September). Advance online publication. DOI: 10.7176/JIEA/9-5-07

Othman, S. B., Bahattab, A. A., Trad, A., & Youssef, H. (2015). Confidentiality and Integrity for Data Aggregation in WSN Using Homomorphic Encryption. *Wireless Personal Communications*, *80*(2), 867–889. DOI: 10.1007/s11277-014-2061-z

Parhamfar, M., & Zabihi, A. 2024. "Next-Gen Energy Solutions: A Brief Study on Boosting Distribution Efficiency with IoE Technology." https://doi.org/DOI: 10.25729/esr.2024.03.009

Putra, K. T., Arrayyan, A. Z., Hayati, N., Firdaus, C. D., Damarjati, C., Bakar, A., & Chen, H.-C. (2024). A Review on the Application of Internet of Medical Things in Wearable Personal Health Monitoring: A Cloud-Edge Artificial Intelligence Approach. *IEEE Access : Practical Innovations, Open Solutions*, *12*, 21437–21452. DOI: 10.1109/ACCESS.2024.3358827

Rafique, W., & Qadir, J. (2024). Internet of Everything Meets the Metaverse: Bridging Physical and Virtual Worlds with Blockchain. *Computer Science Review, 54*(November), 100678. DOI: 10.1016/j.cosrev.2024.100678

Raj, P., Venkatesh, V., & Amirtharajan, R. (2013). Envisioning the cloud-induced transformations in the software engineering discipline. Software Engineering Frameworks for the Cloud Computing Paradigm, 25-53.

Saia, R. (2018). Internet of entities (IoE): a blockchain-based distributed paradigm to security. arXiv preprint arXiv:1808.08809.

Salehi, M., Clark, J., & Mannan, M. (2022, May). Not so immutable: Upgradeability of smart contracts on ethereum. In *International Conference on Financial Cryptography and Data Security* (pp. 539-554). Cham: Springer International Publishing.

Sanwar Hosen, A. S. M. (2020). Blockchain-Based Transaction Validation Protocol for a Secure Distributed IoT Network. *IEEE Access : Practical Innovations, Open Solutions, 8*, 117266–117277. DOI: 10.1109/ACCESS.2020.3004486

Serôdio, C., Cunha, J., Candela, G., Rodriguez, S., Sousa, X. R., & Branco, F. (2023). The 6G ecosystem as support for IoE and private networks: Vision, requirements, and challenges. *Future Internet, 15*(11), 348.

Sguanci, C., Spatafora, R., & Vergani, A. M. (2021). Layer 2 blockchain scaling: A survey. arXiv preprint arXiv:2107.10881.

Shahinzadeh, H., Moradi, J., Gharehpetian, G. B., Nafisi, H., & Abedi, M. (2019, February). Internet of Energy (IoE) in smart power systems. In 2019 5th Conference on Knowledge Based Engineering and Innovation (KBEI) (pp. 627-636). IEEE.

Sharma, A., Suganya, R., Krishna, P. B., Raj, R., & Murugesan, R. K. (2024). Network Efficient Hierarchical Authentication Algorithm for Secure Communication in IoT and IoE. *IEEE Access : Practical Innovations, Open Solutions*.

Shermin, V. (2017). Disrupting Governance with Blockchains and Smart Contracts. *Strategic Change, 26*(5), 499–509. DOI: 10.1002/jsc.2150

Siddiqui, S., Hameed, S., Shah, S. A., Arshad, J., Ahmed, Y., & Draheim, D. (2024). A Smart-Contract-Based Adaptive Security Governance Architecture for Smart City Service Interoperations. *Sustainable Cities and Society, 113*(October), 105717. DOI: 10.1016/j.scs.2024.105717

Singh, A., Parizi, R. M., Zhang, Q., Kim, K. R. C., & Dehghantanha, A. (2020). Blockchain Smart Contracts Formalization: Approaches and Challenges to Address Vulnerabilities. *Computers & Security*, *88*(January), 101654. DOI: 10.1016/j.cose.2019.101654

Sklaroff, J. M. (2017). Smart Contracts and the Cost of Inflexibility. *University of Pennsylvania Law Review*, *166*, •••. https://heinonline.org/HOL/Page?handle=hein.journals/pnlr166&id=267&div=&collection=

Solanki, A. (Ed.). (2023). *Intelligent Systems for IoE Based Smart Cities*. Bentham Science Publishers.

Soltani, S. Z. (2013). *Improving PKI: Solution analysis in case of CA compromisation*. Utrecht University.

Strielkowski, W., Streimikiene, D., Fomina, A., & Semenova, E. (2019). Internet of energy (IoE) and high-renewables electricity system market design. *Energies*, *12*(24), 4790.

Sudharshan, D. (2020). Internet of Everything (IoE). *Marketing in Customer Technology Environments*, (April), 161–208. DOI: 10.1108/978-1-83909-600-620201008

Τσαγδής, A. 2022. "Hardware-Based Security Methods for Internet of Things (IoT), Internet of Everything (IoE) & Cyber-Physical Systems (CPS)," September. https://doi.org/DOI: 10.26265/POLYNOE-2778

Tajjour, S., & Chandel, S. S. (2023). A Comprehensive Review on Sustainable Energy Management Systems for Optimal Operation of Future-Generation of Solar Microgrids. *Sustainable Energy Technologies and Assessments*, *58*(August), 103377. DOI: 10.1016/j.seta.2023.103377

Tyagi, A. K., Aswathy, S. U., Aghila, G., & Sreenath, N. (2021). AARIN: Affordable, Accurate, Reliable and Innovative Mechanism to Protect a Medical Cyber-Physical System Using Blockchain Technology. *International Journal of Intelligent Networks*, *2*(January), 175–183. DOI: 10.1016/j.ijin.2021.09.007

Tyagi, A. K., & Nair, M. (2020). Internet of Everything (IoE) and Internet of Things (IoTs): Threat Analyses, Possible Opportunities for Future. *Journal of Information Assurance and Security*, *15*, 153–177. www.mirlabs.net/jias/index.html

Ugwuanyi, S., Paul, G., & Irvine, J. (2021). Survey of IoT for developing countries: Performance analysis of LoRaWAN and cellular NB-IoT networks. *Electronics (Basel)*, *10*(18), 2224.

Vermesan, O., & Friess, P. (Eds.). (2013). *Internet of things: converging technologies for smart environments and integrated ecosystems*. River publishers.

Vermesan, O., & Friess, P. (2015). *Building the hyperconnected society-internet of things research and innovation value chains, ecosystems and markets*. Taylor & Francis.

Vermesan, O., John, R., Pype, P., Daalderop, G., Ashwathnarayan, M., Bahr, R., Karlsen, T., & Sand, H. E. (2021). Internet of Vehicles – System of Systems Distributed Intelligence for Mobility Applications. *Internet of Things : Engineering Cyber Physical Human Systems*, •••, 93–147. DOI: 10.1007/978-3-030-76493-7_4

Wang, S., Ouyang, L., Yuan, Y., Ni, X., Han, X., & Fei, Y. W. (2019). Blockchain-Enabled Smart Contracts: Architecture, Applications, and Future Trends. *IEEE Transactions on Systems, Man, and Cybernetics. Systems*, *49*(11), 2266–2277. DOI: 10.1109/TSMC.2019.2895123

Wu, X. B., Zou, Z., & Song, D. (2019). *Learn ethereum: build your own decentralized applications with ethereum and smart contracts*. Packt Publishing Ltd.

Xie, J., Tang, H., Huang, T., Yu, F. R., Xie, R., Liu, J., & Liu, Y. (2019). A Survey of Blockchain Technology Applied to Smart Cities: Research Issues and Challenges. *IEEE Communications Surveys and Tutorials*, *21*(3), 2794–2830. DOI: 10.1109/COMST.2019.2899617

Yang, C., Lan, S., Zhao, Z., Zhang, M., Wu, W., & Huang, G. Q. (2023). Edge-Cloud Blockchain and IoE-Enabled Quality Management Platform for Perishable Supply Chain Logistics. *IEEE Internet of Things Journal*, *10*(4), 3264–3275. DOI: 10.1109/JIOT.2022.3142095

Zheng, Z., Xie, S., Hong, N. D., Chen, W., Chen, X., Weng, J., & Imran, M. (2020). An Overview on Smart Contracts: Challenges, Advances and Platforms. *Future Generation Computer Systems*, *105*(April), 475–491. DOI: 10.1016/j.future.2019.12.019

Zou, W., Lo, D., Kochhar, P. S., Xuan, B. D. L., Xia, X., Feng, Y., Chen, Z., & Xu, B. (2021). Smart Contract Development: Challenges and Opportunities. *IEEE Transactions on Software Engineering*, *47*(10), 2084–2106. DOI: 10.1109/TSE.2019.2942301

Chapter 6
Machine Learning-Based Phishing Websites Classification Using Diverse Datasets: An Empirical Analysis

Shahab Haider
https://orcid.org/0000-0001-6802-6133
Ghulam Ishaq Khan Institute of Engineering Sciences and Technology, Pakistan

Bilal Khan
https://orcid.org/0000-0002-6816-3776
University of Engineering and Technology, Mardan, Pakistan

Wahab Khan
City University of Science and Information Technology, Peshawar, Pakistan

Sana Ullah
City University of Science and Information Technology, Peshawar, Pakistan

Zulfiqar Ali
City University of Science and Information Technology, Peshawar, Pakistan

ABSTRACT

Recent technological developments make users vulnerable to several cyber-attacks, where phishing attacks compromise users' sensitive information. To identify these attacks, there are different social techniques, which bring user awareness. However, they are incapable of significantly identifying phishing attacks that demands technology-

DOI: 10.4018/979-8-3373-1424-2.ch006

assisted techniques. The existing literature provides several blacklist-whitelist, fuzzy rule, and Machine Learning (ML) based techniques, where ML techniques are the most efficient. However, there is a lack of comprehensive analysis of ML techniques. To fill this gap, this work presents an in-depth empirical comparative analysis of eleven different ML techniques, including WiSARD, CHIRP, and Ridor that have not been previously analyzed, for phishing attacks' identification. To achieve this aim, this study employs diverse UCI and Mendeley datasets and performs a 10 fold cross validation. Results demonstrate superior performance of J48, with enhanced accuracy and minimized error rate, in comparison with the other eminent techniques.

1. INTRODUCTION

Recent technological advancement in communications enables computers, smartphones, and similar devices to share information through Internet (Awan et al., 2024) and (Khan et al., 2022). This introduces several services, such as digital banking services and e-commerce, to enable user convenience around the world (Rao & Pais, 2019). This give rise to cybercrimes, where attackers consider this as an opportunity to compromise sensitive information including credit cards and login details, etc. (Tan et al., 2016)(Mahajan & Siddavatam, 2018). To this end, phishing websites have gained significant attention of the research community in the recent past (Whittaker & Ryner, 2008). There are various techniques to identify phishing attacks. However, these techniques are not effective enough, as the number of victims are continuously increasing. In 2018, 785,920 unique phishing websites were identified by anti-phishing working group, which is an increase by 69.5% over the last five year (Mahajan & Siddavatam, 2018). Motivations for the phishing attacks include, (i) financial interest, (ii) lack of users' awareness about the use of computers and the Internet, and (iii) these attackers learn from their failed attacks to launch successful attacks in future (Adebowale et al., 2019). Thus, making differentiation among legitimate and phishing websites a challenging task.

Several techniques have been developed to identify such attacks, such as the heuristic, the rule-based, and supervised Machine Learning (ML) techniques (Adebowale et al., 2019)(Babagoli et al., 2019). The author in (Zamir et al., 2020) propose a heuristic framework, to detect malicious activities on different mobile applications linked with e-commerce (Zamir et al., 2020). Furthermore, the work in (Moghimi & Varjani, 2016) aims to protect internet banking from phishing activities using rule-based technique (Chiew et al., 2019). Phishing attacks have put at risk various online businesses around the world, especially, e-commerce. This adversely impact the confidence of companies and their customers, thereby, affecting the company reputation. ML techniques are common to distinguish between legitimate and phishing websites and are considered as effective means of identifying these cyber-attacks. Therefore, there is a need to analyze the ML techniques for their effectiveness to distinguish among phishing and legitimate websites. To this end, we explore the efficiency of different ML techniques for the classification of phishing and legitimate websites. In this study, we analyze eleven ML techniques to find out the best phishing classifiers using two datasets, namely, UCI and Mandaley. These techniques include Average One Dependency Estimator (A1DE), Naïve Bayes (NB), Multilayer Perceptron (MLP), Qualitative Descriptive Analysis (QDA), Support Vector Machine (SVM), WiSARD, Composite Hypercube on Iterated Random Projection (CHIRP), Decision Table (DT), Decision Table Naïve Bayes (DTNB), Ridor, and Decision Tree (J48).

The rest of the paper is organized as follows. Section 2 critically reviews eminent phishing detection techniques. Section 3 details our research methodology, Section 4 includes the results and discussion. Finally, Section 5 concludes this study and provides recommendation of the most effective technique.

2. RELATED WORK

Anti-phishing techniques list down all the known phishing websites and feed them to the browsers' databases to alarm users, thus, protecting them from threats. However, newly developed phishing websites are not detectable through these techniques (Jain & Gupta, 2019) and (Haider et al., 2020), thereby, making it impossible for the browsers to differentiate them from the legitimate ones (Chiew et al., 2019)(Marchal et al., 2016)(Adewole et al., 2019). There are various techniques to identify phishing activities on the Internet for the protection of Internet users from the cyber-attacks that comprises social and technology-assisted solutions. These solutions are detailed below.

2.1 Social Techniques

The following subsections discuss social techniques to combat of phishing attacks.

2.1.1 Legal Solutions

Legal solutions are followed by several countries, where United States of America (USA) is the first to legislate against phishing (Al-Daeef et al., 2017), (Abdelhamid et al., 2014), (Haider et al., 2020) and (Abdelhamid & Thabtah, 2014). In the last decade, Australia, United Kingdom, and USA strengthened their laws against fraud by enacting jail penalties. However, legal solutions are not sufficient to catch and identify phishers (Gupta et al., 2017).

2.1.2 Education

Education creates awareness in users and has turned out to be beneficial, however, such techniques are partially useful against phishing (Abdelhamid & Thabtah, 2014)(Miranda, 2018).

2.2 Technology-Assisted Techniques

The most frequent techniques used for the identification of phishing attacks are heuristic and blacklist techniques (Gautam et al., 2018). A blacklist technique compares a phishing Uniform Resource Locators (URL) with the requested URL. However, it does not deal with all phishing websites, as a new phishing website takes time to be recognized and blacklisted. Conversely, a heuristic technique can identify phishing websites in real-time (Miyamoto et al., 2009). The degree of success depends upon the recognition of the phishing websites and also the timescale of their recognition. Several solutions have been developed, however, most of these are unable to make accurate decisions that result in a plethora of false positives. The following subsections discuss eminent technology-assisted solutions to identify phishing.

2.2.1 Blacklist-Whitelist-Based Techniques

A blacklist technique is a list of websites, thought to be malicious, marked through users voting. Whenever a website is launched, the browser matches it with the blacklist. If the result comes back positive the user is warned not to enter any kind of sensitive information (Abdelhamid et al., 2014), (Haider et al., 2020), (Abbas et al., 2020), and (Haider et al., 2020). The blacklist technique is developed through several solutions, like google safe browsing Microsoft Internet Explorer 9 anti-phishing, and Site Advisor databases. Site Advisor is incapable of identifying newly formulated threats. Moreover, another anti-phishing tool called VeriSign crawls millions of websites to identify cloned phishing websites. One disadvantage of these anti-phishing techniques is that they are always in competition with the attackers. J. Chen and Guo (Guo, 2006) propose the use of Automated Individual WhiteList (AIWL) as an anti-phishing tool based on the trusted websites. AIWL uses NB to trace every login attempt and a website is added to the whitelist on multiple successful logins. Afroz and Greenstadt (Afroz & Greenstadt, 2011) present PhishZoo that builds a profile of the legitimate websites based on fuzzy technique. Profile metrics are used by users to differentiate between malicious and legitimate sites. Several researchers have contended that detection of phishing should be based on the user point of view, as over 90 percent of users remain dependent on the appearance of the website to verify its authenticity (Zamir et al., 2020).

2.2.2 Fuzzy Rule-Based Techniques

The authors in (Zuhair et al., 2016) present a rule-based technique that collect dissimilar features, like security and encryption, domain and identity, source code and javascript, address bar, and social human factor (Zuhair et al., 2016). These features vary for genuine, doubtful, and legitimate websites. Results show a significant association among URLs and domain identities, however, no justification is given as how these attributes are linked (Abdelhamid et al., 2014). A larger set of attributes is used to predict types of websites based upon fuzzy logic. Rules for identification are based upon human experience rather than data mining techniques. Websites are classified as legitimate, highly legitimate, phishing, suspicious, or very phishy. However, there are no details, as how these classifications are formulated to perform the aforementioned task.

2.2.3 Machine Learning Techniques

ML techniques are among the most effective solutions to identify phishing based upon the accuracy of results in text categorization (Abdelhamid et al., 2014) and (Benavides et al., 2020). The work in (Ying & Xuhua, 2006) employs Support Vector Machine (SVM) for the discovery of infrequent and unfamiliar activities, i.e., phishing in websites-based on two variables. The first variable uses the name of a company and the second is identified as page categorizer, which is a representative of the properties relevant to structural feature including abnormal DNS record, abnormal URL, etc. that are hard to replicate. Fette et al, (Fette et al., 2007) compared frequently used ML techniques, like NB, SVM, and decision trees for the detection of phishing emails. A forest technique, namely, Phishing Identification by Learning on Features of Email Received (PILFER), is employed for phishing identification by learning features of the email received. Jain and Gupta (Jain & Gupta, 2019) detect spammed or phishing websites by analyzing the hyperlinks in the source code of websites. The authors in (Perez-Diaz et al., 2020), analyzed the Alternating Direction Method of Multipliers (ADMM) algorithm to identify cheats in electric vehicle aggregators, however, the scope of the work limits it to a single algorithm. Our work aims to identify different kinds of phishing attacks, which can also be adopted in the aforementioned scenario. Lazaridis et al., (Lazaridis et al., 2020) used deep reinforcement learning to identify algorithms that achieve better performance in complex tasks. Contrarily, our work performs a comparative analysis of popular machine learning techniques in complex tasks, such as identification of phishing attacks. The full evaluation of each anomaly detection approach is not simply feasible, conclude in (Freeman et al., 2021). To do this, the authors presented the customized guidelines utilize the characteristics of the time series, such as seasonality, level change concept drift, trends, and missing time steps, to intelligently choose the best anomaly detection algorithms.

2.3 Phishing as a Classification Problem

Classification of websites is based on various features. These features include length of URL, prefix and suffix, names of domain and sub-domains, etc. Initially, context of online security is based on the prior experience of differentiation of phishing websites from the legitimate ones (Jain & Gupta, 2019)(Aburrous et al., 2010). As far as the recent literature is concerned, various researches are focusing on intelligent procedures, such as statistical analysis to distinguish between phishing and legitimate websites (Abdelhamid et al., 2014). Additionally, there are more advanced and developed procedures incorporating statistical analysis of datasets collected from a wide range of sources. In this regard, there are two tools, i.e., data mining and ML that show effectiveness in data analysis in various fields, such as medical, market analysis, and weather forecast, etc. This is due to their ability to provide meaningful information through analysis of large decision making, risk management, and planning. Some important tasks performed through data mining and ML include association rule, regression analysis, multi-label learning, and trend analysis etc. (Abdelhamid, 2015).

ML techniques identify a variable in a particular dataset. The major purpose of classifier is to guess the value of this particular variable in the dataset accuracy with supervised learning (Abdelhamid et al., 2014). In this process, websites are generally classified into different categories, such as legitimate, phishing, and suspicious websites. Features to categorize websites are given specific values that are included in the datasets, obtained from various sources. As phishing websites are dynamic, this issue is considered as a supervised machine learning classification issue. Moreover, Ridor, CHIRP, and WiSARD have not been investigated previously, thus, this study contributes to analyze these techniques for their effectiveness in identification of phishing websites.

3 THE RESEARCH METHODOLOGY

The main focus of this study is to present the performance analysis of various ML techniques for the classification of phishing websites, as shown in Figure 1. These techniques include Average One Dependency Estimator (A1DE), Naïve Bayes (NB), Multilayer Perceptron (MLP), Qualitative Descriptive Analysis (QDA), Support Vector Machine (SVM), WiSARD, Composite Hypercube on Iterated Random Projection (CHIRP), Decision Table (DT), Decision Table Naïve Bayes (DTNB), Ridor, and Decision Tree (J48). The datasets are taken from two different repositories, i.e., the UCI and the Mendeley. Eleven ML techniques are compared on these datasets and the performances are evaluated using Mean Absolute Error (MAE) (Khan et al., 2020), Relative Absolute Error (RAE) (Khan et al., 2020) (Khan et al., n.d.), Root Mean Squared Error (RMSE) (Yildirim, 2017), Root Relative Squared Error (RRSE) (Naseem, Khan, Ahmad, et al., 2020), recall (Rady & Anwar, 2019), precision (Naseem, Khan, Shah, et al., 2020), F-measure (Subasi & Kremic, 2020), Mathew's Correlation Coefficient (MCC) (Naseem, Khan, Ahmad, et al., 2020; Naseem, Khan, Shah, et al., 2020), Receiver Operating Characteristics (ROC) area (Subasi & Kremic, 2020), Precision-Recall Curve (PRC) area (Balogun et al., 2018), and accuracy (Khan et al., 2020).

Figure 1. The research methodology

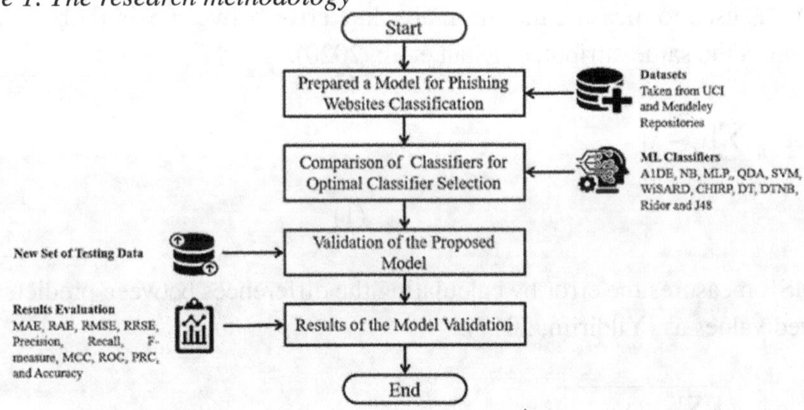

3.1 Datasets

We use two datasets that are obtained from different sources. The first dataset is taken from UCI repository1. Here, we have identified 16 different features from 1353 different websites collected from different sources. Phishing websites are gathered from the Phishtank, whereas legitimate website are collected from Yahoo. A Hypertext Preprocessing (PHP) script (Abdelhamid et al., 2014) divides 1353 websites into legitimate, phishy, and suspicious categories. Out of these websites, 548 sites are classified as legitimate, 702 as phishy, and 103 as suspicious. Similarly, the second dataset is taken from Mendeley2, which is an open source repository. Phishing websites are taken from Phishtank and OpenPhish, and legitimate webpage sources are taken using Common Crawl and Alexa.

3.2 Training and Testing

We perform a 10-fold cross-validation to assess the efficiency of each of the aforementioned classifiers, where the datasets are split in 10 equal subsets Nine subsets are used as training sets, whereas one left is used for testing (Khan et al., 2020) (Naseem, Khan, Ahmad, et al., 2020).

3.3 Performance Assessments Measures

The following subsections detail the performance assessment measures used in this work. We evaluate correctly and incorrectly identified websites for both datasets and computed mean accuracy for each technique in addition to summarizing overall accuracy.

MAE is used to measure the mean absolute error between paired observations that express the same attributes (Khan et al., 2020),

$$MAE = \frac{1}{n}\sum_{i=1}^{n}|x_i - x| \quad (1)$$

RMSE measures the error by calculating the differences between predicted and observed values as (Yildirim, 2017),

$$RMSE = \sqrt{\frac{1}{2}\sum_{j=1}^{n}(y_i - 1)^2} \quad (2)$$

RAE refers to the measures of relative error in a predictor and is evaluated as (Khan et al., 2020) (Khan et al., n.d.),

$$RAE = \frac{\sum_{i=1}^{n}|p_i - a_i|}{\sum_{i=1}^{n}|\overline{a} - a_i|}$$

, (3)

where, p is the predicted target and a is the actual target.

RRSE takes the sum of the squared error and normalizes it by dividing the sum by the total squared error of a simple predictor (Naseem, Khan, Ahmad, et al., 2020),

$$RRSE = \sqrt{\frac{\sum_{j=1}^{n}\left(P_{ij} - T_j\right)^2}{\sum_{j=1}^{n}\left(T_j \_ \bar{T}\right)^2}}$$

. (4)

Precision and Recall are useful for measuring the success of a predictor in unbalanced classes. Precision is the measure of relevancy in the results and recall is the measure of truly relevant returned results (Naseem, Khan, Shah, et al., 2020),

$$Precision = TP/(TP + FP)$$

, (5)

$$Recall = TP/(TP + FN)$$

. (6)

F-measure computes the predictor accuracy by taking weighted harmonic mean of precision and recall as (Subasi & Kremic, 2020),

$$F = \frac{TP}{TP + \frac{1}{2}\left(FP + FN\right)}$$

. (7)

MCC measures the quality through binary classifier as [31] [33],

$$MCC = \frac{TPxTN - FPxFN}{\sqrt{(TP + FP)(TP + FN)(TN + FP)(TN + FN)}}$$

. (8)

ROC curve shows the diagnostic ability of a binary classifier (Subasi & Kremic, 2020).

PRC Curve summarizes the rate of true positives and predictive value of a predictor (Balogun et al., 2018).

4 PERFORMANCE EVALUATION

This section presents the results obtained using the aforementioned set of techniques in Section 3. Results are obtained through Weka version 3.9 running on Microsoft Windows 10 based machine with Intel® Core i5 processor and eight gigabytes memory. Each result obtained is averaged over 20 simulation runs by changing random seed values and keeping the parameters fixed. The following subsection provides in depth analysis of the results obtained.

4.1 Results Analysis

Table 1 details the results for UCI, whereas Table 2 includes the same for Mendeley. The results for UCI show J48 the most effective, as it classifies 1215 out of 1353 websites correctly, whereas NB remains the weakest results with 1107 correct classifications. Similar results can be seen for Mendeley, where out of 10000 websites NB and J48 correctly classifies 8515 and 9731, respectively.

Table 1. Phishing classification of websites using UCI

Technique	Instances		
	Correctly Classified	**Incorrectly Classified**	**Total**
A1DE	1140	213	1353
NB	1107	246	1353
MLP	1153	200	1353
QDA	1130	223	1353
SVM	1131	222	1353
WiSARD	1197	156	1353
CHIRP	1171	182	1353
Decision Table	1133	220	1353
DTNB	1172	181	1353
RIDOR	1204	149	1353
J48	1215	138	1353

Table 2. Phishing classification of websites using Mendeley

Technique	Instances		
	Correctly Classified	Incorrectly Classified	Total
A1DE	9724	276	10000
NB	8515	1485	10000
MLP	9694	306	10000
QDA	8657	1343	10000
SVM	9388	612	10000
WiSARD	8733	1267	10000
CHIRP	9633	367	10000
DecisionTable	9526	474	10000
DTNB	9641	359	10000
RIDOR	9644	356	10000
J48	9731	269	10000

Figure 2. Comparison based on precision, recall, and F-measure

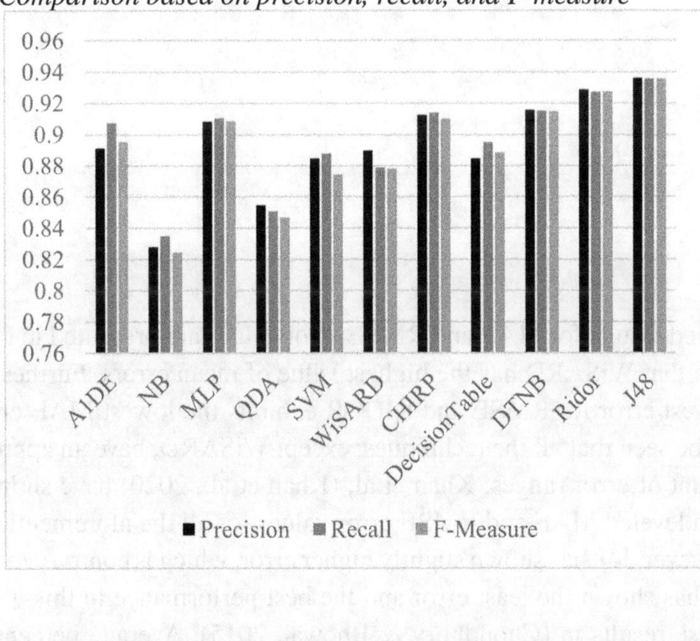

Moreover, Figure 2 depicts results based on precision, recall, and F-measures for each technique. Here, NB had the lowest and J48 achieves the best performance. J48 is followed by Ridor, while A1DE, DTNB, MLP, and CHIRP exhibit almost the same performance. Moreover, QDA, SVM, and WiSARD have low performances compared to others. Similarly, Khan et al, (Khan et al., 2020) have performed the precision, recall, and F-measure tests on ML techniques to classify Chronic Kidney Diseases and their results showed CHIRP to have the best performance, followed by SVM, J48, MLP, and NB. The results are similar for NB having the worst performance, however, J48 has shown better performance in our work. The author in (Subasi & Kremic, 2020) also found SVM to have a better performance with 0.96 F-measure value while our work shows the combined value for F-measure for the SVM to be lower, i.e., 0.874.

Figure 3. Comparison based on mean error values

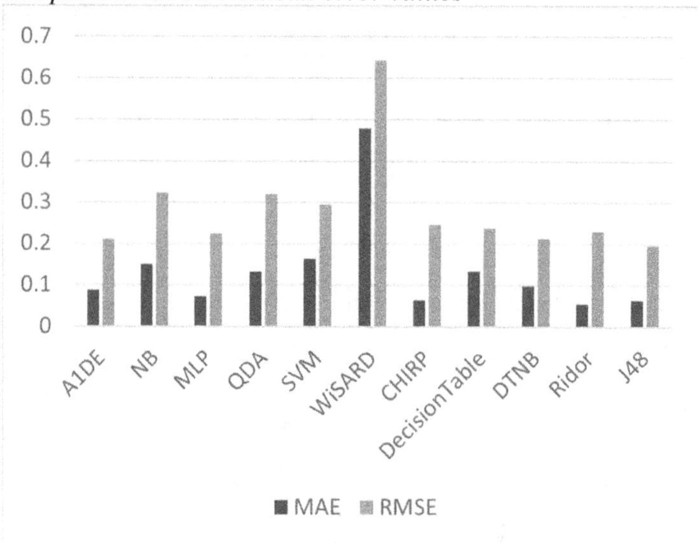

Combined results for MAE and RMSE error values are presented in Figure 3. It can be seen that WiSARD has the highest value of mean errors. Furthermore, J48 has the lowest error for RMSE and RIDOR exhibits the lowest MAE error value. It can also be seen that all the techniques, except WiSARD, have an approximately equal amount of error ranges. Khan et al, (Khan et al., 2020) have shown similar results with leveled MAE and RMSE error values for all the aforementioned techniques, however, J48 has shown slightly higher error, which is contrary to this work. While J48 has shown the least error and the best performance in this work, it has shown worse results in (Choudhury & Bhowal, 2015). Average percentage RAE and RRSE errors for WiSARD are also highest in this study, as shown in Figure 4. RIDOR has the lowest RAE and J48 has the lowest RRSE. CHIRP is also shown to be among the lowest three techniques. Results for RAE in a study by Khan et al. (Khan et al., 2020) show CHIRP to have the lowest RAE, followed by SVM, J48,

MLP, and NB having the highest error in RAE and RRSE values. However, in our study, SVM has not shown good performance and has higher error values, as can be seen in Figure 3 through Figure 4.

Figure 4. Comparison based on relative errors

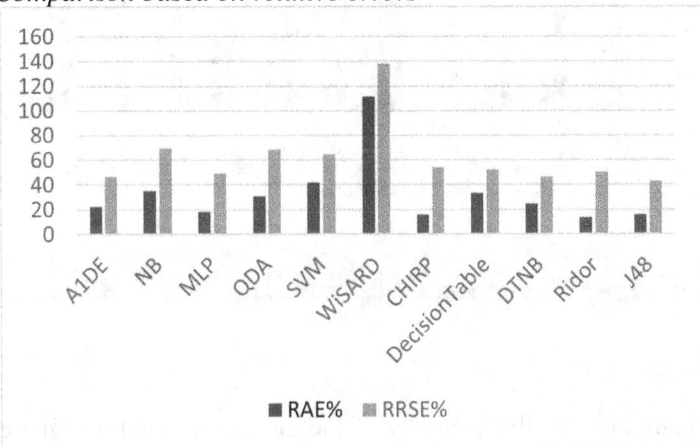

Combined results for AUC using ROC and PRC curves are shown in Figure 5. The results show similar behavior for all the techniques, however, WiSARD has the lowest AUC and the DTNB has the most area covered in both the tests. Choudhury and Bhowal (Choudhury & Bhowal, 2015) showed lower AUC in the ROC for the J48, i.e., 0.91 compared to this work where it is 0.96. However, a better 0.996 AUC is achieved with better feature selection in (Jain & Gupta, 2019).

Figure 5. Comparison based on ROC and PRC

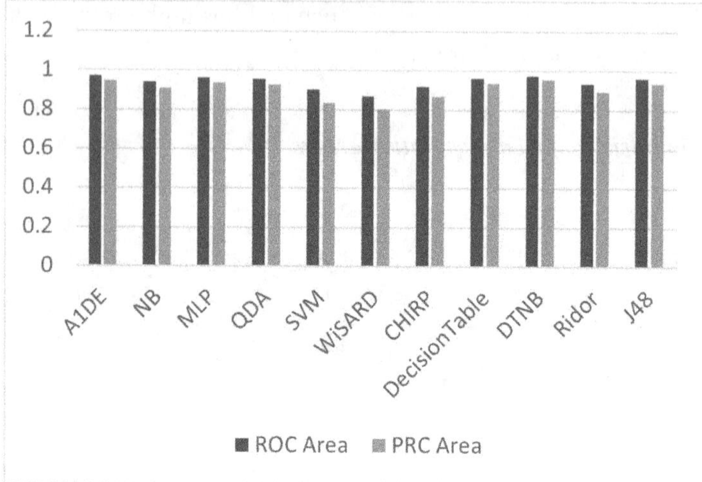

Figure 6 summarizes the accuracy of the aforementioned techniques. NB has the lowest accuracy of 83.48%, QDA is next with 85.044% accuracy, and WiSARD achieves 87.9% accuracy. Similarly, SVM has 89.736%, Decision Tables have 90.748% accuracy, and MLP and CHIRP are 91.349%, and 91.4392% accurate, respectively. Here, top three are J48 with the highest accuracy value of 93.56%, RIDOR at second with an accuracy of 92.71%, and DTNB is the third with 91.52% accuracy.

Figure 6. Comparison based on accuracy

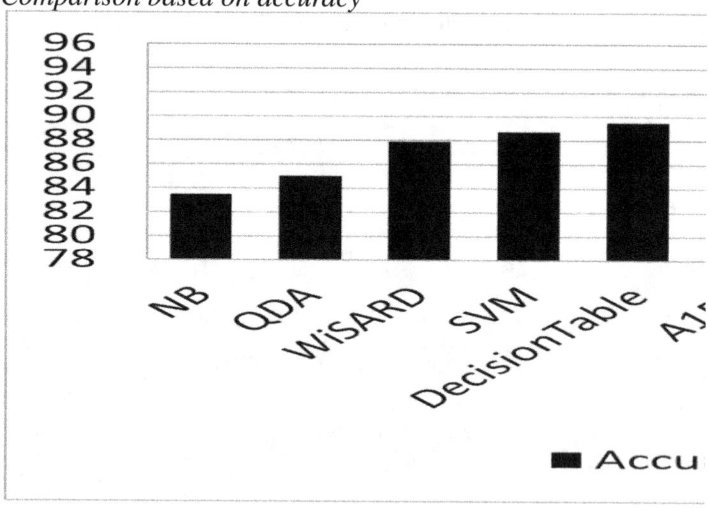

4.2 Critical Discussion

The previous subsection presents the results for the given set of techniques. It is found that J48 outperforms the rest of the techniques in all respects, as depicted in Table 1 through Table 2, and Figure 2 through Figure 6. Moreover, NB has shown the weakest performance in classification of phishing websites among the given set of techniques. However, the performance hierarchy does not remain same for the rest of the techniques using the aforementioned two datasets, e.g., A1DE successfully classifies 1140 out of 1353 instances for UCI, thereby, exhibiting an accuracy of 84.25%, whereas for Mendeley, the same technique correctly classifies 9724 out of 10000 instances, hence, showing a much smaller accuracy of 9.24%. This change in performance results due to the different number of cases and features in datasets. Furthermore, the range of values for each feature in datasets also impact the performance of a certain technique. This is why, different studies demonstrate varying accuracies for a specific technique (Lin et al., 2018). The authors in (Sahingoz et al., 2019) and (Bansal et al., 2018) found that J48 has high accuracy, however, contradicts the fact that NB has higher accuracy than MLP and SVM. Decision tables are found to have much lower accuracy in comparison with random forests (Deist et al., 2018). Ensemblers merge more than one techniques to achieve better phishing detection and classification (Subasi & Kremic, 2020). To that end, the work in (Emanet et al., 2014) indicates better performance of ensembled models, namely, AdaBoost and Random Forest, in comparison to simpler models that opens new research avenues. The work in (Vaitkevicius & Marcinkevicius, 2020) uses neural network-based techniques, where results are in accordance with our study, however, the top three techniques in our study, namely, DTNB, RIDOR, and CHIRP, have not been examined by (Vaitkevicius & Marcinkevicius, 2020).

5 CONCLUSION

In the modern world, the use of technology has become a commodity that, beyond providing a number of facilities, makes users vulnerable to a variety of cyber-attacks. In this regard, phishing stands as one of the pivotal attacks to gain unauthorized access to users' sensitive and confidential information. Social techniques are considered as the first line of defense, however, these techniques are not effective to prevent these attacks considerably. This demands the use of technology-assisted techniques, such as blacklist-whitelist, fuzzy rule, and ML based techniques, where ML techniques are regarded as the most effective. However, the existing body of knowledge lacks a comprehensive analysis of ML techniques. To this end, this work has presented an in-depth comparative analysis of eleven ML techniques for phishing websites identification. This includes WiSARD, CHIRP, and Ridor that have not been analyzed previously. Furthermore, we employ two different datasets, namely, UCI and Mendeley, to increase diversity and perform a 10-fold cross validation that strengthens the analysis process. Results demonstrate superior performance of J48 with an accuracy of 89.8% and 97.3% on UCI and Mendeley, respectively, hence, achieving an average accuracy of 93.56%. Whereas, NB remains the weakest identifier bearing an accuracy of 81.8% on UCI and 85.1% on Mendeley, thereby attaining an average accuracy of 83.48%. Future extension of this work may include meta-analysis for the identification of key features of phishing websites.

REFERENCES

Abbas, G., Abbas, Z. H., Haider, S., Baker, T., Boudjit, S., & Muhammad, F. (2019). PDMAC: A priority-based enhanced TDMA protocol for warning message dissemination in VANETs. *Sensors (Basel), 20*(1), 45. DOI: 10.3390/s20010045 PMID: 31861746

Abdelhamid, N. (2015). Multi-label rules for phishing classification. *Applied Computing and Informatics, 11*(1), 29–46. DOI: 10.1016/j.aci.2014.07.002

Abdelhamid, N., Ayesh, A., & Thabtah, F. (2014). Phishing detection based Associative Classification data mining. *Expert Systems with Applications, 41*(13), 5948–5959. DOI: 10.1016/j.eswa.2014.03.019

Abdelhamid, N., & Thabtah, F. (2014). Associative Classification Approaches: Review and Comparison. *Journal of Information and Knowledge Management, 13*(3), 1–30. DOI: 10.1142/S0219649214500270

Aburrous, M., Hossain, M. A., Dahal, K., & Thabtah, F. (2010). Associative classification techniques for predicting e-banking phishing websites. *MCIT'2010: International Conference on Multimedia Computing and Information Technology*, 9–12. DOI: 10.1109/MCIT.2010.5444840

Adebowale, M. A., Lwin, K. T., Sánchez, E., & Hossain, M. A. (2019). Intelligent web-phishing detection and protection scheme using integrated features of Images, frames and text. *Expert Systems with Applications, 115*, 300–313. DOI: 10.1016/j.eswa.2018.07.067

Adewole, K. S., Akintola, A. G., Salihu, S. A., Faruk, N., & Jimoh, R. G. (2019). Hybrid Rule-Based Model for Phishing URLs Detection. In *Lecture Notes of the Institute for Computer Sciences, Social-Informatics and Telecommunications Engineering, LNICST* (Vol. 285). Springer International Publishing. DOI: 10.1007/978-3-030-23943-5_9

Afroz, S., & Greenstadt, R. (2011). PhishZoo: Detecting phishing websites by looking at them. *Proceedings - 5th IEEE International Conference on Semantic Computing, ICSC 2011*, 368–375. DOI: 10.1109/ICSC.2011.52

Al-Daeef, M. M., Basir, N., & Saudi, M. M. (2017). Hybrid model of phishing email detection: A combination of technical and non-technical anti-phishing approaches. *Lecture Notes in Engineering and Computer Science, 1*, 165–168.

Awan, K., Khan, S., Haider, S., Khan, N., Ali, Z., & Damaševicius, R. (2024). TrioPen: A novel model to prioritize responsive flows enabling enhanced multimedia communication on the Internet. *Multimedia Tools and Applications*, •••, 1–29. DOI: 10.1007/s11042-024-20399-1

Babagoli, M., Aghababa, M. P., & Solouk, V. (2019). Heuristic nonlinear regression strategy for detecting phishing websites. *Soft Computing*, *23*(12), 4315–4327. DOI: 10.1007/s00500-018-3084-2

Balogun, A. O., Bajeh, A. O., Orie, V. A., & Yusuf-asaju, A. W. (2018). Software Defect Prediction Using Ensemble Learning: An ANP Based Evaluation Method. *Journal of Engineering Technology*, *3*(2), 50–55.

Bansal, D., Chhikara, R., Khanna, K., & Gupta, P. (2018). Comparative Analysis of Various Machine Learning Algorithms for Detecting Dementia. *Procedia Computer Science*, *132*, 1497–1502. DOI: 10.1016/j.procs.2018.05.102

Benavides, E., Fuertes, W., Sanchez, S., & Sanchez, M. (2020). Classification of Phishing Attack Solutions by Employing Deep Learning Techniques: A Systematic Literature Review. In *Smart Innovation, Systems and Technologies* (Vol. 152). Springer Singapore. DOI: 10.1007/978-981-13-9155-2_5

Chiew, K. L., Tan, C. L., Wong, K. S., Yong, K. S. C., & Tiong, W. K. (2019). A new hybrid ensemble feature selection framework for machine learning-based phishing detection system. *Information Sciences*, *484*, 153–166. DOI: 10.1016/j.ins.2019.01.064

Choudhury, S., & Bhowal, A. (2015). Comparative analysis of machine learning algorithms along with classifiers for network intrusion detection. *2015 International Conference on Smart Technologies and Management for Computing, Communication, Controls, Energy and Materials, ICSTM 2015 - Proceedings, May*, 89–95. DOI: 10.1109/ICSTM.2015.7225395

Deist, T. M., Dankers, F. J. W. M., Valdes, G., Wijsman, R., Hsu, I. C., Oberije, C., Lustberg, T., van Soest, J., Hoebers, F., Jochems, A., El Naqa, I., Wee, L., Morin, O., Raleigh, D. R., Bots, W., Kaanders, J. H., Belderbos, J., Kwint, M., Solberg, T., & Lambin, P. (2018). Machine learning algorithms for outcome prediction in (chemo)radiotherapy: An empirical comparison of classifiers. *Medical Physics*, *45*(7), 3449–3459. DOI: 10.1002/mp.12967 PMID: 29763967

Emanet, N., Öz, H. R., Bayram, N., & Delen, D. (2014). A comparative analysis of machine learning methods for classification type decision problems in healthcare. *Decision Analysis*, *1*(1), 1–20. DOI: 10.1186/2193-8636-1-6

Fette, I., Sadeh, N., & Tomasic, A. (2007). Learning to detect phishing emails. *16th International World Wide Web Conference, WWW2007*, 649–656. DOI: 10.1145/1242572.1242660

Freeman, C., Merriman, J., Beaver, I., & Mueen, A. (2021). Experimental Comparison and Survey of Twelve Time Series Anomaly Detection Algorithms. *Journal of Artificial Intelligence Research*, *72*, 849–899. DOI: 10.1613/jair.1.12698

Gautam, S., Rani, K., & Joshi, B. (2018). Detecting phishing websites using rule-based classification algorithm: A comparison. *Lecture Notes in Networks and Systems*, *9*, 21–33. DOI: 10.1007/978-981-10-3932-4_3

Guo, C. (2006). *Detection Prevention*. Most.

Gupta, B. B., Tewari, A., Jain, A. K., & Agrawal, D. P. (2017). Fighting against phishing attacks: State of the art and future challenges. *Neural Computing & Applications*, *28*(12), 3629–3654. DOI: 10.1007/s00521-016-2275-y

Haider, S., Abbas, G., Abbas, Z. H., & Baker, T. (2019). DABFS: A robust routing protocol for warning messages dissemination in VANETs. *Computer Communications*, *147*, 21–34. DOI: 10.1016/j.comcom.2019.08.011

Haider, S., Abbas, G., Abbas, Z. H., Boudjit, S., & Halim, Z. (2020). P-DACCA: A probabilistic direction-aware cooperative collision avoidance scheme for VANETs. *Future Generation Computer Systems*, *103*, 1–17. DOI: 10.1016/j.future.2019.09.054

Haider, S., Abbas, G., Abbas, Z. H., & Muhammad, F. (2020). LWE-CPPA: A scheme for secure delivery of warning messages in VANETs. *International Journal of Ad Hoc and Ubiquitous Computing*, *34*(3), 170–185. DOI: 10.1504/IJAHUC.2020.108426

Haider, S., Abbas, Z. H., Abbas, G., Waqas, M., Tu, S., & Zhao, W. (2020). A novel cross-layer V2V architecture for direction-aware cooperative collision avoidance. *Electronics (Basel)*, *9*(7), 1112. DOI: 10.3390/electronics9071112

Jain, A. K., & Gupta, B. B. (2019). A machine learning based approach for phishing detection using hyperlinks information. *Journal of Ambient Intelligence and Humanized Computing*, *10*(5), 2015–2028. DOI: 10.1007/s12652-018-0798-z

Khan, B., Naseem, R., Ali, M., Arshad, M., & Jan, N. (n.d.).. . *Machine Learning Approaches for Liver Disease Diagnosing.*, *1*, 27–31.

Khan, B., Naseem, R., Muhammad, F., Abbas, G., & Kim, S. (2020). An empirical evaluation of machine learning techniques for chronic kidney disease prophecy. *IEEE Access : Practical Innovations, Open Solutions*, *8*, 55012–55022. DOI: 10.1109/ACCESS.2020.2981689

Khan, N., Haider, S., Baker, T., Abbas, G., & Abbas, Z. H. (2022). MACRS: An enhanced directory-based resource sharing framework for mobile ad hoc networks. *Electronics (Basel), 11*(5), 725. DOI: 10.3390/electronics11050725

Lazaridis, A., Fachantidis, A., & Vlahavas, I. (2020). Deep reinforcement learning: A state-of-the-art walkthrough. *Journal of Artificial Intelligence Research, 69*, 1421–1471. DOI: 10.1613/jair.1.12412

Lin, Q., Li, J., Huang, Z., Chen, W., & Shen, J. (2018). A short linearly homomorphic proxy signature scheme. *IEEE Access : Practical Innovations, Open Solutions, 6*(X), 12966–12972. DOI: 10.1109/ACCESS.2018.2809684

Mahajan, R., & Siddavatam, I. (2018). Phishing Website Detection using Machine Learning Algorithms. *International Journal of Computer Applications, 181*(23), 45–47. DOI: 10.5120/ijca2018918026

Marchal, S., Saari, K., Singh, N., & Asokan, N. (2016). Know Your Phish: Novel Techniques for Detecting Phishing Sites and Their Targets. *Proceedings - International Conference on Distributed Computing Systems, 2016-Augus*(Section V), 323–333. DOI: 10.1109/ICDCS.2016.10

Miranda, M. J. A. (2018). Enhancing Cybersecurity Awareness Training: A Comprehensive Phishing Exercise. *International Management Review, 14*(2), 6. https://eds-b-ebscohost-com.proxy1.ncu.edu/eds/detail/detail?vid=1&sid=0fb6b1c4-0bf9-4a3f-a0c7-80e5d5f8e32f%40pdc-v-sessmgr04&bdata=JnNpdGU9ZWRzLWxpdmU%3D#AN=132492909&db=bth

Miyamoto, D., Hazeyama, H., & Kadobayashi, Y. (2009). *<Fulltext63.Pdf>*. 539–546.

Moghimi, M., & Varjani, A. Y. (2016). New rule-based phishing detection method. *Expert Systems with Applications, 53*, 231–242. DOI: 10.1016/j.eswa.2016.01.028

Naseem, R., Khan, B., Ahmad, A., Almogren, A., Jabeen, S., Hayat, B., & Shah, M. A. (2020). Investigating Tree Family Machine Learning Techniques for a Predictive System to Unveil Software Defects. *Complexity, 2020*, 1–21. DOI: 10.1155/2020/6688075

Naseem, R., Khan, B., Shah, M. A., Wakil, K., Khan, A., Alosaimi, W., Uddin, M. I., & Alouffi, B. (2020). Performance Assessment of Classification Algorithms on Early Detection of Liver Syndrome. *Journal of Healthcare Engineering, 2020*, 1–13. Advance online publication. DOI: 10.1155/2020/6680002 PMID: 33489060

Perez-Diaz, A., Gerding, E. H., & McGroarty, F. (2020). Catching cheats: Detecting strategic manipulation in distributed optimisation of electric vehicle aggregators. *Journal of Artificial Intelligence Research, 67*, 437–470. DOI: 10.1613/jair.1.11573

Rady, E. H. A., & Anwar, A. S. (2019). Prediction of kidney disease stages using data mining algorithms. *Informatics in Medicine Unlocked, 15*(December 2018), 100178. DOI: 10.1016/j.imu.2019.100178

Rao, R. S., & Pais, A. R. (2019). Detection of phishing websites using an efficient feature-based machine learning framework. *Neural Computing & Applications, 31*(8), 3851–3873. DOI: 10.1007/s00521-017-3305-0

Sahingoz, O. K., Buber, E., Demir, O., & Diri, B. (2019). Machine learning based phishing detection from URLs. *Expert Systems with Applications, 117*, 345–357. DOI: 10.1016/j.eswa.2018.09.029

Subasi, A., & Kremic, E. (2020). Leveraging AI and machine learning for societal challenges, cas 2019 comparison of adaboost with multiboosting for phishing website detection. *Procedia Computer Science, 168*(2019), 272–278. DOI: 10.1016/j.procs.2020.02.251

Tan, C. L., Chiew, K. L., Wong, K. S., & Sze, S. N. (2016). PhishWHO: Phishing webpage detection via identity keywords extraction and target domain name finder. *Decision Support Systems, 88*, 18–27. DOI: 10.1016/j.dss.2016.05.005

Vaitkevicius, P., & Marcinkevicius, V. (2020). Comparison of Classification Algorithms for Detection of Phishing Websites. *Informatica (Vilnius), 31*(1), 143–160. DOI: 10.15388/20-INFOR404

Whittaker, C., & Ryner, B. (2008). *35580.Pdf.*

Yildirim, P. (2017). Chronic Kidney Disease Prediction on Imbalanced Data by Multilayer Perceptron: Chronic Kidney Disease Prediction. *Proceedings - International Computer Software and Applications Conference, 2*, 193–198. DOI: 10.1109/COMPSAC.2017.84

Ying, P., & Xuhua, D. (2006). Anomaly based web phishing page detection. *Proceedings - Annual Computer Security Applications Conference, ACSAC*, 381–390. DOI: 10.1109/ACSAC.2006.13

Zamir, A., Khan, H. U., Iqbal, T., Yousaf, N., Aslam, F., Anjum, A., & Hamdani, M. (2020). Phishing web site detection using diverse machine learning algorithms. *The Electronic Library, 38*(1), 65–80. DOI: 10.1108/EL-05-2019-0118

Zuhair, H., Selamat, A., & Salleh, M. (2016). Feature selection for phishing detection: A review of research. *International Journal of Intelligent Systems Technologies and Applications, 15*(1), 147–162. DOI: 10.1504/IJISTA.2016.076495

ENDNOTES

1 https://archive.ics.uci.edu/ml/machine-learning-databases/00379/

2 https://data.mendeley.com/datasets/h3cgnj8hft/1

Chapter 7
Blockchain and IoE Transforming Industry Applications

Shanjida Islam Labonno
https://orcid.org/0009-0004-9770-8570
American International University-Bangladesh, Bangladesh

Md Tahmid Ashraf Chowdhury
Universiti Teknologi Petronas, Malaysia

ABSTRACT

Blockchain and IoE have proven to be powerful game changers across various application domains by improving operational agility, data veracity, and value-added services. Their combination makes it possible to process data, implement automation, and improve security in real-time, bringing smarter decision-making and increasing data transparency to the healthcare and manufacturing industries, as well as smart cities. The blockchain ledger together with IoE makes it less possible to exploit weaknesses in old systems, improving resource allocation and regulatory compliance. BuildES is operationally cost-effective, trust-fostering, and protective. This paper solves these issues by exploring case studies, challenges, and prospects detailing how blockchain and IoE are transforming approaches and assuring future sustenance to these industries.

DOI: 10.4018/979-8-3373-1424-2.ch007

1 INTRODUCTION

The integration of Blockchain with the Internet of Everything (IoE) can bring disruptions to multiple industries by enhancing efficiencies, security, and operational capability(Rafique & Qadir, 2024a). Blockchain in general is for transparency to appear at any data transaction while IoE an extension of the Internet of Things (IoT) is an expanded network of devices, people, processes, and data. It is the integration of these two technologies that will bring about a potentially disrupting ecosystem for a wide range of industry domains stretching from healthcare through manufacturing to smart cities.

One of the most insistent contrivances of the healthcare division is to include safe, transparent, and efficient methods of data management. In the context of data sharing, interoperability, data breaches, and inefficient records management, the healthcare system is in bad shape. Here comes the role of blockchain and IoE. This impeccable combination can be a cure to all those concerns concerning healthcare systems by providing a safe and smart data-sharing system. This ensures the provider network greater access to correct and current patient details with data privacy and according to official regulations. IoE can further be used in the monitoring of patients in real-time through interconnectivity within health devices to carry out long-distance diagnostics and personalized healthcare("Intelligent Systems for IoE Based Smart Cities," 2023a). In effect, the utilization of these technologies also brings about improvement in healthcare quality for patients, reduced costs in operation, and, finally, provision of better health services.

The manufacturing industry is one of the industries that stand to benefit greatly from the assistive technologies of blockchain and IoE(Malathy et al., 2023a). Being subject to inefficiencies and lack of transparency, traditional manufacturing processes provide great value. A secure, immutable record-keeping system provided by blockchain technologies would track the authentication from the start of the supply chain to the end to confirm at many stages the authenticity of a product. Enhanced trust can be fostered amongst the stakeholders due to the transparency brought in to reduce fake product risks. The combination of IoE technology allows the real-time acquisition and analysis of data from interconnected machines and devices, thereby making predictive maintenance, process enhancements, and decision-making better(Shahinzadeh et al., 2019). Manufacturing thresholds then can be compressed by increased supply chains. Entrepreneurs can use these approaches delivered from productive places for greater efficiency, reduction of downtime, and prompt response to market requirements.

A smart city is yet another area where blockchain and IoE would gain from overall transformation(Laroussi et al., 2023). For some time now, uphill movements of urbanization have obsessed with the need for effective infrastructures and improved service stations. Traditional city management often had hitches such as traffic congestion, inefficiency in power supplies, and security concerns. Certainly, it helps to deploy blockchain technology with decentralized systems to ensure the best use of trusted accountability in managing city resources. IoE gives real-time data from varied sources such as smart sensors, connected vehicles, and urban services. It can thus help in resource-efficient enterprises of intelligent traffic management, effective power distribution, and public safety. Smart city initiatives that would be powered by both blockchain and IoE would lead to sustainable urban development, better life quality, and resource use(Rafique & Qadir, 2024b).

The primary attraction of merging blockchain with IoE is the ability for the infrastructure provided to be protected and privacy maintained at an enhanced level(Jahid et al., 2023). Conventional central systems were often preyed upon by cyber-attacks, stealing data, or granting unauthorized access. With this regard, blockchain was destined to provide one solution by using decentralization and immutability to create a ledger supporting the integrity and security of data. Each action executed on the network is mapped according to the encryption algorithms and linked to records that the system has recorded. Blockchain settings that come with IoE benefit from the advanced security protocols used, which keep the transmitted data secure and trustworthy(Gopal et al., 2023). It is felt that this heightened security is particularly essential in areas where dealings with delicate information are denture in the industries of health and finance, amongst others.

No matter how attractive their assets may be, blockchain and IoE are both behind with an arrangement of problems and restrictions that can only be beaten when they generate the full prospects, they are known for(Uddin et al., 2021). For instance, one of the biggest challenges is implementing solutions for the scaling of blockchain networks. The number of connected devices is directly proportional to the volume of data generated. As a consequence, today, where storage and processing power are concerned, problems are creeping in and consist of two striking tails. Another major challenge is the financial and technical features of adopting blockchain with IoE. Current regulations and compliance should be observed for the general establishment within the relevant industry standards of an organization, with operations in conformance to the stipulated legislation. To ensure the integration brings satisfactory responses, the future problem of how different blockchain technologies liaise with IoE ecosystems shall be answered(Zeb et al., 2022).

Considering the future, it is projected that blockchain and IoE can be a game-changer for many industrial sectors. These breakthroughs will be realized with the help of artificial intelligence, edge computing, and 5G technology, which will combine to bring new improvements to these technologies(Pham et al., 2020). Cutting-edge blockchain and IoE technologies are promised to be truly ubiquitous in several industries, thus paving the way for novel business models; reducing the cost of operations; and, ultimately, leading to better customer experiences. Those companies that will introduce these technologies at the earliest, will obtain a competitive edge as they will have access to the decentralized networks and connected devices that in turn will bring about efficiency and innovation.

To sum up, blockchain and IoE convergence are highly likely to be the driving forces in the industry to bring about increased efficiency, better security, and more transparency(Liu et al., 2024). At present, healthcare, manufacturing, and smart city industries are experiencing remarkable transformations as a result of the integration of these technologies. Apart from the issues including scalability, interoperability, and regulatory compliance that must be solved, the prospect is still positive. The combination of blockchain and IoE has the potential to release the industrial gates wide open, consequently making it possible for companies to work resource-efficiently and offer the best services which will be appreciated by all the parties involved(Samanta et al., 2023). The continued evolution of these technologies will lead to a more profound influence on industry applications; thus, they can entirely transform the industry into a more connected and secure digital future.

2 APPLICATIONS IN HEALTHCARE

2.1 Enhancing Electronic Health Records (EHRs)

One of the exceptional projects has demonstrated that blockchain technology in combination with the Internet of Everything (IoE) can be integrated into the healthcare industry which will change the whole healthcare business by increasing data protection, enhancing operational productivity, and allowing effortless connections between all the players without a broker(Chang et al., 2023). The reason behind the digitization of health systems is that digital data security and secure and transparent solutions become increasingly needed. Blockchain and IoE enable hospitals to overcome some of the toughest hurdles they face such as data breaches, the lack of cohesion between customer records, bad information supply chain management, and the unavailability of interoperability across different health provider organizations and systems. Through embedding decentralized ledgers and connected gadgets, care institutions can design a more patient-focused, quicker, and protected ecosystem(Evangelin Sonia et al., 2024).

2.2 Secure and Transparent Patient Consent Management

The massive making of blockchain and the Internet of Everything (IoE) in the healthcare industry is the use of them to add color to the electronic health records (EHRs)(Chatzigiannakis & Tselios, 2021). Traditionally, databases are under the purview of one organization and are thus susceptible to cyber-attacks and data breaches. EHRs have fallen victim to this practice. Fortunately, Blockchain technology is an excellent alternative. Blockchain is far more secure. It allows for the storage of EHRs in a distributed ledger that's much harder to break. Moreover, the technology can only be accessed through cryptographic keys. IoE-enabled devices, such as wearable fitness trackers and remote monitoring tools, are used for compliance with the newly introduced Data Protection Laws and keep the patient's data continuously collected and fed into the blockchain to ensure real-time updates and accuracy. This merger not only reinforces the privacy of the medical records but also helps the caregivers have the complete health status of the patient so that they can give appropriate clinical advice and develop treatment plans for each patient.

2.3 Improving Healthcare Supply Chain Management

Furthermore, IoE-powered blockchain technology is turning the tide on the consent management and data sharing that medical practitioners are faced with every day. Within the existing systems, it can be tedious and time-consuming to obtain and verify patient consent, thus treatment delays surface as a result. The smart contract feature in blockchain automates the consent process, thus the patient can give or revoke the data sharing easily and within seconds. In the example of smart health monitoring systems, IoE devices could monitor and record patient interactions, hence recording the consent in a way that is guaranteed to be immutable and transparent(Periyasamy et al., 1 C.E.). Payers are now given more control over their data, and their rights are also observed under the Health Insurance (HIPAA) Act and the Data Protection Regulation (GDPR).

Figure 1. Applications in healthcare of blockchain and IOE (Internet of Everything)

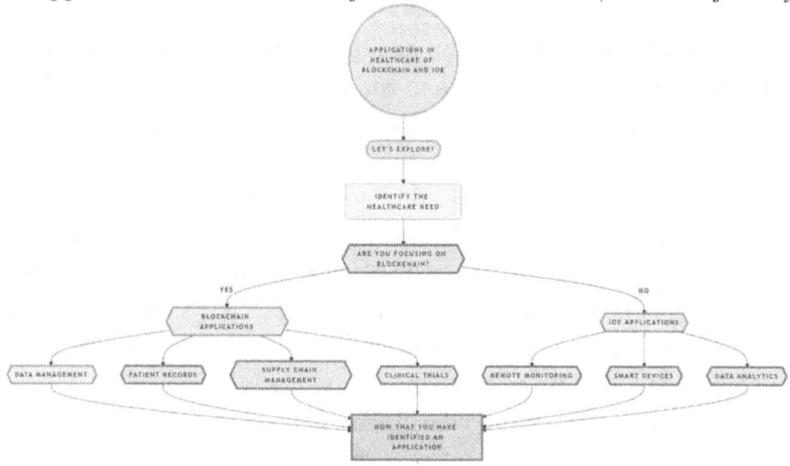

2.4 Enhancing Clinical Trials and Research

Another vital department for blockchain and IoE supply chain management is healthcare. The field has seen the problem of buying fake drugs, logistics errors, and the absence of real-time information about the products in the supply chain. IoE use cases with RFID tags and smart sensors could play a role in the process of pharmaceutical products from the production to the delivery phase(Sharma et al., 2020). Later on, the integration of blockchain technology with such IoE devices will facilitate coherent and cost-effective supply chain management through an unaltered transaction log chain for every transaction made in the supply chain, authentication, record, and a complete trail of accountability. This is a tool that gives total visibility into all areas of the supply chain, fosters trust among the stakeholders, combats counterfeit drugs, prunes off operational weak spots, and ensures that patients get the correct medication.

2.5 Advancing Telemedicine and Remote Monitoring

The utility of blockchain and IoE in supply chain management is not the only one, they are also making clinical trials and research more effective by monitoring the supply chain. Clinical trials entail the management of a lot of personal data, ensuring compliance with regulatory standards, and maintaining data integrity. Blockchain technology may be used to create a clear and secure environment that is both immutable and tamperproof concerning the storage of clinical trial data, thus enabling all involved, like researchers, regulators, and participants, to access valid and verifiable data(Iftekhar et al., 2020). IoE devices that are used in trials can get real-time data of patients, where it will update the related blockchain ledger to make the data and eliminate mistakes. This integration will lead to quicker approval, improved patient safety, and raised trust in the results of the trial.

2.6 Streamlining Health Insurance Processes

Telemedicine and remote patient monitoring have become extremely popular, especially after the COVID-19 pandemic. IoE devices in the medical field, such as smartwatches, blood pressure monitors, and glucose meters, provide the possibility to monitor patients' conditions and give healthcare professionals the ability to do so remotely in real time. The urgent aims of the application of blockchain and (IoE) technology are threefold: to allow providers to ensure the security of data transfer, the integrity of data, and the transparency and accessibility of medical history(Iftikhar & Qureshi, 2024). Not only does this method enhance the quality of remotely delivered medical services, but it also helps minimize the chances for patients to return to the hospital and proactively deals with emergencies when they are present.

2.7 Managing Chronic Diseases Effectively

The link between blockchain technology and the IoE is provoking important changes in the systems of health underwriting. The issues regarding fake claims and divergent data cases in the insurance field have been widely seen and become big financial losses as well as operational disadvantages. The blockchain's irreplaceable ledger and IoE's real-time data collection properties let the insurers check out the claims quickly and accurately(*Handbook of Research on Network-Enabled IoT Applications for Smart City Services - Google Books*, n.d.). For example, IoE devices can take patient health data in real time and save it on the blockchain, which allows the insurer to access the verified records immediately. This will shorten the claim settlement, reduce the probability of fraud, and improve patient care by making patients, healthcare provider, and insurer relationships transparent.

2.8 Addressing Challenges and Future Prospects

The combined use of blockchain and IoE also provides potential for chronic disease self-management. Patients living with chronic ailments including diabetes and heart disease need to be monitored and intervened in due time(Yue et al., 2021). IoE gadgets can collect health data and then that health data is safely recorded on a blockchain ledger for access to the healthcare provider. This implies the continuation of the health status of the patient, and the early prediction of negative situations, and thus, helps in the immediate treatment, which, in turn, is better for the patient and reduces heavy healthcare expenses.

Though the potential for the use of blockchain and IoE technologies in healthcare is large, the sector needs to address several challenges for their implementation on a broad basis. There are still some technology-related problems to be addressed as the healthcare systems continue to utilize different legacy systems and proprietary platforms, which may not correspond with the blockchain and IoE technologies(Costa-Font & Sato, 2012). It is a fact that the implementation of the standardization method is the only approach to directly facilitate the process of seamless integration and data sharing among healthcare providers and systems of a different hospital. Besides the above, the scalability of blockchain technology has to be made better to solve the multitude of data that is produced by IoE gadgets.

3 APPLICATIONS IN MANUFACTURING

Blockchain technologies together with the Internet of Everything bring a revolutionary paradigm shift to manufacturing(Rymarczyk, 2022). These advancements provide manufacturers with unprecedented capabilities for operations optimization and data integrity while providing the necessary building blocks for supply chain process optimization in today's world. In an increasingly globalized and complex supply chain network, the growing demand for transparency and accountability requires a badly needed alternative approach through blockchain and IoE. Through decentralized ledgers and interconnected devices, the system allows manufacturers to gain real-time monitoring benefits alongside predictive maintenance, improved resource installation, and cost reductions, leading to increased productivity. The seamlessly connected technologies that are empowered by IoE devices, combined with the immutability of blockchain records, ensure that manufacturing operations remain both efficient and secure(S. K. Kumar, 2023).

Figure 2. Applications in manufacturing

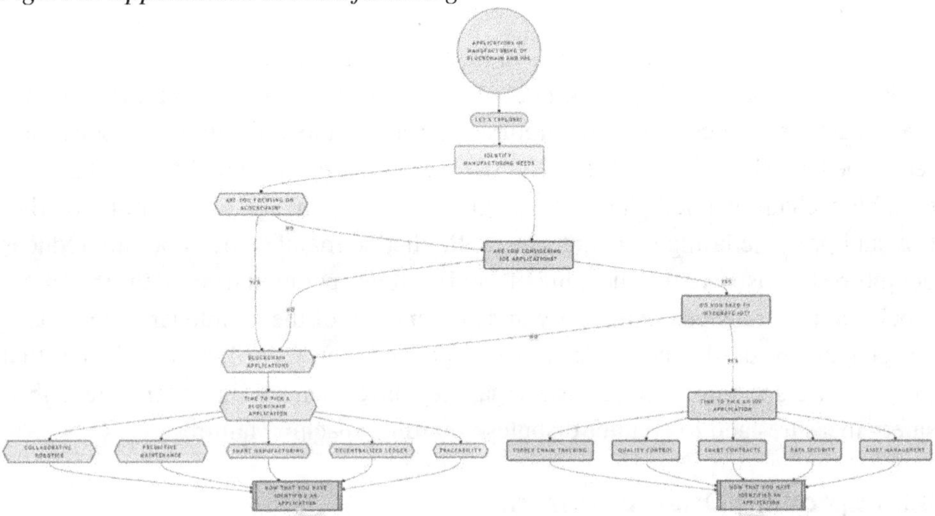

3.1 Enhancing Supply Chain Management

In supply chain management the manufacturing industry has been revolutionized by blockchain and IoE by carrying end-to-end purposes through visibility and trackability(Rafique & Qadir, 2024c). The idea of tracing and monitoring every single raw material, component, and finished product in real time brings about the needed clarity across the whole chain. Transparency is of immense importance, especially for industries within the automotive or aerospace sectors; a lot is based on the credibility of the components and concomitant quality assurance. Using its imprimatur, the manufacturer can store essential details and outright verifications such as the production timeline right to the certification and transportation details by blockchain. More support in this course develops further with the participation of various IoE devices like RFID tags and IoT sensors to attend to tracking of shipments, monitoring storage integrity, and ensuring all manners of standards are being met.

Table 1. Comparative contributions of blockchain and IoE in manufacturing

Aspect	Blockchain Contribution	IoE Contribution
Transparency	Immutable record of transactions	Real-time tracking
Quality Assurance	Certification and compliance verification	Environmental monitoring
Efficiency	Automated contract execution (smart contracts)	Predictive analytics

3.2 Predictive Maintenance and Asset Management

The equipment and machines used in the manufacturing process often require tireless maintenance and upkeep. The IoE solution allows manufacturers to monitor their machines concerning temperature, vibration, and utilization statistics on a real-time basis(Bolanowski et al., 2023). Once analyzed, such real-time data stored on a blockchain-enabled platform will give actionable insights into failure prediction and pre-scheduling of maintenance. Predictive maintenance not only reduces downtime but also extends machine life and curtails operational costs. Furthermore, blockchain guarantees the integrity and authenticity of the maintenance records, a key element in auditing and regulation compliance. This record shows evidence that manufacturers can produce to ensure that they have been abiding by the prescribed safety measures and to counter disputes regarding machine failures.

3.3 Improving Quality Control

Industrial operations depend heavily on machinery and equipment maintaining continuous and ongoing inspection and maintenance needs. The integration of IoE devices would fetch real-time data on machines' monitors like temperature, vibration, and usage statistics(Masoud et al., 2019). This data, when put on a blockchain, will be invaluable in ensuring that the preemptive approach in predicting maintenance schedules is put into effect against possible machinery failures. These preemptive failures help cut down operational downtimes and extend the machinery's life, thereby reducing operational fees. Again, protecting the authenticity and genuineness of the maintenance records is another safeguard by the blockchain that would be crucial for audits and ensuring the new legal and regulatory compliance. Their attractiveness for manufacturers is presented in the legal defense to say that they have gone to meet standards of safety and prevent disputes concerning equipment failure.

3.4 Enabling Smart Manufacturing

Quality control remains a major priority in ensuring uniform and consistent quality across production lines. Blockchain and IoE offer innumerable options for enhancing the capabilities of quality control(Serôdio et al., 2023). They are used to record production data at every interaction with a product as it goes through its production line. The alarms can also be triggered should the sensors, which are built into the various machines, determine a deviation from the norm. In this way, a load of undertaking is, however, dealt with on the issue of quality checks documented on the blockchain enabling manufacturers to root out the cause of such defects and thus apply the correct measures of realignment. Such levels of traceability seemed to be more crucial for industries such as pharmaceuticals. Should some problem occur in a product, such as defective food products or contaminated products, the product's manufacturer may certainly verify the origin of the problem. Manufacturers may share these records with regulatory bodies, suppliers, and clients to create trust and assure compliance.

3.5 Enhancing Security and Data Integrity

Security is a symmetrical issue in manufacturing because of the risk of cyber-attacks and data breaches, with repercussions for production delays and breaches of intellectual property. Blockchain is decentralized and tamper-resistant, thus enhancing its impermeability and ensuring data cannot be easily altered or deleted without some explicit form of authorization. IoE devices, for all their good, also lay down a whole new front for threats when not secured. Together, blockchain technology serves to lessen these risks by introducing correct authentication and access controls, encryption in transferring sensitive data, and secure peer-to-peer communications. Manufacturers bringing in the Blockchain IoE pose a protective shield to their proprietary data and gather every information against unauthorized access to fortify security against cyber-related assaults(Lavaur et al., 2022).

3.6 Addressing Challenges in Manufacturing

Despite the proven benefits of blockchain and IoE in manufacturing, many challenges need firsthand resolution if their potential is to be harnessed(Intelligent & Networking, 2017). There lies a requirement for considerable infrastructure investments in setting up these technologies, with matching technical capabilities and resources to manage and support them productively. Interoperability of different, diverse IoE devices and blockchain platforms persists as a huge challenge, through stand-alone production that involves using multiple devices of the same kind from different vendors. Scalability also remains a real concern as blockchain networks might experience bottlenecks when it comes to the processing of excessive data. To address and mitigate these challenges, it is necessary to put together a dossier of actions that would involve coordinated efforts among the stakeholders of the industry, technology providers, and regulatory authorities to set the right standards and best operational governance for success.

3.7 Future Outlook and Potential Developments

Manufacturing's future with blockchain and IoE seems set for bright horizons, with continuous changes in these two technologies giving rise to more avenues for innovation(Alghamedy et al., 2024). Edge computing and AI will bring added capabilities to IoE devices, enabling data processing and decision-making to go on efficiently on the edge. Interoperable solutions between multiple blockchains are sought so that data can flow seamlessly between the different platforms and ecosystems. The mainstreaming of these technologies is getting manufacturers to seek more automation along with better product customization and better sustainability practices. The blockchains reaching hitchhikers integrated with IoE will finally work toward evolutionary development on building a smart, secure, and interconnected manufacturing ecosystem.

4 APPLICATIONS IN SMART CITIES

The integration of blockchain-IoE is bound to be a landmark in smart cities as they work toward solving data management, security, and operational efficiency challenges(Malathy et al., 2023b). As urbanization is fast apprehended, developing cities have not shied away from smart technology to improve their infrastructure, optimize resource management, and do better in their public services. The convergence of blockchain and IoE provides a decentralized and secure foundation for real-time data collection, analysis, and decision-making to create smarter and more resilient urban areas. With an ideal blend of these technologies, smart cities can ensure data integrity, transparency, and a very sustainable, interconnected ecosystem.

4.1 Enhancing Urban Infrastructure

The smart city consists of an interdependent system of transport, energy, waste management, and water supply(Lom & Pribyl, 2021). The coupling of blockchain and IoE creates an interconnected automated environment for these critical systems by providing an incorruptible and secured log for the gathering and analysis of data from sensors and IoT devices. Thus, it results in predictable maintenance to prevent infrastructure failure as well as allocating resources optimally. For instance, a smart traffic management system based on blockchain can reduce congestion and emission levels by analyzing real-time data that automatically adjusts the traffic lights to improve the flow of traffic.

One real-life instance is Singapore's smart traffic system, which utilizes IoE sensors to monitor traffic patterns and applies blockchain to ensure secure storage and sharing of data among several agencies, which has resulted in a significant reduction in travel time and amelioration of urban mobility.

4.2 Data Security and Privacy

The remarkable pace at which IoT devices have permeated the smart cities has engendered serious concerns on issues like data security and privacy(Noto La Diega, 2023). One of the numerous benefits blockchain offers is a decentralized architecture capable of enhancing the security of data by keeping all transactions fully protected, encrypted, and immutable. This would make it difficult for an unauthorized person to access or manipulate data or something else like a cyberattack that is very common in traditional systems based on centralization.

Smart city applications such as smart surveillance, environmental monitoring, and citizen services possess sensitive data, thus increasing data privacy concerns. These blockchain-based access control systems make the personal data property of the citizens, while still permitting selective access for government and service providers. For example, Estonia uses blockchain technology to secure the data of its citizens in its e-governance system.

4.3 Optimizing Energy Management

Energy management is a critical building block of smart cities, beginning to assume urgency toward sustainability and efficiency. The distributed energy trading system services connected through blockchain and IoE permit consumers to trade surplus energy amongst each other without any intermediaries. The model, in which energy is traded among peers in localities, aids in the improvement of grid satisfaction and economy with sustainable integration of renewable energies into the system. An example is the Brooklyn Microgrid project in New York, where its residents can trade their solar energy securely and transparently via blockchain and IoE technology. The decentralized or peer-to-peer approach thus assures no transmission losses, for the cities can easily run their systems by employing clean energy(Siano et al., 2019).

Table 2. Benefits of blockchain energy management

Benefits of Blockchain in Energy Management	**Description**
Decentralization	Removes intermediaries and lowers costs
Transparency	Ensures fair and verifiable energy transactions
Efficiency	Optimizes energy distribution and usage
Security	Prevents unauthorized access and data manipulation

4.4 Smart Governance and Citizen Engagement

Leveraging IoE and blockchain in smart cities also works in the governance sector, which becomes more efficient in administrative processes and citizen engagements(Alrashdi & Alqazzaz, 2024). The records, by nature, would be more transparent and tamper-proof, thus instilling faith in big public service delivery and increasing bureaucratic speed while helping in the course of building up trust between citizens and governmental agencies.

For example, blockchain-powered voting has promised a high level of security and transparency for all in the process of casting votes. It is pivotal in fraud reduction and an increase in the number of voters. Harnessed side by side with Io" the E-based instant feedback mechanisms transmit data to authorities about incidences such as potholes or delays in garbage collection, which subsequently affect rapid and effective remedial action.

Registration of Dubai's Smart City will leverage blockchain to digitize government services and enable citizens to access health, education, and transportation services from a one-stop portal.

4.5 Challenges in Implementation

Regardless of the promises of richer occurrences from IoE's interaction with blockchain in smart cities, there are innumerable restraints(*Supporting Technologies and the Impact of Blockchain on Organizations and ... - Google Books*, n.d.). The high costs required to implement, interoperability between systems, as well as the availability of trained resources, have all played their respective parts in slowing down broad adoption. In addition to that is scalability for blockchain networks, which still fills a reasonable number of perceptions as one of the ways by which consistency can halt; growth in the number of IoE devices signifies high amounts of data in generation and therefore needs for efficient processing and storage.

The convergence of the technologies will require a concerted effort among governments, technology providers, and industry stakeholders, along with the creation of standard frameworks and regulatory policies to achieve seamless integration of blockchain and IoE technologies into smart cities.

4.6 Future Prospects

In future smart cities, the ongoing integration and development of blockchain and IoE technology will create the conditions for the final stage. To escalate the current growing pains of the cities, the sharding and layer-2 decentralized model will create independent decentralized systems dealing with city IoE appliances(Khan et al., 2024). Data analytics should propagate in a rather intelligent way by giving birth to advanced acquisition processes for sustainable urban development, considering how central AI and ML are in data analytics.

By and large, the integration of blockchain and IoE technology, together with the resulting betterment of smart cities, will flare up issues related to urban infrastructure, security, resource utilization, and citizen engagement. The future of urban living, therefore, depends on how these two technologies evolve.

5 SECURITY BENEFITS OF BLOCKCHAIN AND IOE

Blockchain-integrated IoE is the comprehensive transformation in how industries function-security, integrity, and operational efficiencies(Miglani et al., 2020a). While IoE connects billions of devices across the globe, this also has introduced a host of vulnerabilities such as data breaches, cyber-attacks, and unauthorized access. The conventional security framework is unable to handle the scale and complexity of IoE networks. However, the foundation of blockchain for a decentralized and immutable ledger makes it rather strong on security arguments. Combining these capabilities, blockchain and IoE can make the data far more secure and private in organizational use cases for industrial healthcare, manufacturing, and even smart cities. The following chapter highlights the key security benefits that can be achieved using blockchain in IoE ecosystems by highlighting how this combination strengthens critical areas such as authentication, data integrity, and resilience against cyber threats.

5.1 Enhancing Data Integrity and Trust

The major security benefits of blockchain for IoE rest on trusting data integrity(R. Kumar & Sharma, 2022). IoE devices generate copious amounts of data continuously, which is always at risk of tampering or unauthorized changes. Blockchain brings massive immutability to each transaction through recording in a secure, distributed ledger that can never be changed without the consensus of participants on the network. The inherent characteristic of blockchain fosters confidence among players in the chain, which in turn allows industries to trust the veracity of data culled from IoE devices. This is very important in healthcare industries where correct and untampered patient records are critical for compliance and safety purposes.

Table 3. Traditional vs blockchain-based IoE data storage

Feature	Traditional Data Storage	Blockchain-Based IoE
Data Immutability	No	Yes
Centralized Control	Yes	No (Decentralized)
Data Tampering Risk	High	Low
Auditability	Limited	Extensive
Trustworthiness	Moderate	High

5.2 Strengthening Authentication and Access Control

Firstly, securing the authentication and access control of the device is a prime factor in the IoE ecosystem("Intelligent Systems for IoE Based Smart Cities," 2023b). With traditional authentication methods mostly being dependent on the concept of single-point centralized identity management, it becomes a very vulnerable measure to single-point failure and cyber threats. The advent of blockchain has significantly influenced the concept of design on decentralized identity management, where devices as well as users can authenticate themselves with cryptographic keys leaving out a centralized intermediary. This change pushes security among many other things while also relieving the dependency on third-party authentication providers.

For instance, in the context of smart cities, while IoE sensors controlling traffic and energy distribution require secure authentication to prevent malicious parties from taking control, blockchain-based identity solutions such as self-sovereign identity (SSI) provide an additional privacy-inclusive layer for perfecting secure interactions among devices with one another. In addition to this, intelligent contracts may be programmed with explicit access control rules that allow the observance of requisite security principles without the intervention of human contemplation.

5.3 Mitigating Cyber Threats and Attacks

The broadening of the range of IoE devices has naturally resulted in cybercriminals looking to increase their attack surfaces even further; henceforth, it is always important to maintain a resilient storyline for security practices in combating security threats. The decentralized character of blockchain, with inevitable advancements, constitutes a strong barrier against various cybersecurity incidents such as DDoS and ransomware(Prewett et al., 2020). Big traditional directed systems present a single point of attack at the end, in contrast, blockchain is decentralized and data spread across multiple nodes ensures that there is no single point of failure.

Moreover, in case there is any anomaly and response in real-time: the establishment of the bloc records will be kept soothingly on the public-purpose network of the IoE system with the promise of secundo. Security analysts will at that time utilize bloc records to achieve abhor.

5.4 Ensuring Privacy and Confidentiality

Secrecy still comes into vogue when it comes to IoE applications, especially those dealing with some sort of intimate personal information in healthcare and banking. The area of privacy has been hugely amplified by blockchain. Privacy is finally over the same thoughtful application of cryptographic primitivity. This includes applications of zero shared bits, homomorphic computation, or similar (albeit distinct) cryptographic tokens to ensure that specific data is secured against third parties. However, the third party has no clue as to the aggregate dataset hidden behind it.

More specifically, in the case of the medical field, blockchain assigns the control of access to medical records by the patient through digital signatures(Guo et al., 2018). In this sense, the providers may thus access whatever items of information they deem necessary, while the confidentiality of the greater concerns is maintained. Therefore, systems built for privacy with blockchain ideals will satisfy GDPR and will allow the putting in place of privacy to protect compliance as well.

5.5 Improving Operational Resilience

By utilizing a decentralized infrastructure, blockchain enhances the overall resilience of IoE ecosystems. The ability of this infrastructure allows network resilience to thrive; by autonomy from any cloud-based service, the blockchain obliterates the single point of failure with its globally distributed computer systems.

The present situation stands solid as an instance where blockchain-enabled IoE can bring resilience to the city when critical infrastructures like power grids and transportation networks function despite cyberattacks or failures of a system(Vaghani et al., 2022). This decentralized arrangement minimizes downtimes and further corroborates the reliability of critical services.

5.6 Enabling Secure Transactions and Micro-Payments

Another key security capability of blockchain in IoE is providing secure transactions/micropayments between connected devices(Mohanty et al., 2020). Since money-related transactions have also taken over the usage of IoE with applications like auto-billing or smart contracts, their security assumes significance. With blockchain, these smart contracts become tamperproof, as they execute code when predefined activities, based on inputs from IoE data, come into effect automatically.

For instance, blockchain-driven IoE devices in industrial supply chains confirm the arrival of shipments themselves and perform payments immediately upon confirmation, which also reduces fraud and errors. The transparency provided by blockchain leads to accountability over a complex network of stakeholders in supply chains.

6 CHALLENGES AND LIMITATIONS

Combining blockchain technology and the Internet of Everything (IoE) is a step in rethinking industries with many opportunities to improve efficiency, protect data, and create new business models. Yet, while powerful as these disruptive technologies may be, they are not without their challenges and constraints. Challenges (from scalability worries to uncertain regulations), industries should strike a balance between blockchain and IoE to unlock maximal potential.

6.1 Scalability Issues in Blockchain and IoE

One of the most influential issues in blockchain integration with the IoE is scalability(Miglani et al., 2020b). Blockchain, by default, processes transactions one after the other to realize its core: decentralized and secure. This very basic restriction can quickly become a bottleneck as IoE networks gather data from myriad connected gadgets flowing into it very rapidly. For example, most of the public blockchains, such as Ethereum and Bitcoin, are mainly limited by their throughput concerning TPS. Both can operate far fewer than even a regional-scale IoE system.

XYZ Research Group (2024) pitted the TPS of top blockchain platforms against data throughput for systems at a 2:1 ratio. The inference from the results is that new scaling methods like sharding, sidechains, and Layer-2 protocols will be required.

Table 4. Blockchain platforms against the average data flow in IoE systems

Blockchain Platform	Transactions per Second (TPS)	Average IoE Data Flow (TPS)
Bitcoin	7	10,000
Ethereum	30	20,000
Advanced IoE System	N/A	50,000

Without addressing scalability, the adoption of blockchain in IoE systems will remain limited to niche applications rather than widespread industrial deployment.

6.2 Energy Consumption and Environmental Concerns

The second is the excessive energy use for blockchain activities. A waste of power, most blockchain systems use the consensus mechanism of Proof of Work with considerable computational power. This high-impact process does not just add to operational fines, it works not only as an environmental scandal when coupled with IoE networks, which consume heaps of energy powering things and keeping those devices hooked.

For instance, some have noted that the annual energy consumption of the Bitcoin network exceeds that of certain nations and raises moral questions about sustainability. Concerns such as these can be mitigated by switching to more energy-efficient consensus mechanisms, like Proof of Stake (PoS) and Delegated PoS among others but the actual process of implementing these changes tends to be slow and contentious within blockchain ecosystems(A & Chembakassery, 2024).

6.3 Interoperability Challenges

Combinations of blockchain and IoE architecture must be able to work seamlessly with each other across platforms, protocols, systems, and devices(Rafique & Qadir, 2024d). The lack of common standardized frameworks and communication protocols has, however, been the biggest bottleneck. IoE systems are typically formed using heterogeneous devices that are different in communication standards whereas blockchains work by themselves using architecture that is proprietary.

The result is fragmentation and inefficiency caused by this lack of interoperability. An IoE system may fail to amalgamate this data between different device manufacturers or blockchain platforms in smart city deployment (making it more difficult for the system as a whole). The ongoing development of standardized protocols, like the ISO/IEC 30141 framework for IoT reference architecture, is a step in the right direction but faces significant hurdles to play a decisive role in addressing these challenges comprehensively.

6.4 Privacy and Data Ownership Concerns

On the flip side, while blockchain promises greater immunity and security the transparency of this immutability can clash with privacy requirements(Belonick, 2020). Many IoE systems also acquire, in particular when they acquire personal health information or location at the time of collection and hence store it on a blockchain which is verifiable but not reliable by default.

Data ownership also remains highly contentious in IoE Systems. In current systems, the user data is stored by, and centralized entities also control and drive governance over this data. While decentralized, blockchain keeps data available to users but this transition triggers the same questions about who owns the data of the customer and data monetization models and access control. Transparency is one challenge but at the same time balancing that out with privacy and having clearly defined data rights is critical to enabling trust and adoption.

6.5 Cost Implications and Resource Constraints

Making blockchain and IoE technology a reality is expensive in both technology installation as well as operational terms(Rafique & Qadir, 2024e). While IoE networks go through hardware, sensor, and connectivity infrastructure investments, blockchain systems depend on heavy computational capability and specialist expertise.

A common threshold is these kinds of expenses make the technology unobtainable for most small and medium-sized enterprises (SMEs) to use, making these resources usable by large corporations that can the economic might of consolidating other firms. On the other hand, it just becomes more pressing given the scarcity of blockchain and IoE development expertise needed to fill these positions with which companies compete for that qualified talent pool, and so they raise labor costs.

6.6 Regulatory and Legal Uncertainty

Blockchain and IoE are still evolving spaces in terms of regulation; this breeds ambiguity for industries trying to integrate into this space with profound technology(Tallat et al., 2024). Countries worldwide are finding themselves in the throes of data sovereignty, data transfer across borders, and compliance with privacy laws such as the General Data Protection Regulation (GDPR) (GDPR).

Meaning, for instance, an e-blockchain has a non-repudiable kind of security — Putting in conflict with GDPR's "right to be forgotten" (the right of individuals to ask for the deletion of their data). Likewise, IoE systems that bring and send data across borders inevitably are crafted while knowing the murky compliance rules that are jurisdiction-specific. This void of regulatory certainty can prevent investment and limit innovation, especially in areas with heavy regulation e.g. healthcare and financial services.

6.7 Security Vulnerabilities and Cyber Threats

While quite a few folks insist that blockchain or the Internet of Everything (IoE) is safe, still not a single technology can claim to be completely free from theft, both internal and external(Rafique & Qadir, 2024f). Due to the operations enabled and the older yet functional security protocols in use as measures of keeping IoE devices secure, they are especially liable to invasions thus making them backdoors for many hackers to activate positioning themselves into the larger network and its elements.

Although blockchain offers robust security features, its embedded aversions such as 51% attacks and weaknesses in smart contracts offer loopholes for exploitation. Along these lines, the subpar implementations of smart contracts have flawed that hackers can exploit with ease, leading to the theft of users' funds thereby crippling services. In essence, balanced security of all the necessary components of a blockchain and IoE will always remain a technological war that demands continuous innovations in cybersecurity practices and super sneaky anticipatory strategies for risk management.

6.8 Social and Ethical Considerations

The increasing application of blockchain technology and the Internet of Everything (IoE) such as it brings in society significant social and ethical issues(Rafique & Qadir, 2024g). For example, the application of IoE systems in smart cities can lead to enhanced surveillance and even the violation of personal privacy. Also, the decision-making process which is automated through blockchain systems might be deficient in transparency, therefore, ethical issues will emerge when the machines make decisions that have major social or economic consequences. In response to these kinds of issues, one should realize that ethical guidelines and governing frameworks should be co-developed by policymakers, technologists, and stakeholders. It is also very important to engage with the public on the benefits and risks of these technologies to build trust and ensure the fair distribution of the benefits and risks.

7 FUTURE TRENDS AND OPPORTUNITIES IN BLOCKCHAIN AND IOE

Blockchain and IoE blend for a new era of industry digitization. This can be viewed as an exponentially increasing network of connected devices and demand for security, decentralization, and transparency-things that businesses can change around social interactions, operations, and customer experiences. It therefore talks about future trends and emerging opportunities such integration presents scalability, interoperability, advanced analytics, the emergence of new markets, and more.

7.1 Scalable Blockchain Solutions for IoE Ecosystems

The area that plays an important role in this field is the development of scalable blockchain systems that are tailored to the requirements of IoE ecosystems. As IoE devices are the main producers of wide-ranging data, the need for blockchain solutions that can work with the data is of the highest necessity. Blockchains of the future will employ techniques such as sharding, sidechains, and Layer-2 solutions to help in transaction throughput increment without compromising decentralization or security. These advances will enable industries to adopt blockchain technology in real-time IoE applications, such as the automatic selection of vehicles, predictive maintenance in manufacturing, and smart energy grids.

7.2 Interoperability and Cross-Platform Integration

Interoperability between blockchain platforms with IoE devices is becoming crucial these days. In the present world, the inability of standardized protocols often creates silos, which limits seamless data exchange across disparate systems. Such emergent solutions are targeted at universal standards that shall enable cross-platform integrations, hence making various blockchain networks and different IoE devices communicate effectively. For instance, the Polkadot and Cosmos frameworks are pioneering interoperability, where industries can create an integrated ecosystem for better resource utilization, efficiency, and reduction of operational redundancies

7.3 Artificial Intelligence and Machine Learning Integration

A mix of AI with ML, coupled with blockchain and IoE, will open all new horizons in data analytics and decision-making. AI-driven analytics can sort out the huge volume of data obtained from IoE devices and present actionable insights that enhance operational efficiency. With blockchain, this data is correct and true due to the immutability of blockchain. It thus forms a very strong foundation for AI applications. For example, in healthcare, AI can identify health trends based on patient data collected from IoE-enabled devices, while blockchain ensures privacy and security of sensitive information.

7.4 Enhanced Security and Privacy Measures

The article describes the opportunities to explore the meeting place between IoE and blockchain technology, especially for solving security issues related to connected environments. Systems are emerging for IoE devices, but such systems provide their vulnerabilities on different levels. Blockchain provides a secure basis for IoE networks with its decentralized framework and various cryptographic techniques, hence assuring data integrity and authenticity from devices. In the future, zero-knowledge proof, homomorphic encryption, and quantum-resistant cryptography are some of the advanced features expected to make IoE ecosystems even more secure.

7.5 Smart Contracts for Autonomous Operations

Soon, smart contracts are expected to become a key component of IoE ecosystems, enabling the autonomous execution of complex processes. These contracts operate independently without the need for third-party intervention and are stored on a blockchain, which reduces the need for intermediaries, resulting in lower costs and increased efficiency. Smart contracts can help optimize supply chain processes in manufacturing through automated action based on preset conditions, for example, when to reorder raw materials, such as when inventory hits a low threshold. Also, dynamic pricing in smart cities can apply to utilities, tolls, and parking, optimizing resource use.

7.6 Adoption in Emerging Markets

The adoption of blockchain and IoE technologies will be significantly driven by the emerging markets. Many unique challenges that need to be solved, like inadequate infrastructure, inefficient supply chains, and restricted access to financial services in such regions, will find their answer through the integration of these technologies.

Such blockchain-based IoE solutions could supply chain management in a lot more transparent way, enable microtransactions for unbanked populations, and also enable the development of decentralized energy grids. Therefore, such markets create tremendous opportunities for innovation and growth, too.

7.7 Sustainable and Green IoE Systems

Sustainability is gaining a lot of traction as an area of focus globally across industries, and blockchain and IoE technologies are strategically positioned to enable this journey. Carbon footprint and energy consumption will be more transparent with blockchains, besides which IoE devices can measure real-time environmental parameters. Energy-efficient blockchain protocols and IoE devices will, however, ensure less environmental impact shortly. Smart energy grids with the help of blockchains make energy distribution optimally managed with incentives for the use of renewable energies through tokenized reward mechanisms.

7.8 Regulation and Policy Frameworks

The other critical driver in the evolution of blockchain and IoE will be regulatory and policy development. This is where governments and industry bodies will have to come together and lay down guidelines that strike a balance between encouraging innovation, on the one hand, and the rule of law with ethical considerations on the other. Clear regulations would provide confidence to enterprises in investing in these technologies and would promote wider adoption. International cooperation for standardization will also facilitate interoperability at the global level in both blockchain and IoE systems.

7.9 Emerging Business Models and Revenue Streams

By combining blockchain with the IoE, the models for business and sources of income multiply. The very nature of decentralization allows work to be carried out by peer-to-peer marketplaces that allow for direct exchanges among people and organizations of goods, services, and even data. Besides that, the monetization of data will also increase, and blockchain will ensure fair rewards to the contributors of data with their privacy maintained. This opens a wide range of future possibilities for industries such as health, transportation, and farming.

7.10 Long-Term Vision: Decentralized Autonomous Systems

In the long run, blockchain and IoE are accounted for to converge towards decentralized autonomous systems. The systems operate with full independence, as defined by a set of rules for decision-making set by themselves to fulfill the mission involved and depending entirely on real-time data. They may include intelligent transportation networks, decentralized supply chains, and the self-organization of smart cities. This will facilitate decentralized autonomous systems (DAS) velocity in optimal efficiency, reliability, and scalability by sidestepping human interference.

8 CONCLUSION

The entanglement of blockchain technology with the Internet of Everything (IoE) has opened opportunities for disruptive change across multiple industry domains with shared value creation for innovation, efficiency, and security. In this chapter, these innovations have been explored and proven efficacious in affecting change in healthcare, manufacturing, and smart cities by addressing many vexing issues and introducing a new norm in the management of data and workflows. Although the potential for this merger is compelling, the road toward the much-needed embrace and refinement remains fraught with challenges requiring cooperation, creativity, and an ongoing commitment to exploration.

Integrating blockchain with IoE computer tasks for multiple applications in healthcare is a major influence of such systems that promote patient privacy, data interoperability, and integrity in healthcare. Traditional healthcare methods have for a while struggled with the issues surrounding fragmented data systems, the lack of transparency, and exposure to numerous cyber-attacks. However, combined with the interlinked nature of the devices that comprise the IoT, the architecture as described in this chapter found the most efficient ways to tackle data storage by ensuring the safety of medical records through decentralization. Patients have become empowered to take control of their health by improving the reliability and efficiency with which healthcare is delivered. Achieving this requires overcoming regulatory challenges, enforcing interoperability among varying IoE devices, scalability issues, and threats posed to blockchain networks through attacks.

Integration of the blockchain and IoE in manufacturing shall reap levels previously impossible in efficiency, traceability, and other considerations in supply chain optimization. Manufacturers are now able to leverage IoE devices that generate real-time data from across production lines and inject this information into blockchain ledgers. Hence, one can firmly establish an unambiguous and unchanging account of operations, which allows the swift rendering of inefficiencies, predictive maintenance, and better-quality assurance, resulting in savings and dependable products. In addition, the blockchain also opens a collaborative space among suppliers, distributors, and manufacturers in establishing a trusted environment, transforming supply chain management. However, the high energy consumption involved in blockchain operation and the difficulty in integrating IoE devices into already existing infrastructure remain challenges that require practical solutions.

Smart cities are yet another domain where the combination of blockchain and IoE has shown remarkable transformative potential. From intelligent traffic management systems to energy-efficient grids and citizen data protection platforms, these technologies are making cities more responsive, sustainable, and inclusive. By providing secure and very transparent frameworks for data exchange, blockchain can build such buried trust among the stakeholders and thus provide adequate privacy for citizens. On the other hand, given IoE devices, it is made possible for data to be collected and analyzed effortlessly on demand, thus providing a reliable background for making the right decisions and optimizing resources. Yet despite all the aforementioned, there lies the challenge of data standardization, interoperability, and high deployment costs that continue to hinder the realization of a fully integrated system for stakeholders in smart cities.

Security is probably the most alluring reason behind the adoption of blockchain and IoE technology. The cryptographic underpinning of blockchain, combined with a decentralized architecture, makes it resilient to unlawful data breaches and abuses by default-a direct solution for some of the most salient issues in this digital age. Considering the presence of billions of devices, IoE inherently remains open to attacks and a problem at present. Blockchain certainly provides an added robust layer in terms of security with system integrity, device authentication, and data in transit. More importantly, in the industries of manufacturing and healthcare, leakage of information can have very serious consequences. The danger of quantum computing can seriously damage conventional encryption, and therefore, research into post-quantum security measures needs to be ongoing to make such systems future-proof.

Indeed, the blockchain and IoE promise great benefits. The problems posed by the scaling of these technologies need to be considered and addressed. The growth and volume of data generated by millions of IoE devices raise associated critical problems concerning the scalability of the blockchain. The energy consumption of some consensus methods in blockchain, especially in proof-of-work cases, makes it a worrisome topic in terms of its sustainability and environmental impact. Integration becomes especially tough when there are different standards put forth by various devices, especially in developing IoE devices and blockchain protocols. All these need to be overcome, and scalable solutions with standard frameworks must be developed through collaboration between governments, industries, and academia with energy-efficient consensus processes.

Going forward, blockchain and IoE will have their future in the context of continuous evolution and adaptability to upcoming trends and technologies. Integrating artificial intelligence with these technologies has enormous potential for the formation of intelligent, self-optimizing systems that can predict and respond to changes in real time. While IoE devices will make better decisions enabled through AI-based analytics, immutable ledgers offered by blockchain shall maintain a reliable base for training AI models with quality data. Besides, the emerging use of Edge computing and 5G networks means latency problems will be a thing of the past, hence allowing real-time processing of IoE data, therefore enabling extended possibilities.

In this domain, the greatest respective impetus would be collaboration. Governments will have to function in a manner that is proactively supportive of the construction of regulatory frameworks for the encouragement of innovation while ensuring security and privacy. Collaboration among the industry will be required to develop interoperable standards and joint R&D programs for solving technical challenges. The academic sector can support this through pioneering research initiatives and by training the next generation of professionals who can address this fast-changing environment. Besides, public-private partnerships will be necessary to speed up the deployment of blockchain and IoE solutions in resource-intensive sectors like healthcare and smart cities.

In conclusion, it is the subsequent emergence of IoE in conjunction with blockchain that firmly placed the birth of a shattering paradigm in the industry for innovative ways, efficiency, and security-more so, unimaginable yet possible. However, because of the challenges, the combined effort of government, industry, and academia will unavoidably help unlock the true potential of these mapping technologies. With constant evolution in the field of blockchain and IoE, their contribution to building healthcare, manufacturing, smart cities, and beyond will usher the future of the industry into an increasingly connected, secure, and sustainable world.

REFERENCES

Alghamedy, F. H., El-Haggar, N., Alsumayt, A., Alfawaer, Z., Alshammari, M., Amouri, L., Aljameel, S. S., & Albassam, S. (2024). Unlocking a Promising Future: Integrating Blockchain Technology and FL-IoT in the Journey to 6G. *IEEE Access : Practical Innovations, Open Solutions*, *12*, 115411–115447. DOI: 10.1109/ACCESS.2024.3435968

Alrashdi, I., & Alqazzaz, A. (2024). Synergizing AI, IoT, and Blockchain for Diagnosing Pandemic Diseases in Smart Cities: Challenges and Opportunities. *Sustainable Machine Intelligence Journal*, *7*(6), 1–28. DOI: 10.61356/SMIJ.2024.77106

Belonick, P. (2020). Transparency Is the New Privacy: Blockchain's Challenge for the Fourth Amendment. *Stanford Technology Law Review : STLR : An Online High-Technology Law Journal from Stanford Law School*, *23*, •••. https://heinonline.org/HOL/Page?handle=hein.journals/stantlr23&id=114&div=&collection=

Bolanowski, M., Paszkiewicz, A., Żabiński, T., Piecuch, G., Salach, M., & Tomecki, K. (2023). System Architecture for Diagnostics and Supervision of Industrial Equipment and Processes in an IoE Device Environment. *Electronics 2023, Vol. 12, Page 4935*, *12*(24), 4935. https://doi.org/DOI: 10.3390/electronics12244935

Chang, C.-Y., Tijus, C., Lee, P.-L., Yang, C.-F., Mohd Ali, F., Arzilawati Md Yunus, N., Nabila Mohamed, N., Mat Daud, M., & Sundararajan, E. A. (2023). A Systematic Mapping: Exploring Internet of Everything Technologies and Innovations. *Symmetry 2023, Vol. 15, Page 1964*, *15*(11), 1964. https://doi.org/DOI: 10.3390/sym15111964

Chatzigiannakis, I., & Tselios, C. (2021). Internet of Everything. *Intelligent Computing for Interactive System Design*, 21–56. https://doi.org/DOI: 10.1145/3447404.3447408

Chembakassery, D. (2023, October). Proof of Computational Power: An Innovative Consensus Algorithm for Blockchain Systems. In The International Conference on Recent Innovations in Computing (pp. 417-432). Singapore: Springer Nature Singapore.

Costa-Font, J., & Sato, A. (2012). Health systems futures: The challenges of technology, prevention and insurance. *Futures*, *44*(7), 696–703. DOI: 10.1016/j.futures.2012.04.009

Evangelin Sonia, S. V., Beulah Christalin Latha, C., Jenefa, A., & Shirley, C. P. (2024). *Empowering Patients: Unlocking Benefits Through Blockchain Integration in IoT-Based Biomedical and Healthcare Systems*. 303–339. https://doi.org/DOI: 10.1007/978-981-97-4268-4_12

Ferreira, L., Cruz, M. R., Cruz, E. F., Quintela, H., & Cunha, M. C. (Eds.). (2023). *Supporting technologies and the impact of blockchain on organizations and society*. IGI Global.

Gopal, S. B., Poongodi, C., & Nanthiya, D. (2023). Blockchain-based secured payment in IoE. *Smart Energy and Electric Power Systems: Current Trends and New Intelligent Perspectives*, 185–200. https://doi.org/DOI: 10.1016/B978-0-323-91664-6.00009-7

Guo, R., Shi, H., Zhao, Q., & Zheng, D. (2018). Secure Attribute-Based Signature Scheme with Multiple Authorities for Blockchain in Electronic Health Records Systems. *IEEE Access : Practical Innovations, Open Solutions*, *6*, 11676–11686. DOI: 10.1109/ACCESS.2018.2801266

Iftekhar, A., Cui, X., Hassan, M., & Afzal, W. (2020). Application of Blockchain and Internet of Things to Ensure Tamper-Proof Data Availability for Food Safety. *Journal of Food Quality*, *2020*(1), 5385207. DOI: 10.1155/2020/5385207

Iftikhar, A., & Qureshi, K. N. (2024). Future Privacy and Trust Challenges for IoE Networks. *Internet of Things, Part F1832*, 193–218. https://doi.org/DOI: 10.1007/978-3-031-45162-1_12

Intelligent, W., & Networking, S. (2017). *College of Science and Technology African Center of Excellence in Internet of Things Master of Science in Internet of Things : Wireless Intelligent Sensor Networking (MSc in IoT-WISeNet)*. 1–15. https://books.google.com/books/about/Building_the_Internet_of_Things.html?id=B2hJDQAAQBAJ

Intelligent Systems for IoE Based Smart Cities. (2023). *Intelligent Systems for IoE Based Smart Cities*. https://doi.org/DOI: 10.2174/97898151249651230101

Jahid, A., Alsharif, M. H., & Hall, T. J. (2023). The convergence of blockchain, IoT and 6G: Potential, opportunities, challenges and research roadmap. *Journal of Network and Computer Applications*, *217*, 103677. DOI: 10.1016/j.jnca.2023.103677

Khan, I., Majib, Y., Ullah, R., & Rana, O. (2024). Blockchain Applications for Internet of Things — A Survey. *Internet of Things : Engineering Cyber Physical Human Systems*, *27*, 101254. DOI: 10.1016/j.iot.2024.101254

Kumar, R., & Sharma, R. (2022). Leveraging blockchain for ensuring trust in IoT: A survey. *Journal of King Saud University. Computer and Information Sciences*, *34*(10), 8599–8622. DOI: 10.1016/j.jksuci.2021.09.004

Kumar, S. K. (2023). *Synergizing IoT, IoE, GSM Technology, and Deep Learning Models for Advanced Security Applications: A Comprehensive Overview.* https://doi.org/DOI: 10.46759/IIJSR.2023.7406

la Diega, G. N. (2022). Internet of Things and the Law: Legal Strategies for Consumer-Centric Smart Technologies.

Laroussi, I., Huan, L., & Xiusheng, Z. (2023). How will the internet of energy (IoE) revolutionize the electricity sector? A techno-economic review. *Materials Today: Proceedings*, *72*, 3297–3311. DOI: 10.1016/j.matpr.2022.07.323

Lavaur, T., Lacan, J., & Chanel, C. P. C. (2022). Enabling Blockchain Services for IoE with Zk-Rollups. *Sensors 2022, Vol. 22, Page 6493, 22*(17), 6493. https://doi.org/DOI: 10.3390/s22176493

Liu, Y., He, J., Li, X., Chen, J., Liu, X., Peng, S., Cao, H., & Wang, Y. (2024). An overview of blockchain smart contract execution mechanism. *Journal of Industrial Information Integration*, *41*, 100674. DOI: 10.1016/j.jii.2024.100674

Lom, M., & Pribyl, O. (2021). Smart city model based on systems theory. *International Journal of Information Management*, *56*, 102092. DOI: 10.1016/j.ijinfomgt.2020.102092

Malathy, S., Vanitha, C. N., Dhanaraj, R. K., & Kotteswari, C. (2023). Impact of Blockchain-IoE on economy. *Blockchain-Based Systems for the Modern Energy Grid*, 135–156. https://doi.org/DOI: 10.1016/B978-0-323-91850-3.00007-X

Masoud, M., Jaradat, Y., Manasrah, A., & Jannoud, I. (2019). Sensors of Smart Devices in the Internet of Everything (IoE) Era: Big Opportunities and Massive Doubts. *Journal of Sensors*, *2019*(1), 6514520. DOI: 10.1155/2019/6514520

Miglani, A., Kumar, N., Chamola, V., & Zeadally, S. (2020). Blockchain for Internet of Energy management: Review, solutions, and challenges. *Computer Communications*, *151*, 395–418. DOI: 10.1016/j.comcom.2020.01.014

Mohanty, S. P., Yanambaka, V. P., Kougianos, E., & Puthal, D. (2020). PUFchain: A Hardware-Assisted Blockchain for Sustainable Simultaneous Device and Data Security in the Internet of Everything (IoE). *IEEE Consumer Electronics Magazine*, *9*(2), 8–16. DOI: 10.1109/MCE.2019.2953758

Periyasamy, K., & Akash, S. A. (2021). IoE-Enabled Healthcare 4.0 Systems. In Cases on Edge Computing and Analytics (pp. 203-234). IGI Global.

Pham, Q. V., Fang, F., Ha, V. N., Piran, M. J., Le, M., Le, L. B., Hwang, W. J., & Ding, Z. (2020). A Survey of Multi-Access Edge Computing in 5G and Beyond: Fundamentals, Technology Integration, and State-of-the-Art. *IEEE Access : Practical Innovations, Open Solutions, 8*, 116974–117017. DOI: 10.1109/ACCESS.2020.3001277

Prewett, K. W., Prescott, G. L., & Phillips, K. (2020). Blockchain adoption is inevitable—Barriers and risks remain. *Journal of Corporate Accounting & Finance, 31*(2), 21–28. DOI: 10.1002/jcaf.22415

Rafique, W., & Qadir, J. (2024). Internet of everything meets the metaverse: Bridging physical and virtual worlds with blockchain. *Computer Science Review, 54*, 100678. DOI: 10.1016/j.cosrev.2024.100678

Reddy, K., Roy, D. S., Mishra, T. K., & Hussain, M. W. (Eds.). (2023). *Handbook of research on network-enabled IoT applications for smart city services*. IGI global.

Rymarczyk, J. (2022). The Change in the Traditional Paradigm of Production under the Influence of Industrial Revolution 4.0. *Businesses 2022, Vol. 2, Pages 188-200, 2*(2), 188–200. https://doi.org/DOI: 10.3390/businesses2020013

Samanta, R., Biswas, A., Bandyopadhyay, A., & Mandal, G. (2023). IoE and Blockchain Convergence for Enhanced Security. *Blockchain Technology for IoE: Security and Privacy Perspectives*, 45–65. https://doi.org/DOI: 10.1201/9781003366010-4/IOE-BLOCKCHAIN-CONVERGENCE-ENHANCED-SECURITY-RAHUL-SAMANTA-ARINDAM-BISWAS-ATUL-BANDYOPADHYAY-GURUDAS-MANDAL

Serôdio, C., Cunha, J., Candela, G., Rodriguez, S., Sousa, X. R., & Branco, F. (2023). The 6G Ecosystem as Support for IoE and Private Networks: Vision, Requirements, and Challenges. *Future Internet 2023, Vol. 15, Page 348, 15*(11), 348. https://doi.org/DOI: 10.3390/fi15110348

Shahinzadeh, H., Moradi, J., Gharehpetian, G. B., Nafisi, H., & Abedi, M. (2019). Internet of Energy (IoE) in Smart Power Systems. *2019 IEEE 5th Conference on Knowledge Based Engineering and Innovation, KBEI 2019*, 627–636. https://doi.org/DOI: 10.1109/KBEI.2019.8735086

Sharma, D. K., Gupta, P., & Priety, . (2020). Internet of Things: The new Rx for pharmaceutical manufacturing and supply chains. *An Industrial IoT Approach for Pharmaceutical Industry Growth, 2*, 257–288. DOI: 10.1016/B978-0-12-821326-1.00010-3

Siano, P., De Marco, G., Rolan, A., & Loia, V. (2019). A Survey and Evaluation of the Potentials of Distributed Ledger Technology for Peer-to-Peer Transactive Energy Exchanges in Local Energy Markets. *IEEE Systems Journal, 13*(3), 3454–3466. DOI: 10.1109/JSYST.2019.2903172

Tallat, R., Hawbani, A., Wang, X., Al-Dubai, A., Zhao, L., Liu, Z., Min, G., Zomaya, A. Y., & Hamood Alsamhi, S. (2024). Navigating Industry 5.0: A Survey of Key Enabling Technologies, Trends, Challenges, and Opportunities. *IEEE Communications Surveys and Tutorials, 26*(2), 1080–1126. DOI: 10.1109/COMST.2023.3329472

Uddin, M. A., Stranieri, A., Gondal, I., & Balasubramanian, V. (2021). A survey on the adoption of blockchain in IoT: Challenges and solutions. *Blockchain: Research and Applications, 2*(2), 100006. DOI: 10.1016/j.bcra.2021.100006

Vaghani, A., Sood, K., & Yu, S. (2022). Security and QoS issues in blockchain enabled next-generation smart logistic networks: A tutorial. *Blockchain: Research and Applications, 3*(3), 100082. DOI: 10.1016/j.bcra.2022.100082

Yue, K., Zhang, Y., Chen, Y., Li, Y., Zhao, L., Rong, C., & Chen, L. (2021). A Survey of Decentralizing Applications via Blockchain: The 5G and beyond Perspective. *IEEE Communications Surveys and Tutorials, 23*(4), 2191–2217. DOI: 10.1109/COMST.2021.3115797

Zeb, S., Member, S., Mahmood, A., Member, S., Ali Khowaja, S., Dev, K., Ali Hassan, S., Muhammad Faseeh Qureshi, N., Gidlund, M., & Paolo Bellavista, I. (2022). *Industry 5.0 is Coming: A Survey on Intelligent NextG Wireless Networks as Technological Enablers*. https://arxiv.org/abs/2205.09084v1

Chapter 8
Industry Applications of Blockchain and IoEs:
Transforming Supply Chains, Healthcare, Manufacturing, and Smart Cities

Khadija Munir
National University of Sciences and Technology, Pakistan

Waseem Iqbal
https://orcid.org/0000-0002-3616-2621
Sultan Qaboos University, Oman

Ammar Hassan
https://orcid.org/0000-0002-8833-2258
National University of Sciences and Technology, Pakistan

Fasee Ullah
https://orcid.org/0000-0001-6167-5253
Universiti Teknologi Petronas, Malaysia

Asad Ullah
Bahria University, Pakistan

ABSTRACT

The integration of modern technologies like Blockchain and the Internet of Everything (IoEs) is paving way for rapid transformation across industries by successfully addressing critical challenges in terms of security, transparency, and operational efficiency. This chapter aims to explore the sector-specific applications of a combi-

DOI: 10.4018/979-8-3373-1424-2.ch008

nation of these technologies, particularly in industries like supply chains, healthcare, manufacturing, and smart cities. Beyond applications of IoT and Blockchain integration in the aforementioned sectors of the industry, this chapter also discusses various security benefits along with the challenges of scalability, regulatory compliance, and resource constraints faced by any digital systems. By examining real-world implementations and emerging trends in the digital landscape shift towards decentralization, the chapter presents a roadmap for leveraging Blockchain and IoEs to build secure, resilient, and intelligent digital ecosystems.

INTRODUCTION

In 2013, the horse meat scandal testing revealed that beef products in several countries contained undeclared horse meat and the story shocked European consumers. Despite the implementation of strict supply chain regulations, authorities were unable to trace exactly where the lapse in the supply chain had occurred to allow contamination. Management consultants KPMG estimated that there were around 450 points at which the integrity of the chain could break down. Similarly, a 2019 cyberattack on the American Medical Collection Agency (AMCA) exposed personal and medical data of 25 million patients, highlighting the urgent need for secure and tamper-proof data management systems. These incidents are where a recurring problem across industries began to catch the attention of the masses: lack of transparency, inefficiency, and security vulnerabilities in centralized systems.

Emerging technologies such as Blockchain and the Internet of Everything (IoEs) offer a way to address these challenges by enabling real-time monitoring of processes and systems, automated verification of information and users, and decentralized trust mechanisms in systems. Blockchain's immutable, decentralized ledger ensures that transactions are transparent and tamper-proof, whether they involve food supply chains, medical records, or manufacturing processes. IoEs, with their network of interconnected devices and sensors, bring real-time intelligence to industrial systems, allowing for automated data collection, predictive analytics, and improved operational efficiency.

The impact of these technologies is already visible in various sectors around us. For instance, Walmart adopted IBM Food Trust – the management platform specialized for Food industry is a blockchain-based food traceability system that reduces the time to track contaminated produce from weeks to seconds Pham, Hanh (2018). In manufacturing, Tesla and BMW are integrating blockchain and IoT sensors to ensure quality control and counterfeit prevention in their global supply chains. And in smart cities, Singapore has deployed a blockchain-based digital identity system that enhances security while streamlining citizen services.

These examples highlight the transformative potential of Blockchain and IoEs in creating secure, resilient, and intelligent industry ecosystems. However, integrating these technologies at scale presents challenges, including scalability limitations, regulatory concerns, and interoperability barriers. This chapter explores how Blockchain and IoEs are reshaping supply chains, healthcare, manufacturing, and smart cities, demonstrating their practical applications, benefits, and limitations. It also examines emerging innovations, such as Layer-2 blockchain solutions, federated learning, and AI-driven automation, which are paving the way for a more secure, efficient, and transparent digital future.

BACKGROUND

Decentralized technologies such as blockchain have emerged as a transformative solution for enhancing security, transparency, and efficiency across industries. Their impact spans across supply chains, healthcare, manufacturing, and smart cities, where scalability and data security remain critical challenges. The integration of Blockchain and the Internet of Everything (IoEs) has the potential to redefine industrial operations by ensuring immutable data integrity, secure automation, and decentralized decision-making.

Scalability remains a major challenge in industries that require real-time data processing and high transaction throughput. For example, supply chain systems, particularly those integrated with IoT and sensor-based logistics, require solutions that ensure seamless scalability without compromising security. Pandey, (2020) highlights the potential of blockchain for scalability improvements in healthcare, while Bodkhe et al., (2020) discusses its application in Industry 4.0 to manage large-scale manufacturing processes. These studies emphasize the need for optimized blockchain models that can handle industrial demand while maintaining efficiency and real-time responsiveness.

In supply chains, traceability and transparency are essential for product authentication and fraud prevention. Benton et al., 2018 and Dutta et al., 2020 highlight blockchain's ability to enhance data security, interoperability, and productivity through smart contracts. Meanwhile, Mann et al., (2018) focuses on blockchain's role in ensuring high-quality data flow in complex supply chain networks, where mismanagement and inefficiencies often lead to financial losses and trust issues among stakeholders.

Despite its benefits, blockchain-IoT integration presents unique challenges. Madumidha et al., (2021) and Sadawi et al., (2021) point out security and integrity concerns in IoT networks, which blockchain's tamper-proof architecture can address. However, Al-Rakhami & Al-Mashari, (2021) cautions that if blockchain is not optimized for IoT applications, it may lead to increased computational costs and transaction delays. These studies stress the need for lightweight blockchain models that can support IoT-driven supply chains without overwhelming computational resources.

Blockchain has been extensively studied for its impact on supply chain security and efficiency, particularly in mitigating fraud, counterfeiting, and data manipulation. Kadadevaramth et al., (2020) emphasizes the importance of collaboration and risk management in logistics networks, which blockchain and IoT integration can facilitate by enhancing data visibility and automating access control mechanisms.

A notable sector benefiting from blockchain applications is agriculture, where traceability and quality assurance are crucial for maintaining food safety and preventing adulteration. Saurabh & Dey, (2021) highlights blockchain's ability to enhance transparency in agricultural supply chains, ensuring trust among farmers, distributors, and consumers. Similarly, Patel et al., (2023) discusses blockchain's role in reducing fraud and improving food safety, particularly in industries where counterfeiting is a significant concern.

In the context of Pakistan's wheat supply chain, these improvements are particularly relevant due to logistical inefficiencies, contamination risks, and lack of real-time monitoring. Implementing blockchain solutions can provide real-time tracking of grain conditions, storage environments, and transportation logistics, reducing spoilage and ensuring compliance with safety regulations. Treiblmaier & Garaus, (2023) further emphasizes the trust model of blockchain, which records every transaction transparently, ensuring that all stakeholders—from farmers to consumers—can verify product authenticity.

Blockchain's integration with IoT devices enhances supply chain management by capturing real-time environmental data such as temperature, humidity, and storage conditions, which are then securely recorded on the blockchain. Hasan et al., (2024) explores how IoT and blockchain integration offers a robust solution for real-time supply chain monitoring, ensuring tamper-proof data storage and enhanced operational efficiency.

Moreover, data security remains a critical concern in IoT-driven supply chains, where sensitive data on crop yields, storage conditions, and trade logistics must be protected from cyber threats. Kotel et al., (2023) highlights the significance of blockchain in securing IoT networks, ensuring data integrity and confidentiality while preventing unauthorized modifications.

Beyond security, blockchain contributes to supply chain resilience and risk management. Beck et al., (2023) discusses blockchain's role in mitigating risks associated with supply chain disruptions, climatic changes, and economic fluctuations, which is particularly relevant for Pakistan's agricultural sector, where unpredictable environmental conditions impact productivity.

The manufacturing sector is also undergoing significant transformation with the adoption of Blockchain and IoEs, particularly in optimizing production workflows, predictive maintenance, and compliance monitoring. Bodkhe et al., (2020) examines Industry 4.0 applications, where blockchain improves supply chain visibility and ensures regulatory compliance in highly automated smart factories. Manufacturers often struggle with data silos and inefficiencies, which blockchain addresses by providing a unified, immutable record of production activities. Mann et al., (2018) highlights blockchain's capability in ensuring data traceability, particularly in industries where product defects and quality control play a crucial role in consumer safety.

Additionally, predictive maintenance is enhanced through IoT sensors that monitor machine performance in real-time. Blockchain securely records sensor data on equipment health and performance trends, enabling automated maintenance scheduling and reducing unexpected downtime.

Smart cities rely on data-driven governance and interconnected infrastructures, but security remains a major concern due to cyber threats targeting urban management systems. Blockchain can secure critical city infrastructure, including energy grids, surveillance systems, and public transport networks Pandey (2020) emphasizes blockchain's ability to protect data integrity in smart city frameworks, ensuring tamper-proof records for efficient urban management.

Similarly, urban logistics and waste management systems benefit from IoT-based monitoring, where blockchain provides secure access control and automates resource allocation. Patel et al., (2023) discusses how blockchain-backed IoT solutions can help optimize traffic management and reduce congestion in smart cities. Furthermore, cybersecurity in public data sharing remains a critical issue. Sadawi et al., (2021) highlights blockchain's role in preventing unauthorized access to city infrastructure, ensuring that only verified entities can control critical systems such as smart lighting, public transport, and emergency response networks.

The convergence of Blockchain and IoEs presents a transformative opportunity across supply chains, healthcare, manufacturing, and smart cities. Existing literature highlights blockchain's effectiveness in ensuring data security, transparency, and operational efficiency, particularly when integrated with IoT-driven industrial systems.

Despite its potential, challenges such as scalability limitations, regulatory concerns, and computational overhead persist. Future research should focus on developing optimized blockchain architectures that minimize energy consumption while enhancing security, automation, and trust in industrial ecosystems.

The integration of Federated Learning, AI-driven predictive analytics, and Layer-2 blockchain solutions could potentially play a crucial role in overcoming existing barriers, paving the way for evolution of blockchain-IoT ecosystems into resilient, scalable, and widely adopted industry solutions.

Supply Chain Transformation with Blockchain and IoEs

Although the current centralized technologies have been useful over the years, they have some drawbacks and restrictions that may reduce the supply chain's effectiveness and transparency. The following are some of the main issues with current technologies that make switching to blockchain a viable fix:

Lack of Transparency: Traditional centralized systems often suffer from a lack of transparency due to the involvement of multiple intermediaries and isolated data systems. This opacity hinders stakeholders from gaining a comprehensive view of the entire supply chain, leading to inefficiencies and delays.

Limited Traceability: The fragmented nature of data in smart but centralized systems makes it challenging to track the origin and journey of wheat through the supply chain. This limitation can obscure the source of fraud, compliance issues, or quality concerns.

Data Inconsistencies: When different parties maintain separate records, data discrepancies can arise, leading to conflicting information and errors. These inconsistencies can result in delays and disputes in supply chain operations.

Vulnerability to Fraud: Centralized systems are susceptible to data tampering and fraud. Unauthorized modifications to records and lack of transparency can allow the introduction of counterfeit production, leading to substantial financial losses and damage to brand reputation.

Inefficient Contract Management: Traditional contract management often relies on manual processes, leading to delays and additional administrative burdens. This inefficiency can slow down the overall pace and agility of the supply chain.

Prolonged Settlement Processes: Traditional payment systems, with their numerous intermediaries and extended clearance times, can delay financial transaction settlements. These delays might affect cash flow and the liquidity of the supply chain.

Complex Compliance Procedures: Adhering to regulations and standards can be a cumbersome and time-consuming process, especially when multiple parties have different reporting requirements.

1. Enhancing Transparency and Fraud Prevention in Supply Chains

The global supply chain has long been plagued by inefficiencies, counterfeiting, and a lack of transparency (Almabrok, 2023). Traditional supply chain tracking methods often fail to ensure the authenticity of goods due to information asymmetry and weak enforcement mechanisms. While governments have implemented various enforcement measures to curb counterfeiting, such as border inspections and legal penalties, these efforts have proven insufficient in fully addressing the problem as the impacts of counterfeiting have been increasingly profound on global supply chains (Zelong Yi, 2020). The increasing scale of global trade, complex supply networks, and sophisticated counterfeit techniques make it difficult for authorities to detect and eliminate fraudulent products entirely.

Blockchain technology, when integrated with the Internet of Everything (IoEs), presents a transformational solution to these challenges. By providing decentralized, tamper-proof ledgers, blockchain ensures that every transaction, from manufacturing to retail, is transparently recorded and verifiable. This approach significantly reduces the risk of counterfeit goods infiltrating supply chains and enables consumers to verify product authenticity in real-time. Additionally, IoT-enabled sensors can provide real-time updates on a product's journey, ensuring compliance with storage conditions, transportation protocols, and quality control.

2. Real-time Tracking with IoT Sensors

One of the most critical aspects of supply chain security is ensuring continuous monitoring and traceability of goods as they move through different stakeholders. Traditionally, companies have relied on paper-based records, centralized databases, and RFID tags to track products, but these systems are often vulnerable to tampering, data corruption, or errors.

By integrating IoT sensors with blockchain, companies can create a secure and real-time tracking system that continuously updates the location, status, and environmental conditions of shipments. For example, in pharmaceutical supply chains, IoT temperature sensors can ensure that vaccines or other temperature-sensitive drugs are stored under the required conditions throughout their journey. The data from these sensors is hashed and stored on the blockchain, preventing any unauthorized modifications.

- **Location Tracking:** GPS-enabled IoT devices record precise shipment locations, ensuring real-time visibility of product movement.
- **Environmental Monitoring**: Sensors track temperature, humidity, and exposure to external contaminants, ensuring product quality is maintained.
- **Tamper Detection:** Blockchain-based smart contracts alert stakeholders if unauthorized access or deviations occur during transportation.

IoT-powered blockchain systems, in a nutshell enable manufacturers, distributors, and retailers to eliminate information asymmetry (Moulding, R., 2019) ensuring that all parties involved in the supply chain have access to real-time, verifiable data.

3. Blockchain's Role in Eliminating Counterfeit Goods

Counterfeiting is a multi-billion-dollar problem that affects industries ranging from luxury fashion and electronics to pharmaceuticals and food products. The intrinsic value of brand names creates incentives for counterfeiters to produce fake goods that closely resemble authentic products. In many cases, consumers unknowingly purchase counterfeit products due to a lack of transparency and verifiable product information.

Despite government crackdowns on counterfeit markets, counterfeiting persists because:

- Weak government enforcement in certain regions allows counterfeiters to operate with minimal consequences (Carsten Fink, 2016).
- Consumers often struggle to distinguish between authentic and fake products due to information asymmetry.
- Current authentication methods, such as RFID tags, can be tampered with or copied, making them unreliable.

Blockchain disrupts this landscape by offering immutable, tamper-proof product authentication mechanisms (Hubert Pun). Companies can issue unique digital certificates or QR codes linked to blockchain records, ensuring that only genuine products are recorded on the ledger. Consumers can scan a product's blockchain-verified QR code at the point of sale (Jiang et. Al, 2023) to check its origin, manufacturing details, and distribution history.

Brands such as Prada, LVMH, and Cartier have launched the AURA blockchain to authenticate luxury products (Kshetri, 2024). Consumers can verify the entire history of a handbag or watch simply by scanning a QR code. Pharmaceutical companies leverage blockchain to prevent counterfeit drugs from entering the supply chain. Pfizer and Moderna use blockchain-based track-and-trace solutions to ensure COVID-19 vaccines are not tampered with during distribution. Anita, N., 2022 proposed an anonymous anti-counterfeit system whereas Pham et al., (2019) has proposed an Ethereum based anti-counterfeit supply chain framework shown in Figure 1 as follows:

Figure 1. Overview of a proposed anti-counterfeit system based on Ethereum

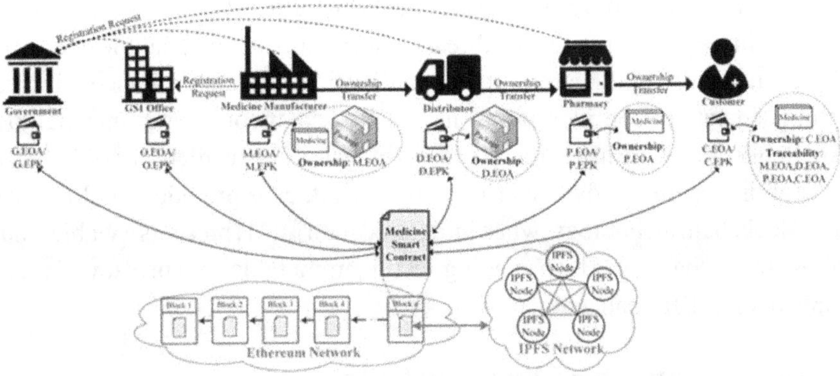

4. Smart Contracts for Secure Access Control in Supply Chains

One of the biggest security concerns in supply chains is unauthorized access to sensitive products and transaction data (Hassjia, 2020). Traditional access control mechanisms rely on centralized databases, which are vulnerable to hacking, insider threats, and data leaks. Blockchain-based smart contracts once deployed, offer an innovative approach to managing secure and decentralized access control in supply chain networks (Hassan et al., 2023).

Smart contracts enable:

- **Automated Role-Based Access Control (RBAC):** Stakeholders such as manufacturers, distributors, retailers, and regulators receive customized access permissions based on their role in the supply chain (S. Tiwari, 2023).
- **Tamper-Proof Transaction Logs:** Each interaction, whether it's a shipment update, product verification, or quality inspection, is securely recorded on the blockchain and cannot be altered retroactively.
- **Fraud Prevention via Automated Authentication:** Only authorized supply chain participants can issue product updates, reducing the risk of counterfeit infiltration.

Blockchain and IoEs in Healthcare

The healthcare industry is undergoing an increase in amounts of health data and venture capital, with connected medical devices, electronic health records (EHRs), and telemedicine platforms becoming integral to patient care (Hermes, S, 2020). The Internet of Healthcare Things (IoHT) plays a crucial role in enabling real-time patient monitoring, automated diagnostics, and secure data sharing. However, the sensitive nature of health data, combined with the increasing use of IoHT devices, makes the industry highly vulnerable to cyber threats, data breaches, and unauthorized access.

Cyberattacks on healthcare systems can have severe consequences, including compromised patient confidentiality, altered medical records, and financial losses. The challenge lies in ensuring the security, integrity, and availability of health data while enabling seamless data sharing across healthcare providers and regulatory bodies. Blockchain technology, when integrated with IoHT, presents a viable solution to address these challenges by providing secure, immutable, and privacy-preserving mechanisms for data management.

2. Blockchain and IoHT Integration for Secure Health Data Management

Previously the data in healthcare ecosystems was being kept in relational databases and dealt with Structured Query Language. But such centralized systems have shortcomings that can be overcome using decentralized systems (Kuo, TT, 2017). The integration of blockchain and IoHT in healthcare introduces a decentralized framework that enhances data security, provenance, and real-time decision-making. This approach ensures that sensitive medical data is securely stored, shared, and verified without compromising patient privacy (Singh, S., 2021). Key benefits of blockchain-IoHT integration in healthcare include:

- **Immutability and Data Provenance**: Goel, U., Ruhl, R., & Zavarsky, P. (2019) discuss that blockchain ensures that patient records remain tamper-proof, preserving a transparent and verifiable history of medical data transactions.
- **Decentralized Access Control**: Smart contracts define role-based permissions for healthcare providers, patients, and regulatory authorities, ensuring that only authorized users can access sensitive health records.
- **Privacy-Preserving Data Sharing**: Off-chain storage mechanisms, combined with homomorphic encryption and differential privacy techniques, enable secure data sharing while protecting patient confidentiality.

3. Blockchain-IoHT Applications in Healthcare

A. Secure Electronic Health Records (EHRs)

Traditional centralized healthcare systems rely on cloud-based or on-premises storage for managing patient records (Boppana, 2019). These systems are vulnerable to hacking, insider threats, and single points of failure. Blockchain-based decentralized EHRs allow patients and healthcare providers to securely access medical history while preventing unauthorized modifications or tampering.

In blockchain-integrated healthcare systems:

- IoHT devices (e.g., wearable health trackers, smart diagnostic tools) collect patient vitals in real time.
- The data is securely encrypted and stored off-chain, with blockchain storing hash-based references to ensure tamper-proof provenance. (Rahman, M., 2020)
- Smart contracts enable secure access control, allowing doctors, researchers, and insurers to access data with patient consent.

B. COVID-19 Monitoring and Health Status Verification

The COVID-19 pandemic underscored the need for secure health status tracking systems that maintain patient privacy (Małagocka, K. 2024), while enabling efficient contact tracing and symptom monitoring (Khurshid A, 2020) In response, blockchain-based health credentialing systems were developed to ensure that COVID-19 test results, vaccination records, and health status information could be securely shared.

Figure 2. IOHT based health status verification system

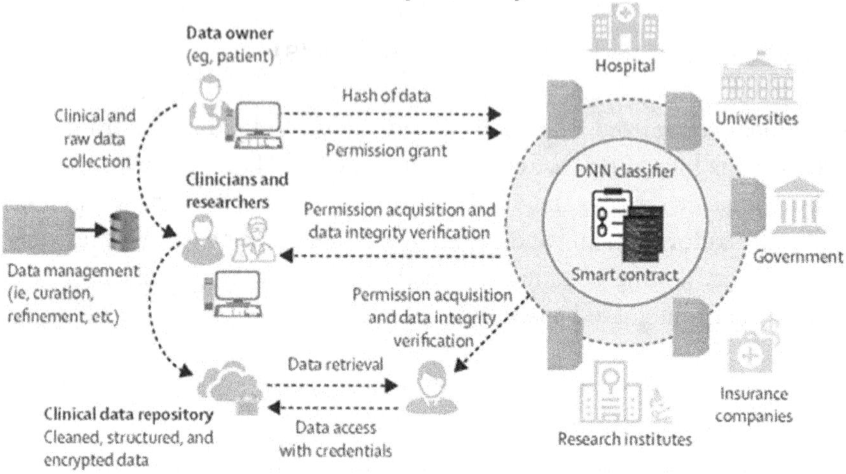

An example of a blockchain-IoHT-based health status verification system (Ng, W. Y., Tan, T.-E., 2021) operates as follows:

- IoHT sensors collect COVID-19-related health data (e.g., temperature, oxygen levels) from wearable devices and edge nodes.
- The data is processed at the edge, encrypted, and stored in a decentralized format to prevent unauthorized access.
- A medical authority dApp generates a QR code-based health profile for each individual, allowing secure verification at public venues without exposing personal health data.
- The system enables biometric authentication (e.g., facial recognition) for verifying health status while preventing identity fraud.

C. Counterfeit Drug Prevention and Supply Chain Transparency

The pharmaceutical industry faces a rising threat of counterfeit drugs, which pose significant risks to patient health and safety. Blockchain-IoHT solutions provide end-to-end traceability for the pharmaceutical supply chain, ensuring that only authenticated drugs reach consumers (Sharma, N, 2024).

A blockchain-powered drug supply chain system works by:

- Assigning unique digital identifiers to pharmaceutical batches.
- Tracking drug movement through IoHT-enabled logistics sensors to verify storage conditions (e.g., temperature, humidity).

- Recording each transaction (manufacturing, distribution, retail) on an immutable blockchain ledger.
- Enabling instant verification of a drug's authenticity through blockchain-backed scanning systems at pharmacies and hospitals (Pawar, V, 2023).

This solution reduces the risk of counterfeit drugs, enhances compliance with regulatory standards, and improves patient safety.

D. Federated Learning and Blockchain for Secure Medical AI

AI-powered diagnostic tools and predictive healthcare models rely on vast amounts of patient data for training. However, sharing raw medical data with centralized AI models introduces privacy risks and regulatory concerns. Federated Learning (FL), combined with blockchain, enables privacy-preserving AI model training across multiple healthcare institutions without exposing sensitive data.

- IoHT edge devices locally train AI models on private patient data, instead of transmitting data to central servers.
- The aggregated model updates (instead of raw data) are shared via a permissioned blockchain network, ensuring data provenance and integrity.
- Secure enclave computing environments (e.g., Intel SGX) further protect model parameters from cyber threats.

4. Cybersecurity Challenges and Solutions in Blockchain-IoHT Healthcare

Key Security Risks in Healthcare IoHT

While blockchain provides enhanced security, several challenges persist in implementing large-scale blockchain-IoHT healthcare systems:

- **Scalability**: Handling vast amounts of real-time health data from millions of IoHT devices poses challenges for blockchain networks.
- **Regulatory Compliance**: Adhering to HIPAA, GDPR, and other data privacy regulations requires careful implementation of role-based access controls.
- **Computational Overhead**: Blockchain-based encryption and consensus mechanisms must be optimized to prevent delays in real-time healthcare monitoring.

- **Hybrid Blockchain Architectures**: Combining on-chain smart contract execution with off-chain secure data storage (e.g., IPFS) improves scalability and efficiency.
- **Zero-Knowledge Proofs (ZKPs) and Homomorphic Encryption**: These cryptographic techniques enable secure multi-party computations without exposing raw health data.
- **AI-Driven Threat Detection**: Federated learning-based security models help detect anomalous activity and cyber threats in healthcare networks without violating patient privacy.

5. Future Outlook

Blockchain-IoHT integration is revolutionizing healthcare security, patient data management, and medical AI applications. By ensuring data integrity, privacy, and accessibility, blockchain facilitates trusted healthcare ecosystems while addressing security vulnerabilities.

Future advancements in Layer-2 blockchain scaling, quantum-safe cryptography, and AI-driven anomaly detection will further enhance the security of IoHT-driven healthcare solutions. As adoption grows, these technologies will play a crucial role in shaping the next generation of secure, patient-centric healthcare systems.

SMART MANUFACTURING WITH BLOCKCHAIN AND IOE

Industry 4.0 represents a change from the centralized scheduled manufacturing to a dynamic and decentralized one, to improve the product quality, individualization, and system flexibility (A. Zarreh, 2020). The shift therefore from a traditional manufacturing process into an interconnected ecosystem involves IoT-enabled smart factories that leverage the power of real-time data to attain improved decision-making and operational efficiency. However, in order to achieve that, conventional centralized systems fall short owing to their security vulnerabilities, data silos, and inefficient resource allocation. Therefore, an integration of Blockchain and the Internet of Everything (IoE) comes forth as a promise of a decentralized, secure, and transparent solution to address these challenges ubiquitous to conventional systems, ensuring data integrity, automation, and trust in manufacturing processes.

1. Eliminating Data Silos and Improving Quality Control

One of the biggest hurdles in smart manufacturing is the lack of interoperability between different systems, leading to fragmented data storage across multiple platforms. Manufacturers often struggle to synchronize data across supply chains, production lines, and quality control units. Blockchain offers a tamper-proof distributed ledger that ensures all stakeholders, including suppliers, manufacturers, and logistics providers, have access to verified real-time data.

For instance, a smart automotive assembly plant implementing blockchain-based data sharing can significantly reduce defects by ensuring every part is authentically sourced and meets compliance standards. If a batch of faulty sensors is identified, blockchain allows for immediate tracking of affected vehicles, ensuring faster recalls and minimizing risks.

2. IoT Sensors for Equipment Monitoring

IoT sensors play a crucial role in predictive maintenance by monitoring industrial machines in real time. Traditional maintenance approaches are often reactive, leading to unexpected breakdowns, costly downtime, and inefficient resource allocation. By integrating IoT with blockchain, manufacturers can achieve secure and immutable logging of machine health data, allowing predictive analytics to optimize performance.

Consider a steel manufacturing plant where IoT sensors are installed on heat-treatment furnaces to monitor temperature, pressure, and wear-and-tear. The sensor data is recorded on the blockchain, ensuring real-time access and transparency across different departments. If an anomaly is detected, smart contracts automatically schedule maintenance before a critical failure occurs, preventing downtime and financial losses.

3. Blockchain-Based Compliance and Maintenance Logs

Compliance with safety and regulatory standards is essential in industries such as aerospace, pharmaceuticals, and food manufacturing. Blockchain-based compliance frameworks ensure that regulatory bodies, auditors, and manufacturers have immutable records of machine performance, safety inspections, and material certifications.

For example, in pharmaceutical manufacturing, IoT sensors track environmental conditions (e.g., temperature, humidity) in drug storage facilities. The recorded data is stored on the blockchain, ensuring that any tampering attempt is immediately detected and flagged. This enhances regulatory compliance and minimizes the risk of counterfeit drugs entering the market.

Similarly, in aircraft manufacturing, blockchain ensures that each component's quality checks, certifications, and maintenance logs are securely stored, preventing fraudulent alterations and enhancing aviation safety.

4. Example: Optimizing Car Manufacturing with Blockchain and IoT

A real-world example of blockchain and IoT in action is seen in car manufacturing. Companies like BMW and Tesla have started using blockchain-secured smart contracts to improve efficiency in their supply chains and production processes. Shahbazi and Byun (2021) have proposed a Smart Manufacturing Real-Time Analysis and utilized Blockhain and cloud in the demonstrated prototype.

Figure 3. Proposed smart integrated system

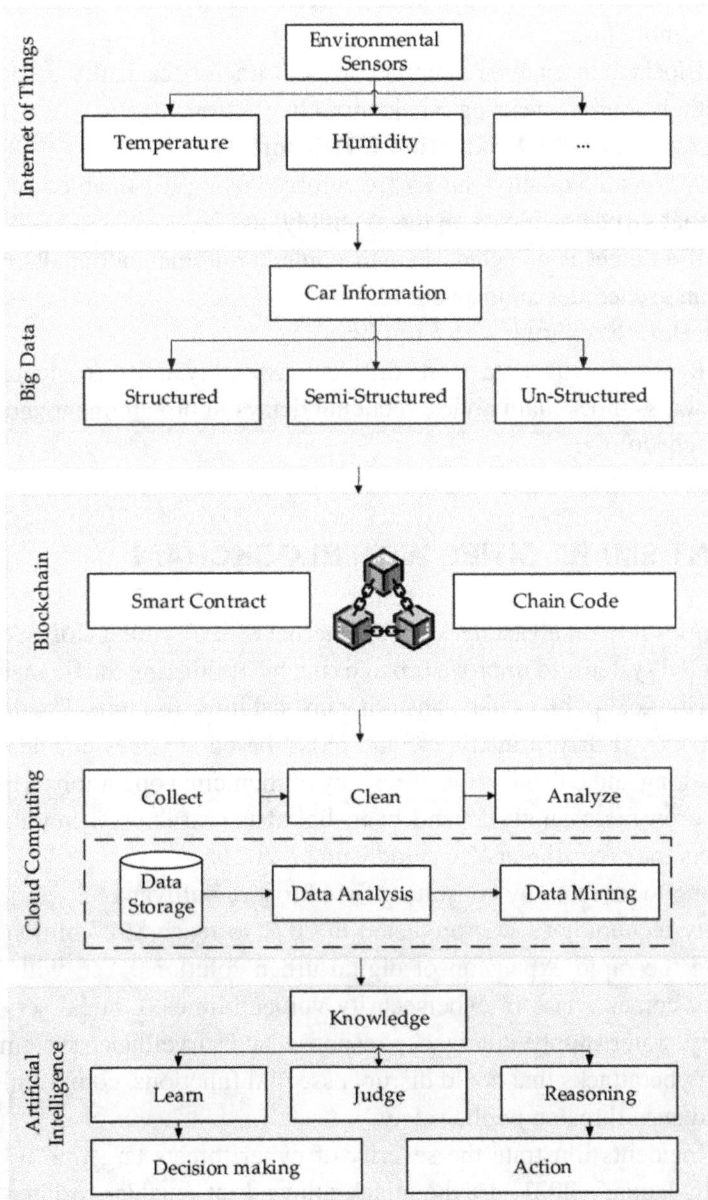

1. **Component Tracking & Authentication**:

- Each car component (batteries, sensors, tires) is assigned a unique blockchain record, preventing counterfeit parts from entering the assembly line.
- Blockchain enables manufacturers to trace back faulty components to their source, ensuring quick corrective action.

2. **Smart Contracts for Production Efficiency**:
   - Automated quality checks are enforced using IoT-enabled robotic arms that inspect vehicles on the assembly line.
   - If a defect is detected, a smart contract automatically halts production and schedules an inspection.
3. **Secure Data Exchange with Suppliers**:
   - Real-time IoT data from different assembly units is securely shared across blockchain nodes, reducing delays in procurement and assembly scheduling.

EFFICIENT SMART CITIES WITH BLOCKCHAIN

Smart cities rely on a vast network of Internet of Everything (IoE) devices and interconnected systems to improve urban living by optimizing traffic management, energy distribution, public safety, and other critical infrastructure. The deployment of IoT sensors, AI-driven analytics, and cloud-based services enables real-time decision-making and enhances the efficiency of municipal operations. However, as these cities grow increasingly dependent on digital infrastructures, they also become prime targets for cyber threats (Aravind Kumar, 2021).

According to research by consulting firm Frost & Sullivan in 2020, investment in smart city technologies was projected in 2021 to reach $327 billion by 2025, highlighting the rapid expansion of digital urban solutions. Yet, with increased connectivity comes a rise in cybersecurity vulnerabilities. Critical services such as electricity, water supply, emergency response, and surveillance systems are susceptible to cyberattacks that could disrupt essential functions, compromise citizen privacy, and even threaten public safety.

Recent incidents illustrate the severity of cyber threats targeting urban infrastructure. In January 2021, a cyberattack allowed an outsider to alter chemical concentrations in a local water supply system, posing a significant public health risk. Additionally, ransomware attacks have locked city staff out of essential municipal networks, effectively halting operations until payments were made to restore access. As cities continue integrating digital technologies, the urgency to develop robust cybersecurity frameworks cannot be overstated.

1. Role of Blockchain and IoEs in Smart Cities

To address these vulnerabilities, integrating blockchain technology with IoEs offers a promising solution. Blockchain's decentralized, immutable, and transparent nature ensures that data integrity is maintained across smart city infrastructures. By eliminating single points of failure and enhancing access control mechanisms, blockchain strengthens cybersecurity while enabling secure and efficient urban services.

Key benefits of blockchain-IoE integration in smart cities include:

- **Immutable Data Storage**: Prevents unauthorized modifications to critical records such as traffic management logs, energy consumption reports, and public safety data.
- **Decentralized Identity Management**: Eliminates reliance on centralized authentication systems, reducing the risk of data breaches and identity fraud.
- **Secure Data Sharing:** Blockchain enables privacy-preserving data exchange among government agencies, ensuring sensitive information is protected from unauthorized access or manipulation.

By leveraging these properties, smart cities can enhance operational resilience while safeguarding against cyber threats that could compromise essential services.

2. Critical Applications of Blockchain-IoE in Smart Cities

A. Traffic Management and Smart Infrastructure

Modern cities face increasing challenges in managing traffic congestion, public transportation efficiency, and road safety. IoE-enabled sensors embedded in roadways and traffic lights generate real-time data on vehicle movement, congestion levels, and accident-prone areas. However, without proper security mechanisms, these systems are vulnerable to attacks that could manipulate traffic signals or disable monitoring functions.

Blockchain integration provides tamper-proof logging of traffic data, ensuring that real-time updates remain accurate and unaltered. Smart contracts enable automated, decentralized control of traffic signals, optimizing urban mobility without relying on centralized authorities that could be compromised. Additionally, blockchain-powered toll systems allow for fraud-free, automated transactions, reducing the risk of financial exploitation.

B. Secure Energy and Water Management

Smart grids and IoT-enabled water distribution networks are essential for sustainable resource management in modern cities. However, cyberattacks targeting these systems could lead to widespread power outages, water contamination, or manipulated billing records.

Blockchain's immutable ledger and decentralized structure ensure that energy distribution records remain tamper-proof, preventing malicious actors from altering grid parameters. IoE sensors integrated with blockchain can detect anomalies in water quality, leakages, and unauthorized access, allowing authorities to respond proactively to potential threats. Additionally, blockchain-based tokenized energy credits incentivize renewable energy adoption, enabling citizens and businesses to trade surplus energy securely.

C. Surveillance and Public Safety

Public surveillance systems, including CCTV cameras, biometric access controls, and emergency alert mechanisms, are critical for maintaining urban security. However, these systems are also susceptible to cyberattacks that could compromise video footage, disable emergency response systems, or manipulate security alerts.

Figure 4. Threat model in smart public safety system

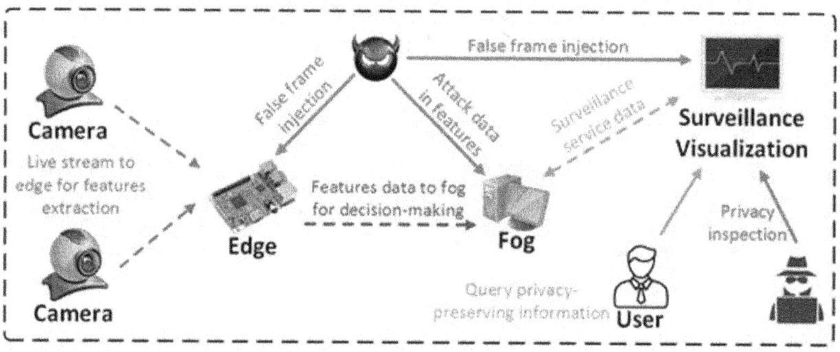

Xu et al., (2020) has provided a Threat model in smart public safety system in Figure 4. Blockchain-integrated IoE solutions enhance surveillance security by ensuring tamper-proof storage of video recordings. In the event of a cyberattack, blockchain-based forensic logs enable rapid identification of breaches, ensuring swift countermeasures. Smart contract-powered emergency response systems prevent false alerts and unauthorized overrides, ensuring only verified signals trigger citywide security responses.

3. Key Cybersecurity Threats in Smart Cities

While blockchain and IoEs offer transformative benefits, several cybersecurity risks still pose challenges to their widespread adoption. The most pressing threats include:

- **Ransomware Attacks:** Cybercriminals can infiltrate municipal databases, encrypt vital information, and demand ransoms, disrupting critical services.
- **IoT-Based DDoS Attacks:** Malicious actors can exploit IoT devices in smart cities to overwhelm municipal servers, causing system failures.
- **Insider and Nation-State Threats:** Disruptions to traffic signals, power grids, and emergency networks could be orchestrated by internal threats or hostile entities, jeopardizing public safety.

Blockchain as a Cybersecurity Solution for Smart cities

By incorporating blockchain security mechanisms, cities can mitigate these risks through:

- **Decentralized Authentication:** Eliminating reliance on single centralized authorities prevents widespread security breaches.
- **Smart Contract-Based Security Policies:** Automated security protocols enforce strict access control, reducing unauthorized system access.
- **Federated Learning for AI-Driven Threat Detection:** Instead of sharing raw data, federated learning allows AI models to analyze cyber threats securely without exposing sensitive information.

4. Future of Decentralization in Smart Cities

The future of smart cities lies in the seamless integration of decentralized technologies, such as blockchain and the Internet of Everything (IoE), to create secure, efficient, and sustainable urban environments. As cities grow smarter and more interconnected, the need for robust, scalable, and transparent systems becomes paramount. A useful method for determining vulnerabilities to online attacks in smart home systems flaws is simulations (Riaz et al., 2024). Most of such flaws can be covered by using decentralized systems. Decentralization offers a transformative approach to addressing these challenges, enabling cities to operate more autonomously while ensuring data integrity, security, and citizen trust. Below, we explore the key trends and innovations shaping the future of decentralization in smart cities. Further research directions must be taken up in different streams under the integration of IoT, Industry 4.0, and smart cities, to explore maximum potential impact of this combination of technologies (Ahmed et al., 2025).

A. Layer-2 Blockchain Scaling Solutions

One of the most significant challenges in implementing blockchain technology in smart cities is scalability. Traditional blockchain networks, such as Ethereum, often face limitations in transaction speed and cost, making them unsuitable for large-scale urban applications. To address this, Layer-2 scaling solutions are emerging as a game-changer. These solutions, including rollups, sidechains, and state channels, operate on top of the main blockchain, enabling faster and cheaper transactions without compromising security.

- **Rollups:** By bundling multiple transactions into a single batch, rollups significantly reduce the load on the main blockchain, enhancing scalability and efficiency.
- Sidechains: Independent blockchains that run parallel to the main chain, sidechains allow for customized solutions tailored to specific smart city applications, such as energy trading or traffic management.
- State Channels: These enable off-chain transactions between parties, reducing congestion on the main blockchain while maintaining security through periodic on-chain settlements.

B. AI-Powered Predictive Analytics

As smart cities become increasingly reliant on data-driven decision-making, the role of artificial intelligence (AI) in enhancing cybersecurity and operational efficiency cannot be overstated. AI-powered predictive analytics will be instrumental in identifying and mitigating cyber threats in real time, ensuring the resilience of smart city infrastructure.

Real-Time Threat Detection: AI algorithms can analyze vast amounts of data from IoE devices to detect anomalies and potential cyberattacks, such as Distributed Denial of Service (DDoS) attacks or data breaches.

Predictive Maintenance: By analyzing data from sensors embedded in urban infrastructure, AI can predict equipment failures or maintenance needs, reducing downtime and costs.

Traffic Optimization: AI can process real-time traffic data to optimize traffic flow, reduce congestion, and improve public transportation efficiency.

C. Cross-Sector Collaborations

The success of decentralized smart cities depends on collaboration between governments, industries, and academia. Cross-sector partnerships will drive the development of standardized security protocols and regulatory frameworks, ensuring interoperability and data security across different systems and applications.

- **Public-Private Partnerships**: Governments and private companies can collaborate to develop and implement decentralized solutions for energy management, waste disposal, and public safety.
- **Academic Research**: Universities and research institutions can contribute by exploring innovative applications of blockchain and IoE, such as privacy-preserving technologies and quantum-resistant cryptography.
- **Global Standards:** International organizations can play a key role in establishing global standards for decentralized systems, ensuring consistency and security across borders.

D. Decentralized Energy Management

One of the most promising applications of decentralization in smart cities is peer-to-peer (P2P) energy trading. Blockchain enables residents to buy and sell renewable energy generated by solar panels or wind turbines, creating a decentralized energy grid.

Energy Efficiency: IoE devices monitor energy consumption in real time, optimizing distribution and reducing waste.

Empowering Consumers: Decentralized energy systems give consumers greater control over their energy usage and costs, promoting sustainability.

Resilience: A decentralized energy grid is less vulnerable to single points of failure, ensuring a more resilient power supply. As renewable energy adoption grows, decentralized energy management will play a crucial role in creating sustainable and self-sufficient smart cities.

E. Privacy-Preserving Technologies

As smart cities collect and process vast amounts of data, ensuring citizen privacy is a top priority. Decentralized technologies, combined with privacy-preserving techniques, can address these concerns.

Zero-Knowledge Proofs: These cryptographic techniques allow data to be verified without revealing the underlying information, ensuring privacy while maintaining transparency.

Federated Learning: This AI approach enables devices to collaboratively learn from data without sharing it, protecting user privacy.

F. Intelligent Transportation Systems

Decentralization will revolutionize urban transportation by enabling intelligent transportation systems (ITS) that are secure, efficient, and autonomous.

- **Vehicle-to-Everything (V2X) Communication:** Blockchain ensures secure communication between vehicles, infrastructure, and pedestrians, reducing accidents and improving traffic flow.
- **Autonomous Vehicles:** Decentralized systems can facilitate the safe operation of autonomous vehicles by providing real-time data on road conditions and traffic.
- **Smart Parking:** IoE sensors and blockchain can optimize parking space allocation, reducing congestion and emissions.

Security, Compliance, and Automation Benefits

When it comes to integrating blockchain technology and the Internet of Everything (IoE) into industries like supply chains, healthcare, manufacturing, and smart cities, the benefits are hard to ignore. These technologies don't just add a layer of efficiency, they fundamentally change how we think about security, compliance, and automation. Let's break it down.

A. Immutability, Decentralization, and Fraud Prevention

One of the primary features of blockchain is its immutability. Once data is recorded on the blockchain, it has no room for edits, no deletions at any user's behest. Hence, the immutability alone makes blockchain a game-changer for industries where trust and transparency are not negotiable.

- **Immutability:** In a supply chain system where every step—from raw materials to the finished product—is recorded on a blockchain. No one can tamper with the data, which means no hidden errors will go unrecognized because of a digital paper trail that can't be shredded.
- **Decentralization:** Unlike traditional systems where one entity holds all the power, blockchain spreads control across a network. This makes it hard for bad actors to manipulate the system. If one node goes down or gets hacked,

the rest of the network remains operational without fail or compromise on credibility.

- **Fraud Prevention:** In most pharmaceuticals, for example, counterfeit drugs are a massive problem, but blockchain can track every pill from the factory to the pharmacy. If something in the records shows any discrepancy, it's easy to figure out immediately owing to the decentralized nature of the system.

B. Smart Contracts utility for regulatory compliance

If blockchain serves as the backbone of a digital system, smart contracts are the muscles. These acts as self-executing code automate processes, ensure there's no middlemen, and make sure every stakeholder acts according to the rules laid in the contract.

- **Automated Transactions:** If a shipment of goods arrives at its destination, and the payment is automatically released. The principle of no invoices, no delays, and no arguments makes the utility of smart contracts in supply chains very powerful.
- **Conditional Logic:** In healthcare, smart contracts can ensure patient data is only shared when specific conditions are met, for instance, getting the patient's consent. It's not only efficient but also ethical.
- **Streamlined Processes:** In manufacturing, smart contracts can handle every part of the process from inventory management to quality control. If a machine breaks down, the system can automatically order replacement parts.

C. Simplified Audits and Regulatory Compliance

Compliance is a huge problem even if regulations are put in place by governing bodies. But blockchain makes it relatively less difficult to execute by providing a transparent, auditable record of every transaction.

- **Transparent Records:** Auditors love blockchain because it gives them a clear, real-time view of what's happening. No more digging through piles of paperwork or chasing down missing documents. Everything is right there, on the ledger.
- **Automated Reporting:** Smart contracts can generate reports for regulators automatically. This facility of automation in reporting not only saves user's time but also reduces the risk of human error.

- **Data Integrity:** In industries like healthcare, where regulations like GDPR and HIPAA are strict, blockchain ensures that patient data is accurate and secure. It's a win-win for businesses and regulators.

D. Enhanced Cybersecurity

In a world where cyberattacks are becoming more sophisticated, blockchain and IoE offer a much-needed layer of protection.

- **Secure Data Sharing:** IoE devices generate tons of data in small periods of time, and blockchain ensures that it's shared securely.
- **Encryption:** Every piece of data on the blockchain is encrypted, making it virtually impossible for unauthorized users to access it.
- **Decentralized Identity (DID):** With blockchain-based identity systems, users have control over their personal data. This reduces the risk of identity theft and gives people peace of mind.

E. **Real-Time Monitoring and Alerts**

One of the prominent benefits of combining blockchain and IoE is the ability to monitor systems in real time. Here's how it's beneficial for your operations:

- Supply Chain Monitoring: Sensors can detect if a shipment of food is getting too warm or if a package has been opened. If something's wrong, the system sends an alert immediately.
- Healthcare Monitoring: Wearable devices can track a patient's vital signs and notify doctors if something seems off. It's proactive healthcare at its best.
- Manufacturing Quality Control: If a machine starts acting up, sensors can flag the issue before it causes a breakdown. This not only saves time but also prevents costly delays.

F. Cost Efficiency and Operational Excellence

At the end of the day, businesses want to save money and run smoothly. Blockchain and IoE deliver on both fronts.

- **Reduced Fraud:** By preventing fraud, organizations can avoid financial losses and protect their reputation. It's like having an insurance policy that actually works.

- **Lower Administrative Costs:** Smart contracts cut out the middleman, reducing paperwork and administrative overhead. It's efficiency without the hassle.
- **Improved Efficiency:** Real-time monitoring and automated processes mean fewer mistakes and faster operations. It's like upgrading from a bicycle to a sports car.

CHALLENGES AND FUTURE DIRECTIONS

The integration of Blockchain and the Internet of Everything (IoEs) across industries has demonstrated significant potential in enhancing security, transparency, and operational efficiency. However, despite these advantages, several key challenges persist that hinder their widespread adoption. Addressing these issues requires technological advancements, regulatory adaptations, and cost-effective solutions. This section explores the major challenges faced in implementing Blockchain and IoEs, followed by a discussion on emerging solutions that aim to improve scalability, reduce costs, and facilitate smoother integration into existing industrial frameworks.

1. Scalability, Operational Costs, and Regulatory Concerns

A. Scalability and Performance Bottlenecks

One of the primary challenges in blockchain adoption is scalability. Public blockchains, such as Ethereum and Bitcoin, face high transaction processing times and network congestion due to their reliance on consensus mechanisms like Proof-of-Work (PoW) or Proof-of-Stake (PoS). In large-scale industrial applications, such as real-time supply chain tracking or smart city infrastructure, the current blockchain framework struggles to handle high transaction volumes efficiently. The computational demands of blockchain networks can also lead to increased latency, making real-time decision-making difficult in IoEs-driven ecosystems.

B. Operational and Implementation Costs

The financial implications of blockchain integration in IoEs remain a significant barrier. High energy consumption, particularly in PoW-based blockchains, contributes to substantial operational costs. Additionally, deploying blockchain infrastructure, including smart contract development, security audits, and maintenance, requires specialized expertise and resources. Small and medium-sized enterprises (SMEs), which could benefit significantly from blockchain-driven automation and security, often lack the financial resources to implement such solutions at scale.

C. Regulatory and Compliance Challenges

Governments and regulatory bodies are still developing legal frameworks to govern blockchain applications across industries. Issues such as data privacy laws (e.g., GDPR), smart contract enforceability, and cross-border digital transactions pose regulatory challenges. In sectors like healthcare and finance, where data confidentiality and regulatory compliance are paramount, blockchain adoption is met with concerns about legal liability and jurisdictional inconsistencies. Without clear, standardized regulations, organizations may be hesitant to fully integrate blockchain and IoEs into their operations.

2. Emerging Solutions: Layer-2 Blockchains and AI-Driven IoEs

To address these challenges, researchers and industry leaders are exploring innovative solutions that enhance blockchain scalability, reduce operational costs, and align with regulatory requirements.

A. Layer-2 Blockchain Solutions for Scalability

Layer-2 scaling solutions, such as Rollups (Optimistic and ZK-Rollups) and state channels, are being developed to improve blockchain throughput without compromising security. These solutions offload transactions from the main blockchain while maintaining decentralization and data integrity, making them well-suited for high-frequency industrial applications. For example, supply chain management systems leveraging Layer-2 networks can execute smart contract-based transactions faster and more cost-effectively than traditional Layer-1 blockchains.

B. AI-Driven IoEs for Cost Optimization

The convergence of Artificial Intelligence (AI) with IoEs is transforming how data is managed in blockchain-powered ecosystems. AI-driven predictive analytics and machine learning algorithms can optimize data verification, transaction processing, and resource allocation, thereby reducing energy and computational costs. For instance, in smart manufacturing, AI-integrated IoEs can predict machine failures, allowing blockchain smart contracts to trigger automated maintenance processes, improving efficiency while minimizing downtime and expenses.

C. Regulatory Sandboxes and Blockchain Governance Models

To navigate regulatory uncertainties, governments and organizations are increasingly adopting regulatory sandboxes—controlled environments where blockchain applications can be tested before large-scale deployment. Additionally, Decentralized Autonomous Organizations (DAOs) and blockchain governance models are being developed to ensure compliance and enhance transparency in decision-making processes. These models offer flexibility for businesses to adapt to regulatory requirements while retaining the benefits of decentralization and automation.

CONCLUSION

Key Findings and Industry Impact

The integration of Blockchain and the Internet of Everything (IoEs) is fundamentally transforming industries by enhancing security, transparency, and operational efficiency. In supply chains, these technologies provide end-to-end traceability, fraud prevention, and automation, significantly reducing counterfeiting risks while ensuring regulatory compliance. The healthcare sector benefits from tamper-proof electronic health records, secure IoT-based patient monitoring, and enhanced drug authentication, addressing data privacy and security concerns. Similarly, in manufacturing, IoT sensors optimize production efficiency by monitoring equipment health in real-time, while blockchain ensures immutable compliance logs and quality control. For smart cities, these technologies enable secure data management, improve cybersecurity frameworks, and support energy-efficient urban systems, strengthening resilience against cyber threats.

Despite these advancements, challenges such as scalability limitations, regulatory concerns, and computational overhead persist. However, emerging solutions, including Layer-2 blockchain protocols, AI-driven automation, and federated learning, are addressing these constraints, paving the way for more scalable and cost-effective adoption across industries.

Adoption Strategies and Future Prospects

To fully realize the potential of Blockchain-IoEs integration, industries must adopt strategic approaches tailored to their specific needs. Ensuring scalability through optimized blockchain architectures, such as hybrid models and sidechains, will be crucial for handling high transaction volumes efficiently. In a few novel cases, Software Defined Networks (SDNs) are being used to fill gaps in IoT architecture implementation, as proposed by Iqbal et al. (2020). Collaboration with policymakers and regulatory bodies is equally important to establish clear legal frameworks and standards that support decentralized systems while maintaining compliance with data privacy regulations. Additionally, fostering interoperability between blockchain and IoT platforms will enable seamless data exchange, reducing fragmentation in industrial ecosystems.

As these technologies continue to evolve, their impact on industries will become more profound. The future of Blockchain-IoEs integration lies in automating industrial operations through smart contracts, enabling secure and decentralized identity management, and leveraging AI for predictive analytics and fraud detection. Furthermore, decentralized energy systems and peer-to-peer energy trading will contribute to more sustainable smart cities, ensuring efficient resource management and enhanced environmental resilience.

The convergence of Blockchain and IoEs represents a transformative shift toward secure, intelligent, and decentralized digital ecosystems. While challenges remain, continuous innovation in scalability, cybersecurity, and regulatory compliance will drive widespread adoption. As industries increasingly rely on these technologies, they will unlock new levels of efficiency, security, and automation, shaping a future where digital trust and operational resilience become the foundation of global industrial systems.

REFERENCES

Ahmed, W., Iqbal, W., Hassan, A., Ahmad, A., Ullah, F., & Srivastava, G. (2025). Elevating e-health excellence with IOTA distributed ledger technology: Sustaining data integrity in next-gen fog-driven systems. *Future Generation Computer Systems*, •••, 107755.

Al-Rakhami, M. S., & Al-Mashari, M. (2021). A blockchain-based trust model for the Internet of Things supply chain management. *Sensors (Basel)*, *21*(5), 1759. Advance online publication. DOI: 10.3390/s21051759 PMID: 33806319

Almabrok, H. A. (2023). Blockchain for Supply Chain Management: To Enhance Transparency, Traceability, and Efficiency. [AJAPAS]. *African Journal of Advanced Pure and Applied Sciences*, 2(4), 239–253.

Anita, N., Vijayalakshmi, M., & Shalinie, S. M. (2022). Blockchain-based anonymous anti-counterfeit supply chain framework. *Sadhana*, *47*(4), 208. DOI: 10.1007/s12046-022-01984-2

Ayub Khan, A., Laghari, A. A., Shaikh, Z. A., Dacko-Pikiewicz, Z., & Kot, S. (2022). Internet of Things (IoT) Security With Blockchain Technology: A State-of-the-Art Review. *IEEE Access : Practical Innovations, Open Solutions*, *10*, 122679–122695. DOI: 10.1109/ACCESS.2022.3223370

Beck, J., Birkel, H., Spieske, A., & Gebhardt, M. (2023). Will the blockchain solve the supply chain resilience challenges? Insights from a systematic literature review. *Computers & Industrial Engineering*, *185*, 109623. Advance online publication. DOI: 10.1016/j.cie.2023.109623

Benton, M. C., Radziwill, N. M., Purritano, A. W., & Gerhart, C. J. (2018). Blockchain for Supply Chain: Improving Transparency and Efficiency Simultaneously. Software Quality Professional, 20(3).

. Blika, A., Palmos, S., Doukas, G., Lamprou, V., Pelekis, S., Kontoulis, M., Ntanos, C., & Askounis, D. (n.d.). *Received XX Month, XXXX; revised XX Month, XXXX; accepted XX Month, XXXX; Date of publication XX Month Federated Learning For Enhanced Cybersecurity And Trustworthiness In 5G and 6G Networks: A Comprehensive Survey*. https://doi.org/DOI: 10.1109/OJCOMS.2024.011100

Bodkhe, U., Tanwar, S., Parekh, K., Khanpara, P., Tyagi, S., Kumar, N., & Alazab, M.et al. (2020). Blockchain for Industry 4.0: A Comprehensive Review. *IEEE Access : Practical Innovations, Open Solutions*, *8*, 79764–79800. DOI: 10.1109/ACCESS.2020.2988579

. Boppana, V. R. (2019). *Cybersecurity Challenges in Cloud Migration for Healthcare*.

Dutta, P., Choi, T.-M., Somani, S., & Butala, R.et al. (2020). Blockchain technology in supply chain operations: Applications, challenges and research opportunities. *Transportation Research Part E, Logistics and Transportation Review*, *142*, 102067. Advance online publication. DOI: 10.1016/j.tre.2020.102067 PMID: 33013183

Fink, C., Maskus, K. E., & Qian, Y. (2016). The Economic Effects of Counterfeiting and Piracy: A Review and Implications for Developing Countries. *The World Bank Research Observer*, *31*(1), 1–28. DOI: 10.1093/wbro/lkv010

Frick, K. T., Abreu, G. M., Malkin, N., Pan, A., & Post, A. E. (2021). The cybersecurity risks of smart city technologies: What do the experts think. White Paper, CLTC White Paper Series; UC Berkeley: Berkeley, CA, USA.

Goel, U., Ruhl, R., & Zavarsky, P. (2019). Using healthcare authority and patient blockchains to develop a tamper-proof record tracking system. *2019 IEEE 5th International Conference on Cloud Computing and Intelligence Systems (CCIS)*, 409–414. https://doi.org/DOI: 10.1109/CCIS48116.2019.9071601

Hasan, H. R., Musamih, A., Salah, K., Jayaraman, R., Omar, M., Arshad, J., & Boscovic, D.et al. (2024). Smart agriculture assurance: IoT and blockchain for trusted sustainable produce. *Computers and Electronics in Agriculture*, *224*, 109184. Advance online publication. DOI: 10.1016/j.compag.2024.109184

Hassan, A., Makhdoom, I., Iqbal, W., Ahmad, A., & Raza, A. (2023). From trust to truth: Advancements in mitigating the blockchain oracle problem. *Journal of Network and Computer Applications*, *217*, 103672. DOI: 10.1016/j.jnca.2023.103672

Hassija, V., Chamola, V., Gupta, V., & Jain, S. (2020). A survey on supply chain security: Application areas, security threats, and solution architectures. *IEEE Internet of Things Journal*.

Iqbal, W., Abbas, H., Daneshmand, M., Rauf, B., & Bangash, Y. A. (2020). An In-Depth Analysis of IoT Security Requirements, Challenges, and Their Countermeasures via Software-Defined Security. *IEEE Internet of Things Journal*, *7*(10), 10250-10276. *Article*, *9099839*. Advance online publication. DOI: 10.1109/JIOT.2020.2997651

Jiang, J. Y., Elmaghraby, W. J., & Moon, K. (2023). An Empirical Study of Blockchain-Driven Transparency in a Consumer Marketplace. *The Wharton School Research Paper*, 1–69.

Jiang, Y., Ma, B., Wang, X., Yu, G., Yu, P., Wang, Z., Ni, W., & Liu, R. P. (2024). Blockchained Federated Learning for Internet of Things: A Comprehensive Survey. *ACM Computing Surveys*, *56*(10), 1–37. Advance online publication. DOI: 10.1145/3659099

Kadadevaramth, R. S., Sharath, D., Ravishankar, B., & Kumar, P. M. (2020, February). A Review and development of research framework on Technological Adoption of Blockchain and IoT in Supply Chain Network Optimization. In *2020 International Conference on Mainstreaming Block Chain Implementation (ICOMBI)* (pp. 1-8). IEEE.

Kalusivalingam, A. K., Sharma, A., Patel, N., & Singh, V. (2021). Enhancing smart city development with ai: Leveraging machine learning algorithms and iot-driven data analytics. *International Journal of Artificial Intelligence and Machine Learning*, *2*(3).

Khurshid, A. (2020). Applying Blockchain Technology to Address the Crisis of Trust During the COVID-19 Pandemic. *JMIR Medical Informatics*, *8*(9), e20477. DOI: 10.2196/20477 PMID: 32903197

Kotel, S., Sbiaa, F., Kamoun, R. M., & Hamel, L.et al. (2023). A blockchain-based approach for secure IoT. *Procedia Computer Science*, *225*, 3876–3886. DOI: 10.1016/j.procs.2023.10.383

Kshetri, N. (2024). *Securing Trust and Exclusivity: The Role of Blockchain in Luxury Brand Strategies*. 1–39.

Kuo, T. T., Kim, H. E., & Ohno-Machado, L. (2017). Blockchain distributed ledger technologies for biomedical and health care applications. *Journal of the American Medical Informatics Association : JAMIA*, *24*(6), 1211–1220. DOI: 10.1093/jamia/ocx068 PMID: 29016974

Leng, J., Ye, S., Zhou, M., Zhao, J. L., Liu, Q., Guo, W., Cao, W., & Fu, L. (2021). Blockchain-Secured Smart Manufacturing in Industry 4.0: A Survey. *IEEE Transactions on Systems, Man, and Cybernetics. Systems*, *51*(1), 237–252. DOI: 10.1109/TSMC.2020.3040789

Madumidha, S. SivaRanjani, P., & Venmuhilan, B. (2023). Integrating Blockchain and IoT in supply chain management: a framework for transparency and traceability. In Research Anthology on Convergence of Blockchain, Internet of Things, and Security (pp. 291-313). IGI Global.

Małagocka, K. (2024). Navigating Digital Privacy and Surveillance: Post-Covid Regulatory and Theoretical Insights. *Politics and Governance*, *12*, 8572. Advance online publication. DOI: 10.17645/pag.8572

Mann, S., Potdar, V., Gajavilli, R. S., & Chandan, A. (2018, December). Blockchain technology for supply chain traceability, transparency and data provenance. In *Proceedings of the 2018 international conference on blockchain technology and application* (pp. 22-26).

Moulding, R. (2019). *The promise of Blockchain and its impact on relationships between actors in the supply chain: A theory-based research framework.*

Ng, W. Y., Tan, T.-E., Movva, P. V. H., Fang, A. H. S., Yeo, K.-K., Ho, D., Foo, F. S. S., Xiao, Z., Sun, K., Wong, T. Y., Sia, A. T.-H., & Ting, D. S. W. (2021). Blockchain applications in health care for COVID-19 and beyond: A systematic review. *The Lancet. Digital Health, 3*(12), e819–e829. DOI: 10.1016/S2589-7500(21)00210-7 PMID: 34654686

Pandey, C. (2020). Scalability challenges and opportunities in blockchain-based systems: A systematic review. [TURCOMAT]. *Turkish Journal of Computer and Mathematics Education, 11*(3), 2022–2031. DOI: 10.17762/turcomat.v11i3.13599

Patel, M., Brahmbhatt, A. B. J. N., & Singh, V. (2023). Blockchain technology in food safety and traceability concern to livestock products. *Heliyon, 9*(6), e16526. Advance online publication. DOI: 10.1016/j.heliyon.2023.e16526 PMID: 37265625

Pawar, V., Manoj, G., Sagar, G. V. A., Abirami, M., Priya, P. S., & Sahoo, A. K. (2023). *Smart distribution network for healthcare goods in hospitals.*

Pham, H. (2018). *The Impact of Blockchain Technology on the Improvement of Food Supply Chain Management: Transparency and Traceability: A Case Study of Walmart and Atria.*

Pun, H., Swaminathan, J. M., & Hou, P. (2024). Blockchain Adoption for Combating Deceptive Counterfeits. *Production and Operations Management, 30*(4), 864–882. Advance online publication. DOI: 10.1111/poms.13348

Rahman, M. A., Hossain, M. S., Islam, M. S., Alrajeh, N. A., & Muhammad, G. (2020). Secure and provenance enhanced Internet of Health Things framework: A blockchain managed federated learning approach. *IEEE Access : Practical Innovations, Open Solutions, 8*, 205071–205087. DOI: 10.1109/ACCESS.2020.3037474 PMID: 34192116

Riaz, A., Iqbal, W., Islam, F. U., Hassan, M., Tariq, R., Chehri, A., & Madni, A. F. (2025). S2H-securing smart homes: A blockchain-based preservation approach. *Internet of Things : Engineering Cyber Physical Human Systems*, •••, 101523.

Sadawi, A., Hassan, M. S., & Ndiaye, M. (2021). A survey on the integration of blockchain with IoT to enhance performance and eliminate challenges. *IEEE Access : Practical Innovations, Open Solutions*, *9*, 54478–54497. DOI: 10.1109/ACCESS.2021.3070555

Saurabh, S., & Dey, K. (2021). Blockchain technology adoption, architecture, and sustainable agri-food supply chains. *Journal of Cleaner Production*, *284*, 124731. Advance online publication. DOI: 10.1016/j.jclepro.2020.124731

Sharma, N., & Rohilla, R. (2024). A multilevel authentication-based blockchain powered medicine anti-counterfeiting for reliable IoT supply chain management. *The Journal of Supercomputing*, *80*(4), 4870–4913. DOI: 10.1007/s11227-023-05654-w

Singh, S., Bhatt, P., Sharma, S. K., & Rabiu, S. (2021). Digital transformation in healthcare: Innovation and technologies. In *Blockchain for Healthcare Systems* (pp. 61–79). CRC Press. DOI: 10.1201/9781003141471-5

Tiwari, S., Sharma, P., Choi, T. M., & Lim, A. (2023). Blockchain and third-party logistics for global supply chain operations: Stakeholders' perspectives and decision roadmap. *Transportation Research Part E, Logistics and Transportation Review*, *170*, 103012.

Treiblmaier, H., & Garaus, M. (2023). Using blockchain to signal quality in the food supply chain: The impact on consumer purchase intentions and the moderating effect of brand familiarity. *International Journal of Information Management*, *68*, 102514. Advance online publication. DOI: 10.1016/j.ijinfomgt.2022.102514

. Xu, R., Nikouei, S. Y., Nagothu, D., Fitwi, A., & Chen, Y. (2020). BlendSPS: A blockchain-enabled decentralized smart public safety system

Yi, Z., Yu, M., & Cheung, K. L. (2020). Impacts of Counterfeiting on a Global Supply Chain. *Manufacturing & Service Operations Management*, *24*(1), 159–178. DOI: 10.1287/msom.2020.0912

Zarreh, A., Wan, H., Lee, Y., Saygin, C., & Janahi, R. A. (2020). Risk assessment for cyber security of manufacturing systems: A game theory approach. *Procedia Manufacturing*, *38*, 605–612. DOI: 10.1016/j.promfg.2020.01.077

Chapter 9
MediBlock:
A Consent-Based EHR Sharing System

Rachana Yogesh Patil
https://orcid.org/0000-0001-9973-6998
Pimpri Chinchwad College of Engineering, India

Yogesh Patil
D.Y. Patil College of Engineering, India

ABSTRACT

Electronic Health Records (EHRs) contain vital patient health information, but their secure and efficient management remains a challenge. Blockchain technology has the potential to resolve these issues by providing a decentralised, secure, and immutable EHR ledger. This paper investigates the use of blockchain for EHR administration and proposes a framework for the implementation of a blockchain-based EHR system. Our proposed architecture consists of a decentralised network of nodes for storing and sharing EHRs, smart contracts for enforcing access control and consent management, and a consensus algorithm for guaranteeing the integrity and validity of the EHRs. We discuss the prospective advantages of using blockchain for EHR administration, such as increased security, privacy, and interoperability, as well as the obstacles that must be overcome to ensure the successful implementation of a blockchain-based EHR system.

DOI: 10.4018/979-8-3373-1424-2.ch009

INTRODUCTION

Electronic Health Records (EHRs) are crucial because they contain vital patient health, medical history, and treatment information. EHRs provide healthcare providers with a comprehensive view of patient health, enabling them to make educated decisions regarding patient treatment, (Ajayi, Abouali, & Saadawi, 2020). EHRs can also aid in reducing medical errors, enhancing patient outcomes, and enhancing healthcare delivery efficiency, (Wang *et al.*, 2019).

Epic is the most popular EHR system in the United States and is utilized by numerous institutions and healthcare systems. It includes clinical documentation, medication administration, order entry, and a patient portal. Cerner is a well-known EHR system that includes order entry, clinical decision support, medication administration, and a patient portal, (Xu *et al.*, 20210. Allscripts is a popular EHR system among small and medium-sized healthcare providers, as it offers electronic prescribing, clinical decision support, and a patient portal. Meditech is a typical EHR system utilized in rural areas, with features including clinical documentation, order input, and patient portal, (Patil, Karati, & Patil, 2024) (Deore *et al.*, 2021). Athenahealth is an EHR system specifically designed for small and medium-sized healthcare providers, offering features such as clinical documentation, order entry, electronic prescribing, and patient portal. All of these EHR systems are user-friendly and can be adapted to meet the specific requirements of healthcare providers, (Sarode *et al.*, 2022). However, they encounter obstacles such as data privacy and security concerns, interoperability issues, and the requirement for ongoing maintenance and support, (Deore *et al.*, 2022).

In this chapter we are trying to propose a system for managing EHR using IPFS, a decentralised database and an access control for the records with patient's consent so that privacy of the patient will be maintained and possibility for information mishandling can be reduced to very low numbers. Blockchain being a decentralized ledger we can add all the information transfers as transactions on a chain to keep records of information sharing. A system where the patient sends access to the doctor while consultation and revoke in between if accepted by mistake. The doctor can upload reports and prescriptions. Access will be revoked after the doctor submits his reports. In this case the doctor will be awarded with a consultation fees.

1.1 Evolution of Blockchain in Healthcare

The journey of blockchain in healthcare has been nothing short of transformative. From its initial conception in cryptocurrency to its application in the medical field, blockchain has gradually carved out a crucial role in securing, sharing, and managing healthcare data.

2015-2016: Early Blockchain Pilots in Healthcare

In the early days, blockchain was mostly theoretical in healthcare, with pilots focusing on securing HER, (Tandon *et al.,* 2020). These early projects aimed to demonstrate blockchain's potential to address longstanding issues of data privacy, security, and ownership. While still in its infancy, these efforts laid the foundation for a future where healthcare data could be shared more securely and efficiently.

2017-2018: Interoperability and Smart Contracts

As the technology matured, the focus shifted to overcoming one of the most significant challenges in healthcare: interoperability. Blockchain made it possible for disparate healthcare systems to securely share patient data across platforms, breaking down data silos, (Patil & Bannore, 20220. Smart contracts, a major breakthrough, automated patient consent processes, allowing individuals to control who accesses their health data. This was a significant leap toward giving patients more control over their healthcare information.

2020: Blockchain in Pandemic Data Sharing

When the COVID-19 pandemic struck, the need for secure, real-time sharing of health data became more urgent than ever. Blockchain stepped in to facilitate the safe exchange of critical information, such as vaccination records and testing results. This period showed the world how blockchain could quickly adapt to unprecedented situations and ensure that sensitive data was protected while enabling global cooperation in managing public health, (Chang & Chen, 2020) (Yadav, Singh, Kushwaha, 2023).

2021-2023: Widespread Adoption and Integration

By 2021, blockchain was no longer just a promising concept but an integral part of healthcare systems worldwide. Its ability to provide secure, real-time access to health records across various institutions improved the efficiency and coordination of care, (Patil & Patil, 2022). Healthcare providers were now able to access critical patient information quickly and securely, which was especially vital in emergencies. Compliance with regulations like HIPAA and GDPR also became seamless, further solidifying blockchain's place in healthcare.

Figure 1. Evolution of blockchain in healthcare

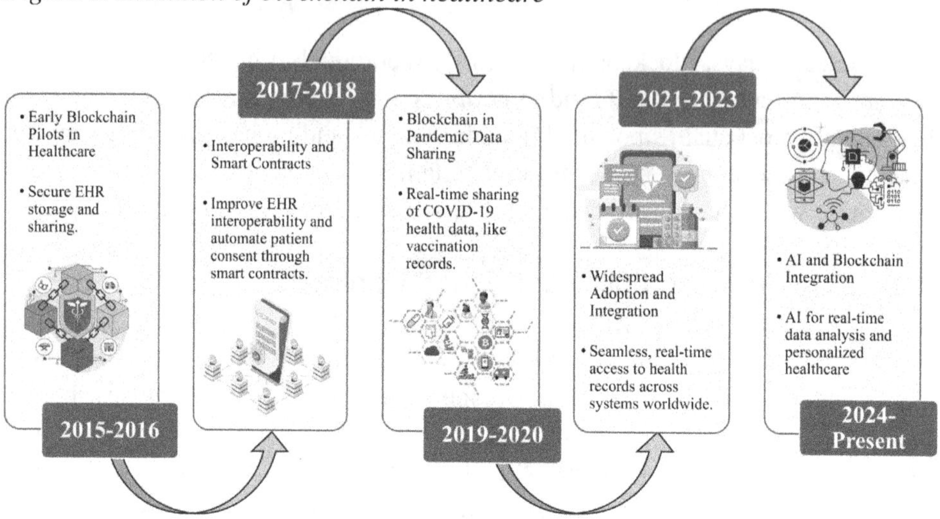

2024-Present: AI and Blockchain Integration

Looking ahead, the integration of blockchain with Artificial Intelligence is poised to revolutionize healthcare further. Blockchain's secure and transparent infrastructure supports AI by providing reliable data for analysis, (Borse *et al.,* 2022). This synergy enables real-time data-driven decisions, allowing healthcare providers to offer more personalized treatment options. By combining the security of blockchain with the predictive capabilities of AI, we are stepping into an era of smarter, more efficient healthcare systems.

Looking at the evolution of blockchain in healthcare as described in Figure 1, it's clear that technology has moved from an experimental phase to becoming a core element of the industry. Each milestone represents a response to real-world challenges be it security, data sharing, or regulatory compliance and each step has brought tangible improvements in the way we handle healthcare data.

What's particularly striking is how quickly blockchain adapted to the global crisis presented by the COVID-19 pandemic, showing its resilience and potential to provide quick, secure solutions when the world needed them most. Now, as blockchain continues to merge with AI, the future of healthcare looks even more promising, with enhanced patient care, personalized medicine, and streamlined operations on the horizon.

2 LITERATURE REVIEW

Electronic health records (EHRs) hold delicate patient data that has to be handled with care to protect privacy and security, (Bannore, Patil, & Devane, 2022). A potential strategy to improve patient control over their health data and safeguard their privacy is consent-based EHR sharing. This study examines the idea of consent-based EHR exchange and emphasizes the contribution of blockchain technology to the creation of a safe and open system, (Patil *et al.*, 2023). With consent-based EHR sharing, patients may directly manage their consent preferences because to blockchain's decentralized and irreversible properties. Patients have the ability to allow or withdraw access to their EHRs for particular healthcare institutions or providers, (Patil, Patil, & Bannore, 2023) (Mahamuni et al., 2022). To enforce consent regulations and ensure that the asking entity has secured the patient's consent before accessing the EHRs, blockchain-based smart contracts are deployed. This strategy guarantees openness, responsibility, and patience.

The authors propose a solution based on blockchain technology to assure the integrity and consistency of shared health data, (Ajayi, Abouali, & Saadawi, 2020). Their solution includes a standard format for exchanging electronic health records (EHRs), the detection of malevolent activities on stored and shared EHRs, and the facilitation of secure EHR exchange between different healthcare systems. The proposed architecture is designed to protect against both external and internal threats and is capable of validating the integrity and consistency of EHR requests and responses. The system retains verified EHRs perpetually in a distributed ledger and securely shares them with other healthcare systems upon request. In addition, the proposed architecture is robust enough to accommodate real-time additions of new healthcare systems to the network.

In research work, (Jaiman & Urovi, 2020), the dynamic consent model for health data sharing using blockchain technology is a promising approach to addressing some of the problems associated with conventional data-sharing methods. This model respects individual consent and ensures accountability for all participants in the data-sharing platform by granting them control over their own data and allowing them to set conditions for its use. The use of blockchain technology offers a secure, decentralized platform for data sharing and permits the maintenance of a transaction history. This implies that all data usage can be monitored, and permission can be modified or removed on demand. Additionally, the model is GDPR-compliant, indicating that it satisfies the requirements of the EU General Data Protection Regulation. The solution can represent and standardize user consent and match it to data requester statement queries by combining two consent representation models. Overall, the dynamic consent model for health data sharing using blockchain technology is a promising solution for assuring data privacy and security and facilitating effective data sharing in the healthcare industry.

TP-HER (Cao *et al.,* 2019) is a secure and attack-resistant administration system for electronic health records (EHR). The system establishes a secure channel between the patient, hospital, and designated physicians using a password-based authentication mechanism. The patient generates warrants to delegate to physicians, which indicates the identities of delegated physicians, their diagnosing period, and other supplementary information. During the course of a patient's treatment, EHRs are generated and incorporated into an Ethereum transaction. In the case of a single doctor, the doctor is responsible for the EHRs she/he generates, whereas in the case of multiple doctors, each doctor is responsible for the EHRs generated by the preceding doctor. Consideration is given to the timeliness of EHRs, and the system utilizes the timestamp of the Ethereum block containing the transaction to ascertain when EHRs were generated. The security of TP-EHR relies heavily on the security of the Ethereum blockchain, and the system implies that an adversary without a significant portion of the network's computational capacity cannot fork Ethereum and therefore cannot compromise TP-security. EHR's Even if the cloud server conspires with a malevolent doctor to tamper with outsourced EHRs, it cannot alter the corresponding Ethereum blockchain transaction.

A blockchain-secured PHR (Rahman *et al.*, 2019) (Personal Health Record) is a patient-centric platform for storing health-related information securely. Using blockchain technology, this method ensures that access to PHR is securely authorized and that all PHR-related actions are transparently recorded on the blockchain. The content of the PHR is stored in an off-chain database, which is more scalable and effective than storing data directly on the blockchain. The blockchain ensures that only authorized users can access PHR and that all PHR-related actions are recorded and tamper-resistant. A blockchain-secured PHR is distinguished by the fact that patients have complete control over who can access their health information. Only with the patient's permission can healthcare professionals' access PHR, ensuring that patients have complete control over their own health information. However, once permission is granted, the healthcare professional is able to view the patient's complete medical record, ensuring that all pertinent information is accessible to provide the best care possible.

Rahman *et al.* (2019) outlines a system for managing electronic medical records securely that combines IPFS and blockchain technologies. The suggested architecture provides a decentralized, unchangeable, and transparent solution to the problems with the integrity and security of information in conventional healthcare systems. The study makes a contribution to the area of handling health care information and offers perceptions into the possibilities of cutting-edge technology for protecting private data.

MedRec focuses on enhancing privacy and security in TMIS (Traditional Medical Information Systems) and e-medical records by utilizing blockchain technology, (Ekblaw *et al.,* 2016). This solution incorporates private and consortium blockchains to ensure secure, scalable medical data sharing. It relies on three-factor authentication, PRE (Proxy Re-encryption), PEKS (Public Key Encryption with Keyword Search), and encryption to secure data access. With permissioned access and PRE for secure third-party sharing, MedRec addresses the challenges of data privacy, immutability, and secure access. Scalability is supported, though it comes with overhead from the encryption mechanisms used.

MeDShare is a blockchain-based solution designed to enable secure and trustless sharing of medical data among cloud service providers, (Xia *et al.,* 2017). It utilizes permissioned blockchain technology, likely leveraging Hyperledger Fabric, to control access to sensitive health data. Smart contracts regulate the sharing of data and enforce access control mechanisms, ensuring that only authorized entities can retrieve and share information. This approach improves scalability through its permissioned design, and the solution focuses on providing privacy, security, and trust among healthcare providers. However, it has limitations related to real-world deployment and blockchain scalability.

Zhang and Lin (2018) proposes a consortium blockchain-based approach for secure and privacy-preserving medical data sharing in e-health systems. It leverages Ethereum-based or similar blockchain platforms for secure data exchange among multiple healthcare institutions. Smart contracts are employed to enforce permissions and control access, ensuring that only authorized parties can access sensitive health data. Consortium design supports scalability, though potential issues such as performance, cost, and privacy concerns related to governance may arise. The focus of this solution is on privacy, security, integrity, and building trust among participants in the healthcare network.

Table 1. Different blockchain types with their platforms and networks

Aspect	(Ajayi et al., 2020)	(Jaiman &Urovi, 2020)	(Cao et al., 2019)	(Rahman et al., 2019)	(Ekblaw et al., 2016)	(Xia et al., 2017)	(Zhang & Lin, 2018)
Objective	Integrity of shared EHRs	Dynamic consent for secure sharing	Attack-resistant EHR administration	Secure patient-centric health storage	Enhance privacy/security in TMIS and e-medical records	Secure and trust-less medical data sharing	Consortium-based secure medical data sharing
Blockchain Type	Consortium	Public	Private	Private	Private & Consortium	Permissioned	Consortium
Platform Used	Hyperledger Fabric	Ethereum	Polkadot	Hyperledger Fabric	Not specified	Hyperledger Fabric (assumed)	Ethereum-based or similar blockchain

continued on following page

Table 1. Continued

Aspect	(Ajayi et al., 2020)	(Jaiman &Urovi, 2020)	(Cao et al., 2019)	(Rahman et al., 2019)	(Ekblaw et al., 2016)	(Xia et al., 2017)	(Zhang & Lin, 2018)
Network	Private Test Network	Ethereum Mainnet	Private Test Network	Not Applicable	Not specified	Theoretical, not deployed	Private consortium network
Security Measures	Protection against internal/ external threats	GDPR compliance, accountability	Prevents attacks using Ethereum's security	Tamper-resistant, authorized access only	Three-factor auth, PRE, PEKS, encryption	Encryption, blockchain for immutability, access control	Encryption, blockchain for immutability, smart contracts
Data Access Control	Secure sharing upon request	Fine-grained consent control	Delegated access via warrants	Patient-authorized access	Permissioned access, PRE for third-party sharing	Smart contracts control data sharing	Smart contracts enforce access permissions
Scalability	Real-time healthcare system additions	Not discussed	Relies on Ethereum scalability	Off-chain database for storage	Scalable with overhead from PRE/PEKS	Improved scalability with permissioned design	Consortium design supports scalability
Advantages	- Perpetual storage - Real-time system addition	- Privacy - Dynamic permissions - Accountability	- Robust security - Scalable	- Patient-centric - Scalable	- Metadata publishing - Trust-less data sharing	Privacy, integrity, trust among providers	Privacy, security, integrity, trust among providers
Limitations	Scalability not addressed	Relies on accurate consent modeling	Heavy reliance on Ethereum's security	Risk of over-disclosure of patient data	Not specified	Real-world deployment issues, blockchain scalability	Potential performance issues, cost, privacy concerns

Recent studies on blockchain-based EHR systems, such as MedRec, MeDShare, and TP-HER, have demonstrated the potential of decentralized platforms in addressing privacy, security, and interoperability challenges in healthcare. MedRec focuses on enhancing privacy through private and consortium blockchains, while MeDShare utilizes permissioned blockchain to enable trust-less sharing of medical data among cloud providers. Similarly, TP-HER employs Ethereum blockchain for secure and attack-resistant EHR management. However, these systems face limitations such as scalability issues, high computational overhead, and restricted dynamic consent mechanisms. By leveraging IPFS for scalable storage and integrating dynamic, GDPR-compliant patient consent models, the proposed MediBlock framework addresses these shortcomings, ensuring enhanced privacy, fine-grained access control, and efficient data sharing across healthcare systems.

Patients have greater power over their medical data by utilizing blockchain technology for permission-based EHR sharing, guaranteeing that their privacy is protected, and that data access only occurs with their explicit authorization, (Patil, Patil, & Bannore, 2024) (Patil, 2024). Both consumers and healthcare providers gain from the EHR sharing process' increased reliability thanks to the blockchain's openness, security, and accountability. While consent-based EHR sharing via blockchain provides considerable benefits in terms of privacy and control, it's crucial to keep in mind that there are still obstacles to be addressed, including scalability, interoperability, and compliance with regulations. In order to realize the full potential of the blockchain technology in healthcare data exchange, ongoing research and development efforts are concentrated on overcoming these difficulties.

3. PROPOSED SYSTEM

The proposed system aims to address the growing need for secure, transparent, and efficient access to EHRs by leveraging blockchain technology and decentralized storage. Traditional methods of storing and sharing health records often raise concerns about data privacy, security, and interoperability between healthcare providers. By integrating blockchain with smart contracts and InterPlanetary File System (IPFS), this system ensures that patient data remains under the patient's control while enabling authorized entities, such as doctors, hospitals, and insurance companies, to securely access health information. The architecture is designed to provide a streamlined process for requesting, granting, and recording consent for accessing health records, ensuring a transparent and tamper-proof system for managing sensitive health data.

Figure 2. Architecture of proposed system

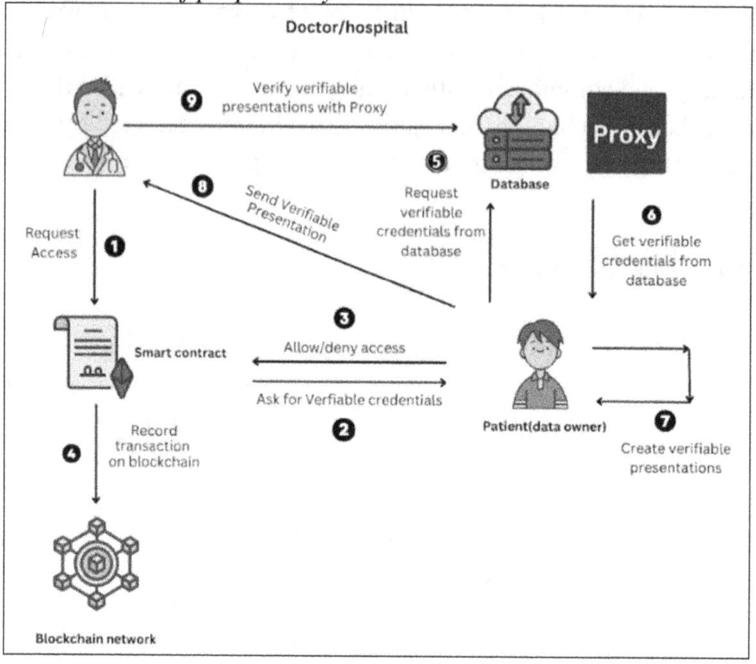

The architecture of the proposed system as described in Figure 2 follows these steps:

- **Request for Data Access:** The concerned doctor, hospital, or insurance company requests access to the patient's health data. This request is made through a smart contract deployed on the blockchain network, ensuring a transparent and secure method of initiating data access.
- **Patient Notification:** Upon receiving the access request, a notification is sent to the patient. This notification includes details about the requestor (doctor, hospital, or insurance company) and their request to access the patient's health records.
- **Patient Consent:** The patient reviews the request and has the option to either allow or deny access to their health records. Once the patient responds, the entire transaction, including the patient's decision, is recorded on the Ethereum blockchain, ensuring an immutable and transparent record of consent.
- **Granting Access:** If the patient grants permission, the requested party is provided with access to the health records. This access is managed securely through the blockchain, ensuring that only authorized entities can view the patient's data.

- **Accessing Health Records:** The requested party can access the health records by using the unique address or ID provided by the patient. This ensures that the specific health record is retrieved, maintaining confidentiality and ensuring the integrity of the data.
- **Decentralized Database via IPFS:** The health records are stored in a decentralized manner using IPFS. Unlike traditional cloud databases that use an address for data retrieval, IPFS uses a Content Identifier (CID) to uniquely identify and locate the data. When the patient receives granted access, they provide the CID to the requesting party. Using this CID, the IPFS server retrieves the specific health record, ensuring data integrity and security.

This system combines blockchain's transparency and security with IPFS's decentralized storage to provide a robust and efficient method for managing patient data access, ensuring that health records are accessed securely with patient consent.

Figure 3. Sequence diagram of the system

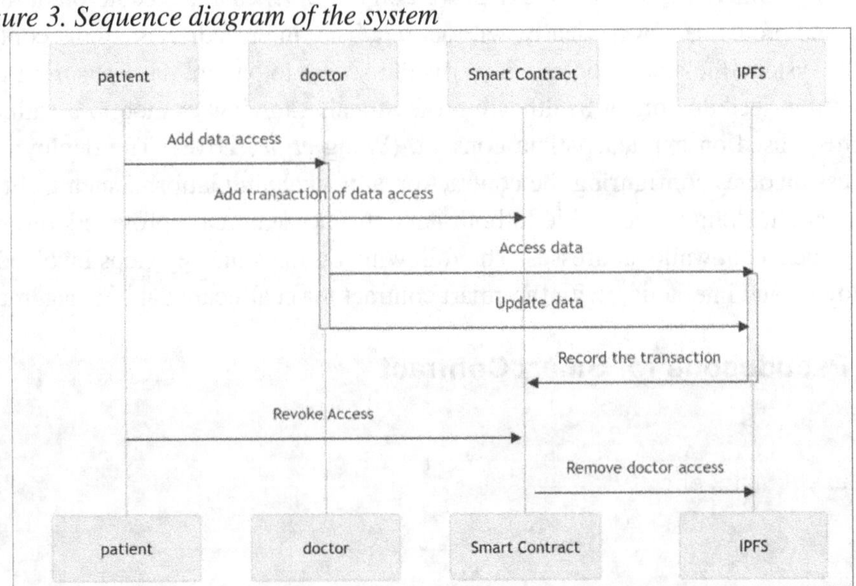

The sequence of the project, as illustrated in Figure 3, follows these steps:

- **Patient Grants Access:** Initially, the patient grants access to their data to the doctor, allowing them to view the necessary health information.
- **Transaction Stored on Blockchain:** A transaction is created and stored on the blockchain, ensuring that the consent and access request are securely recorded.

- **Data Displayed on Doctor's Dashboard:** The patient's health data is retrieved from IPFS and displayed on the doctor's dashboard, making it easily accessible for review and analysis.
- **Doctor Updates Health Records:** The doctor reviews the data and can add additional information regarding the patient's diagnosis or treatment plan into the database, enriching the record with new medical insights.
- **Submission and Revocation of Access:** Once the doctor submits the updated information, access to the data is revoked, ensuring that the doctor no longer has access. Additionally, the doctor is awarded the consultation fees.

4. SMART CONTRACT DEPLOYMENT

The deployment of the smart contract is a crucial step in ensuring that the proposed healthcare data sharing system operates securely and efficiently, (Zou *et al.,* 2019). Smart contracts, once deployed on the blockchain, execute predefined rules and protocols automatically, without requiring intermediaries. In the context of this system, the smart contract governs the access to patient data, ensuring that only authorized doctors or healthcare professionals can view or modify a patient's records, based on explicit patient consent, (Wang *et al.,* 2018). The deployment process involves configuring the contract on a blockchain platform, such as Ethereum, and making it accessible to both patients and healthcare providers through their blockchain wallet addresses. The following outlines the key steps involved in deploying and interacting with the smart contract for healthcare data management.

4.1 Pseudocode for Smart Contract

```
struct Patient {

string name;

uint age;

address[] doctorAccessList;
```

```
string diagnosis;

string record;

}

struct Doctor {

string name;

uint age;

address[] patientDataAccessList;

}

mapping(address => Patient) public patients;

mapping(address => Doctor) public doctors;

function add_user(address user, string memory name, uint
age, string memory role) public {

if (keccak256(abi.encodePacked(role)) == keccak256("doc-
tor")) {

doctors);
```

```
} else if (keccak256(abi.encodePacked(role)) == kec-
cak256("patient")) {

patients, "", "");

}

}

function permit_access(address patient, address doctor) pub-
lic {

patients[patient].doctorAccessList.push(doctor);

doctors[doctor].patientDataAccessList.push(patient);

}

function revoke_access(address patient, address doctor) pub-
lic {

for (uint i = 0; i < patients[patient].doctorAccessList.
length; i++) {

if (patients[patient].doctorAccessList[i] == doctor) {

delete patients[patient].doctorAccessList[i];
```

```
    }

    }

    for (uint j = 0; j < doctors[doctor].patientDataAccessList.
length; j++) {

    if (doctors[doctor].patientDataAccessList[j] == patient) {

    delete doctors[doctor].patientDataAccessList[j];

    }

    }

    }

    function submit_diagnosis(address patient, address doctor,
string memory diagnosis) public {

    patients[patient].diagnosis = diagnosis;

    uint fee = 2 ether; // Example consultation fee

    // Transfer consultation fee from patient to doctor

    payable(doctor).transfer(fee);
```

```
}

function get_hash(address patient) public view returns
(string memory) {

return patients[patient].record;

}

function set_hash(address patient, string memory hash) pub-
lic {

patients[patient].record = hash;

}
```

The smart contract consists of two primary structs: Patient and Doctor, which are designed to store relevant details about the patients and healthcare professionals involved in the system. Mappings are used to associate user addresses (from their Metamask wallets) with the corresponding Patient and Doctor structs, ensuring that the smart contract can efficiently track access rights and interactions.

4.2 Functions of the Smart Contract

- **add_user(address user, string memory name, uint age, string memory role):** Registers a user (either a doctor or a patient) based on the specified **role**. The appropriate struct (either Patient or Doctor) is populated with the user's name, age, and other relevant details.
- **permit_access(address patient, address doctor):** Allows the patient to grant access to their health records to a specific doctor. This function adds the doctor's address to the doctorAccessList in the Patient struct and adds the patient's address to the patientDataAccessList in the Doctor struct.
- **revoke_access(address patient, address doctor):** Allows the patient to revoke access to their data from a specific doctor. This function removes the

doctor's address from the doctorAccessList in the Patient struct and removes the patient's address from the patientDataAccessList in the Doctor struct.

- **submit_diagnosis(address patient, address doctor, string memory diagnosis):** Enables a doctor to submit a diagnosis for a specific patient. Upon submission, a consultation fee (e.g., 2 ether) is transferred from the patient's account to the doctor's account as compensation for the consultation.
- **get_hash(address patient):** Retrieves the IPFS hash of the patient's data, which is stored in the record field of the Patient struct. This hash points to the actual health data stored on the decentralized IPFS network.
- **set_hash(address patient, string memory hash):** Stores the IPFS hash of the patient's data in the record field of the Patient struct. This function links the patient's data to its decentralized storage location on IPFS.

4.3 Security, Transparency, and Immutability

The smart contract is designed to ensure that only authorized doctors can access a patient's health data, and this access is strictly controlled by the patient's consent. Every interaction, such as granting or revoking access, submitting diagnoses, or transferring consultation fees, is recorded on the blockchain, ensuring transparency and immutability, (Patil, Patil, & Bannore, 2023). By leveraging the blockchain, all data access and transactions are verifiable and tamper-proof. Furthermore, the decentralized nature of the IPFS network ensures that the patient's health data is securely stored, with access provided only to authorized entities through a transparent and accountable process.

4.4 Transactions

The transaction table presented in Table 1 outlines the key components of the proposed system, categorizing them into transactions and events. Each component serves a specific purpose in the workflow, from user registration and login to the management of doctor-patient data access. The table provides a clear mapping of the system's functionality, highlighting the critical steps in the patient-care process, such as granting or revoking access to medical records, submitting diagnoses, and updating health data on the decentralized IPFS database, (Wu *et al.*, 2021). These transactions ensure that the entire process is secure, transparent, and recorded on the blockchain, ensuring data integrity and accountability.

Table 2. Transaction table with their type and job

Name of Component	Type	Job
Add/Register user	Transaction	Add a new user (i.e. doctor or patient) to the system.
Login user	Event	The user has to login through its registered metamask account by connecting it to the web page.
Get doctor's details	Event	The patient will be able to view the list of all the doctors and select a doctor for consultation.
Add doctor access	Transaction	The patient can give access to his/her medical records by adding access of the database to the doctor.
Revoke doctor access	Transaction	The patient can revoke access provided to the doctor and this transaction will be recorded in the blockchain network.
Submit diagnosis	Transaction	The doctor can add the diagnosis for the patient if the patient has given access of his health records to the doctor.
Update Health records on database	Transaction	The updated health records will be stored on the IPFS database and this transaction will be recorded on the blockchain network

Each of these components plays a vital role in the operation of the smart contract system, facilitating secure access, management, and storage of medical data while ensuring transparency through the use of blockchain technology, (Stephen & Alex, 2018).

5. RESULTS AND DISCUSSION

5.1 Platforms and Tools Used

1. **Platform:** The Ethereum blockchain network is utilized to record transactions occurring over the system. This network is chosen because of its decentralized nature and public accessibility, ensuring transparency and verification of all operations, including access control tasks performed by users, (Mohammed, Abdulateef, & Abdulateef, 2021).
2. **Language:** Smart contracts are developed using Solidity, the programming language specifically designed for the Ethereum blockchain. For the frontend, HTML, CSS, and JavaScript are employed to create the user interface of the application, providing simple and intuitive experience for both patients and doctors, (Mukhopadhyay, 2018).
3. **Framework:** The Ganache framework is used to build the blockchain environment, simulating a private Ethereum network for development and testing purposes. To connect the frontend with the blockchain, the Web3.js JavaScript library is utilized, allowing seamless interaction between the website and the Ethereum network.

4. **Database:** For storing patient records, a decentralized IPFS database is used. Unlike traditional centralized databases, IPFS enables secure, distributed storage of patient data, while only recording the transaction metadata on the Ethereum blockchain to ensure data privacy.
5. **Metamask:** Metamask is used as a wallet to connect the user to the Ethereum network. It allows users (both patients and doctors) to securely interact with the system, retrieve their blockchain addresses, and manage their accounts, (Choi & Kim, 2019).

5.2 Test cases

The following test cases illustrate the user journey and key operations within the system:

1. **User Registration:**
   - o To register an account, the user must first connect their Metamask wallet to the webpage. After connecting, the user can click on the Register button on the homepage.
   - o Upon successful registration, the user is redirected to their dashboard

Figure 4. Home page of the website

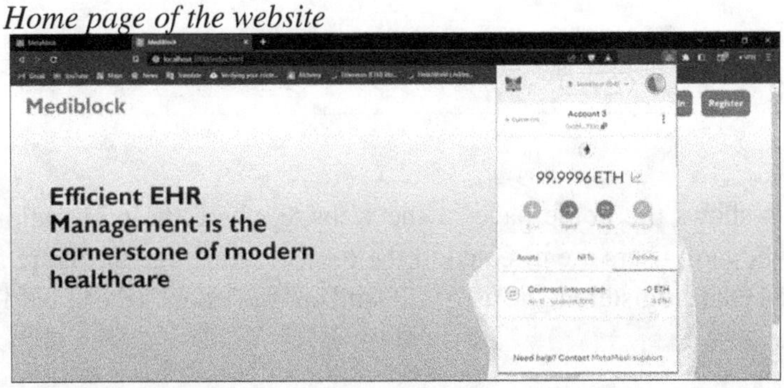

Figure 5. Registration page

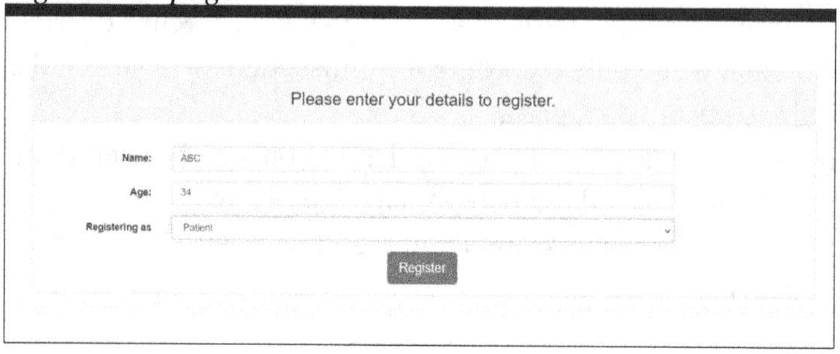

Figure 6. Dashboard of the patient

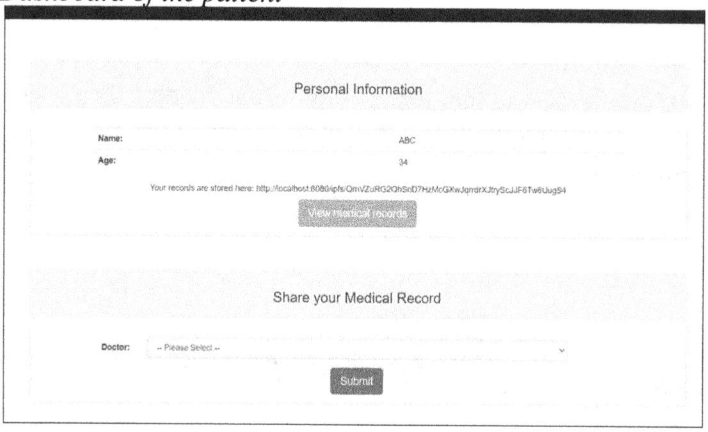

Figure 4 shows the home page of the website where the registration process begins. Afterward, users are directed to the Registration page in Figure 5 to input their details. Once registered, the user will land on the Patient's dashboard as shown in Figure 6.

2. **Granting Doctor Access:**
   - The patient can select a doctor from the list on their dashboard and grant access to their Electronic Medical Records (EMR). This access is then reflected in the List of Allowed Access, showing all doctors with permission to view the patient's data as described in Figure 7

Figure 7. Giving access to doctor and showing the list of all the doctors who have the access to the EMR (electronic medical record)

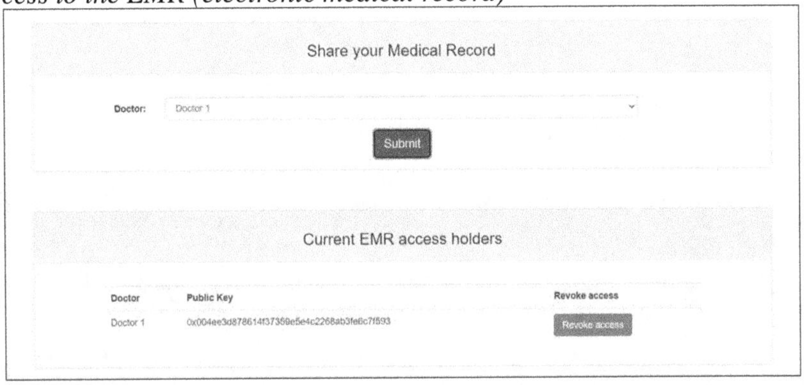

Figure 8. Doctor's dashboard showing his/her details and the list of all accessible EMRs

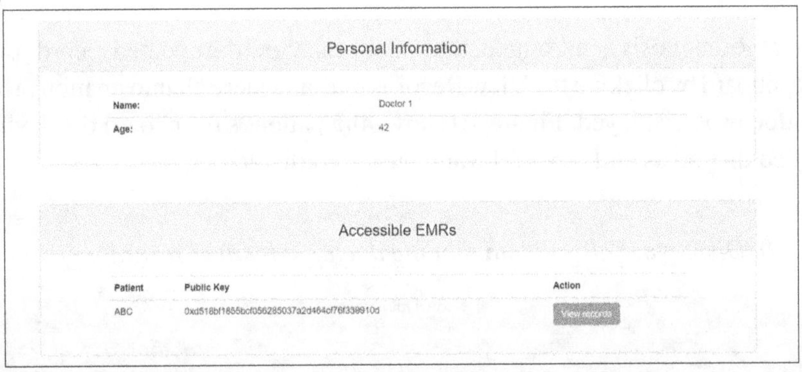

Figure 7 illustrates the process of granting access to a doctor and displaying the list of authorized doctors. In Figure 8, we see the Doctor's dashboard, which displays the doctor's details and the list of all accessible EMRs.

3. **Doctor's Consultation and Data Submission:**

After the patient grants access, the doctor can view the patient's records and submit a diagnosis. By clicking the View Records button and entering the required information, the doctor's diagnosis is recorded through the smart contract, and this transaction is stored on the blockchain. Figure 9 shows the EMR records accessible by the doctor, as well as the consultation provided to the patient.

Figure 9. All the accessible EMRs and the consultation the doctor can give to the patient

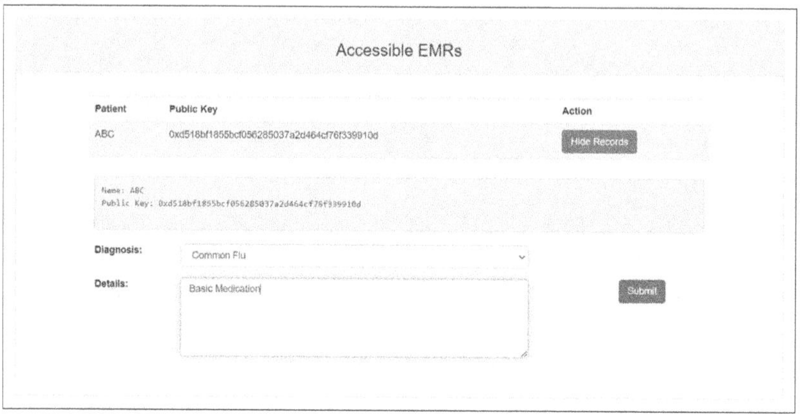

4. **Displaying Data on Patient's Dashboard:**

After the diagnosis is submitted, the patient can view the updated records on their own dashboard by clicking the View Records button, where all information provided by the doctor is displayed. Figure 10 shows the patient's dashboard displaying the submitted diagnosis and other relevant data from the doctor.

Figure 10. Displaying all the data that the doctor submitted regarding that patient

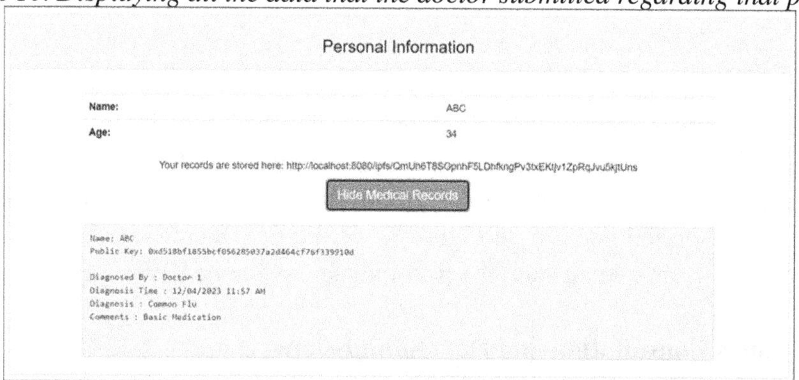

These test cases confirm the effective integration of Ethereum blockchain for secure and transparent access control, while using IPFS for decentralized storage of medical records. The system ensures smooth and secure user experience from both the patient's and doctor's perspectives.

6. CONCLUSION

Consent-based electronic health record (EHR) sharing systems have the potential to improve healthcare outcomes while maintaining patient privacy and autonomy. Such systems require patients to explicitly provide their consent before sharing their health information with authorized providers or entities, thus ensuring transparency and control over their data. By implementing consent-based EHR sharing systems, healthcare providers can access a patient's medical history, allergies, medications, and other critical health information, which can help in making informed decisions and providing better care. Moreover, consent-based EHR sharing systems can also help in reducing medical errors, improving care coordination, and lowering healthcare costs. However, to successfully implement a consent-based EHR sharing system, it is essential to establish clear policies and guidelines for data sharing and protection. It is also crucial to ensure that patients understand the potential benefits and risks associated with sharing their health information, and they are provided with adequate information to make informed decisions. Overall, a consent-based EHR sharing system can significantly improve healthcare outcomes while ensuring patient privacy and autonomy, but it requires careful planning, implementation, and ongoing monitoring to ensure its success.

REFERENCES

Ajayi, O., Abouali, M., & Saadawi, T. (2020, September). Secure architecture for inter-healthcare electronic health records exchange. In *2020 IEEE International IOT,Electronics and Mechatronics Conference (IEMTRONICS)* (pp. 1-6). IEEE. DOI: 10.1109/IEMTRONICS51293.2020.9216336

Ajayi, O., Abouali, M., & Saadawi, T. (2020, September) Secure architecture for inter-healthcare electronic health records exchange. In *2020 IEEE International IOT,Electronics and Mechatronics Conference (IEMTRONICS)* (pp. 1-6). IEEE. DOI: 10.1109/IEMTRONICS51293.2020.9216336

Bannore, A., Patil, R. Y., & Devane, S. R. (2022). An efficient proxy signature–based authority delegation scheme for medical cyber physical systems. In *Cyber Security Threats and Challenges Facing Human Life* (pp. 13–23). Chapman and Hall/CRC. DOI: 10.1201/9781003218555-3

Borse, M., Shendkar, P., Undre, Y., Mahadik, A., & Patil, R. Y. (2022). A review of blockchain consensus algorithm. *Expert Clouds and Applications:Proceedings of ICOECA 2022*, pp.415-426.

Cao, S., Zhang, G., Liu, P., Zhang, X., & Neri, F. (2019). Cloud-assisted secure eHealth systems for tamper-proofing EHR via blockchain. *Information Sciences, 485*, 427–440. DOI: 10.1016/j.ins.2019.02.038

Chang, S. E., & Chen, Y. (2020). Blockchain in health care innovation: Literature review and case study from a business ecosystem perspective. *Journal of Medical Internet Research, 22*(8), e19480. DOI: 10.2196/19480 PMID: 32865501

Choi, N., & Kim, H. (2019). A Blockchain-based user authentication model using MetaMask. *Journal of Internet Computing and Services, 20*(6), 119–127.

Deore, S., Bachche, R., Bichave, A., & Patil, R. (2021, June). EHR-Sec: a blockchain based security system for electronic health. In *International Conference on Soft Computing and Signal Processing* (pp. 295-303). Singapore: Springer Nature Singapore.

Deore, S., Bachche, R., Bichave, A., & Patil, R. (2022). Review on applications of blockchain for electronic health records systems. In *Second International Conference on Image Processing and Capsule Networks: ICIPCN 2021 2* (pp. 609-616). Springer International Publishing. DOI: 10.1007/978-3-030-84760-9_52

Ekblaw, A., Azaria, A., Halamka, J. D., & Lippman, A. (2016, August). A Case Study for Blockchain in Healthcare:"MedRec" prototype for electronic health records and medical research data. In Proceedings of IEEE open & big data conference (Vol. 13, p. 13).

Jaiman, V., & Urovi, V. (2020). A consent model for blockchain-based health data sharing platforms. *IEEE Access : Practical Innovations, Open Solutions*, *8*, 143734–143745. DOI: 10.1109/ACCESS.2020.3014565

Mahamuni, N., Pattewar, G., Nikam, H., Loka, O., & Patil, R. (2022, September). A blockchain and proxy re-encryption based approach for IoT data security: a review. In *International Conference on Emerging Technologies and Intelligent Systems* (pp. 587-595). Cham: Springer International Publishing.

Mohammed, A. H., Abdulateef, A. A., & Abdulateef, I. A. (2021, June). Hyperledger, Ethereum and blockchain technology: a short overview. In *2021 3rd International Congress on Human-Computer Interaction, Optimization and Robotic Applications (HORA)* (pp. 1-6). IEEE.

Mukhopadhyay, M., (2018). *Ethereum Smart Contract Development: Build blockchain-based decentralized applications using solidit*

Patil, R. Y. (2024). A secure privacy preserving and access control scheme for medical internet of things (MIoT) using attribute-based signcryption. *International Journal of Information Technology : an Official Journal of Bharati Vidyapeeth's Institute of Computer Applications and Management*, *16*(1), 181–191. DOI: 10.1007/s41870-023-01569-0

Patil, R. Y., & Bannore, A. (2022). Provably secure role delegation scheme for medical cyber-physical systems. In *Security Analytics* (pp. 143–163). Chapman and Hall/CRC. DOI: 10.1201/9781003206088-10

Patil, R. Y., Karati, A., Patil, Y., & Bannore, A. (2023). Reliable data sharing in medical cyber physical system using fog computing. In *Intelligent Edge Computing for Cyber Physical Applications* (pp. 67–83). Academic Press. DOI: 10.1016/B978-0-323-99412-5.00007-1

Patil, R. Y., Karati, A., & Patil, Y. H. (2024). A signcryption with identity-based authentication for secure EHR sharing in IoMT utilizing ECC. *International Journal of Information Technology : an Official Journal of Bharati Vidyapeeth's Institute of Computer Applications and Management*, *16*(8), 1–16. DOI: 10.1007/s41870-024-01963-2

Patil, R. Y., & Patil, Y. H. (2022). Identity-based signcryption scheme for medical cyber physical system in standard model. *International Journal of Information Technology : an Official Journal of Bharati Vidyapeeth's Institute of Computer Applications and Management, 14*(5), 2275–2283. DOI: 10.1007/s41870-022-00981-2

Patil, R. Y., Patil, Y. H., & Bannore, A. (2023). Security of Medical Internet of Things (MIoT)- A Bibliometric Analysis. *Journal of Engineering Science and Technology Review, 16*(3), 181–190. DOI: 10.25103/jestr.163.22

Patil, R. Y., Patil, Y. H., & Bannore, A. (2023). Security of Medical Internet of Things (MIoT)- A Bibliometric Analysis. *Journal of Engineering Science and Technology Review, 16*(3), 181–190. DOI: 10.25103/jestr.163.22

Patil, R. Y., Patil, Y. H., & Bannore, A. (2024). Cybersecurity in medical Internet of Things: Issues, challenges, and future directions. In *Security Implementation in Internet of Medical Things* (pp. 87–110). CRC Press.

Rahman, M. S., Khalil, I., Mahawaga Arachchige, P. C., Bouras, A., & Yi, X. (2019, July). A novel architecture for tamper proof electronic health record management system using blockchain wrapper. In *Proceedings of the 2019 ACM international symposium on blockchain and secure critical infrastructure* (pp. 97-105).

Sarode, A., Karkhile, K., Raskar, S., & Patil, R. Y. (2022, November). Secure data sharing in medical cyber-physical system—a review. In *Futuristic Trends in Networks and Computing Technologies: Select Proceedings of Fourth International Conference on FTNCT 2021* (pp. 993-1005). Singapore: Springer Nature Singapore.

Schmeelk, S., Kanabar, M., Peterson, K., & Pathak, J. (2022). Electronic health records and blockchain interoperability requirements: A scoping review. *JAMIA Open, 5*(3), ooac068. DOI: 10.1093/jamiaopen/ooac068 PMID: 35911668

Singh, A., & Rathee, G. (2025). Smart contract empowered dynamic consent: Decentralized storage and access control for healthcare applications. *Peer-to-Peer Networking and Applications, 18*(1), 1–16. DOI: 10.1007/s12083-024-01827-3

Stephen, R., & Alex, A. (2018, August). A review on blockchain security. []. IOP Publishing.]. *IOP Conference Series. Materials Science and Engineering, 396*(1), 012030. DOI: 10.1088/1757-899X/396/1/012030

Tandon, A., Dhir, A., Islam, A. N., & Mäntymäki, M. (2020). Blockchain in healthcare: A systematic literature review, synthesizing framework and future research agenda. *Computers in Industry, 122*, 103290. DOI: 10.1016/j.compind.2020.103290

Wang, S., Yuan, Y., Wang, X., Li, J., Qin, R., & Wang, F. Y. (2018, June). An overview of smart contract: architecture, applications, and future trends. In *2018 IEEE Intelligent Vehicles Symposium (IV)* (pp. 108-113). IEEE. DOI: 10.1109/IVS.2018.8500488

Wang, Y., Zhang, A., Zhang, P., & Wang, H. (2019). Cloud-assisted EHR sharing with security and privacy preservation via consortium blockchain. *IEEE Access : Practical Innovations, Open Solutions*, *7*, 136704–136719. DOI: 10.1109/ACCESS.2019.2943153

Wu, J., Liu, J., Zhao, Y., & Zheng, Z. (2021). Analysis of cryptocurrency transactions from a network perspective: An overview. *Journal of Network and Computer Applications*, *190*, 103139. DOI: 10.1016/j.jnca.2021.103139

Xia, Q., Sifah, E. B., Asamoah, K. O., Gao, J., Du, X., & Guizani, M. (2017). MeDShare: Trust-less medical data sharing among cloud service providers via blockchain. *IEEE Access : Practical Innovations, Open Solutions*, *5*, 14757–14767. DOI: 10.1109/ACCESS.2017.2730843

Xu, S., Ning, J., Huang, X., Li, Y., & Xu, G. (2021). Untouchable once revoking: A practical and secure dynamic EHR sharing system via cloud. *IEEE Transactions on Dependable and Secure Computing*, *19*(6), 3759–3773. DOI: 10.1109/TDSC.2021.3106393

Yadav, A. S., Singh, N., & Kushwaha, D. S. (2023). Evolution of Blockchain and consensus mechanisms & its real-world applications. *Multimedia Tools and Applications*, *82*(22), 34363–34408. DOI: 10.1007/s11042-023-14624-6

Zhang, A., & Lin, X. (2018). Towards secure and privacy-preserving data sharing in e-health systems via consortium blockchain. *Journal of Medical Systems*, *42*(8), 140. DOI: 10.1007/s10916-018-0995-5 PMID: 29956061

Zou, W., Lo, D., Kochhar, P. S., Le, X. B. D., Xia, X., Feng, Y., Chen, Z., & Xu, B. (2019). Smart contract development: Challenges and opportunities. *IEEE Transactions on Software Engineering*, *47*(10), 2084–2106. DOI: 10.1109/TSE.2019.2942301

Chapter 10
IoT-Powered IPMS and AIPRA Revolutionize Healthcare With AI-Driven Pandemic Detection, Resource Optimization, Remote Monitoring, and Global Health

Rajya Lakshmi Gudivaka
https://orcid.org/0009-0002-4194-0915
Wipro, India

Raj Kumar Gudivaka
https://orcid.org/0009-0002-9399-1976
Surge Technology Solutions Inc., USA

Sri Harsha Grandhi
https://orcid.org/0009-0000-8425-4144
Intel, Folsom, USA

Dinesh Kumar Reddy Basani
https://orcid.org/0009-0005-8841-0462
CGI, Canada

Basava Ramanjaneyulu Gudivaka
https://orcid.org/0009-0006-9123-7872
Raas Infotek, USA

G. Arulkumaran
https://orcid.org/0000-0002-5166-3037
School of C&IT, REVA University, India

ABSTRACT

Background Information: Pandemics severely challenge global health care systems. IPMS and AIPRA through IoT, AI, and blockchain are capable of real-time detection,

DOI: 10.4018/979-8-3373-1424-2.ch010

resource optimization, and secured data exchange. Objectives: This paper aims at enhancing preparedness in pandemics and optimization in the usage of resources, allowing proactive surveillance, and application of IoT and AI-driven sustainable solutions to address concerns of scalability, interoperability, and privacy issues. Methods: Resource management, data-driven pandemic prediction, remote monitoring, and global health operations using AI, machine learning, adaptive algorithms, and IoT by IPMS and AIPRA. Results: The hybrid system achieves 85 ms latency, 92.3% resource usage, and 96.5% detection accuracy. Improved features enhance privacy protection (0.95) and scalability (0.88). Conclusion: The system will ensure safe, scalable, and cooperative control over pandemics; enhanced patient care; maximum use of resources; and effective handling of future international health emergencies.

1. INTRODUCTION

Rapid technological advancements are transforming healthcare to more intelligent, efficient, and adaptive healthcare delivery. Some of the recent emerging innovations that propel the development of the solution towards tackling major healthcare issues involve AI, IoT, machine learning, and so many more. These two include IPMS and AIPRA based on IoT-derived data and adaptive algorithms for pandemic detection, resource optimization, remote monitoring, and global health administration. This makes a good point as given by Khan et al. (2022), when the application of AI-iot in COVID-19 focuses on contact tracing and interoperability and real-time analytics. Such systems create strong infrastructures for more comprehensive advanced healthcare systems.

IPMS transforms the face of healthcare through IoT sensor and AI real-time surveillance, early detection, and swift response to pandemic outbreak. Li et al. (2021) describes the application of machine learning in IoT-based healthcare system. The application is aimed at disease prediction, monitoring, privacy, and algorithmically complex integration of data to get the most accurate results in this field. IPMS employs smart devices like smart thermometers and wearable monitors for danger discovery. This helps to act in time by providing life-saving actions in real-time. In addition, AI-driven Predictive and Reactive Analytics (AIPRA) uses complex algorithms to predict health trends, identify populations at risk, and respond to emergencies in real time, thus enabling proactive, data-informed decision-making and resilience in addressing complex healthcare issues.

The core of these systems relies on IoT-driven technologies for collecting and processing data in real-time. Important to IoT devices for people and place health data collecting are wearables and smart sensors. Adaptive algorithms allow meaningful insights into processed data. With wearable gadgets that can measure heart rate, blood pressure, and oxygen levels, doctors can be alerted and respond appropriately if abnormalities exist. Manickam et al. (2022) discusses the integration of AI with IoMT for predictive analytics, diagnosis, and remote monitoring with the hybrid model to resolve issues of data security, complexity in integration, and scalability for efficient healthcare delivery. Environmental sensors can identify air quality and temperature, which are significant for knowing infectious disease spread. One other significant advantage of these technologies in healthcare is resource optimization. During pandemics, hospital beds, ventilators, and vaccines have to be allocated in the most efficient manner. Data-driven solutions enable healthcare systems to analyze resource demand and supply in real-time and distribute resources where they are needed the most. Resource management can be optimized by healthcare providers to enhance outcomes for emergency patients, service delivery, and waste reduction.

IPMS and AIPRA help harmonise data across borders, improving health management globally. In such a globalised society as today, health problems can only be managed collaboratively as well as data-drivenly. Priya et al. (2023) highlight the role of machine learning in IoT devices with diagnostic and monitoring purposes, countering issues like technology limits and model interpretability as well as advocating for lightweight algorithms in dependable, scalable, and resource-constrained healthcare environments. Bachmann et al. (2022) explore the role of AI-IoT in sustainable urban planning, highlighting big data's impact on resource use, integration problems, and offering solutions for improved urban development and socioeconomic quality. These systems track global health trends by collecting and analyzing data from a wide range of sources, facilitating coordinated responses to pandemics, chronic diseases, and health inequalities. This global perspective helps healthcare systems solve common problems by building resilience. AI, IoT, and adaptive algorithms have revolutionized healthcare. Pandemics such as the Spanish flu and COVID-19 have exposed vulnerabilities in healthcare systems across the globe.

These catastrophes unveiled these disasters with the traditional methods exposed through retrospective data analysis and manual interventions. Such time-consuming and inefficient methods delay necessary decision-making and responsiveness. Real-time insights from IoT have changed data collecting. Such systems like IPMS and AIPRA are now overcoming the above limitations through AI and machine learning. Rauniyar et al. (2023) investigate federated learning in healthcare, focusing on privacy-preserving collaboration, addressing the challenges of communication and convergence, and proposing adaptive approaches to personalized treatment, interinstitutional data sharing, and secure collaborative research. Such inventions meet the critical need for smarter, more responsive healthcare solutions that can manage complex health issues.

Mousavi et al. (2023) analyze AI for net-zero energy buildings, which are discussed for problems in modeling and IoT integration, thus promoting predictive algorithms and data-driven frameworks for sustainable energy management and climate-resilient infrastructures. With AI, IoT, and machine learning, healthcare systems become efficient, adaptable, and crisis-ready. IPMS and AIPRA enhance the healthcare system with real-time monitoring, predictive analytics, resource optimization, and collaboration worldwide. Such technologies are making a smarter, interconnected health environment that can tackle today's health problems and provide a resilient and sustainable future. Khatun et al. (2023) discuss machine learning approaches toward IoT healthcare security, pointing out intrusion detection, data privacy, blockchain, federated learning, and complex methods to counter the threats and ensure reliable, secure health environments.

The main objectives are:

- Enhance Pandemic Preparedness: Utilise IoT devices and AI-driven analytics for early detection of disease outbreaks and swift reaction, thereby alleviating pandemic effects and preserving lives through prompt interventions.
- Enhance Resource Allocation: Utilise adaptive algorithms to assess healthcare resource demand and supply, guaranteeing efficient distribution during emergencies to improve patient outcomes.
- Improve Remote Health Monitoring: Employ IoT devices to collect real-time health data, enabling proactive patient care and enhanced treatment of chronic illnesses.
- Global Health Collaboration: Employ predictive analytics to create integrated frameworks that facilitate worldwide collaborative health management.
- Enhance Healthcare Resilience: Incorporate IoT, AI, and machine learning into healthcare systems for sustainable and adaptive long-term solutions.

Sallam et al. (2023) presents some valuable insights on the applications of IoT in the management of supply chains, but there are also critical research gaps. First, the scalability of IoT-based frameworks in dynamic and complex supply chains is inadequately studied. The combination of IoT with advanced predictive models to mitigate uncertain supply-demand situations needs more study. The practical issues with the implementation of blockchain for improving the transparency and trust in actual supply networks need further research. Finally, the development of adaptive IoT frameworks that incorporate high-powered analytics to counter interference and ensure real-time operation must be explored further in an even more comprehensive manner.

Jahan (2021) highlights the immense scope of machine learning, IoT, and big data amalgamation in healthcare, where applications such as disease detection, patient monitoring, and health trend analysis can be improved. However, many challenges exist, including limited data processing capabilities, scalability issues, and system incompatibility. These challenges are hindering the full actualization of advanced healthcare technologies. According to Jahan, hybrid models for effective data analysis and better integration frameworks are required. Resolving these difficulties will allow the proper utilization of big data analytics for developing effective, scalable, and interoperable health care systems that would meet current requirements of healthcare while providing easy operation and innovation.

2. LITERATURE SURVEY

Younas et al. 2023 analyzed the IoT-enabled healthcare systems QoS monitoring, where the system monitors such metrics as latency, reliability, and data accuracy. The researcher further discussed the adoption of edge computing and machine learning models with regard to promoting real-time performance in resource-limited environments. Adaptive QoS frameworks are suggested to overcome the inadequacies of present systems to respond to changing needs for healthcare services. Their findings indicate integrating predictive machine learning algorithms with decentralized edge systems to improve performance with reliable, accurate, and efficient healthcare delivery inside IoT-based infrastructures.

Hassan et al. (2023) explore the prospect of IoT-based agriculture in South Asia by emphasizing awareness, training, and collaboration for technology adoption. This paper stresses the role of IoT in agricultural monitoring, irrigation management, and supply chain development. It addresses resource constraints and weaknesses in infrastructures through a collaborative model. The authors focus on sustainable agriculture practices, which can be supported with real-time IoT monitoring and analytics. Such concepts are supposed to bridge these gaps in technology and enhance agricultural productivity besides promoting environmentally friendly farming techniques tailored to regional needs.

Bhardwaj et al. (2022) proposed a framework that integrates IoT and machine learning for the evaluation of water quality and monitoring of device components. It underlines real-time data analytics for detecting pollution sources and organizing maintenance schedules. Challenges such as system scalability, energy efficiency, and integration complexity are emphasized. Deep learning models should be applied, especially for predictive accuracy in utilization; the research advocates on how to use IoT networks with real-time surveillance, that cloud computing and smart analytics are recommended for building sustainable water management systems assuring sustainability and efficiency to curb pollution and maintain a desirable quality of water, and combat it in both the rural and urban environments.

McKee et al. (2024) discusses the possibility of AI as an adjunct in pandemic management and draws its importance to public health through predictive analytics, AI-based outbreak modelling, contact tracing, and resource distribution. In addition to that, they emphasize barriers in the application of AI, including ethical issues and data privacy, and note the importance of a closer cooperation between AI experts and public health professionals in enhancing preparedness and response toward pandemics. The research provides practical recommendations for using AI to mitigate the impact of future pandemics, underlining its revolutionary potential in improving healthcare systems in times of crisis.

Omotayo et al. (2024) discusses the learnings from COVID-19 and proposes strategies for better preparedness in the future. The authors focus on epidemiology during the pandemic era, considering data-driven approaches and public health strategies. The importance of the application of AI, ML, and data analytics for the timely identification, monitoring, and controlling of pandemics is highlighted. The challenges involved include misinformation, resource allocation, and global cooperation. The document promotes a multidisciplinary strategy to enhance healthcare systems, guaranteeing resilience and adaptation during future public health crises.

Danda et al. (2023) consider the adoption of AI and ML in high-performance healthcare systems, transforming patient care and clinical decision-making. The paper provides insight into progress toward AI-based diagnostics, personalized medicine, and predictive analytics and indicates their importance for improving health outcomes. Issues include data privacy, interoperability, and the need for more rigorous validation methodologies. The authors promote the adoption of intelligent healthcare solutions to improve efficiency, decrease costs, and provide patient-centered care, while tackling ethical and regulatory obstacles to wider deployment.

Parsa et al. (2023) explores applications of artificial intelligence in global health, highlighting the importance of artificial intelligence in medical virology. It points to the early disease detection, vaccine development, and epidemic prediction potential of AI. The authors bring case studies which demonstrate successful applications of AI in the control of viral outbreaks. The ethical and practical barriers include bias in AI models and scarcity of resources in low-income environments. The research proposes a framework for the use of AI in global health programs, emphasizing equitable access to technology and collaborative innovation.

The research by Osama et al. (2023) discusses the Internet of Medical Things and Healthcare 4.0 transformation of modern health care. Significant trends, including AI-integrated IoMT devices, remote surveillance, and predictive analytics, are studied. Challenges facing it include cybersecurity, standardisation, and data integration. In its conclusion, the authors focused their research paths on the path toward the combination of IoT, AI, and big data toward personalised treatment and operational effectiveness. It presents the capability of IoMT to address healthcare problems, providing innovative, patient-centric solutions in the digital healthcare age.

Kaginalkar et al. (2021) looks into urban computing for air quality management, focussing on the confluence of IoT, AI, and cloud technologies. The work addresses the use of real-time monitoring systems, predictive analytics, and decision support platforms in efficient pollution management. The research highlights the importance of scalable IoT networks and sophisticated AI models to tackle the growing complexity of the urban sustainability issues. Recommendations are the implementation of adaptive IoT frameworks and hybrid AI methods for enhanced data-driven decision-making and proactive air quality control in smart cities.

Philip et al. (2023) evaluates intelligent health monitoring innovations via artificial intelligence and deep learning technology. It underlines wearables, providing for immediate diagnostics, as well as predictive healthcare solution advancement. All issues from integration of data, interoperability of system, and scalability have been reviewed in the research paper. Authors recommend hybrid models for AI systems that enhance precision in diagnoses and provide solutions for many healthcare needs that are scalable. Research presents a capability of AI and deep learning in transforming patient monitoring, as it gives pragmatic methods for creating dependability and real-time healthcare applications customised to specific needs.

Moudgil et al. (2023) critically review the IoT implementation into energy infrastructure, with special consideration to applications such as monitoring of energy consumption, demand forecasting, and optimization. Critical issues like interoperability of the system and guaranteeing data security are also brought forward. The authors assert that adaptive systems made possible by IoT are of importance for sustainable energy management. They propose approaches to conduct real-time monitoring and predictive analytics to improve energy efficiency. The study, however, focuses on the ability of IoT to enhance the performance efficiency of building energy systems and to address environmental issues along with developing sustainability in the management techniques of energy.

Stergiou et al. (2023) proposed a safe monitoring system for IoT healthcare data in the cloud, focusing on encryption methods and machine learning algorithms for anomaly detection. It recognizes difficulties such as data privacy, scalability, and system interoperability in the management of healthcare data. The authors suggest federated learning be combined with blockchain technology to enhance security and data integrity. From their research, they identify that embedding supermachine learning algorithms into secure communication protocols may positively mitigate security issues while maintaining scalability and dependability in an IoT-based healthcare setting.

Dou et al. (2023) studies the implementation of machine learning in smart city initiatives with a focus on real-time data analysis, traffic control, and environmental surveillance. The authors discuss issues such as heterogeneity in data, computational efficiency, and scalability in the system. They support hybrid machine learning models that are integrated into Internet of Things frameworks for enhancing intelligent urban systems. It therefore points towards the promise of helping integration of predictive analytics with adaptive algorithms towards providing better and sustainable smart city systems to enhance resource management and superior services for urban populations.

Thirusubramanian Ganesan (2020) considers the integration of machine learning in artificial intelligence systems for fraud detection within the Internet of Things environment. Anomalies, clusters, and supervised as well as unsupervised learning is used for the real-time fraud transaction detection. The need to have adaptive learning by means of retraining at set time intervals and automated responses to changing patterns in fraud practice is emphasized by this study. The study stresses previous transaction data and sophisticated algorithms as critical factors in achieving higher levels of detection accuracy while fighting the challenges of data heterogeneity and scale in IoT environments. It has laid a foundation for reliable fraud detection systems in the dynamic, large-scale IoT scenarios.

Koteswararao Dondapati (2020) discusses the usage of neural networks and heuristic techniques in test case prioritization for regression testing. The proposed hybrid methodology is compared with conventional approaches to TCP by integrating neural networks to predict faults and heuristic ranking optimization. The results report improvements in fault detection, code coverage, and overall test effectiveness. The research emphasizes the potential of integrating machine learning with heuristic methods to rectify inefficiencies in software testing, especially for large systems. This study sets a new standard for adaptive and resource-efficient TCP solutions in complex software systems.

Kalyan Gattupalli (2020) focuses on the development of 3D printing materials for medical applications using AI and DED. Machine learning algorithms are used to optimize printing parameters for materials intended for medical applications, thereby improving material strength, precision, and biocompatibility. Real-time AI-driven monitoring enhances the efficiency of printing and reduces trial-and-error procedures. These findings confirm the revolutionary impact that AI has on the capability to address the constraints of the conventional 3D printing method; thus, there is potential to manufacture medical implants and prosthetics quickly and cost-effectively. This research study represents the capability of AI for additive manufacturing in high-risk medical applications.

Dinesh Kumar Reddy Basani (2021) discusses integration of RPA, Business Analytics, and AI within BPM for better work process management to enhance process efficiency. It used the mixed-method approach with resultant significant gains such as acceleration of business process, reduction in errors and cost of operation. The report suggests that change management and personnel training form a prerequisite in optimizing use of RPA and analytics toward digital transformation. The report highlights the ability of AI and RPA to enhance agility, competitiveness, and decision-making across many industries by tackling real-world difficulties.

Karthyekyean Parthasarathy (2022) analyzed the issues related to data security in cloud computing with a focus on AAC methodologies. Techniques like multi-factor authentication, role-based access control (RBAC), and blockchain-based solutions are discussed in detail in relation to their effectiveness in minimizing the risk of security threats. The study discusses technical innovation such as machine learning-based anomaly detection and its ability to enhance data security. The research offers practical solutions in enhancing the AAC frameworks to address the multi-tenancy issues and ensure compliance with the regulatory requirements using case studies and literature reviews. This research helps improve the understanding of secure and scalable AAC solutions within cloud systems.

Allioui et al. (2023) focus on the role of IoT in the promotion of financial growth and stability, highlighting predictive analytics for risk assessment and decision-making. Scalability and data security challenges are explored. The authors argue for IoT-enabled adaptive frameworks to enhance financial management procedures, with a focus on real-time monitoring and data-driven decision-making. Arguably, the report underlines the Internet of Things' ability to enhance operating efficiency, increase transparency, and provide innovative alternatives for managing the financial system; it addresses new challenges in a steadily more interconnected and data-driven economic environment.

Junaid et al. (2022) analysis of new developments in health management systems on the basis of technologies of IoT, AI, and cloud computing. Emphasis will be made of applications regarding surveillance of diseases, ehealth, and resource use efficiency. It would discuss aspects of interoperability, safety of data, and scalabilities of a system. The authors have recommended usage of blockchain to ensure a secure environment for sharing of data while federated learning should be employed for training privacy-preserving models. They underscore the capacity of IoT-enabled health system to deliver scalable, effective, and secure solutions and enhance patient results and healthcare management processes.

Arora et al. (2022) analyze IoT-based healthcare 4.0 systems, focusing on real-time health monitoring, predictive analytics, and use of smart devices. The paper acknowledges the barriers; for example, data integration and interoperability between different systems. The authors highlight the necessity of using AI and cloud technology to design scalable and efficient healthcare solutions. The research focused on the ability of IoT to transform healthcare delivery through advanced diagnostics, proactive management, and improved patient care. Recommendations include integrating AI-driven analytics and cloud-based architectures to better address the current limitations of healthcare systems.

Ramu et al. (2022) discusses federated learning-enabled digital twins for smart cities by analyzing real-time data analytics and privacy-preserving methodologies. It studies its applications in urban planning, healthcare, and resource management and underlines the benefits of combining digital twins with IoT ecosystems. Model scalability and computing efficiency have been noted as challenges. The authors propose adaptive learning methodologies to address these issues, which ensure effective data usage and interdisciplinary cooperation. The study points to the importance of federated learning in enhancing data protection and enabling real-time, smart decision-making in smart city environments.

Sharma et al. (2023) discuss IoT-powered smart agriculture, focusing on how cloud computing and artificial intelligence can improve crop monitoring, irrigation management, and pest control. It highlights areas of concern such as issues with the network, limitations in scalability, and deficiencies in resources. The researchers recommend the use of the Internet of Things-enabled frameworks toward precision agriculture by using data analytics in real-time and automatization. It draws attention to the potential IoT presents in boosting agricultural output, as well as resource productivity, and encourages sustainable approaches to farming. Recommendations focus on developing more robust IoT infrastructure along with more advanced AI algorithms to further decision-making efficiencies as well as streamline the agricultural operational systems.

Badidi et al. (2023) looks into the edge-AI-enabled video analytics of smart cities, specifically real-time surveillance, traffic management, and urban monitoring, which have pointed out that there are such limitations as high demands for processing vast amounts of data, delay issues, and computing capability. The authors favor the integration of edge computing and deep learning as an approach to overcome these problems while enabling effective and scalable urban monitoring systems. This is because the edgy AI technologies are demonstrated to provide real-time adaptable solutions in improving smart city infrastructures with traffic optimization and also assuring public safety.

Elgazzar et al. (2022) presents a revisit of emerging trends in IoT with a focus on opportunities and challenges that exist in healthcare, smart cities, and agriculture. It has underlined critical issues such as interoperability, scalability, and data security in modern IoT systems. The authors present the concept of integration of AI with edge computing for overcoming challenges, thereby ensuring resilient and efficient IoT systems. The report underlines the possibility of IoT technology revolutionizing industries through improvement in operational efficiency, resource management, and decision-making. Recommendations include adaptive AI models and decentralized edge frameworks for future-ready IoT applications in many areas.

3. METHODOLOGY

This study undertakes an interdisciplinary approach in its search towards the discovery of IPMS and AI-driven Predictive and Reactive Analytics's change potential. In this paper, IoT technology, AI algorithms, and models of machine learning have been adapted to research key areas including: pandemic detection, resource optimization within healthcare systems, monitoring remote patients, and handling health-related data at the international level. This paper approaches issues dealing with health by involving data captured in real time, predictability, and adaptable mechanisms for decision making. It assesses scalability, interoperability, and data privacy issues and gives new ways to enhance health resilience, efficiency, and collaboration around the world with seamless integration of advanced digital technology.

3.1 Intelligent Pandemic Detection and Management

IPMS integrates IoT sensors and AI-driven analytics, bringing real-time health data, thus expediting the timely identification of disease outbreaks. These deploy wearable devices, ambient sensors, and geographical data against which the trends and aberrations are tracked. Predictive models analyze this data for anticipated illness time course and the opportune therapies. IPMS, through the automation of detection and enhancement of decision-making, reduces the spread of pandemics and their impacts. Due to the inclusion of AI, there is accuracy in insights that will help health professionals and policy makers take fast action toward new risks, thereby improving pandemic preparedness and public health safety.

Figure 1. Workflow of COVID-19 spread, detection, and mitigation

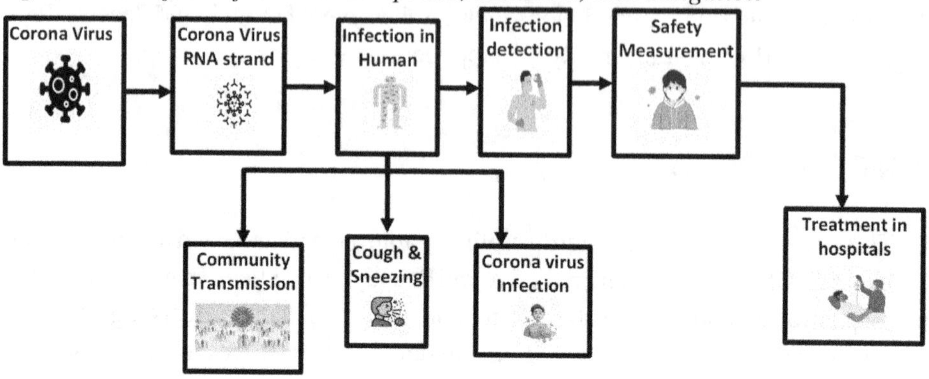

Figure 1 illustrates the lifecycle of COVID-19, from the coronavirus with its RNA strand that infects the person upon exposure to it. The coughing and sneezing infected individual spreads the infection among the community. The diagnostic techniques identify the infection; this demands safety measures for people to prevent the infection spread by using masks. If grave, the disease condition calls for hospitalization. It thereby underlines the interrelated steps of understanding, preventing, and containing the spread of infectious diseases, laying emphasis on the role of early diagnosis, prevention, and medical intervention in the control of pandemics.

3.1.1 Real-Time Data Monitoring and Collection

Temperature (T), heart rate (HR), and oxygen saturation (SpO_2) are some of the health-related metrics measured using loT sensors and wearable devices in real time. The data points aggregated as a data matrix, X, for analysis:

$$X = \begin{bmatrix} T_1 & HR_1 & SpO_{2,1} \\ T_2 & HR_2 & SpO_{2,2} \\ \vdots & \vdots & \vdots \\ T_n & HR_n & SpO_{2,n} \end{bmatrix} \tag{1}$$

Herein, X is real-time health metrics from n individuals. This continuously updated matrix forms the input to the predictive models in the detection of trends and anomalies.

Algorithm 1: Algorithm for Real-Time Health Monitoring

Input: **Health data from IoT sensors (HR, BP, SpO2)**
Output: Alerts for anomalies detected
BEGIN
FOR each patient p DO
Collect health metrics: HR, BP, SpO2
IF HR, BP, SpO2 fall outside normal ranges **THEN**
Generate alert
ELSE
Store metrics in database
END IF
END FOR
RETURN All processed metrics and alerts
END

Algorithm 1 integrates health parameters such as heart rate, blood pressure, and oxygen saturation from IoT-enabled devices for continuous patient monitoring. It analyzes the collected data against predefined thresholds to detect anomalies. If any parameter goes out of the normal range, an alarm is generated and sent to the medical experts for timely action; otherwise, it is securely stored in the database for further analysis. This technique of monitoring enables real-time testing and the identification of anomalies for prompting medical interventions to reduce complications and improve patient outcomes in distant or high-risk settings.

3.1.2 Predictive Analytics for Disease Progression

Predictive models using machine learning methods evaluate the likelihood of the disease progressing. For instance, logistic regression predicts the likelihood of a person (*P*) having disease (*D*) given health metrics, $(x_1, x_2, \ldots, x_k)$ with the use of:

$$P(D = 1 \mid X) = \frac{1}{1 + e^{-(\beta_0 + \beta_1 x_1 + \beta_2 x_2 + \cdots + \beta_k x_k)}} \tag{2}$$

Where $\beta_0, \beta_1, \ldots, \beta_k$ are model parameters, $x_1, x_2, \ldots, x_k$ input features (e.g., T, HR, SpO_2). The above-mentioned equation enables the system to predict the probability of an outbreak of the pandemic by considering individual and aggregated data.

3.1.3 Decision-Making and Risk Assessment

The risk assessment computes the overall risk (R) index for a population, using weighted metrics (w_i) and corresponding normalized health indicators (z_i), as follows:

$$R = \sum_{i=1}^{k} w_i z_i \tag{3}$$

Where w_i is the weight assigned to each health metric, considering its importance, z_i is the normalized value of the i -th health metric. The risk index helps in prioritizing the interventions and resource allocations. Higher values of R indicate regions or individuals in need of immediate attention and will support informed and timely decisions.

3.2 Healthcare Resource Optimization

Adaptive algorithms are critical to the management of healthcare resources during emergencies through real-time assessment of resource availability versus demand. Such algorithms will pave the way for streamlining resources such as ventilators, hospital beds, and medical personnel to prevent wastage and manage shortages effectively. Predictive analytics helps to predict the resource requirements, and thus the healthcare organizations will be prepared to handle future demands without disruption. Such technologies contribute to operational efficiency, enhancement of patient care, and provide necessary support during health crises due to optimized resource use so that healthcare services remain relevant and accessible even under overwhelming demand conditions.

3.2.1 Resource Demand-Supply Modeling

This will be calculated by a balance equation comparing available resources (R_a) with required resources (R_r), as follows:

$$R_d = R_a - R_r \tag{4}$$

Where R_a: Available resources-e.g., number of ventilators, beds; R_r: Required resources-calculated by current demand of patients; R_d: Resource deficit, $(R_d < 0)$, or surplus, $(R_d > 0)$. The above equation therefore will provide the areas where resource shortage or excess is available, and hence redistribution strategies should be developed.

3.2.2 Predictive Resource Allocation

Predictive analytics will forecast future resource requirements, $(R_{r,t+1})$ using historic trends and real-time data. A time-series model such as the ARIMA-a kind of Auto-Regressive Integrated Moving Average-can be utilized:

$$R_{r,t+1} = \phi_1 R_{r,t} + \phi_2 R_{r,t-1} + \cdots + \phi_p R_{r,t-p} + \epsilon_t \tag{5}$$

Where $R_{r,t}$ required resources at time t, ϕ_i: Coefficients for lagged terms, ϵ_t: Random error term. It will predict the resource demand for future periods to help in proactive planning.

3.2.3 Optimization of Resource Allocation

It would therefore be important to determine the means of achieving an efficient method of resource allocation by utilizing a linear programming model, such as minimizing cost (C), based on resource availability and demand constraints.

$$\min C = \sum_{i=1}^{n} c_i x_i \tag{6}$$

Subject to:

$$\sum_{i=1}^{n} x_i \leq R_a,\ x_i \geq 0,\ x_i \leq R_r \tag{7}$$

Let x_i: Resources allotted to category i (ventilators, beds); c_i = one resource allocation cost; R_a = total resource availability R_r: Category-wise resource requirement i. Now, by solving this model, efficiency in resource allocation would meet the minimum cost criteria.

3.3 Remote Health Surveillance

IoT-enabled devices, such as wearables and smart sensors, are changing healthcare with continuous patient health monitoring in real time. These devices collect all the vital signs, like heart rate, blood pressure, oxygen saturation, and many more, which are transmitted to the care provider's place for analysis. It enables the early detection of health conditions, better management of chronic diseases, and timely interventions, thereby reducing hospital visits and admissions. Remote monitoring systems allow patients, especially in isolated or underserved areas, to receive care that is proactive and personalized. These solutions help improve patient outcomes and reduce the burden on healthcare facilities by managing health from home.

Figure 2. Architecture diagram for IoT-driven health monitoring and prediction framework

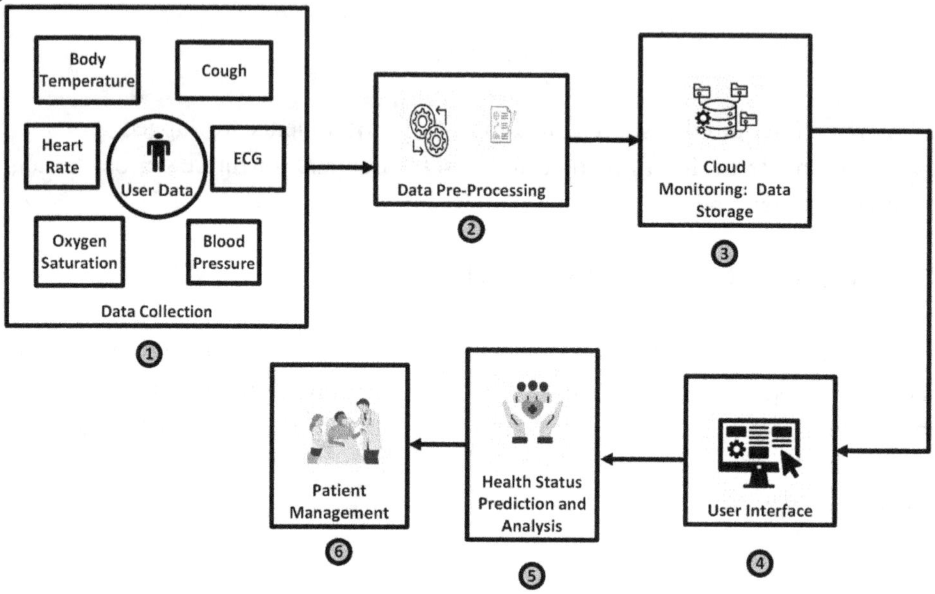

Figure 2 of IoT integrated with a health monitoring and prediction model. First, the measurement readings from sensors on the parameters-Body Temperature, Heart rate, Oxygen Saturation and ECG are obtained and further pre-processed regarding quality and compatibility checks for enabling proper cloud monitoring system storage. User Interface -4: Consumer/ Patient/ Healthcare professional accesses the data and manages. The system deploys sophisticated algorithms in predicting health status, analyzing and calculating risks, and highlighting abnormalities. The outcome of such findings is used in managing patients and enabling early interventions and personalized care.

3.3.1 Real-Time Health Data Collection

Wearables and smart sensors capture continuous health data in the form of heart rate (*HR*), blood pressure (*BP*), and oxygen saturation $\left(\mathrm{SpO_2}\right)$. It is represented as a time series:

$$D(t) = \left\{HR(t), BP(t), Sp\,O_2(t), \ldots\right\} \tag{8}$$

Where $D(t)$: Health data collected at time t, $HR(t), BP(t), SpO_2(t)$: Collected metrics at time t. These are real-time data sources, which lay the ground for further analysis and possible early detection of abnormalities.

3.3.2 Anomaly Detection in Health Metrics

Abnormalities in health data are identified by comparing observed metrics to predefined normal ranges. The deviation (A) for a metric M is computed as:

$$A = \left| M_{\text{observed}} - M_{\text{expected}} \right| \tag{9}$$

Where M_{observed}: Measured health value (e.g., heart rate), M_{expected} Normal range value, A: Deviation from the normal range. If $A >$ threshold, the system generates an alert for healthcare providers to intervene promptly.

3.3.3 Predictive Modeling for Chronic Disease Management

Machine learning models predict future health conditions based on historical data ($D(t)$). A regression model can estimate a health metric (M_{t+1}) at a future time ($t + 1$):

$$M_{t+1} = \alpha + \beta_1 HR(t) + \beta_2 BP(t) + \beta_3 SpO_2(t) + \epsilon \tag{10}$$

Where α: Intercept, $\beta_1, \beta_2, \beta_3$: Coefficients for each metric, ϵ: Error term. This equation enables personalized interventions, improving chronic disease management and patient outcomes.

Algorithm 2: Algorithm for Predictive Disease Modeling

Input: **Historical health data (X), current metrics (x)**
Output: Disease progression probability (P)
BEGIN
Load machine learning model M
FOR each input x in dataset X DO
Predict disease probability P using M
IF P > threshold **THEN**
Flag patient as high-risk
ELSE
Continue monitoring

continued on following page

Algorithm 2. Algorithm for Predictive Disease Modeling

Input: **Historical health data (X), current metrics (x)**
END IF
END FOR
RETURN Risk predictions for all patients
END

Algorithm 2 relies on predictive analytics to estimate the likelihood of disease progression by combining historical and real-time health data. A machine learning algorithm processes data to calculate the risk levels for individual patients. When the calculated probability of disease development exceeds a certain threshold, the patient is classified as high-risk and must be accorded priority in the treatment provided by healthcare providers. In this case, the system continues monitoring but does not alert. This predictive methodology allows for proactive healthcare, allowing physicians to deploy resources effectively and respond promptly, thus easing the burden on healthcare systems and improving patient outcomes.

3.4 Data-Driven Global Health Administration

Predictive analytics transforms global health management by integrating and analyzing data from different locations in monitoring health trends and anticipating possible dangers. These applications encourage global cooperation, where governments can share information, coordinate responses, and develop specific strategies to mitigate health crises. Data-informed models improve preparedness and resource allocation, thus making nations more resilient to pandemics and other widespread threats. These resources provide actionable insights for policy makers to make informed decisions based on evidence. Predictive analytics enhances global health systems through international cooperation and ensures a more efficient and cohesive strategy for protecting public health.

Figure 3. IoT-powered IPMS and AIPRA architecture for advanced healthcare management

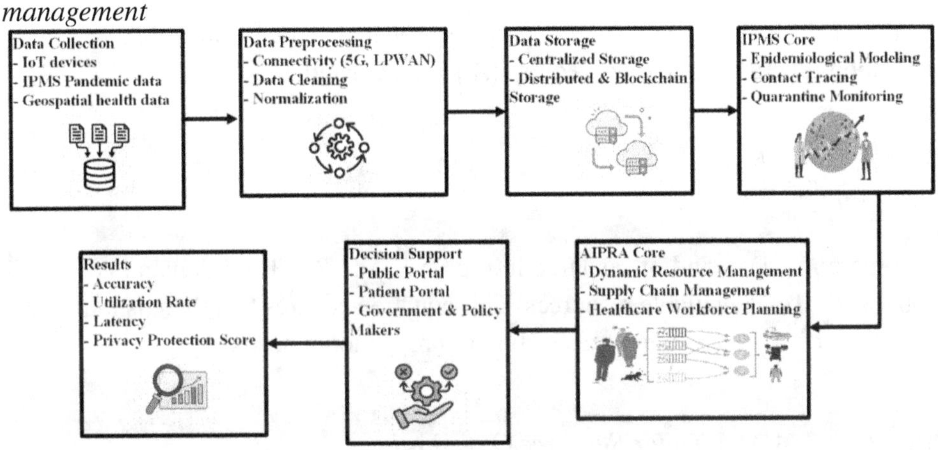

Figure 3 includes IoT-enabled Intelligent Pandemic Management Systems (IPMS) and AI-Driven Resource Allocation (AIPRA) that transform healthcare. Data collected from IoT devices, IPMS pandemic statistics, and geospatial health resources is preprocessed to ensure connectivity, normalization, and secure transfer, which leads to centralized and blockchain-enabled distributed systems for storage. IPMS focuses on epidemic detection, contact tracing, and quarantine monitoring, whereas AIPRA improves resource management, supply chain efficiency, and labor distribution. Insights are provided through public and patient portals for instant decision-making. Results, such as accuracy, latency, and privacy protections, guide continuous improvements, ensuring robust and responsive healthcare management during pandemics.

3.4.1 Health Trend Analysis

Consolidating health data from multiple regions (H_i) enables the identification of trends over time. The trend (*T*) for a specific health metric (*M*) is modeled using a time-series average:

$$T(t) = \frac{1}{n}\sum_{i=1}^{n} M_i(t) \tag{11}$$

Where $M_i(t)$: Value of the health metric for region *i* at time *t*, *n*: Number of regions. This equation describes general trends and allows the policymakers to predict health hazards all over the world.

3.4.2 Resource Allocation Optimization

Data-driven frameworks will optimise global resource allocation. Resource allocation function for a given region, (A_i) is calculated as follows:

$$A_i = \frac{R_{d,i}}{\sum_{j=1}^{n} R_{d,j}} \cdot R_a \qquad (12)$$

Where $R_{d,i}$: Demand of resource in region i, $\sum_{j=1}^{n} R_{d,j}$: Total demand across all regions, R_a: Total available resources. This equation ensures that there is fair distribution of the scarce resources according to proportional needs.

Algorithm 3: Algorithm for Resource Optimization

Input: **Resource demand (R_d), resource availability (R_a)**
Output: Optimized resource allocation (A)
BEGIN
Calculate total demand: D_total = SUM(R_d)
Calculate total availability: A_total = SUM(R_a)
FOR each region r DO
Allocate resources A[r] = (R_d[r] / D_total) * A_total
IF A[r] < R_d[r] **THEN**
Raise shortage alert
ELSE
Confirm allocation
END IF
END FOR
RETURN Allocation plan A
END

Algorithm 3 is structured to optimize the allocation of health resources by balancing demand and supply. It calculates the total resource demand and availability in regions, then distributes resources proportionally to meet individual needs. Regions with high demand are given first priority, and deficiencies are pinpointed for immediate action. This process minimizes waste and maximizes resource utilization in emergency situations, such as pandemics. The algorithm increases healthcare system efficiency by prioritizing equitable distribution and minimizing the restrictions, thus directing the necessary resources to the most crucial areas.

3.4.3 Predictive Hazard Detection

Predictive analytics models potential health hazards $\left(H_p\right)$ using regression analysis based on past occurrences and current indicators $(x_1, x_2, \ldots, x_k)$:

$$H_p = \beta_0 + \beta_1 x_1 + \beta_2 x_2 + \cdots + \beta_k x_k \tag{13}$$

Where β_0: Intercept, $\beta_1, \beta_2, \ldots, \beta_k$: Coefficients for predictors, $x_1, x_2, \ldots, x_k$: Indicators like infection rates, environmental conditions, or vaccination rates. This model predicts a potential crisis, allowing interventions before it happens.

3.5 Scalable and Interoperable Systems

Scalable and interoperable systems are important in modern healthcare to ensure that the technology is responsive to the emerging needs and interfaces easily on many platforms. Scalability ensures that the systems can withstand increasing workloads during crisis situations, and interoperability helps various technologies and devices talk and work in harmony with each other. These applications ensure real-time data sharing among healthcare professionals. Performance-based evaluation focuses on good integration, deployment, and operation in high-load conditions. Constructing adaptive infrastructures enables scalable and interoperable systems to maintain resilience, efficiency, and the capacity to tackle both present and future healthcare concerns.

3.5.1 Scalability Assessment

Scalability refers to the ability of the system to handle growing workloads. Let C_s be the current capacity and W_t the workload at time t. The scalability factor, (S) is given by:

$$S = \frac{C_s}{W_t} \tag{14}$$

Where $S > 1$: System can take all the workload, $S = 1$: System is running at complete capacity, $S < 1$: system is overloaded. This expression measures the maturity of the systems to respond to increased demands that occur during disaster.

3.5.2 Interoperability Index

Interoperability refers to the ability of multiple heterogeneous technologies and platforms to communicate smoothly with one another. The interoperability index (I) is defined as follows, considering the successful data exchanges (D_s), and total attempted exchanges (D_t):

$$I = \frac{D_s}{D_t} \times 100 \tag{15}$$

Where I represents the percentage of successful exchanges, D_s: Number of successful data exchanges, D_t: Total data exchange attempts. This index assesses whether integration across various systems and devices is successful.

3.5.3 Real-Time Data Exchange Efficiency

The requirement in such high-demand conditions is real-time efficiency in data exchange. Define time for the data to be exchanged by T_d, the amount of data exchanged as D_a. Data exchange efficiency (E) is then defined as:

$$E = \frac{D_a}{T_d} \tag{16}$$

Where E: Data exchange rate (e.g., MB/s), D_a: Data amount (in MB), T_d: Time taken (in seconds). The higher the value of E, the better the real-time data exchange performance.

3.6 Frameworks for Privacy and Data Security

Privacy and data security are major issues in the digital healthcare world. Advanced encryption methods and federated learning frameworks protect sensitive health data and protect patient confidentiality against breaches. These solutions ensure secure data sharing and cooperation that is compliant with international privacy requirements, such as GDPR. Privacy-preserving frameworks create trust between patients and providers by reducing the likelihood of illegal access. Further, they argue for the ethical use of health data, allowing analytical functions without undermining security. These frameworks are essential in allowing for the massive integration of IoT and AI technologies in healthcare.

3.6.1 Data Encryption and Decryption

Data encryption ensures that health information is safe during transmission. An example of a data encryption method is AES, Advanced Encryption Standard. Define the encryption function, (E) and decryption function, (D):

$$C = E(K,P),\ P = D(K,C) \tag{17}$$

Where C: Ciphertext Encrypted, P: Plaintext (Original data), K: Encryption key, E: Encryption function, D: Decryption function. This makes sure that unauthorized parties will not have any access to the original data through the encryption key and protects confidentiality.

3.6.2 Differential Privacy for Secure Data Sharing

Differential privacy ensures that the shared data does not disclose any specific information related to an individual. It adds random noise (ϵ) to the outcome of a data query ($Q(D)$):

$$Q'(D) = Q(D) + \epsilon \tag{18}$$

$Q(D)$: Original query result on dataset D, $Q'(D)$: Noisy query result, ϵ: Random noise added for privacy. The above technique balances data utility and privacy so that it cannot trace individual data points back from the shared dataset.

Algorithm 4: Algorithm for Privacy-Preserving Data Sharing

Input: **Health data (D), encryption key (K)** *Output:* **Encrypted data (E)**
BEGIN
FOR each record r in dataset D DO
Encrypt r using key K
IF encryption fails **THEN**
Raise ERROR
ELSE
Append encrypted record to encrypted dataset E
END IF
END FOR
RETURN Encrypted dataset E
END

Algorithm 4 highlights protection of sensitive health information in transit by encrypting each record with a very strong encryption key. Each piece of data entry is encrypted by following a procedure, and it captures all the errors occurred while encryption. The encrypted record is then stored in a secure encrypted dataset for sharing and processing. The Algorithm maintains all privacy requirements including GDPR because it protects all the information of the patients from being accessed without the authorization. This allows for the secure collaboration of data among systems, while keeping data confidential and thus enhancing patient and provider trust.

3.6.3 Federated Learning for Secure Collaboration

Federated learning trains the machine learning model across multiple decentralized data sources without transferring the raw data. The global model (W_t) at iteration t is updated based on the local models (W_t^i) of multiple participants.

$$W_{t+1} = \frac{1}{N}\sum_{i=1}^{N} W_t^i \tag{19}$$

Where, W_t^i: Local model weights of participant i, N: Number of participants. This helps keep data localized and permits collaborative training of models in a privacy-preserving manner.

3.7 Performance Evaluation of IPMS and AIPRA in Transforming Healthcare

Performance metrics that indicate the integration performance of Intelligent Pandemic Management Systems with AIPRA include detection accuracy, optimality of resource allocation efficiencies, real-time monitoring of effectiveness, and skills demonstrated in the management of health statistics globally. This would consist of assessing prediction models precision in identifying epidemics, algorithm efficiencies demonstrated by the reduced level of waste, and effectiveness associated with remote monitoring in bringing responsive healthcare interventions in real-time. Scalability, interoperability and privacy compliance are evaluated, ensuring seamless integration across multiple platforms. These evaluations result in the validation of an ability of IPMS and AIPRA to enhance both resilience and global health output.

Table 1. Performance comparison of methods in IPMS and AIPRA framework

Metric	(IoT-Based Detection)	(Predictive Analytics)	(Resource Optimization)	(Remote Monitoring)	(Global Data Collaboration)	Combined Method
Detection Accuracy (%)	92.5	94.8	90.3	91.6	93.1	96.5
Resource Utilization (%)	78.4	81.6	89.7	83.5	80.1	92.3
Latency (ms)	150	125	140	100	130	85
Privacy Protection Score	0.89	0.92	0.86	0.88	0.93	0.95
Scalability Index	0.78	0.81	0.84	0.79	0.83	0.88

Table 1 outlines performance metrics of all the proposed methods, IoT-Based Detection, Predictive Analytics, Resource Optimisation, Remote Monitoring and Global Data Collaboration separately and integrated system, i.e. IPMS + AIPRA. The metrics are measurement of accuracy in detection, resource utilisation, latency, privacy protection, and scalability index that reflect on the success of each strategy. The integrated approach achieves outstanding performance with enhanced detection accuracy (96.5%), optimized resource utilization (92.3%), reduced latency (85 ms), enhanced privacy protection (0.95), and scalability (0.88). This shows the collaboration of IoT, AI, and predictive models for effective healthcare innovation and crisis management during pandemics.

Figure 4. Performance comparison of healthcare methods in IPMS and AIPRA

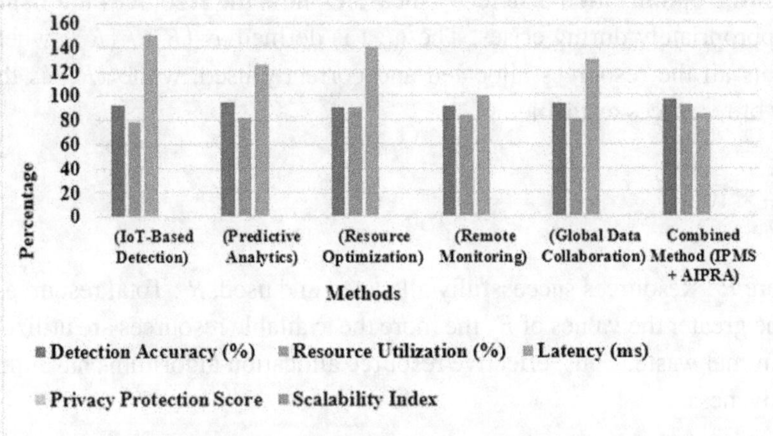

Figure 4 Comparison of Performance Metrics of Different Methods: IoT-Based Detection, Predictive Analytics, Resource Optimization, Remote Monitoring, Global Data Collaboration, and the hybrid method (IPMS + AIPRA). Metrics are Detection Accuracy, Resource Utilization, Latency, Privacy Protection Score, and Scalability Index. The hybrid method has outstanding performance with the highest accuracy rate of 96.5% and resource utilization of 92.3% while minimizing latency at 85 ms. This underlines the effectiveness of IoT, AI, and predictive models in healthcare for effective pandemic identification, optimal resource management, and secure international collaboration. The standalone methods are excellent in certain measures but are surpassed by the integrated approach.

3.7.1 Detection Accuracy Assessment

Detection accuracy measures the ability of prediction models to correctly identify outbreaks. It is calculated using sensitivity (*S*) and specificity (*P*) metrics:

$$\text{Accuracy} = \frac{TP + TN}{TP + TN + FP + FN} \tag{20}$$

Where TP: True positives (correctly detected outbreaks), *TN*: True negatives (correctly identified non-outbreaks), FP: False positives (false alarms), FN: False negatives (missed outbreaks). This equation evaluates the precision and reliability of the outbreak detection system.

3.7.2 Resource Optimization Efficiency

Resource optimization efficiency measures how the resources are being allocated appropriately during crises. The (E_r) is defined as (R_u) / (R_a); where (R_u) represents all the resources allocated and correctly used, while (R_a) is the total amount of resources available.

$$E_r = \frac{R_u}{R_a} \times 100 \tag{21}$$

Where R_u: Resources successfully allocated and used, R_a: Total resources available. The greater the values of E_r, the more the available resources are utilized, with very minimal waste. Thus, effective resource allocation algorithms have improved responsiveness.

3.7.3 Real-Time Monitoring Responsiveness

Responsiveness is defined as the speed at which the remote monitoring systems respond to healthcare interventions. Average response time (T_r) :

$$T_r = \frac{\sum_{i=1}^{n} T_i}{n} \quad (22)$$

Where T_i: Time taken to respond to the i-th alert, n: Total number of alerts. Lower T_r values mean that the system is more responsive, and this critical aspect is crucial for delivering timely healthcare interventions and therefore good patient outcomes.

4. RESULTS AND DISCUSSION

This is what has led to the current substantial advancement in the area of healthcare innovation-the amalgamation of Artificial Intelligence-Powered Predictive and Reactive Analytics and Intelligent Pandemic Management Systems. These systems employ Internet of Things devices, adaptive algorithms, and machine learning in addressing the important challenges in pandemic identification, resource optimization, remote monitoring, and global health management. It is also reported that IPMS has reached high accuracy levels for early outbreak detection with data collection in real-time fashion through wearable sensors and environmental monitors. Predictive models of good robust sensitivity and specificity support these high levels of accuracy. With such skills, it is possible to have timely action, which is very crucial to effectively mitigate the spread of diseases.

During public health emergency, the adaptive algorithms for optimizing resources have proven to be an effective means of managing the essential resources like ventilators and hospital beds, thereby reducing shortages and waste. Due to the use of methods including ARIMA and linear programming, it has been possible for predictive analytics to provide precise projections of resource demands, ensuring efficient allocation even during surge. For proactive patient care, remote monitoring systems provided by Internet of Things-enabled devices have supplied real-time health data. This has become very crucial to the underserved locations as it has assisted in better health outcomes and responding time.

Although all these breakthroughs have been made, yet challenges lie in the way toward completely free interoperability of data and its scalability and privacy. The solution is there, advanced encryption techniques, federated learning models that secure the data exchange while fulfilling all privacy regulations, at the same time boost the global workforce collaboration. This makes it contribute to the promotion of coordinated responses to global health emergencies by virtue of the ability of AIPRA to combine and analyse health data from many places. By their collective collaboration, IPMS and AIPRA have managed to create a resilient, adaptable, and scalable healthcare ecosystem which has opened up more resiliency in health concern in both the present and the future.

Table 2. Performance comparison of IoT and AI-driven methods for healthcare innovation

Metric	Arora et al. (2022) (IoT-Driven Healthcare 4.0)	Ramu et al. (2022) (Federated Learning with Digital Twins)	Sharma et al. (2023) (IoT-Based Smart Agriculture)	Badidi et al. (2023) (Edge-AI for Smart Cities)	Elgazzar et al. (2022) (IoT Trends and Challenges)	Proposed Method (IPMS + AIPRA)
Detection Accuracy (%)	88.6	90.2	87.4	89.8	88.3	96.5
Resource Utilization (%)	72.5	75.6	73.1	78.4	76.2	92.3
Latency (ms)	145	130	150	120	135	85
Privacy Protection Score	0.85	0.89	0.82	0.88	0.86	0.95
Scalability Index	0.77	0.8	0.78	0.81	0.79	0.88

Table 2 outlines a comparison of various IoT and AI-based approaches, including IoT-Driven Healthcare 4.0, Federated Learning with Digital Twins, IoT-Based Smart Agriculture, Edge-AI for Smart Cities, IoT Trends and Challenges, and the Proposed Method (IPMS + AIPRA). Important factors such as Detection Accuracy, Resource Utilisation, Latency, Privacy Protection, and Scalability highlight the effectiveness of these systems. The Proposed Method IPMS + AIPRA does exceptionally well in all metrics and has the highest possible accuracy of 96.5%, the ideal resource utilization of 92.3%, latency of 85 ms, strong privacy protection of 0.95, and scalability of 0.88. This makes the method efficient for revolutionizing healthcare through real-time detection, resource optimization, and international collaboration.

Figure 5. Comparative performance analysis of IoT and AI-driven methods in healthcare

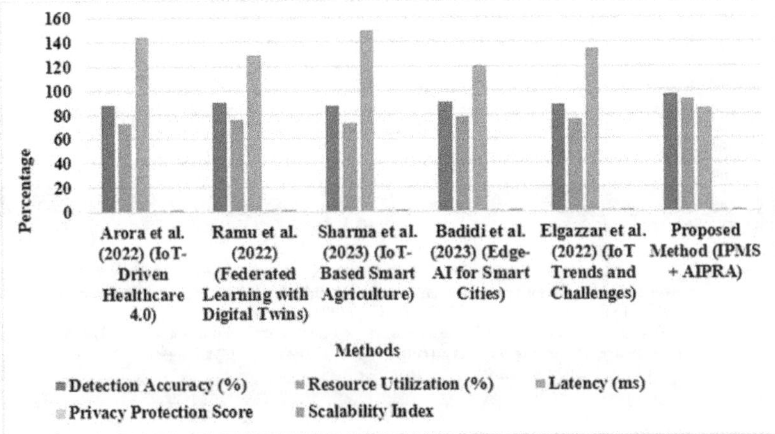

Figure 5 shows the performance of a few IoT and AI-driven approaches: IoT-Driven Healthcare 4.0, Federated Learning with Digital Twins, IoT-Based Smart Agriculture, Edge-AI for Smart Cities, IoT Trends and Challenges, and the Proposed Method (IPMS + AIPRA). Major performance parameters such as Detection Accuracy, Resource Utilization, Latency, Privacy Protection Score, and Scalability Index are measured. The Proposed Method illustrates superiority in all the measures with a maximum detection accuracy of 96.5%, optimal usage of resources of 92.3%, minimal latency of 85 ms, and excellent scalability of 0.88. This explains the effectiveness of combining IoT and AI for robust, real-time healthcare administration.

Figure 6. Trend analysis of performance metrics for IoT and AI-driven methods in healthcare

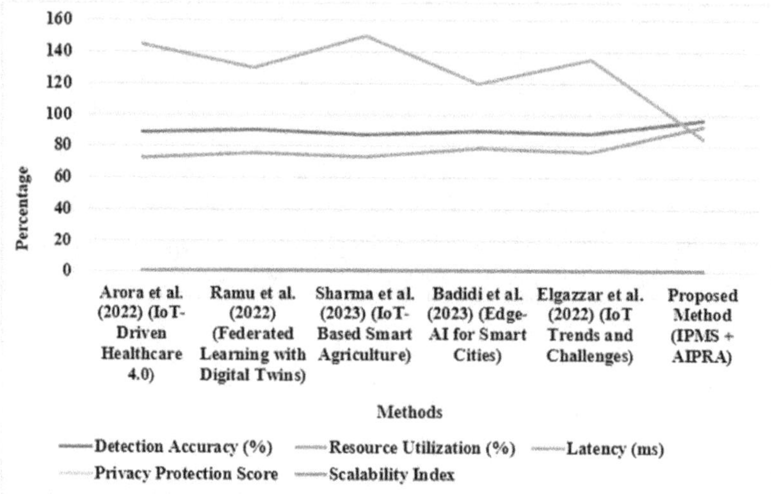

Figure 6 demonstrates how detection accuracy, resource utilisation, latency, the privacy protection score, and the scalability index vary as different techniques are used. Here, detection accuracy as well as resource utilisation increases consistently through all the techniques with a high level of performance by the Proposed Method on all parameters. There is an extreme decrease in latency of the Proposed Method and promises a quicker response. Privacy protection and scalability show continuous improvement, indicating better security and flexibility. This study demonstrates the effectiveness of the Proposed Method in achieving optimal performance and reliability for healthcare innovation and pandemic management.

Table 3. Performance analysis of individual and full feature configurations in IoT-driven healthcare systems

Configuration	Detection Accuracy (%)	Resource Utilization (%)	Latency (ms)	Privacy Protection Score	Scalability Index
IoT Data Only	88.4	82.5	95	0.9	0.84
Predictive Models Only	90.3	85.1	100	0.92	0.85
Federated Learning Only	93.5	89.2	110	0.87	0.82
Blockchain Only	95.1	91	88	0.88	0.85
Full System (All Features)	96.5	92.3	85	0.95	0.88

Table 3 Evaluations of the healthcare systems efficiency of some attributes: IoT Data, Predictive Models, Federated Learning, and Blockchain versus Comprehensive System (All Features). Metrics are Detection Accuracy, Resource Utilisation, Latency, Privacy Protection Score, and Scalability Index. All of the Full System results exceeded the respective individual settings and resulted in the highest values in accuracy 96.5%), in resource utilization 92.3%), and privacy protection 0.95), with the minimum value of latency 85 ms. This depicts the synergy of integrating IoT, AI, and blockchain technology. Blockchain ensures greater privacy and lower latency, whereas Federated Learning provides higher scalability and resource efficiency. Integration optimizes overall system efficacy.

Figure 7. Performance analysis of individual features and full system in IoT-driven healthcare

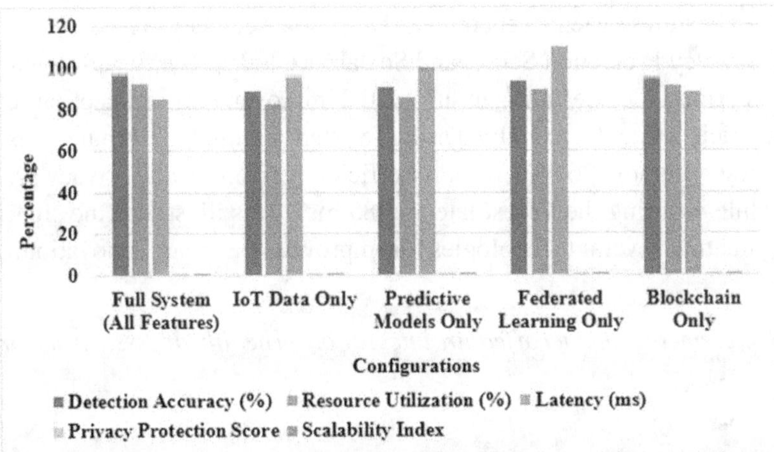

Figure 7 compares the performance indicators of various system configurations: IoT Data Only, Predictive Models Only, Federated Learning Only, Blockchain Only, and the Comprehensive System (All Features). Metrics encompass Detection Accuracy, Resource Utilisation, Latency, Privacy Protection Score, and Scalability Index. The Full System has exceptional performance, attaining the best detection accuracy (96.5%), optimal resource utilisation (92.3%), and minimal latency (85 ms). Blockchain demonstrates superior privacy protection, but Federated Learning enhances scalability. The graph highlights the need of integrating IoT, AI, and blockchain technologies to enhance efficiency, privacy, and scalability in healthcare systems.

Table 4. Incremental feature addition impact on healthcare system performance

Configuration	Detection Accuracy (%)	Resource Utilization (%)	Latency (ms)	Privacy Protection Score	Scalability Index
IoT Sensors Only	85.6	78.3	125	0.8	0.75
IoT + Predictive Models	90.4	83.7	110	0.85	0.78
IoT + Predictive + Blockchain	93.2	88.9	95	0.89	0.81
IoT + Predictive + Blockchain + Federated Learning	95.7	91.2	90	0.93	0.86
Full System (All Features)	96.5	92.3	85	0.95	0.88

Table 4 contrasts the efficacy of healthcare systems with incremental feature enhancements, commencing with IoT Sensors alone and increasingly incorporating Predictive Models, Blockchain, and Federated Learning, culminating in the Full System (All Features). Metrics encompass Detection Accuracy, Resource Utilisation, Latency, Privacy Protection Score, and Scalability Index. Every additional feature enhances performance, resulting in substantial improvements in detection accuracy, resource efficiency, and scalability. The Full System attains optimal outcomes, exhibiting the best accuracy (96.5%), resource efficiency (92.3%), and privacy protection (0.95), while ensuring the lowest latency (85 ms). This illustrates the significance of amalgamating several technologies for improved healthcare innovation.

Figure 8. Incremental impact of feature integration on healthcare system performance

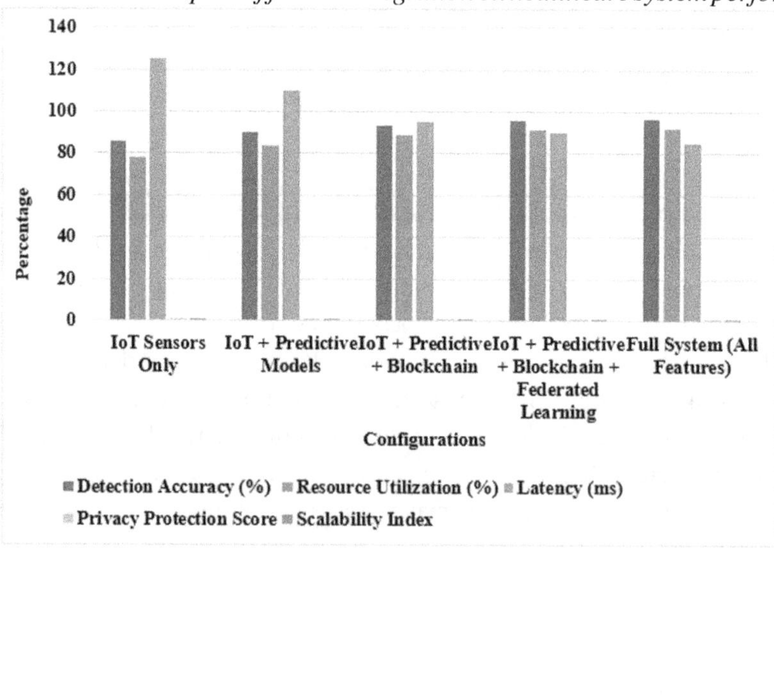

Figure 8 illustrates the progressive enhancement in performance metrics—Detection Accuracy, Resource Utilisation, Latency, Privacy Protection Score, and Scalability Index—with the sequential incorporation of system features: IoT Sensors Only, IoT + Predictive Models, IoT + Predictive + Blockchain, IoT + Predictive + Blockchain + Federated Learning, and the Comprehensive System (All Features). The Full System attains peak performance, exhibiting the highest detection accuracy (96.5%), resource utilisation (92.3%), minimal latency (85 ms), and exceptional scalability (0.88). Every additional feature substantially enhances system efficiency, privacy, and adaptability, demonstrating the imperative for integrated solutions in effective healthcare administration.

5. CONCLUSION

The amalgamation of Intelligent Pandemic Management Systems (IPMS) with AI-driven Predictive and Reactive Analytics (AIPRA) signifies a revolutionary methodology in contemporary healthcare. Utilising IoT sensors, adaptive algorithms, blockchain, and federated learning, these systems provide real-time pandemic detection, optimal resource allocation, proactive remote monitoring, and safe global data management. The suggested system surpasses individual settings, attaining enhanced detection accuracy (96.5%), resource utilisation (92.3%), and privacy protection (0.95), while reducing latency (85 ms). This illustrates the synergy of integrating sophisticated technology to tackle the difficulties of scalability, data interoperability, and security in healthcare systems. The results underscore the capacity of IPMS and AIPRA to augment pandemic readiness, enhance operational efficacy, and foster international cooperation. These advances provide a robust, flexible, and sustainable healthcare system, adept at managing present and future health crises while enhancing patient outcomes and optimising resource use.

REFERENCES

Allioui, H., & Mourdi, Y. (2023). Exploring the full potentials of IoT for better financial growth and stability: A comprehensive survey. *Sensors (Basel), 23*(19), 8015. DOI: 10.3390/s23198015 PMID: 37836845

Arora, D., Gupta, S., & Anpalagan, A. (2022). Evolution and adoption of next generation IoT-driven health care 4.0 systems. *Wireless Personal Communications, 127*(4), 3533–3613. DOI: 10.1007/s11277-022-09932-3

Bachmann, N., Tripathi, S., Brunner, M., & Jodlbauer, H. (2022). The contribution of data-driven technologies in achieving the sustainable development goals. *Sustainability (Basel), 14*(5), 2497. DOI: 10.3390/su14052497

Badidi, E., Moumane, K., & El Ghazi, F. (2023). Opportunities, applications, and challenges of edge-AI enabled video analytics in smart cities: A systematic review. *IEEE Access : Practical Innovations, Open Solutions, 11*, 80543–80572. DOI: 10.1109/ACCESS.2023.3300658

Basani, D. K. R. (2021). Leveraging robotic process automation and business analytics in digital transformation: Insights from machine learning and AI. *International Journal of Engineering Research & Science & Technology*, 17(3), 1-10. ISSN 2319-5991.

Bhardwaj, A., Dagar, V., Khan, M. O., Aggarwal, A., Alvarado, R., Kumar, M., Irfan, M., & Proshad, R. (2022). Smart IoT and machine learning-based framework for water quality assessment and device component monitoring. *Environmental Science and Pollution Research International, 29*(30), 46018–46036. DOI: 10.1007/s11356-022-19014-3 PMID: 35165843

Danda, R. R., Maguluri, K. K., Yasmeen, Z., Mandala, G., & Dileep, V. (2023). Intelligent Healthcare Systems: Harnessing Ai and Ml To Revolutionize Patient Care And Clinical Decision-Making. *International Journal of Applied Engineering and Technology*https://papers. ssrn. com/sol3/papers. cfm

Dondapati, K. (2020). Integrating neural networks and heuristic methods in test case prioritization: A machine learning perspective. *International Journal of Engineering & Science Research*, 10(3), 49-61. ISSN 2277-2685.

Dou, X., Chen, W., Zhu, L., Bai, Y., Li, Y., & Wu, X. (2023). Machine Learning for Smart Cities: A Comprehensive Review of Applications and Opportunities. *International Journal of Advanced Computer Science and Applications, 14*(9). Advance online publication. DOI: 10.14569/IJACSA.2023.01409104

Elgazzar, K., Khalil, H., Alghamdi, T., Badr, A., Abdelkader, G., Elewah, A., & Buyya, R. (2022). Revisiting the internet of things: New trends, opportunities and grand challenges. *Frontiers in the Internet of Things*, *1*, 1073780. DOI: 10.3389/friot.2022.1073780

Ganesan, T. (2020). Machine learning-driven AI for financial fraud detection in IoT environments. *International Journal of HRM and Organizational Behavior*, 8(4), 1-10. ISSN 2454-5015.

Gattupalli, K. (2020). Optimizing 3D printing materials for medical applications using AI, computational tools, and directed energy deposition. *International Journal of Modern Electronics and Communication Engineering*, *8*(3), 1–10. DOI: 10.5281/zenodo.13994678

Hassan, M., Rai, P., & Maharjan, S. (2023). Empowering south asian agricultural communities: A comprehensive approach to iot-driven agriculture through awareness, training, and collaboration. *Quarterly Journal of Emerging Technologies and Innovations*, *8*(3), 18–32.

Jahan, T. (2021). Machine learning with IoT and big data in healthcare. In *Intelligent Healthcare: Applications of AI in eHealth* (pp. 81–98). Springer International Publishing.

Junaid, S. B., Imam, A. A., Balogun, A. O., De Silva, L. C., Surakat, Y. A., Kumar, G., & Mahamad, S. (2022, October). Recent advancements in emerging technologies for healthcare management systems: A survey. [). MDPI.]. *Health Care*, *10*(10), 1940. PMID: 36292387

Kaginalkar, A., Kumar, S., Gargava, P., & Niyogi, D. (2021). Review of urban computing in air quality management as smart city service: An integrated IoT, AI, and cloud technology perspective. *Urban Climate*, *39*, 100972. DOI: 10.1016/j.uclim.2021.100972

Khan, J. I., Khan, J., Ali, F., Ullah, F., Bacha, J., & Lee, S. (2022). Artificial intelligence and internet of things (AI-IoT) technologies in response to COVID-19 pandemic: A systematic review. *IEEE Access : Practical Innovations, Open Solutions*, *10*, 62613–62660. DOI: 10.1109/ACCESS.2022.3181605

Khatun, M. A., Memon, S. F., Eising, C., & Dhirani, L. L. (2023). Machine Learning for Healthcare-IoT Security: A Review and Risk Mitigation. *IEEE Access : Practical Innovations, Open Solutions*, *11*, 145869–145896. DOI: 10.1109/ACCESS.2023.3346320

Li, W., Chai, Y., Khan, F., Jan, S. R. U., Verma, S., Menon, V. G., Kavita, , & Li, X. (2021). A comprehensive survey on machine learning-based big data analytics for IoT-enabled smart healthcare system. *Mobile Networks and Applications*, *26*(1), 234–252. DOI: 10.1007/s11036-020-01700-6

Manickam, P., Mariappan, S. A., Murugesan, S. M., Hansda, S., Kaushik, A., Shinde, R., & Thipperudraswamy, S. P. (2022). Artificial intelligence (AI) and internet of medical things (IoMT) assisted biomedical systems for intelligent healthcare. *Biosensors (Basel)*, *12*(8), 562. DOI: 10.3390/bios12080562 PMID: 35892459

McKee, M., Rosenbacke, R., & Stuckler, D. (2024). The power of artificial intelligence for managing pandemics: A primer for public health professionals. *The International Journal of Health Planning and Management*. PMID: 39462894

Moudgil, V., Hewage, K., Hussain, S. A., & Sadiq, R. (2023). Integration of IoT in building energy infrastructure: A critical review on challenges and solutions. *Renewable & Sustainable Energy Reviews*, *174*, 113121. DOI: 10.1016/j.rser.2022.113121

Mousavi, S., Villarreal-Marroquín, M. G., Hajiaghaei-Keshteli, M., & Smith, N. R. (2023). Data-driven prediction and optimization toward net-zero and positive-energy buildings: A systematic review. *Building and Environment*, *242*, 110578. DOI: 10.1016/j.buildenv.2023.110578

Omotayo, O., Muonde, M., Olorunsogo, T. O., Ogugua, J. O., & Maduka, C. P. (2024). Pandemic epidemiology: A comprehensive review of covid-19 lessons and future healthcare preparedness. *International Medical Science Research Journal*, *4*(1), 89–107. DOI: 10.51594/imsrj.v4i1.739

Osama, M., Ateya, A. A., Sayed, M. S., Hammad, M., Pławiak, P., Abd El-Latif, A. A., & Elsayed, R. A. (2023). Internet of medical things and healthcare 4.0: Trends, requirements, challenges, and research directions. *Sensors (Basel)*, *23*(17), 7435. DOI: 10.3390/s23177435 PMID: 37687891

Parsa, A. D., Hakkim, S., Vinnakota, D., Mahmud, I., Bulsari, S., Dehghani, L., & Kabir, R. (2023). Artificial Intelligence for Global Healthcare. In *Artificial Intelligence in Medical Virology* (pp. 1–21). Springer Nature Singapore. DOI: 10.1007/978-981-99-0369-6_1

Parthasarathy, K. (2022). Examining cloud computing's data security problems and solutions: Authentication and access control (AAC). *Journal of Science and Technology*, 7(12), 1-10. ISSN 2456-5660.

Philip, J., Gandhimathi, S. K., Chalichalamala, S., Karnam, B., Chandanapalli, S. B., & Chennupalli, S. (2023). Smart Health Monitoring Using Deep Learning and Artificial Intelligence. *Revue d'Intelligence Artificielle*, *37*(2), 451–464. DOI: 10.18280/ria.370222

Priya, S. S., Al-Fatlawy, M. H., Khare, N., Mahalakshmi, V., & Ganesh, S. S. (2023, December). Machine and Deep Learning Classifications for IoT-Enabled Healthcare Devices. In *2023 4th International Conference on Computation, Automation and Knowledge Management (ICCAKM)* (pp. 01-07). IEEE. DOI: 10.1109/ICCAKM58659.2023.10449617

Ramu, S. P., Boopalan, P., Pham, Q. V., Maddikunta, P. K. R., Huynh-The, T., Alazab, M., Nguyen, T. T., & Gadekallu, T. R. (2022). Federated learning enabled digital twins for smart cities: Concepts, recent advances, and future directions. *Sustainable Cities and Society*, *79*, 103663. DOI: 10.1016/j.scs.2021.103663

Rauniyar, A., Hagos, D. H., Jha, D., Håkegård, J. E., Bagci, U., Rawat, D. B., & Vlassov, V. (2023). Federated learning for medical applications: A taxonomy, current trends, challenges, and future research directions. *IEEE Internet of Things Journal*.

Sallam, K., Mohamed, M., & Mohamed, A. W. (2023). Internet of Things (IoT) in supply chain management: Challenges, opportunities, and best practices. *Sustainable Machine Intelligence Journal*, *2*, 3–1. DOI: 10.61185/SMIJ.2023.22103

Sharma, S. K., Sharma, A. K., Sharma, S., Shukla, K., & Ishaan, I. (2023). IoT-Based Smart Agriculture. In *Convergence of Cloud Computing, AI, and Agricultural Science* (pp. 137-151). IGI Global. DOI: 10.4018/979-8-3693-0200-2.ch007

Stergiou, C. L., Plageras, A. P., Memos, V. A., Koidou, M. P., & Psannis, K. E. (2023). Secure Monitoring System for IoT Healthcare Data in the Cloud. *Applied Sciences (Basel, Switzerland)*, *14*(1), 120. DOI: 10.3390/app14010120

Younas, M. I., Iqbal, M. J., Aziz, A., & Sodhro, A. H. (2023). Toward QoS monitoring in IoT edge devices driven healthcare—A systematic literature review. *Sensors (Basel)*, *23*(21), 8885. DOI: 10.3390/s23218885 PMID: 37960584

Chapter 11
Smart Water Governance With Blockchain Technology:
Blockchain Water Management

Bannishikha Banerjee
https://orcid.org/0000-0003-4848-8749
Amity University, Kolkata, India

Ujan Sen
https://orcid.org/0009-0008-0870-1123
Amity University, Kolkata, India

Siddhanta Pramanik
Amity University, Kolkata, India

Aryan Banerjee
Amity University, Kolkata, India

ABSTRACT

Effective water management is essential to address the growing pressures of population increase, climate change, and resource scarcity. However, traditional water management approaches often face challenges such as inefficiency, lack of transparency, and difficulties in ensuring accountability. Blockchain technology, known for its decentralized and immutable ledger system, offers promising solutions to these persistent issues. This chapter examines the potential of blockchain in transforming water management systems by enabling secure, transparent, and efficient processes. By leveraging blockchain, water-related data—including usage, quality, and distribution—can be recorded in a tamper-proof manner, reducing inefficiencies

DOI: 10.4018/979-8-3373-1424-2.ch011

and enhancing trust among stakeholders.

I. INTRODUCTION

Water is an indispensable resource that serves as the foundation for life, economic activity, and ecological stability. The critical nature of water for human survival cannot be overstated—its importance stretches beyond just consumption for daily life to include its essential role in industrial, agricultural, and energy sectors. As the world's population continues to grow, so does the demand for water. This increasing demand, combined with the effects of climate change, highlights the urgency for sustainable water management strategies to ensure that this vital resource remains available for future generations.

Water is pivotal in multiple sectors of the economy, particularly in agriculture. Irrigation, for instance, accounts for the largest share of water consumption worldwide, utilizing over 70% of all freshwater resources, (Pimentel *et al.*, 1997). According to the Food and Agriculture Organization (FAO), more than three-quarters of the global freshwater used annually is allocated for agricultural purposes, (Postel, 2014). As water scarcity becomes a more pressing issue, the need for more efficient and equitable management practices becomes even more apparent. Effective water resource management is essential to balance the growing demand for water with its sustainable availability.

The Urgency of Efficient Water Resource Management

The rapid growth in global water demand is driven by factors such as population growth, urbanization, economic development, and climate change. According to the United Nations, the global population is projected to reach 9.7 billion by 2050, which will undoubtedly increase water demand. This heightened demand, coupled with unpredictable weather patterns due to climate change, puts immense pressure on available freshwater resources. In many parts of the world, water is becoming increasingly scarce, and the need for efficient and equitable water management has never been more critical, (Jagtap *et al.*, 2022).

In many regions, water rights and entitlements are poorly defined or managed, leading to inefficient allocation and sometimes even conflicts over water use. Proper governance of water resources, particularly in terms of the legal and economic frameworks that regulate access, can help ensure that water is allocated in the most efficient and equitable manner. One of the most promising approaches to achieving this goal is through the trading of water rights.

The Concept of Water Rights and Water Rights Trading

The concept of water rights is rooted in the broader framework of property rights, which defines ownership and control over natural resources, (Chen, Cao, & Li, 20210. Water rights refer to the legal entitlements that grant individuals or entities the authority to use water for specific purposes, whether for personal consumption, agricultural irrigation, industrial use, or ecological preservation. These rights can be transferable, allowing for the reallocation of water between different users in response to changing needs.

Water rights trading is a practice where the entitlements to use water are treated as economic assets. This practice allows individuals or entities to buy and sell water rights, enabling the redistribution of water based on demand. Water rights trading first gained traction in developed nations, particularly in the United States, Australia, and Chile, where strong legal frameworks and well-established markets facilitated the exchange of water rights. Over time, other regions have adopted similar systems, with varying degrees of success, tailored to their unique socio-economic and environmental conditions, (Grantham & Viers, 2014) (Delorit, Parker, & Block, 2019).

Water rights trading aims to improve the efficiency of water resource allocation by enabling the transfer of water from lower-value uses to higher-value uses. For example, water that would otherwise be used inefficiently in agriculture can be sold to industrial or urban users who can put it to more productive use. This approach ensures that water is allocated where it provides the greatest economic benefit and minimizes waste.

Water Rights Trading Systems: Global Trends and Practices

The legal and institutional frameworks for water rights trading have evolved in different ways across the globe. In developed countries such as the United States, Australia, and New Zealand, water markets have become integral parts of water resource management. These nations have established comprehensive regulatory frameworks that define how water rights can be traded and ensure that these markets function effectively. For instance, in the United States, water rights trading is governed by both state and federal laws, and each state has its own system for managing water entitlements, (Ge, Wu, & Chen, 2017).

In Australia, the government has implemented a national water trading scheme that enables the transfer of water rights between regions and sectors. This system is one of the most advanced in the world and has helped to improve the efficiency of water use, especially in regions that face chronic water scarcity, such as the Murray-Darling Basin. Australia's experience with water rights trading has shown that, with the right legal and institutional structures in place, water markets can play a crucial role in ensuring that water is used sustainably and equitably, (Yli-Huumo *et al.,* 2016).

In contrast, many developing countries are still in the early stages of implementing water rights trading systems. While these nations recognize the importance of managing water resources more efficiently, they often face challenges related to legal infrastructure, governance, and institutional capacity. In regions with weak governance structures or complex social dynamics, the establishment of water markets can be difficult. However, there are examples of progress, such as the introduction of water rights trading systems in parts of Africa and Latin America. These emerging markets are still in the pilot stages but offer promising insights into how water trading can be adapted to diverse contexts, (Saberi *et al.,* 2019).

The Role of Governance in Water Rights Trading

The success of water rights trading is heavily dependent on the quality of governance that underpins these systems. In order for water markets to function effectively, there must be clear legal frameworks that define the ownership and transferability of water rights. Additionally, water trading systems must be governed by principles of equity and sustainability to ensure that water is distributed in a fair and responsible manner, (Predescu *et al.*, 2021).

One of the main goals of water rights trading is to achieve a more efficient allocation of water. This involves allowing water to flow from lower-value uses to higher-value uses, where it can generate greater economic benefits. For example, water that was originally allocated for agricultural use in a region with declining crop yields may be more effectively used in industrial processes or urban centers with growing water needs. Trading systems facilitate such reallocations by creating a marketplace for water rights, where buyers and sellers can negotiate and transact based on their water needs, (Mahmoud *et al.,* 2021).

However, for these markets to function equitably, it is important that the interests of marginalized or vulnerable groups, such as small-scale farmers or indigenous communities, are protected. A well-designed water rights trading system must consider the social implications of water redistribution and ensure that access to water is not restricted to those with greater economic power. Furthermore, the environmental impact of water transactions should be carefully monitored to avoid over-exploitation of water resources in ecologically sensitive areas, (Chohan, 2019).

Economic and Ecological Impacts of Water Rights Trading

Water rights trading not only offers a means of improving economic efficiency but also has significant ecological benefits. One of the key advantages of water trading is that it provides an incentive for users to adopt water-saving technologies and practices. Since water rights are typically allocated based on historical use, those who consume water inefficiently can be incentivized to reduce their usage in order to retain or sell their water rights, (Jagtap *et al.*, 2021).

For instance, in regions facing severe water scarcity, such as parts of the western United States and Australia, water rights trading has led to the adoption of more efficient irrigation practices and the development of water-saving technologies. These technologies, such as drip irrigation systems and soil moisture sensors, allow farmers to use water more efficiently, thereby increasing agricultural productivity while reducing water consumption. By creating a market-driven incentive for conservation, water rights trading promotes sustainable water management practices across all sectors, (Banerjee & Patel, 2016).

On the ecological side, water rights trading has the potential to improve the health of freshwater ecosystems by reallocating water to environmental uses, such as maintaining river flow or preserving wetlands. For example, water that was previously used for agriculture can be transferred to environmental uses, helping to restore ecosystems and preserve biodiversity, (Nakamoto, 2008). In many cases, governments and environmental organizations have participated in water rights markets to secure water for environmental purposes, ensuring that ecosystems have sufficient water to thrive.

The Challenges and Future of Water Rights Trading

While water rights trading holds significant promise for improving water resource management, there are also challenges that must be addressed. One of the main concerns is ensuring that the legal and institutional frameworks governing water markets are robust enough to prevent misuse or exploitation. In some cases, water rights trading has been criticized for exacerbating inequalities, with wealthier individuals or corporations buying up water rights and leaving poorer communities without access to this essential resource, (Zheng *et al.*, 2018).

Furthermore, the impact of climate change on water availability poses a major challenge to water rights trading. As weather patterns become more unpredictable, the availability of water resources may fluctuate, leading to volatility in water markets. This can create uncertainty for both buyers and sellers and may undermine the stability of water rights systems. It is therefore essential that water rights trading systems are flexible enough to adapt to changing environmental conditions and that stakeholders are adequately prepared to manage these changes, (Banerjee *et al.,* 2020).

Looking to the future, it is likely that the role of water rights trading will continue to grow, particularly in regions where water scarcity is becoming more acute. As the global population increases and climate change exacerbates water shortages, it will be crucial to adopt innovative approaches to water management. Water rights trading, when implemented with sound governance and appropriate legal structures, can help to ensure that water is allocated efficiently, equitably, and sustainably, (Thakur *et al.,* 2021).

Water rights trading presents a viable solution to the growing global challenge of managing limited water resources. By enabling the redistribution of water to where it is most needed, water rights trading can improve both economic and ecological outcomes. However, for these systems to function effectively, they must be underpinned by strong legal frameworks, robust governance structures, and principles of equity and sustainability. When implemented correctly, water rights trading can promote efficient water use, encourage conservation, and ensure the equitable distribution of this vital resource. As water scarcity becomes an increasingly urgent issue, water rights trading offers a promising path toward sustainable and resilient water management for the future.

Figure 1. Integrated water management

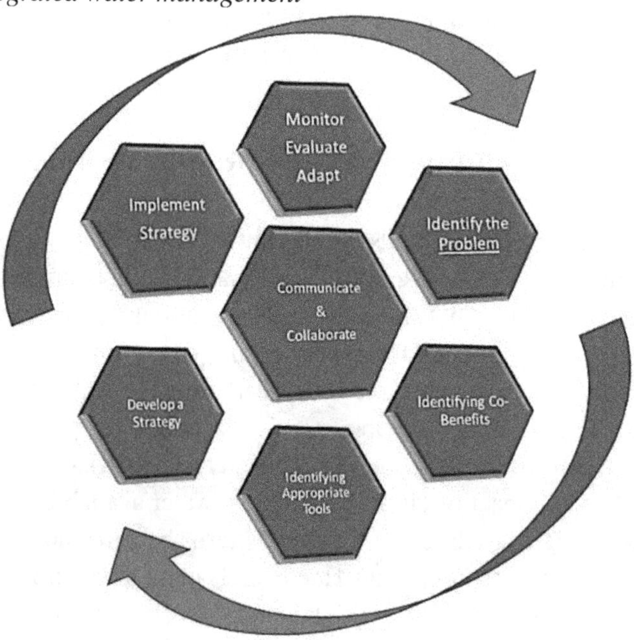

II. ROLE OF BLOCKCHAIN

To ensure that all stakeholders associated with a transaction are acknowledged within the system and that the transactional data remains immutable, secure, and robust, blockchain technology employs advanced security measures within a decentralized framework. This decentralized framework is designed to maintain transparency, accountability, and resilience, which are essential for building trust in the system. Blockchain achieves these objectives through a combination of various security mechanisms such as hash structures, asymmetric encryption, digital signatures, and encrypted certificates. Each of these tools plays a pivotal role in maintaining data integrity, making it highly resistant to tampering and unauthorized changes. This is especially critical in today's digital world, where security breaches and data manipulation can result in severe financial and reputational damage. The strength of blockchain lies in its ability to mitigate such risks effectively by utilizing a combination of cryptographic techniques and a distributed ledger system, (Banerjee & Saha, 2022).

The foundation of blockchain's security lies in its cryptographic principles. Blockchain uses a hash structure, which is a one-way mathematical function that transforms input data into a fixed-length output known as a hash value. The use of cryptographic hashing ensures that even a small change in the input data will result in a drastically different hash, making it virtually impossible to alter the data without detection. This feature plays a crucial role in securing the integrity of transactional data, as it links each block of data to the one before it, forming a chain that becomes progressively more secure the more blocks are added. As new blocks are added to the blockchain, each subsequent block is cryptographically linked to the previous one, creating an immutable record of transactions that cannot be altered once confirmed, (Torky & Hassanein, 2020). The hash of each block is uniquely tied to the data it contains, further strengthening the integrity of the entire blockchain. This chain of blocks, once confirmed, cannot be altered or deleted, ensuring the integrity of all historical records.

In addition to hashing, blockchain incorporates asymmetric encryption, which utilizes a pair of keys—a public key and a private key—for secure data transmission. The public key is used to encrypt data, while the private key is used to decrypt it. This ensures that only the holder of the private key can decrypt the data that has been encrypted using their public key, enhancing confidentiality and security. By using asymmetric encryption, blockchain systems ensure that sensitive information, such as personal details or transaction data, can only be accessed by authorized parties, (Nayal *et al.*, 2021). This encryption scheme prevents unauthorized access, making it difficult for malicious actors to eavesdrop on communication or alter transaction data in transit. Furthermore, asymmetric encryption ensures that data is securely transmitted even over unsecured networks, which is especially important in today's interconnected digital ecosystem.

Digital signatures also play a critical role in ensuring authenticity and integrity. A digital signature, created using a private key, acts as proof of ownership and verifies that the transaction was indeed authorized by the rightful party. The digital signature verifies the sender's identity and ensures that the contents of the message have not been tampered with during transmission. In a blockchain system, each participant is provided with a private key, which they use to sign their transactions. This ensures that only the authorized participant can initiate a transaction and that the transaction cannot be altered without invalidating the signature, (Pincheira *et al.,* 2021). Digital signatures also provide non-repudiation, meaning that once a transaction is signed and recorded on the blockchain, the participant cannot deny their involvement in the transaction. This increases accountability and reduces the likelihood of fraudulent activities.

Furthermore, encrypted certificates are used to further strengthen the blockchain's security architecture. These certificates serve as an additional layer of authentication, ensuring that only authorized entities can interact with the system. This prevents unauthorized access and manipulation of data, safeguarding the system against potential attacks or fraud. Encrypted certificates are particularly useful in blockchain applications where identity verification is critical, such as in healthcare, finance, and legal services. These certificates provide a secure mechanism for verifying the identity of participants in the blockchain network, ensuring that only trusted entities are allowed to interact with the system, (Banerjee, Jani, & Shah, 2021).

The decentralized nature of blockchain also contributes significantly to its security. Unlike traditional centralized systems where data is stored on a single server or database, blockchain's decentralized structure distributes data across multiple nodes in a network. Each node holds a copy of the entire blockchain, which is continuously updated with new transactions. This ensures that there is no single point of failure in the system, making it far less vulnerable to cyberattacks or data breaches. Since all participants in the blockchain network have access to the same copy of the ledger, there is no need to rely on a central authority to validate transactions. This reduces the risk of corruption, manipulation, or unauthorized access to the data. Additionally, the decentralized network uses consensus mechanisms, such as Proof of Work or Proof of Stake, to validate and confirm transactions. These mechanisms require multiple nodes to agree on the validity of a transaction before it is added to the blockchain, further reducing the risk of fraud or manipulation, (Saha, Banerjee, & Joshi, 2022).

The decentralized structure not only enhances security but also ensures the system's reliability and robustness. Since all nodes in the network must reach a consensus before any changes are made, it becomes nearly impossible for a malicious actor to alter the data without gaining control over a significant portion of the network. This consensus-based validation process guarantees that the data stored on the blockchain is accurate and trustworthy, as it has been validated by multiple independent nodes, (Biswas *et al.,* 2024). The distributed nature of blockchain also makes it more resilient to attacks. Even if one node or a small group of nodes is compromised, the integrity of the overall system remains intact, as other nodes can continue to validate and store transactions.

One of the most significant advantages of blockchain technology lies in its verifiable and immutable characteristics. Once a transaction is recorded on the blockchain, it cannot be changed or erased. This immutability is crucial for maintaining a transparent and tamper-proof record of all transactions. This feature makes blockchain highly suitable for applications where data integrity and transparency are paramount, such as financial transactions, supply chain management, and legal agreements. By ensuring that all records are permanent and cannot be altered retroactively, blockchain instills confidence in its users, making it a valuable tool for businesses and organizations across various sectors, (Bhat *et al.,* 2022).

The verifiability and immutability of blockchain also make it particularly relevant for organizational leadership and resource management. In the context of supply chain management, for example, blockchain allows for the secure and transparent tracking of goods as they move through the supply chain. Each transaction or movement of goods is recorded on the blockchain, creating an immutable and verifiable history of the product's journey from the manufacturer to the consumer. This ensures that all stakeholders can trust the authenticity of the product and its provenance, reducing the risk of fraud or counterfeit goods. Furthermore, by providing a transparent and traceable record, blockchain helps businesses comply with regulatory requirements and industry standards, promoting ethical practices throughout the supply chain, (Banerjee, Jani, & Shah, 2021).

Another critical area where blockchain is proving its value is in environmental resource management. The integration of blockchain with other technologies, such as the Internet of Things (IoT) and cloud computing, has the potential to revolutionize ecological stewardship projects. IoT devices can collect real-time data on environmental conditions, such as air quality, water usage, and energy consumption. This data can then be securely recorded on the blockchain, creating a transparent and immutable record of environmental metrics. This integration allows for more effective monitoring, management, and tracking of environmental resources, creating new opportunities for sustainable practices and helping organizations meet their sustainability goals, (Khan *et al.,* 2022).

For example, blockchain can be used to track the provenance of sustainable products, such as certified organic goods, ensuring that they are produced and transported in accordance with environmental standards. By recording every step of the product's journey on the blockchain, consumers can verify that the product is genuinely sustainable, while businesses can demonstrate their commitment to ethical practices. Additionally, the use of blockchain in combination with IoT can help organizations monitor and reduce their carbon footprint. By tracking energy usage and emissions in real-time, blockchain can provide businesses with the data they need to optimize their operations, reduce waste, and minimize their environmental impact.

One area where blockchain is already showing significant promise is in the management of energy systems, particularly in the context of renewable energy, (Kumarathunga, Calheiros, & Ginige, 2022). Traditional energy grids are often inefficient and prone to waste, as they rely on centralized control and fail to take advantage of decentralized energy sources such as solar panels or wind turbines. Blockchain has the potential to modernize the energy sector by enabling peer-to-peer energy trading, where individuals or households can buy and sell excess energy generated from renewable sources. By using blockchain to facilitate these transactions, households can manage their energy consumption more efficiently, reduce waste, and lower their utility costs. This creates a more sustainable energy model, where renewable energy is optimized and waste is minimized.

By modernizing the local renewable energy market with distributed ledger technology, blockchain empowers households to take greater control of their energy management. It allows for a more transparent and decentralized energy market where consumers and producers can interact directly, without the need for intermediaries. This reduces costs, increases efficiency, and encourages the adoption of renewable energy sources. In addition, blockchain can be used to track and verify the origin of renewable energy, ensuring that it meets sustainability standards and can be certified as green energy. This has the potential to drive further investment in renewable energy infrastructure and help reduce reliance on fossil fuels, (Patel, Ucchula, & Banerjee, 2013) (Song *et al.*, 2022).

In conclusion, blockchain technology offers a robust, secure, and transparent framework for managing data and transactions. Its combination of cryptographic techniques, decentralized structure, and consensus mechanisms ensures that data remains immutable, verifiable, and tamper-proof. The integration of blockchain with other technologies such as IoT and cloud computing further enhances its potential to drive sustainable practices and improve resource management across various sectors. From optimizing energy consumption to ensuring the traceability of sustainable products, blockchain is proving to be a transformative tool for enhancing operational efficiency, transparency, and sustainability in today's world. Its potential to revolutionize industries ranging from supply chain management to environmental stewardship makes it a powerful tool for the future of business and society. Moreover, as blockchain continues to evolve and expand its applications, it is likely to play an even more pivotal role in shaping the future of technological innovation and sustainability, (Banerjee, Hazra, & Sarkar, 2024).

Furthermore, encrypted certificates are used to further strengthen the blockchain's security architecture. These certificates serve as an additional layer of authentication, ensuring that only authorized entities can interact with the system. This prevents unauthorized access and manipulation of data, safeguarding the system against potential attacks or fraud.

The decentralized nature of blockchain also contributes significantly to its security. Unlike traditional centralized systems where data is stored on a single server or database, blockchain's decentralized structure distributes data across multiple nodes in a network. Each node holds a copy of the entire blockchain, which is continuously updated with new transactions. This ensures that there is no single point of failure in the system, making it far less vulnerable to cyberattacks or data breaches. Additionally, the decentralized network uses consensus mechanisms, such as Proof of Work or Proof of Stake, to validate and confirm transactions. These mechanisms require multiple nodes to agree on the validity of a transaction before it is added to the blockchain, further reducing the risk of fraud or manipulation, (Zeng *et al.*, 2021).

The decentralized structure not only enhances security but also ensures the system's reliability and robustness. Since all nodes in the network must reach a consensus before any changes are made, it becomes nearly impossible for a malicious actor to alter the data without gaining control over a significant portion of the network. This consensus-based validation process guarantees that the data stored on the blockchain is accurate and trustworthy, as it has been validated by multiple independent nodes.

One of the most significant advantages of blockchain technology lies in its verifiable and immutable characteristics. Once a transaction is recorded on the blockchain, it cannot be changed or erased. This immutability is crucial for maintaining a transparent and tamper-proof record of all transactions. This feature makes blockchain highly suitable for applications where data integrity and transparency are paramount, such as financial transactions, supply chain management, and legal agreements. By ensuring that all records are permanent and cannot be altered retroactively, blockchain instills confidence in its users, making it a valuable tool for businesses and organizations across various sectors.

The verifiability and immutability of blockchain also make it particularly relevant for organizational leadership and resource management. In the context of supply chain management, for example, blockchain allows for the secure and transparent tracking of goods as they move through the supply chain. Each transaction or movement of goods is recorded on the blockchain, creating an immutable and verifiable history of the product's journey from the manufacturer to the consumer. This ensures that all stakeholders can trust the authenticity of the product and its provenance, reducing the risk of fraud or counterfeit goods, (Banerjee & Sarkar, 2024).

Another critical area where blockchain is proving its value is in environmental resource management. The integration of blockchain with other technologies, such as the Internet of Things (IoT) and cloud computing, has the potential to revolutionize ecological stewardship projects. IoT devices can collect real-time data on environmental conditions, such as air quality, water usage, and energy consumption. This data can then be securely recorded on the blockchain, creating a transparent and immutable record of environmental metrics. This integration allows for more effective monitoring, management, and tracking of environmental resources, creating new opportunities for sustainable practices and helping organizations meet their sustainability goals.

For example, blockchain can be used to track the provenance of sustainable products, such as certified organic goods, ensuring that they are produced and transported in accordance with environmental standards. By recording every step of the product's journey on the blockchain, consumers can verify that the product is genuinely sustainable, while businesses can demonstrate their commitment to ethical practices. Additionally, the use of blockchain in combination with IoT can help organizations monitor and reduce their carbon footprint. By tracking energy usage and emissions in real-time, blockchain can provide businesses with the data they need to optimize their operations, reduce waste, and minimize their environmental impact, (Faisal *et al.*, 2014).

One area where blockchain is already showing significant promise is in the management of energy systems, particularly in the context of renewable energy. Traditional energy grids are often inefficient and prone to waste, as they rely on centralized control and fail to take advantage of decentralized energy sources such as solar panels or wind turbines. Blockchain has the potential to modernize the energy sector by enabling peer-to-peer energy trading, where individuals or households can buy and sell excess energy generated from renewable sources. By using blockchain to facilitate these transactions, households can manage their energy consumption more efficiently, reduce waste, and lower their utility costs. This creates a more sustainable energy model, where renewable energy is optimized and waste is minimized.

In the context of residential energy systems, blockchain can play a transformative role by allowing users to monitor their energy usage in real-time and make adjustments based on their consumption patterns. For example, a household could sell excess solar energy back to the grid or to other households, using blockchain as a secure and transparent platform for the transaction. This would not only increase the efficiency of the energy system but also incentivize individuals to invest in renewable energy sources, as they could earn income from selling excess energy.

By modernizing the local renewable energy market with distributed ledger technology, blockchain empowers households to take greater control of their energy management. It allows for a more transparent and decentralized energy market where consumers and producers can interact directly, without the need for intermediaries. This reduces costs, increases efficiency, and encourages the adoption of renewable energy sources. In addition, blockchain can be used to track and verify the origin of renewable energy, ensuring that it meets sustainability standards and can be certified as green energy. This has the potential to drive further investment in renewable energy infrastructure and help reduce reliance on fossil fuels, (Banerjee, 2024).

In conclusion, blockchain technology offers a robust, secure, and transparent framework for managing data and transactions. Its combination of cryptographic techniques, decentralized structure, and consensus mechanisms ensures that data remains immutable, verifiable, and tamper-proof. The integration of blockchain with other technologies such as IoT and cloud computing further enhances its potential to drive sustainable practices and improve resource management across various sectors. From optimizing energy consumption to ensuring the traceability of sustainable products, blockchain is proving to be a transformative tool for enhancing operational efficiency, transparency, and sustainability in today's world. Its potential to revolutionize industries ranging from supply chain management to environmental stewardship makes it a powerful tool for the future of business and society.

In the context of water resource management, blockchain offers several specific benefits, particularly when applied to groundwater asset transactions. The following key advantages highlight its impact:

- Automated evaluation of transactions: Blockchain enables the seamless and automatic assessment of water resource exchanges using smart contracts, reducing the need for manual intervention, (Mukherjee & Banerjee, 2024).
- Decentralized trading mechanism: Parties involved in water rights transactions can independently negotiate and compete within a secure and transparent blockchain framework, eliminating reliance on centralized authorities.
- Immutable metadata: The transactional metadata stored within the blockchain ecosystem is both irrevocable and easily identifiable. This eliminates the need for analog-based recognition or manual recordkeeping, streamlining the management process, (Banerjee, Jani, & Shah, 2021).
- Elimination of intermediaries: Blockchain removes the necessity of third-party evaluators for water entitlement agreements. This not only reduces costs but also enhances trust and efficiency in transactions.

The use of blockchain in water resource management also supports broader sustainability goals. By ensuring transparency and accountability in the allocation and exchange of water resources, blockchain helps mitigate disputes and fosters collaborative resource sharing. Figure 2 illustrates blockchain's role in enhancing water management processes, while Table 2 outlines the key features of blockchain technology and its applications.

Beyond its direct applications in water management, blockchain holds implications for a wide array of industries. Its ability to provide a decentralized, secure, and tamper-proof record system makes it a valuable tool for governance, finance, and supply chain management. For example, in agriculture, blockchain can be used to track water usage and ensure compliance with regulations, promoting more sustainable practices. Similarly, in urban planning, blockchain can facilitate the efficient allocation of utilities, improving resource distribution in densely populated areas, (Banerjee, 2024).

When integrated with IoT, blockchain enhances data collection and analysis, enabling real-time monitoring of water systems. Sensors connected to IoT devices can provide accurate data on water flow, quality, and usage, which is then securely stored and processed on the blockchain. This integration offers unprecedented visibility into resource management, empowering decision-makers to implement data-driven policies. The distributed nature of blockchain ensures that information is accessible to all authorized parties, fostering transparency and collaboration. Moreover, its cryptographic security features protect sensitive data, reducing the risk of cyber threats. These attributes make blockchain a powerful tool for building trust among stakeholders, a critical factor in managing shared resources like water.

In conclusion, blockchain technology has the potential to revolutionize the management of natural resources, including water. Its secure, decentralized, and transparent framework offers significant advantages, from automating resource allocation to eliminating intermediaries in transactions. When combined with IoT and cloud technologies, blockchain creates a comprehensive system for monitoring and managing environmental resources effectively. As shown in Figure 2, blockchain's role in water management is multifaceted, providing solutions that enhance sustainability, efficiency, and accountability. By leveraging the unique features of blockchain, stakeholders can address the challenges of resource scarcity and pave the way for more equitable and sustainable resource management practices.

Figure 2. Blockchain for sustainable water management

Table 1. Features of blockchain

Decentralization	A decentralized application (DApp) allows for autonomous operation based on predefined requirements by utilizing smart contracts. Since blockchain operates in a decentralized manner, each node or cluster within the network functions independently, ensuring that the system remains operational even if individual components fail, (Ge, Wu, & Chen, 2017). This structure of decentralization reduces data reliance and minimizes latency, which improves the efficiency of the overall process. By eliminating the risk of a single point of failure, the system ensures continuous uptime and fosters robust oversight, making the DApp more reliable and secure. This decentralized approach enables greater scalability and resilience, as the application can maintain operations even when some parts of the network experience issues. Additionally, decentralization promotes transparency, as all transactions and processes are recorded on a distributed ledger, accessible to all network participants. This level of openness and autonomy empowers users while reducing the need for intermediaries, further enhancing the overall efficiency and trustworthiness of the application. Ultimately, DApps offer a more secure and efficient alternative to traditional centralized systems by leveraging blockchain technology and smart contracts.
Forgery Resistance	Virtual signatures play a crucial role in smart contracts by verifying the integrity of data and ensuring the reliability of the distributed ledger. Once a transaction or interaction is recorded in a decentralized application (DApp), it becomes immutable, meaning it cannot be modified or altered, even by the parties involved, including the beneficiary, (Saberi *et al.*, 2019). This immutability feature ensures that the system remains transparent and trustworthy, as all actions are permanently logged on the blockchain. By utilizing virtual signatures, DApps maintain a high level of security and accountability, preventing unauthorized changes and ensuring that all parties comply with the terms of the contract. This mechanism also fosters confidence in the decentralized system, as it eliminates the possibility of tampering or manipulation of data after execution.
Transparency	Genuine users always have uninterrupted access to the exchange and its related data, ensuring that they can interact with the system and retrieve necessary information whenever required, (Mahmoud *et al.*, 2021). This continuous accessibility is crucial for maintaining transparency, trust, and seamless user experience in decentralized applications.
Self-execution	When the predefined conditions are met, commercial transactions related to the components within the ecosystem occur automatically, without the need for a third-party intermediary, (Jagtap *et al.*, 2021). This process is facilitated by smart contracts, which are self-executing agreements that operate on blockchain technology. By eliminating intermediaries, these transactions become more efficient, cost-effective, and secure. The system ensures that all parties adhere to the agreed-upon terms, while also promoting transparency, as all actions are recorded on a decentralized ledger. This approach reduces the risk of fraud or manipulation, fostering greater trust and reliability in the ecosystem.

continued on following page

Table 1. Continued

Openness	Traditional organizations typically operate with a top-down hierarchical structure, where a central authority or a few essential agencies hold the power to enforce rules and ensure that responsibilities are met. This structure relies on a clearly defined chain of command to direct decisions, maintain order, and ensure accountability. However, this centralized model can be inflexible and may limit the input of lower-level members. It can also lead to inefficiencies, as decisions are often slow and bottlenecked at the top. In contrast, decentralized systems challenge and transform this rigid hierarchy by distributing authority across the network. Rather than a few individuals or agencies holding all the power, each member of a decentralized organization is granted the ability to participate actively in decision-making. This includes submitting suggestions, casting votes, and directly influencing policy. This collaborative approach fosters a more inclusive environment where diverse perspectives are valued, and decisions can be made more efficiently and democratically. Decentralization encourages innovation, as members are empowered to propose new ideas and solutions without waiting for approval from a centralized authority. Furthermore, it helps eliminate bottlenecks that typically slow down processes in hierarchical organizations. This system is not only more adaptive but also ensures a higher level of engagement and commitment from all participants, as they feel a sense of ownership over the decisions made. Ultimately, decentralization promotes a flatter organizational structure, where power and decision-making are distributed equally among members, resulting in a more agile, transparent, and responsive system. This model is especially effective in environments that require flexibility, innovation, and the active participation of all stakeholders, (Nakamoto, 2008).

continued on following page

Table 1. Continued

Incentives	Tokens are digital assets issued by decentralized initiatives, typically within a blockchain-based ecosystem. These tokens serve as a means of representing value, ownership, or rights within the decentralized network. They can be designed for various purposes, such as facilitating transactions, rewarding participants, or providing access to certain features within the ecosystem. The exchange of tokens on the blockchain plays a key role in enabling right holders to realize and exercise their rights, as well as to receive rewards for their contributions to the network. This process is integral to the functioning of decentralized organizations and applications. In decentralized systems, the use of tokens helps establish a direct relationship between the participants and the platform. Tokens can represent various forms of value, such as voting rights, staking capabilities, or even ownership in the form of equity. By issuing tokens, decentralized projects ensure that all stakeholders—whether they are users, developers, or investors—have a tangible and verifiable stake in the success of the initiative. These tokens are exchanged on the blockchain, which provides a transparent and immutable ledger, ensuring that all transactions are securely recorded and verified by the network. The exchange of tokens not only enables the realization of rights but also incentivizes stakeholders to participate actively in the system. For example, in a decentralized finance (DeFi) ecosystem, users may receive tokens as rewards for providing liquidity to the platform. Similarly, token holders in decentralized governance systems may have the ability to vote on proposals, making decisions that impact the direction of the project. This creates a dynamic system where participants are encouraged to contribute and collaborate, knowing that their actions are directly rewarded. Through the use of tokenized systems, decentralized initiatives can foster broad-scale collaboration among various stakeholders. The token exchange mechanism encourages interactions between participants, as they can trade, stake, or vote using their tokens, creating a vibrant, participatory ecosystem. Collaboration becomes more effective as participants are incentivized to work together toward shared goals, such as the development of new features, expansion of the network, or improving the overall ecosystem. Furthermore, the decentralized nature of these tokens ensures that power is distributed among all participants, rather than being concentrated in the hands of a few central authorities. One of the significant advantages of tokenization in decentralized systems is the ability to optimize the utilization of assets within the organization. Traditional organizations often face inefficiencies due to centralized decision-making processes, lack of transparency, or mismanagement of resources. In contrast, decentralized networks can ensure that assets—whether financial, intellectual, or human—are used optimally, thanks to the transparent nature of blockchain technology. Through tokenized systems, assets can be tracked, traded, or allocated in ways that maximize their utility. For instance, in a decentralized marketplace, assets such as data, intellectual property, or computing power can be tokenized and exchanged in a transparent manner. This allows stakeholders to derive maximum value from their assets while ensuring fair compensation for their contributions. By enabling frictionless exchange and incentivizing collaboration, token-based systems help drive the efficient use of resources across the network. In summary, tokens issued by decentralized initiatives provide a powerful mechanism for enabling right holders to access their rights, receive rewards, and actively participate in the ecosystem. The exchange of tokens fosters collaboration and optimizes the utilization of assets, ultimately contributing to the success and sustainability of decentralized organizations. By leveraging blockchain technology, these systems offer enhanced transparency, security, and efficiency, ensuring that all participants are fairly rewarded for their contributions and that resources are used to their full potential, (Zheng *et al.*, 2018).

Table 1 highlights the key features of blockchain technology and its potential applications for sustainable water management. By leveraging these features, water management systems can transition from traditional administrative frameworks to more dynamic, decentralized, and efficient organizational models. One such approach involves transforming the watershed neighborhood administrative unit into a water supply enterprise or a water consumption association. This model integrates independent financing irrigation districts, a common organizational framework that has significantly improved the management and operational mechanisms of irrigation systems, (Banerjee, 2024).

The transformation of irrigation management systems into self-sustaining entities marks a shift towards decentralized governance in water resource management. Water supply enterprises, under this model, assume responsibility for designing, operating, and maintaining water distribution systems. A key feature of these enterprises is their independence in decision-making and financial operations. By maintaining separate financial records and adhering to market-driven financial principles, these entities achieve self-sufficiency and autonomy. Such a model demonstrates how decentralization can enhance efficiency and responsiveness in water resource management.

Self-supporting irrigation districts exemplify a viable model for decentralization, offering several advantages for sustainable water management. These districts operate based on agreements established through water consumption initiatives, where fees are determined by the volume of water used, (Enescu *et al.*, 2020). This approach not only incentivizes responsible water usage but also promotes transparency and accountability. Blockchain technology plays a pivotal role in this transformation by ensuring that all data related to water transactions are immutable, secure, and automatically updated in real-time according to the rules and system changes of the decentralized framework.

Blockchain's decentralized nature provides several benefits that enhance the efficiency and reliability of water management systems. One of the primary advantages is the ability to share expertise and information among all stakeholders. This feature fosters a collaborative environment where knowledge exchange can improve decision-making and problem-solving processes. By enabling all participants to access the same reliable and transparent data, blockchain facilitates the creation of a favorable trade ecosystem for water resources, (Banerjee, Jani, & Shah, 2021).

The use of blockchain also addresses critical challenges in water rights management, particularly the issue of information asymmetry. In traditional systems, disparities in access to information can lead to inefficiencies and conflicts over resource allocation. Blockchain's dynamic, real-time data dissemination capabilities ensure that all stakeholders have equal access to accurate and up-to-date information. Additionally, its comprehensive network access enables parties on either side of water rights transactions to collaborate effectively. This collaboration helps develop practical solutions to overcome information imbalances and supports the efficient distribution of resources, (Yahaya *et al.*, 2020).

The decentralization enabled by blockchain technology also transforms the financial and operational frameworks of water management systems. By integrating smart contracts, water supply enterprises can automate various processes, such as fee collection and allocation of resources. Smart contracts are self-executing agreements with terms encoded directly into the blockchain. These contracts eliminate the need for intermediaries, reducing costs and enhancing efficiency. Moreover, they ensure compliance with predefined rules, providing a transparent and secure mechanism for managing water transactions.

Another significant benefit of blockchain in water management is its ability to ensure the traceability and transparency of transactions. The immutability of blockchain records ensures that all transactions are permanently recorded and cannot be altered retrospectively. This feature is particularly important for maintaining trust among stakeholders, as it provides a verifiable audit trail for all activities. For example, water supply enterprises can use blockchain to track the allocation and usage of water resources, ensuring that all parties adhere to agreed-upon terms.

Blockchain technology also supports the development of decentralized water markets, where stakeholders can trade water rights in a secure and transparent environment. These markets enable the reallocation of water resources to areas with the highest demand, promoting efficient use and reducing wastage. By providing a platform for trading water rights, blockchain helps balance supply and demand, ensuring that resources are distributed equitably and sustainably.

Furthermore, the integration of blockchain with other emerging technologies, such as the Internet of Things (IoT) and artificial intelligence (AI), enhances its potential applications in water management. IoT devices can be used to monitor water usage, quality, and availability in real-time. This data can be securely stored on the blockchain, providing stakeholders with a comprehensive view of resource conditions. AI algorithms can analyze this data to identify trends and optimize resource allocation, further improving the efficiency of water management systems.

In addition to its technical advantages, blockchain also has broader implications for governance and policy-making in water management. By providing a decentralized and transparent platform, blockchain empowers local communities to take an active role in managing their water resources. This participatory approach ensures that decisions are made collaboratively and reflect the needs and priorities of all stakeholders. Moreover, blockchain's ability to provide real-time data and insights supports evidence-based policy-making, enabling governments to implement more effective and targeted interventions, (Mehta *et al.,* 2021).

Despite its numerous advantages, the implementation of blockchain in water management is not without challenges. The technology requires significant investments in infrastructure and expertise, which may be a barrier for resource-constrained regions. Additionally, the integration of blockchain with existing systems and processes requires careful planning and coordination. Policymakers and stakeholders must address these challenges to fully realize the potential of blockchain in transforming water management systems, (Leeuwen *et al.,* 2020).

In conclusion, blockchain technology offers a transformative approach to sustainable water management by enhancing transparency, efficiency, and collaboration. Through the decentralization of water management systems, blockchain enables the creation of self-sustaining entities that are financially and operationally autonomous. By addressing information asymmetry and fostering real-time collaboration, blockchain supports the equitable distribution of water resources. Furthermore, its integration with emerging technologies, such as IoT and AI, expands its potential applications and provides innovative solutions to complex water management challenges. As illustrated in Table 1, the features of blockchain provide a robust foundation for developing sustainable and efficient water management systems. With careful planning and collaboration, blockchain can play a pivotal role in addressing the growing global demand for water and ensuring the long-term sustainability of this vital resource.

III. FUTURE SCOPE OF BLOCKCHAIN

The Future Scope of Blockchain in Managing Water Resources

As the global population continues to rise and climate change intensifies, water scarcity and mismanagement have emerged as pressing challenges. Innovative solutions are critical to ensure the sustainable management of water resources, (Banerjee, 2019). Blockchain technology, with its ability to enhance transparency, accountability, and efficiency, holds immense potential to transform the water sector. This article explores the future scope of blockchain in managing water resources, emphasizing its applications, advantages, and the hurdles that need to be overcome for widespread adoption.

Understanding Blockchain Technology

Blockchain is a decentralized and distributed ledger technology designed to securely record transactions across multiple nodes in a network. The defining feature of blockchain is its immutability; once a transaction is recorded, it cannot be altered without consensus among the network participants, (Patel, Ucchula, & Banerjee, 2013). This inherent transparency and security make blockchain highly adaptable across sectors, from finance and supply chain management to energy and, more recently, water resource management, (Banerjee, 2019).

Challenges in Water Resource Management

Water scarcity, inefficient distribution systems, contamination, and inequitable access to clean water are some of the critical issues facing global water management. Traditional systems often lack transparency, leading to mismanagement and corruption. Data fragmentation further compounds these challenges, as water resource data is frequently isolated across different agencies and regions, preventing comprehensive analysis and informed decision-making, (Aoun *et al.*, 2021). Furthermore, the lack of reliable real-time monitoring systems limits the ability to address problems proactively. These challenges call for robust technological solutions that ensure equitable and efficient use of water resources.

Key Applications of Blockchain in Water Resource Management

Blockchain technology offers several innovative applications that can address these challenges and redefine water management practices.

1. Water Quality Monitoring

Blockchain can enhance real-time monitoring of water quality by integrating data from IoT-enabled sensors deployed in water bodies. This data, stored on a blockchain, is tamper-proof and accessible to stakeholders such as government agencies, NGOs, and the public, (Mehta *et al.*, 2021). The transparency ensures accountability and allows prompt interventions when water quality deviates from acceptable standards. For instance, blockchain can facilitate early detection of pollutants, enabling authorities to act swiftly to prevent health hazards. Case studies from cities like Singapore have shown the potential for such systems to revolutionize urban water quality monitoring.

2. Water Trading and Rights Management

In areas where water scarcity is a major concern, blockchain can simplify the trading of water rights. Smart contracts—self-executing digital agreements with predefined terms—can automate transactions between parties, ensuring transparency and reducing the need for intermediaries, (Bordel *et al.*, 2019). By enabling efficient allocation based on real-time demand and supply, blockchain facilitates the optimal utilization of water resources. This system can particularly benefit agricultural sectors, where irrigation demands account for the majority of water usage. Pilot projects in Australia have demonstrated the feasibility of blockchain-based water rights trading, reducing administrative overhead and ensuring equitable access to water.

3. Supply Chain Transparency

Blockchain can be used to track the entire water supply chain, from the source to the end consumer. This allows stakeholders to verify the origin, quality, and treatment processes of water, (Patek, Ucchula, & Banerjee, 2014). Such transparency builds trust among consumers and ensures compliance with health and safety regulations. For example, urban water utilities can use blockchain to provide consumers with a verified record of water purification processes, thereby enhancing public confidence.

4. Decentralized Water Management

Blockchain enables the decentralization of water resource management, empowering local communities to take an active role in decision-making. Through blockchain-based platforms, communities can collectively manage water usage, pricing, and infrastructure maintenance, (Banerjee, 2024). This participatory approach promotes sustainable practices and ensures that decisions reflect local needs and priorities. Examples from rural India illustrate how community-led water management initiatives can benefit from decentralized governance supported by blockchain.

5. Efficient Billing Systems

Blockchain can revolutionize billing systems for water utilities by integrating smart meters with blockchain networks. These meters can record water consumption in real time, and the data can be securely stored and processed for billing, (Mukherjee & Banerjee, 2024). This approach reduces errors, resolves disputes over billing discrepancies, and enhances revenue collection for utilities. The resulting financial stability can support infrastructure development and maintenance. Pilot programs in South Korea have shown the efficiency of blockchain-based billing systems in reducing fraud and improving transparency.

Benefits of Blockchain in Water Management

The adoption of blockchain technology in the water sector offers several key benefits:

1. Increased Transparency

Blockchain provides an immutable record of transactions, which is crucial for combating corruption and ensuring fair resource allocation, (Banerjee, 2024a). Transparency fosters trust among stakeholders and supports better governance of water resources. For instance, international water-sharing agreements could be managed more effectively with blockchain, reducing disputes between nations over shared resources.

2. Enhanced Data Security

Blockchain's decentralized architecture makes it highly resistant to hacking and data breaches. Sensitive information related to water quality, allocation, and consumption can be securely stored, reducing risks associated with data tampering, (Banerjee, 2024b). This is particularly vital in ensuring that public health data remains reliable.

3. Improved Operational Efficiency

By automating processes such as billing and rights trading through smart contracts, blockchain reduces administrative burdens and streamlines operations. This efficiency translates into cost savings for utilities and improved service delivery for consumers, (Enescu *et al.,* 2020).

4. Empowered Stakeholders

Blockchain platforms encourage stakeholder participation by providing equal access to information. Communities can use these platforms to actively engage in water management, fostering accountability and sustainable practices, (Banerjee, Jani, & Shah, 2021).

Challenges to Blockchain Implementation in Water Management

While the potential of blockchain is significant, several obstacles must be addressed to enable its successful integration into water management systems:

1. Technical Barriers

The implementation of blockchain requires substantial technical expertise and infrastructure. Many water utilities, particularly in developing countries, may lack the resources to adopt this technology, (Yahaya *et al.,* 2020). Training programs and investments in capacity-building will be essential to overcome these barriers.

2. Regulatory Challenges

The regulatory environment surrounding blockchain is still evolving. Governments must establish clear policies to govern its use while addressing concerns about data privacy, security, and consumer protection, (Mehta *et al.,* 2021). Successful implementation in countries like Estonia, which has adopted blockchain for public services, serves as a model for water management regulation.

3. Stakeholder Resistance

For blockchain initiatives to succeed, stakeholders—including governments, water utilities, and local communities—must be convinced of its benefits. Building awareness and addressing skepticism through education and advocacy are essential, (Leeuwen *et al.,* 2020).

4. Interoperability Issues

Different blockchain platforms often lack compatibility, hindering data sharing and collaboration. Developing standards for interoperability will be crucial for creating cohesive water management networks, (Banerjee, 2019).

Future Prospects of Blockchain in Water Management

The future of blockchain in managing water resources looks promising, with several emerging trends and innovations on the horizon:

1. Integration with Artificial Intelligence (AI)

Combining blockchain with AI can enhance water resource management by enabling predictive analytics. AI algorithms can analyze blockchain-stored data to forecast water demand, detect potential quality issues, and optimize resource allocation, (Aoun *et al.,* 2021). This integration can be particularly useful for regions prone to droughts.

2. Development of Global Water Resource Networks

Blockchain can facilitate the creation of global networks for water management, enabling cross-border collaboration on shared water resources. Such networks can address transboundary water disputes and promote sustainable practices at an international level.

3. Public-Private Partnerships

Collaboration between governments and private enterprises can drive the development of tailored blockchain applications for local water management needs. These partnerships can also provide the financial and technical resources necessary for large-scale implementation.

4. Educational Initiatives

Raising awareness about blockchain's potential in water management is critical. Training programs for water resource managers, policymakers, and community leaders can help build the capacity needed for successful implementation.

5. Smart City Integration

Blockchain can play a vital role in the water management systems of smart cities. By integrating with IoT devices, blockchain can enable real-time monitoring and management of water distribution networks, ensuring efficient use of resources in urban areas.

6. Circular Water Economy

Blockchain can support the development of a circular water economy, where wastewater is treated and reused sustainably. By tracking water usage and treatment processes, blockchain ensures accountability and promotes the efficient reuse of resources.

Blockchain technology represents a transformative solution to the complex challenges of water resource management. Its ability to enhance transparency, security, and efficiency makes it an invaluable tool for addressing water scarcity, improving distribution systems, and fostering sustainable practices. By enabling decentralized management, blockchain empowers local communities and promotes equitable resource allocation.

However, realizing the full potential of blockchain requires overcoming technical, regulatory, and stakeholder-related challenges. Investments in infrastructure, capacity building, and policy development are essential to pave the way for blockchain's widespread adoption in the water sector.

As innovations such as AI integration and global water networks emerge, the scope of blockchain in managing water resources will continue to expand. With collaboration among governments, private enterprises, and communities, blockchain can play a pivotal role in ensuring the sustainable management of this vital resource, securing a water-rich future for generations to come.

IV. APPLICATIONS OF BLOCKCHAIN

Blockchain technology has gained significant traction across various industries for its ability to provide secure, transparent, and decentralized solutions. In water resource management, blockchain offers innovative applications that address critical challenges like inefficiency, waste, and lack of transparency, (Banerjee, Hazra, & Sarkar, 2024).

One of the most promising applications is in water usage monitoring and management. Blockchain enables the real-time tracking of water consumption through smart meters. These meters record usage data on the blockchain, ensuring accuracy and transparency. This technology can help reduce water wastage by encouraging sustainable practices and enabling authorities to implement fair pricing models based on consumption.

Another application lies in water quality monitoring. Blockchain can be used to store and share data collected from sensors monitoring water sources. This creates an immutable record of water quality parameters, making it easier to identify contamination and respond quickly to potential hazards. The decentralized nature of blockchain also ensures that this data is tamper-proof, boosting trust among stakeholders, (Song *et al.*, 2022).

Supply chain management in water distribution is another area where blockchain is making an impact. From sourcing and treatment to distribution, blockchain can provide end-to-end transparency, ensuring accountability at each stage. This is particularly beneficial in regions where water theft or mismanagement is a concern.

Additionally, blockchain can facilitate smart contracts for water trading and allocation. In areas with limited water resources, blockchain-powered smart contracts enable efficient trading between users while ensuring compliance with predefined rules and regulations. This can help optimize resource allocation and promote equitable distribution, (Mukherjee & Banerjee, 2024).

Finally, blockchain enhances community participation by empowering individuals to access data and participate in decision-making processes. This democratization fosters better water governance and sustainable practices.

By integrating blockchain into water resource management, stakeholders can ensure transparency, efficiency, and sustainability in managing this vital resource.

V. CONCLUSIONS AND FUTURE WORK

The management of water resources heavily relies on the proper allocation and regulation of water rights. To achieve ecological and economic stability, it is essential to manage the trading of water entitlements with a scientific approach. Blockchain technology, a groundbreaking development in modern technological innovation, offers promising opportunities despite being in the early stages of adoption. Its potential for transforming water resource management has garnered significant interest in recent discussions. In the context of water trading, blockchain technology can serve as a tool to enhance governance and transparency. By utilizing the decentralized nature of blockchain, a consensus-based alliance chain can effectively balance decentralization and operational efficiency. This approach could pave the way for a blockchain-based marketplace for trading irrigation water leases. Such a system could provide unalterable and readily accessible information on various transaction parameters, including the trade date, water volume, quality status, usage duration, and specific trade regulations. By embedding these details within an immutable blockchain ledger, the system ensures reliability and minimizes the risk of data manipulation. The integration of blockchain into water trading infrastructure can lead to the automation of processes, thereby increasing efficiency. Smart contracts, an integral component of blockchain technology, offer a transformative way to facilitate the trading of water rights. These self-executing contracts enable automated verification processes, eliminating the need for time-consuming manual inspections of agreements. Furthermore, they empower trading parties to negotiate and compete independently, fostering a fair and efficient marketplace. Another advantage of blockchain technology is its ability to securely and traceably store water license data across a decentralized network of servers. This ensures that transaction records remain accessible and tamper-proof, enhancing data security and transparency. As the reliance on manual processes diminishes, operational costs decrease, and the accuracy of data handling improves. Consequently, blockchain can help address the informational asymmetries that often hinder the efficient functioning of water rights trading. Decentralized applications (dApps) powered by blockchain further amplify user engagement by providing incentives that align with socio-economic objectives. These applications offer a dynamic and adaptable framework for encouraging participation, which is critical for the success of any trading platform. By leveraging blockchain's unique capabilities, stakeholders can foster a more inclusive and transparent environment for managing water resources.

REFERENCES

Aoun, A., Ibrahim, H., Ghandour, M., & Ilinca, A. (2021). Blockchain-Enabled Energy Demand Side Management Cap and Trade Model. *Energies*, *14*(24), 8600. DOI: 10.3390/en14248600

Banerjee, B., (2019). Avalanche effect: A judgement parameter of strength in symmetric key block ciphers. International journal of engineering development and research, 7(2), pp.116-121.

Banerjee, B. (2024). Blockchain 2030: Revolutionizing the Future of Digital Trust. *International Research Journal of Scientific Studies*, *1*(1), 13–18.

Banerjee, B. (2024). Quantum Horizons: Shaping the Future of Computing. *International Research Journal of Scientific Studies*, *1*(1), 7–12.

Banerjee, B. (2024). Next-Gen Computing: Exploring Industry 4.0. *International Research Journal of Scientific Studies*, *1*(1), 1–6.

Banerjee, B., Hazra, D., & Sarkar, D. (2024). IoT-Enabled Water Quality Management System for Rural Areas of Bharuch District. In *Water Informatics: Challenges and Solutions Using State of Art Technologies* (pp. 33–47). Springer Nature Singapore. DOI: 10.1007/978-981-97-1518-3_3

Banerjee, B., Jani, A., & Shah, N. (2021). Digital Image Encryption Using Double Crossover Approach for SARS-CoV-2 Infected Lungs in a Blockchain Framework. *Frontiers in Blockchain*, *4*, 771241. DOI: 10.3389/fbloc.2021.771241

Banerjee, B., Jani, A., & Shah, N. (2021). A genetic blockchain approach for securing smart vehicles in quantum era. In *Vehicular Communications for Smart Cars* (pp. 85–108). CRC Press. DOI: 10.1201/9781315110905-5

Banerjee, B., Jani, A., & Shah, N. (2021). *Asymmetric Confidentiality in Blockchain Embedded Smart Grids in Galois Field*. Frontiers in Blockchain. DOI: 10.3389/fbloc.2021.770074

Banerjee, B., Jani, A., Shah, N., & Patel, A. (2020). Post Quantum Security Enhancement Scheme in IoT Blockchain Framework. *GIS Sci. J*, *7*(6), 664–672.

Banerjee, B., & Patel, J. T. (2016). A Symmetric Key Block Cipher to Provide Confidentiality in Wireless Sensor Networks. INFOCOMP Journal of Computer Science, 15(1), 12–18. Retrieved from https://infocomp.dcc.ufla.br/index.php/infocomp/article/view/515

Banerjee, B., & Saha, G. 2022. Emotion Independent Face Recognition-Based Security Protocol in IoT-Enabled Devices. In Cloud IoT (pp. 199218). Chapman and Hall/CRC. DOI: 10.1201/9781003155577-18

Banerjee, B., & Sarkar, D. (2024). Blockchain-Based Quantum Resistant Electoral Management System for the Post-Pandemic Era. In Ensuring Security and End-to-End Visibility Through Blockchain and Digital Twins (pp. 102-115). IGI Global. DOI: 10.4018/979-8-3693-3494-2.ch006

Bhat, S. A., Huang, N. F., Sofi, I. B., & Sultan, M. (2022). Agriculture-Food Supply Chain Management Based on Blockchain and IoT: A Narrative on Enterprise Blockchain Interoperability. *Agriculture*, *12*(1), 40. DOI: 10.3390/agriculture12010040

Biswas, N., Santra, D., Banerjee, B., & Biswas, S. (2024). Harnessing the Power of Machine Learning for Parkinson's Disease Detection. In *AIoT and Smart Sensing Technologies for Smart Devices* (pp. 140–155). IGI Global. DOI: 10.4018/979-8-3693-0786-1.ch008

Bordel, B., Martin, D., Alcarria, R., & Robles, T. A Blockchain-based Water Control System for the Automatic Management of Irrigation Communities. In *Proceedings of the 2019 IEEE International Conference on Consumer Electronics (ICCE)*, Las Vegas, NV, USA, 11–13 January 2019. DOI: 10.1109/ICCE.2019.8661940

Chen, S. J., Cao, Y. Y., & Li, J. (2021). The Effect of Water Rights Trading Policy on Water Resource Utilization Efficiency: Evidence from a Quasi-Natural Experiment in China. *Sustainability (Basel)*, *13*(9), 5281. DOI: 10.3390/su13095281

Chohan, U. W. (2019). Blockchain and environmental sustainability: case of IBM's blockchain water management. Notes on the 21st Century (CBRI).

Delorit, J. D., Parker, D. P., & Block, P. J. (2019). An agro-economic approach to framing perennial farm-scale water resources demand management for water rights markets. *Agricultural Water Management*, *218*, 68–81. DOI: 10.1016/j.agwat.2019.03.029

Enescu, F. M., Bizon, N., Onu, A., Răboacă, M. S., Thounthong, P., Mazare, A. G., & erban, G. (2020). S, erban, G. Implementing Blockchain Technology in Irrigation Systems That Integrate Photovoltaic Energy Generation Systems. *Sustainability (Basel)*, *12*(4), 1540. DOI: 10.3390/su12041540

Faisal, M. A., Aung, Z., Williams, J. R., & Sanchez, A. (2014). Data-stream-based intrusion detection system for advanced metering infrastructure in smart grid: A feasibility study. *IEEE Systems Journal*, *2014*(9), 31–44.

Ge, M., Wu, F. P., & Chen, X. P. (2017). A Coupled Allocation for Regional Initial Water Rights in Dalinghe Basin, China. *Sustainability (Basel), 9*(3), 428. DOI: 10.3390/su9030428

Grantham, T. E., & Viers, J. H. (2014). 100 years of California's water rights system: Patterns, trends and uncertainty. *Environmental Research Letters, 9*(8), 084012. DOI: 10.1088/1748-9326/9/8/084012

Jagtap, S., Skouteris, G., Choudhari, V., & Rahimifard, S. (2022). Improving Water Efficiency in the Beverage Industry with the Internet of Things. In Bhatt, C., Kumar, N., Bashir, A., & Alazab, M. (Eds.), *Implementing Data Analytics and Architectures for Next Generation Wireless Communications* (pp. 18–26). IGI Global. DOI: 10.4018/978-1-7998-6988-7.ch002

Jagtap, S., Skouteris, G., Choudhari, V., Rahimifard, S., & Duong, L. N. K. (2021). An Internet of Things Approach for Water Efficiency: A Case Study of the Beverage Factory. *Sustainability (Basel), 13*(6), 3343. DOI: 10.3390/su13063343

Khan, A. A., Shaikh, Z. A., Belinskaja, L., Baitenova, L., Vlasova, Y., Gerzelieva, Z., Laghari, A. A., Abro, A. A., & Barykin, S. (2022). A Blockchain and Metaheuristic-Enabled Distributed Architecture for Smart Agricultural Analysis and Ledger Preservation Solution: A Collaborative Approach. *Applied Sciences (Basel, Switzerland), 12*(3), 1487. DOI: 10.3390/app12031487

Kumarathunga, M., Calheiros, R. N., & Ginige, A. (2022). Smart Agricultural Futures Market: Blockchain Technology as a Trust Enabler between Smallholder Farmers and Buyers. *Sustainability (Basel), 14*(5), 2916. DOI: 10.3390/su14052916

Leeuwen, G., AlSkaif, T., Gibescu, M., & van Sark, W. (2020). An integrated blockchain- based energy management platform with bilateral trading for microgrid communities. *Applied Energy, 263*, 114613. DOI: 10.1016/j.apenergy.2020.114613

Mahmoud, H. H., Wu, W. Y., & Wang, Y. H. (2021). WDSchain: A Toolbox for Enhancing the Security Using Blockchain Technology in Water Distribution System. *Water (Basel), 13*(14), 1944. DOI: 10.3390/w13141944

Mehta, D., Tanwar, S., Bodkhe, U., Shukla, A., & Kumar, N. (2021). Blockchain-based royalty contract transactions scheme for Industry 4.0 supply-chain management. *Information Processing & Management, 58*(4), 102586. DOI: 10.1016/j.ipm.2021.102586

Mukherjee, S., & Banerjee, B. (2024). Latest Developments in Artificial Intelligence: Enhancing Creativity and Productivity. *International Research Journal of Scientific Studies, 1*(1), 19–23.

Nakamoto, S. (2008). *Bitcoin: A peer-to-peer electronic cash system*. Decentralized Business Review., Available online https://nakamotoinstitute.org/bitcoin/

Nayal, K., Raut, R. D., Narkhede, B. E., Priyadarshinee, P., Panchal, G. B., & Gedam, V. V. (2021). Antecedents for blockchain technologyenabled sustainable agriculture supply chain. *Annals of Operations Research*, •••, 1–45. PMID: 34898788

Patel, M. K., Uchhula, V., & Banerjee, B., (2014). Comparative Evaluation of AODV, DSDV and AOMDV based on end-to-end delay and routing overhead using Network Simulator.

Patel, M. K., Uchhula, V. V., & Banerjee, B. (2013). Comparative Analysis of Routing Protocols in MANET Based on Packet Delivery Ratio using NS2. *International Journal of Advanced Research in Computer Science and Software Engineering*, *3*(11), 172–177.

Pimentel, D., Houser, J., Preiss, E., White, O., Fang, H., Mesnick, L., Troy, B., Stephanie, T., Jerrod, S., & Sharon, A. (1997). Water Resources: Agriculture, the Environment, and Society. *Bioscience*, *47*(2), 97–106. DOI: 10.2307/1313020

Pincheira, M., Vecchio, M., Giaffreda, R., & Kanhere, S. S. (2021). Cost-effective IoT devices as trustworthy data sources for a blockchainbased water management system in precision agriculture. *Computers and Electronics in Agriculture*, *180*, 105889. DOI: 10.1016/j.compag.2020.105889

Postel, S. (2014). *The Last Oasis: Facing Water Scarcity*. Routledge. DOI: 10.4324/9781315070346

Predescu, A., Arsene, D., Pahon u, B., Mocanu, M., & Chiru, C. (2021). Pahont,u, B.; Mocanu, M.; Chiru, C. A Serious Gaming Approach for Crowdsensing in Urban Water Infrastructure with Blockchain Support. *Applied Sciences (Basel, Switzerland)*, *11*(4), 1449. DOI: 10.3390/app11041449

Saberi, S., Kouhizadeh, M., Sarkis, J., & Shen, L. (2019). Blockchain technology and its relationships to sustainable supply chain management. *International Journal of Production Research*, *57*(7), 2117–2135. DOI: 10.1080/00207543.2018.1533261

Saha, G., Banerjee, B., & Joshi, F. M. (2022). Predictive Edge Computing of SST Time-Series-Based Marine Warning System using Cloud Computing Infrastructure. In *Cloud IoT* (pp. 59–74). Chapman and Hall/CRC. DOI: 10.1201/9781003155577-7

Song, L., Luo, Y., Chang, Z., Jin, C., & Nicolas, M. (2022). Blockchain Adoption in Agricultural Supply Chain for Better Sustainability: A Game Theory Perspective. *Sustainability (Basel)*, *14*(3), 1470. DOI: 10.3390/su14031470

Thakur, T., Mehra, A., Hassija, V., Chamola, V., Srinivas, R., Gupta, K. K., & Singh, A. P. (2021). Smart water conservation through a machine learning and blockchain-enabled decentralized edge computing network. *Applied Soft Computing*, *106*, 107274. DOI: 10.1016/j.asoc.2021.107274

Torky, M., & Hassanein, A. E. (2020). Integrating blockchain and the internet of things in precision agriculture: Analysis, opportunities, and challenges. *Computers and Electronics in Agriculture*, *178*, 105476. DOI: 10.1016/j.compag.2020.105476

Yahaya, A. S., Javaid, N., Alzahrani, F. A., Rehman, A., Ullah, I., Shahid, A., & Shafiq, M. (2020). Blockchain Based Sustainable Local Energy Trading Considering Home Energy Management and Demurrage Mechanism. *Sustainability (Basel)*, *12*(8), 3385. DOI: 10.3390/su12083385

Yli-Huumo, J., Ko, D., Choi, S., Park, S., & Smolander, K. (2016). Where Is Current Research on Blockchain Technology? A Systematic Review. *PLoS One*, *11*(10), e0163477. DOI: 10.1371/journal.pone.0163477 PMID: 27695049

Zeng, H., Dhiman, G., Sharma, A., Sharma, A., & Tselykh, A. (2021). An IoT and Blockchain-based approach for the smart water management system in agriculture. *Expert Systems: International Journal of Knowledge Engineering and Neural Networks*, •••, e12892.

Zheng, Z. B., Xie, S., Dai, H. N., Chen, X., & Wang, H. (2018). Blockchain challenges and opportunities: A survey. *International Journal of Web and Grid Services*, *14*(4), 352–375. DOI: 10.1504/IJWGS.2018.095647

Chapter 12

Exploring the Potential of Blockchain-Embedded Smart Grids in Quantum Era: Blockchain Embedded Smart Grids

Bannishikha Banerjee
https://orcid.org/0000-0003-4848-8749
Amity University, Kolkata, India

Sreejita Sikdar
Amity University, Kolkata, India

Pratyay Khastagir
https://orcid.org/0009-0009-0613-4257
Amity University, Kolkata, India

Arshiya Dutta
Amity University, Kolkata, India

Shumaila A. Rahim
Amity University, Kolkata, India

Indraneel Mukhopadhyay
Amity University, Kolkata, India

ABSTRACT

To integrate green and renewable energy into traditional power systems, the concept of a "smart grid" has been introduced. The "Internet of Energy" is emerging as a way to provide energy information anytime, anywhere, with the goal of creating a sustainable society in the quantum age. The traditional centralized grid faces challenges in managing growing connections, prompting a shift toward decentralized smart grids. Blockchain, with its transparency and security, offers a promising solution for smart grid frameworks, particularly in the quantum era. This study reviews blockchain's role in smart grids, focusing on addressing security issues. It discusses current research, practical applications, and the challenges of using blockchain to improve smart grid safety.

DOI: 10.4018/979-8-3373-1424-2.ch012

I. INTRODUCTION

The proliferation of Internet of Things (IoT) devices and advancements in technology have led to an increased demand for power. This demand has prompted a global evaluation of a wide range of both small and large-scale power generation and distribution solutions. Additionally, the growing need for sustainable and renewable energy across various sectors is driving the need for adaptable power generation methods. The future energy system requirements are guided by three fundamental principles: Decarbonization, Decentralization, and Digitalization, (Andoni *et al.*, 2019). These principles serve as the foundation for the European Commission's Energy Union Package, (European Commission (EU), 2021). The concept of the Internet of Energy (IoE) (Shahzad *et al.*, 2020) has emerged as a result of the development of low-voltage power generation and distribution systems. The Internet of Energy (IoE) offers numerous benefits, such as enhancing energy generation, distribution, and consumption through intelligent and automated tools that facilitate secure data exchange among various stakeholders, (Mollah *et al.*, 2020). IoE is designed as an inclusive network, where all energy sources are treated with equal importance, (Banerjee, Jani, & Shah, 2021). As per the National Institute of Standards and Technology (NIST) (Wang & Su, 2020), within the realm of smart grids, a "smart grid domain" refers to a higher-level category that encompasses organizations, buildings, individuals, systems, devices, or other entities with shared objectives of exchanging, storing, processing, and managing information required for the smart grid. These domains encompass generation, transmission, distribution, consumption, operation, service provision, and market aspects. In examining the interplay among distinct smart grid sectors derived from Wang and Su (2020), we find that the generation domain is tasked with producing energy through diverse means. Meanwhile, service providers are the key players in governing the energy flow and managing energy distribution, operations, and trading. The term "customers" encompasses a wide array of components, including but not limited to Advanced Metering Infrastructures (AMI), automation stations, demand response systems, intelligent appliances, sensors, connected devices, supervisory control and data acquisition (SCADA) systems, electric vehicles, and home energy management solutions, as detailed in Pillitteri and Brewer (2014). These elements collectively contribute to the overall functionality and effectiveness of the smart grid.

By creating two-way communication between utility suppliers and customers, the AMI makes it easier to gather, monitor, and analyse data on energy usage. Smart metres, the AMI centre, and the communication network are the three main parts of AMI. Electricity use is recorded and tracked by smart metres, which also provide real-time data to the AMI centre. The AMI centre functions as a server in charge of overseeing data systems. Multiple communication protocols are employed to facilitate communication among household appliances, smart meters, and the AMI center, (El Mrabet *et al.*, 2018). By monitoring, managing, and regulating the power grid, the SCADA system plays a crucial part in the functioning of energy systems. The real-time control, increased operational effectiveness, improved grid stability, and seamless interaction with upcoming distributed database technologies and renewable energy systems are the key features of the intelligent power grid. Additionally, localised microgrid systems that provide environmentally friendly electricity and lessen dependency on centralised energy sources and high-voltage governmental or corporate power facilities might be classified as smart grids. To achieve intelligence, six fundamental prerequisites have been identified for the smart grid, (Faisal *et al.,* 2014). To begin with, managing consumer data empowers consumers by providing them with dependable and frequent updates regarding their electricity usage. Next, adaptation and generation technologies play a crucial role in achieving a harmonious equilibrium between energy supply and demand. This progress has also made it easier to incorporate renewable energy sources, electric vehicles, two-way communication, as well as automated and self-sustaining systems that engage consumers, (Ourahou *et al.,* 2020).

The prevailing trend in the development and expansion of microgrids renders the traditional approach of centrally controlled intelligent grid management, control, and operation obsolete and challenging to implement. The production and dissemination of fossil-free energy are subject to fluctuations due to factors such as weather conditions, energy source availability, geographical locations, existing infrastructure, and energy demand. These variances, coupled with the decentralization of the energy system, necessitate contemporary and adaptable management and operational systems, alongside innovative energy storage solutions, (Banerjee *et al.,* 2020). Furthermore, it is crucial to comprehend the art of harmonizing power generation and distribution in accordance with seasonal demand fluctuations. The extent of energy losses can be significantly attributed to the length of power transmission lines. The integration of microgrid and renewable infrastructure in energy generation and distribution can substantially mitigate these energy losses while simultaneously contributing to environmental preservation, (Salkuti, 2020). The introduction of an electricity market has the potential to serve as a driving force behind the expansion of microgrid production, offering the opportunity to boost generator revenues while concurrently reducing consumption expenses, (Mattila *et al.,* 2016). The prevailing challenge revolves around the establishment of well-coordinated and systematically automated controls for the production and distribution of these microgrids, particularly as the number of prosumers continues to rise. Existing technologies and accomplishments within the energy sector are ill-suited for the unique characteristics of microgrids. Consequently, numerous stakeholders within the energy industry are advocating for the use of blockchain technology (Konashevych, 2016) to facilitate power transactions within microgrids. This endeavor aims to encourage local utilization of distributed generation (DG), foster decentralized grid management, and promote peer-to-peer (P2P) power trading, (Mattila *et al.,* 2016).

A. Smart Grids

The increasing demand for distributed renewable energy sources has emerged as a crucial response to the challenges posed by climate change, aiming to balance the production, distribution, transmission, and consumption of energy in a more sustainable way. Renewable energy technologies, including wind, solar, and biomass, have become central to this transition, offering viable alternatives to traditional fossil fuel-based systems.

In the contemporary landscape, there is a growing trend of connecting small-scale generators, such as residential solar panels or community-based wind farms, to the conventional electric grid. Historically, energy production has been dominated by large-scale centralized systems, relying heavily on fossil fuels such as coal and natural gas, or hydropower. These energy sources typically necessitate significant investments at the state or corporate level, making it difficult for smaller players to enter the energy market. However, recent technological innovations have paved the way for private enterprises, small businesses, and even individuals to engage in low-voltage renewable electricity generation. This shift is transforming the energy landscape, allowing for greater participation in the generation and consumption of renewable energy, and contributing to the decentralization of the energy system, (Konashevych, 2016).

The case of Sweden exemplifies the trend toward decentralized renewable energy generation. In 2020, the country installed 65,819 solar panels and 4,333 wind turbines, marking a significant increase in renewable energy capacity compared to previous years. This growth is impressive, with an annual surge of about 40% in renewable energy generation from 2016 to 2020. Such progress highlights the importance of renewable energy in Sweden's energy strategy, which is committed to achieving 100% reliance on renewable energy by 2040. This ambitious target reflects the government's determination to reduce carbon emissions, decrease reliance on fossil fuels, and promote sustainable energy solutions. The widespread adoption of decentralized renewable energy technologies is considered essential for meeting this goal, as it allows for the generation and distribution of low-voltage, emission-free energy across a broad range of applications, from residential to industrial sectors, (Banerjee & Saha, 2022).

Globally, the momentum behind renewable energy expansion continues to build. In 2020, 87 governments around the world set renewable energy targets for 2030, with a combined goal to introduce 721 gigawatts of new renewable capacity, primarily from wind, solar, and other non-hydro renewable technologies. These targets are indicative of a global shift toward a cleaner, more sustainable energy future, and they reflect the increasing recognition of renewable energy as a key component of climate change mitigation efforts. As the world moves toward these ambitious renewable energy goals, there is an increasing need for systems that can integrate and coordinate the various energy sources to ensure stability and reliability.

The challenge of integrating decentralized renewable energy sources into existing energy systems lies in the complexity of coordinating the various sources and managing their output effectively. Traditional energy systems are highly regulated and centralized, with well-established protocols for energy distribution. However, the integration of small-scale, intermittent renewable sources, such as wind and solar, into these systems presents challenges in terms of balancing supply and demand, managing fluctuations in power generation, and ensuring the stability of the grid. Additionally, renewable energy sources often require different levels of infrastructure and technologies to ensure that they can be effectively connected to and coordinated with the central grid, (Xue *et al.*, 2017).

One promising solution to these challenges is the integration of microgrids, which are localized energy systems that can operate independently or in conjunction with the main grid. Microgrids are designed to generate, store, and distribute renewable energy within a specific geographic area, such as a neighborhood or community. These systems can incorporate a wide range of distributed generation (DG) units, including solar panels, wind turbines, biomass, fuel cells, and even traditional power sources such as natural gas or coal. By providing localized energy generation and storage, microgrids reduce the reliance on centralized systems, which can be vulnerable to disruptions such as blackouts or natural disasters. Moreover, they offer a more flexible and resilient way to manage energy demand and supply, as they can be dynamically adjusted based on local conditions, (Yuan & Wang, 2016).

Research has highlighted the operational challenges associated with microgrid systems, particularly in terms of achieving power balance and ensuring effective communication among the various distributed generation units. For example, fluctuations in wind and solar energy generation can create imbalances in supply and demand, which must be addressed to maintain grid stability. Additionally, the coordination of different types of energy sources—ranging from renewable technologies such as wind and solar to traditional fossil fuel-based generators—requires sophisticated control systems and communication technologies, (Davis *et al.*, 2018). Many of these systems are still in the early stages of development and require further refinement to ensure their operational integrity and efficiency.

A key component of successful microgrid integration is the ability to communicate and exchange data with the central grid. By connecting microgrids with the larger grid, it is possible to create a more unified and efficient energy system that can leverage the strengths of both decentralized and centralized energy generation. For example, when renewable energy generation is high and local demand is low, excess energy from microgrids can be fed back into the central grid, helping to stabilize the overall energy supply. Similarly, during periods of low renewable generation, microgrids can draw power from the central grid to meet local demand. This integration creates a more flexible and resilient energy system that can better respond to fluctuations in both supply and demand.

The development of advanced data exchange systems and automation technologies will play a crucial role in facilitating the integration of microgrids with the larger energy grid. These systems will allow for real-time monitoring and control of energy generation, distribution, and consumption, enabling more efficient decision-making and ensuring the stability of both the microgrid and the central grid, (Energimyndigheten, 2020). In particular, the use of smart grid technologies, such as sensors, communication networks, and advanced analytics, will enable better coordination and optimization of energy flows across multiple sources. This will help to address issues such as power imbalances, energy losses, and system inefficiencies, ensuring that energy is delivered in the most efficient and cost-effective manner.

Despite the potential benefits of decentralized renewable energy systems, several barriers to their widespread adoption remain. One significant challenge is the regulatory and policy landscape, which can vary significantly across regions. In some countries, the regulatory framework may be insufficient to support the integration of microgrids and distributed energy systems into the main grid. For example, in many regions, utility companies may have limited incentives to invest in the necessary infrastructure to connect decentralized energy systems to the grid, as they may not see a direct financial benefit from such investments. Additionally, existing grid infrastructure may not be designed to accommodate the fluctuations in energy generation associated with renewable sources, making upgrades and investments in new technologies essential, (Ajadi *et al.,* 2020).

Another challenge is the financial cost of implementing decentralized renewable energy systems, including microgrids. While the cost of renewable energy technologies has decreased significantly in recent years, the initial investment required for the installation of microgrid systems can still be prohibitively expensive for some communities and businesses. To address this issue, governments and financial institutions will need to provide greater support through incentives, subsidies, or financing mechanisms to make these systems more accessible to a broader range of stakeholders, (Hannan *et al.,* 2020).

The growing demand for decentralized renewable energy sources represents a vital step toward addressing the challenges of climate change and reducing dependence on fossil fuels. As technological advancements continue to make renewable energy systems more affordable and accessible, the integration of microgrids and distributed energy generation into the larger grid will become increasingly important. However, to achieve this goal, significant efforts will be required to overcome the technical, regulatory, and financial barriers that currently hinder the widespread adoption of these systems. Through continued research, innovation, and policy support, it is possible to create a more sustainable and resilient energy system that can meet the needs of both today's and tomorrow's generations.

B. Blockchain Embedded Smart Grids

Blockchain technology, recognized for its decentralized and secure framework that underpins information exchange, has made notable strides in various sectors. One sector where blockchain's application is beginning to gain traction is the energy industry. Despite its relatively recent development in this area, the application of blockchain in the energy sector shows immense potential for transforming how data is exchanged, monitored, and secured among diverse stakeholders. The focus on improving transparency, efficiency, and security in energy transactions aligns with blockchain's inherent capabilities. Although the full potential of blockchain technology in the energy sector is still unfolding, an increasing body of research, projects, and industry initiatives suggests that it could play a crucial role in optimizing energy management, particularly in the context of smart grids and distributed energy resources, (Banerjee, Jani, & Shah, 2021).

In the context of the energy sector, blockchain technology's decentralized nature offers significant advantages over traditional systems. The energy industry has traditionally relied on central authorities to manage the flow of electricity and the associated data, often resulting in inefficiencies, high costs, and risks related to privacy and security. However, blockchain, by enabling secure and transparent transactions in a decentralized manner, can address these challenges. The technology ensures that data related to energy generation, distribution, and consumption is securely recorded, verified, and shared among relevant stakeholders without the need for intermediaries.

One of the most promising applications of blockchain in the energy sector is its role in microgrid energy trading. Microgrids, which are localized networks of energy production and consumption, are becoming increasingly important as the global energy landscape shifts toward renewable sources. Blockchain technology can facilitate energy trading within microgrids by enabling peer-to-peer transactions. Through smart contracts and blockchain-based platforms, individuals and organizations within the microgrid can trade energy in a secure, transparent, and efficient manner. This not only enhances energy trading but also empowers consumers by providing them with more control over their energy usage and production. Several blockchain-based frameworks have already been proposed and implemented to enable such energy trading in microgrids, demonstrating the practical applications of blockchain in this domain, (Banerjee, Jani, & Shah, 2021b).

Moreover, blockchain's potential extends beyond microgrid trading to the creation of distributed energy markets, where energy pricing and distribution are decentralized. Traditional energy markets rely on central entities to set prices and manage distribution. With blockchain, the pricing mechanisms can be automated and managed using smart contracts, creating a more transparent and fair system. Research has also explored the use of Ethereum-based energy trading systems, which enable communication between smart meters in households and distribution system operators (DSOs). These systems offer a decentralized way to monitor energy usage, adjust pricing in real-time, and ensure efficient distribution across the grid.

Alongside blockchain, other technologies such as wireless sensor networks (WSNs) and the Internet of Things (IoT) offer potential solutions to the challenges of privacy and security in energy management. IoT devices can gather real-time data on energy consumption and production, which can then be analyzed to optimize the operation of smart grids. The integration of WSNs and IoT with blockchain technology creates a robust framework for secure and efficient data aggregation. These technologies enable intelligent systems to monitor and interact with each other, improving overall energy production and consumption. Additionally, these systems can help optimize grid operations by providing real-time insights into grid status and performance, (Badal *et al.,* 2019).

As the energy sector continues to evolve, the need for a unified platform that can manage, operate, and control smart grids becomes more apparent. Smart grids, which integrate renewable energy sources, distributed generation (DG) units, and advanced communication technologies, require a reliable system to ensure proper communication among all involved components. The integration of DG units into the main grid requires robust communication protocols to maintain stability, particularly in terms of voltage and frequency control. Blockchain's role in managing this communication can enhance the performance and reliability of smart grids by ensuring secure, transparent, and real-time data exchange between stakeholders.

One of the key challenges in smart grid operations is fostering collaboration among diverse stakeholders, including energy producers, consumers, regulators, and operators. Blockchain technology can play a crucial role in promoting stakeholder collaboration by enabling transparent and secure interactions. Through decentralized platforms, stakeholders can access real-time data, verify transactions, and engage in fair and transparent energy trading without the need for a centralized authority. This fosters trust among participants and creates an ecosystem where information is readily available, making it easier to coordinate efforts and resolve issues, (Alladi *et al.,* 2019).

Another critical aspect of smart grid operations is data analysis and management. The vast amounts of data generated by smart meters, sensors, and IoT devices in smart grids require efficient management and analysis. Blockchain can facilitate data management by ensuring the integrity and security of the data, making it tamper-proof and verifiable. This enables accurate and reliable data analysis, which is essential for optimizing grid performance, predicting energy demand, and identifying potential issues before they become critical. By using blockchain to manage data securely, smart grids can operate more efficiently and ensure that energy distribution is aligned with demand.

Grid imbalances, such as mismatches between energy supply and demand, are a significant challenge in smart grid management. These imbalances can lead to inefficiencies, increased costs, and potential system failures. Blockchain can help address grid imbalances by enabling real-time monitoring and automated adjustments through smart contracts. Smart contracts can automatically trigger actions based on predefined conditions, such as redistributing energy from one part of the grid to another when an imbalance is detected. This decentralized approach to grid management allows for faster and more efficient responses to imbalances, reducing the risk of blackouts and improving overall grid stability, (Di Silvestre *et al.,* 2020).

Decentralization of grid management and operations is another key area where blockchain can have a profound impact. Traditional grid management relies on central entities that control the flow of energy and make decisions on behalf of the entire system. Blockchain's decentralized nature enables distributed decision-making, where individual stakeholders can autonomously make decisions based on the information available to them. This can lead to a more resilient and flexible grid, where decisions are made locally but are coordinated across the entire system. Decentralized grid management can also empower consumers by giving them more control over their energy usage and production, (Foti & Vavalis, 2021).

Security and privacy are crucial concerns in smart grid operations, as the integration of digital technologies exposes the grid to cyber threats and data breaches. Blockchain technology offers a robust solution to these challenges by providing secure and tamper-proof data storage and transaction mechanisms. The decentralized nature of blockchain ensures that there is no single point of failure, making it more resistant to attacks. Additionally, blockchain's use of cryptographic techniques ensures that only authorized parties can access sensitive data, protecting the privacy of consumers and operators. By enhancing security and privacy, blockchain can help build trust in smart grid systems and encourage greater adoption of these technologies.

While blockchain holds significant promise for smart grid operations, its implementation is not without challenges. The energy sector is complex, and the integration of blockchain technology into existing systems requires careful planning and coordination. Legal, regulatory, and technical hurdles must be overcome to ensure that blockchain-based solutions comply with industry standards and can be seamlessly integrated into the existing energy infrastructure. Furthermore, the scalability of blockchain networks must be considered to ensure that they can handle the large amounts of data generated by smart grids without compromising performance, (Hussain, Farooq, & Ustun, 2019).

Despite these challenges, the potential benefits of blockchain in smart grid management make it an area of intense research and development. The ability to foster stakeholder collaboration, improve data management, address grid imbalances, decentralize operations, and enhance security and privacy is transformative for the energy sector. As blockchain technology continues to evolve, it is likely that its application in the energy sector will expand, leading to more efficient, secure, and transparent energy systems, (Li *et al.,* 2019).

The integration of blockchain technology into the management, operation, and control of smart grids offers numerous advantages. Blockchain's decentralized and secure framework enables efficient energy trading, enhances stakeholder collaboration, improves data analysis and management, addresses grid imbalances, and strengthens security and privacy measures. By leveraging the strengths of blockchain, smart grids can become more resilient, efficient, and flexible, paving the way for a more sustainable and decentralized energy future. As the energy sector continues to evolve, blockchain technology will play an increasingly important role in shaping the future of energy management and distribution. The need for further research and development in this field is essential to fully unlock the potential of blockchain and realize its transformative impact on the energy sector.

Table 1. Existing smart grid vs blockchain smart grid

Aspect of Smart Grid	Existing Smart Grid	Blockchain Smart Grid
Transition in Power Sources	Transitioned to use sustainable sources and grid integration	Moving towards a decentralized framework by coordinating distributed energy resources
Focus	Initially focused on integrating innovative detection and control into the traditional grid	Emphasizes ongoing monitoring, automated control, and optimization
Intermediation and Markets	Depended on intermediaries and integrated markets	Supports multiple users in generating and sharing energy through distributions
Communication Technologies	Relied on advanced communication technologies	Predominantly utilizes the Energy Internet for seamless energy and data sharing
Communication Direction	Bi-directional communications	Supports advanced plug-and-play functionalities

continued on following page

Table 1. Continued

Aspect of Smart Grid	Existing Smart Grid	Blockchain Smart Grid
Computational and Communication Costs	Faced heavy computational and communication costs	Costs are distributed among network entities
Network Expansion Options	Limited options for network expansion	Offers the flexibility to expand rapidly with numerous availabilities
Vulnerability to Single Points of Failure	Vulnerable to single points of failure	Demonstrates resilience against single points of failure
Integration with Energy Networks	Primarily integrated with electric energy networks	Integrated with various energy networks
Dependency on Regional Grid Control	Dependent on regional grid control	Facilitates smooth access to extensive distributed energy resources

C. Blockchain in Quantum Era

Quantum computing has emerged as one of the most transformative technologies of the 21st century, captivating the imagination of researchers, engineers, and organizations around the globe. With the promise of solving complex problems that are currently beyond the reach of classical computers, quantum computing is poised to revolutionize fields such as cryptography, materials science, and artificial intelligence. While the principles of quantum mechanics, which form the foundation of quantum computing, have been studied for over a century, the application of these principles to practical computing systems is a relatively recent development. In fact, the journey from theoretical physics to quantum computing as a viable technology has been long and complex, marked by significant milestones and breakthroughs, (Li *et al.*, 2019).

The origins of quantum computing date back to the late 1970s and early 1980s, a period during which foundational research began to bring quantum mechanics from the realm of abstract theory into the domain of practical computation. The groundwork for quantum computing was laid by a number of pioneering researchers, among whom Paul Benioff stands out for his contributions. In 1979, Benioff, a scientist at Argonne National Labs, published a seminal paper that introduced the idea of a quantum mechanical model for a computer. His work provided the first theoretical framework for the quantum Turing machine, which became the foundation for later developments in quantum computing. Benioff's research was groundbreaking in suggesting that a quantum computer, which could operate according to the principles of quantum mechanics, was not only theoretically possible but also potentially feasible. This insight laid the foundation for a new paradigm in computation, one that would eventually lead to the development of practical quantum computers, (Kappagantu & Daniel, 2018).

As quantum mechanics became more integrated into the study of computation, researchers began to recognize the immense potential of quantum systems to solve problems that classical computers could not efficiently handle. Quantum computing leverages the unique properties of quantum mechanics, such as superposition and entanglement, to process information in fundamentally different ways from classical computers. Unlike classical bits, which represent either a 0 or a 1, quantum bits (qubits) can exist in multiple states simultaneously due to the principle of superposition. This allows quantum computers to perform certain types of calculations much faster than classical computers, making them particularly well-suited for tasks involving large-scale data processing, optimization, and cryptographic analysis, (Musleh, Yao, & Muyeen, 2019).

The theoretical foundations of quantum computing were further solidified in the 1980s and 1990s by key contributions from figures such as Richard Feynman, David Deutsch, and Peter Shor. Feynman, in particular, played a pivotal role in illustrating the inherent limitations of classical computers in simulating quantum systems, thus highlighting the need for a new type of computer capable of exploiting quantum mechanics. Deutsch's work expanded on Feynman's ideas by proposing a universal quantum computer, one that could simulate any physical process governed by quantum mechanics. Shor's algorithm, introduced in the mid-1990s, provided a concrete example of a problem that quantum computers could solve exponentially faster than classical computers: integer factorization. This breakthrough demonstrated the potential of quantum computing to outperform classical systems in specific areas, particularly in the field of cryptography, (Hamouda, Nassar, & Salama, 2020).

Fast forward to the present day, and nearly every major technology company is investing heavily in the development of quantum computing technologies. Companies such as IBM, Google, Microsoft, and Intel are leading the charge in creating quantum computers and exploring their practical applications. IBM, for instance, has been at the forefront of quantum computing research and has made significant strides in making quantum computing accessible to the public. Through its Quantum Experience platform, IBM allows users to experiment with quantum algorithms on real quantum processors, providing an early glimpse into the potential of quantum computing. IBM's Quantum Gate Model, which forms the basis for its quantum computing systems, is one of the most advanced quantum computing frameworks currently available.

Google, too, has made significant progress in the field of quantum computing, achieving a major milestone in 2019 with the announcement of quantum supremacy. This term refers to the point at which a quantum computer performs a calculation that would be practically impossible for a classical computer to complete in a reasonable amount of time. Google's achievement, which involved using its quantum processor Sycamore to solve a specific problem faster than the world's most powerful supercomputers, marked a critical step in proving the viability of quantum computing for real-world applications. Microsoft, on the other hand, has focused on developing a topological quantum computing approach, which aims to overcome some of the challenges associated with qubit stability and error correction, (Massola, Denzler, & Christen, 2020).

While the field of quantum computing has made tremendous progress, there are still significant challenges that need to be addressed before quantum computers can become practical for widespread use. One of the key challenges is scalability. Current quantum computers are limited in the number of qubits they can manage, and as the number of qubits increases, so does the complexity of maintaining their coherence and minimizing errors. Quantum error correction, which involves designing algorithms to detect and correct errors in quantum computations, is an area of active research and is considered one of the major hurdles to building large-scale quantum computers. Additionally, quantum computers require extremely low temperatures to operate, which adds another layer of complexity to their design and maintenance.

Despite these challenges, the potential of quantum computing is immense, particularly in areas such as cryptography, materials science, and artificial intelligence. One of the most exciting implications of quantum computing is its potential to disrupt the field of cybersecurity. The rise of blockchain technology, which has been hailed for its ability to provide secure, transparent, and tamper-proof transactions, is particularly vulnerable to the advent of practical quantum computers. Blockchain relies on cryptographic algorithms, such as RSA and elliptic curve cryptography, which are based on the computational difficulty of factoring large numbers and solving discrete logarithm problems. These cryptographic systems are secure because they are extremely difficult for classical computers to break. However, quantum computers, with their ability to perform certain calculations exponentially faster than classical systems, could potentially crack these encryption schemes, rendering current blockchain security protocols vulnerable, (Banerjee, 2019).

The implications of this for the blockchain ecosystem are profound. If quantum computers can break the cryptographic foundations of blockchain, it could lead to a situation where the security of blockchain-based systems is compromised. This would have far-reaching consequences for applications that rely on blockchain, including cryptocurrencies, supply chain management, and digital identity verification. For example, smart contracts, which are self-executing contracts with the terms of the agreement directly written into code, could become vulnerable to exploitation by quantum-enabled attackers. The entire integrity of the blockchain network could be undermined, as attackers might be able to manipulate transaction records or forge digital signatures, (Cheng, Zeng, & Huang, 2017).

Recognizing the potential threat posed by quantum computing, researchers in the field of cryptography are already exploring quantum-resistant algorithms designed to withstand the computational power of quantum computers. These post-quantum cryptographic algorithms are being developed with the goal of ensuring that blockchain systems can remain secure even in a world with quantum computers. NIST (National Institute of Standards and Technology) is leading efforts to standardize post-quantum cryptographic algorithms, with a focus on identifying cryptographic schemes that are resistant to attacks by quantum computers. These efforts are critical for ensuring the long-term security and viability of blockchain technology.

In addition to its potential to disrupt blockchain security, quantum computing also has the potential to enhance blockchain in other ways. For instance, quantum computing could be used to improve the efficiency of blockchain consensus algorithms. Blockchain relies on consensus mechanisms, such as proof-of-work and proof-of-stake, to validate transactions and maintain the integrity of the network. These mechanisms, while secure, can be computationally intensive and require significant energy consumption. Quantum computers could potentially accelerate the validation process by solving certain computational problems more efficiently than classical computers. This could lead to faster transaction processing and reduced energy consumption, making blockchain technology more scalable and environmentally friendly, (Galici *et al.,* 2021).

Another potential application of quantum computing in blockchain is in the area of secure multi-party computation. Quantum cryptography, particularly quantum key distribution (QKD), is a technique that uses the principles of quantum mechanics to enable secure communication between parties. QKD leverages the properties of quantum entanglement to detect eavesdropping and ensure the security of communication channels. By integrating quantum cryptography with blockchain, it may be possible to create ultra-secure blockchain networks that are resistant to both classical and quantum attacks. This could pave the way for more secure and privacy-preserving applications of blockchain, such as secure voting systems, confidential financial transactions, and private data sharing.

While the relationship between quantum computing and blockchain is still evolving, it is clear that the two technologies will have a profound impact on each other. As quantum computing advances, it will undoubtedly present both challenges and opportunities for blockchain technology. On the one hand, quantum computers could threaten the security of blockchain by breaking traditional cryptographic algorithms. On the other hand, quantum computing could also enhance blockchain by enabling more efficient consensus mechanisms, faster transaction processing, and ultra-secure communication channels. The race to develop quantum-resistant blockchain systems and explore the synergies between quantum computing and blockchain is already underway, and the future of these technologies will likely be shaped by their interaction, (Banerjee & Patel, 2016).

In conclusion, quantum computing represents a revolutionary shift in computing technology, with the potential to transform numerous industries and fields. While there are significant challenges to overcome, the progress made in recent years has been remarkable, with companies such as IBM, Google, and Microsoft leading the way. However, the advent of practical quantum computers poses a significant threat to the security of blockchain technology, which relies on cryptographic systems that could be vulnerable to quantum attacks. As a result, there is an urgent need for the development of quantum-resistant algorithms and quantum-enhanced blockchain systems to ensure the continued security and viability of blockchain in the quantum era. The interplay between quantum computing and blockchain will shape the future of both technologies, and their combined potential promises to drive innovation in areas ranging from cybersecurity to decentralized finance.

II. CHALLENGES FOR MANAGEMENT, CONTROL AND OPERATIONS ON SMART GRID

Quantum computing has emerged as one of the most promising technologies in recent years, drawing significant attention due to its potential to revolutionize multiple industries. Although the theory of quantum mechanics has been around for over a century, its application in computing is a more recent development. The foundations of quantum computing were laid in the 1970s and 1980s, with early contributions by researchers like Paul Benioff, who proposed the idea of a quantum Turing machine in 1979, suggesting the possibility of a quantum computer. This theoretical groundwork marked the beginning of a new era in computing, (Patel, Ucchula, & Banerjee, 2013).

Quantum computers are built on the principles of quantum mechanics, particularly concepts like superposition and entanglement. While classical computers use bits that can represent either a 0 or a 1, quantum computers use qubits, which can represent both 0 and 1 simultaneously due to superposition. This ability allows quantum computers to process vast amounts of data at once, making them exponentially faster than classical computers for certain types of calculations. Quantum entanglement, another key quantum property, enables qubits to be linked in ways that allow them to work together more efficiently, even over long distances.

Today, companies like IBM, Google, and Microsoft are heavily invested in the development of quantum computing technologies. IBM, for example, has made quantum computing more accessible through its Quantum Experience platform, allowing users to experiment with quantum algorithms on real processors. Google made headlines in 2019 by achieving quantum supremacy, demonstrating that their quantum processor, Sycamore, could solve a specific problem faster than the world's most powerful supercomputers. These advancements represent important steps toward the practical application of quantum computing, (Saha, Banerjee, & Joshi, 2022).

However, the rise of quantum computing also presents challenges, particularly in the area of cybersecurity. Many existing cryptographic systems, including those used in blockchain technology, rely on mathematical problems that are difficult for classical computers to solve but could be easily cracked by a sufficiently powerful quantum computer. Blockchain, known for its ability to provide secure and transparent transactions, could be vulnerable to quantum attacks once quantum computers become more capable. This presents a significant concern for industries relying on blockchain for secure data management and digital transactions.

In response to these challenges, researchers are exploring quantum-resistant cryptographic algorithms that can withstand the power of quantum computers. Efforts are being led by organizations like NIST, which is working to standardize algorithms that will secure data in a post-quantum world. These advancements are essential for ensuring the continued integrity of blockchain technology and other cryptographic systems as quantum computers become more powerful, (Unahalekhaka & Sripakarach, 2020).

On the other hand, quantum computing also has the potential to enhance blockchain technology. Quantum computers could help speed up consensus algorithms used in blockchain networks, improving transaction processing and reducing energy consumption. Furthermore, quantum cryptography, particularly quantum key distribution, offers the possibility of ultra-secure communication channels, which could be integrated into blockchain systems to increase privacy and security.

Quantum computing represents a transformative technology with the potential to both challenge and enhance existing systems like blockchain. While quantum computers pose a threat to current cryptographic protocols, ongoing research into quantum-resistant algorithms and quantum-enhanced blockchain systems will play a critical role in securing the future of both technologies. As quantum computing continues to advance, its relationship with blockchain will shape the future of cybersecurity, decentralized finance, and many other sectors.

A. Collaboration between Stakeholders

Modern technologies, high investments, lack of accurate information, etc. complicate the coordination between actors in the energy sector. The current smart grid system faces the problem of energy balancing, especially when different actors are involved in the processes of generation, distribution, trading, and consumption. While much of the literature focuses on the technical aspects of the smart grid challenges, collaboration between stakeholders is equally important and needs to be properly addressed, (Biswas *et al.,* 2024). Energy suppliers and traders typically request an estimated amount of energy from generators based on their demand analysis. Such an estimate can be inaccurate due to several factors: expansion of the region, population growth, environmental factors, and increase in microgrid generators in the area. This can lead to high distribution losses, unbalanced voltage and frequency loads, and consequent power outages. In addition, some microgrids, such as solar systems, produce more energy during the warm summer months when energy demand is lowest. A modern data exchange system between the stakeholders could pave the way to store the excess produced energy in a local hydrogen gas or battery without affecting the main grid infrastructure. Therefore, it is important to establish close cooperation between relevant players such as generators, distributors, retailers, consumers, and regulators to facilitate grid management.

B. Controlling Grid Imbalance

Imbalances in power generation and consumption can stem from a combination of physical and technical issues. Disruptions in network components, such as insulation faults or impaired cables, external interference from third parties, acts of vandalism, as well as natural phenomena like wind or storms, can collectively contribute to disruptions in the equilibrium of power supply. Technical issues, such as malicious attacks, deviations in frequency, overloads, losses in synchronization, and voltage fluctuations, can also be contributing factors to power imbalances, (Banerjee, Hazra, & Sarkar, 2024). Voltage variations present another potential complication for grid stability. For instance, a photovoltaic (PV) power plant generates excess energy during the sunniest part of the day when demand is typically lower, leading to a situation where the PV power plant produces more electricity than the grid can accommodate, resulting in Reverse Power Flow (RPF) into the transmission grid, (Hannan et al., 2020) (Banerjee, Jani, & Shah, 2021) (Banerjee, Jani, & Shah, 2021) (Badal *et al.,* 2019). As a result, it is imperative to maintain control and monitoring of power supply during each period. A study discussed in Alladi *et al.* (2019) explored the emerging challenges associated with voltage control in the smart grid. To address these challenges, all stakeholders must adapt their approaches to power generation, distribution, and consumption to regulate both active and reactive power, (Faisal *et al.,* 2014). However, this task becomes increasingly complex due to the multitude of power generation methods and the various regulatory requirements in place.

C. Data Analysis and Management

The current management of data in smart grids encounters several challenges, including issues related to the quality of data aggregation, security, compliance control, standardization, and the efficiency of the management system, (Di Silvestre, 2020). A substantial volume of data is continually generated and exchanged among various stakeholders, (Alladi *et al.,* 2019). The reliability and consistency of incoming data streams, such as weather forecasts and power generation status, play a pivotal role in enabling operators to effectively supervise and govern the grid system, (Banerjee, 2019). This information proves invaluable in preventing abrupt and unforeseen disruptions in the power supply. Furthermore, this extensive dataset can serve multiple purposes in grid operations, including generating alerts, forecasting demand, estimating power generation, adjusting pricing, and more. Given the involvement of multiple smart grid domains in the data collection process, the dataset tends to be quite substantial. For example, adopting an Advanced Metering Infrastructure that collects data every 10 minutes instead of monthly intervals can amplify the data analysis workload by more than 4000 times. Moreover, there exists a regulatory mandate to furnish accurate data as frequently as possible, which presents a considerable challenge, (Patel, Ucchula, & Banerjee, 2013). The application of modern, automated, and secure data processing technologies holds the potential to enhance data management, storage, and reporting capabilities within the smart grid infrastructure.

D. Decentralizing Grid Management and Operation

The decentralization of grid operations empowers stakeholders to locally control and manage their data. Operating a smart grid in a decentralized context represents a vital area of research. Research efforts are focused on demand-side control and optimizing grid operations, (Foti & Vavalis, 2021). The decentralization of grid operations is facilitated through the deployment of distributed automation devices such as phasor management units (PMUs), remote terminal units (RTUs), SCADA systems, and smart meters, which are utilized for data collection and monitoring. In Ourahou *et al.* (2020), research delved into distributed automation strategies for electric power distribution systems, exploring their advantages and challenges. Additionally, there was consideration given to employing high-resolution sensors capable of providing real-time data and enhancing the visibility of the distribution system operator beyond the confines of substation assets. Furthermore, there exist challenges pertaining to the coordinated and cost-efficient integration of distributed smart grid systems, generation resources, and demand response capabilities, (Saha, Banerjee, & Joshi, 2022). These challenges add complexity to the management and operation of distributed energy resources. It is imperative to undertake further efforts aimed at facilitating coordination between stakeholders operating in both decentralized and centralized capacities.

E. Security and Privacy

Although the decentralization of smart grid operation and management offers numerous advantages, it simultaneously presents security and privacy concerns. In contemporary power systems, the SCADA module gathers data from remote terminals, transmitting and storing it in plain text at the main control center. This centralized data collection and storage approach is susceptible to cyberattacks. Cybersecurity stands as one of the most formidable challenges for the current smart grid. Over time, numerous cyberattacks have occurred, (Davis *et al.,* 2018). Attackers employ a four-step process—Exploration, Scanning, Exploitation, and Maintaining Access (Energimyndigheten, 2020)—to seize control. Various attacks on smart grids are documented, including the jabbing attack, where an attacker installs a rogue smart power meter, leading to false data transmission and subsequent desynchronization and power interruptions. The puppet attack initiates a signal to the node, allowing the attacker to take control of the node and transmit additional signals into the network, thereby destabilizing the smart meter network. Another example is the stack smashing attack, which compromises the network's application layer and exposes sensitive data. Conversely, an experimental attack renders the smart grid layer susceptible to DoS (Denial of Service) attacks, (Kappagantu & Daniel, 2018). A comprehensive exploration of attack methodologies, detection methods, and countermeasures can be found in Pillitteri and Brewer (2021).

III. BLOCKCHAIN FOR SMART GRID MANAGEMENT, CONTROL AND OPERATION

Blockchain provides a novel response to these issues by reducing the complexities associated with data management, promoting equitable incentive systems, reducing regulatory expenses, addressing technical concerns, lowering transaction fees among decentralized nodes, enhancing the speed of resources, and mitigating price adjustment challenges. Furthermore, it can enhance transparency among stakeholders, guarantee the security and confidentiality of data, streamline energy supply chains, and reduce distribution losses. The utilization of blockchain in the energy sector represents an active field of research and development, as indicated by recent developments, (Banerjee & Sarkar, 2024). Nevertheless, a majority of these applications have not advanced beyond the experimental pilot phase. A noteworthy case in point is the Brooklyn Microgrid project, (Hannan *et al.,* 2020), which enables local users of solar energy to engage in data exchange through blockchain technology. Another illustrative instance is the Electron project in the UK, (Banerjee, Jani, & Shah, 2021), which leverages a blockchain-based platform to facilitate the involvement of grid operators, systems, local energy markets, and distributed energy sources in various grid optimization markets featuring different energy assets. This demonstrates the global recognition of the potential applications of blockchain technology in the energy sector. For a comprehensive compilation of initiatives by companies aiming to integrate blockchain within the energy sector, please refer to Banerjee (2024). Historically, energy generation, distribution, and control have predominantly been the domain of financially robust corporations. The implementation of Advanced Metering Infrastructures (AMI) facilitates bidirectional communication among generators, distributors, retailers, and consumers, thereby allowing the transition from conventional infrastructure to a smart grid. Furthermore, smart systems like Wireless Sensor Networks (WSNs), the Internet of Things (IoT), Virtual Power Plants (VPPs), and other sophisticated control systems enable the fine-tuning of power generation and consumption. These advanced technologies collectively contribute to the enhancement of the power grid, rendering it more intelligent, efficient, and automated, (Ajadi *et al.,* 2020) (Badal *et al.,* 2019). The following figures (Figure 1, 2 and 3) shows the block structure, the chain structure, and the asset transfer mechanism. In smart grid the blockchain process is employed to transfer monetary assets against power.

Figure 1. Block structure

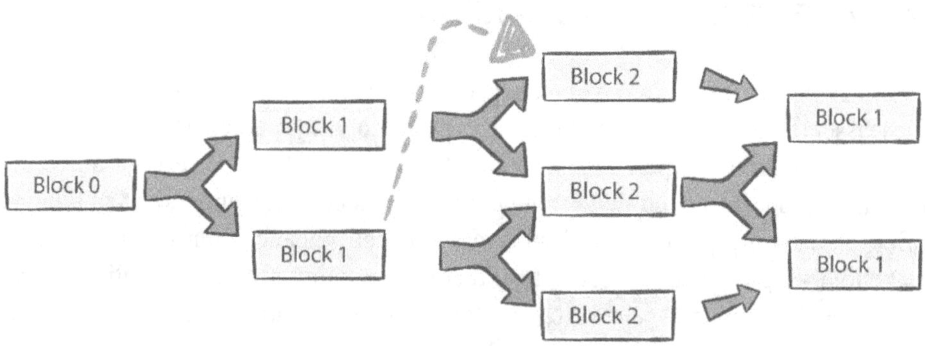

Figure 2. Blockchain

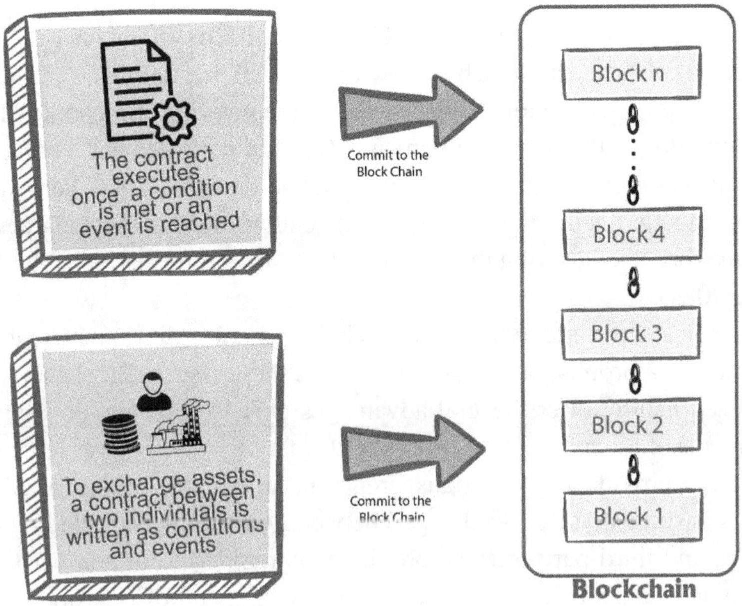

Figure 3. Asset exchange between parties

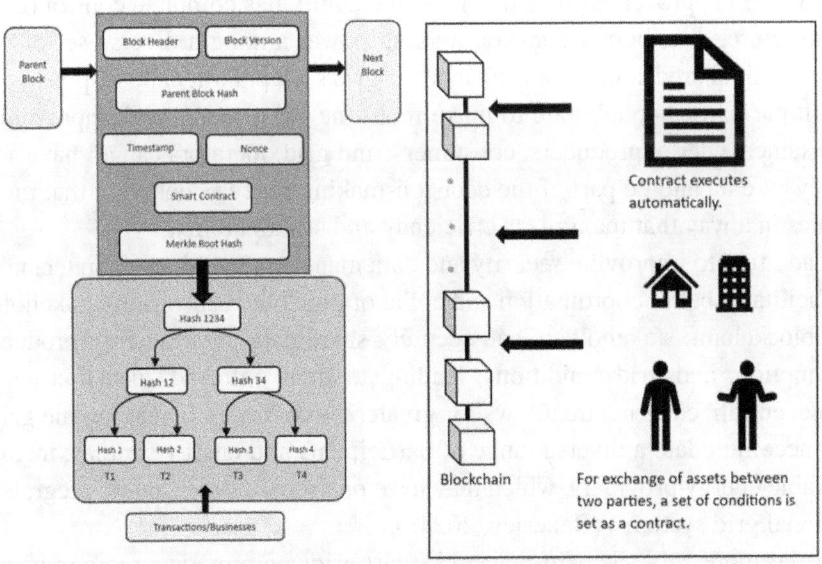

Traditional smart grid operations have largely relied on centralized control and management systems, which, while effective in certain contexts, expose the grid infrastructure to various vulnerabilities. These centralized systems are typically more susceptible to cyberattacks, data breaches, and operational failures, as a single point of failure can disrupt the entire grid. Moreover, the growing complexity of modern energy networks, with increasing demands for data management, access control, and security, has created significant operational bottlenecks. These bottlenecks can hinder the smooth functioning of the grid, especially when managing large amounts of real-time data and ensuring the security of sensitive information, (Mukherjee & Banerjee, 2024).

In recent years, the integration of blockchain technology into smart grid systems has emerged as a promising solution to address these issues. Blockchain, with its decentralized nature, offers several advantages over the conventional centralized approach. One of the most significant benefits of a blockchain-powered smart grid is its ability to provide a secure, transparent, and immutable ledger for all transactions. This ensures that data exchanged between stakeholders, including utilities, consumers, and third-party service providers, is tamper-proof and verifiable. By utilizing blockchain's consensus mechanisms, such as proof of work or proof of stake, the smart grid can achieve a higher level of security and resilience against cyberattacks, (Banerjee, 2024b).

Table 2 illustrates a comparative analysis of the benefits of a decentralized blockchain-powered smart grid versus a centralized grid management system. The decentralized approach ensures that no single entity has complete control over the infrastructure, distributing decision-making power among a diverse set of stakeholders. This shared control can enhance the grid's adaptability and responsiveness, as multiple parties collaborate to make real-time adjustments and improvements. For instance, energy producers, consumers, and grid operators can all have access to relevant data and be part of the decision-making process, ensuring that the grid operates in a way that maximizes efficiency and sustainability.

In addition to improving security and data management, blockchain technology also facilitates better coordination and collaboration between various stakeholders. With blockchain, stakeholders can securely share data about energy production, consumption, and grid conditions, leading to more informed decision-making. This decentralized structure allows for greater flexibility in managing the grid, as it can accommodate a diverse range of participants and energy sources, including renewable energy providers, which may have previously struggled to integrate into traditional grid systems, (Banerjee, 2024c).

Furthermore, a blockchain-powered smart grid can provide a more transparent and trustworthy platform for energy transactions. Consumers, for example, can track the flow of energy from production to consumption, ensuring that they are paying fair prices and contributing to sustainable energy practices. The immutable nature of blockchain records also helps prevent fraud and ensures the integrity of the data.

The shift from a centralized to a decentralized, blockchain-powered smart grid offers numerous advantages, including enhanced security, improved data management, and better stakeholder collaboration. By distributing control and fostering greater transparency, blockchain can help create a more resilient, efficient, and equitable energy grid, addressing many of the challenges associated with traditional smart grid systems.

Table 2. Blockchain based solutions to address the challenges of smart grids

Blockchain Application Areas	Blockchain-Based Solutions to Address the Challenges	Ref.
Collaboration between stakeholders	✓ Fosters trust and transparency between stakeholders and the public. ✓ Automates monitoring and maintenance of the smart grid. ✓ Enables resource allocation and tracking of environmental indicators. ✓ Enhances the efficiency of renewable energy sources. ✓ Advances the digitalization of the grid and sanctions new applications for the power system. ✓ Empowers microgrid prosumers to play a significant role in the management and operation of the smart grid.	Banerjee & Saha (2022)
Controlling Grid Imbalance	✓ Regulating voltage and ensuring equitable production distribution among distributed generation units. ✓ Facilitating a temperature-safe system to safeguard customer data collected and transmitted to the smart grid.	Xue *et al.*, 2017) (Yuan & Wang (2016)
Data—Analysis and Management	✓ Safeguarding the authenticity and accuracy of aggregated data. ✓ Developing unalterable data structures resistant to modification, featuring high scalability, and accommodating microtransactions. ✓ Elevating the architecture of the power management system for real-time monitoring of power consumption. ✓ Implementing secure data aggregation through encryption. ✓ Enabling a multi-dimensional data aggregation control mechanism for the smart grid. ✓ Establishing a decentralized aggregation mechanism to manage transactions among various smart meters.	Banerjee, Jani, & Shah (2021) (Badal *et al.*, 2019)

continued on following page

Table 2. Continued

Blockchain Application Areas	Blockchain-Based Solutions to Address the Challenges	Ref.
Decentralizing grid management and operations	✓ Strengthening authentication and non-repudiation measures. ✓ Enabling power management processes without relying on a trusted intermediary. ✓ Involvement in distributed computing to alleviate the computational burden on Virtual Power Plants (VPPs). ✓ Promoting decentralization. ✓ Amplifying transparency, digitizing the grid, and facilitating novel applications for the power system. ✓ Assisting advanced metering infrastructure control systems to enhance operational efficiency, optimal planning, and efficient trading. ✓ Enabling traceable energy management on the smart grid.	Alladi *et al.*, 2019) (Di Silvestre *et al.*, 2020) (Li *et al.*,2019)
Security and privacy	✓ Creating rigid data structures that cannot be modified. ✓ Improving cybersecurity and privacy in smart grid systems. ✓ Enhancing security, privacy, information security, and access control. ✓ Addressing localization and provenance concerns. ✓ Resolving issues related to real-time performance, elevated transaction expenses, and information security. ✓ Promptly identifying adversarial nodes.	Kappagantu & Daniel (2018) (Musleh, Yao, & Muyeen, 2019)

Blockchain technology has the potential to address these challenges by offering a decentralized platform that allows all participants to equitably share information. This technology has the capacity to empower all participants to collectively establish a platform without necessitating any form of trust, (Kappagantu & Daniel, 2018). The integration of blockchain within the energy sector offers numerous advantages, including the encouragement of decentralized low-voltage energy system production and distribution, (Badal *et al.,* 2019). Furthermore, it facilitates streamlined multi-tier systems, (Banerjee, Jani, & Shah, 2021), where energy producers, distribution system operators, transmission system operators, and consumers can engage in direct communication to enhance operational efficiency. Additionally, when coupled with smart contracts, blockchain empowers efficient management of the smart grid, (Hussain, Farooq, & Ustun, 2019). By employing pre-established consensus rules, smart contracts broadcast signals to all nodes, thereby guaranteeing the validity of transactions. This automated process enables precise control of all energy storage movements, ultimately enhancing the equilibrium between supply and demand, (Li *et al.,* 2019). Additionally, blockchain can effectively capture, archive, and disseminate all energy transactions, ensuring decentralized security for all energy-related flows and business operations, (Banerjee, Jani, & Shah, 2021).

IV. ROLE OF BLOCKCHAIN IN IOT, AI AND EDGE COMPUTING

The Internet of Things (IoT), Artificial Intelligence (AI), and Edge Computing are interconnected yet distinct technologies, each playing a vital role in modern innovation. IoT refers to the network of physical devices that collect and share data through the internet. These devices enhance automation, real-time monitoring, and remote control across industries. However, IoT's data generation capabilities depend on intelligent analysis, where AI steps in. AI processes and interprets the vast volumes of data generated by IoT, enabling predictions, decision-making, and process optimization.

Edge Computing complements IoT and AI by decentralizing data processing. Instead of sending data to centralized cloud servers, Edge Computing processes it near the source. This reduces latency, enhances real-time responses, and minimizes bandwidth usage. For example, in healthcare, IoT devices collect patient data, AI analyzes it, and Edge Computing ensures rapid processing during emergencies.

Blockchain technology impacts these domains by addressing critical challenges like security, privacy, and data integrity. IoT devices often face vulnerabilities due to limited security mechanisms, making them targets for cyberattacks. Blockchain provides a decentralized framework, where transactions are securely recorded, ensuring tamper-proof data sharing. In AI, blockchain enhances trust by verifying the integrity of datasets and algorithms, reducing biases and ensuring transparency. Similarly, in Edge Computing, blockchain ensures secure communication between devices and nodes, creating a robust system for real-time data processing without compromising security.

The convergence of IoT, AI, and Edge Computing, strengthened by blockchain, is revolutionizing industries like healthcare, logistics, and manufacturing. Blockchain's decentralized nature not only secures interactions between these technologies but also fosters trust, making it a pivotal enabler in the digital transformation era. Together, they unlock a future of secure, efficient, and intelligent systems.

V. CONCLUSION AND FUTURE WORK

Smart grid systems driven by blockchain technology have the capability to function autonomously, following predefined consensus mechanisms, all without the need for human intervention, intermediaries, or centralized authorization. Moreover, they offer effective data aggregation methods to address privacy and security issues within the grid. This study comprehensively investigates the utilization of blockchain-based solutions in the governance, regulation, and functioning of smart grid systems. This paper concentrates on the non-financial uses of blockchain technology within the energy sector, delineating the challenges into five primary domains: collaborative engagement among stakeholders, rectifying grid imbalances, refining data management and operational processes, the decentralization of grid operations, and enhancing security and privacy. Through an extensive examination, analysis, and comparison with existing literature, this study pinpoints supplementary challenges and emphasizes prospective avenues for future research within these five domains. Various existing technologies employ diverse blockchain architectures tailored to specific application contexts, showcasing the technology's potential in facilitating the management and operation of smart grid infrastructure. Nonetheless, instances of actual technology implementations for grid management, control, and operations, as found in the literature, remain infrequent and confined to specific regions. This reveals a deficiency in systematic technological solutions for the comprehensive management, control, and operation of smart grids. Addressing this challenge necessitates the dismantling of the current grid management, control, and operational frameworks, followed by the systematic formulation, design, and creation of a dedicated blockchain application system. This should be achieved through the integration of the blockchain's technical strengths. Given the challenges in modifying blockchain system architecture and the enduring nature of online data storage, it becomes imperative to possess a comprehensive grasp of the existing power grid's structure, operational aspects, and technical management. Furthermore, a thorough understanding of the forthcoming business and commercial growth within the smart grid sector, along with reasonably accurate predictions regarding system technology and business trends, constitute critical prerequisites for the design and development of an exceptionally dependable, scalable, enduring, and open blockchain system.

REFERENCES

Ajadi, T., Cuming, V., Boyle, R., Strahan, D., Kimmel, M., Logan, M., & McCrone, A. (2020). Global Trends in Renewable Energy Investment. https://www.fs-unep-centre.org/wp-content/uploads/2020/06/GTR_2020.pdf (accessed on 23 December 2021).

Alladi, T., Chamola, V., Rodrigues, J. J., & Kozlov, S. A. (2019). Blockchain in smart grids: A review on different use cases. *Sensors (Basel)*, *19*(22), 4862. DOI: 10.3390/s19224862 PMID: 31717262

Andoni, M., Robu, V., Flynn, D., Abram, S., Geach, D., Jenkins, D., McCallum, P., & Peacock, A. (2019). Blockchain technology in the energy sector: A systematic review of challenges and opportunities. *Renewable & Sustainable Energy Reviews*, *100*, 143–174. DOI: 10.1016/j.rser.2018.10.014

Badal, F. R., Das, P., Sarker, S. K., & Das, S. K. (2019). A survey on control issues in renewable energy integration and microgrid. *Prot. Control. Mod. Power Syst.*, *4*(1), 8. DOI: 10.1186/s41601-019-0122-8

Banerjee, B., (2019). Avalanche effect: A judgement parameter of strength in symmetric key block ciphers. International journal of engineering development and research, 7(2), pp.116-121.

Banerjee, B. (2024). Blockchain 2030: Revolutionizing the Future of Digital Trust. *International Research Journal of Scientific Studies*, *1*(1), 13–18.

Banerjee, B. (2024). Quantum Horizons: Shaping the Future of Computing. *International Research Journal of Scientific Studies*, *1*(1), 7–12.

Banerjee, B. (2024). Next-Gen Computing: Exploring Industry 4.0. *International Research Journal of Scientific Studies*, *1*(1), 1–6.

Banerjee, B., Hazra, D., & Sarkar, D. (2024). IoT-Enabled Water Quality Management System for Rural Areas of Bharuch District. In *Water Informatics: Challenges and Solutions Using State of Art Technologies* (pp. 33–47). Springer Nature Singapore. DOI: 10.1007/978-981-97-1518-3_3

Banerjee, B., Jani, A., & Shah, N. (2021). *Asymmetric Confidentiality in Blockchain Embedded Smart Grids in Galois Field.* Frontiers in Blockchain. DOI: 10.3389/fbloc.2021.770074

Banerjee, B., Jani, A., & Shah, N. (2021). Digital Image Encryption Using Double Crossover Approach for SARS-CoV-2 Infected Lungs in a Blockchain Framework. *Frontiers in Blockchain*, *4*, 771241. DOI: 10.3389/fbloc.2021.771241

Banerjee, B., Jani, A., & Shah, N. (2021). A genetic blockchain approach for securing smart vehicles in quantum era. In *Vehicular Communications for Smart Cars* (pp. 85–108). CRC Press. DOI: 10.1201/9781315110905-5

Banerjee, B., Jani, A., Shah, N., & Patel, A. (2020). Post Quantum Security Enhancement Scheme in IoT Blockchain Framework. *GIS Sci. J*, *7*(6), 664–672.

Banerjee, B., & Patel, J. T. (2016). A Symmetric Key Block Cipher to Provide Confidentiality in Wireless Sensor Networks. INFOCOMP Journal of Computer Science, 15(1), 12–18. Retrieved from https://infocomp.dcc.ufla.br/index.php/infocomp/article/view/515

Banerjee, B., & Saha, G. (2022). Emotion Independent Face Recognition-Based Security Protocol in IoT-Enabled Devices. In Cloud IoT (pp. 199-218). Chapman and Hall/CRC. DOI: 10.1201/9781003155577-18

Banerjee, B., & Sarkar, D. (2024). Blockchain-Based Quantum Resistant Electoral Management System for the Post-Pandemic Era. In Ensuring Security and End-to-End Visibility Through Blockchain and Digital Twins (pp. 102-115). IGI Global. DOI: 10.4018/979-8-3693-3494-2.ch006

Biswas, N., Santra, D., Banerjee, B., & Biswas, S. (2024). Harnessing the Power of Machine Learning for Parkinson's Disease Detection. In *AIoT and Smart Sensing Technologies for Smart Devices* (pp. 140–155). IGI Global. DOI: 10.4018/979-8-3693-0786-1.ch008

Cheng, S., Zeng, B., & Huang, Y. Z. (2017, November). Research on application model of blockchain technology in distributed electricity market. []). IOP Publishing.]. *IOP Conference Series. Earth and Environmental Science*, *93*(1), 012065.

Davis, S. J., Lewis, N. S., Shaner, M., Aggarwal, S., Arent, D., Azevedo, I. L., Benson, S. M., Bradley, T., Brouwer, J., & Caldeira, K.. (2018). Net-zero emissions energy systems. *Science*, *360*(6396), 6396. DOI: 10.1126/science.aas9793 PMID: 29954954

Di Silvestre, M. L., Gallo, P., Guerrero, J. M., Musca, R., Sanseverino, E. R., Sciumè, G., Vasquez, J. C., & Zizzo, G. (2020). Blockchain for power systems: Current trends and future applications. *Renewable & Sustainable Energy Reviews*, *119*, 109585. DOI: 10.1016/j.rser.2019.109585

El Mrabet, Z., Kaabouch, N., El Ghazi, H., & El Ghazi, H. (2018). Cyber-security in smart grid: Survey and challenges. *Computers & Electrical Engineering*, *67*, 469–482. DOI: 10.1016/j.compeleceng.2018.01.015

Energimyndigheten. 2020. Available online: https://www.energimyndigheten.se/statistik/den-officiella-statistiken/ statistikprodukter/natanslutna-solcellsanlaggningar/ (accessed on 23 November 2021).

Faisal, M. A., Aung, Z., Williams, J. R., & Sanchez, A. (2014). Data-stream-based intrusion detection system for advanced metering infrastructure in smart grid: A feasibility study. *IEEE Systems Journal*, *9*(1), 31–44. DOI: 10.1109/JSYST.2013.2294120

Foti, M., & Vavalis, M. (2021). What can blockchain do for power grids? *Blockchain: Res. Appl.*, *2*, 100008.

Galici, M., Mureddu, M., Ghiani, E., Celli, G., Pilo, F., Porcu, P., & Canetto, B. (2021). Energy Blockchain for Public Energy Communities. [CrossRef]. *Applied Sciences (Basel, Switzerland)*, *11*(8), 3457. DOI: 10.3390/app11083457

Hamouda, M. R., Nassar, M. E., & Salama, M. M. A. (2020). A Novel Energy Trading Framework Using Adapted Blockchain Technology. *IEEE Transactions on Smart Grid*, *12*(3), 2165–2175. DOI: 10.1109/TSG.2020.3045662

Hannan, M. A., Tan, S. Y., Al-Shetwi, A. Q., Jern, K. P., & Begum, R. A. (2020). Optimized controller for renewable energy sources integration into microgrid: Functions, constraints, and suggestions. *Journal of Cleaner Production*, *256*, 120419. DOI: 10.1016/j.jclepro.2020.120419

Hussain, S. S., Farooq, S. M., & Ustun, T. S. (2019, March). Implementation of blockchain technology for energy trading with smart meters. In 2019 Innovations in Power and Advanced Computing Technologies (i-PACT) (Vol. 1, pp. 1-5). IEEE.

Kappagantu, R., & Daniel, S. A. (2018). Challenges and issues of smart grid implementation: A case of Indian scenario. *Journal of Electrical Systems and Information Technology*, *5*(3), 453–467. DOI: 10.1016/j.jesit.2018.01.002

Konashevych, O. I. (2016). Advantages and current issues of blockchain use in microgrids. *Electron. Model.*, *38*(2), 93–104. DOI: 10.15407/emodel.38.02.093

Li, Y., Teng, Y., Cao, R., & Li, N. (2019, October). Research on coordination control system of virtual power plant based on blockchain. In 2019 IEEE 8th International Conference on Advanced Power System Automation and Protection (APAP) (pp. 1377-1383). IEEE.

Mattila, J., Seppälä, T., Naucler, C., Stahl, R., Tikkanen, M., Bådenlid, A., & Seppälä, J. (2016). Industrial blockchain platforms: An exercise in use case development in the energy industry (No. 43). ETLA Working Papers.

Mazzola, L., Denzler, A., & Christen, R. (2020). Towards a Peer-to-Peer energy market: an overview. arXiv preprint arXiv:2003.07940.

Mollah, M. B., Zhao, J., Niyato, D., Lam, K. Y., Zhang, X., Ghias, A. M., Koh, L. H., & Yang, L. (2020). Blockchain for future smart grid: A comprehensive survey. *IEEE Internet of Things Journal, 8*(1), 18–43. DOI: 10.1109/JIOT.2020.2993601

Mukherjee, S., & Banerjee, B. (2024). Latest Developments in Artificial Intelligence: Enhancing Creativity and Productivity. *International Research Journal of Scientific Studies, 1*(1), 19–23.

Musleh, A. S., Yao, G., & Muyeen, S. M. (2019). Blockchain applications in smart grid–review and frameworks. *IEEE Access : Practical Innovations, Open Solutions, 7*, 86746–86757.

Ourahou, M., Ayrir, W., Hassouni, B. E., & Haddi, A. (2020). Review on smart grid control and reliability in presence of renewable energies: Challenges and prospects. *Mathematics and Computers in Simulation, 167*, 19–31. DOI: 10.1016/j.matcom.2018.11.009

Patel, M. K., Uchhula, V. V., & Banerjee, B. (2013). Comparative Analysis of Routing Protocols in MANET Based on Packet Delivery Ratio using NS2. *International Journal of Advanced Research in Computer Science and Software Engineering, 3*(11), 172–177.

Pillitteri, V.; Brewer, T. (2014). Guidelines for Smart Grid Cybersecurity, NIST Interagency/Internal Report (NISTIR); National Institute of Standards and Technology: Gaithersburg, MD, USA,. Available online: (accessed on 17 September 2021).DOI: 10.6028/NIST.IR.7628r1

Saha, G., Banerjee, B., & Joshi, F. M. (2022). Predictive Edge Computing of SST Time-Series-Based Marine Warning System using Cloud Computing Infrastructure. In *Cloud IoT* (pp. 59–74). Chapman and Hall/CRC. DOI: 10.1201/9781003155577-7

Salkuti, S. R. (2020). Challenges, issues and opportunities for the development of smart grid. [IJECE]. *International Journal of Electrical and Computer Engineering, 10*(2), 1179–1186. DOI: 10.11591/ijece.v10i2.pp1179-1186

Shahzad, Y., Javed, H., Farman, H., Ahmad, J., Jan, B., & Zubair, M. (2020). Internet of energy: Opportunities, applications, architectures and challenges in smart industries. *Computers & Electrical Engineering, 86*, 106739. DOI: 10.1016/j.compeleceng.2020.106739

Unahalekhaka, P., & Sripakarach, P. (2020). Reduction of reverse power flow using the appropriate size and installation position of a BESS for a PV power plant. *IEEE Access : Practical Innovations, Open Solutions*, *8*, 102897–102906.

Wang, Q., & Su, M. (2020). Integrating blockchain technology into the energy sector—From theory of blockchain to research and application of energy blockchain. *Computer Science Review*, *37*, 100275. DOI: 10.1016/j.cosrev.2020.100275

Xue, L., Teng, Y., Zhang, Z., Li, J., Wang, K., & Huang, Q. (2017, September). Blockchain technology for electricity market in microgrid. In 2017 2nd International Conference on Power and Renewable Energy (ICPRE) (pp. 704-708). IEEE.

Yuan, Y., & Wang, F. Y. (2016). Blockchain: The state of the art and future trends. *Acta Automatica Sinica (Beijing)*, *42*, 481–494.

Chapter 13
Regulation and Innovation in Financial Markets:
The Impact of Fintech on Traditional Banking and Financial Systems Blockchain Technology

Daksh Agarwal
https://orcid.org/0009-0003-9045-1322
Christ University, India

Shruti Ranjan
Christ University, India

ABSTRACT

In this chapter, we present the underlying technical principles of distributed ledger technology (DLT) and blockchain technology and outline their practical applications in FinTech. In the recent years, DLT and blockchain technologies in general and cryptocurrencies, in particular, have attracted substantial attention from both researchers and practitioners due to their unique technological features such as the lack of centralized control and high level of anonymity. Because of the disruptive nature, DLT and blockchain have led to the evolution of decentralized applications in multiple domains such as finance, health care, supply chains etc. In this chapter, we first outline basic principles and foundations underpinning the DLT and blockchain technologies. Second, we discuss several applications in the FinTech domain such as cryptocurrencies, smart contracts, risk management, corporate finance, governance, crowdfunding, and derivative markets.

DOI: 10.4018/979-8-3373-1424-2.ch013

INTRODUCTION

This Includes Blockchain Technology, Cryptocurrencies And Decentralized Finance (DeFi)

Throughout history, technology and financial innovation have always gone hand-in-hand. In several decades, these developments have led to a transformation of the financial sector, giving rise to new products and services and business models. They have also played a role in the disruption of traditional financial systems and disintermediation. This journey can be traced back a little over a decade, with the global Financial Crisis (GFC) of 2008 proving to be a watershed moment that challenged the trust between consumers and financial institutions, and banks in particular. The erosion of trust was not limited to retail and investment banks, but also extended to other centralized organizations, including central banks

Many FinTech companies started to flourish in the result to GFC. It used to have the sleek, fresh, homegrown high-tech culture of the bubbly startup being built, and these companies provided novel, decentralized processes to establish trust and served as substitutes for the fiat currency system. Distributed Ledger Technologies (DLT), which have no centralized control and offer a great level of anonymity, are the substance of this FinTech revolution. Their distinctive attributes enable decentralized applications in numerous fields, including healthcare, supply chains, and, most importantly, finance. In this chapter, we explore the building blocks of DLT and blockchain, their real-world use cases and the transformational impact they can have in the world of FinTech.

Technology Evolution in Finans:

Milestones: The financial sector is undergoing a major overhaul, driven by the rapid evolution of technology (World Bank, 2019 (Natarajan et al., 2019)). It includes the improvement of current services and the development of new financial products. In particular, blockchain technology came into its own with the introduction of Bitcoin in 2009. Bitcoin is the first decentralized cryptocurrency, announced by an anonymous entity called (Satoshi Nakamoto, 2008) as a new breed of digital cash. By 2020 Bitcoin had become the largest cryptocurrency by market cap at over $100 billion.

A key feature of Bitcoin is its ability to preserve currency value without centralized oversight or governmental intervention. It is done via a public distributed ledger that is based on blockchain technology and where every transaction is entered in a transparent way. Bitcoin was initially underrated as a potential, mere niche, (European Central Bank 2012; ECB 2015)dismissing research showing impact. That scepticism has changed course, however, in recent years as financial institutions started to examine, and implement, blockchain and DLT in their own businesses.

Evolving Beyond Bitcoin: From Cryptocurrencies to...

Besides Bitcoin, hundreds of cryptocurrencies have appeared, with a combined market capitalization of several hundred billion dollars. Cryptocurrencies were thought to be speculative investments when they first entered the market, but they soon uncovered a technology with the potential to revolutionize various facets of life: the blockchain. Outside of finance, use cases for blockchain technology include power generation, healthcare (e.g. producing a verifiable digital ID for remote patients), education (e.g. for smart diplomas), government operations (e.g. smart contracts), supply chain management (e.g. for food safety), and transportation (e.g. for digital registries to manage vehicles much like chassis numbers do today). This level of adoption demonstrates the flexibility and potential of blockchain technology to drive innovation in a wide range of industries.

But, the rise of cryptocurrencies and blockchain also brings challenges. Some people and institutions have had massive financial gains, but there have also been financial losses, such as the bankruptcies of cryptocurrency exchanges (Szostek, 2019). This tension highlights the importance of finding a middle ground between harnessing the potential of blockchain and navigating its vulnerabilities.

Blockchain Technology: A Platform for Innovation

There is a lot of interest in blockchain technology by governments, academia, enterprises, and financial institutions due to its disruptive nature. Seizing its potential, the European Union established the EU Blockchain Observatory and Forum in 2018. This initiative was to encourage collaboration between member states, raise awareness and educate about the new technology, and showcase developments in the field of blockchain. It's nice to know that industry recognizes the potential of blockchain and is working towards addressing the challenges presented by it.

However, the anonymity of cryptocurrencies has raised red flags with regulators. The anonymity, scalability, and ease of use of cryptocurrencies make them one of the most popular means of money laundering and cybercrime (Sun Yin et al., 2019). As a result, authorities around the world are seeking to establish guidelines and frameworks for these to ensure that blockchain and DLT are used responsibly.

DLT and Blockchain in FinTech Explained

Understanding the technology and guiding principles behind DLT and blockchain is crucial to fully appreciate how these technologies are transforming the FinTech landscape. DLT acts as a decentralized ledger wherein each transaction is recorded on several nodes, promoting transparency, security, and immutability. Blockchain, one type of a DLT, organizes data in structured blocks that are chronologically linked to form a secure and verifiable chain of records.

There is a huge range of usages of such technologies in FinTech. Blockchain also facilitates secure and transparent transactions, decreasing the necessity for middlemen and lowering costs. It also streamlines cross-border payments, increases supply chain transparency, and enables smart contracts—self-executing legal contracts with agreed-upon terms. These abilities could potentially disrupt conventional banking and financial institutions, creating increased efficiency and larger access.

Legal and Regulatory Considerations

Although the technological advantages of blockchain and DLT are unquestionable, they bring many important legal and regulatory questions related to their adoption. Finding the right balance will be a challenge for governments and regulators as they work to promote innovation while also addressing concerns about privacy, security, and financial system stability. These might include the development of clear legal guidelines for blockchain technology, addressing data privacy and protection issues, and ensuring adherence to anti-money laundering (AML) and know-your-customer (KYC) regulations.

In this respect, eventually, the European Union has a head start, establishing a consist counterbalance for a coherent blockchain & DLT framework in all of its member states. This is key for facilitating the adoption of these technologies in a way that is in concordance with the objectives of society and the economy.

Structure of the Book and Key Themes

To this end, this chapter is structured in different sections that cover the impact that Blockchain and DLT have in relation to FinTech. In Section 2, we discuss the basics of DLT and blockchain namely, their basic principles, components, and functionalities. 3. Section 3: Various FinTech Applications and Analysis of Applicability of Blockchain. The fourth section of the interview addresses the legal and regulatory side of blockchain and DLT, including existing initiatives and potential hurdles. Lastly, Section 5 wraps-up with thoughts on market heuristics surrounding the uptake of these technologies and long-term implications for the FinTech industry.

Principles Behind Distributed Ledger Technologies (DLT) and Blockchain

The rise of blockchain technology has marked a significant shift in how data, transactions, and trust are managed in digital ecosystems. Its innovative and disruptive potential has given rise to numerous decentralized applications, including cryptocurrencies, smart contracts, and decentralized finance (DeFi). The introduction of Bitcoin in 2009 by an anonymous entity under the pseudonym Satoshi Nakamoto served as the foundation for the blockchain revolution. Today, Bitcoin remains the largest cryptocurrency, boasting a market capitalization exceeding $200 billion. Despite its groundbreaking nature, Bitcoin's technical underpinnings and the broader foundations of blockchain technology trace their origins to concepts and research from the 1980s and 1990s. This chapter explores the principles and technical components of Distributed Ledger Technologies (DLT) and blockchain, their structures, and their implications for the FinTech landscape.

Distributed Ledger Technologies (DLT) and Blockchain

Distributed Ledger Technology (DLT) is a system where data is replicated, shared, and synchronized across multiple sites, institutions, or geographies, allowing transactions to have public witnesses. According to Rauchs et al. (2018), DLT operates in an environment without a central operator or authority, even in potentially adversarial conditions. Its foundation lies in distributed computing principles, with applications ranging from finance to healthcare, supply chain management, and beyond. Blockchain, a subset of DLT, gained prominence with the launch of Bitcoin and is characterized by its decentralized structure, tamper-proof records, and cryptographic security mechanisms.

Blockchain operates as a distributed data structure that ensures the integrity and immutability of transactions. Transactions are grouped into blocks, each containing a timestamp, transaction data, and a cryptographic hash of the previous block. This chain of blocks, secured by cryptographic algorithms, ensures data integrity and provides transparency. Blockchain networks achieve consensus through distributed algorithms, enabling trust among participants without a central authority.

Key Technical Components of Blockchain Technology

To understand blockchain's transformative power, it is essential to examine its underlying technical components and principles.

Distributed Ledger

The distributed ledger is the cornerstone of blockchain technology. Unlike centralized ledgers managed by a single authority, distributed ledgers are collectively maintained by participants in a decentralized environment. These ledgers ensure transparency and reduce the risk of manipulation, as all participants hold identical copies of the ledger.

A distributed ledger must possess certain characteristics to function effectively:

Immutability: Data, once recorded, cannot be altered or deleted. Only new entries can be added, preserving the integrity of the ledger.

Verifiability: Cryptographic digests allow for the verification of ledger states without requiring the entire dataset.

Decentralization: Peer-to-peer networks ensure data is stored and managed across multiple nodes, eliminating single points of failure.

The ledger achieves consensus through protocols that validate and agree on the accuracy of transactions before adding them to the blockchain.

Hash Functions

Hash functions are cryptographic tools that ensure data integrity and security. A hash function converts input data into a fixed-size string of characters, which serves as a digital fingerprint of the data. The properties of hash functions include:

Determinism: The same input always produces the same hash.

Efficiency: Hashes are generated quickly.

Collision Resistance: Different inputs produce unique hashes.

Preimage Resistance: It is computationally infeasible to reverse-engineer the input from its hash.

Blockchain uses hash functions like SHA-256, which is widely implemented in Bitcoin. Hashing organizes and links data within blockchain blocks, with the Merkle Tree structure summarizing transactions in a secure and efficient manner.

Digital Signatures

Digital signatures ensure the authenticity and non-repudiation of transactions in blockchain networks. These cryptographic mechanisms use asymmetric key pairs: a private key for signing and a public key for verification. The key properties of digital signatures include:

Authenticity: Verifies the sender of a transaction.

Integrity: Ensures the transaction has not been altered.

Non-repudiation: Prevents the sender from denying their actions.

In Bitcoin, the Elliptic Curve Digital Signature Algorithm (ECDSA) is used to generate key pairs, enabling secure and efficient transaction verification.

Digital Timestamping

The concept of digital timestamping addresses the need to verify the chronological order of transactions. Proposed in the 1990s, digital timestamping links documents or transactions using cryptographic hashes, creating a chain of records. Each transaction includes a timestamp and is linked to its predecessor, ensuring a verifiable sequence. This concept underpins blockchain's tamper-resistant data structure, with Merkle Trees enhancing efficiency and security.

Fault Tolerance

Blockchain systems must be resilient to faults and malicious actors in a decentralized environment. Fault tolerance mechanisms ensure the consistency and reliability of the distributed ledger. Byzantine Fault Tolerance (BFT) is a key principle, enabling consensus among nodes even in the presence of malicious participants. Protocols like Practical Byzantine Fault Tolerance (PBFT) and Paxos have influenced blockchain's fault tolerance mechanisms.

Consensus Protocols

Consensus protocols are vital for establishing trust and agreement in blockchain networks. They ensure that all nodes agree on the validity of transactions before adding them to the ledger. Common consensus mechanisms include:

Proof of Work (PoW): Participants solve complex cryptographic puzzles to validate transactions. This energy-intensive mechanism underpins Bitcoin and prevents tampering by making attacks costly.

Proof of Stake (PoS): Validators are chosen based on their ownership or stake in the network, reducing energy consumption and incentivizing honest behavior.

Other Mechanisms: Variants like Proof of Authority (PoA), Proof of Burn, and Delegated Proof of Stake (DPoS) cater to specific use cases and trade-offs between decentralization, security, and scalability.

Smart Contracts

Smart contracts are self-executing agreements with terms directly written into code. These contracts automate processes and eliminate intermediaries, reducing costs and increasing efficiency. First conceptualized by Nick Szabo in the 1990s, smart contracts are particularly powerful in combination with blockchain, enabling tamper-proof and automated execution of agreements.

Smart contracts are used in various applications, including tokenized assets, decentralized finance platforms, and supply chain management. They allow for programmable money, where funds are automatically transferred based on predefined conditions.

Public vs. Permissioned Blockchains

Blockchain networks can be categorized as public or permissioned based on their access and governance structures:

Public Blockchains: Open to all participants, these networks, like Bitcoin and Ethereum, operate in a permissionless environment. Anyone can join, validate transactions, and participate in consensus. Public blockchains emphasize decentralization but may face scalability and energy efficiency challenges.

Permissioned Blockchains: Access is restricted to authorized participants, and governance is centralized or semi-centralized. Examples include Hyperledger Fabric and Corda. Permissioned blockchains prioritize efficiency and privacy, making them suitable for enterprise applications.

Characteristics of Blockchain Technology

The orchestration of the above principles and components results in several defining characteristics of blockchain technology:

Decentralization: Eliminates reliance on centralized authorities, fostering trust among participants.

Transparency: Ensures that all transactions are visible and verifiable by network participants.

Immutability: Preserves the integrity of data by preventing unauthorized modifications.

Security: Leverages cryptographic methods to protect data from tampering and unauthorized access.

Efficiency: Reduces transaction costs and processing times by automating processes and removing intermediaries.

CONCLUSION

Distributed Ledger Technologies and blockchain represent a paradigm shift in how data, trust, and transactions are managed. By combining decentralization, cryptographic security, and consensus mechanisms, these technologies enable innovative solutions across industries. From cryptocurrencies and smart contracts to decentralized finance and supply chain optimization, the applications of blockchain are vast and transformative.

Understanding the principles behind DLT and blockchain is essential for leveraging their potential in FinTech and beyond. As these technologies continue to evolve, their adoption will be shaped by advancements in scalability, regulatory frameworks, and integration with existing systems. Blockchain's foundational concepts, rooted in decades of research, have paved the way for a more decentralized, transparent, and efficient digital economy. as shown Tab. 1.

Table 1. Characteristics of the Blockchain

Immutability	Data written to database cannot be changed or deleted without consensus leading to data integrity
Decentralization	No single point of failure/control achieved by decentralized architecture and a distributed database
Transparency	All data sent through the blockchain is visible to all network participants
Pseudonymity	The identity of data senders and receivers is unknown
Chronology	Every transaction is time-stamped and can be traced back

Applications of Distributed Ledger Technology (DLT) in FinTech

Distributed Ledger Technology (DLT), more commonly known as blockchain, has emerged as a revolutionary concept in the financial technology (FinTech) sector. This technology, known for its decentralized, secure, and immutable nature, has found significant applications in FinTech and is poised to redefine financial processes and systems in the years to come. Below, we delve into key applications of DLT in the FinTech domain, particularly focusing on cryptocurrencies and the challenges they face in achieving widespread adoption.

2.1 Cryptocurrencies

The inception of cryptocurrencies marked a turning point in digital finance. After several unsuccessful attempts in the 1990s to create a decentralized, censorship-resistant, and secure digital currency—such as b-money, Hashcash, and Bitgold—the release of the Bitcoin whitepaper in 2008 by an anonymous individual or group using the pseudonym Satoshi Nakamoto finally laid the foundation for modern cryptocurrencies. This whitepaper outlined the technical workings of blockchain, providing the blueprint for a system based on decentralized peer-to-peer (P2P) transactions (Nakamoto, 2008).

In 2009, Bitcoin became operational, and Hal Finney, a key contributor, mined the first bitcoins and performed the first P2P blockchain transaction with Nakamoto (Chohan, 2017). Bitcoin's rise coincided with the 2008 financial crisis, positioning it as an alternative to traditional banking systems. Despite its promise of financial liberation, Bitcoin initially gained traction as a payment method in black markets due to its pseudonymous nature—a reputation it continues to contend with.

By 2020, the cryptocurrency market cap reached $335 billion, with the top 20 cryptocurrencies comprising 90% of the total value. However, it wasn't until 2014 that the financial industry began to recognize blockchain's potential beyond cryptocurrencies, seeing it as a tool to address systemic inefficiencies, corruption, and transparency issues. The technology has since evolved, incorporating advances in cryptography, networking, and economics to make it more applicable to the financial sector (Treleaven et al., 2017).

While the future of cryptocurrencies appears promising, several challenges hinder their widespread adoption, including cyber risks, transaction delays, scalability issues, and high volatility. The sections below discuss these challenges and the ongoing efforts to address them.

3.1.1 Cyber Risks

Blockchain's design makes it inherently resistant to tampering, as data is linked using hash pointers, ensuring that any modifications are detectable. However, the security of private keys and hashing algorithms can still be points of vulnerability. For instance, the IOTA project, which facilitates payments across interconnected devices using its cryptocurrency, faced criticism for using an internally developed hash function, Curl-P-27, that had significant security lapses (Heilman et al., 2019).

These lapses, including the absence of a robust seed generator for wallet keys, led to losses totaling $4 million in IOTA cryptocurrency.

Such incidents highlight the importance of using well-established, open-source cryptographic functions rather than proprietary, unverified algorithms. Organizations like MIT's Digital Currency Initiative (DCI) advocate for rigorous cryptoanalysis and security audits conducted by firms such as SmartDec, OpenZeppelin, and Chainsecurity. These measures are crucial for building trust and ensuring the safety of blockchain-based systems.

3.1.2 Transaction Delays and Scalability

Scalability remains a significant bottleneck for cryptocurrencies due to their reliance on consensus mechanisms in decentralized systems. For instance, Bitcoin's Proof of Work (PoW) protocol processes only seven transactions per second, while Ethereum's native network handles four transactions per second (Dalvit, 2020). This is far slower than traditional payment systems like Visa, which can process thousands of transactions per second.

Innovations in consensus algorithms aim to overcome these limitations. Techniques like Zero-Knowledge Proofs (ZKP) (Goldwasser et al., 1989) and ZK-STARKS (Ben-Sasson et al., 2019) have demonstrated potential for significantly faster transaction processing. StarkWare, a company comprising experts from ConsenSys, Coinbase, and Intel Capital, has developed a payment system on Ethereum called Stark that enables 9,000 trades and 18,000 payments per second. Such advancements could enhance the scalability and usability of cryptocurrencies, making them more viable for mainstream financial applications.

3.1.3 Volatility

One of the most significant barriers to cryptocurrency adoption is price volatility. The unpredictable nature of cryptocurrency prices has deterred many users and businesses from relying on them for everyday transactions. To address this issue, stablecoins have emerged as a solution.

Stablecoins are cryptocurrencies designed to minimize volatility by pegging their value to an underlying asset or basket of assets. These assets can include fiat currencies, other cryptocurrencies, or commodities. The pegging mechanism is implemented either on-chain through smart contracts or off-chain via financial institutions.

Tether, the largest stablecoin by market capitalization, reached a valuation of over $18 billion in 2020. However, it has faced scrutiny for its lack of transparency and insufficient documentation to verify its claimed 1:1 backing ratio. In contrast,

Maker's DAI stablecoin has gained credibility for its decentralized and transparent approach. The DAI operates on the Ethereum blockchain and is backed by collateral deposited into smart contracts. Users can generate DAI by depositing assets into these contracts, creating a self-regulated system managed by its users.

This innovative model not only ensures transparency but also mitigates volatility, making DAI a reliable stablecoin for various financial applications. As the market continues to mature, stablecoins are likely to play a pivotal role in bridging the gap between traditional finance and blockchain-based systems.

1.1. Corporate Finance & Governance

The public's interest in blockchain technology goes beyond just building alternative monetary systems. A study on industry trends by Cambridge Centre for Alternative Finance (CCAF) in 2019 demonstrated that 43% of enterprise blockchain networks in operation or under testing are in the Financial Services) Rauchs et al., 2019). This especially includes already existent service providers working with the technology, use cases go beyond the accounting but also encompass the wider networks of interaction, such as supply chain tracking, trading infrastructure, and document certifying (Rauchs et al. 2019, 10). The other 63%, which translates into three systems, are scattered throughout various sectors from government, media, manufacturing, energy and health.

As stated in a report from OECD (Akgiray, 2019) blockchain makes sense for financial applications including capital markets, where the entire ecosystem can be scaled; payment systems, whether cross-border or intra-national; over-the-counter trading that includes trading full cycles of bonds derivates (futures), commodities, and other illiquid assets; and trade finance where processes today take several weeks and can be significantly shortened by avoiding intermediary steps, additional tasks and paperwork (Akgiray, 2019, p. 15). The distance they go, and where they end up using different parts of blockchain technology or even building whole infrastructures is limited by the capacity and ambition of the distinct projects. Largely hinges as to what type of consensus the system will primarily be based on, and whether this system will be multi-party or act as a driver for transformation of processes As. The first case is where the control throughout the network is not centralised, and therefore agree-agreed upon over the data, while the second does not work with that direction, only utilising bits and pieces of DLT technologies in order solve or improve we suppose a business case. Yes, unless you are a truly distributed system (both data and authority), you're still an internal enterprise blockchain, for a practical reason, not an ideal one. According to Rauchs et al (2019, p.19), 67 enterprise blockchain systems were studied, and only 3% of these were multi-party consensus networks, 20% planned to be, while the remaining 77% were just using the system to restructure their internal workings. Internal systems certainly matter — the majority of new services and business models will be a product of such a project.

1.2. Financial Accounting

Both blockchain and DLT are ledger-based technologies, where distributed ledger constructs are being used to record transactions and as such, by design it is an accounting methodology. By its foundational decentralization and distributed nature, it completely transforms the making, preservation and updating of fiscal records. Through kind of universal entry bookkeeping, all entries are identically and permanently shared with everyone participating. These are propagation, which allows live updates to the entire system to be shared, permanence, which is defined by the consensus mechanism determining what change can and cannot be made (only adding something is allowed, deleting and changing is not), and programmability, or smart contract, which allows for program code to be stored with the transaction entries So, really, accounting has to do with measuring, sharing and analyzing financial information. It's to determine or define ownership and responsibility or so that the best way to allocate resources can be planned. The entire accounting profession can use blockchain and DLT to its advantage — this technology reduces the cost of keeping up and auditing ledgers as it grants total assurance that information is factual. A better coherence would allow accountants to focus their minds on strategic decision-making and value estimation rather than the recording process; blockchain would never eliminate the subjective decision making that is so crucial for our economy. Along with increasing the scope: bringing value coming from measuring previously unmeasured, unnoticed data, for example proof of ownership.

There is no novel attempt to add transparency to accounting information. In addition, the International Financial Reporting Standards (IFRS, 2020) have been advocating trust and transparency to the world's financial markets and the law firm has received increased attention against unlawful auditing. Since the 80s Tripple-entry bookkeeping has also been touted as a means for opening up to outside users (Ijiri, 1986) by allowing any third party to read a shared cryptographic receipt of the transaction between two parties. Since then, this term has become synonymous with blockchain (Tyra, 2014) and several projects have emerged.

The most influential players in the accounting field are the Big Four accounting firms: Deloitte, PwC, EY and KPMG, and all have been highly active on the R&D scene in the blockchain sector for the past two years, forming teams like Deloitte's Rubix, Fintech strategy-consulting platforms like PwC's Denovo, business systems like EY's Ops Chain and collaborations with tech suppliers like KMPG' partnership with Guardtime. There are also smaller initiatives, startups, and research spinning out enterprise blockchain solutions for the financial sector, such as the zkLedger

(Adeyanju, 2017), Pacio (Ajello, 2014), Request Network (Akgiray, 2019), Ledgerium (Ali, Clarke, & McCorry, 2015). To illustrate how a blockchain and DLT based financial accounting can work, we use the example of

Ledgerium. Ledgerium is Australian based company established in the year 2018, constructing a ledger Luca, a up cloud based knowledge recording payment transactions people on both sides using blockchain. Its product is in a partner testing phase which allows select companies to test its technology for testing their external auditing cheaply. In practice, when company A needs to pay company B for that service done and uses its accounting service, say Xero, a favourite of Australians. It then sends a Hash and the invoice details with the invoice to Luca, and this invoice is encrypted with the public key of company B, B corp will receive a request of it, and can verify the transaction and can accept the transaction by requesting Hash. This will then be stamped on the common ledger held by the two parties, and Luca will automatically ping the bank to settle the financial transaction, and add the payment once completed. Auditors may then use the hashes of transactions or each party's actions to prove their veracity.

1.3. Accounting and Regulatory Compliance

To me, the area that comes into immediate focus is reporting and the compliance there where there has always been hope related to the legal quality of the accounting with the immutable aspect of a blockchain hitting the right note. There are two part of confidence in capital markets, that is transparency and monitoring. The transparency comes in the form of standards and regulations companies must comply, while monitoring occurs through the regulatory agencies who enforce fairness. This is where blockchain comes in, whereby it could allow for greater visibility for both these processes, enabling companies to become more transparent and allowing for easier monitoring. In 2018 a US government guidance (ASC 606) issued specifically on how revenue is recognized when including use of contract, and earlier companies that had investigated smart contracts made it easier to comply in undertaking exploratory work on products and services (Lewtan et al., 2018).

With regulations such as the ASC 606, businesses that utilize new, and often more complex, business models will be able to more effectively track their revenue stream, through blockchain-enabled services. As such, video game publishers are no longer very much concerned about their point-of-sale/marketplace, but their end-users when creating long term relationships: their games may come with deluxe versions, all including purchasable content downloads, coins and in-game, and continuous bug-fixes, etc. Alternatively, users can purchase these items separately, at an increased cost per item. In a blockchain-setup, the end-user gets a unique serial number, and the reseller gets to attach one at the point of sales. Sales will be refered back to the customer while a token will be issued with value price assigned from the smartcontract and encrypted onto the ledger its the revenue of the company. The tokens will combine with downloaded updates, new content, or in-game currency, and while the endincome appears as 'total sum', each new element will be traceable.

Molina-Jimenez et al. Julyi, Shen, & Szachną, challenge the architecture of these blockchain systems (2018b) in their exploratory study with hybrid architecture for smart contract components since, online and off-line systems have disadvantages: pure permission-less and truly democratic blockchain platforms can be limited in scalability, speed, costly, etc., off-line systems will need corruptible third parties. Depending on the type of operation, we could afford trust, transparency, throughput, response time, and cost through a service; This service is a Smart Contract. There is no uniform scenario, and you will need to match each blockchain platform (for example Ethereum or Hyperledger) correct pair to the off-line processing. In a Cambridge Computer Lab experiment, they used the Rinkeby tenet of the Ethereum Blockchain for the on-blockchain portion, and for the off-line portion, used the Contract Compliance Checker tool, thus simulating a hybrid model (Molina-Jimenez et al., 2018a). These can read one another now and the outcome demonstrated that the architecture is implementable (given that the off-blockchain component utilizes standard APIs that can communicate with those utilized by blockchains).

1.4. Crowdfunding, Peer-to-Peer Lending & ICOs

In 2017 the digital version of an IPO started gaining in popularity, Initial Coin Offerings (ICOs), garnering over five billion USD in investments to blockchain based projects for that year alone, (Adeyanju, 2017).

ICO is decentralised fundraising: any project before issuing its token, these tokens can be bought at a specified price; individuals and companies then pay them, generally in the form of Bitcoin (BTC) or Ether (ETH). After the minimum sell of tokens has been reached to fund the project it can be started, built and opened for holders of the tokens to use them for services on the platform. Stand-alone tokens have a divide across platforms, in that some you can only use as a currency and are exchangeable by the public, others can be used to pay for different services, others represent assets in and of themselves, (Ajello, 2014).

Similar to any investment class, especially new ones, the vast majority of ICOs are in the same vein as the game-changers ("game changers"), but rather actual scams, including no intentions of completing the projects' objectives (Dowlat and Hodapp, 2018). Of course, ICOs also have their advantages, as well-regulated crowdfunding-platforms can be avoided, trusted support can be gained for smaller-scale initiatives, value can be created jointly and maybe very fast. Several ICOs were put on hold due to a huge amount of interest (Filecoin, Tezoz, and Brave) (Adeyanju, 2017). A decentralized web browser is a decentralized web browser that distinguishes its users from excessive data, as was started by the former CEO of Mozilla Firefox (Akgiray, 2019); it allows users to pay out their most frequently used websites to encourage an add-free internet; so far it has raised 35 million USD in 30 seconds, (Akgiray, 2019). The ban followed a freeze period across the market, as the heavy-handed regulation was expected, with recent offerings beginning to slowly wear away the restrictions.

Any financial risk-averse entity has all the right to wait for a proper legal frame, and it is only recently (ESMA, 2019) (The European Securities and Markets Authority) published its advice, concluding things like "Given the diversity of these crypto-assets, many of which also exhibit hybrid features, ESMA considers that there is no 'one size fits all' approach to legal qualification. (ESMA, 2019, p. 9). This implies that even after a launch, a significant amount of time must be spent on certification and approval, as tokens are evaluated on a caseby-case basis. Today the current price of entry for having a regulatory compliant ICO may become very expensive; an OECD (Ali, Clarke, & McCorry, 2015) analysis indicated that costs associated with performing third-party security audits, marketing the advantages, and manipulating other requirements range between 50.000–500.000 USD.

Nonetheless the projects that have emerged and continue to do so demonstrate that the technology can substantially underpin financial services as a sequel to improved: workflow and management, contractual relationships and security (Weber, 2019). Through their platform systems online, crowdfunding mechanisms have also evolved from ICOS, and channel investment within larger projects or a collective group of individuals. The project may be associated with a financial return (e.g. equity or interest) or non-financial remuneration or with emotional impact. Crowdfunding based platforms where DLT is being represented are donation based (BlockBonds), match-funding (GOTEO), equity crowdfunding ecosystems

(RealMarket), and more. New versions continue to arise like WHIRL, an up-start service launched in 2018 to match surpluses on a "pay it forward" basis. In which, here a new project can only be started after the founder(s) have supported other projects, and so leading to a virtuous cycle of generosity, and good reputation (Baber, 2019).

1.5. Derivative Market and the Smart Contracts

Tokens are considered the most promising application of crypto according to author Shermin Voshgmir in the book "Token Economics" (Locklin, 2019), and after ICO coins are security tokens so they do have a well-defined purpose: compliance. These are a securities which is based on or derived from an underlying asset or a collection of underlying assets, which are the stocks, bonds, interest rates, currencies, etc. And these instruments are interlaced with smart contracts to the asset and token, these financial instruments can represent the fractions of the total value of an asset and are tradeable. In fact, according to the European Securities and Markets Authority, security tokens are also capable of being classified as transfer such as securities under the MiFID directive, but the classification of each case is up to the individual member states (ESMA, 2019, p. 4). The report underlines the especially no disruption risk of traditional securities trading services, and the European Central Bank also has been looking into some possible use-cases (ESMA, 2019).

By simplifying the process of emission, while at the same time greatly shortening the clearing and settlement, such processes can also be simplified on the institutional level. And this is also likely where the biggest opportunity lies; in financial institutions adopting the smart contracts to generate liquidity in a decentralized manner, bypassing the need for fourth-party governance. It may thus reduce significantly the cost of both investors and issuers, and consequently not only affect the transaction process but also the nature of the trading and exchanges (EU Commission, 2019).

A primary venue for active testing of blockchain-based models are national stock exchanges where security exchanges and clearing houses have been doing research. ASX plan to Replace the Designed Platform CHESS on Blockchain Technology In 2017 Australia Stock Exchange (ASX) started planning to replace its widely recognized platform CHESS by blockchain technology by a startup named Digital Asset Holdings. The initiative is being developed on top of the open-source smart contract language DAML, and was expected to be deployed back in 2019 but is still ongoing and with more partners to collaborate with. Projects at national stock exchanges in Japan, Korea and India have been trail-blazing testing on the technology for trading low liquidity, shares of start-ups and know-your-customer data protocols respectively (OECD, 2018). Many banks and exchanges are conducting new experiments with different varieties of money experimenting with how tokenized assets can be available for trade and transaction and have been issued by a digital central bank such as (SIX and the Swiss National Bank). However, these are still happening on an exploratory level for now as the volatility and scalability issues of the blockchain and crypto are preventing mass-scale adoption. Also, formal regulation and legal remedies (based on securities law) are still lagging behind, leaving the situation in a state of the unknown. (CFPB), on the comparison between DLT and blockchain.

The innovations and technology surrounding the cryptocurrencies and blockchain-based applications such as smart contracts etc., have drawn a considerable amount of attention from researchers in the law discipline, especially with respect to the regulation and governance of these technologies and with respect to them. Table 1 presents in detail the relevant extant literature research on the legal aspects of Blockchain regulation, compliance and governance.

As reported in Table 1, the state-of-the-art research discourse on blockchain regulation consists of dual poles of dominant streams that are opposite yet complementary: frugal regulation vs. holistic regulation. The stream of research studies (Kleiman, 2013; Ajello, 2014; Lin, 2016) most concerned with money laundering and digital crime through cryptocurrencies and their implications for the economy and society of the countries, aims at setting up clear and strict rules, compliance protocols and guidance frameworks for the cryptocurrency industry. In contrast, extensive research considers blockchain to be a very disruptive and innovative technology and advocates much less restrictive regulation, avoiding the attempt to, in other words, curb or impede the growth of series of recommendations for examples as to amend the current legal provisions if needed to enable a functional regulation model. Furthermore, without hampering the innovation of cryptocurrencies, a correct regulatory model will enable them to self-regulate in a vaguely considered regulatory structure and while revealing the actors in case of needs (money laundering for example) help cryptocurrencies to overcome their bad reputation and quite possibly revolutionize organizations.

Apart from cryptocurrencies such as Bitcoin, previous research is also focused on the regulation and compliance with respect to the applicability of blockchain and DLTs for several use cases, such as digital-asset transfers (Kiviat, 2015), property rights (Arrun˜ada, 2018), cryptosecurities (Lee, 2016), derivatives markets (Surujnath, 2017), electronic contracts (Sklaroff, 2017), records management (Franks, 2020) etc. for financial, accounting and other administrative domains. Similar to its stance in its cryptocurrency work, however, the work from the law disciplines added that developing practical applications in these areas via the blockchain could add some support to the transparency of the application areas because hidden secrecy is eliminated and offers a route to more efficient document and authorship verification, title transfers, and contract enforcement. And just one example of the vast number of research about regulation and governance of blockchain (Young, 2018) proposed the smart constitution or decentralized blockchainbased governance implementation that will allow the government to act in accordance to smart constitution laws transparently and also prohibits to act outside of its mandate. Considering there is a rich amount of discourse around the existing body of literature on regulation and compliance, it could be beneficial to the provider of trusted third-party services to the end-consumers, as it becomes evident that the regulators of governmental agencies as a whole would need to balance their regulatory and compliance paradigms for cryptocurrencies with the responsibility of ensuring that it does not turn into an un-accountable overearring to law abiding citizens wishing to transact with cryptocurrencies and DLTs within the scope of legal limits.

Table 2. Research on regulatory initiatives of blockchain & DLTs

Article	Primary Theme	Main Arguments
Kleiman (2013)	Regulation	Cryptocurrencies can be potential security and economic threat and argues for establishing clear jurisdictional lines and regulations for the virtual currency industry.
Turpin (2014)	Regulation (favorable)	Argues for regulation, but is in favour of embracing the new technology. Recommends that governments should further study and regulate Bitcoin, but without attempting to stop or slow the growth of the currency itself and without attacking otherwise law-abiding citizens who transact in Bitcoins.
Ajello (2014)	Regulation, Money Laundering	Is concerned with Bitcoin's money laundering and its economic and social consequences. Advocates for more stringent regulations and argues that cryptocurrencies deserve greater attention from regulators and law enforcement officials.
McLeod (2014)	Regulation	Argues for regulation, but suggests to amend the existing legal provisions in an amicable way to create a workable regulatory model for cryptocurrencies.
Sonderegger (2015)	Regulation (favorable)	Suggests that given Bitcoin's ideological and technological underpinnings, it requires a degree of regulatory freedom to succeed. Argues that proper regulation will not stifle innovation but will allow it to self-regulate within a vaguely defined regulatory framework.
Kiviat (2015)	Digital Assets, Regulation (favorable)	Argues that the true value of technology lies in its potential to facilitate more efficient digital-asset transfers and advocates that policymakers must carefully define the specific activities that they seek to regulate.
Tsukerman (2015)	Regulation (favorable)	Claims that unmasking actors on the blockchain will help Bitcoin shed its infamous reputation and that Bitcoins must be brought into the light and seen as a useful currency, and not simply as the refuge of dark web inhabitants.
Colombo (2016)	Regulation (favorable)	Argues that responsibility of regulators and lawmakers is to establish rules that safeguard consumers and markets without hindering growth and innovation. Opines that it will be difficult to get right when dealing with something as new and alien (to fiat currency regulatory apparatus) as virtual currency.
Lin (2016)	Cybersecurity, Compliance	Focuses on the challenges of financial cybersecurity, technology integration, compliance, and the role of humans in the future of modern finance.

Table 3. Research on regulatory initiatives of blockchain & DLTs (cont.)

Article	Primary Theme	Main Arguments & Recommendations
Lee (2016)	Cyber Securities and Stock Markets	Argues that blockchain will create crypto securities that will allow the public to verify transactions if they want, which will remove some of the hidden secrecy surrounding much of the high frequency and dark pool trading occurring today.
Gabison (2016)	Regulation, Accountability	Argues for the need for policymakers to reinvestigate several laws and rights for blockchain. Fears that lack of accountability to a policing authority, users can be exposed to attacks and allows potential transfers that finance criminal activities.
Christopher (2016)	Enforcement and Trust	Argues that Bitcoin requires more trust than is generally understood and both currency and payment systems benefit from the involvement of trusted intermediaries in response to problems and crises.
Rosner and Kang (2016)	Flexible Regu- lation	Argues for a flexible and principles-based approach to amend current regulatory frameworks to account for modern technological realities. Claims that the cryptocurrency Ripple's advantages suggest that users will increasingly use these systems in place of traditional payment processes.
Shackelford and Myers (2017)	Cyber Security, Regulation	Examines blockchains through the lens of polycentric governance to ascertain what could be done to build trust in distributed systems and ultimately promote cyber peace. Assessment is that it will take many years to build sustainable blockchain system by involving by numerous stakeholders and policymakers.
Guo (2017)	Patents for blockchain technology	Discusses whether trade secret or copyright protection should apply to protect the claims and uses of blockchain technology and states that only time will tell if blockchain technology can be claimed as intellectual property or be used in court.
Reyes (2017)	Crypto-legal structures	Advocates for usage of blockchain technologies for legal systems (crypto law) and argues that crypto law could offer a legal discourse to serve more rapidly, more efficiently, more transparently, and in creative ways, that may encourage increased civic engagement.
Ross (2017)	Regulation, National char- ter	Claims that regulatory emphasis on the threat posed by cryptocurrencies has created a hostile environment to innovation. Advises establishing a national charter for FinTechs to absorb the full potential of blockchain technology.
Surujnath (2017)	Derivatives Markets	Advocates that blockchains with self-executing smart-contracts provide compelling opportunities in derivatives markets and that they can reduce dependency on central counterparties that are exposed to large amounts of credit risk.

Table 4. Research on regulatory initiatives of blockchain & DLTs (cont.)

Article	Primary Theme	Main Arguments & Recommendations
Sklaroff (2017)	Smart vs Semantic contracts	Argues that semantic contracts offer two forms of flexibility: linguistic ambiguity and enforcement discretion, which are important in the contracting process and therefore smart contracting will impose more costs.
Arrun˜ada (2018)	Smart contracts for Property rights	Argues that intermediaries' role is crucial in the processes of firms' strategies and contracting and therefore it can not be replaced by blockchain but argues for private blockchains for archiving purposes within standard registration systems.
Morgan (2018)	Open-minded Regulation	Argues for the regulation of cryptocurrencies with a more open-minded approach to promote truly informed policy decisions as opposed to irrational and poor investment decisions.
Young (2018)	Smart Constitution, Smart Social Contract	Advocates for a smart constitution, to make the government operates transparently and unable to operate outside of its mandate and also argues that "When something is codified, and connected to the blockchain, *code is law*. When the code is the law, any entity tied to it is powerless to act outside of the code. This will ensure that governments stay within their expressed powers." Young (2018).
SUCIU et al. (2019)	Regulation for crypto-based business	Explored the initiatives for the regulation of crypto-based businesses such as ICOs in the UK, Estonia and Switzerland and found out that these are the friendly companies when it comes to doing digital businesses.
(Franks, 2020)	Records management	Presents several opportunities and challenges in terms of using DLT for records management and information governance.
(Priem, 2020)	Policy debate on regulation of DLTs	Explored which regulatory barriers need to be removed for full adoption of DLTs and also the challenges & risks related to DLT systems are also identified, in addition to a good summarization of the regulatory initiatives in EU for the DLTs.

CONCLUSION

In this chapter, we examined the basic principles and concepts of DLT and blockchain technologies, focusing on some essential components, including hash functions, digital signatures, and digital timestamping. These elements are the building blocks for DLT and blockchain frameworks, providing the technical architecture upon which those technologies are built. We have also covered consensus protocols and fault tolerance, which are crucial concepts for any blockchain as they provide a way to reach agreement in a decentralized and distributed environment. In addition to this, a detailed lecture was offered on how DLT and blockchain technologies are revolutionising FinTech solutions as well. Finally, we presented a summary of the current research programs and ongoing work within the regulatory and legal environment of blockchain and DLT.

Regulation

In the past few years, the lead for systematic measures towards blockchain utilisation increases especially in light of cryptocurrencies. Cryptocurrencies are often associated with illegal activities because of their high level of anonymity (Sun Yin et al., 2019). The most extreme example of this can be the downfall of Silk Road, an illegal online marketplace (Christin, 2013). More than this example, several reports and articles document, Bitcoin being used to facilitate terrorist financing, thefts, frauds, and ransomware attacks (Hout and Bingham, 2013; Martin, 2014a). These problems have attracted attention from financial regulators, law enforcement agencies, intelligence activities and companies inside the Bitcoin blockchain ecosystem. Types of cryptocurrency include Bitcoin (Ali et al., 2015; Böhme et al., 2015)Stakeholders are tracking the technical progress, economic consequences, and societal integration of such cryptocurrency.

These challenges have led to a demand for the implementation of regulation to help combat the illicit use of cryptocurrencies and other blockchain-based applications. While there is no widely agreed upon regulation concerning cryptocurrencies and blockchain, there have been several initiatives considered in relation to possible forms of regulation. For example, regulators like the UK Financial Conduct Authority (2017) and the Financial Stability Board (2018) are already investigating whether new regulations are needed or whether current regimes could be modified to better suit the distinctive features of blockchain technology. Such efforts look to reduce the risks of blockchain while capturing its best potential.

However, most regulators are yet to proceed with caution, following a "wait-and-watch" policy. This cautious approach is due to blockchain technology being new and evolving constantly. The interests of regulators and legal authorities are thus directed to identifying and solving the problems and obstacles hindering the implementation of blockchain technology effectiveness today. Thorough investigations into these issues are necessary before creating comprehensive regulatory frameworks. A rushed regulatory approach risks stifling innovation, but a thoughtful, adaptive framework can enable responsible development and use of blockchain technologies.

Market Adoption

Although technological development is important, it is just one element that will ensure successful market deployment of DLT-based FinTech goods and services. The adoption process will depend on multiple factors, such as transaction efficiency and energy consumption, as well as regulatory challenges posed by both cybersecurity threats and criminal exploitation. Indeed, some of these challenges can be tackled through advancements in DLT, but DLT alone cannot suffice.

The market landscape is further shaped by entrenched interests and established players in the financial sector. Because they deal frequently with such markets and participants, these stakeholders are well placed to take advantage of these market characteristics, which typically offer relatively standardized terms and established inter-institutional operations. Consequently, they can be more resistant to the integration of revolutionary technologies such as blockchain or DLT that threaten to displace established financial flows.

Notwithstanding such obstacles, the interaction between technology and financial service innovations will continue to be important for the development of FinTech. DLT has a chance to establish itself as an alternative to more traditional systems by resolving problems like lack of scalability, energy inefficiency, and cybersecurity risks. In addition, they should still look for innovative solutions in the financial services ranging from blockchain—these have the potential to win over traditional players due to their clear advantages in reducing costs, increasing efficiency, and improving security.

Similarly, the adoption of DLT and blockchain technologies also relies on the engagement of multiple stakeholders such as technology developers, financial institutions, regulatory authorities, and end-users. By working together, this can enhance trust, promote innovation and ultimately facilitate smooth integration of DLT-powered solutions into the traditional financial practices.

Final Thoughts

To conclude, the synergy between technology-driven progress and service evolution will persist as a defining force in the FinTech space. Many advances have been made in developing DLT and blockchain technology but there is still some way to go. Navigating these challenges will require continued engagement between stakeholders, evidence-based policy responses, and a focus on enabling innovation. With advancements being made in the area continually, the impact that DLT can have on the finance sector, and even broader, is potentially limitless.

REFERENCES

Adeyanju, C. (2017). How a loyalty program on blockchain works, explained. https://cointelegraph.com/explained/how-a-loyalty-program-on-blockchain-works -explained.

Akgiray, V. (2019). The potential for blockchain technology in corporate governance.

Ali, S. T. (2015, March). Bitcoin: perils of an unregulated global P2P currency (Transcript of Discussion). In Cambridge international workshop on security protocols (pp. 294-306). Cham: Springer International Publishing.

Andreas, M. (2014). *Antonopoulos. Mastering Bitcoin: unlocking digital cryptocurrencies*. O'Reilly Media, Inc.

Arrun˜ada, B. (2018). Blockchain's struggle to deliver impersonal exchange. *Minnesota Journal of Law, Science & Technology*, *19*(1), 55.

Baber, H. (2019). Blockchain-based crowdfunding: A 'pay-it-forward' model of whirl. [IJRTE]. *International Journal of Recent Technology and Engineering*, *8*(3), 2277–3878.

Back, A. (2002). Hashcash-a denial of service counter-measure.

Bank, E. C. (2015). *Virtual currency schemes-a further analysis. Technical report, Tech. rep*. European Central Bank.

Bayer, D. (1993). Stuart Haber, and W Scott Stornetta. Improving the efficiency and reliability of digital time-stamping. In *Sequences Ii* (pp. 329–334). Springer. DOI: 10.1007/978-1-4613-9323-8_24

Ben-Sasson, E., Bentov, I., Horesh, Y., & Riabzev, M. (2019). Scalable zero knowledge with no trusted setup. In Advances in Cryptology–CRYPTO 2019: 39th Annual International Cryptology Conference, Santa Barbara, CA, USA, August 18–22, 2019 [Springer International Publishing.]. *Proceedings*, *39*(Part III), 701–732.

B¨ohme, R., Christin, N., Edelman, B., & Moore, T. (2015). Bitcoin: Economics, technology, and governance. *The Journal of Economic Perspectives*, *29*(2), 213–238. DOI: 10.1257/jep.29.2.213

Carla, L. (2017). Reyes. Conceptualizing cryptolaw. *Nebraska Law Review*, *96*(2), 384.

Carter, J. L., & Wegman, M. N. (1977, May). Universal classes of hash functions. In *Proceedings of the ninth annual ACM symposium on Theory of computing* (pp. 106-112).

Castro, M., Liskov, B., ... Practical byzantine fault tolerance. In *OSDI*, volume 99, pages 173–186, 1999.

Chohan, U. W. (2022). A history of bitcoin. Available at *SSRN* 3047875.

Christin, N. (2013, May). Traveling the Silk Road: A measurement analysis of a large anonymous online marketplace. In *Proceedings of the 22nd international conference on World Wide Web* (pp. 213-224).

Christina Marta, S. U. C. I. U., Christian, N. A. S. U. L. E. A., & Diana Florentina, N. A. S. U. L. E. A. (2019). *Towards developing a friendlier regulatory framework for blockchain-based businesses*. Economic Convergence in European Union.

Christopher, C. M. (2016). The bridging model: Exploring the roles of trust and enforcement in banking, bitcoin, and the blockchain. *Nev. LJ*, *17*, 139.

Commission, E. U. (2019). *Potential use cases for innovative technologies in securities posttrading. Technical report*. European Central Bank.

Dalvit, L. (2020). Ethereum: a new record of transactions per second thanks to istanbul. https://en.cryptonomist.ch/2020/01/07/ethereum-transactions-per -second-istanbul/,.

Damgård, I. B. (1989, August). A design principle for hash functions. In Conference on the Theory and Application of Cryptology (pp. 416-427). New York, NY: Springer New York.

Don Johnson, A. M., & Vanstone, S. (2001). The elliptic curve digital signature algorithm (ecdsa). *International Journal of Information Security*, *1*(1), 36–63. DOI: 10.1007/s102070100002

European Central Bank. (2012). *Virtual currency schemes. EC Bank, Virtual Currency Schemes (h*. European Central Bank.

Faber, B., Michelet, G., Weidmann, N., Mukkamala, R. R., & Vatrapu, R. (2019). BPDIMS: A blockchain-based personal data and identity management system. In The 52nd Hawaii International Conference on System Sciences. HISS 2019: HISS 2019 (pp. 6855-6864). Hawaii International Conference on System Sciences (HICSS).

Financial Conduct Authority. (2017). *Discussion paper on distributed ledger technology. Technical report*. Financial Conduct Authority.

Financial Stability Board. (2018). *Crypto-assets: report to the g20 on the work of the fsb and standardsetting bodies. Technical report*. Financial Stability Board.

Gabison, G. (2016). Policy considerations for the blockchain technology public and private applications. *Science and Technology Law Review*, *19*, 327.

Gennaio, E. S. M. A. (2019). *Advice, initial coin offerings and crypto-assets. Technical report*. European Securities and Markets Authority.

Goldwasser, S., Micali, S., & Rackoff, C. (1989). The knowledge complexity of interactive proof systems. *SIAM Journal on Computing*, *18*(1), 186–208. DOI: 10.1137/0218012

Guo, A. (2017). Blockchain receipts: Patentability and admissibility in court. *ChicagoKent Journal of Intellectual Property*, *16*(2), 440.

Gustavus, J. (1994). *Simmons. Contemporary cryptology: The science of information integrity*. IEEE press.

Haber, S., & Stornetta, W. S. (1991). *How to time-stamp a digital document*. Springer Berlin Heidelberg.

Heilman, E., Narula, N., Tanzer, G., Lovejoy, J., Colavita, M., Virza, M., & Dryja, T. (2019). Cryptanalysis of curl-p and other attacks on the iota cryptocurrency. Cryptology ePrint Archive.

IFRS. (2020). List of ifrs standards list of ifrs standards. https://www.ifrs.org/issued-standards/list-of-standards/.

Ijiri, Y. (1986). A framework for triple-entry bookkeeping. *The Accounting Review*, •••, 745–759.

Jared, A. (2013). Kleiman. Beyond the silk road: Unregulated decentralized virtual currencies continue to endanger us national security and welfare. *American University National Security Law Brief*, *4*(1), 59.

Jeremy, M. (2017). Sklaroff. Smart contracts and the cost of inflexibility. *University of Pennsylvania Law Review*, *166*, 263.

Jonathan, B. (2014). Turpin. Bitcoin: The economic case for a global, virtual currency operating in an unexplored legal framework. *Indiana Journal of Global Legal Studies*, *21*(1), 335–368. DOI: 10.2979/indjglolegstu.21.1.335

Lamport, L. (2001). Paxos made simple. ACM SIGACT News (Distributed Computing Column) 32, 4 (Whole Number 121, December 2001), 51-58.

Lamport, L. (2019). The part-time parliament. In *Concurrency: the Works of Leslie Lamport* (pp. 277–317). ACM Books. DOI: 10.1145/3335772.3335939

Lamport, L., Shostak, R., & Pease, M. (1982). The byzantine generals problem. [TOPLAS]. *ACM Transactions on Programming Languages and Systems*, *4*(3), 382–401. DOI: 10.1145/357172.357176

Lee, L. (2016). New kids on the blockchain: How bitcoin's technology could reinvent the stock market. *Hastings Business Law Journal, 12*(2), 81.

Lewtan, J., McManus, J., & Roohani, S. Blockchain: Opportunity to improve financial reporting and corporate governance. In *Hawai'i Accounting Research Conference (HARC)*, 2018.

Locklin, S. (2019). *Token economics. Technical report.* Brave Software.

Martin, J. (2014). Lost on the Silk Road: Online drug distribution and the 'cryptomarket'. *Criminology & Criminal Justice, 14*(3), 351–367.

Martin, J. (2014a). *Drugs on the dark net: How cryptomarkets are transforming the global trade in illicit drugs*. Springer. DOI: 10.1057/9781137399052

McLeod, P. (2013). Taxing and regulating bitcoin: The government's game of catch up. *CommLaw Conspectus, 22*, 379.

Merkle, R. C. (1989, August). One way hash functions and DES. In Conference on the Theory and Application of Cryptology (pp. 428-446). New York, NY: Springer New York.

Merkle, R. C. (2019). Protocols for public key cryptosystems. In *Secure communications and asymmetric cryptosystems* (pp. 73–104). Routledge.

Molina-Jimenez, C., Sfyrakis, I., Solaiman, E., Ng, I., Wong, M. W., Chun, A., & Crowcroft, J. (2018, November). Implementation of smart contracts using hybrid architectures with on and off–blockchain components. In 2018 IEEE 8th International Symposium on Cloud and Service Computing (SC2) (pp. 83-90). IEEE.

Molina-Jimenez, C., Solaiman, E., Sfyrakis, I., Ng, I., & Crowcroft, J. (2019). On and off-blockchain enforcement of smart contracts. In Euro-Par 2018: Parallel Processing Workshops: Euro-Par 2018 International Workshops, Turin, Italy, August 27-28, 2018, Revised Selected Papers 24 (pp. 342-354). Springer International Publishing.

Morgan, J. S. (2017). What I learned trading cryptocurrencies while studying the law. *U. Miami Int'l & Comp. L. Rev., 25*, 159.

Morris, J. (2015). *Dworkin. Sha-3 standard: Permutation-based hash and extendable-output functions. Technical report, National Institute of Standards and Technology.* NIST.

Nakamoto, S. (2008). Bitcoin: A peer-to-peer electronic cash system.

Narayanan, A., & Clark, J. (2017). Bitcoin's academic pedigree. *Communications of the ACM, 60*(12), 36–45.

Narayanan, A., & Clark, J. (2017). Bitcoin's academic pedigree. *Communications of the ACM*, *60*(12), 36–45.

Natarajan, H., Krause, S., & Gradstein, H. (2017). Distributed ledger technology and blockchain.

Nicholas, J. (2014). Ajello. Fitting a square peg in a round hole: Bitcoin, money laundering, and the fifth amendment privilege against self-incrimination. *Brooklyn Law Review*, *80*(2), 435.

OECD. (2018). *The potential for blockchain technology in public equity markets in asia. Technical report.* OECD CAPITAL MARKETSERIES.

Patricia, C. (2020). Franks. Implications of blockchain distributed ledger technology for records management and information governance programs. *Records Management Journal*.

Penard, W., & Van Werkhoven, T. (2008). On the secure hash algorithm family. Cryptography in context, 1-18.

Priem, R. (2020). Distributed ledger technology for securities clearing and settlement: Benefits, risks, and regulatory implications. *Financial Innovation*, *6*(1), 1–25. DOI: 10.1186/s40854-019-0169-6

Prikhodko, P., Izumchenko, E., Aliper, A., Romantsov, K., & Zhebrak, A.. (2018). Converging blockchain and next-generation artificial intelligence technologies to decentralize and accelerate biomedical research and healthcare. *Oncotarget*, *9*(5), 5665–5690. DOI: 10.18632/oncotarget.22345 PMID: 29464026

Rauchs, M. (2019). *Apolline Blandin, Keith Bear, and Stephen B McKeon. 2nd global enterprise blockchain benchmarking study. Technical report, Cambridge Centre for Alternative Finance*. CCAF.

Rauchs, M., Glidden, A., Gordon, B., Pieters, G. C., Recanatini, M., Rostand, F., & Zhang, B. Z. (2018). Distributed ledger technology systems: A conceptual framework. Available at *SSRN* 3230013.

Ronald, J. (2016). Colombo. Bitcoin: Hype or harbinger. *Journal of International Business and Law*, *16*(1), 1.

Ronald, L. (1978). Rivest, Adi Shamir, and Len Adleman. A method for obtaining digital signatures and public-key cryptosystems. *Communications of the ACM*, *21*(2), 120–126. DOI: 10.1145/359340.359342

Rosner, M. T., & Kang, A. (2015). Understanding and regulating twenty-first century payment systems: The ripple case study. *Michigan Law Review*, *114*, 649.

Ross, E. S. (2016). Nobody puts blockchain in a corner: The disruptive role of blockchain technology in the financial services industry and current regulatory issues. *Cath. UJL & Tech*, *25*, 353.

Shackelford, S. J., & Myers, S. (2017). Block-by-block: Leveraging the power of blockchain technology to build trust and promote cyber peace. *Yale JL & Tech.*, *19*, 334.

Sonderegger, D. (2015). A regulatory and economic perplexity: Bitcoin needs just a bit of regulation. *Wash. UJL & Pol'y*, *47*, 175.

Sun Yin, H. H., Langenheldt, K., Harlev, M., Mukkamala, R. R., & Vatrapu, R. (2019). Regulating cryptocurrencies: A supervised machine learning approach to de-anonymizing the bitcoin blockchain. *Journal of Management Information Systems*, *36*(1), 37–73. DOI: 10.1080/07421222.2018.1550550

Surujnath, R. (2017). Off the chain: A guide to blockchain derivatives markets and the implications on systemic risk. *Fordham Journal of Corporate & Financial Law*, *22*(2), 257.

Swan, M. (2015). *Blockchain: Blueprint for a new economy*. O'Reilly Media, Inc.

Szabo, N. (1997). Formalizing and securing relationships on public networks. *First Monday*.

Szostek, D. (2019). *Blockchain and the Law*. Nomos Verlag. DOI: 10.5771/9783845298290

Tom, C. W. (2016). Lin. Compliance, technology, and modern finance. *Brooklyn Journal of Corporate. Financial & Commercial Law*, *11*(1), 159.

Treleaven, P., Brown, R. G., & Yang, D. (2017). Blockchain technology in finance. *Computer*, *50*(9), 14–17. DOI: 10.1109/MC.2017.3571047

Trevor, I. (2015). Kiviat. Beyond bitcoin: Issues in regulating blockchain tranactions. *Duke Law Journal*, *65*, 569.

Tsukerman, M. (2015). The block is hot: A survey of the state of bitcoin regulation and suggestions for the future. *Berkeley Technology Law Journal*, *30*(4), 1127.

Tyra, J. M. (2014). Triple entry bookkeeping with bitcoin. Bitcoin magazine, 2014.

Van Hout, M. C., & Bingham, T. (2013). 'Silk Road', the virtual drug marketplace: A single case study of user experiences. *The International Journal on Drug Policy*, *24*(5), 385–391.

Wang, W., Hoang, D. T., Hu, P., Xiong, Z., Niyato, D., Wang, P., Wen, Y., & Kim, D. I. (2019). A survey on consensus mechanisms and mining strategy management in blockchain networks. *IEEE Access : Practical Innovations, Open Solutions, 7*, 22328–22370. DOI: 10.1109/ACCESS.2019.2896108

Weber, C. (2019). *Exploring dlt and blockchain for alternative finance: A collection of case studies. Tech. rep., Technical report.* European Crowdfunding Network.

Xu, L., & Bruck, J. (2007, September). Highly available distributed storage systems. In Workshop on wide area networks and high performance computing (pp. 307-330). London: Springer London.

Young, S. (2018). Enforcing constitutional rights through computer code. *Catholic University Journal of Law and Technology*, *26*(1), 1.

Compilation of References

Aazam, M., Zeadally, S., & Harras, K. A. (2018, May). Fog computing architecture, evaluation, and future research directions. *IEEE Communications Magazine*, *56*(5), 46–52. DOI: 10.1109/MCOM.2018.1700707

Abbas, G., Abbas, Z. H., Haider, S., Baker, T., Boudjit, S., & Muhammad, F. (2019). PDMAC: A priority-based enhanced TDMA protocol for warning message dissemination in VANETs. *Sensors (Basel)*, *20*(1), 45. DOI: 10.3390/s20010045 PMID: 31861746

Abdalla, R. S., Mahbub, S. A., Mokhtar, R. A., Ali, E. S., & Saeed, R. A. (2021). IoE Design Principles and Architecture. *Internet of Energy for Smart Cities*, 145–170. https://doi.org/DOI: 10.1201/9781003047315-6

Abdelhamid, N. (2015). Multi-label rules for phishing classification. *Applied Computing and Informatics*, *11*(1), 29–46. DOI: 10.1016/j.aci.2014.07.002

Abdelhamid, N., Ayesh, A., & Thabtah, F. (2014). Phishing detection based Associative Classification data mining. *Expert Systems with Applications*, *41*(13), 5948–5959. DOI: 10.1016/j.eswa.2014.03.019

Abdelhamid, N., & Thabtah, F. (2014). Associative Classification Approaches: Review and Comparison. *Journal of Information and Knowledge Management*, *13*(3), 1–30. DOI: 10.1142/S0219649214500270

Abid, A., Cheikhrouhou, S., Kallel, S., & Jmaiel, M. (2025). A privacy-preserving traceability system for self-sovereign identity-based inter-organizational business processes. *Computer Standards & Interfaces*, *92*, 103930. DOI: 10.1016/j.csi.2024.103930

Aburrous, M., Hossain, M. A., Dahal, K., & Thabtah, F. (2010). Associative classification techniques for predicting e-banking phishing websites. *MCIT'2010: International Conference on Multimedia Computing and Information Technology*, 9–12. DOI: 10.1109/MCIT.2010.5444840

Adebowale, M. A., Lwin, K. T., Sánchez, E., & Hossain, M. A. (2019). Intelligent web-phishing detection and protection scheme using integrated features of Images, frames and text. *Expert Systems with Applications*, *115*, 300–313. DOI: 10.1016/j.eswa.2018.07.067

Adeniyi, A. E., Jimoh, R. G., Awotunde, J. B., Aworinde, H. O., Falola, P. B., & Ninan, D. O. (2024). Blockchain for secured cybersecurity in emerging healthcare systems. *Cybersecurity in Emerging Healthcare Systems*, 335–361. DOI: 10.1049/PBHE064E_ch11

Adewole, K. S., Akintola, A. G., Salihu, S. A., Faruk, N., & Jimoh, R. G. (2019). Hybrid Rule-Based Model for Phishing URLs Detection. In *Lecture Notes of the Institute for Computer Sciences, Social-Informatics and Telecommunications Engineering, LNICST* (Vol. 285). Springer International Publishing. DOI: 10.1007/978-3-030-23943-5_9

Adeyanju, C. (2017). How a loyalty program on blockchain works, explained. https://cointelegraph.com/explained/how-a-loyalty-program-on-blockchain-works-explained.

Afrin, N., & Pathak, A. (2023). Blockchain-Powered Security and Transparency in Supply Chain: Exploring Traceability and Authenticity through Smart Contracts. *International Journal of Computer Applications*, *185*(49), 975–8887. DOI: 10.5120/ijca2023923318

Afroz, S., & Greenstadt, R. (2011). PhishZoo: Detecting phishing websites by looking at them. *Proceedings - 5th IEEE International Conference on Semantic Computing, ICSC 2011*, 368–375. DOI: 10.1109/ICSC.2011.52

Ahmed, S. F., Alam, M. S., Afrin, S., Rafa, S. J., Taher, S. B., Kabir, M., Muyeen, S. M., & Gandomi, A. H. (2024). Toward a Secure 5G-Enabled Internet of Things: A Survey on Requirements, Privacy, Security, Challenges, and Opportunities. *IEEE Access : Practical Innovations, Open Solutions*, *12*, 13125–13145. DOI: 10.1109/ACCESS.2024.3352508

Ahmed, W., Iqbal, W., Hassan, A., Ahmad, A., Ullah, F., & Srivastava, G. (2025). Elevating e-health excellence with IOTA distributed ledger technology: Sustaining data integrity in next-gen fog-driven systems. *Future Generation Computer Systems*, •••, 107755.

Ajadi, T., Cuming, V., Boyle, R., Strahan, D., Kimmel, M., Logan, M., & McCrone, A. (2020). Global Trends in Renewable Energy Investment. https://www.fs-unep-centre.org/wp-content/uploads/2020/06/GTR_2020.pdf (accessed on 23 December 2021).

Ajayi, O., Abouali, M., & Saadawi, T. (2020, September). Secure architecture for inter-healthcare electronic health records exchange. In *2020 IEEE International IOT,Electronics and Mechatronics Conference (IEMTRONICS)* (pp. 1-6). IEEE. DOI: 10.1109/IEMTRONICS51293.2020.9216336

Akan, O. B., Dinc, E., Kuscu, M., Cetinkaya, O., & Bilgin, B. A. (2023). Internet of Everything (IoE) - From Molecules to the Universe. *IEEE Communications Magazine*, *61*(10), 122–128. DOI: 10.1109/MCOM.001.2200594

Akgiray, V. (2019). The potential for blockchain technology in corporate governance.

Akkaoui, R., Stefanov, A., Palensky, P., & Epema, D. H. J. (2022). A Taxonomy and Lessons Learned From Blockchain Adoption Within the Internet of Energy Paradigm. *IEEE Access : Practical Innovations, Open Solutions*, *10*, 106708–106739. DOI: 10.1109/ACCESS.2022.3212148

Al Sadawi, A., Hassan, M. S., & Ndiaye, M. (2021). A Survey on the Integration of Blockchain with IoT to Enhance Performance and Eliminate Challenges. *IEEE Access : Practical Innovations, Open Solutions*, *9*, 54478–54497. DOI: 10.1109/ACCESS.2021.3070555

Al-Daeef, M. M., Basir, N., & Saudi, M. M. (2017). Hybrid model of phishing email detection: A combination of technical and non-technical anti-phishing approaches. *Lecture Notes in Engineering and Computer Science*, *1*, 165–168.

Alghamedy, F. H., El-Haggar, N., Alsumayt, A., Alfawaer, Z., Alshammari, M., Amouri, L., Aljameel, S. S., & Albassam, S. (2024). Unlocking a Promising Future: Integrating Blockchain Technology and FL-IoT in the Journey to 6G. *IEEE Access : Practical Innovations, Open Solutions*, *12*, 115411–115447. DOI: 10.1109/ACCESS.2024.3435968

Alharthi, M. K., Moria, K. M., Alghazzawi, D. M., & Tayeb, H. O. (2022). Epileptic disorder detection of seizures using EEG signals. *Sensors (Basel)*, *22*(17), 6592. DOI: 10.3390/s22176592 PMID: 36081048

Ali, S. T. (2015, March). Bitcoin: perils of an unregulated global P2P currency (Transcript of Discussion). In Cambridge international workshop on security protocols (pp. 294-306). Cham: Springer International Publishing.

Alladi, T., Chamola, V., Rodrigues, J. J., & Kozlov, S. A. (2019). Blockchain in smart grids: A review on different use cases. *Sensors (Basel)*, *19*(22), 4862. DOI: 10.3390/s19224862 PMID: 31717262

Allioui, H. ;, Mourdi, Y., Allioui, H., & Mourdi, Y. (2023). Exploring the Full Potentials of IoT for Better Financial Growth and Stability: A Comprehensive Survey. *Sensors 2023, Vol. 23, Page 8015, 23*(19), 8015. https://doi.org/DOI: 10.3390/s23198015

Almabrok, H. A. (2023). Blockchain for Supply Chain Management: To Enhance Transparency, Traceability, and Efficiency. [AJAPAS]. *African Journal of Advanced Pure and Applied Sciences*, *2*(4), 239–253.

Al-Rakhami, M. S., & Al-Mashari, M. (2021). A blockchain-based trust model for the Internet of Things supply chain management. *Sensors (Basel)*, *21*(5), 1759. Advance online publication. DOI: 10.3390/s21051759 PMID: 33806319

Alrashdi, I., & Alqazzaz, A. (2024). Synergizing AI, IoT, and Blockchain for Diagnosing Pandemic Diseases in Smart Cities: Challenges and Opportunities. *Sustainable Machine Intelligence Journal*, *7*(6), 1–28. DOI: 10.61356/SMIJ.2024.77106

Al-Shahwani, H. I. W., Mijwil, M. M., Doshi, R., Hiran, K. K., & Bala, I. (2024). Evaluating Antivirus Effectiveness Against Malware in Ascending Order for Increasing Blockchain Endpoint Protection. 150–166. doi:: DOI: 10.4018/979-8-3693-1131-8.ch008

Andoni, M., Robu, V., Flynn, D., Abram, S., Geach, D., Jenkins, D., McCallum, P., & Peacock, A. (2019). Blockchain technology in the energy sector: A systematic review of challenges and opportunities. *Renewable & Sustainable Energy Reviews*, *100*, 143–174. DOI: 10.1016/j.rser.2018.10.014

Andreas, M. (2014). *Antonopoulos. Mastering Bitcoin: unlocking digital cryptocurrencies*. O'Reilly Media, Inc.

Anita, N., Vijayalakshmi, M., & Shalinie, S. M. (2022). Blockchain-based anonymous anti-counterfeit supply chain framework. *Sadhana*, *47*(4), 208. DOI: 10.1007/s12046-022-01984-2

Antonios, P., Konstantinos, K., & Christos, G. (2023a). A Systematic Review on Semantic Interoperability in the IoE-Enabled Smart Cities. *Internet of Things : Engineering Cyber Physical Human Systems*, *22*(July), 100754. DOI: 10.1016/j.iot.2023.100754

Aoun, A., Ibrahim, H., Ghandour, M., & Ilinca, A. (2021). Blockchain-Enabled Energy Demand Side Management Cap and Trade Model. *Energies*, *14*(24), 8600. DOI: 10.3390/en14248600

Arefkhani, R., Husain, A. J., Tech, M., & Student, C. (n.d.). *Optimized Resource Allocation in Blockchain Fog-based IOE*. Retrieved February 7, 2025, from www.ijert.org

Arif, M., Aslam, N., Khan, Z. A., & Aurangzeb, K. (2020). Fog Computing for Secure and Efficient Data Processing in IoT Networks. *IEEE Transactions on Industrial Informatics*, *16*(5), 3120–3130.

Arora, D., Gupta, S., & Anpalagan, A. (2022). Evolution and adoption of next generation IoT-driven health care 4.0 systems. *Wireless Personal Communications*, *127*(4), 3533–3613. DOI: 10.1007/s11277-022-09932-3

Arrun˜ada, B. (2018). Blockchain's struggle to deliver impersonal exchange. *Minnesota Journal of Law, Science & Technology*, *19*(1), 55.

Atzori, L., Iera, A., & Morabito, G. (2010). Internet of Things (IoT): A Vision, Architectural Challenges and Applications. *IEEE Transactions on Industrial Informatics*, *7*(4), 469–476.

Awan, K., Khan, S., Haider, S., Khan, N., Ali, Z., & Damaševicius, R. (2024). TrioPen: A novel model to prioritize responsive flows enabling enhanced multimedia communication on the Internet. *Multimedia Tools and Applications*, •••, 1–29. DOI: 10.1007/s11042-024-20399-1

Ayub Khan, A., Laghari, A. A., Shaikh, Z. A., Dacko-Pikiewicz, Z., & Kot, S. (2022). Internet of Things (IoT) Security With Blockchain Technology: A State-of-the-Art Review. *IEEE Access : Practical Innovations, Open Solutions*, *10*, 122679–122695. DOI: 10.1109/ACCESS.2022.3223370

B¨ohme, R., Christin, N., Edelman, B., & Moore, T. (2015). Bitcoin: Economics, technology, and governance. *The Journal of Economic Perspectives*, *29*(2), 213–238. DOI: 10.1257/jep.29.2.213

Baazeem, R. (2024). Multilayered Framework for Enhancing Data Confidentiality, Integrity, and Threat Detection through Blockchain, Advanced Cryptography, and Machine Learning. [IJCNA]. *International Journal of Computer Networks and Applications*, *11*(5). Advance online publication. DOI: 10.22247/ijcna/2024/36

Babagoli, M., Aghababa, M. P., & Solouk, V. (2019). Heuristic nonlinear regression strategy for detecting phishing websites. *Soft Computing*, *23*(12), 4315–4327. DOI: 10.1007/s00500-018-3084-2

Babar, A. Z., & Akan, O. B. (2024). *Sustainable and Precision Agriculture with the Internet of Everything (IoE)*. https://arxiv.org/abs/2404.06341v3

Babbar, H., Rani, S., Bouachir, O., & Aloqaily, M. (2023). From Massive IoT Toward IoE: Evolution of Energy Efficient Autonomous Wireless Networks. *IEEE Communications Standards Magazine*, *7*(2), 32–39. DOI: 10.1109/MCOMSTD.0001.2100116

Baber, H. (2019). Blockchain-based crowdfunding: A 'pay-it-forward'model of whirl. [IJRTE]. *International Journal of Recent Technology and Engineering*, *8*(3), 2277–3878.

Bachmann, N., Tripathi, S., Brunner, M., & Jodlbauer, H. (2022). The contribution of data-driven technologies in achieving the sustainable development goals. *Sustainability (Basel)*, *14*(5), 2497. DOI: 10.3390/su14052497

Back, A. (2002). Hashcash-a denial of service counter-measure.

Badal, F. R., Das, P., Sarker, S. K., & Das, S. K. (2019). A survey on control issues in renewable energy integration and microgrid. *Prot. Control. Mod. Power Syst.*, *4*(1), 8. DOI: 10.1186/s41601-019-0122-8

Badidi, E., Moumane, K., & El Ghazi, F. (2023). Opportunities, applications, and challenges of edge-AI enabled video analytics in smart cities: A systematic review. *IEEE Access : Practical Innovations, Open Solutions*, *11*, 80543–80572. DOI: 10.1109/ACCESS.2023.3300658

Bagchi, S., Abdelzaher, T. F., Govindan, R., Shenoy, P., Atrey, A., Ghosh, P., & Xu, R. (2020). New frontiers in IoT: Networking, systems, reliability, and security challenges. *IEEE Internet of Things Journal*, *7*(12), 11330–11346.

Bagirovs, E. (2024). Applications of post-quantum cryptography. European Conference on cyber Warfare and Security, 23(1), 49-57. https://doi.org/DOI: 10.34190/eccws.23.1.2247

Balogun, A. O., Bajeh, A. O., Orie, V. A., & Yusuf-asaju, A. W. (2018). Software Defect Prediction Using Ensemble Learning: An ANP Based Evaluation Method. *Journal of Engineering Technology*, *3*(2), 50–55.

Bandaranayake, B. 2014. "Fraud and Corruption Control at Education System Level." Http://Dx.Doi.Org/10.1177/1555458914549669 17 (4): 34–53. https://doi.org/DOI: 10.1177/1555458914549669

Banerjee, B., & Patel, J. T. (2016). A Symmetric Key Block Cipher to Provide Confidentiality in Wireless Sensor Networks. INFOCOMP Journal of Computer Science, 15(1), 12–18. Retrieved from https://infocomp.dcc.ufla.br/index.php/infocomp/article/view/515

Banerjee, B., & Saha, G. 2022. Emotion Independent Face Recognition-Based Security Protocol in IoT-Enabled Devices. In Cloud IoT (pp. 199218). Chapman and Hall/CRC. DOI: 10.1201/9781003155577-18

Banerjee, B., & Sarkar, D. (2024). Blockchain-Based Quantum Resistant Electoral Management System for the Post-Pandemic Era. In Ensuring Security and End-to-End Visibility Through Blockchain and Digital Twins (pp. 102-115). IGI Global. DOI: 10.4018/979-8-3693-3494-2.ch006

Banerjee, B., (2019). Avalanche effect: A judgement parameter of strength in symmetric key block ciphers. International journal of engineering development and research, 7(2), pp.116-121.

Banerjee, B. (2024). Blockchain 2030: Revolutionizing the Future of Digital Trust. *International Research Journal of Scientific Studies*, *1*(1), 13–18.

Banerjee, B. (2024). Next-Gen Computing: Exploring Industry 4.0. *International Research Journal of Scientific Studies*, *1*(1), 1–6.

Banerjee, B. (2024). Quantum Horizons: Shaping the Future of Computing. *International Research Journal of Scientific Studies*, *1*(1), 7–12.

Banerjee, B., Hazra, D., & Sarkar, D. (2024). IoT-Enabled Water Quality Management System for Rural Areas of Bharuch District. In *Water Informatics: Challenges and Solutions Using State of Art Technologies* (pp. 33–47). Springer Nature Singapore. DOI: 10.1007/978-981-97-1518-3_3

Banerjee, B., Jani, A., & Shah, N. (2021). A genetic blockchain approach for securing smart vehicles in quantum era. In *Vehicular Communications for Smart Cars* (pp. 85–108). CRC Press. DOI: 10.1201/9781315110905-5

Banerjee, B., Jani, A., & Shah, N. (2021). *Asymmetric Confidentiality in Blockchain Embedded Smart Grids in Galois Field*. Frontiers in Blockchain. DOI: 10.3389/fbloc.2021.770074

Banerjee, B., Jani, A., & Shah, N. (2021). Digital Image Encryption Using Double Crossover Approach for SARS-CoV-2 Infected Lungs in a Blockchain Framework. *Frontiers in Blockchain*, *4*, 771241. DOI: 10.3389/fbloc.2021.771241

Banerjee, B., Jani, A., Shah, N., & Patel, A. (2020). Post Quantum Security Enhancement Scheme in IoT Blockchain Framework. *GIS Sci. J*, *7*(6), 664–672.

Bank, E. C. (2015). *Virtual currency schemes-a further analysis. Technical report, Tech. rep*. European Central Bank.

Bannore, A., Patil, R. Y., & Devane, S. R. (2022). An efficient proxy signature–based authority delegation scheme for medical cyber physical systems. In *Cyber Security Threats and Challenges Facing Human Life* (pp. 13–23). Chapman and Hall/CRC. DOI: 10.1201/9781003218555-3

Bansal, D., Chhikara, R., Khanna, K., & Gupta, P. (2018). Comparative Analysis of Various Machine Learning Algorithms for Detecting Dementia. *Procedia Computer Science, 132*, 1497–1502. DOI: 10.1016/j.procs.2018.05.102

Basani, D. K. R. (2021). Leveraging robotic process automation and business analytics in digital transformation: Insights from machine learning and AI. *International Journal of Engineering Research & Science & Technology*, 17(3), 1-10. ISSN 2319-5991.

Bayer, D. (1993). Stuart Haber, and W Scott Stornetta. Improving the efficiency and reliability of digital time-stamping. In *Sequences Ii* (pp. 329–334). Springer. DOI: 10.1007/978-1-4613-9323-8_24

Beck, J., Birkel, H., Spieske, A., & Gebhardt, M. (2023). Will the blockchain solve the supply chain resilience challenges? Insights from a systematic literature review. *Computers & Industrial Engineering, 185*, 109623. Advance online publication. DOI: 10.1016/j.cie.2023.109623

Belonick, P. (2020). Transparency Is the New Privacy: Blockchain's Challenge for the Fourth Amendment. *Stanford Technology Law Review : STLR : An Online High-Technology Law Journal from Stanford Law School, 23*, •••. https://heinonline.org/HOL/Page?handle=hein.journals/stantlr23&id=114&div=&collection=

Benavides, E., Fuertes, W., Sanchez, S., & Sanchez, M. (2020). Classification of Phishing Attack Solutions by Employing Deep Learning Techniques: A Systematic Literature Review. In *Smart Innovation, Systems and Technologies* (Vol. 152). Springer Singapore. DOI: 10.1007/978-981-13-9155-2_5

Ben-Sasson, E., Bentov, I., Horesh, Y., & Riabzev, M. (2019). Scalable zero knowledge with no trusted setup. In Advances in Cryptology–CRYPTO 2019: 39th Annual International Cryptology Conference, Santa Barbara, CA, USA, August 18–22, 2019 [Springer International Publishing.]. *Proceedings, 39*(Part III), 701–732.

Benton, M. C., Radziwill, N. M., Purritano, A. W., & Gerhart, C. J. (2018). Blockchain for Supply Chain: Improving Transparency and Efficiency Simultaneously. Software Quality Professional, 20(3).

Bhardwaj, A., Dagar, V., Khan, M. O., Aggarwal, A., Alvarado, R., Kumar, M., Irfan, M., & Proshad, R. (2022). Smart IoT and machine learning-based framework for water quality assessment and device component monitoring. *Environmental Science and Pollution Research International, 29*(30), 46018–46036. DOI: 10.1007/s11356-022-19014-3 PMID: 35165843

Bhat, S. A., Huang, N. F., Sofi, I. B., & Sultan, M. (2022). Agriculture-Food Supply Chain Management Based on Blockchain and IoT: A Narrative on Enterprise Blockchain Interoperability. *Agriculture*, *12*(1), 40. DOI: 10.3390/agriculture12010040

Bhavsingh, M., Samunnisa, K., & Mallareddy, A. (2024). Enhancing efficiency and security in mtc environments: A novel strategy for dynamic grouping and streamlined management. *Emerg. Technol. Eng. J.*, *1*(1), 43–56. DOI: 10.53898/etej2024114

Bhushan, B., Sahoo, C., Sinha, P., & Khamparia, A. (2020). Unification of Blockchain and Internet of Things (BIoT): requirements, working model, challenges and future directions. *Wireless Networks 2020 27:1*, *27*(1), 55–90. https://doi.org/DOI: 10.1007/s11276-020-02445-6

Biswas, N., Santra, D., Banerjee, B., & Biswas, S. (2024). Harnessing the Power of Machine Learning for Parkinson's Disease Detection. In *AIoT and Smart Sensing Technologies for Smart Devices* (pp. 140–155). IGI Global. DOI: 10.4018/979-8-3693-0786-1.ch008

Blumberg, D. M., & Rau-Chaplin, M. S. (2016). Security and Privacy in the Internet of Things: Current State and Future Directions. *Telecommunications Policy*, *41*(1), 76–96.

Bodkhe, U., Tanwar, S., Parekh, K., Khanpara, P., Tyagi, S., Kumar, N., & Alazab, M. (2020). Blockchain for Industry 4.0: A comprehensive review. *IEEE Access : Practical Innovations, Open Solutions*, *8*, 79764–79800. DOI: 10.1109/ACCESS.2020.2988579

Boison, D. K., Malcalm, E., Antwi-Boampong, A., & Hiran, K. K. (2022). Assessing Factors Affecting the Blockchain Adoption in Public Procurement Delivery in Ghana: A Correlational Study Using UTAUT2 Theoretical Framework. *International Journal of Ambient Computing and Intelligence*, *13*(1), 1–13. DOI: 10.4018/ijaci.314568

Bolanowski, M., Paszkiewicz, A., Żabiński, T., Piecuch, G., Salach, M., & Tomecki, K. (2023). System Architecture for Diagnostics and Supervision of Industrial Equipment and Processes in an IoE Device Environment. *Electronics 2023, Vol. 12, Page 4935*, *12*(24), 4935. https://doi.org/DOI: 10.3390/electronics12244935

Bordel, B., Martin, D., Alcarria, R., & Robles, T. A Blockchain-based Water Control System for the Automatic Management of Irrigation Communities. In *Proceedings of the 2019 IEEE International Conference on Consumer Electronics (ICCE)*, Las Vegas, NV, USA, 11–13 January 2019. DOI: 10.1109/ICCE.2019.8661940

Borse, M., Shendkar, P., Undre, Y., Mahadik, A., & Patil, R. Y. (2022). A review of blockchain consensus algorithm. *Expert Clouds and Applications:Proceedings of ICOECA 2022*, pp.415-426.

Brennecke, M., Guggenberger, T., Schellinger, B., & Urbach, N. (2022). the de-central bank in decentralized finance: a case study of makerdao.. https://doi.org/ DOI: 10.24251/HICSS.2022.737

Brun, A., Sudheer, B., & Goud, K. 2023. "Implementation of IoT Technologies in Manufacturing Process." https://www.politesi.polimi.it/handle/10589/139316

Cao, S., Zhang, G., Liu, P., Zhang, X., & Neri, F. (2019). Cloud-assisted secure eHealth systems for tamper-proofing EHR via blockchain. *Information Sciences*, *485*, 427–440. DOI: 10.1016/j.ins.2019.02.038

Carla, L. (2017). Reyes. Conceptualizing cryptolaw. *Nebraska Law Review*, *96*(2), 384.

Carter, J. L., & Wegman, M. N. (1977, May). Universal classes of hash functions. In *Proceedings of the ninth annual ACM symposium on Theory of computing* (pp. 106-112).

Castro, M., Liskov, B., ... Practical byzantine fault tolerance. In *OSDI*, volume 99, pages 173–186, 1999.

Chang, C.-Y., Tijus, C., Lee, P.-L., Yang, C.-F., Mohd Ali, F., Arzilawati Md Yunus, N., Nabila Mohamed, N., Mat Daud, M., & Sundararajan, E. A. (2023). A Systematic Mapping: Exploring Internet of Everything Technologies and Innovations. *Symmetry 2023, Vol. 15, Page 1964, 15*(11), 1964. https://doi.org/DOI: 10.3390/sym15111964

Chang, S. E., & Chen, Y. (2020). Blockchain in health care innovation: Literature review and case study from a business ecosystem perspective. *Journal of Medical Internet Research*, *22*(8), e19480. DOI: 10.2196/19480 PMID: 32865501

Chatzigiannakis, I., & Tselios, C. (2021). Internet of Everything. *Intelligent Computing for Interactive System Design*, (February), 21–56. DOI: 10.1145/3447404.3447408

Chembakassery, D. (2023, October). Proof of Computational Power: An Innovative Consensus Algorithm for Blockchain Systems. In The International Conference on Recent Innovations in Computing (pp. 417-432). Singapore: Springer Nature Singapore.

Cheng, S., Zeng, B., & Huang, Y. Z. (2017, November). Research on application model of blockchain technology in distributed electricity market. [). IOP Publishing.]. *IOP Conference Series. Earth and Environmental Science*, *93*(1), 012065.

Chen, S. J., Cao, Y. Y., & Li, J. (2021). The Effect of Water Rights Trading Policy on Water Resource Utilization Efficiency: Evidence from a Quasi-Natural Experiment in China. *Sustainability (Basel), 13*(9), 5281. DOI: 10.3390/su13095281

Chiew, K. L., Tan, C. L., Wong, K. S., Yong, K. S. C., & Tiong, W. K. (2019). A new hybrid ensemble feature selection framework for machine learning-based phishing detection system. *Information Sciences, 484*, 153–166. DOI: 10.1016/j.ins.2019.01.064

Chohan, U. W. (2019). Blockchain and environmental sustainability: case of IBM's blockchain water management. Notes on the 21st Century (CBRI).

Chohan, U. W. (2022). A history of bitcoin. Available at *SSRN* 3047875.

Choi, N., & Kim, H. (2019). A Blockchain-based user authentication model using MetaMask. *Journal of Internet Computing and Services, 20*(6), 119–127.

Choudhury, S., & Bhowal, A. (2015). Comparative analysis of machine learning algorithms along with classifiers for network intrusion detection. *2015 International Conference on Smart Technologies and Management for Computing, Communication, Controls, Energy and Materials, ICSTM 2015 - Proceedings, May*, 89–95. DOI: 10.1109/ICSTM.2015.7225395

Christina Marta, S. U. C. I. U., Christian, N. A. S. U. L. E. A., & Diana Florentina, N. A. S. U. L. E. A. (2019). *Towards developing a friendlier regulatory framework for blockchain-based businesses*. Economic Convergence in European Union.

Christin, N. (2013, May). Traveling the Silk Road: A measurement analysis of a large anonymous online marketplace. In *Proceedings of the 22nd international conference on World Wide Web* (pp. 213-224).

Christopher, C. M. (2016). The bridging model: Exploring the roles of trust and enforcement in banking, bitcoin, and the blockchain. *Nev. LJ, 17*, 139.

Civas, M., Cetinkaya, O., Kuscu, M., & Akan, O. B. (2021). Universal Transceivers: Opportunities and Future Directions for the Internet of Everything (IoE). *Frontiers in Communications and Networks, 2*, 733664. DOI: 10.3389/frcmn.2021.733664

Commission, E. U. (2019). *Potential use cases for innovative technologies in securities posttrading. Technical report*. European Central Bank.

Costa-Font, J., & Sato, A. (2012). Health systems futures: The challenges of technology, prevention and insurance. *Futures, 44*(7), 696–703. DOI: 10.1016/j.futures.2012.04.009

Cuccuru, P. (2017). Beyond Bitcoin: An Early Overview on Smart Contracts. *International Journal of Law and Information Technology*, *25*(3), 179–195. DOI: 10.1093/ijlit/eax003

D'Onfro, D. (2020). Smart Contracts and the Illusion of Automated Enforcement. *Washington University Journal of Law and Policy*, *61*, •••. https://heinonline.org/HOL/Page?handle=hein.journals/wajlp61&id=185&div=&collection=

da Costa, V. C. F., Oliveira, L. F., & de Souza, J. (2021). A collaborative approach to support interoperability and awareness of Internet of Everything (IoE) enablers. *Proceedings of the 2021 IEEE International Conference on Human-Machine Systems, ICHMS 2021*. https://doi.org/DOI: 10.1109/ICHMS53169.2021.9582657

Dalvit, L. (2020). Ethereum: a new record of transactions per second thanks to istanbul. https://en.cryptonomist.ch/2020/01/07/ethereum-transactions-per -second-istanbul/,.

Damgård, I. B. (1989, August). A design principle for hash functions. In Conference on the Theory and Application of Cryptology (pp. 416-427). New York, NY: Springer New York.

Danda, R. R., Maguluri, K. K., Yasmeen, Z., Mandala, G., & Dileep, V. (2023). Intelligent Healthcare Systems: Harnessing Ai and Ml To Revolutionize Patient Care And Clinical Decision-Making. *International Journal of Applied Engineering and Technology*https://papers. ssrn. com/sol3/papers. cfm

Das, P., Chitra Jain, A., & Singh, M. (2024). Toward a Trusted Smart City Ecosystem : IoE and Blockchain-Enabled Cognitive Frameworks for Shared Business Services. *Industrial Internet of Things Security*, (October), 208–228. DOI: 10.1201/9781003466284-11

David, Anne, Tan Yigitcanlar, Rita Yi Man Li, Juan M. Corchado, Pauline Hope Cheong, Karen Mossberger, and Rashid Mehmood. 2023. "Understanding Local Government Digital Technology Adoption Strategies: A PRISMA Review." *Sustainability 2023, Vol. 15, Page 9645* 15 (12): 9645. https://doi.org/.DOI: 10.3390/su15129645

Davis, S. J., Lewis, N. S., Shaner, M., Aggarwal, S., Arent, D., Azevedo, I. L., Benson, S. M., Bradley, T., Brouwer, J., & Caldeira, K.. (2018). Net-zero emissions energy systems. *Science*, *360*(6396), 6396. DOI: 10.1126/science.aas9793 PMID: 29954954

De Guimarães, J. C. F., Severo, E. A., Felix Júnior, L. A., Da Costa, W. P. L. B., & Salmoria, F. T. (2020). Governance and quality of life in smart cities: Towards sustainable development goals. *Journal of Cleaner Production*, *253*, 119926. DOI: 10.1016/j.jclepro.2019.119926

Deist, T. M., Dankers, F. J. W. M., Valdes, G., Wijsman, R., Hsu, I. C., Oberije, C., Lustberg, T., van Soest, J., Hoebers, F., Jochems, A., El Naqa, I., Wee, L., Morin, O., Raleigh, D. R., Bots, W., Kaanders, J. H., Belderbos, J., Kwint, M., Solberg, T., & Lambin, P. (2018). Machine learning algorithms for outcome prediction in (chemo)radiotherapy: An empirical comparison of classifiers. *Medical Physics, 45*(7), 3449–3459. DOI: 10.1002/mp.12967 PMID: 29763967

Delorit, J. D., Parker, D. P., & Block, P. J. (2019). An agro-economic approach to framing perennial farm-scale water resources demand management for water rights markets. *Agricultural Water Management, 218*, 68–81. DOI: 10.1016/j.agwat.2019.03.029

Deore, S., Bachche, R., Bichave, A., & Patil, R. (2021, June). EHR-Sec: a block-chain based security system for electronic health. In *International Conference on Soft Computing and Signal Processing* (pp. 295-303). Singapore: Springer Nature Singapore.

Deore, S., Bachche, R., Bichave, A., & Patil, R. (2022). Review on applications of blockchain for electronic health records systems. In *Second International Conference on Image Processing and Capsule Networks: ICIPCN 2021 2* (pp. 609-616). Springer International Publishing. DOI: 10.1007/978-3-030-84760-9_52

Dhanalakshmi, J., & Pandeeswari, N. (2024). Blockchain Enabled Security and Integrity in Cloud Computing. *8th International Conference on I-SMAC (IoT in Social, Mobile, Analytics and Cloud), I-SMAC 2024 - Proceedings*, 1076–1082. DOI: 10.1109/I-SMAC61858.2024.10714885

Di Silvestre, M. L., Gallo, P., Guerrero, J. M., Musca, R., Sanseverino, E. R., Sciumè, G., Vasquez, J. C., & Zizzo, G. (2020). Blockchain for power systems: Current trends and future applications. *Renewable & Sustainable Energy Reviews, 119*, 109585. DOI: 10.1016/j.rser.2019.109585

Diro, A., Zhou, L., Saini, A., Kaisar, S., & Hiep, P. C. (2024). Leveraging Zero Knowledge Proofs for Blockchain-Based Identity Sharing: A Survey of Advancements, Challenges and Opportunities. *Journal of Information Security and Applications, 80*(February), 103678. DOI: 10.1016/j.jisa.2023.103678

Don Johnson, A. M., & Vanstone, S. (2001). The elliptic curve digital signature algorithm (ecdsa). *International Journal of Information Security, 1*(1), 36–63. DOI: 10.1007/s102070100002

Dondapati, K. (2020). Integrating neural networks and heuristic methods in test case prioritization: A machine learning perspective. *International Journal of Engineering & Science Research*, 10(3), 49-61. ISSN 2277-2685.

Dou, X., Chen, W., Zhu, L., Bai, Y., Li, Y., & Wu, X. (2023). Machine Learning for Smart Cities: A Comprehensive Review of Applications and Opportunities. *International Journal of Advanced Computer Science and Applications, 14*(9). Advance online publication. DOI: 10.14569/IJACSA.2023.01409104

Dutta, P., Choi, T.-M., Somani, S., & Butala, R.et al. (2020). Blockchain technology in supply chain operations: Applications, challenges and research opportunities. *Transportation Research Part E, Logistics and Transportation Review, 142*, 102067. Advance online publication. DOI: 10.1016/j.tre.2020.102067 PMID: 33013183

Ekblaw, A., Azaria, A., Halamka, J. D., & Lippman, A. (2016, August). A Case Study for Blockchain in Healthcare:"MedRec" prototype for electronic health records and medical research data. In Proceedings of IEEE open & big data conference (Vol. 13, p. 13).

El Mrabet, Z., Kaabouch, N., El Ghazi, H., & El Ghazi, H. (2018). Cyber-security in smart grid: Survey and challenges. *Computers & Electrical Engineering, 67*, 469–482. DOI: 10.1016/j.compeleceng.2018.01.015

Elgazzar, K., Khalil, H., Alghamdi, T., Badr, A., Abdelkader, G., Elewah, A., & Buyya, R. (2022). Revisiting the internet of things: New trends, opportunities and grand challenges. *Frontiers in the Internet of Things, 1*, 1073780. DOI: 10.3389/friot.2022.1073780

El-Hoiy, A. A. A., & El-Hennawy, M. I. (2017). LoRaWAN: A Low-Power Wide-Area Network Protocol for Internet of Things Applications. *IEEE Access : Practical Innovations, Open Solutions, 5*, 16774–16787.

Emanet, N., Öz, H. R., Bayram, N., & Delen, D. (2014). A comparative analysis of machine learning methods for classification type decision problems in healthcare. *Decision Analysis, 1*(1), 1–20. DOI: 10.1186/2193-8636-1-6

Energimyndigheten. 2020. Available online: https://www.energimyndigheten.se/statistik/den-officiella-statistiken/ statistikprodukter/natanslutna-solcellsanlaggningar/ (accessed on 23 November 2021).

Enescu, F. M., Bizon, N., Onu, A., Răboacă, M. S., Thounthong, P., Mazare, A. G., & erban, G. (2020). S,erban, G. Implementing Blockchain Technology in Irrigation Systems That Integrate Photovoltaic Energy Generation Systems. *Sustainability (Basel), 12*(4), 1540. DOI: 10.3390/su12041540

European Central Bank. (2012). *Virtual currency schemes. EC Bank, Virtual Currency Schemes (h.* European Central Bank.

Evangelin Sonia, S. V., Beulah Christalin Latha, C., Jenefa, A., & Shirley, C. P. (2024). *Empowering Patients: Unlocking Benefits Through Blockchain Integration in IoT-Based Biomedical and Healthcare Systems*. 303–339. https://doi.org/DOI: 10.1007/978-981-97-4268-4_12

Faber, B., Michelet, G., Weidmann, N., Mukkamala, R. R., & Vatrapu, R. (2019). BPDIMS: A blockchain-based personal data and identity management system. In The 52nd Hawaii International Conference on System Sciences. HISS 2019: HISS 2019 (pp. 6855-6864). Hawaii International Conference on System Sciences (HICSS).

Faisal, M. A., Aung, Z., Williams, J. R., & Sanchez, A. (2014). Data-stream-based intrusion detection system for advanced metering infrastructure in smart grid: A feasibility study. *IEEE Systems Journal, 2014*(9), 31–44.

Fang, H., & Qian, Q. (2021). Privacy preserving machine learning with homomorphic encryption and federated learning. *Future Internet, 13*(4), 94. DOI: 10.3390/fi13040094

Farias da Costa, V. C., Oliveira, L., & de Souza, J. (2021). Internet of everything (IoE) taxonomies: A survey and a novel knowledge-based taxonomy. *Sensors (Basel), 21*(2), 568.

Ferreira, L., Cruz, M. R., Cruz, E. F., Quintela, H., & Cunha, M. C. (Eds.). (2023). *Supporting technologies and the impact of blockchain on organizations and society*. IGI Global.

Fette, I., Sadeh, N., & Tomasic, A. (2007). Learning to detect phishing emails. *16th International World Wide Web Conference, WWW2007*, 649–656. DOI: 10.1145/1242572.1242660

Financial Conduct Authority. (2017). *Discussion paper on distributed ledger technology. Technical report*. Financial Conduct Authority.

Financial Stability Board. (2018). *Crypto-assets: report to the g20 on the work of the fsb and standardsetting bodies. Technical report*. Financial Stability Board.

Fink, C., Maskus, K. E., & Qian, Y. (2016). The Economic Effects of Counterfeiting and Piracy: A Review and Implications for Developing Countries. *The World Bank Research Observer, 31*(1), 1–28. DOI: 10.1093/wbro/lkv010

Foti, M., & Vavalis, M. (2021). What can blockchain do for power grids? *Blockchain: Res. Appl.*, 2, 100008.

Fowdur, T. P., Hurbungs, V., & Babooram, L. (2024). Leveraging the Power of Blockchain in Industry 4.0 and Intelligent Real-Time Systems for Achieving the SDGs. *Artificial Intelligence, Engineering Systems and Sustainable Development: Driving the UN SDGs*, 109–121. https://doi.org/DOI: 10.1108/978-1-83753-540-820241009/FULL/XML

Freeman, C., Merriman, J., Beaver, I., & Mueen, A. (2021). Experimental Comparison and Survey of Twelve Time Series Anomaly Detection Algorithms. *Journal of Artificial Intelligence Research*, *72*, 849–899. DOI: 10.1613/jair.1.12698

Frick, K. T., Abreu, G. M., Malkin, N., Pan, A., & Post, A. E. (2021). The cybersecurity risks of smart city technologies: What do the experts think. White Paper, CLTC White Paper Series; UC Berkeley: Berkeley, CA, USA.

Friess, P., & Vermesan, O. (2015). Building the Hyperconnected Society- Internet of Things Research and Innovation Value Chains, Ecosystems and Markets. *Building the Hyperconnected Society- Internet of Things Research and Innovation Value Chains. Ecosystems and Markets*, *332*. Advance online publication. DOI: 10.1201/9781003337454

Gabison, G. (2016). Policy considerations for the blockchain technology public and private applications. *Science and Technology Law Review*, *19*, 327.

Galici, M., Mureddu, M., Ghiani, E., Celli, G., Pilo, F., Porcu, P., & Canetto, B. (2021). Energy Blockchain for Public Energy Communities. [CrossRef]. *Applied Sciences (Basel, Switzerland)*, *11*(8), 3457. DOI: 10.3390/app11083457

Ganesan, T. (2020). Machine learning-driven AI for financial fraud detection in IoT environments. *International Journal of HRM and Organizational Behavior*, 8(4), 1-10. ISSN 2454-5015.

Gartner, M. (2023). Influencable autonomy and predictable freedom in the IoE.

Gattupalli, K. (2020). Optimizing 3D printing materials for medical applications using AI, computational tools, and directed energy deposition. *International Journal of Modern Electronics and Communication Engineering*, *8*(3), 1–10. DOI: 10.5281/zenodo.13994678

Gautam, S., Rani, K., & Joshi, B. (2018). Detecting phishing websites using rule-based classification algorithm: A comparison. *Lecture Notes in Networks and Systems*, *9*, 21–33. DOI: 10.1007/978-981-10-3932-4_3

Gbadebo, Ayoade., Erick, Bauman., Latifur, Khan., Kevin, W., Hamlen. (2019). Smart Contract Defense through Bytecode Rewriting. 384-389. DOI: 10.1109/Blockchain.2019.00059

Ge, M., Wu, F. P., & Chen, X. P. (2017). A Coupled Allocation for Regional Initial Water Rights in Dalinghe Basin, China. *Sustainability (Basel)*, *9*(3), 428. DOI: 10.3390/su9030428

Gennaio, E. S. M. A. (2019). *Advice, initial coin offerings and crypto-assets. Technical report.* European Securities and Markets Authority.

Goel, U., Ruhl, R., & Zavarsky, P. (2019). Using healthcare authority and patient blockchains to develop a tamper-proof record tracking system. *2019 IEEE 5th International Conference on Cloud Computing and Intelligence Systems (CCIS)*, 409–414. https://doi.org/DOI: 10.1109/CCIS48116.2019.9071601

Goldwasser, S., Micali, S., & Rackoff, C. (1989). The knowledge complexity of interactive proof systems. *SIAM Journal on Computing*, *18*(1), 186–208. DOI: 10.1137/0218012

Gopal, S. B., Poongodi, C., & Nanthiya, D. (2023). Blockchain-based secured payment in IoE. *Smart Energy and Electric Power Systems: Current Trends and New Intelligent Perspectives*, 185–200. https://doi.org/DOI: 10.1016/B978-0-323-91664-6.00009-7

Gostin, L. O., Levit, L. A., & Nass, S. J. (Eds.). (2009). *Beyond the HIPAA privacy rule: enhancing privacy, improving health through research.*

Gourisetti, S. N. G., Sebastian-Cardenas, D. J., Bhattarai, B., Wang, P., Widergren, S., Borkum, M., & Randall, A. (2021). Blockchain Smart Contract Reference Framework and Program Logic Architecture for Transactive Energy Systems. *Applied Energy*, *304*(December), 117860. DOI: 10.1016/j.apenergy.2021.117860

Governatori, G., Idelberger, F., Milosevic, Z., Riveret, R., Sartor, G., & Xu, X. (2018). On Legal Contracts, Imperative and Declarative Smart Contracts, and Blockchain Systems. *Artificial Intelligence and Law*, *26*(4), 377–409. DOI: 10.1007/s10506-018-9223-3

Grantham, T. E., & Viers, J. H. (2014). 100 years of California's water rights system: Patterns, trends and uncertainty. *Environmental Research Letters*, *9*(8), 084012. DOI: 10.1088/1748-9326/9/8/084012

Gubbi, J., Buyya, R., Marusic, S., & Palaniswami, M. (2013). Internet of Things (IoT): A Vision, Architectural Elements, and Future Directions. *Future Generation Computer Systems*, *29*(7), 1645–1660. DOI: 10.1016/j.future.2013.01.010

Guo, A. (2017). Blockchain receipts: Patentability and admissibility in court. *ChicagoKent Journal of Intellectual Property*, *16*(2), 440.

Guo, C. (2006). *Detection Prevention*. Most.

Guo, R., Shi, H., Zhao, Q., & Zheng, D. (2018). Secure Attribute-Based Signature Scheme with Multiple Authorities for Blockchain in Electronic Health Records Systems. *IEEE Access : Practical Innovations, Open Solutions*, *6*, 11676–11686. DOI: 10.1109/ACCESS.2018.2801266

Gupta, B. B., Tewari, A., Jain, A. K., & Agrawal, D. P. (2017). Fighting against phishing attacks: State of the art and future challenges. *Neural Computing & Applications*, *28*(12), 3629–3654. DOI: 10.1007/s00521-016-2275-y

Gupta, H., Dastjerdi, A. V., Ghosh, S. K., & Buyya, R. (2017). iFogSim: A toolkit for modeling and simulation of resource management techniques in the Internet of Things, edge and fog computing environments. *Software, Practice & Experience*, *47*(9), 1275–1296. DOI: 10.1002/spe.2509

Gustavus, J. (1994). *Simmons. Contemporary cryptology: The science of information integrity*. IEEE press.

Haber, S., & Stornetta, W. S. (1991). *How to time-stamp a digital document*. Springer Berlin Heidelberg.

Habib, G., Sharma, S., Ibrahim, S., Ahmad, I., Qureshi, S., & Ishfaq, M. (2022). Blockchain Technology: Benefits, Challenges, Applications, and Integration of Blockchain Technology with Cloud Computing. *Future Internet 2022, Vol. 14, Page 341, 14*(11), 341. DOI: 10.3390/fi14110341

Haider, S., Abbas, G., Abbas, Z. H., & Baker, T. (2019). DABFS: A robust routing protocol for warning messages dissemination in VANETs. *Computer Communications, 147*, 21–34. DOI: 10.1016/j.comcom.2019.08.011

Haider, S., Abbas, G., Abbas, Z. H., Boudjit, S., & Halim, Z. (2020). P-DACCA: A probabilistic direction-aware cooperative collision avoidance scheme for VANETs. *Future Generation Computer Systems, 103*, 1–17. DOI: 10.1016/j.future.2019.09.054

Haider, S., Abbas, G., Abbas, Z. H., & Muhammad, F. (2020). LWE-CPPA: A scheme for secure delivery of warning messages in VANETs. *International Journal of Ad Hoc and Ubiquitous Computing*, *34*(3), 170–185. DOI: 10.1504/IJAHUC.2020.108426

Haider, S., Abbas, Z. H., Abbas, G., Waqas, M., Tu, S., & Zhao, W. (2020). A novel cross-layer V2V architecture for direction-aware cooperative collision avoidance. *Electronics (Basel)*, *9*(7), 1112. DOI: 10.3390/electronics9071112

Hakiri, A., Gokhale, A., Ben Yahia, S., & Mellouli, N. (2024). A comprehensive survey on digital twin for future networks and emerging Internet of Things industry. *Computer Networks, 244*, 110350. DOI: 10.1016/j.comnet.2024.110350

Hammi, M. T., Bellot, P., & Serhrouchni, A. (2018). BCTrust: A decentralized authentication blockchain-based mechanism. *IEEE Wireless Communications and Networking Conference, WCNC, 2018-April*, 1–6. https://doi.org/DOI: 10.1109/WCNC.2018.8376948

Hamouda, M. R., Nassar, M. E., & Salama, M. M. A. (2020). A Novel Energy Trading Framework Using Adapted Blockchain Technology. *IEEE Transactions on Smart Grid, 12*(3), 2165–2175. DOI: 10.1109/TSG.2020.3045662

Han, R., Yu, J., Lin, H., Chen, S., & Esteves-Veríssimo, P. (2021). On the Security and Performance of Blockchain Sharding. *Cryptology EPrint Archive*. https://eprint.iacr.org/2021/1276

Hannan, M. A., Tan, S. Y., Al-Shetwi, A. Q., Jern, K. P., & Begum, R. A. (2020). Optimized controller for renewable energy sources integration into microgrid: Functions, constraints, and suggestions. *Journal of Cleaner Production, 256*, 120419. DOI: 10.1016/j.jclepro.2020.120419

Haoyang, A., & Debiao, H. (2024). Efficient Certificateless Online/Offline Signcryption Scheme Without Bilinear Pairing for Smart Home Consumer Electronics. *IEEE Transactions on Consumer Electronics, 70*(1), 4005–4015. DOI: 10.1109/TCE.2023.3307697

Harder, E. F. H. (2017). The future of contracts in a digital economy: The impact of smart contracts on transaction costs in financial markets (Master's thesis, University of Twente).

Hasan, H. R., Musamih, A., Salah, K., Jayaraman, R., Omar, M., Arshad, J., & Boscovic, D.et al. (2024). Smart agriculture assurance: IoT and blockchain for trusted sustainable produce. *Computers and Electronics in Agriculture, 224*, 109184. Advance online publication. DOI: 10.1016/j.compag.2024.109184

Hassan, A., Makhdoom, I., Iqbal, W., Ahmad, A., & Raza, A. (2023). From trust to truth: Advancements in mitigating the blockchain oracle problem. *Journal of Network and Computer Applications, 217*, 103672. DOI: 10.1016/j.jnca.2023.103672

Hassan, M., Rai, P., & Maharjan, S. (2023). Empowering south asian agricultural communities: A comprehensive approach to iot-driven agriculture through awareness, training, and collaboration. *Quarterly Journal of Emerging Technologies and Innovations, 8*(3), 18–32.

Hassija, V., Chamola, V., Gupta, V., & Jain, S. (2020). A survey on supply chain security: Application areas, security threats, and solution architectures. *IEEE Internet of Things Journal.*

Hazra, R., Chatterjee, P., Singh, Y., Podder, G., & Das, T. (2024). Data Encryption and Secure Communication Protocols. In Strategies for E-Commerce Data Security: Cloud, Blockchain, AI, and Machine Learning (pp. 546-570). IGI Global.

Heilman, E., Narula, N., Tanzer, G., Lovejoy, J., Colavita, M., Virza, M., & Dryja, T. (2019). Cryptanalysis of curl-p and other attacks on the iota cryptocurrency. Cryptology ePrint Archive.

Hiran, K. K., Doshi, R., & Patel, M. (2024a). Applications of Virtual and Augmented Reality for Health and Wellbeing. *Applications of Virtual and Augmented Reality for Health and Wellbeing*, 1–353. DOI: 10.4018/979-8-3693-1123-3

Hiran, K. K., Doshi, R., & Patel, M. (2024b). Modern technology in healthcare and medical education: Blockchain, IoT, AR, and VR. *Modern Technology in Healthcare and Medical Education: Blockchain, IoT, AR, and VR*, 1–310. DOI: 10.4018/979-8-3693-5493-3

Hiran, K. K., Doshi, R., & Rathi, R. (2014). Security & privacy issues of cloud & grid computing networks. *Security & Privacy Issues of Cloud & Grid Computing NetworksArticle in International Journal on Computational Science & Applications*, *4*(1), 83–91. Advance online publication. DOI: 10.5121/ijcsa.2014.4108

Hossain, R., Md, F. A. N., Islam, A., Rakin, T. M., & Al-Amin, M. (2024). A Comprehensive Analysis of Blockchain Technology and Consensus Protocols Across Multilayered Framework. *IEEE Access : Practical Innovations, Open Solutions*, *12*, 63087–63129. DOI: 10.1109/ACCESS.2024.3395536

Hussain, S. S., Farooq, S. M., & Ustun, T. S. (2019, March). Implementation of blockchain technology for energy trading with smart meters. In 2019 Innovations in Power and Advanced Computing Technologies (i-PACT) (Vol. 1, pp. 1-5). IEEE.

Ibrahim, R. F., Abu Al-Haija, Q., & Ahmad, A. (2022). DDoS Attack Prevention for Internet of Thing Devices Using Ethereum Blockchain Technology. *Sensors 2022, Vol. 22, Page 6806, 22*(18), 6806. DOI: 10.3390/s22186806

IFRS. (2020). List of ifrs standards list of ifrs standards. https://www.ifrs.org/issued-standards/list-of-standards/.

Iftekhar, A., Cui, X., Hassan, M., & Afzal, W. (2020). Application of Blockchain and Internet of Things to Ensure Tamper-Proof Data Availability for Food Safety. *Journal of Food Quality*, *2020*(1), 5385207. DOI: 10.1155/2020/5385207

Iftikhar, A., & Qureshi, K. N. (2024). Future Privacy and Trust Challenges for IoE Networks. *Internet of Things, Part F1832*, 193–218. https://doi.org/DOI: 10.1007/978-3-031-45162-1_12

Iftikhar, A., & Qureshi, K. N. (2023). Future privacy and trust challenges for IoE networks. In *Cybersecurity Vigilance and Security Engineering of Internet of Everything* (pp. 193–218). Springer Nature Switzerland.

Ijiri, Y. (1986). A framework for triple-entry bookkeeping. *The Accounting Review*, •••, 745–759.

Ilbiz, E., & Durst, S. (2019). The Appropriation of Blockchain for Small and Medium-sized Enterprises. *Journal of Innovation Management*, *7*(1), 26–45. DOI: 10.24840/2183-0606_007.001_0004

Imoize, A. L., Adedeji, O., Tandiya, N., & Shetty, S. (2021). 6G Enabled Smart Infrastructure for Sustainable Society: Opportunities, Challenges, and Research Roadmap. *Sensors 2021, Vol. 21, Page 1709, 21*(5), 1709. https://doi.org/DOI: 10.3390/s21051709

Inclusive Fintech: Blockchain, Cryptocurrency And Ico - David Kuo Chuen Lee, Linda Low - Google Books. (n.d.). Retrieved February 7, 2025, from https://books.google.com.my/books?hl=en&lr=&id=HCpjDwAAQBAJ&oi=fnd&pg=PR5&dq=Blockchain+and+IoE+will+change+the+way+industries+operate+and+make+transactions+infinitely+more+effective,+transparent,+and+secure&ots=ip4uuRl7Ru&sig=lXN4Pid0Eoa9Qwt8GnleCueSig0&redir_esc=y#v=onepage&q&f=false

Intelligent Systems for IoE Based Smart Cities. (2023). *Intelligent Systems for IoE Based Smart Cities*. https://doi.org/DOI: 10.2174/97898151249651230101

Intelligent, W., & Networking, S. (2017). *College of Science and Technology African Center of Excellence in Internet of Things Master of Science in Internet of Things : Wireless Intelligent Sensor Networking (MSc in IoT-WISeNet)*. 1–15. https://books.google.com/books/about/Building_the_Internet_of_Things.html?id=B2hJDQAAQBAJ

Internet of Things: Converging Technologies for Smart Environments and ... - Google Books. (n.d.). Retrieved February 5, 2025, from https://books.google.com.my/books?hl=en&lr=&id=rHYGZ0wxLP0C&oi=fnd&pg=PR1&dq=The+Internet+of+Everything+is+a+complete+transformation+when+it+comes+to+how+people,+processes,+data+and+devices+join+together+to+create+one+grand+interconnected+ecosystem&ots=N_FsvVywDj&sig=mD1qXt7RGotNnn07VSFN8kwpPxk&redir_esc=y#v=onepage&q&f=false

Iqbal, W., Abbas, H., Daneshmand, M., Rauf, B., & Bangash, Y. A. (2020). An In-Depth Analysis of IoT Security Requirements, Challenges, and Their Countermeasures via Software-Defined Security. *IEEE Internet of Things Journal, 7*(10), 10250-10276. *Article, 9099839*. Advance online publication. DOI: 10.1109/JIOT.2020.2997651

Ismail, F. S. M., Mushtaque, S. G. M., & Adane, D. (1 C.E.). Struggles, Potential, and Research Angles in the Amalgamation of Blockchain Technology With 6G Networks. Https://Services.Igi-Global.Com/Resolvedoi/Resolve.Aspx?Doi=10.4018/978-1-6684-5376-6.Ch007, 167–196. https://doi.org/DOI: 10.4018/978-1-6684-5376-6.ch007

Jafar, Q. (2019). digital currency generation using hash function and digital signature (digcur). *Al-Nahrain Journal of Science, 22*(2), 68–77. DOI: 10.22401/ANJS.22.2.09

Jagtap, S., Skouteris, G., Choudhari, V., & Rahimifard, S. (2022). Improving Water Efficiency in the Beverage Industry with the Internet of Things. In Bhatt, C., Kumar, N., Bashir, A., & Alazab, M. (Eds.), *Implementing Data Analytics and Architectures for Next Generation Wireless Communications* (pp. 18–26). IGI Global. DOI: 10.4018/978-1-7998-6988-7.ch002

Jagtap, S., Skouteris, G., Choudhari, V., Rahimifard, S., & Duong, L. N. K. (2021). An Internet of Things Approach for Water Efficiency: A Case Study of the Beverage Factory. *Sustainability (Basel), 13*(6), 3343. DOI: 10.3390/su13063343

Jahan, T. (2021). Machine learning with IoT and big data in healthcare. In *Intelligent Healthcare: Applications of AI in eHealth* (pp. 81–98). Springer International Publishing.

Jahid, A., Alsharif, M. H., & Hall, T. J. (2023). The convergence of blockchain, IoT and 6G: Potential, opportunities, challenges and research roadmap. *Journal of Network and Computer Applications, 217*, 103677. DOI: 10.1016/j.jnca.2023.103677

Jaiman, V., & Urovi, V. (2020). A consent model for blockchain-based health data sharing platforms. *IEEE Access : Practical Innovations, Open Solutions, 8*, 143734–143745. DOI: 10.1109/ACCESS.2020.3014565

Jain, R. K., Hiran, K., & Paliwal, G. (2012). QUANTUM CRYPTOGRAPHY: A NEW GENERATION OF INFORMATION SECURITY SYSTEM. *International Journal of Computers and Distributed Systems*Www.Ijcdsonline.Com, *2*. https://www.researchgate.net/publication/320404164

Jain, A. K., & Gupta, B. B. (2019). A machine learning based approach for phishing detection using hyperlinks information. *Journal of Ambient Intelligence and Humanized Computing, 10*(5), 2015–2028. DOI: 10.1007/s12652-018-0798-z

Jared, A. (2013). Kleiman. Beyond the silk road: Unregulated decentralized virtual currencies continue to endanger us national security and welfare. *American University National Security Law Brief, 4*(1), 59.

Javaid, M., Haleem, A., Singh, R. P., Suman, R., & Khan, S. (2022). A review of Blockchain Technology applications for financial services. *BenchCouncil Transactions on Benchmarks. Standards and Evaluations, 2*(3), 100073. DOI: 10.1016/j.tbench.2022.100073

Javed, I. T., & Qureshi, K. N. (2024). Role of Blockchain for IoE Infrastructures and Applications. *Internet of Things, Part F1832*, 127–139. https://doi.org/DOI: 10.1007/978-3-031-45162-1_8

Jeremy, M. (2017). Sklaroff. Smart contracts and the cost of inflexibility. *University of Pennsylvania Law Review, 166*, 263.

Jiang, J. Y., Elmaghraby, W. J., & Moon, K. (2023). An Empirical Study of Blockchain-Driven Transparency in a Consumer Marketplace. *The Wharton School Research Paper*, 1–69.

Jiang, Y., Ma, B., Wang, X., Yu, G., Yu, P., Wang, Z., Ni, W., & Liu, R. P. (2024). Blockchained Federated Learning for Internet of Things: A Comprehensive Survey. *ACM Computing Surveys, 56*(10), 1–37. Advance online publication. DOI: 10.1145/3659099

Jindal, A., Kumar, N., & Aujla, G. S. (Eds.). (2021). *Internet of Energy for Smart Cities: Machine Learning Models and Techniques*. CRC Press.

Jonathan, B. (2014). Turpin. Bitcoin: The economic case for a global, virtual currency operating in an unexplored legal framework. *Indiana Journal of Global Legal Studies, 21*(1), 335–368. DOI: 10.2979/indjglolegstu.21.1.335

Junaid, S. B., Imam, A. A., Balogun, A. O., De Silva, L. C., Surakat, Y. A., Kumar, G., & Mahamad, S. (2022, October). Recent advancements in emerging technologies for healthcare management systems: A survey. []. MDPI.]. *Health Care, 10*(10), 1940. PMID: 36292387

Kadadevaramth, R. S., Sharath, D., Ravishankar, B., & Kumar, P. M. (2020, February). A Review and development of research framework on Technological Adoption of Blockchain and IoT in Supply Chain Network Optimization. In *2020 International Conference on Mainstreaming Block Chain Implementation (ICOMBI)* (pp. 1-8). IEEE.

Kaginalkar, A., Kumar, S., Gargava, P., & Niyogi, D. (2021). Review of urban computing in air quality management as smart city service: An integrated IoT, AI, and cloud technology perspective. *Urban Climate*, *39*, 100972. DOI: 10.1016/j.uclim.2021.100972

Kairouz, P., ... (2019). "Advances and Open Problems in Federated Learning." *arXiv preprint arXiv:1912.04977*.

Kalusivalingam, A. K., Sharma, A., Patel, N., & Singh, V. (2021). Enhancing smart city development with ai: Leveraging machine learning algorithms and iot-driven data analytics. *International Journal of Artificial Intelligence and Machine Learning*, *2*(3).

Kambourakis, G., Neisse, R., & Nai-Fovino, I. (2021). *Information security in the age of EU-Institutions digitalisation, a landscape analysis*. European Commission, Joint Research Centre.

Kaneko, Y., Saito, T., & Kikuchi, H. (2015). cryptographic operation load-balancing between cryptographic module and cpu., 698-705. https://doi.org/DOI: 10.1109/AINA.2015.256

Kappagantu, R., & Daniel, S. A. (2018). Challenges and issues of smart grid implementation: A case of Indian scenario. *Journal of Electrical Systems and Information Technology*, *5*(3), 453–467. DOI: 10.1016/j.jesit.2018.01.002

Kelliher, D. (2013). An investigation into the effects of iPad/tablet device use in special education and in particular in the case of a student with Williams Syndrome: a case study approach (Doctoral dissertation, University of Limerick).

Khalil, M. I., Jhanjhi, N. Z., Humayun, M., Sivanesan, S. K., Masud, M., & Hossain, M. S. (2021). Hybrid smart grid with sustainable energy efficient resources for smart cities. *Sustainable Energy Technologies and Assessments*, *46*, 101211. DOI: 10.1016/j.seta.2021.101211

Khan, A. A., Shaikh, Z. A., Belinskaja, L., Baitenova, L., Vlasova, Y., Gerzelieva, Z., Laghari, A. A., Abro, A. A., & Barykin, S. (2022). A Blockchain and Metaheuristic-Enabled Distributed Architecture for Smart Agricultural Analysis and Ledger Preservation Solution: A Collaborative Approach. *Applied Sciences (Basel, Switzerland)*, *12*(3), 1487. DOI: 10.3390/app12031487

Khan, B., Naseem, R., Ali, M., Arshad, M., & Jan, N. (n.d.).. . *Machine Learning Approaches for Liver Disease Diagnosing.*, *1*, 27–31.

Khan, B., Naseem, R., Muhammad, F., Abbas, G., & Kim, S. (2020). An empirical evaluation of machine learning techniques for chronic kidney disease prophecy. *IEEE Access : Practical Innovations, Open Solutions*, *8*, 55012–55022. DOI: 10.1109/ACCESS.2020.2981689

Khan, I., Majib, Y., Ullah, R., & Rana, O. (2024). Blockchain Applications for Internet of Things — A Survey. *Internet of Things : Engineering Cyber Physical Human Systems*, *27*, 101254. DOI: 10.1016/j.iot.2024.101254

Khan, J. I., Khan, J., Ali, F., Ullah, F., Bacha, J., & Lee, S. (2022). Artificial intelligence and internet of things (AI-IoT) technologies in response to COVID-19 pandemic: A systematic review. *IEEE Access : Practical Innovations, Open Solutions*, *10*, 62613–62660. DOI: 10.1109/ACCESS.2022.3181605

Khan, M. A., Ashraf, M. U., & Shafiq, M. (2020). Machine Learning-Based Anomaly Detection for Securing Fog-Based IoT Systems. *IEEE Access : Practical Innovations, Open Solutions*, *8*, 121551–121563.

Khan, M. A., & Salah, K. (2018). IoT security: Review, blockchain solutions, and open challenges. *Future Generation Computer Systems*, *82*, 395–411. DOI: 10.1016/j.future.2017.11.022

Khan, N., Haider, S., Baker, T., Abbas, G., & Abbas, Z. H. (2022). MACRS: An enhanced directory-based resource sharing framework for mobile ad hoc networks. *Electronics (Basel)*, *11*(5), 725. DOI: 10.3390/electronics11050725

Khan, S. N., Loukil, F., Ghedira-Guegan, C., Benkhelifa, E., & Bani-Hani, A. (2021). Blockchain Smart Contracts: Applications, Challenges, and Future Trends. *Peer-to-Peer Networking and Applications*, *14*(5), 2901–2925. DOI: 10.1007/s12083-021-01127-0 PMID: 33897937

Khare, S. K., Bajaj, V., & Acharya, U. R. (2021). PDCNNet: An Automatic Framework for the detection of parkinson's disease using EEG signals'. *IEEE Sensors Journal*, *21*(15), 17017–17024. DOI: 10.1109/JSEN.2021.3080135

Khatun, M. A., Memon, S. F., Eising, C., & Dhirani, L. L. (2023). Machine Learning for Healthcare-IoT Security: A Review and Risk Mitigation. *IEEE Access : Practical Innovations, Open Solutions*, *11*, 145869–145896. DOI: 10.1109/ACCESS.2023.3346320

Khazanchi, D., Vyas, A. K., Hiran, K. K., & Padmanaban, S. (2021). Blockchain 3.0 for sustainable development. *Blockchain 3.0 for Sustainable Development*, 1–158. https://doi.org/DOI: 10.1515/9783110702507/EPUB

Khurshid, A. (2020). Applying Blockchain Technology to Address the Crisis of Trust During the COVID-19 Pandemic. *JMIR Medical Informatics*, *8*(9), e20477. DOI: 10.2196/20477 PMID: 32903197

Kim, S., Yun, S., Lee, E., Bae, S., & Lee, I. (2020). Fast packet inspection for end-to-end encryption. *Electronics (Basel)*, *9*(11), 1937. DOI: 10.3390/electronics9111937

Kirli, D., Couraud, B., Robu, V., Salgado-Bravo, M., Norbu, S., Andoni, M., Antonopoulos, I., Negrete-Pincetic, M., Flynn, D., & Kiprakis, A. (2022). Smart contracts in energy systems: A systematic review of fundamental approaches and implementations. *Renewable & Sustainable Energy Reviews*, *158*, 112013. DOI: 10.1016/j.rser.2021.112013

Knight, B. (2022). The classroom as a complex adaptive system (CAS): Credible framing, useful metaphor or mis-designation? *International Journal of Complexity in Education*, *3*(1). https://uwe-repository.worktribe.com/output/8809354/the-classroom-as-a-complex-adaptive-system-cas-credible-framing-useful-metaphor-or-mis-designation

Konashevych, O. I. (2016). Advantages and current issues of blockchain use in microgrids. *Electron. Model.*, *38*(2), 93–104. DOI: 10.15407/emodel.38.02.093

Korneeva, E., Olinder, N., & Strielkowski, W. (2021). Consumer attitudes to the smart home technologies and the internet of things (IOT). *Energies*, *14*(23), 7913.

Kotel, S., Sbiaa, F., Kamoun, R. M., & Hamel, L.et al. (2023). A blockchain-based approach for secure IoT. *Procedia Computer Science*, *225*, 3876–3886. DOI: 10.1016/j.procs.2023.10.383

Kshetri, N. (2024). *Securing Trust and Exclusivity: The Role of Blockchain in Luxury Brand Strategies*. 1–39.

Kumar, S. K. (2023). *Synergizing IoT, IoE, GSM Technology, and Deep Learning Models for Advanced Security Applications: A Comprehensive Overview*. https://doi.org/DOI: 10.46759/IIJSR.2023.7406

Kumar, A., Ottaviani, C., Gill, S., & Buyya, R. (2021). securing the future internet of things with post-quantum cryptography. *Security and Privacy*, *5*(2), e200. Advance online publication. DOI: 10.1002/spy2.200

Kumar, A., Tripathi, A., & Sharma, S. (2021). Lightweight Cryptography for Resource-Constrained IoT Devices: A Survey and Comparative Analysis. *IEEE Internet of Things Journal*, *8*(6), 5398–5413.

Kumarathunga, M., Calheiros, R. N., & Ginige, A. (2022). Smart Agricultural Futures Market: Blockchain Technology as a Trust Enabler between Smallholder Farmers and Buyers. *Sustainability (Basel)*, *14*(5), 2916. DOI: 10.3390/su14052916

Kumar, R., & Sharma, R. (2022). Leveraging blockchain for ensuring trust in IoT: A survey. *Journal of King Saud University. Computer and Information Sciences*, *34*(10), 8599–8622. DOI: 10.1016/j.jksuci.2021.09.004

Kundu, D. (2019). Blockchain and Trust in a Smart City. Https://Doi.Org/10.1177/0975425319832392, *10*(1), 31–43. https://doi.org/DOI: 10.1177/0975425319832392

Kuo, T. T., Kim, H. E., & Ohno-Machado, L. (2017). Blockchain distributed ledger technologies for biomedical and health care applications. *Journal of the American Medical Informatics Association : JAMIA*, *24*(6), 1211–1220. DOI: 10.1093/jamia/ocx068 PMID: 29016974

Kurniawan, H., & Mambo, M.Kurniawan and Mambo. (2022). Homomorphic Encryption-Based Federated Privacy Preservation for Deep Active Learning. *Entropy (Basel, Switzerland)*, *24*(11), 1545. Advance online publication. DOI: 10.3390/e24111545 PMID: 36359635

Kushwaha, S. S., Joshi, S., Singh, D., Kaur, M., & Lee, H. N. (2022). Systematic Review of Security Vulnerabilities in Ethereum Blockchain Smart Contract. *IEEE Access : Practical Innovations, Open Solutions*, *10*, 6605–6621. DOI: 10.1109/ACCESS.2021.3140091

Kuznetsov, O., Rusnak, A., Yezhov, A., Kanonik, D., Kuznetsova, K., & Karashchuk, S. (2024). Enhanced security and efficiency in blockchain with aggregated zero-knowledge proof mechanisms. *IEEE Access : Practical Innovations, Open Solutions*, *•••*, 1–1. DOI: 10.1109/ACCESS.2024.3384705

la Diega, G. N. (2022). Internet of Things and the Law: Legal Strategies for Consumer-Centric Smart Technologies.

Lamport, L. (2001). Paxos made simple. ACM SIGACT News (Distributed Computing Column) 32, 4 (Whole Number 121, December 2001), 51-58.

Lamport, L. (2019). The part-time parliament. In *Concurrency: the Works of Leslie Lamport* (pp. 277–317). ACM Books. DOI: 10.1145/3335772.3335939

Lamport, L., Shostak, R., & Pease, M. (1982). The byzantine generals problem. [TOPLAS]. *ACM Transactions on Programming Languages and Systems*, *4*(3), 382–401. DOI: 10.1145/357172.357176

Langley, D. J., van Doorn, J., Ng, I. C. L., Stieglitz, S., Lazovik, A., & Boonstra, A. (2021). The Internet of Everything: Smart Things and Their Impact on Business Models. *Journal of Business Research, 122*(January), 853–863. DOI: 10.1016/j.jbusres.2019.12.035

Lara-Nino, C., Diaz-Perez, A., & Morales-Sandoval, M. (2018). Energy and area costs of lightweight cryptographic algorithms for authenticated encryption in wsn. *Security and Communication Networks, 2018*, 1–14. DOI: 10.1155/2018/5087065

Laroussi, I., Huan, L., & Xiusheng, Z. (2023). How will the internet of energy (IoE) revolutionize the electricity sector? A techno-economic review. *Materials Today: Proceedings, 72*, 3297–3311. DOI: 10.1016/j.matpr.2022.07.323

Lavaur, T., Lacan, J., & Chanel, C. P. C. (2022). Enabling Blockchain Services for IoE with Zk-Rollups. *Sensors 2022, Vol. 22, Page 6493, 22*(17), 6493. https://doi.org/DOI: 10.3390/s22176493

Lavaur, T., Lacan, J., & Chanel, C. (2022). Enabling blockchain services for ioe with zk-rollups. https://doi.org/DOI: 10.20944/preprints202208.0023.v1

Lavaur, T., Lacan, J., & Chanel, C. P. (2022). Enabling blockchain services for ioe with zk-rollups. *Sensors (Basel), 22*(17), 6493.

Lazaridis, A., Fachantidis, A., & Vlahavas, I. (2020). Deep reinforcement learning: A state-of-the-art walkthrough. *Journal of Artificial Intelligence Research, 69*, 1421–1471. DOI: 10.1613/jair.1.12412

Lee, L. (2016). New kids on the blockchain: How bitcoin's technology could reinvent the stock market. *Hastings Business Law Journal, 12*(2), 81.

Leeuwen, G., AlSkaif, T., Gibescu, M., & van Sark, W. (2020). An integrated blockchain- based energy management platform with bilateral trading for microgrid communities. *Applied Energy, 263*, 114613. DOI: 10.1016/j.apenergy.2020.114613

Leng, J., Ye, S., Zhou, M., Zhao, J. L., Liu, Q., Guo, W., Cao, W., & Fu, L. (2021). Blockchain-Secured Smart Manufacturing in Industry 4.0: A Survey. *IEEE Transactions on Systems, Man, and Cybernetics. Systems, 51*(1), 237–252. DOI: 10.1109/TSMC.2020.3040789

Leong, W. Y., Leong, Y. Z., & Leong, W. S. (2024). Enhancing Blockchain Security. *IEEE Symposium on Wireless Technology and Applications, ISWTA*, 108–112. DOI: 10.1109/ISWTA62130.2024.10651753

Lewtan, J., McManus, J., & Roohani, S. Blockchain: Opportunity to improve financial reporting and corporate governance. In *Hawai'i Accounting Research Conference (HARC)*, 2018.

Li, Y., Teng, Y., Cao, R., & Li, N. (2019, October). Research on coordination control system of virtual power plant based on blockchain. In 2019 IEEE 8th International Conference on Advanced Power System Automation and Protection (APAP) (pp. 1377-1383). IEEE.

Lin, Q., Li, J., Huang, Z., Chen, W., & Shen, J. (2018). A short linearly homomorphic proxy signature scheme. *IEEE Access : Practical Innovations, Open Solutions*, *6*(X), 12966–12972. DOI: 10.1109/ACCESS.2018.2809684

Lin, S. Y., Zhang, L., Li, J., Ji, L., & Sun, Y. (2022). A Survey of Application Research Based on Blockchain Smart Contract. *Wireless Networks*, *28*(2), 635–690. DOI: 10.1007/s11276-021-02874-x

Liu, J., & Liu, Z. (2019). A Survey on Security Verification of Blockchain Smart Contracts. *IEEE Access : Practical Innovations, Open Solutions*, *7*, 77894–77904. DOI: 10.1109/ACCESS.2019.2921624

Liu, L., Ren, S., Wang, C., & Zhang, Y. (2021). Secure and Efficient Resource Management in Fog-Based IoT Networks. *IEEE Transactions on Network Science and Engineering*, *2*(2), 205–218.

Liu, L., Tsai, W. T., Md, Z. A. B., Peng, H., & Liu, M. (2022). Blockchain-Enabled Fraud Discovery through Abnormal Smart Contract Detection on Ethereum. *Future Generation Computer Systems*, *128*(March), 158–166. DOI: 10.1016/j.future.2021.08.023

Liu, Y., He, J., Li, X., Chen, J., Liu, X., Peng, S., Cao, H., & Wang, Y. (2024a). An Overview of Blockchain Smart Contract Execution Mechanism. *Journal of Industrial Information Integration*, *41*(September), 100674. DOI: 10.1016/j.jii.2024.100674

Li, W., Chai, Y., Khan, F., Jan, S. R. U., Verma, S., Menon, V. G., Kavita, , & Li, X. (2021). A comprehensive survey on machine learning-based big data analytics for IoT-enabled smart healthcare system. *Mobile Networks and Applications*, *26*(1), 234–252. DOI: 10.1007/s11036-020-01700-6

Li, Y., Li, Z., Li, X., & Lin, X. (2020). Multi-Layered Security Architecture for Industrial IoT Systems. *IEEE Transactions on Industrial Electronics*, *67*(11), 8912–8922.

Lo, Y., & Medda, F. (2020). uniswap and the rise of the decentralized exchange. SSRN Electronic Journal. https://doi.org/DOI: 10.2139/ssrn.3715398

Locklin, S. (2019). *Token economics. Technical report*. Brave Software.

Lom, M., & Pribyl, O. (2021). Smart city model based on systems theory. *International Journal of Information Management*, *56*, 102092. DOI: 10.1016/j.ijinfomgt.2020.102092

Lu, W., Li, Z., Li, Y., & Xu, X. (2021). Blockchain-Based Trust Management for Fog Computing in IoT Networks. *IEEE Internet of Things Journal*, *8*(5), 3401–3412.

Lyon, D. (2014). Surveillance, Snowden, and Big Data: Capacities, Consequences. *Big Data & Society*, *1*(2), 2053951714541861. Advance online publication. Http://Dx.Doi.Org/10.1177/2053951714541861. DOI: 10.1177/2053951714541861

Macrinici, D., Cartofeanu, C., & Gao, S. (2018). Smart Contract Applications within Blockchain Technology: A Systematic Mapping Study. *Telematics and Informatics*, *35*(8), 2337–2354. DOI: 10.1016/j.tele.2018.10.004

Madumidha, S. SivaRanjani, P., & Venmuhilan, B. (2023). Integrating Blockchain and IoT in supply chain management: a framework for transparency and traceability. In Research Anthology on Convergence of Blockchain, Internet of Things, and Security (pp. 291-313). IGI Global.

Mahajan, R., & Siddavatam, I. (2018). Phishing Website Detection using Machine Learning Algorithms. *International Journal of Computer Applications*, *181*(23), 45–47. DOI: 10.5120/ijca2018918026

Mahamuni, N., Pattewar, G., Nikam, H., Loka, O., & Patil, R. (2022, September). A blockchain and proxy re-encryption based approach for IoT data security: a review. In *International Conference on Emerging Technologies and Intelligent Systems* (pp. 587-595). Cham: Springer International Publishing.

Mahato, S., & Paul, S. (2018). *Electroencephalogram (EEG) signal analysis for diagnosis of major depressive disorder (MDD): A Review*. Nanoelectronics, Circuits and Communication Systems., DOI: 10.1007/978-981-13-0776-8_30

Mahmood, M. S., & Al Dabagh, N. B. (2023). Blockchain technology and internet of things: Review, challenge and security concern. *International Journal of Electrical and Computer Engineering*, *13*(1), 718–735. DOI: 10.11591/ijece.v13i1.pp718-735

Mahmoud, H. H., Wu, W. Y., & Wang, Y. H. (2021). WDSchain: A Toolbox for Enhancing the Security Using Blockchain Technology in Water Distribution System. *Water (Basel)*, *13*(14), 1944. DOI: 10.3390/w13141944

Majeed, A., Haq, A. U., Jamal, A., Bhana, R., Banigo, F., & Baadel, S. (2016a). Internet of everything (IoE) exploiting organisational inside threats: Global network of smart devices (GNSD). *ISSE 2016 - 2016 International Symposium on Systems Engineering - Proceedings Papers*. https://doi.org/DOI: 10.1109/SysEng.2016.7753152

Majeed, A., Bhana, R., Haq, A. U., & Williams, M.-L. (2016). "Devising a Secure Architecture of Internet of Everything (IoE) to Avoid the Data Exploitation in Cross Culture Communications." *IJACSA). International Journal of Advanced Computer Science and Applications*, *7*(4). Advance online publication. www.ijacsa.thesai.org. DOI: 10.14569/IJACSA.2016.070443

Majeed, A., Haq, A. U., Jamal, A., Bhana, R., Banigo, F., & Baadel, S. (2016, October). Internet of everything (IoE) exploiting organisational inside threats: Global network of smart devices (GNSD). In *2016 IEEE International Symposium on Systems Engineering (ISSE)* (pp. 1-7). IEEE.

Makani, S., Pittala, R., Alsayed, E., Aloqaily, M., & Jararweh, Y. (2022). A survey of blockchain applications in sustainable and smart cities. *Cluster Computing*, *25*(6), 3915–3936. DOI: 10.1007/s10586-022-03625-z

Małagocka, K. (2024). Navigating Digital Privacy and Surveillance: Post-Covid Regulatory and Theoretical Insights. *Politics and Governance*, *12*, 8572. Advance online publication. DOI: 10.17645/pag.8572

Malathi, K. (n.d.). *Improved Dynamic Regression Framework for Effective Data Management in Wireless Networks on Cloud-assisted Internet of Everything Platform*. https://doi.org/DOI: 10.58346/JISIS.2024.I2.011

Malathy, S., Vanitha, C. N., Dhanaraj, R. K., & Kotteswari, C. (2023). Impact of Blockchain-IoE on economy. *Blockchain-Based Systems for the Modern Energy Grid*, 135–156. https://doi.org/DOI: 10.1016/B978-0-323-91850-3.00007-X

Manickam, P., Mariappan, S. A., Murugesan, S. M., Hansda, S., Kaushik, A., Shinde, R., & Thipperudraswamy, S. P. (2022). Artificial intelligence (AI) and internet of medical things (IoMT) assisted biomedical systems for intelligent healthcare. *Biosensors (Basel)*, *12*(8), 562. DOI: 10.3390/bios12080562 PMID: 35892459

Mann, S., Potdar, V., Gajavilli, R. S., & Chandan, A. (2018, December). Blockchain technology for supply chain traceability, transparency and data provenance. In *Proceedings of the 2018 international conference on blockchain technology and application* (pp. 22-26).

Marchal, S., Saari, K., Singh, N., & Asokan, N. (2016). Know Your Phish: Novel Techniques for Detecting Phishing Sites and Their Targets. *Proceedings - International Conference on Distributed Computing Systems, 2016-Augus*(Section V), 323–333. DOI: 10.1109/ICDCS.2016.10

Márquez-Sánchez, S., Calvo-Gallego, J., Erbad, A., Ibrar, M., Fernandez, J. H., Houchati, M., & Corchado, J. M. (2023). Enhancing building energy management: Adaptive edge computing for optimized efficiency and inhabitant comfort. *Electronics (Basel), 12*(19), 4179.

Martin, J. (2014). Lost on the Silk Road: Online drug distribution and the 'cryptomarket'. *Criminology & Criminal Justice, 14*(3), 351–367.

Martin, J. (2014a). *Drugs on the dark net: How cryptomarkets are transforming the global trade in illicit drugs*. Springer. DOI: 10.1057/9781137399052

Masoud, M., Jaradat, Y., Manasrah, A., & Jannoud, I. (2019). Sensors of Smart Devices in the Internet of Everything (IoE) Era: Big Opportunities and Massive Doubts. *Journal of Sensors, 2019*(1), 6514520. DOI: 10.1155/2019/6514520

Mathur, N., & Sinha, S. (2023). Security Model and Access Control Mechanisms for Attack Mitigation in IoE. *Blockchain Technology for IoE: Security and Privacy Perspectives*, (January), 67–100. DOI: 10.1201/9781003366010-6

Mattila, J., Seppälä, T., Naucler, C., Stahl, R., Tikkanen, M., Bådenlid, A., & Seppälä, J. (2016). Industrial blockchain platforms: An exercise in use case development in the energy industry (No. 43). ETLA Working Papers.

Mazzola, L., Denzler, A., & Christen, R. (2020). Towards a Peer-to-Peer energy market: an overview. arXiv preprint arXiv:2003.07940.

McKee, M., Rosenbacke, R., & Stuckler, D. (2024). The power of artificial intelligence for managing pandemics: A primer for public health professionals. *The International Journal of Health Planning and Management*. PMID: 39462894

McKinney, S. A., Landy, R., & Wilka, R. (2017). "Smart Contracts, Blockchain, and the Next Frontier of Transactional Law." *Washington Journal of Law, Technology & Arts* 13. https://heinonline.org/HOL/Page?handle=hein.journals/washjolta13&id=321&div=&collection=

McLeod, P. (2013). Taxing and regulating bitcoin: The government's game of catch up. *CommLaw Conspectus, 22*, 379.

Mehta, D., Tanwar, S., Bodkhe, U., Shukla, A., & Kumar, N. (2021). Blockchain-based royalty contract transactions scheme for Industry 4.0 supply-chain management. *Information Processing & Management, 58*(4), 102586. DOI: 10.1016/j.ipm.2021.102586

Merkle, R. C. (1989, August). One way hash functions and DES. In Conference on the Theory and Application of Cryptology (pp. 428-446). New York, NY: Springer New York.

Merkle, R. C. (2019). Protocols for public key cryptosystems. In *Secure communications and asymmetric cryptosystems* (pp. 73–104). Routledge.

Meydani, A., Shahinzadeh, H., Ramezani, A., Gharehpetian, G. B., & Tanwar, S. (2024). "Analysis of the Cybersecurity and Privacy Protection of Blockchain-Empowered Internet of Energy (IoE)." *Proceeding of 8th International Conference on Smart Cities, Internet of Things and Applications, SCIoT 2024*, 213–28. https://doi.org/DOI: 10.1109/SCIoT62588.2024.10570124

Miglani, A., Kumar, N., Chamola, V., & Zeadally, S. (2020). Blockchain for Internet of Energy management: Review, solutions, and challenges. *Computer Communications, 151*, 395–418. DOI: 10.1016/j.comcom.2020.01.014

Mik, E. (2017). Smart Contracts: Terminology, Technical Limitations and Real World Complexity. *Law, Innovation and Technology, 9*(2), 269–300. DOI: 10.1080/17579961.2017.1378468

Miranda, M. J. A. (2018). Enhancing Cybersecurity Awareness Training: A Comprehensive Phishing Exercise. *International Management Review, 14*(2), 6. https://eds-b-ebscohost-com.proxy1.ncu.edu/eds/detail/detail?vid=1&sid=0fb6b1c4-0bf9-4a3f-a0c7-80e5d5f8e32f%40pdc-v-sessmgr04&bdata=JnNpdGU9ZWRzLWxpdmU%3D#AN=132492909&db=bth

Mishra, P., & Singh, G. (2023). Energy Management Systems in Sustainable Smart Cities Based on the Internet of Energy: A Technical Review. *Energies 2023, Vol. 16, Page 6903, 16*(19), 6903. https://doi.org/DOI: 10.3390/en16196903

Mishra, P., & Singh, G. (2023). Energy management systems in sustainable smart cities based on the internet of energy: A technical review. *Energies, 16*(19), 6903.

Miyamoto, D., Hazeyama, H., & Kadobayashi, Y. (2009). *<Fulltext63.Pdf>*. 539–546.

Mogadem, M. M., Li, Y., & Meheretie, D. L. (2022). A Survey on Internet of Energy Security: Related Fields, Challenges, Threats and Emerging Technologies. *Cluster Computing, 25*(4), 2449–2485. DOI: 10.1007/s10586-021-03423-z

Moghimi, M., & Varjani, A. Y. (2016). New rule-based phishing detection method. *Expert Systems with Applications*, *53*, 231–242. DOI: 10.1016/j.eswa.2016.01.028

Mohammed, A. H., Abdulateef, A. A., & Abdulateef, I. A. (2021, June). Hyperledger, Ethereum and blockchain technology: a short overview. In *2021 3rd International Congress on Human-Computer Interaction, Optimization and Robotic Applications (HORA)* (pp. 1-6). IEEE.

Mohanty, S. P., Yanambaka, V. P., Kougianos, E., & Puthal, D. (2020). PUFchain: A Hardware-Assisted Blockchain for Sustainable Simultaneous Device and Data Security in the Internet of Everything (IoE). *IEEE Consumer Electronics Magazine*, *9*(2), 8–16. DOI: 10.1109/MCE.2019.2953758

Molina-Jimenez, C., Sfyrakis, I., Solaiman, E., Ng, I., Wong, M. W., Chun, A., & Crowcroft, J. (2018, November). Implementation of smart contracts using hybrid architectures with on and off–blockchain components. In 2018 IEEE 8th International Symposium on Cloud and Service Computing (SC2) (pp. 83-90). IEEE.

Molina-Jimenez, C., Solaiman, E., Sfyrakis, I., Ng, I., & Crowcroft, J. (2019). On and off-blockchain enforcement of smart contracts. In Euro-Par 2018: Parallel Processing Workshops: Euro-Par 2018 International Workshops, Turin, Italy, August 27-28, 2018, Revised Selected Papers 24 (pp. 342-354). Springer International Publishing.

Mollah, M. B., Zhao, J., Niyato, D., Lam, K. Y., Zhang, X., Ghias, A. M., Koh, L. H., & Yang, L. (2020). Blockchain for future smart grid: A comprehensive survey. *IEEE Internet of Things Journal*, *8*(1), 18–43. DOI: 10.1109/JIOT.2020.2993601

Morgan, J. S. (2017). What I learned trading cryptocurrencies while studying the law. *U. Miami Int'l & Comp. L. Rev.*, *25*, 159.

Morris, J. (2015). *Dworkin. Sha-3 standard: Permutation-based hash and extendable-output functions. Technical report, National Institute of Standards and Technology.* NIST.

Moudgil, V., Hewage, K., Hussain, S. A., & Sadiq, R. (2023). Integration of IoT in building energy infrastructure: A critical review on challenges and solutions. *Renewable & Sustainable Energy Reviews*, *174*, 113121. DOI: 10.1016/j.rser.2022.113121

Moulding, R. (2019). *The promise of Blockchain and its impact on relationships between actors in the supply chain: A theory-based research framework.*

Mousavi, S., Villarreal-Marroquín, M. G., Hajiaghaei-Keshteli, M., & Smith, N. R. (2023). Data-driven prediction and optimization toward net-zero and positive-energy buildings: A systematic review. *Building and Environment*, *242*, 110578. DOI: 10.1016/j.buildenv.2023.110578

Mukherjee, S., & Banerjee, B. (2024). Latest Developments in Artificial Intelligence: Enhancing Creativity and Productivity. *International Research Journal of Scientific Studies*, *1*(1), 19–23.

Mukhopadhyay, M., (2018). *Ethereum Smart Contract Development: Build blockchain-based decentralized applications using solidit*

Musleh, A. S., Yao, G., & Muyeen, S. M. (2019). Blockchain applications in smart grid–review and frameworks. *IEEE Access : Practical Innovations, Open Solutions*, *7*, 86746–86757.

Nakamoto, S. (2008). Bitcoin: A peer-to-peer electronic cash system.

Nakamoto, S. (2008). *Bitcoin: A peer-to-peer electronic cash system*. Decentralized Business Review., Available online https://nakamotoinstitute.org/bitcoin/

Náñez Alonso, S. L., Jorge-vázquez, J., Echarte Fernández, M. Á., & Reier Forradellas, R. F. (2021). Cryptocurrency Mining from an Economic and Environmental Perspective. Analysis of the Most and Least Sustainable Countries. *Energies 2021, Vol. 14, Page 4254, 14*(14), 4254. https://doi.org/DOI: 10.3390/en14144254

Narayanan, A., & Clark, J. (2017). Bitcoin's academic pedigree. *Communications of the ACM*, *60*(12), 36–45.

Naseem, R., Khan, B., Ahmad, A., Almogren, A., Jabeen, S., Hayat, B., & Shah, M. A. (2020). Investigating Tree Family Machine Learning Techniques for a Predictive System to Unveil Software Defects. *Complexity*, *2020*, 1–21. DOI: 10.1155/2020/6688075

Naseem, R., Khan, B., Shah, M. A., Wakil, K., Khan, A., Alosaimi, W., Uddin, M. I., & Alouffi, B. (2020). Performance Assessment of Classification Algorithms on Early Detection of Liver Syndrome. *Journal of Healthcare Engineering*, *2020*, 1–13. Advance online publication. DOI: 10.1155/2020/6680002 PMID: 33489060

Nasir, N. M., Hassan, S., & Zaini, K. M. (2024). *Securing Permissioned Blockchain-based Systems: An Analysis on the Significance of Consensus Mechanisms*. IEEE., DOI: 10.1109/ACCESS.2024.3465869

Natarajan, H., Krause, S., & Gradstein, H. (2017). Distributed ledger technology and blockchain.

Nayal, K., Raut, R. D., Narkhede, B. E., Priyadarshinee, P., Panchal, G. B., & Gedam, V. V. (2021). Antecedents for blockchain technologyenabled sustainable agriculture supply chain. *Annals of Operations Research*, •••, 1–45. PMID: 34898788

Ng, W. Y., Tan, T.-E., Movva, P. V. H., Fang, A. H. S., Yeo, K.-K., Ho, D., Foo, F. S. S., Xiao, Z., Sun, K., Wong, T. Y., Sia, A. T.-H., & Ting, D. S. W. (2021). Blockchain applications in health care for COVID-19 and beyond: A systematic review. *The Lancet. Digital Health*, *3*(12), e819–e829. DOI: 10.1016/S2589-7500(21)00210-7 PMID: 34654686

Nicholas, J. (2014). Ajello. Fitting a square peg in a round hole: Bitcoin, money laundering, and the fifth amendment privilege against self-incrimination. *Brooklyn Law Review*, *80*(2), 435.

Nofal, R. A., Tran, N., Garcia, C., Liu, Y., & Dezfouli, B. (2019, November). A comprehensive empirical analysis of tls handshake and record layer on iot platforms. In *Proceedings of the 22nd International ACM Conference on Modeling, Analysis and Simulation of Wireless and Mobile Systems* (pp. 61-70).

Nti, I., Gyamfi, E., & Osei, M. (2017). Effective cryptographic technique for securing cloud storage systems. *International Journal of Applied Information Systems*, *12*(4), 19–25. DOI: 10.5120/ijais2017451696

Nwakeze, Osita, Miracle. (2024). The Importance of Network Security in Protecting Sensitive Data and Information. International journal of research and innovation in applied science, IX(VI):259-270. DOI: 10.51584/IJRIAS.2024.906024

Nzuva, S. M. (2019). Smart Contracts Implementation, Applications, Benefits, and Limitations. *Journal of Information Engineering and Applications*, (September). Advance online publication. DOI: 10.7176/JIEA/9-5-07

Oduor, X., & Omariba, Z. B. (2022). Application of cryptography in enhancing privacy of personal data in medical services. *International Journal of Communication and Information Technology*, *3*(1), 16–21. DOI: 10.33545/2707661X.2022.v3.i1a.41

OECD. (2018). *The potential for blockchain technology in public equity markets in asia. Technical report.* OECD CAPITAL MARKETSERIES.

Omotayo, O., Muonde, M., Olorunsogo, T. O., Ogugua, J. O., & Maduka, C. P. (2024). Pandemic epidemiology: A comprehensive review of covid-19 lessons and future healthcare preparedness. *International Medical Science Research Journal*, *4*(1), 89–107. DOI: 10.51594/imsrj.v4i1.739

Osama, M., Ateya, A. A., Sayed, M. S., Hammad, M., Pławiak, P., Abd El-Latif, A. A., & Elsayed, R. A. (2023). Internet of medical things and healthcare 4.0: Trends, requirements, challenges, and research directions. *Sensors (Basel)*, *23*(17), 7435. DOI: 10.3390/s23177435 PMID: 37687891

Othman, S. B., Bahattab, A. A., Trad, A., & Youssef, H. (2015). Confidentiality and Integrity for Data Aggregation in WSN Using Homomorphic Encryption. *Wireless Personal Communications*, *80*(2), 867–889. DOI: 10.1007/s11277-014-2061-z

Ourahou, M., Ayrir, W., Hassouni, B. E., & Haddi, A. (2020). Review on smart grid control and reliability in presence of renewable energies: Challenges and prospects. *Mathematics and Computers in Simulation*, *167*, 19–31. DOI: 10.1016/j.matcom.2018.11.009

Pandey, C. (2020). Scalability challenges and opportunities in blockchain-based systems: A systematic review. [TURCOMAT]. *Turkish Journal of Computer and Mathematics Education*, *11*(3), 2022–2031. DOI: 10.17762/turcomat.v11i3.13599

Parhamfar, M., & Zabihi, A. 2024. "Next-Gen Energy Solutions: A Brief Study on Boosting Distribution Efficiency with IoE Technology." https://doi.org/DOI: 10.25729/esr.2024.03.009

Parsa, A. D., Hakkim, S., Vinnakota, D., Mahmud, I., Bulsari, S., Dehghani, L., & Kabir, R. (2023). Artificial Intelligence for Global Healthcare. In *Artificial Intelligence in Medical Virology* (pp. 1–21). Springer Nature Singapore. DOI: 10.1007/978-981-99-0369-6_1

Parthasarathy, K. (2022). Examining cloud computing's data security problems and solutions: Authentication and access control (AAC). *Journal of Science and Technology*, 7(12), 1-10. ISSN 2456-5660.

Patel, M. K., Uchhula, V., & Banerjee, B., (2014). Comparative Evaluation of AODV, DSDV and AOMDV based on end-to-end delay and routing overhead using Network Simulator.

Patel, M. K., Uchhula, V. V., & Banerjee, B. (2013). Comparative Analysis of Routing Protocols in MANET Based on Packet Delivery Ratio using NS2. *International Journal of Advanced Research in Computer Science and Software Engineering*, *3*(11), 172–177.

Patel, M., Brahmbhatt, A. B. J. N., & Singh, V. (2023). Blockchain technology in food safety and traceability concern to livestock products. *Heliyon*, *9*(6), e16526. Advance online publication. DOI: 10.1016/j.heliyon.2023.e16526 PMID: 37265625

Patil, R. Y. (2024). A secure privacy preserving and access control scheme for medical internet of things (MIoT) using attribute-based signcryption. *International Journal of Information Technology : an Official Journal of Bharati Vidyapeeth's Institute of Computer Applications and Management*, *16*(1), 181–191. DOI: 10.1007/s41870-023-01569-0

Patil, R. Y., & Bannore, A. (2022). Provably secure role delegation scheme for medical cyber-physical systems. In *Security Analytics* (pp. 143–163). Chapman and Hall/CRC. DOI: 10.1201/9781003206088-10

Patil, R. Y., Karati, A., & Patil, Y. H. (2024). A signcryption with identity-based authentication for secure EHR sharing in IoMT utilizing ECC. *International Journal of Information Technology : an Official Journal of Bharati Vidyapeeth's Institute of Computer Applications and Management*, *16*(8), 1–16. DOI: 10.1007/s41870-024-01963-2

Patil, R. Y., Karati, A., Patil, Y., & Bannore, A. (2023). Reliable data sharing in medical cyber physical system using fog computing. In *Intelligent Edge Computing for Cyber Physical Applications* (pp. 67–83). Academic Press. DOI: 10.1016/B978-0-323-99412-5.00007-1

Patil, R. Y., & Patil, Y. H. (2022). Identity-based signcryption scheme for medical cyber physical system in standard model. *International Journal of Information Technology : an Official Journal of Bharati Vidyapeeth's Institute of Computer Applications and Management*, *14*(5), 2275–2283. DOI: 10.1007/s41870-022-00981-2

Patil, R. Y., Patil, Y. H., & Bannore, A. (2023). Security of Medical Internet of Things (MIoT)- A Bibliometric Analysis. *Journal of Engineering Science and Technology Review*, *16*(3), 181–190. DOI: 10.25103/jestr.163.22

Patil, R. Y., Patil, Y. H., & Bannore, A. (2024). Cybersecurity in medical Internet of Things: Issues, challenges, and future directions. In *Security Implementation in Internet of Medical Things* (pp. 87–110). CRC Press.

Patricia, C. (2020). Franks. Implications of blockchain distributed ledger technology for records management and information governance programs. *Records Management Journal*.

Pawar, V., Manoj, G., Sagar, G. V. A., Abirami, M., Priya, P. S., & Sahoo, A. K. (2023). *Smart distribution network for healthcare goods in hospitals*.

Peivandizadeh, A., & Adarbah, Y., H., Molavi, B., Mohajerzadeh, A., & H. Al-Badi, A. (2024). A Secure Key Exchange and Authentication Scheme for Securing Communications in the Internet of Things Environment. *Future Internet*, *16*(10), 357.

Penard, W., & Van Werkhoven, T. (2008). On the secure hash algorithm family. Cryptography in context, 1-18.

Pengkun, Li., Jinshu, Su., Xiaofeng, Wang. (2020). iTLS: Lightweight Transport-Layer Security Protocol for IoT With Minimal Latency and Perfect Forward Secrecy. IEEE Internet of Things Journal, 7(8):6828-6841. DOI: 10.1109/JIOT.2020.2988126

Perez-Diaz, A., Gerding, E. H., & McGroarty, F. (2020). Catching cheats: Detecting strategic manipulation in distributed optimisation of electric vehicle aggregators. *Journal of Artificial Intelligence Research*, *67*, 437–470. DOI: 10.1613/jair.1.11573

Periyasamy, K., & Akash, S. A. (2021). IoE-Enabled Healthcare 4.0 Systems. In Cases on Edge Computing and Analytics (pp. 203-234). IGI Global.

Pfisterer, D., & Römer, K. (2009). Message Queue Telemetry Transport (MQTT): A Publish/Subscribe Protocol for the Internet of Things. *IEEE Communications Magazine*, *47*(1), 10–19.

Pham, H. (2018). *The Impact of Blockchain Technology on the Improvement of Food Supply Chain Management: Transparency and Traceability: A Case Study of Walmart and Atria*.

Pham, Q. V., Fang, F., Ha, V. N., Piran, M. J., Le, M., Le, L. B., Hwang, W. J., & Ding, Z. (2020). A Survey of Multi-Access Edge Computing in 5G and Beyond: Fundamentals, Technology Integration, and State-of-the-Art. *IEEE Access : Practical Innovations, Open Solutions*, *8*, 116974–117017. DOI: 10.1109/ACCESS.2020.3001277

Philip, J., Gandhimathi, S. K., Chalichalamala, S., Karnam, B., Chandanapalli, S. B., & Chennupalli, S. (2023). Smart Health Monitoring Using Deep Learning and Artificial Intelligence. *Revue d'Intelligence Artificielle*, *37*(2), 451–464. DOI: 10.18280/ria.370222

Pillitteri, V.; Brewer, T. (2014). Guidelines for Smart Grid Cybersecurity, NIST Interagency/Internal Report (NISTIR); National Institute of Standards and Technology: Gaithersburg, MD, USA,. Available online: (accessed on 17 September 2021).DOI: 10.6028/NIST.IR.7628r1

Pimentel, D., Houser, J., Preiss, E., White, O., Fang, H., Mesnick, L., Troy, B., Stephanie, T., Jerrod, S., & Sharon, A. (1997). Water Resources: Agriculture, the Environment, and Society. *Bioscience*, *47*(2), 97–106. DOI: 10.2307/1313020

Pincheira, M., Vecchio, M., Giaffreda, R., & Kanhere, S. S. (2021). Cost-effective IoT devices as trustworthy data sources for a blockchainbased water management system in precision agriculture. *Computers and Electronics in Agriculture*, *180*, 105889. DOI: 10.1016/j.compag.2020.105889

Pooja, G., Dhawane., P., Navghare., Dr., Sampada, Mashirkar., Nikita, Y., Kapadnis., Dipika, D, Raigar., Kimaya, Urane. (2024). Cryptography in Network Security: a Mini Review. Communications on Applied Nonlinear Analysis, DOI: 10.52783/cana.v32.1960

Popoola, O., Rodrigues, M., Marchang, J., Shenfield, A., Ikpehai, A., & Popoola, J. (2024). A critical literature review of security and privacy in smart home healthcare schemes adopting IoT & blockchain: Problems, challenges and solutions. *Blockchain: Research and Applications*, *5*(2), 100178. Advance online publication. DOI: 10.1016/j.bcra.2023.100178

Postel, S. (2014). *The Last Oasis: Facing Water Scarcity*. Routledge. DOI: 10.4324/9781315070346

Predescu, A., Arsene, D., Pahon u, B., Mocanu, M., & Chiru, C. (2021). Pahont,u, B.; Mocanu, M.; Chiru, C. A Serious Gaming Approach for Crowdsensing in Urban Water Infrastructure with Blockchain Support. *Applied Sciences (Basel, Switzerland)*, *11*(4), 1449. DOI: 10.3390/app11041449

Prewett, K. W., Prescott, G. L., & Phillips, K. (2020). Blockchain adoption is inevitable—Barriers and risks remain. *Journal of Corporate Accounting & Finance*, *31*(2), 21–28. DOI: 10.1002/jcaf.22415

Priem, R. (2020). Distributed ledger technology for securities clearing and settlement: Benefits, risks, and regulatory implications. *Financial Innovation*, *6*(1), 1–25. DOI: 10.1186/s40854-019-0169-6

Prikhodko, P., Izumchenko, E., Aliper, A., Romantsov, K., & Zhebrak, A.. (2018). Converging blockchain and next-generation artificial intelligence technologies to decentralize and accelerate biomedical research and healthcare. *Oncotarget*, *9*(5), 5665–5690. DOI: 10.18632/oncotarget.22345 PMID: 29464026

Priya, S. S., Al-Fatlawy, M. H., Khare, N., Mahalakshmi, V., & Ganesh, S. S. (2023, December). Machine and Deep Learning Classifications for IoT-Enabled Healthcare Devices. In *2023 4th International Conference on Computation, Automation and Knowledge Management (ICCAKM)* (pp. 01-07). IEEE. DOI: 10.1109/ICCAKM58659.2023.10449617

Pun, H., Swaminathan, J. M., & Hou, P. (2024). Blockchain Adoption for Combating Deceptive Counterfeits. *Production and Operations Management*, *30*(4), 864–882. Advance online publication. DOI: 10.1111/poms.13348

Putra, K. T., Arrayyan, A. Z., Hayati, N., Firdaus, C. D., Damarjati, C., Bakar, A., & Chen, H.-C. (2024). A Review on the Application of Internet of Medical Things in Wearable Personal Health Monitoring: A Cloud-Edge Artificial Intelligence Approach. *IEEE Access : Practical Innovations, Open Solutions*, *12*, 21437–21452. DOI: 10.1109/ACCESS.2024.3358827

Qamar, A., Javed, T., & Beg, M. (2021). Detecting compliance of privacy policies with data protection laws. https://doi.org//arxiv.2102.12362DOI: 10.48550

Rady, E. H. A., & Anwar, A. S. (2019). Prediction of kidney disease stages using data mining algorithms. *Informatics in Medicine Unlocked, 15*(December 2018), 100178. DOI: 10.1016/j.imu.2019.100178

Rafique, W., & Qadir, J. (2024). Internet of everything meets the metaverse: Bridging physical and virtual worlds with blockchain. *Computer Science Review, 54*, 100678. DOI: 10.1016/j.cosrev.2024.100678

Rahman, M. A., Hossain, M. S., Islam, M. S., Alrajeh, N. A., & Muhammad, G. (2020). Secure and provenance enhanced Internet of Health Things framework: A blockchain managed federated learning approach. *IEEE Access : Practical Innovations, Open Solutions, 8*, 205071–205087. DOI: 10.1109/ACCESS.2020.3037474 PMID: 34192116

Rahman, M. S., Khalil, I., Mahawaga Arachchige, P. C., Bouras, A., & Yi, X. (2019, July). A novel architecture for tamper proof electronic health record management system using blockchain wrapper. In *Proceedings of the 2019 ACM international symposium on blockchain and secure critical infrastructure* (pp. 97-105).

Raj, P., Venkatesh, V., & Amirtharajan, R. (2013). Envisioning the cloud-induced transformations in the software engineering discipline. Software Engineering Frameworks for the Cloud Computing Paradigm, 25-53.

Ramsay, S. (2018). *The General Data ProtectionRegulation vs. The Blockchain : A legal study on the compatibility between blockchain technology and the GDPR*. https://urn.kb.se/resolve?urn=urn:nbn:se:su:diva-157498

Ramu, S. P., Boopalan, P., Pham, Q. V., Maddikunta, P. K. R., Huynh-The, T., Alazab, M., Nguyen, T. T., & Gadekallu, T. R. (2022). Federated learning enabled digital twins for smart cities: Concepts, recent advances, and future directions. *Sustainable Cities and Society, 79*, 103663. DOI: 10.1016/j.scs.2021.103663

Rana, M. T., Numan, M., Yousif, M., Hussain, T., Khan, A. Z., & Zhao, X. (2024). Enhancing sustainability in electric mobility: Exploring blockchain applications for secure EV charging and energy management. *Computers & Electrical Engineering, 119*, 109503. DOI: 10.1016/j.compeleceng.2024.109503

Rao, R. S., & Pais, A. R. (2019). Detection of phishing websites using an efficient feature-based machine learning framework. *Neural Computing & Applications, 31*(8), 3851–3873. DOI: 10.1007/s00521-017-3305-0

Rauchs, M. (2019). *Apolline Blandin, Keith Bear, and Stephen B McKeon. 2nd global enterprise blockchain benchmarking study. Technical report, Cambridge Centre for Alternative Finance*. CCAF.

Rauchs, M., Glidden, A., Gordon, B., Pieters, G. C., Recanatini, M., Rostand, F., & Zhang, B. Z. (2018). Distributed ledger technology systems: A conceptual framework. Available at *SSRN* 3230013.

Rauniyar, A., Hagos, D. H., Jha, D., Håkegård, J. E., Bagci, U., Rawat, D. B., & Vlassov, V. (2023). Federated learning for medical applications: A taxonomy, current trends, challenges, and future research directions. *IEEE Internet of Things Journal*.

Rayes, A., & Salam, S. (2022). Internet of Things from Hype to Reality: The Road to Digitization: Third Edition. *Internet of Things from Hype to Reality: The Road to Digitization: Third Edition*, 1–451. https://doi.org/DOI: 10.1007/978-3-030-90158-5/COVER

Reddy, K. S., Agarwal, K., & Tyagi, A. K. (2021). Beyond Things: A Systematic Study of Internet of Everything. *Advances in Intelligent Systems and Computing, 1180 AISC*, 226–242. https://doi.org/DOI: 10.1007/978-3-030-49339-4_23

Reddy, K., Roy, D. S., Mishra, T. K., & Hussain, M. W. (Eds.). (2023). *Handbook of research on network-enabled IoT applications for smart city services*. IGI global.

Riaz, A., Iqbal, W., Islam, F. U., Hassan, M., Tariq, R., Chehri, A., & Madni, A. F. (2025). S2H-securing smart homes: A blockchain-based preservation approach. *Internet of Things : Engineering Cyber Physical Human Systems*, •••, 101523.

Rijal, S., & Saranani, F. (2023). The Role of Blockchain Technology in Increasing Economic Transparency and Public Trust. [TACIT]. *Technology and Society Perspectives*, *1*(2), 56–67. DOI: 10.61100/tacit.v1i2.51

Ronald, J. (2016). Colombo. Bitcoin: Hype or harbinger. *Journal of International Business and Law*, *16*(1), 1.

Ronald, L. (1978). Rivest, Adi Shamir, and Len Adleman. A method for obtaining digital signatures and public-key cryptosystems. *Communications of the ACM*, *21*(2), 120–126. DOI: 10.1145/359340.359342

Rosner, M. T., & Kang, A. (2015). Understanding and regulating twenty-first century payment systems: The ripple case study. *Michigan Law Review*, *114*, 649.

Ross, E. S. (2016). Nobody puts blockchain in a corner: The disruptive role of blockchain technology in the financial services industry and current regulatory issues. *Cath. UJL & Tech*, *25*, 353.

Rymarczyk, J. (2022). The Change in the Traditional Paradigm of Production under the Influence of Industrial Revolution 4.0. *Businesses 2022, Vol. 2, Pages 188-200, 2*(2), 188–200. https://doi.org/DOI: 10.3390/businesses2020013

Saberi, S., Kouhizadeh, M., Sarkis, J., & Shen, L. (2019). Blockchain technology and its relationships to sustainable supply chain management. *International Journal of Production Research, 57*(7), 2117–2135. DOI: 10.1080/00207543.2018.1533261

Saha, G., Banerjee, B., & Joshi, F. M. (2022). Predictive Edge Computing of SST Time-Series-Based Marine Warning System using Cloud Computing Infrastructure. In *Cloud IoT* (pp. 59–74). Chapman and Hall/CRC. DOI: 10.1201/9781003155577-7

Sahingoz, O. K., Buber, E., Demir, O., & Diri, B. (2019). Machine learning based phishing detection from URLs. *Expert Systems with Applications, 117*, 345–357. DOI: 10.1016/j.eswa.2018.09.029

Saia, R. (2018). Internet of entities (IoE): a blockchain-based distributed paradigm to security. arXiv preprint arXiv:1808.08809.

Saia, R., Carta, S., Recupero, D. R., & Fenu, G. (2019a). Internet of entities (IoE): A blockchain-based distributed paradigm for data exchange between wireless-based devices. *SENSORNETS 2019 - Proceedings of the 8th International Conference on Sensor Networks*, 77–84. https://doi.org/DOI: 10.5220/0007379600770084

Saini, H. K., Jain, K. L., Hiran, K. K., & Bhati, A. (2021). Paradigms to make smart city using blockchain. In *Blockchain 3.0 for Sustainable Development*.

Salehi, M., Clark, J., & Mannan, M. (2022, May). Not so immutable: Upgradeability of smart contracts on ethereum. In *International Conference on Financial Cryptography and Data Security* (pp. 539-554). Cham: Springer International Publishing.

Salih, A., & Abdulrazzaq, M. (2023). cyber security: Performance analysis and challenges for cyber attacks detection. *Indonesian Journal of Electrical Engineering and Computer Science, 31*(3), 1763. DOI: 10.11591/ijeecs.v31.i3.pp1763-1775

Salkuti, S. R. (2020). Challenges, issues and opportunities for the development of smart grid. [IJECE]. *International Journal of Electrical and Computer Engineering, 10*(2), 1179–1186. DOI: 10.11591/ijece.v10i2.pp1179-1186

Sallam, K., Mohamed, M., & Mohamed, A. W. (2023). Internet of Things (IoT) in supply chain management: Challenges, opportunities, and best practices. *Sustainable Machine Intelligence Journal, 2*, 3–1. DOI: 10.61185/SMIJ.2023.22103

Sam, D., Jayanthi, K., Tiwari, R., Ebenezer, A. S., Kanmani, S. D., & Sheeba, A. (2023). Blockchain in internet of entities - issues and challenges. *Blockchain-Based Systems for the Modern Energy Grid*, 83–99. https://doi.org/DOI: 10.1016/B978-0-323-91850-3.00012-3

Samanta, R., Biswas, A., Bandyopadhyay, A., & Mandal, G. (2023). IoE and Blockchain Convergence for Enhanced Security. *Blockchain Technology for IoE: Security and Privacy Perspectives*, 45–65. https://doi.org/DOI: 10.1201/9781003366010-4/IOE-BLOCKCHAIN-CONVERGENCE-ENHANCED-SECURITY-RAHUL-SAMANTA-ARINDAM-BISWAS-ATUL-BANDYOPADHYAY-GURUDAS-MANDAL

Sanwar Hosen, A. S. M. (2020). Blockchain-Based Transaction Validation Protocol for a Secure Distributed IoT Network. *IEEE Access : Practical Innovations, Open Solutions*, *8*, 117266–117277. DOI: 10.1109/ACCESS.2020.3004486

Sarode, A., Karkhile, K., Raskar, S., & Patil, R. Y. (2022, November). Secure data sharing in medical cyber-physical system—a review. In *Futuristic Trends in Networks and Computing Technologies: Select Proceedings of Fourth International Conference on FTNCT 2021* (pp. 993-1005). Singapore: Springer Nature Singapore.

Saurabh, S., & Dey, K. (2021). Blockchain technology adoption, architecture, and sustainable agri-food supply chains. *Journal of Cleaner Production*, *284*, 124731. Advance online publication. DOI: 10.1016/j.jclepro.2020.124731

Schmeelk, S., Kanabar, M., Peterson, K., & Pathak, J. (2022). Electronic health records and blockchain interoperability requirements: A scoping review. *JAMIA Open*, *5*(3), ooac068. DOI: 10.1093/jamiaopen/ooac068 PMID: 35911668

Schnäbe, H., Greer, D. C., & Zanella, A. (2014). Constrained Application Protocol (CoAP): A Transport Protocol for the Internet of Things. *IEEE Internet of Things Journal*, *1*(1), 112–126.

Serôdio, C., Cunha, J., Candela, G., Rodriguez, S., Sousa, X. R., & Branco, F. (2023). The 6G Ecosystem as Support for IoE and Private Networks: Vision, Requirements, and Challenges. *Future Internet 2023, Vol. 15, Page 348*, *15*(11), 348. https://doi.org/DOI: 10.3390/fi15110348

Serôdio, C., Cunha, J., Candela, G., Rodriguez, S., Sousa, X. R., & Branco, F. (2023). The 6G ecosystem as support for IoE and private networks: Vision, requirements, and challenges. *Future Internet*, *15*(11), 348.

Sguanci, C., Spatafora, R., & Vergani, A. M. (2021). Layer 2 blockchain scaling: A survey. arXiv preprint arXiv:2107.10881.

Shackelford, S. J., & Myers, S. (2017). Block-by-block: Leveraging the power of blockchain technology to build trust and promote cyber peace. *Yale JL & Tech.*, *19*, 334.

Shahinzadeh, H., Moradi, J., Gharehpetian, G. B., Nafisi, H., & Abedi, M. (2019). Internet of Energy (IoE) in Smart Power Systems. *2019 IEEE 5th Conference on Knowledge Based Engineering and Innovation, KBEI 2019*, 627–636. https://doi.org/DOI: 10.1109/KBEI.2019.8735086

Shahinzadeh, H., Moradi, J., Gharehpetian, G. B., Nafisi, H., & Abedi, M. (2019, February). Internet of Energy (IoE) in smart power systems. In 2019 5th Conference on Knowledge Based Engineering and Innovation (KBEI) (pp. 627-636). IEEE.

Shahzad, Y., Javed, H., Farman, H., Ahmad, J., Jan, B., & Zubair, M. (2020). Internet of energy: Opportunities, applications, architectures and challenges in smart industries. *Computers & Electrical Engineering*, *86*, 106739. DOI: 10.1016/j.compeleceng.2020.106739

Sharma, P., Sharma, I., Pamecha, S., & Hiran, K. K. (2023). Green Currency Based on Blockchain Technology for Sustainable Development. Https://Services.Igi-Global.Com/Resolvedoi/Resolve.Aspx?Doi=10.4018/978-1-6684-5072-7.Ch005, 102–118. DOI: 10.4018/978-1-6684-5072-7.ch005

Sharma, S. K., Sharma, A. K., Sharma, S., Shukla, K., & Ishaan, I. (2023). IoT-Based Smart Agriculture. In *Convergence of Cloud Computing, AI, and Agricultural Science* (pp. 137-151). IGI Global. DOI: 10.4018/979-8-3693-0200-2.ch007

Sharma, A., Suganya, R., Krishna, P. B., Raj, R., & Murugesan, R. K. (2024). Network Efficient Hierarchical Authentication Algorithm for Secure Communication in IoT and IoE. *IEEE Access : Practical Innovations, Open Solutions*.

Sharma, D. K., Gupta, P., & Priety, . (2020). Internet of Things: The new Rx for pharmaceutical manufacturing and supply chains. *An Industrial IoT Approach for Pharmaceutical Industry Growth*, 2, 257–288. DOI: 10.1016/B978-0-12-821326-1.00010-3

Sharma, D., Tilwari, V., & Pack, S. (2024). An overview for Designing 6G Networks: Technologies, Spectrum Management, Enhanced Air Interface and AI/ML Optimization. *IEEE Internet of Things Journal*. Advance online publication. DOI: 10.1109/JIOT.2024.3505617

Sharma, N., & Rohilla, R. (2024). A multilevel authentication-based blockchain powered medicine anti-counterfeiting for reliable IoT supply chain management. *The Journal of Supercomputing*, *80*(4), 4870–4913. DOI: 10.1007/s11227-023-05654-w

Sharma, P., Jindal, R., & Borah, M. D. (2021). Blockchain-based decentralized architecture for cloud storage system. *Journal of Information Security and Applications, 62*, 102970. DOI: 10.1016/j.jisa.2021.102970

Shermin, V. (2017). Disrupting Governance with Blockchains and Smart Contracts. *Strategic Change, 26*(5), 499–509. DOI: 10.1002/jsc.2150

Shoetan, P. O., & Familoni, B. T. (2024). Blockchain's impact on financial security and efficiency beyond cryptocurrency uses. *International Journal of Management & Entrepreneurship Research, 6*(4), 1211–1235.

Shrivas, M., Bansal, A., Hiran, K. K., & Doshi, R. (2022). *Advancements in quantum blockchain with real-time applications*. IGI Global. DOI: 10.4018/978-1-6684-5072-7

Siano, P., De Marco, G., Rolan, A., & Loia, V. (2019). A Survey and Evaluation of the Potentials of Distributed Ledger Technology for Peer-to-Peer Transactive Energy Exchanges in Local Energy Markets. *IEEE Systems Journal, 13*(3), 3454–3466. DOI: 10.1109/JSYST.2019.2903172

Siddiki Abir, M. A. B., Chowdhury, M. Z., & Jang, Y. M. (2023). Software-Defined UAV Networks for 6G Systems: Requirements, Opportunities, Emerging Techniques, Challenges, and Research Directions. *IEEE Open Journal of the Communications Society, 4*, 2487–2547. DOI: 10.1109/OJCOMS.2023.3323200

Siddiqui, S., Hameed, S., Shah, S. A., Arshad, J., Ahmed, Y., & Draheim, D. (2024). A Smart-Contract-Based Adaptive Security Governance Architecture for Smart City Service Interoperations. *Sustainable Cities and Society, 113*(October), 105717. DOI: 10.1016/j.scs.2024.105717

Singh, A., Parizi, R. M., Zhang, Q., Kim, K. R. C., & Dehghantanha, A. (2020). Blockchain Smart Contracts Formalization: Approaches and Challenges to Address Vulnerabilities. *Computers & Security, 88*(January), 101654. DOI: 10.1016/j.cose.2019.101654

Singh, A., & Rathee, G. (2025). Smart contract empowered dynamic consent: Decentralized storage and access control for healthcare applications. *Peer-to-Peer Networking and Applications, 18*(1), 1–16. DOI: 10.1007/s12083-024-01827-3

Singh, D. S. (2024). Decentralized finance (DeFi): Exploring the role of blockchain and cryptocurrency in financial ecosystems. *International Research Journal of Modernization in Engineering Technology and Science*, •••, 5.

Singh, S., Bhatt, P., Sharma, S. K., & Rabiu, S. (2021). Digital transformation in healthcare: Innovation and technologies. In *Blockchain for Healthcare Systems* (pp. 61–79). CRC Press. DOI: 10.1201/9781003141471-5

Siyal, A. A., Junejo, A. Z., Zawish, M., Ahmed, K., Khalil, A., & Soursou, G. (2019). Applications of Blockchain Technology in Medicine and Healthcare: Challenges and Future Perspectives. *Cryptography 2019, Vol. 3, Page 3, 3*(1), 3. https://doi.org/ DOI: 10.3390/cryptography3010003

Sklaroff, J. M. (2017). Smart Contracts and the Cost of Inflexibility. *University of Pennsylvania Law Review, 166*, •••. https://heinonline.org/HOL/Page?handle=hein .journals/pnlr166&id=267&div=&collection=

Sklavos, N. (2012). cryptographic hardware & embedded systems for communications.. https://doi.org/DOI: 10.1109/ESTEL.2012.6400096

Solanki, A. (Ed.). (2023). *Intelligent Systems for IoE Based Smart Cities*. Bentham Science Publishers.

Soltani, S. Z. (2013). *Improving PKI: Solution analysis in case of CA compromisation*. Utrecht University.

Sonderegger, D. (2015). A regulatory and economic perplexity: Bitcoin needs just a bit of regulation. *Wash. UJL & Pol'y, 47*, 175.

Song, L., Luo, Y., Chang, Z., Jin, C., & Nicolas, M. (2022). Blockchain Adoption in Agricultural Supply Chain for Better Sustainability: A Game Theory Perspective. *Sustainability (Basel), 14*(3), 1470. DOI: 10.3390/su14031470

Sonko, S. (2024). quantum cryptography and u.s. digital security: a comprehensive review: investigating the potential of quantum technologies in creating unbreakable encryption and their future in national security. *Computer Science & It Research Journal, 5*(2), 390–414. DOI: 10.51594/csitrj.v5i2.790

Stephen, R., & Alex, A. (2018, August). A review on blockchain security. [). IOP Publishing.]. *IOP Conference Series. Materials Science and Engineering, 396*(1), 012030. DOI: 10.1088/1757-899X/396/1/012030

Stergiou, C. L., Plageras, A. P., Memos, V. A., Koidou, M. P., & Psannis, K. E. (2023). Secure Monitoring System for IoT Healthcare Data in the Cloud. *Applied Sciences (Basel, Switzerland), 14*(1), 120. DOI: 10.3390/app14010120

Strielkowski, W., Streimikiene, D., Fomina, A., & Semenova, E. (2019). Internet of energy (IoE) and high-renewables electricity system market design. *Energies, 12*(24), 4790.

Subasi, A., & Kremic, E. (2020). Leveraging AI and machine learning for societal challenges, cas 2019 comparison of adaboost with multiboosting for phishing website detection. *Procedia Computer Science, 168*(2019), 272–278. DOI: 10.1016/j.procs.2020.02.251

Sudharshan, D. (2020). Internet of Everything (IoE). *Marketing in Customer Technology Environments*, (April), 161–208. DOI: 10.1108/978-1-83909-600-620201008

Sun Yin, H. H., Langenheldt, K., Harlev, M., Mukkamala, R. R., & Vatrapu, R. (2019). Regulating cryptocurrencies: A supervised machine learning approach to de-anonymizing the bitcoin blockchain. *Journal of Management Information Systems, 36*(1), 37–73. DOI: 10.1080/07421222.2018.1550550

Sun, J., Cao, R., Zhou, M., Hussain, W., Wang, B., Xue, J., & Xiang, J. (2021). A hybrid deep neural network for classification of schizophrenia using EEG Data. *Scientific Reports, 11*(1), 4706. Advance online publication. DOI: 10.1038/s41598-021-83350-6 PMID: 33633134

Surujnath, R. (2017). Off the chain: A guide to blockchain derivatives markets and the implications on systemic risk. *Fordham Journal of Corporate & Financial Law, 22*(2), 257.

Swan, M. (2015). *Blockchain: Blueprint for a new economy.* O'Reilly Media, Inc.

Szabo, N. (1997). Formalizing and securing relationships on public networks. *First Monday.*

Szostek, D. (2019). *Blockchain and the Law.* Nomos Verlag. DOI: 10.5771/9783845298290

Tajjour, S., & Chandel, S. S. (2023). A Comprehensive Review on Sustainable Energy Management Systems for Optimal Operation of Future-Generation of Solar Microgrids. *Sustainable Energy Technologies and Assessments, 58*(August), 103377. DOI: 10.1016/j.seta.2023.103377

Tallat, R., Hawbani, A., Wang, X., Al-Dubai, A., Zhao, L., Liu, Z., Min, G., Zomaya, A. Y., & Hamood Alsamhi, S. (2024). Navigating Industry 5.0: A Survey of Key Enabling Technologies, Trends, Challenges, and Opportunities. *IEEE Communications Surveys and Tutorials, 26*(2), 1080–1126. DOI: 10.1109/COMST.2023.3329472

Tan, C. L., Chiew, K. L., Wong, K. S., & Sze, S. N. (2016). PhishWHO: Phishing webpage detection via identity keywords extraction and target domain name finder. *Decision Support Systems, 88*, 18–27. DOI: 10.1016/j.dss.2016.05.005

Tandon, A., Dhir, A., Islam, A. N., & Mäntymäki, M. (2020). Blockchain in healthcare: A systematic literature review, synthesizing framework and future research agenda. *Computers in Industry, 122*, 103290. DOI: 10.1016/j.compind.2020.103290

Taylor, A., Raleigh, N. A. B., Kurki, S., Ferreira-Aulu, M. B., & Wilenius, M. (2019). *PRECURSORS TO A "GOOD" BIOECONOMY IN 2125: MAKING SENSE OF BIOECONOMY & JUSTICE HORIZONS First Foresight Report of the BioEcoJust Project.*

Technolab Zignuts. (2018, May 23). *Understanding of Blockchain Architecture: How It Works & How to Build - Zignuts Technolab.* https://www.zignuts.com/blog/how-blockchain-architecture-works-basic-understanding-of-blockchain-and-its-architecture

Thakur, T., Mehra, A., Hassija, V., Chamola, V., Srinivas, R., Gupta, K. K., & Singh, A. P. (2021). Smart water conservation through a machine learning and blockchain-enabled decentralized edge computing network. *Applied Soft Computing, 106*, 107274. DOI: 10.1016/j.asoc.2021.107274

Thesis, P. D., Luis González Ramírez, P., & Lloret Mauri Jesús Tomás Gironés Valencia, J. (2022). *Interconnection Architecture of Proximity Smart IoE-Networks with Centralised Management.* https://doi.org/DOI: 10.4995/Thesis/10251/181892

Tiwari, S., Sharma, P., Choi, T. M., & Lim, A. (2023). Blockchain and third-party logistics for global supply chain operations: Stakeholders' perspectives and decision roadmap. *Transportation Research Part E, Logistics and Transportation Review, 170*, 103012.

Tkachuk, R. V., Ilie, D., Robert, R., Kebande, V., & Tutschku, K. (2023). Towards efficient privacy and trust in decentralized blockchain-based peer-to-peer renewable energy marketplace. *Sustainable Energy. Grids and Networks, 35*, 101146. DOI: 10.1016/j.segan.2023.101146

Tom, C. W. (2016). Lin. Compliance, technology, and modern finance. *Brooklyn Journal of Corporate. Financial & Commercial Law, 11*(1), 159.

Torky, M., & Hassanein, A. E. (2020). Integrating blockchain and the internet of things in precision agriculture: Analysis, opportunities, and challenges. *Computers and Electronics in Agriculture, 178*, 105476. DOI: 10.1016/j.compag.2020.105476

Touati, F., Tariq, H., Crescini, D., & Ben Mnaouer, A. (2018). Development of Prototype for IoT and IoE Scalable Infrastructures, Architectures and Platforms. *Lecture Notes in Computer Science (Including Subseries Lecture Notes in Artificial Intelligence and Lecture Notes in Bioinformatics), 11277 LNCS*, 202–216. https://doi.org/DOI: 10.1007/978-3-030-02849-7_18

Treiblmaier, H., & Garaus, M. (2023). Using blockchain to signal quality in the food supply chain: The impact on consumer purchase intentions and the moderating effect of brand familiarity. *International Journal of Information Management*, *68*, 102514. Advance online publication. DOI: 10.1016/j.ijinfomgt.2022.102514

Treleaven, P., Brown, R. G., & Yang, D. (2017). Blockchain technology in finance. *Computer*, *50*(9), 14–17. DOI: 10.1109/MC.2017.3571047

Trevor, I. (2015). Kiviat. Beyond bitcoin: Issues in regulating blockchain tranactions. *Duke Law Journal*, *65*, 569.

Tsukerman, M. (2015). The block is hot: A survey of the state of bitcoin regulation and suggestions for the future. *Berkeley Technology Law Journal*, *30*(4), 1127.

Tyagi, A. K., Aswathy, S. U., Aghila, G., & Sreenath, N. (2021). AARIN: Affordable, Accurate, Reliable and Innovative Mechanism to Protect a Medical Cyber-Physical System Using Blockchain Technology. *International Journal of Intelligent Networks*, *2*(January), 175–183. DOI: 10.1016/j.ijin.2021.09.007

Tyagi, A. K., Dananjayan, S., Agarwal, D., & Thariq Ahmed, H. F. (2023). Blockchain—Internet of Things applications: Opportunities and challenges for industry 4.0 and society 5.0. *Sensors (Basel)*, *23*(2), 947.

Tyagi, A. K., & Nair, M. (2020a). Internet of Everything (IoE) and Internet of Things (IoTs): Threat Analyses, Possible Opportunities for Future. *Journal of Information Assurance and Security*, *15*, 153–177. www.mirlabs.net/jias/index.html

Tyra, J. M. (2014). Triple entry bookkeeping with bitcoin. Bitcoin magazine, 2014.

Tzinos, I., Limniotis, K., & Kolokotronis, N. (2022). Evaluating the performance of post-quantum secure algorithms in the tls protocol. Journal of Surveillance security and Safety, 3(3), 101-127. https://doi.org/DOI: 10.20517/jsss.2022.15

Τσαγδής, A. 2022. "Hardware-Based Security Methods for Internet of Things (IoT), Internet of Everything (IoE) & Cyber-Physical Systems (CPS)," September. https://doi.org/DOI: 10.26265/POLYNOE-2778

Uddin, M. A., Stranieri, A., Gondal, I., & Balasubramanian, V. (2021). A survey on the adoption of blockchain in IoT: Challenges and solutions. *Blockchain: Research and Applications*, *2*(2), 100006. DOI: 10.1016/j.bcra.2021.100006

Ugwuanyi, S., Paul, G., & Irvine, J. (2021). Survey of IoT for developing countries: Performance analysis of LoRaWAN and cellular NB-IoT networks. *Electronics (Basel)*, *10*(18), 2224.

Umapathi, V., Murugaiah, M., & Doshi, R. (2024). *Bio-Inspired Optimization Techniques in Blockchain Systems*. IGI Global., DOI: 10.4018/979-8-3693-1131-8

Unahalekhaka, P., & Sripakarach, P. (2020). Reduction of reverse power flow using the appropriate size and installation position of a BESS for a PV power plant. *IEEE Access : Practical Innovations, Open Solutions*, *8*, 102897–102906.

Unogwu, O. J., Doshi, R., Hiran, K. K., & Mijwil, M. M. (2022). Introduction to Quantum-Resistant Blockchain. Https://Services.Igi-Global.Com/Resolvedoi/Resolve.Aspx?Doi=10.4018/978-1-6684-5072-7.Ch002, 36–55. DOI: 10.4018/978-1-6684-5072-7.ch002

Upadhyay, N. (2020). Demystifying blockchain: A critical analysis of challenges, applications and opportunities. *International Journal of Information Management*, *54*, 102120. DOI: 10.1016/j.ijinfomgt.2020.102120

Urs, W. (2023). *Thomas, Lugrin*. Hash Functions., DOI: 10.1007/978-3-031-33386-6_5

Vaghani, A., Sood, K., & Yu, S. (2022). Security and QoS issues in blockchain enabled next-generation smart logistic networks: A tutorial. *Blockchain: Research and Applications*, *3*(3), 100082. DOI: 10.1016/j.bcra.2022.100082

Vaitkevicius, P., & Marcinkevicius, V. (2020). Comparison of Classification Algorithms for Detection of Phishing Websites. *Informatica (Vilnius)*, *31*(1), 143–160. DOI: 10.15388/20-INFOR404

Van Hout, M. C., & Bingham, T. (2013). 'Silk Road', the virtual drug marketplace: A single case study of user experiences. *The International Journal on Drug Policy*, *24*(5), 385–391.

Vashishth, T. K., Sharma, V., Kumar, B., Sharma, K. K., Chaudhary, S., & Panwar, R. (2025). Blockchain for Securing Federated Learning Systems: Enhancing Privacy and Trust. Model Optimization Methods for Efficient and Edge AI: Federated Learning Architectures, Frameworks and Applications, 299-320.

Verma, A., Bhattacharya, P., Madhani, N., Trivedi, C., Bhushan, B., Tanwar, S., Sharma, G., Bokoro, P. N., & Sharma, R. (2022). Blockchain for Industry 5.0: Vision, Opportunities, Key Enablers, and Future Directions. *IEEE Access : Practical Innovations, Open Solutions, 10*, 69160–69199. DOI: 10.1109/ACCESS.2022.3186892

Vermesan, O., & Friess, P. (2015). *Building the hyperconnected society-internet of things research and innovation value chains, ecosystems and markets*. Taylor & Francis.

Vermesan, O., & Friess, P. (Eds.). (2013). *Internet of things: converging technologies for smart environments and integrated ecosystems*. River publishers.

Vermesan, O., John, R., Pype, P., Daalderop, G., Ashwathnarayan, M., Bahr, R., Karlsen, T., & Sand, H. E. (2021). Internet of Vehicles – System of Systems Distributed Intelligence for Mobility Applications. *Internet of Things : Engineering Cyber Physical Human Systems*, •••, 93–147. DOI: 10.1007/978-3-030-76493-7_4

Vithalkar, P. (2024). cryptographic protocols resilient to quantum attacks: advancements in post-quantum cryptography. cana, 31(3s), 520-532. https://doi.org/DOI: 10.52783/cana.v31.805

Wang, H., Zhang, Y., Zomaya, A., & Li, S. (2022). Lightweight and Efficient Intrusion Detection System for Fog-Based IoT Networks. *IEEE Transactions on Dependable and Secure Computing*, *19*(7), 1545–1558.

Wang, J., Zhang, X., Zhang, Y., & Li, Z. (2023). Multi-Agent Reinforcement Learning for Dynamic Security Management in Fog-IoT Networks. *IEEE Transactions on Emerging Topics in Computational Intelligence*, *7*(4), 1238–1250.

Wang, Q., & Su, M. (2020). Integrating blockchain technology into the energy sector—From theory of blockchain to research and application of energy blockchain. *Computer Science Review*, *37*, 100275. DOI: 10.1016/j.cosrev.2020.100275

Wang, S., Ouyang, L., Yuan, Y., Ni, X., Han, X., & Fei, Y. W. (2019). Blockchain-Enabled Smart Contracts: Architecture, Applications, and Future Trends. *IEEE Transactions on Systems, Man, and Cybernetics. Systems*, *49*(11), 2266–2277. DOI: 10.1109/TSMC.2019.2895123

Wang, S., Yuan, Y., Wang, X., Li, J., Qin, R., & Wang, F. Y. (2018, June). An overview of smart contract: architecture, applications, and future trends. In *2018 IEEE Intelligent Vehicles Symposium (IV)* (pp. 108-113). IEEE. DOI: 10.1109/IVS.2018.8500488

Wang, W., Hoang, D. T., Hu, P., Xiong, Z., Niyato, D., Wang, P., Wen, Y., & Kim, D. I. (2019). A survey on consensus mechanisms and mining strategy management in blockchain networks. *IEEE Access : Practical Innovations, Open Solutions*, *7*, 22328–22370. DOI: 10.1109/ACCESS.2019.2896108

Wang, Y., Zhang, A., Zhang, P., & Wang, H. (2019). Cloud-assisted EHR sharing with security and privacy preservation via consortium blockchain. *IEEE Access : Practical Innovations, Open Solutions*, *7*, 136704–136719. DOI: 10.1109/ACCESS.2019.2943153

Weber, C. (2019). *Exploring dlt and blockchain for alternative finance: A collection of case studies. Tech. rep., Technical report*. European Crowdfunding Network.

Weihong, W. (2024). Poster: I Know What Crypto You Got Last Summer: A Study on Web3 Wallet. *Security and Privacy*, *1-2*, 1–2. Advance online publication. DOI: 10.1109/BRAINS63024.2024.10732070

Wenhua, Z., Qamar, F., Abdali, T., Hassan, R., Jafri, S., & Nguy n, Q. (2023). Blockchain technology: Security issues, healthcare applications, challenges and future trends. *Electronics (Basel)*, *12*(3), 546. DOI: 10.3390/electronics12030546

Whittaker, C., & Ryner, B. (2008). *35580.Pdf.*

Wu, J., Liu, J., Zhao, Y., & Zheng, Z. (2021). Analysis of cryptocurrency transactions from a network perspective: An overview. *Journal of Network and Computer Applications*, *190*, 103139. DOI: 10.1016/j.jnca.2021.103139

Wu, X. B., Zou, Z., & Song, D. (2019). *Learn ethereum: build your own decentralized applications with ethereum and smart contracts*. Packt Publishing Ltd.

Wu, Y., Li, Y., Li, X., & Li, Z. (2022). Privacy-Preserving and Secure Data Aggregation in Fog Computing for IoT Applications. *IEEE Transactions on Parallel and Distributed Systems*, *33*(8), 1864–1877.

Wylde, V., Rawindaran, N., Lawrence, J., Balasubramanian, R., Prakash, · Edmond, Jayal, A., Khan, I., Hewage, C., & Platts, J. (2022). Cybersecurity, Data Privacy and Blockchain: A Review. *SN Computer Science 2022 3:2*, *3*(2), 1–12. https://doi.org/DOI: 10.1007/s42979-022-01020-4

Xia, Q., Sifah, E. B., Asamoah, K. O., Gao, J., Du, X., & Guizani, M. (2017). MeDShare: Trust-less medical data sharing among cloud service providers via blockchain. *IEEE Access : Practical Innovations, Open Solutions*, *5*, 14757–14767. DOI: 10.1109/ACCESS.2017.2730843

Xie, J., Tang, H., Huang, T., Yu, F. R., Xie, R., Liu, J., & Liu, Y. (2019). A Survey of Blockchain Technology Applied to Smart Cities: Research Issues and Challenges. *IEEE Communications Surveys and Tutorials*, *21*(3), 2794–2830. DOI: 10.1109/COMST.2019.2899617

Xu, L., & Bruck, J. (2007, September). Highly available distributed storage systems. In Workshop on wide area networks and high performance computing (pp. 307-330). London: Springer London.

Xue, L., Teng, Y., Zhang, Z., Li, J., Wang, K., & Huang, Q. (2017, September). Blockchain technology for electricity market in microgrid. In 2017 2nd International Conference on Power and Renewable Energy (ICPRE) (pp. 704-708). IEEE.

Xu, H., Klaine, P. V., Onireti, O., Cao, B., Imran, M., & Zhang, L. (2020). Blockchain-enabled resource management and sharing for 6G communications. *Digital Communications and Networks*, *6*(3), 261–269. DOI: 10.1016/j.dcan.2020.06.002

Xu, S., Ning, J., Huang, X., Li, Y., & Xu, G. (2021). Untouchable once revoking: A practical and secure dynamic EHR sharing system via cloud. *IEEE Transactions on Dependable and Secure Computing*, *19*(6), 3759–3773. DOI: 10.1109/TDSC.2021.3106393

Yadav, A. S., Singh, N., & Kushwaha, D. S. (2023). Evolution of Blockchain and consensus mechanisms & its real-world applications. *Multimedia Tools and Applications*, *82*(22), 34363–34408. DOI: 10.1007/s11042-023-14624-6

Yahaya, A. S., Javaid, N., Alzahrani, F. A., Rehman, A., Ullah, I., Shahid, A., & Shafiq, M. (2020). Blockchain Based Sustainable Local Energy Trading Considering Home Energy Management and Demurrage Mechanism. *Sustainability (Basel)*, *12*(8), 3385. DOI: 10.3390/su12083385

Yang, C., Lan, S., Zhao, Z., Zhang, M., Wu, W., & Huang, G. Q. (2023). Edge-Cloud Blockchain and IoE-Enabled Quality Management Platform for Perishable Supply Chain Logistics. *IEEE Internet of Things Journal*, *10*(4), 3264–3275. DOI: 10.1109/JIOT.2022.3142095

Yang, J., Wen, J., Jiang, B., & Wang, H. (2020). Blockchain-based sharing and tamper-proof framework of big data networking. *IEEE Network*, *34*(4), 62–67. DOI: 10.1109/MNET.011.1900374

Yengkhom, A., & Mukhopadhyay, D. (2022). A survey on various applications of internet of things on blockchain platform. *Blockchain for IoT*, 21–48. https://doi.org/DOI: 10.1201/9781003188247-2/SURVEY-VARIOUS-APPLICATIONS-INTERNET-THINGS-BLOCKCHAIN-PLATFORM-ARCHANA-YENGKHOM-DEBARKA-MUKHOPADHYAY

Yildirim, P. (2017). Chronic Kidney Disease Prediction on Imbalanced Data by Multilayer Perceptron: Chronic Kidney Disease Prediction. *Proceedings - International Computer Software and Applications Conference, 2*, 193–198. DOI: 10.1109/COMPSAC.2017.84

Ying, P., & Xuhua, D. (2006). Anomaly based web phishing page detection. *Proceedings - Annual Computer Security Applications Conference, ACSAC*, 381–390. DOI: 10.1109/ACSAC.2006.13

Yi, Z., Yu, M., & Cheung, K. L. (2020). Impacts of Counterfeiting on a Global Supply Chain. *Manufacturing & Service Operations Management, 24*(1), 159–178. DOI: 10.1287/msom.2020.0912

Yli-Huumo, J., Ko, D., Choi, S., Park, S., & Smolander, K. (2016). Where Is Current Research on Blockchain Technology? A Systematic Review. *PLoS One, 11*(10), e0163477. DOI: 10.1371/journal.pone.0163477 PMID: 27695049

Younas, M. I., Iqbal, M. J., Aziz, A., & Sodhro, A. H. (2023). Toward QoS monitoring in IoT edge devices driven healthcare—A systematic literature review. *Sensors (Basel), 23*(21), 8885. DOI: 10.3390/s23218885 PMID: 37960584

Young, S. (2018). Enforcing constitutional rights through computer code. *Catholic University Journal of Law and Technology, 26*(1), 1.

Youssef, A. B., Dutta, P. K., Doshi, R., & Sajnani, M. (Eds.). (2024). *AI, Blockchain, and Metaverse in Hospitality and Tourism Industry 4.0: Case Studies and Analysis*. CRC Press.

Yuan, Y., & Wang, F. Y. (2016). Blockchain: The state of the art and future trends. *Acta Automatica Sinica (Beijing), 42*, 481–494.

Yue, K., Zhang, Y., Chen, Y., Li, Y., Zhao, L., Rong, C., & Chen, L. (2021). A Survey of Decentralizing Applications via Blockchain: The 5G and beyond Perspective. *IEEE Communications Surveys and Tutorials, 23*(4), 2191–2217. DOI: 10.1109/COMST.2021.3115797

Yunakovsky, S., Kot, M., Pozhar, N., Nabokov, D., Kudinov, M., Guglya, A., Kiktenko, E. O., Kolycheva, E., Borisov, A., & Fedorov, A. (2021). Towards security recommendations for public-key infrastructures for production environments in the post-quantum era. *EPJ Quantum Technology*, *8*(1), 14. Advance online publication. DOI: 10.1140/epjqt/s40507-021-00104-z

Zamir, A., Khan, H. U., Iqbal, T., Yousaf, N., Aslam, F., Anjum, A., & Hamdani, M. (2020). Phishing web site detection using diverse machine learning algorithms. *The Electronic Library*, *38*(1), 65–80. DOI: 10.1108/EL-05-2019-0118

Zarreh, A., Wan, H., Lee, Y., Saygin, C., & Janahi, R. A. (2020). Risk assessment for cyber security of manufacturing systems: A game theory approach. *Procedia Manufacturing*, *38*, 605–612. DOI: 10.1016/j.promfg.2020.01.077

Zeb, S., Member, S., Mahmood, A., Member, S., Ali Khowaja, S., Dev, K., Ali Hassan, S., Muhammad Faseeh Qureshi, N., Gidlund, M., & Paolo Bellavista, I. (2022). *Industry 5.0 is Coming: A Survey on Intelligent NextG Wireless Networks as Technological Enablers*. https://arxiv.org/abs/2205.09084v1

Zeng, H., Dhiman, G., Sharma, A., Sharma, A., & Tselykh, A. (2021). An IoT and Blockchain-based approach for the smart water management system in agriculture. *Expert Systems: International Journal of Knowledge Engineering and Neural Networks*, •••, e12892.

Zhang, A., & Lin, X. (2018). Towards secure and privacy-preserving data sharing in e-health systems via consortium blockchain. *Journal of Medical Systems*, *42*(8), 140. DOI: 10.1007/s10916-018-0995-5 PMID: 29956061

Zhang, D., Li, Z., Zhang, J., & Gu, L. (2019). Anomaly Detection and Intrusion Prevention in Fog-Based IoT Networks: A Survey. *IEEE Access : Practical Innovations, Open Solutions*, *7*, 113067–113082.

Zheng, Z., Xie, S., Dai, H., Chen, X., & Wang, H. (2017). An Overview of Blockchain Technology: Architecture, Consensus, and Future Trends. *Proceedings - 2017 IEEE 6th International Congress on Big Data, BigData Congress 2017*, 557–564. DOI: 10.1109/BigDataCongress.2017.85

Zheng, Z. B., Xie, S., Dai, H. N., Chen, X., & Wang, H. (2018). Blockchain challenges and opportunities: A survey. *International Journal of Web and Grid Services*, *14*(4), 352–375. DOI: 10.1504/IJWGS.2018.095647

Zheng, Z., Xie, S., Hong, N. D., Chen, W., Chen, X., Weng, J., & Imran, M. (2020). An Overview on Smart Contracts: Challenges, Advances and Platforms. *Future Generation Computer Systems*, *105*(April), 475–491. DOI: 10.1016/j.future.2019.12.019

Zou, W., Lo, D., Kochhar, P. S., Xuan, B. D. L., Xia, X., Feng, Y., Chen, Z., & Xu, B. (2021). Smart Contract Development: Challenges and Opportunities. *IEEE Transactions on Software Engineering*, *47*(10), 2084–2106. DOI: 10.1109/TSE.2019.2942301

Zuhair, H., Selamat, A., & Salleh, M. (2016). Feature selection for phishing detection: A review of research. *International Journal of Intelligent Systems Technologies and Applications*, *15*(1), 147–162. DOI: 10.1504/IJISTA.2016.076495

About the Contributors

Fasee Ullah graduated from Universiti Teknologi Malaysia (UTM), Malaysia, Faculty of computing in 2017. Dr. Fasee has also completed the postdoctoral fellowship from the University of Macau (2019-2021), which is the academic talented program of the Government of Macau. Currently, he is working as Associate Professor at the department of Computer & Information Sciences, Universiti Teknologi PETRONAS, Perak, Malaysia. He has published many research papers in reputed impact factor journals and conferences. Dr. Fasee is the recipient of the Chancellor Award and the Best Student Award at UTM during his PhD, for his excellent research contributions to wireless communication and health monitoring. His research areas included are Wireless Body Area Network, Wireless Sensor Networks, Cloud Security, Smart hash security designing, smart cities, Big data analytics, Machine learning, deep learning and internet of things. He is currently providing reviewing services to IEEE Transactions on computers, Transactions on Network Science and Engineering, IEEE Transactions on Cloud Computing, IEEE Access, IEEE Sensor Journal, ACM, and International Journal of Distributed Sensor Networks.

Arfat Ahmad Khan received the B.Eng. de- gree in electrical engineering from the University of Lahore, Pakistan, in 2013, the M.Eng. degree in electrical engineering from the Government College University Lahore, Pakistan, in 2015, and the Ph.D. degree in telecommunication and com- puter engineering from the Suranaree University of Technology, Thailand, in 2018. From 2014 to 2016, he was an RF Engineer with Etisalat, United Arab Emirates. From 2018 to 2022, he worked as a Lecturer and a Senior Researcher with the Suranaree University of Technology. He is currently working as a Senior Lecturer and a Researcher at Khon Kaen University, Thailand. He has published more than 50 high impact factored research articles in reputed journals, such as IEEE transactions, Elsevier, etc. His research interests include optimization and stochastic pro- cesses, wireless sensor networks,

Machine, deep and federated learning for intelligent systems, such as Agriculture, Internet Security, Image processing, etc., and the advance wireless communications.

Asad Ullah Dedicated and accomplished computer science professional with expertise in Artificial Intelligence. Adept at conducting cutting-edge research, delivering engaging lectures, and mentoring students to foster their academic and professional growth. Committed to advancing the field of computer science through innovative research contributions and educational excellence. Proven leadership abilities in academic administration and collaborative research initiatives.

***

Zulfiqar Ali is working as Assistant Professor of Computer Science. His filed of interests include software testing, and requirement engineering.

K. Aravinthan is an Assistant Professor and Research Advisor at AMC, Vallam, Thanjavur, Tamil Nadu, India. He is a reviewer from ASTESJ-Science and Technology/Engineering. He holds a B.Sc. (Physics) and MCA from A.V.V.M. Sri Pushpam College Poondi, Bharathidasan University, Tamil Nadu, India. He also holds an MBA (HRM) from Annamalai University, Tamil Nadu, India, and a Ph.D. (CS) from Bharathidasan University. He has published numerous books and research papers in international publications and journals.

Ruchi Doshi is having more than 18 years of academic, research and software development experience in Asia and Africa. Currently she is working as research supervisor at the Azteca University, Mexico and Adjunct Professor at the Jyoti Vidyapeeth Women's University, Jaipur, Rajasthan, India. She worked in the BlueCrest University College, Liberia,West Africa as Registrar and Head, Examination; BlueCrest University College, Ghana, Africa; Amity University, Rajasthan, India; Trimax IT Infrastructure & Services, Udaipur, India. She worked as a Founder Chair, Women in Engineering (WIE) and Secretary Position in the IEEE Liberia Subsection. She worked with Ministry of Higher Education (MoHE) in Liberia and Ghana for the Degree approvals and accreditations processes. She is interested in the field of Machine Learning and Cloud computing framework development. She has published numerous research papers in peer-reviewed international journals and conferences. She is a Reviewer, Advisor, Ambassador and Editorial board member of various reputed International Journals and Conferences.

Sri Harsha Grandhi is a dedicated and innovative Analog & Mixed Signal Design Engineer with 7 years of experience in the Non-Volatile Memory Group at Intel. Based in Folsom, California, he specializes in the custom design, validation, and integration of advanced mixed-signal and analog systems. Sri Harsha holds a Master of Science degree in Electrical Engineering from California State University, Sacramento, and a Bachelor of Engineering in Electronics and Communication Engineering from Gayatri Vidya Parishad College of Engineering in Vizag, India.

Basava Ramanjaneyulu Gudivaka is a highly experienced professional with over 11 years in Design and Development, specializing in Robotic Process Automation (RPA) for over 8 years. Certified in UiPath, Openspan/Pega Robotics, Automation Anywhere, and Blue Prism, Basava excels in problem-solving, technical leadership, and solution design.

Raj Kumar Gudivaka has a total of 4.4 years of IT experience, with over 3 years dedicated to RPA (Robotic Process Automation) implementation, focusing on MS Power Automate Desktop Flows and Automation Anywhere (Version 11 & A360). Raj collaborates with teams and Business Analysts to understand requirements, ensuring that bots align with process mapping guidelines. They create work plans, specifications, and programs following development procedures and utilize code repository tools like GitHub and GitLab for version control.

Rajya Lakshmi Gudivaka possesses knowledge in RPA (UiPath, Power Automate), particularly in building RPA solutions using UiPath. They are skilled in end-to-end automation solutions, encompassing analysis, designing, development, testing, and deployment. Their understanding of RPA best practices and familiarity with UiPath Orchestrator for robot deployment and management underscores their proficiency in automation technologies

Shahab Haider is working as Assistant Professor of Computer Science. His field of interests include Wireless sensor networks, Software engineering, and MANETs.

Ammar Hassan did Telecommunications Engineering from the National University of Science and Technology, Pakistan in 2012, a Masters in Computer Science (MCS) from Virtual University of Pakistan in 2019 and Masters in Information Security from National University of Science and Technology in 2023. He holds multiple technical certifications from EC Council, Microsoft, Cisco, and Huawei including CEH(Master), MOS(Access), CSCU, CCENT, HCNP(R&S), and HCNA(Security). He is a master trainer for Certified Ethical Hacking Certification. Currently, he is serving as a lecturer in Department of Information Security, National University of Science and Technology.

Mohammad Ahsanul Islam I am a software engineer and researcher specializing in blockchain technology, data science, and artificial intelligence. My work focuses on developing scalable, high-performance backend systems using Java and Spring Boot while exploring innovative applications of emerging technologies in research and industry. My research interests span distributed ledger technologies, smart contracts, AI-driven automation, and data-driven decision-making. I am particularly focused on leveraging blockchain for security and transparency, harnessing data science for predictive insights, and applying AI to optimize complex systems. Through my research, I aim to contribute to the advancement of these fields by developing novel frameworks and methodologies that address real-world challenges. As a researcher and author, I am committed to bridging the gap between academia and industry by publishing scholarly work and collaborating on interdisciplinary projects. I aim to contribute to the growing body of knowledge in emerging technologies while fostering innovation and practical adoption.

Swati Jeevan is a versatile professional with extensive experience spanning data analytics, academic leadership, and technology education. Currently Senior Lecturer in SRH International College, Heidelberg, Germany and Specialist Lecturer in Data Analytics at the Berlin School of Business & Innovation in Berlin. She imparts expertise in Python, R, and SQL, preparing students for real-world data challenges. Swati has held various roles, including Vice-Dean of the Faculty of Economics & Business Administration and Shift-Leads Manager in technology-driven environments. Her entrepreneurial experience includes running a training institute and her technical acumen extends to Microsoft Office Suite, PowerBI, and programming languages. Academically, she studying Ph.D. in Information Technology, an M.A. in Innovation & Entrepreneurship, and an M.Sc. in IT, reflecting her commitment to lifelong learning and innovation. Swati is also a published author and speaker, contributing to conferences on AI and business intelligence. Residing in Heidelberg, Germany, she is an active member of professional networks like IEEE and certified as a Blockchain Expert by the Blockchain Council.

M. M. Kamruzzaman (Senior Member, IEEE) received the B.E. and M.S. degrees in computer science and engineering and the Ph.D. degree in information and communication technology. He worked as a Postdoctoral Research Fellow at Shenzhen University, China. He is currently working as Associate Professor in the Department of Computer Science, College of Computer and Information Science, Jouf University, Saudi Arabia. His research interests include 5G, 6G, artificial intelligence, image processing, remote sensing, GIS, cloud computing, and big data. He is serving as a member of editorial board for several international journals. He is also serving as a TPC member and a reviewer for few international journals and conferences.

Khadija Munir is a cybersecurity researcher with a keen interest in IT security, blockchain, and malware analysis. Her research interests lie in secure software engineering, static analysis, and reverse engineering.

N Saranya received her PhD degree in electronics and communication engineering from PSG College of Technology, under Anna University, India in 2020, and the ME degree in wireless communication From PSG College of Technology, India, in 2015. She is currently working as assistant professor in the Department of Electronics and Communication Engineering, Sri Manakula Vinayagar Engineering College, Puducherry. Her research area involves antennas, RF and microwave circuit design and wireless power Transmission, wireless security.

P.Raja completed in Bachelor of Engineering with the specialization of Electronics and Communication Engineering at Madras University, Master of Technology with the Speclization of Microelectronics and VLSI Design at IIT Madras and Completed Doctoral Program in Electronics and Communication Engineering at Pondicherry University. He working as a professor in the Department of Electronics and Communication Engineering, Sri Manakula Vinayagar Engineering College, Puducherry, India. He has two decades of teaching experience. His research area is VLSI Design, Signal Processing and Wireless Communication. He is a Professional Membership of the Indian Society for Technical Education and Institute of Electrical and Electronics Engineers, The Institution of Engineers (India) and The Institution of Engineers (India). He also received Excellent Professional Achievement Award (Class1)" from Society of Professional Engineers (India).

Dinesh Kumar Reddy Basani is a seasoned RPA Developer with a background in Computer Science, holding a Master's degree from Northwestern Polytechnic University (2016). With extensive experience in RPA development and having previously worked as a Pega Developer from 2016 to 2018, Dinesh has a proven track record of automating time-consuming manual tasks efficiently.

Wanglen Soram is working as an Assistant Professor in the Computer Engineering Department at Marwadi University, Rajkot, Gujarat, India.

Index

A

B

C

D

E

F

H

I

L

M

N

O

P

Q

R

S

T

V

W

www.ingramcontent.com/pod-product-compliance
Lightning Source LLC
LaVergne TN
LVHW080348011026
849161LV00009B/2232